Books by Paul Johnson

Civilizations of the Holy Land   1979
The Civilization of Ancient Egypt   1978
Enemies of Society   1977
A History of Christianity   1976
A Place in History   1975
Pope John 23rd   1974
Elizabeth I: A Study in Power and Intellect   1974
The Offshore Islanders: From Roman Occupation
  to European Entry   1972

A HISTORY OF CHRISTIANITY

PAUL JOHNSON

A History
of Christianity

A TOUCHSTONE BOOK
Published by Simon & Schuster
New York London Toronto Sydney

This edition specially printed for Borders Books by Simon & Schuster, Inc.

2005 Borders Books

ISBN 0-7432-8203-5

Printed and bound in the United States of America

07 08 09 10 M 9 8 7 6 5 4 3

To
Marigold

My constant helpmate,
wisest counsellor,
and best friend.

CONTENTS

PROLOGUE

It is now almost 2000 years since the birth of Jesus Christ set in motion the chain of events which led to the creation of the Christian faith and its diffusion throughout the world. During these two millennia Christianity has, perhaps, proved more influential in shaping human destiny than any other institutional philosophy, but there are now signs that its period of predominance is drawing to a close, thereby inviting a retrospect and a balance sheet. In this book I have attempted to survey the whole history in one volume. This involves much compression and selection, but it has the advantage of providing new and illuminating perspectives, and of demonstrating how the varied themes of Christianity repeat and modulate themselves through the centuries. It draws on the published results of a vast amount of research which has been conducted during the past twenty years on a number of notable episodes in Christian history, and it aims to present the salient facts as modern scholars see and interpret them.

It is, then, a work of history. You may ask: is it possible to write of Christianity with the requisite degree of historical detachment? In 1913 Ernst Troeltsch argued persuasively that sceptical and critical methods of historical research were incompatible with Christian belief; many historians and most religious sociologists would agree with him. There is, to be sure, an apparent conflict. Christianity is essentially a historical religion. It bases its claims on the historical facts it asserts. If these are demolished it is nothing. Can a Christian, then, examine the truth of these facts with the same objectivity he would display towards any other phenomenon? Can he be expected to dig the grave of his own faith if that is the way his investigations seem to point? In the past, very few Christian scholars have had the courage or the confidence to place the unhampered pursuit of truth before any other consideration. Almost all have drawn the line somewhere. Yet how futile their defensive efforts have proved! How ridiculous their sacrifice of integrity seems in retrospect! We laugh at John Henry Newman because, to protect his students, he kept his copy of *The Age of Reason* locked up in his safe. And we feel uncomfortable when Bishop Stubbs, once Regius Professor of Modern History at Oxford, triumphantly records – as he did in a public lecture – his first meeting with the historian John Richard Green: 'I knew by description the sort of man I was to meet: I recognised him as he got into the Wells carriage, holding in his hand a volume of Renan. I said to myself, "If I can hinder, he shall not read that book." We sat opposite and fell immediately into conversation. . . . He came to me at Navestock afterwards, and that volume of Renan found its way into my waste-paper basket.' Stubbs had condemned Renan's *Vie de Jésus* without reading it, and the whole point of his anecdote was that he had persuaded Green to do the same. So one historian corrupted another, and Christianity was shamed in both.

For Christianity, by identifying truth with faith, must teach – and, properly understood, does teach – that any interference with the truth is immoral. A Christian with faith has nothing to fear from the facts; a Christian historian who draws the line limiting the field of enquiry at any point whatsoever, is admitting the limits of his faith. And of course he is also destroying the nature of his religion, which is a progressive revelation of truth. So the Christian, according to my understanding, should not be inhibited in the smallest degree from following the line of truth; indeed, he is positively bound to follow it. He should be, in fact, freer than the non-Christian, who is precommitted by his own rejection. At all events, I have sought to present the facts of Christian history as truthfully and nakedly as I am able, and to leave the rest to the reader.

Iver, Buckinghamshire 1975

PART ONE

The Rise and Rescue of the Jesus Sect
(50 BC–AD 250)

SOME TIME ABOUT THE MIDDLE of the first century AD, and very likely in the year 49, Paul of Tarsus travelled south from Antioch to Jerusalem and there met the surviving followers of Jesus of Nazareth, who had been crucified about sixteen years before. This Apostolic Conference, or Council of Jerusalem, is the first political act in the history of Christianity and the starting-point from which we can seek to reconstruct the nature of Jesus's teaching and the origins of the religion and church he brought into being.

We have two near-contemporary accounts of this Council. One, dating from the next decade, was dictated by Paul himself in his letter to the Christian congregations of Galatia in Asia Minor. The second is later and comes from a number of sources or eye-witness accounts assembled in Luke's Acts of the Apostles. It is a bland, quasi-official report of a dispute in the Church and its satisfactory resolution. Let us take this second version first. It relates that 'fierce dissension and controversy' had arisen in Antioch because 'certain persons', from Jerusalem and Judea, in flat contradiction to the teaching of Paul, had been telling converts to Christianity that they could not be saved unless they underwent the Jewish ritual of circumcision. As a result, Paul, his colleague Barnabas, and others from the mission to the gentiles in Antioch, travelled to Jerusalem to consult with 'the apostles and elders'.

There they had a mixed reception. They were welcomed by 'the church and the apostles and the elders'; but 'some of the Pharisaic party who had become believers' insisted that Paul was wrong and that all converts must not only be circumcized but taught to keep the Jewish law of Moses. There was 'a long debate', followed by speeches by Peter, who supported Paul, by Paul himself and Barnabas, and a summing up by James, the younger brother of Jesus. He put forward a compromise which was apparently adopted 'with the agreement of the whole Church'. Under this, Paul and his colleagues were to be sent back to Antioch accompanied by a Jerusalem delegation bearing a letter. The letter set out the terms of the compromise: converts need not submit to circumcision but they must observe certain precepts in the Jewish law in matters of diet and sexual conduct. Luke's record in Acts states that this half-way position was arrived at 'unanimously', and that when the decision was conveyed to the Antioch congregation, 'all rejoiced'. The Jerusalem delegates were thus able to return to Jerusalem, having solved the problem, and Paul carried on with his mission.

This, then, is the account of the first council of the Church as presented by a consensus document, what one might call an eirenic and ecumenical version, designed to present the new religion as a mystical body with a co-ordinated and unified life of its own, moving to inevitable and predestined conclusions. Acts, indeed, says specifically that the ruling of the Council was 'the decision of the Holy Spirit'. No wonder it was accepted unanimously! No wonder that 'all' in Antioch 'rejoiced at the encouragement it brought'.

Paul's version, however, presents quite a different picture. And his is not merely an eye-witness account, but an account by the chief and central participant, perhaps the only one who grasped the magnitude of the issues at stake. Paul is not interested in smoothing the ragged edges of controversy. He is presenting a case to men and women whose spiritual lives are dominated by the issues confronting the elders in that room in Jerusalem. His purpose is not eirenic or ecumenical, still less diplomatic. He is a man burning to tell the truth and to imprint it like fire in the minds of his readers. In the apochryphal *Acts of Paul,* written perhaps a hundred years after his death, the tradition of his physical appearance is vividly preserved: '. . . a little man with a big, bold head. His legs were crooked, but his bearing was noble. His eyebrows grew close together and he had a big nose. A man who breathed friendliness.' He himself says that his appearance was unimpressive. He was, he admits, no orator; not, in externals, a charismatic leader. But the authentic letters which survive him radiate the inner charisma: they have the ineffaceable imprint of a massive personality, eager, adventurous, tireless, voluble, a man who struggles heroically for the truth and then delivers it in uncontrollable excitement, hurrying ahead of his powers of articulation. Not a man easy to work with, or confute in argument, or rebuke into silence, or to advance a compromise: a dangerous, angular, unforgettable man, breathing friendliness, indeed, but creating monstrous difficulties and declining to resolve them by any sacrifice of the truth.

Moreover, Paul was quite sure he had got the truth. He has no reference to the Holy Spirit endorsing, or even advancing, the compromise solution as presented by Luke. In his Galatians letter, a few sentences before his version of the Jerusalem Council, he dismisses, as it were, any idea of a conciliar system directing the affairs of the Church, any appeal to the judgment of mortal men sitting in council. 'I must make it clear to you, my friends,' he writes, 'that the gospel you heard me preach is no human invention. I did not take it over from any man; no man taught it me; I received it through a revelation of Jesus Christ.' Hence, when he comes to describe the council and its consequences he writes exactly as he feels, in harsh, concrete and unambiguous terms. His Council is not a gathering of inspired pneumatics, operating in accordance with infallible guidance from the spirit, but a human conference of weak and vulnerable men, of whom he alone had a divine mandate. How, as Paul saw it, could it be otherwise? Jewish elements were wrecking his mission in Antioch, which he was conducting on the express instructions of God, 'who had set me apart from birth and called me through his grace, chose to reveal his Son to me and through me, in order that I might proclaim him among the gentiles'. To defeat them, therefore, he went to Jerusalem 'because it had been revealed by God that I should do so'. He saw the leaders of the Jerusalem Christians, 'the men of repute', as he terms them, 'at a private interview'. These men, James, Christ's brother, the Apostles Peter and John, 'those reputed pillars of our society', were inclined to accept the gospel as Paul taught it and to acknowledge his credentials as an apostle and teacher of Christ's doctrine. They divided up the missionary territory, 'agreeing that we should go to the gentiles while they went to the Jews'. All they asked was that Paul should ensure that his gentile congregations should provide financial support for the Jerusalem Church, 'which was the very thing I made it my business to do.' Having reached this bargain, Paul and the pillars 'shook hands on it'. There is no mention that Paul made concessions on doctrine. On the contrary, he complains that enforcing circumcision on converts had hitherto been 'urged' as a sop to 'certain sham-Christians, interlopers who had stolen in to spy upon the liberty we enjoy in the fellowship of Jesus Christ'. But 'not for a moment did I yield to their dictation.' He was 'determined on the full truth of the gospel'. Unfortunately, continues Paul, his apparent victory at Jerusalem did not end the matter. The 'pillars', who had contracted to stand firm against the Jewish 'sham-Christians', in return for financial support, did not do so. When Peter later came to Antioch, he was prepared at first to treat gentile Christians as religious and racial equals and eat his meals with them; but then, when emissaries from James arrived in the city, he 'drew back and began to hold aloof, because he was afraid of the advocates of circumcision'. Peter was 'clearly in the wrong'. Paul told him so 'to his face'. Alas, others showed the 'same lack of principle', even Barnabas, who 'played false like the rest'. Paul writes in a context in which the battle, far from being won, is continuing and becoming more intense; and he gives the distinct impression that he fears it could be lost.

Paul writes with passion, urgency and fear. He disagrees with the account in Acts not merely because he sees the facts differently but because he has an altogether more radical idea of their importance. For Luke, the Jerusalem Council is an ecclesiastical incident. For Paul, it is part of the greatest struggle ever waged. What lies behind it are two unresolved questions. Had Jesus Christ founded a new religion, the true one at last? Or, to put it another way, was he God or man? If Paul is vindicated, Christianity is born. If he is overruled, the teachings of Jesus become nothing more than the hallmarks of a Jewish sect, doomed to be submerged in the mainstream of an ancient creed.

To demonstrate why Paul's analysis was substantially correct, and the dispute the first great turning point in the history of Christianity, we must first examine the relationship between Judaism and the world of the first century AD. By the time of Christ, the Roman republic, which had been doubling in size with every generation, had expanded to encompass the whole of the Mediterranean theatre. It was in some respects a liberal empire, bearing the marks of its origins. This was a new, indeed unique, conjunction in world history: an empire which imposed stability and so made possible freedom of trade and communications throughout a vast area, yet did not seek to regiment ideas or inhibit their exchange and propagation. The Roman law could be brutal and was always relentless, but it still operated over a comparatively limited area of human conduct. Many fields of economic and cultural activity lay outside its scope. Moreover, even where the law prescribed, it was not always assiduous. Roman law tended to sleep unless infractions were brought to its attention by the external signs of disorder: vociferous complaints, breaches of the peace, riots. Then it warned, and if its warnings went unheeded, acted with ferocity until silence was reimposed; afterwards, it would sleep again. Within Roman rule, a sensible and circumspect man, however antinomian his views, could survive and flourish, and even propagate them; it was one very important reason why Rome was able to extend and perpetuate itself.

In particular, Rome was tolerant towards the two great philosophical and religious cultures which confronted it in the central and eastern Mediterranean: Hellenism and Judaism. Rome's own republican religion was ancient but primitive and jejune. It was a religion of State, concerned with civil virtues and outward observance. It was administered by paid government functionaries and its purposes and style were indistinguishable from those of the State. It did not touch the heart or impose burdens on a man's credulity. Cicero and other intellectuals defended it on no higher grounds than that it was an aid to public decorum. Of course, being a state religion, it modified itself as the forms of government changed. When the republic failed, the new emperor became, *ex officio*, the *pontifex maximus*. Imperialism was an eastern idea; and it carried with it the notion of quasi-divine powers invested in the ruler. Accordingly, after the death of Caesar, the Roman senate usually voted the deification of an emperor, provided he had been successul and admired; a witness would swear he had seen the dead man's soul wing to heaven from the funeral pyre. But the system which linked divinity to government was observed more in the letter than the spirit; sometimes not even in the letter. Emperors who claimed divinity in their lifetimes – Caligula, Nero, Domitian – were not so honoured once they were safely dead; and the compulsory veneration of a living emperor was more likely to be enforced in the provinces than in Rome. Even in the provinces the public sacrifices were simply a routine genuflection to government; on the vast majority of Rome's citizens and subjects they imposed no burden of conscience.

The State's compulsory but marginal civic creed thus left ample freedom for the psyche within the empire. Every man could have and practise a second religion if he chose. Or, to put it another way, the mandatory civic cult made possible freedom of worship. The choice was enormous. There were some cults of specific Roman origin and taste. Then, all the subject peoples who had been absorbed into the empire had their own gods and goddesses; they often won adherents because they were not identified with the State and their native ceremonies and priests had exotic glamour. The religious scene was constantly shifting. All, and especially the well-to-do, were encouraged to participate in it by the very nature of the educational system, which was identified with no cult but was in a sense the domicile of all. The empirical quest for religious truth was inseparable from any other form of knowledge. Theology was part of philosophy, or *vice versa*; and rhetoric, the art of proof and disproof, was the handmaiden of both. The common language of the empire was Greek and it was especially the tongue of business, education, and truth-seeking. And Greek, as a language and as a culture, was transforming the Roman world-view of religious experience. Greek religion, like Roman, had been in origin a series of city-cults, public demonstrations of fear, respect and gratitude towards the home-gods of the city-state. Alexander's creation of a Hellenic empire had transformed the city-states into a vast territorial unit, in which the free citizen was no longer, as a rule, directly involved in government. He thus had time, opportunity, and above all motive to develop his private sphere and explore his own individual and personal responsibilities. Philosophy began to direct itself increasingly to intimate conduct. Thus, under the impulse of the Greek genius, an age of personal religion opened. What had hitherto been purely a matter of tribal, racial, city, state or – in the loosest sense – social conformity now became a matter of individual concern. Who am I? Where am I going? What do I believe? What, then, must I do? These questions were being asked increasingly, and not only by Greeks. The Romans were undergoing a similar process of emancipation from all-demanding civic duty. Indeed, one could say that the world-empire itself freed multitudes from the burdens of public concern and gave them leisure to study their navels. In the schools, the stress was increasingly on moral teaching, chiefly Stoic in origin. Lists of vices and virtues, and the duties of fathers to children, husbands to wives, masters to slaves – and *vice versa* – were compiled.

But this, of course, was mere ethics, not essentially different from municipal codes of behaviour. The schools did not, or could not, answer many questions now regarded as fundamental and urgent, questions which revolved around the nature of the soul and its future, and its relationship to the universe and eternity. And once such questions were asked, and recorded as having been asked, they would not go away: civilization was maturing. In the Middle Ages, Christian metaphysicians were to portray the Greeks in the decades before Christ as struggling manfully but blindly towards a knowledge of God, trying, as it were, to conjure up Jesus out of the thin Athenian air, to invent Christianity out of their poor pagan heads. In a sense, this supposition is right: the world was intellectually ready for Christianity. It was waiting for God. But it is unlikely the Hellenic world could have produced such a system from its own resources. Its intellectual weapons were various and powerful. It had a theory of nature and a cosmology of sorts. It had logic and mathematics, the rudiments of an empirical science. It could develop methodologies. But it lacked the imagination to relate history to speculation, to produce that startling blend of the real and the ideal which is the religious dynamic. The Greek culture was an intellectual machine for the elucidation and transformation of religious ideas. You put in a theological concept and it emerged in a highly sophisticated form, communicable to the entire civilized world. But Greece could not, or at any rate did not, produce the ideas themselves. These came from the east, from Babylon, Persia, Egypt, mostly tribal or national cults in origin, later liberated from time and place by transformation into cults attached to individual deities. These gods and goddesses lost their localities, changed their names, amalgamated themselves with other, once-national or tribal gods, and then, in turn, moved westwards and were syncretized with the gods of Greece and Rome: thus the Baal of Dolichenus was identified with Zeus and Jupiter, Isis with Ishtar and Aphrodite. By the time of Christ there were hundreds of such cults, perhaps thousands of sub-cults. There were cults for all races, classes and tastes, cults for every trade and situation in life. A new form of religious community appeared for the first time in history: not a nation celebrating its patriotic cult, but a voluntary group, in which social, racial and national distinctions were transcended: men and women coming together just as individuals, before their god.

Thus the religious climate, though infinitely various, was no longer wholly bewildering: it was beginning to clear. Indeed, these new forms of voluntary religious association had a tendency to develop in certain particular and significant directions. The new gods were increasingly seen as 'Lords' and their worshippers as servants; there was a growth of the ruler-cult, with the king-god as saviour and his enthronement as the dawn of civilization. Above all, there was a marked tendency towards monotheism. More and more men were looking not just for a god, but God, *the* God. In the strongly syncretist Hellenic world, where the effort to reconcile religions was most persistent and successful, the gnostic cults which were now emerging, and which offered new keys to the universe, were based on the necessity of monotheism, even though they assumed a dualistic universe operated by rival forces of good and evil. So the religious scene was moving, progressing all the time. What it lacked was any kind of stability. It became increasingly less likely that an educated man would support the cult of his parents, let alone his grandparents; or even that he would fail to change his cult once, perhaps twice, in his life. And, perhaps less noticeably, the cults themselves were in constant osmosis. We do not know enough about the time to provide complete explanations for this constant and ubiquitous religious flux. But it is obvious enough that the old city and national creeds were now hopelessly obsolete except as aids to public decorum, and the oriental mystery cults, though syncretized and rendered sophisticated by the Hellenic philosophical machine, still could not provide a satisfactory account of man and his future. There were huge gaps and anomalies in all the systems. And the frantic efforts to plug them produced disintegration, and so yet more change.

It is at this point in the argument that we see the crucial relevance of the Jewish impingement on the Roman world. For the Jews not merely had a god; they had God. They had been monotheists for at least two millennia. They had resisted with infinite fortitude and sometimes with grievous suffering, the temptations and ravages of eastern polytheistic systems. It is true that their god was originally tribal, and more recently national; in fact he was still national, and since he was closely and intimately associated with the Temple in Jerusalem, he was in some way municipal too. But Judaism was also, and very much so, an interior religion, pressing closely and heavily on the individual, who was burdened with a multitude of injunctions and prohibitions which posed acute problems of interpretation and scruple. The practising Jew was essentially *homo religiosus* as well as a functionary of a patriotic cult. The two aspects might even conflict, for Pompey was able to breach the walls of Jerusalem in 65 BC primarily because the stricter elements among the Jewish defenders refused to bear arms on the sabbath.

It could be said, in fact, that the power and dynamism of the Jewish faith transcended the military capacity of the Jewish people. The Jewish state might, and did, succumb to empires, but its religious expression survived, flourished and violently resisted cultural assimilation or change. Judaism was greater than the sum of its parts. Its angular will to survive was the key to recent Jewish history. Like other Middle-eastern states, Jewish Palestine had fallen to Alexander of Macedon and then had become a prize in the dynastic struggles which followed his death in 323 BC. It had eventually fallen to the Graeco-oriental monarchy of the Seleucids, but had successfully resisted Hellenization. The attempt by the Seleucid king, Antiochus Epiphanes, in 168 BC, to impose Hellenic norms on Jerusalem, and especially on the Temple, had provoked armed revolt. There was then, and there remained throughout this period, a Hellenizing party among the Jews, anxious to submit to the cultural processing-machine. But it never formed the majority, and it was to the majority that the Maccabean brothers appealed against the Seleucids, seizing Jerusalem, and cleansing the Temple of Greek impurities in 165 BC. This bitter religious war inevitably strengthened the connection in the Jewish mind between history, religion, and the future aspirations of the people and the individual, no real distinction being drawn between national destiny and a personal eternity of happiness. But the connection was variously interpreted and rival predictions and theories jostled each other in the sacred books. The oldest of the Maccabean writings in the Old Testament, opposing the revolt led by the brothers, is the Book of Daniel, which foretells the fall of empires through the agency of God, not man: 'one like a son of man' will come on the clouds of heaven, embodying the apocalyptic hope of the Jews, and accompanied by a general resurrection of the dead. By contrast, the first book of Maccabees insists that God helps those who help themselves. Its successor, by Jason of Cyrene, emphasizes the transcendent power of God and reverts to the idea of a bodily resurrection and the potency of miracles.

The Jews, then, were unanimous in seeing history as a reflection of God's activity. The past was not a series of haphazard events but unrolled remorselessly according to a divine plan which was also a blueprint and code of instructions for the future. But the blueprint was cloudy; the code uncracked; or, rather, there were rival and constantly changing systems for cracking it. And, since the Jews could not agree on how to interpret their past or how to prepare for the future, they tended to be equally divided on what they should do at present. Jewish opinion was a powerful force, but an exceptionally volatile and fragmented one. Jewish politics were the politics of division and faction. After the Maccabean revolt, the Jews had kings who were also high priests, accorded recognition by an expanding Roman empire, but rivalries of scriptural interpretation led to irreconcilable disputes over policies, successions, claims, descents. There was a strong element in the Jewish priesthood and society which regarded Rome as the least of various evils, and it was this faction which invited Pompey's intervention in 65 BC.

Granted a stable political framework, the Jewish potential was enormous. The Jews could not provide stability for themselves and the Romans did not find it easy either, chiefly because they could not decide on the constitutional status of their acquisition, a recurrent problem in their empire. Confronted with a stiff-necked subordinate people, with a strong cultural tradition of its own, they always hesitated to impose direct rule, except *in extremis*, preferring, instead, to work with a local 'strong man', personally attached to Rome, who could deal with his subjects in their own vernacular of law and custom; such a man could be rewarded (and contained) if successful, dropped and replaced if he failed. Thus Judea was placed under the new province of Syria, ruled by a governor in Antioch and local authority was entrusted to ethnarchs, recognized as 'kings' if they proved themselves sufficiently durable and ruthless. Under the Syrian province, Herod, who seized the Judean throne in 43 BC, was confirmed as 'King of the Jews' four years later, and granted Roman approval and protection. Herod was the type of man with whom Rome preferred to deal, to the point where they accepted and endorsed his arrangement for dividing his kingdom after his death among three sons, Archelaus, who got Judea, Herod Philip, and Herod Antipas. The division was not entirely successful, for in AD 6 Judea had to be placed in direct Roman custody under a succession of procurators; and in the 60s, the system as a whole blew up, in a disastrous revolt and bloody reprisal, the cycle repeating itself in the next century, until Rome, in exasperation, razed Jerusalem to the ground and rebuilt it as a pagan city. The Romans never solved the Palestine problem.

Nevertheless, especially in its early decades under Herod the Great, Rome's relationship with the Jews was fruitful. There was already a huge Jewish diaspora, especially in the great cities of the eastern Mediterranean – Alexandria, Antioch, Tarsus, Ephesus, and so forth. Rome itself had a large and rich Jewish colony. During the Herodian years, the diaspora expanded and flourished. The empire gave the Jews equality of economic opportunity and freedom of movement for goods and persons. They formed wealthy communities wherever the Romans had imposed stability. And in Herod they had a munificent and powerful patron. To many Jews he was suspect and some refused to recognize him as a Jew at all – not on account of his voluptuous and exceptionally violent private life, but because of his Hellenic attachments. But Herod was unquestionably generous to the Jews. In Jerusalem, he rebuilt the Temple on twice the scale of Solomon. This huge and magnificent enterprise was still uncompleted at Herod's death in 4 BC, and was finished in Jesus's lifetime. It was large and expensive even by the standards of Graeco-Roman architecture, and one of the great tourist sights of the empire: an impressive symbol of a fierce, living, expanding religion. Herod was equally generous to the diaspora Jews. In all the big cities he provided them with community centres and he endowed and built scores of synagogues, the new type of ecclesiastical institution, prototype of the Christian basilica, where services were held for the dispersed. In the great Roman cities, the Jewish communities gave an impression of wealth, increasing power, self-confidence and success. Within the Roman system, they were exceptionally privileged. Many of the diaspora Jews were already Roman citizens, and all Jews, since the days of Julius Caesar, who greatly admired them, enjoyed rights of association. This meant they could meet to hold religious services, community dinners and feasts, and for every kind of social and charitable purpose. The Romans recognized the strength of Jewish religious feelings by, in effect, exempting them from observance of the state religion. In place of emperor-worship, the Jews were allowed to show their respect for the state by offering sacrifices on the emperor's behalf. This was a unique concession. The wonder is that it was not more resented. But the diaspora Jews were, on the whole, admired and imitated, rather than envied. They were not in the least self-effacing. They could, when they chose, play a leading role in municipal politics, especially in Egypt, where they were perhaps over a million strong. Some had notable careers in the imperial service. Among these there were passionate admirers of the Roman system, like the historian Josephus, or the philosopher Philo. While the Jews of Judea, and still more so of semi-Jewish areas like Galilee, tended to be poor, backward, obscurantist, narrow-minded, fundamentalist, uncultured and xenophobic, the diaspora Jews were expansive, rich, cosmopolitan, well-adjusted to Roman norms and to Hellenic culture, Greek-speaking, literate and open to ideas.

They were also, in notable contrast to the Palestine Jews, anxious to spread their religion. In general, diaspora Jews were proselytizers, often passionately so. Throughout this period some Jews at least had universalist aims, and hoped that Israel would be 'the light of the gentiles'. The Greek adaptation of the Old Testament, or Septuagint, which was composed in Alexandria and was widely used in diaspora communities, has an expansionist and missionary flavour quite alien to the original. And there were in all probability catechisms

and manuals for aspiring converts, reflecting the liberal-mindedness and
large-heartedness of the diaspora Jew to the gentile. Philo, too, projected in his
philosophy the concept of a gentile mission and wrote joyfully: 'There is not a
single Greek or barbarian city, not a single people, to which the custom of
Sabbath observance has not spread, or in which the feast days, the kindling of
the lights, and many of our prohibitions about food are not heeded.' This
claim was generally true. Though it is impossible to present accurate figures, it
is clear that by the time of Christ the diaspora Jews greatly outnumbered the
settled Jews of Palestine: perhaps by as many as 4.5 million to 1 million. Those
attached in some way to the Jewish faith formed a significant proportion of the
total population of the empire and in Egypt, where they were most strongly
entrenched, one in every seven or eight inhabitants was a Jew. A large
proportion of these people were not Jewish by race. Nor were they full Jews in
the religious sense: that is, few of them were circumcized or expected to obey
the law in all its rigour. Most of them were *noachides*, or God-fearers. They
recognized and worshipped the Jewish God and they were permitted to mingle
with synagogue worshippers to learn Jewish law and customs – exactly like the
future Christian catechumens. But, unlike the catechumens, they were not
generally expected to become full Jews; they had intermediate status of
various kinds. On the other hand, they seemed to have played a full role in
Jewish social arrangements. Indeed, this was a great part of the appeal of
diaspora Judaism. The Jews, with their long and assured tradition of
monotheism, had much to offer to a world looking for a sure, single god, but
their ethics were in some ways even more attractive than their theology. The
Jews were admired for their stable family life, for their attachment to chastity
while avoiding the excesses of celibacy, for the impressive relationships they
sustained between children and parents, for the peculiar value they attached to
human life, for their abhorrence of theft and their scrupulosity in business.
But even more striking was their system of communal charity. They had
always been accustomed to remit funds to Jerusalem for the upkeep of the
Temple and the relief of the poor. During the Herodian period they also
developed, in the big diaspora cities, elaborate welfare services for the
indigent, the poor, the sick, widows and orphans, prisoners and incurables.
These arrangements were much talked about and even imitated; and, of
course, they became a leading feature of the earliest Christian communities
and a principal reason for the spread of Christianity in the cities. On the eve
of the Christian mission they produced converts to Judaism from all classes,
including the highest: Nero's empress, Poppaea, and her court circle, were
almost certainly God-fearers, and King Izates II of Adiabene on the Upper
Tigris embraced a form of Judaism with all his house. There were probably
other exalted converts. Certainly many authors, including Seneca, Tacitus,
Suetonius, Horace and Juvenal, testify to successful Jewish missionary
activity in the period before the fall of Jerusalem.

Was there a real possibility that Judaism might become the world religion in an age which longed for one? Or, to put it another way, if Christianity had not intervened, capitalized on many of the advantages of Judaism, and taken over its proselytizing role, might Judaism have continued to spread until it captured the empire? That was the way some Jews in the diaspora certainly wished to go; the same Jews, of course, who embraced Christianity when the opportunity arose. But plainly Judaism could not become a world religion without agonizing changes in its teaching and organization. It bore the marks of its tribal origins in more than a notional sense. The priests were supposed to be descendants of the tribe of Aaron, temple-attendants of Levi, kings and rulers of David, and so forth. These rules were not always observed and exact heredity was a matter of guesswork, imagination or downright fraud, but manifest breaches were always resented and frequently led to violence and schism over generations. Then, too, there was the obstacle of circumcision, on which no compromise seemed possible within the Judaic framework; and the monstrous ramifications of a legal system which had elaborated itself over many generations. The Jewish scriptures, formidable in bulk and often of impenetrable obscurity, gave employment in Palestine to a vast cottage industry of scribes and lawyers, both amateur and professional, filling whole libraries with their commentaries, enmeshing the Jewish world in a web of canon law, luxuriant with its internal conflicts and its mutual exclusions, too complex for any one mind to comprehend, bread and butter for a proliferating clergy and an infinite series of traps for the righteous. The ultimate success of a Gentile mission would depend on the scale and hardihood of the demolition work carried out on this labyrinth of Mosaic jurisprudence.

And where would the demolition stop? Must it not be extended to the Temple itself, whose very existence as the geographical pivot of the faith anchored it firmly in place and history, and thus denied its universality? The Temple, now, in Herod's version, rising triumphantly over Jerusalem, was an ocular reminder that Judaism was about Jews and their history – not about anyone else. Other gods flew in across the deserts from the East without much difficulty, jettisoning the inconvenient and embarassing accretions from their past, changing, as it were, their accents and manners as well as their names. But the God of the Jews was still alive and roaring in his Temple, demanding blood, making no attempt to conceal his racial and primitive origins. Herod's fabric was elegant, modern, sophisticated – he had, indeed, added some Hellenic decorative effects much resented by fundamentalist Jews who constantly sought to destroy them – but nothing could hide the essential business of the Temple, which was the ritual slaughter, consumption and combustion of sacrificial cattle on a gigantic scale. The place was as vast as a small city. There were literally thousands of priests, attendants, temple-soldiers and minions. To the unprepared visitor, the dignity and charity of Jewish diaspora life, the thoughtful comments and homilies of the Alexandrian synagogue, was quite lost amid the smoke of the pyres, the bellows of terrified beasts, the sluices of blood, the abattoir stench, the unconcealed and

unconcealable machinery of tribal religion inflated by modern wealth to an
industrial scale. Sophisticated Romans who knew the Judaism of the diaspora
found it hard to understand the hostility towards the Jews shown by colonial
officials who, behind a heavily-armed escort, had witnessed Jerusalem at
festival time. Diaspora Judaism, liberal and outward-minded, contained the
matrix of a universal religion, but only if it could be cut off from its
barbarous origins; and how could so thick and sinewy an umbilical cord be
severed?

In a sense, the same problem and tension could be felt within Palestine
Judaism. Jews were aware of the huge dynamic within their faith and of the
almost intolerable restraints from the past which bound and emasculated it.
Able, industrious, God-fearing, they felt bitter and frustrated by their
manifest inability to solve their political problems. There was a yawning gap
between their religious pretensions, their historical claims, their elect status,
on the one hand, and the ugly reality of poverty and subservience to the *kittim*.
Was there not something monstrously wrong with a nation which complained
bitterly of Roman taxation and misrule, yet insisted that the empire was at
least preferable to the mess the Jews would make of it themselves? To what
extent was the disjunction between Jewish aspiration and performance the
responsibility of a fallacious religious analysis and prognosis? These questions and others, constantly asked, never satisfactorily answered, kept the
Jewish world on the brink of a perpetual reformation. In some ways Judaism
was highly unstable, and it was certainly fissiparous. It had gaps. The Jews
took their theory of nature from the Greeks. There is no proper cosmology in
the Old Testament; it was not entirely clear to the Jews where exactly God was
in relation to man, in either space or time. Satan rarely made his appearance so
could not be regarded as the causal agent of sin, and only a few Jews accepted
the oriental explanation of twin worlds of good and evil, forever battling. All
Jews acknowledged angels, intermediate beings in strict hierarchical order.
But they did not really have a theory of God. God *did* things: created the
world, guided it, chose Israel, laid down the law; but it was not clear why he
existed or what his ultimate purpose and ambition was. He appeared
eccentric, sometimes motiveless. Nor was he all-powerful since, as judge, he
was bound by his own law. In a sense, then, the law was God; there was thus
no room for grace and a man could save himself only by his good works. His
relationship with God, therefore, was a purely legalistic one. This might have
been tolerable had the law been clear. But most of it was not statute but case-
law. It did not lay down instructions for daily life but was a comprehensive
collection of possible instances, with extensive discussion. A great deal of it
was concerned with the Temple itself. Some of it was archaic, irrelevant; much
of the rest was open to violent disagreement.

Quarrels over varied approaches to the law were compounded by rival
interpretations of the post-Maccabean situation. Palestine Judaism was not a
unitary religion but a collection of sects: it is possible, even from the

fragmentary sources, to ennumerate as many as twenty-four.* All the sects were monotheistic, of course, and all accepted the law in some form. But agreement went no further. The Samaritans had broken the connection with the Temple and had their own sanctuary on Mount Gerizim; many would not allow them to be Jews at all. On the other hand, the Essenes did not recognize the Temple either and they were agreed to be one of the purest and strictest sects. There was no ruling orthodoxy: that is, hieratic power was not identified with the prevailing tendency. The high priesthood, under the procuratorship, was in the hands of Sadducee aristocrats, who supported and upheld the Roman occupation. They were rich, conservative, linked among themselves by complex family alliances, had large estates and saw Roman rule underpinning all these things more securely than a national kingship. We do not know much about their teaching, since Judaism achieved a high degree of Pharisaic unity after the destruction of the Temple in 70 AD, and Sadducee traditions were not preserved. But they do not seem to have believed in life after death or the intervention of providence. Their religion was defective and in some respects quite impracticable, since they interpreted the law literally without any allowance for historical change, so they could have no popular following. They were, in fact, a class of collaborators, ruling the colony through the High Council of Jerusalem, which sat on the Temple Mount, and was referred to as the Sanhedrin. The Romans upheld the powers of the Council and when necessary enforced Jewish cult rules, such as the exclusion of Gentiles from the Temple. They addressed their official letters to the 'rulers, senate and people of the Jerusalemites', thus giving the Sanhedrin the status of an elective municipality in a major city. In fact, throughout this period it was little more than the family circle of Annas, the high priest, who was appointed by the procurator and removable at will.

True, its seventy members, priests, elders and scribes, included a good many Pharisees, who can be described as the middle-class popular party. They were there for convenience, and of necessity, for the overwhelming majority of lawyers were Pharisees. But the two factions disagreed on virtually every issue; in fact the prosecution of Christ is one of the few occasions on which Sadducees and Pharisees are recorded as having worked together. There were many schools among the Pharisees, but most held no brief for the Romans; they were, in varying degrees, nationalists, and some were Zealots, prepared to rise with violence when the scriptures seemed to command it. Josephus describes them as 'a party of Jews who seem to be more religious than the others, and explain the laws with more minute care'. He adds that they used

* Jesus's mission took place during a period of intense flux and variety in the Jewish world, expressed, for instance, in rival methods of interpreting the scriptures. Thus Philo's exegesis was allegorical, the Sadducees' literal, the Pharisees' hermeneutic and expository; the *Jubilees* and other works followed a narrative method, and in the *Thanksgiving Hymns* of the Qumran the method is imitative. Jesus's method was indirect, but it may be that he was much influenced by liberal Pharaseeism. For Jesus's place in the spectrum of early first-century Jewish religious controversy, see John Bowker, *Targums and Rabbinical Literature* (Cambridge, 1969), and his *Jesus and the Pharisees* (Cambridge, 1973).

tradition to interpret scripture and the laws in a sensible manner. They were in fact working canon lawyers and casuists. They rejected the strict and defeatist immobility of the Sadducees and beavered away with great learning and ingenuity to make observance of the law possible in a rapidly changing society. Without them the Judaic system could not be made to work at all. Of course the casuistic effort often placed them in an unfavourable light, but they could also be presented as empiricists, serious but friendly and human. When Jesus said that the sabbath was made for man, not man for the sabbath, he was quoting a Pharisaic formula; and when he announced his 'great commandment' he was giving a heightened version of a saying taught by one of the liberal Pharisee rabbis, Hillel. The Pharisees were many and ubiquitous (not least in the diaspora); their activities were almost coextensive with the Jewish nation as a whole. Anyone operating among the Jews had to take up a posture towards them. And in some ways their teaching was satisfactory. They were quite clear there was life after death. The righteous would rise again. The wicked would be eternally punished. But wickedness, of course, was determined by infractions of the law, a burden the Pharisees could (up to a point) ease, explain and justify but never remove. Even God, it seemed, could not remove the law. Thus life was a series of daily court-cases, settled on technicalities, whose ethical quality was not improved by the fact that anything *not* specifically forbidden by the law was licit.

Even so, there were sects in Jewish society who regarded the ruling priestly groups in Jerusalem as hopelessly corrupt and compromised, and who sought by direct action to restore the theocratic state in all its purity. One such had formed itself, from among descendants of the high-priest Zadoc, and from the priestly tribe of Aaron, around the middle of the second century BC. Their leader was an unidentified Temple official referred to as the Teacher of Righteousness, and their chief grievance was the appointment of a high priest from outside the priestly tribes. Having failed to win their point they left the Temple and set up an alternative and purified focus of worship in the desert near the Dead Sea. The Essene sect, as it was called, had existed for about 150 years by the time of Jesus's birth and was an important and respected movement in Judaism. Josephus says that there were about 4,000 Essenes (as opposed to 6,000 Pharisees); there were groups of them in all Jewish towns, and various desert settlements or camps in Syria and Egypt, as well as in Palestine. But their chief centre, where about 200 of them lived, was at Qumran.

It is one of the ironies of history that the Essenes, in their concern for the purity of the Temple, stumbled on a theological concept which made the Temple no longer significant as a physical and geographic fact, and thus opened the way to the universalist principle. The founders of the Essenes, as priests, were a closed hereditary group, born not made: their holiness was directly derived from the Temple, since Yahweh himself dwelt there, with his presence, or *shekinah*, in the Holy of Holies, from whence holiness spread in concentric circles with diminishing intensity. When they moved to Qumran, they took enormous pains to preserve the purity of their status and devotions. Indeed they seemed to have hoped that, by presenting themselves as a super-pure elect within an elect, they could eventually strike a new covenant with God. In the meantime they observed the Temple laws with extra care. We know their rules from the scrolls which have been recovered from caves near the Dead Sea; and their efforts to achieve the maximum of ritual purity by endless lustrations are reflected in the elaborate plumbing arrangements which have been identified at the Qumran site. Like the Temple priests, only more so, the Essene functionaries had to wear special garments, which were constantly changed and washed; they had to be careful not to touch anything polluted, and to take ceremonial baths. They had to be without physical blemish, following Leviticus: 'For no one who has a blemish shall draw near, a man blind or lame or one who has a mutilated face or a limb too long. . . .' Those described as weak or blemished occupied inferior roles. The Qumran priests performed blessings and cursings, and read out proclamations, in exactly the same way as the Temple priests.

The Qumran monastery, in fact, was an alternative Temple, set up to carry on its essential function until the real one should be purified and restored. But what began as a temporary arrangement acquired in course of time a new institutional significance. The mere act of dislocation to the desert implied that the presence of God was no longer bound to the physical Temple in Jerusalem. What 'attracted' God was, rather, the existence and worship of the pure Israel represented by the undefiled community of Essenes. Indeed, there could be 'Temples' wherever Essenes were gathered together, provided they were scrupulous in their purification ceremonies. Thus what constituted the Temple was no longer geography and stone, but the very existence of the community: the Temple had become spiritualized, a symbol, a 'human Temple' of men. The Temple is not the building, but the worshippers, that is, the Church. Once this concept is married to the quite different, but contemporary, concept of the Pharisee synagogue, that is, a building which may be sited anywhere in the world where the faithful gather to worship and hear scripture explained, then we are very close to the primitive idea of the Christian community. Indeed, the new Qumran concept is strongly reflected in Paul: 'For we are the Temple of the living God . . . Since we have these promises, beloved, let us cleanse ourselves from every defilement of body and spirit, and make holiness perfect in the fear of God' (2 Cor. 6:16ff). Or again, to the congregation at Corinth: 'Do you not know that you are God's Temple, and that God's spirit dwells in you? If anyone destroys God's Temple, God will destroy him. For God's Temple is holy, and that [temple] you are.' In his letter to the Ephesians, Paul writes of the heavenly edifice built on the foundations of the apostles and the prophets, Christ Jesus being the chief corner-stone, and later Christian writers complete the image, first found in Qumran texts; thus, 1 Pet. 2:3–6: 'Come to him, to that living stone, rejected of men but in God's sight chosen and precious; and like living stones be yourselves built up into a spiritual house, to be a holy priesthood, to offer spiritual sacrifices acceptable to God through Jesus Christ.'

By this last stage, of course, the community has replaced not only the Temple but the priesthood and their sacrifices. The Essenes travelled only a very limited way down this decisive road to universalism. In many ways they were still dominated by the idea of the real, physical Temple and its actual sacrifices of animal flesh. But they threw out another concept which was later used to provide an escape from the old sacrificial idea. From Temple practice, the Essenes at Qumran and elsewhere developed the regular practice of a sacral meal of bread and wine, which at Qumran took place in the main meeting-hall, or Hall of the Covenant, of the monastery. It was preceded by purification rites, special robes were worn, and the meal was presided over by a priest who blessed the elements and was the first to eat and drink them. The meal was an anticipation, it seems, of the perfect ritual in the heavenly Temple. Thus we have here the concept of a symbolic sacrifice, later applied by and to Jesus, which eventually allowed the Christians to break away completely from the Temple cult and its daily sacrifices and so free themselves from Jewish history and Palestine geography.

Nevertheless, it is quite wrong to present the Essene cult as Christianity without Jesus. Among other Jewish sects, the Temple was being spiritualized, if much more slowly. Between the Maccabean period and the destruction of the Temple in AD 70, the law was gradually displacing the Temple as the central focus of religion; the influence of the priests was diminishing and the scribes, chiefly Pharisees, were emerging as popular leaders, preparing the way for the age of the rabbis. The earliest Christians had greater difficulty than the Essenes in freeing themselves from the Temple, as we shall see. Moreover, though it is possible to isolate certain Essene ideas which were later Christianized, many of their other concepts were very different. In some ways they were a backward and obscurantist group, rigid, bigoted, and liable to express their convictions in bloodshed and hatred. They had a communal life and shared their goods, at any rate in their monastic camps, but like many other poor, humble and convinced believers, they were grotesquely and theoretically intolerant. Their literature includes some striking and edifying hymns, but it centres round far more menacing documents, which are in effect disciplinary and training manuals, culminating in an actual war-plan, based on Roman military methods, in which Essene priests are to lead a purified and reinvigorated Israel to a final victory. The Essenes were, in fact, members of an extremist apocalyptic-eschatological sect, who expected their triumph to come soon. Their interpretation of the events which created their Qumran mission, of the whole of Jewish history, and their very careful and selective exegesis of the scriptures, is essentially violent, militaristic and racial. Their ideas are marked by the narrowest kind of exclusiveness. The individual is nothing; the pure community (and a community by birth and race) is all.

Jerusalem and its wicked priests are the enemies; but then, so are all the Gentiles. In due course the Son of Light, led by the Essenes, will fight a war against the Sons of Darkness, who have compromised with the non-elect world; after the battle has been won, following the war-plan, a king will be restored to the throne and the purified Israel will live in the manner of Zadok. All the lucky ones, who will live for ever, will be Israelite by birth. The bad Jews and the Gentiles will all be dead. That is the plan for human history, devised by God, and shortly to be enacted.

The Essenes had no matrix for a world-religion; far from it. Rather their monastery and their other cells, were incubators for extremists, Zealots, men of violence and *enragés*. The excavations at Qumran show that the monastery became a centre of resistance during the war of AD 66–70, and was stormed and burned by the Roman army. This annihilation marked the end of the Essenes as a separate sect – inevitably so, since they were exploring a stream of Jewish religious and political thought which led nowhere but to destruction. But the Essene monasteries, cells and city-groups were schools of more than Zealots. Their importance in the history of Christianity lies in the fact that they provided experimental centres – religious universities, indeed – which lay outside the mainstream of Jewish teaching as practised in Jerusalem. In their ultra-conformity, they were essentially nonconformist and antinomial. A man might enter an Essene community a pious, conformist Jew and emerge a Zealot; or he might go there for Zealous reasons and become a hermit. Or he might produce entirely novel ideas, or seize upon some aspect of Essene teaching and practice and develop it in a radically new direction. Thus the Essene movement was a powerful contribution to the fundamental instability of Judaism during this period. And the sense of crisis was deepening. It entered an acute phase after Judea was directly annexed by the Roman state and thus made liable to Roman fiscal procedures. These proved to be much less popular than the pro-Roman party had anticipated; it has been calculated that in first century Palestine, Roman and Jewish taxes together may have reached as much as 25 per cent (non-progressive) of incomes, in an economy which in some respects and in some areas was not far above the subsistence level.

Palestine was thus soaked in politico-religious apocalypticism. Irredentist politics and religious extremism were inextricably mixed. All Palestinian Jews to some extent believed in a Messianic solution. There were, it is true, many different doctrines of the Messiah but the variations were matters of detail and all rested on the unitary belief that foreign oppressors would be driven out and God alone would rule Israel. Thus a man who criticized the Romans was making a religious statement and a man who insisted on the highest degree of ritual purity was playing politics. In the opening decades of the first century AD the example of the Essenes led to the appearance of a number of baptist movements in the Jordan Valley. The whole area, from the Lake of Genasseret down to the Dead Sea itself was alive with holy eccentrics. Many had been to Qumran, and there imbibed the prevailing obsession with ritual purity and the use of holy water as a therapy and cleansing process. It is, in fact, significant that Philo calls the Essene *theraputae*: to ordinary observers it was the most obvious and striking aspect of their teaching. We can be almost certain that John the Baptist was, or had been, an Essene monk. He was recruiting not so much for the monastery but for the broader movement of the élite within the élite, carrying the cleansing and purifying process into the world outside, and thus hastening the apocalyptic moment when the war against the Sons of Darkness would begin.

The Baptist is thus the link between the general reformist and noncon-formist movement in Judaism and Jesus himself. Unfortunately, in terms of actual historical knowledge, he is a very weak link. In some ways he is a completely mysterious figure. His function, in the history of Christianity, was to attach elements of the Essene teaching to a consistent view of Jewish eschatology. John was an impatient man, as well as a wild-looking one: the Messiah was not merely coming – he was here! The apocalypse was rolling fast towards the people, so now was the time to repent and prepare. And then, in due course, Jesus appeared and was identified. This is the first glimpse, admittedly a vivid one, we get of John. There is one other glimpse, equally vivid, some years later, when he fell foul of Herod Antipas and lost his head. The rest is darkness. The second most important person in the history of Christianity remains enigmatic. Yet the synoptic gospels, and still more the Gospel according to John, emphasize the importance of the Baptist in the mission of Jesus. He is the operative agent who sets the whole thing in motion. The three synoptic writers, and the editor of John's gospel, working within a different stream of knowledge, are clearly using very powerful oral traditions, or even written documents, dealing specifically with the Baptist's work. Somewhere, behind our sources, or behind the sources of our sources, there was once the whole story of the Baptist as related by a follower or lieutenant. But the earliest Christian historians selected only what they regarded as strictly relevant to their purpose, and now the rest is irrecoverably lost. Our only non-Christian source, Josephus, shows that John was at one time an Essene. His account of John's teaching, such as it is, accords closely with the Qumran Manual of Discipline; and of course his actual appearance is directly related to Essene prophecies, which it resembles in important details, as did his prophecies and sayings. But John was also moving away from Essene concepts, in the direction of what became Christianity. His baptism ceremony, unlike the repeated bathing-rites of the Essenes, is a once and for all affair (but he was not unique in this). Secondly, John thought God would intervene, admittedly in wrathful mood, without the assistance of the Essene army and its war-plan. John was not militaristic. Most important of all, he had broken away from the absolute exclusiveness of the Essenes, teaching that God's special favours were to be offered to the entire Jewish people, not just to the sect. John was not yet a universalist, but he was moving in that direction. He was, in short, a carrier, bringing certain key Essene doctrines out of their narrow, bellicose, racist and sectarian framework, and proclaiming them in a wider world.

The logic of this analysis, then, is that the Baptist was in a sense Jesus's teacher, and that the pupil improved on, expanded and transformed his master's ideas. But it is at this point that our evidence breaks down. If anything, it points in another direction. John did not claim to teach the Messiah, merely to identify him; indeed, he specifically rejected any master-pupil relationship. The fact that Jesus was baptized by John does not imply any inferiority, submission or acknowledgement of higher wisdom. The trouble is that we do not know precisely what John taught. We do not know his history or education. We do not even know whether he had a complete theology or cosmology of his own, whether his eschatology was limited to the crude Messianism reflected in the gospels, or, as seems more likely, was elaborate and sophisticated. We do not even know his concept of Jesus's status: it was obviously high, but how high – the key question? And anyway, how close were their contacts? How well did they know each other? How much, if anything, did either teach each other? Why did the Baptist make secret inquiries about Jesus's mission and receive mysterious replies? The exotic story of the Baptist's end, shorn of its romantic details, places him in a highly political posture and it is interesting that Herod Antipas did not like Jesus either. Was there, then, a political connection between these two religious innovators?

Our ignorance of the Baptist inevitably clouds our view of the uniqueness of Jesus. Indeed, the historical problem of the Baptist, baffling as it is, serves merely as an introduction to the much greater problem of Jesus. There can, at least, be absolutely no doubt about his historical existence. Unfortunately, the *Antiquities* of Josephus (published about AD 93), so useful about other related topics, is virtually silent on the point. Josephus was a Hellenized Jew, a Romanophile, indeed a Roman general and historian whose work received imperial subsidies. The manuscript chain coming down to us inevitably passed through Christian control. Since Josephus was strongly opposed to Jewish irredentism, or any other sectarian movement which gave trouble to the authorities, he clearly adopted an anti-Christian posture. But this has been tampered with. Thus, he mentions the judicial murder of James by the high priest Ananias in AD 62, and calls James the brother 'of Jesus, the so-called Christ', in a way to suggest that he has already given an account of Jesus and his mission. But what has actually come down to us is a passage which describes Jesus as a wise man, a lover of truth, much beloved by his followers; it accepts his miracles and resurrection and hints strongly at his divinity. The passage is plainly a non-too-ingenious Christian invention and what Josephus actually wrote has gone. Attempts to reconstruct it have not so far won general acceptance. The inference from Josephus is that Jesus was a Jewish sectarian with messianic claims and a substantial following which had survived his extinction: a nuisance to the empire, in fact. This view is reflected

in other non-Christian references, which are few but clearly confirm Jesus's
historicity. Tacitus, in his *Annals*, writing of the fire of Rome in 64, refers to
'the detestable superstition' of Christianity, to 'Christus, the founder of this
sect', and to his crucifixion 'in the reign of Tiberius by the Procurator Pontius
Pilate' – though it is not clear whether he got this last from Christian or official
sources. Pliny the Younger, writing in 112, says the sect 'sang a hymn to Christ
as a God', and refused to curse Christ; only renegades were willing to do so.
The earliest reference, by Suetonius, which implies that Christians were
known at Rome even in the reign of Claudius, AD 41–54, is unfortunately
garbled: he writes of Jews being expelled from Rome because 'they were
constantly rioting at the instigation of Chrestus'. Did he think 'Chrestus' was
still alive at the time? Anyway, he, and every other source referring to earliest
Christianity, treat Jesus Christ as an actual, historical person.

When we turn to the earliest Christian sources, we enter a terrifying
jungle of scholarly contradictions. All were writing evangelism or theology
rather than history, even when, like Luke in his gospel, they assume the
literary manners of a historian and seek to anchor the events of Jesus's life in
secular chronology. Moreover, all the documents have a long pre-history
before they reached written form. Their evaluation was a source of acute
puzzlement to thoughtful Christians even in the earliest decades of the second
century and probably before. Indeed, the puzzles began as soon as any
Christian had access to more than one account or source, written or oral. This
was happening increasingly by the closing decades of the first century, for oral
accounts continued to circulate long after the earliest written gospels
appeared in the two decades 60–80, and were attaining written form well into
the second century. The canonical documents (let alone those later judged
apochryphal) thus overlap with the earliest writings of the Church Fathers.
They are products of the early Church and they are tainted in the sense that
they reflect ecclesiastical controversy as well as evangelistic motivation, the
difficulties of reducing oral descriptions of mysterious concepts to writing,
and a variety of linguistic traps. The four gospels declared canonical, for
instance, were circulated, but not necessarily first written, in colloquial Greek;
but Matthew was almost certainly translated from Hebrew, and all four were
either *thought* in Aramaic, or transcriptions from tales which were Aramaic in
original circulation, yet which drew on Hebrew quotations and, to a lesser
extent, on Hellenic or Hellenized concepts. The possibilities for misunderstanding are infinite. Moreover, we cannot assume that the gospels we have
reflect the earliest oral traditions. The prologue to Luke makes it clear that
they are based on earlier written accounts, themselves derived from the words
of eye-witnesses: Luke is thus the third or possibly even fourth link along a
chain stretching back two generations. The first Christian to comment on the
problem was Papias, Bishop of Hierapolis, who flourished in the first decades
of the second century. The fourth-century historian Bishop Eusebius of
Caesarea, through whose compilations Papias survives at all, remarks

irritably: 'Clearly he was very weak of intellect.' Yet on this subject, at least, he makes sense: '. . . if ever any man came who had been a follower of the elders, I would inquire about the sayings of the elders; what Andrew said, or Peter, or Philip, or Thomas or James, or John or Matthew, or any other of the Lord's disciples; and what Aristion says and John the Elder, who are disciples of the Lord. For I did not consider I got so much profit from the contents of books as from the utterances of a living and abiding voice.' By Papias's day, indeed, knowledge of the authorship of the canonical gospels, and the manner in which they were composed, is already confused; what he has to say about Mark and Matthew is shaky tradition. But he gives us a useful hint that at that stage the oral chain, less full of pitfalls, was still preferable to the written one. By the time Irenaeus, Bishop of Lyons, wrote at the end of the second century, the oral tradition has gone for good. He has to put his trust in the canonical writing and does so in full confidence; but what he says about their authorship and emergence is, in part at least, manifest nonsense. In short, by the end of the second century, a well-informed ecclesiastic like Irenaeus, professionally engaged in putting down heresy and establishing the truth, knew no more about the origins of the gospels than we do; rather less, in fact.

This is a depressing qualification we must bear constantly in mind: the sheer ignorance of even those figures quite close in time to Jesus. The earliest Christian document is Paul's first Epistle to the Thessalonians, which can plausibly be dated to about AD 51. Paul was writing in the fifties and early sixties; his authentic epistles (Romans, 1 and 2 Corinthians, Galatians, Philippians, 1 Thessalonians and Philemon) are in an evidential sense straightforward written documents; there is no oral tradition behind them and the editing process is minimal – indeed some of them may have been circulated or 'published' in edited form even during Paul's lifetime. Paul is the first witness to Jesus, the start of any historical inquiry. He is the writer who gets closest to the actual Messiah. But there is nevertheless an unbridgeable gap of several years between Jesus's death (*circa* AD 30–33) and Paul's first contacts with the Christian circle, for though Paul was in Jerusalem at the time of Stephen's death in 36, he did not return, as a Christian, until two years later. This chronological gap was quite adequate to cloud everything connected with the historical Jesus, as men, dazzled by the fact of the Resurrection, thought back from this to the Jesus they had known and reconstructed him in their minds. Paul got there too late in the day; the well of truth had already been muddied. We probably know more about the Jesus of history than he did, despite the intervals of nearly 2,000 years. This is one chief reason why Paul, who was obsessed by truth, tells us so little about Jesus the man. He says only that he was a Jew, born under the law, of Davidic descent, was betrayed, crucified, buried and rose again. He rationalizes his silence and, as it were, defends his ignorance (or uncertainty about the true facts) by remarking (2 Cor. 5:16): 'With us, therefore, worldly standards have ceased to count in our estimate of any man; even if once they counted in our understanding of Christ, they do so now no longer.' He cannot present himself as a disciple of the historical Jesus. On the contrary, he was commissioned apostle by the risen Lord. His Jesus is the son of God, pre-existent and supernatural, who accepted the form of a 'servant' so that he could identify himself as man and be available for his sacrificial role. The only details of Jesus's life which matter, for Paul's strictly theological purposes, are the proof of manhood and the crucifixion. He also has to show, and he does so in impressive detail, that Christ rose again and appeared to many people, including himself. Here Paul becomes a historian and an eyewitness: he is our prime documentary proof that the very earliest Christians believed Christ rose from the dead and walked the earth.

Paul's authentic epistles, therefore, are thus strict primary sources. Of course they do not go very far. He probably had no Christian documents, though primitive Christian writings were circulating towards the end of his life. Where he does deal with events, however, we get the picture direct, as he saw it, heard it or believed it; there is no distorting editorial lens and no generational interval, erosive of truth, between oral and written composition. It is a different matter with the canonical gospels. Though presented as historical narratives, their origins are complex and their reliability variable. Their starting-point, in all probability, were Jesus's efforts to train his followers as teachers by ordering them to learn by heart key passages in his sermons. This process, interrupted by his death, was resumed with intensity after his resurrection and now centred round the narrative of his passion, which was learnt in various polished forms and used not only as a continuous evangelical story but as the centrepiece of the earliest liturgical services. The second major element was what we call the Sermon on the Mount, or 'great sermon', which also seems to have achieved a definite form at a very early stage, and was probably memorized by disciples while Jesus was still engaged in his ministry. At some stage individual sayings of Jesus were written down, and later gathered into groups, or into a whole book. Papias refers to a 'book of oracles' which was probably such a collection of Jesus's words, and forms (after Paul's epistles) the earliest Christian manuscript. Then, in the decade of the sixties, the progressive elimination of the first generation of Christians, the actual eye-witnesses, followed by persecution and war, which caused the dispersal of the Jerusalem circle, provided an urgent incentive to record Jesus's teaching in imperishable shape. Mark, from the circle of Peter, first created the gospel as a literary form. From a remark by Papias we deduce that he accompanied Peter on mission, towards the end of his life, giving simultaneous translation of Peter's Aramaic sermons in colloquial Greek. His gospel, written soon after Peter's death, is a major effort to order and rationalize a number of difficult elements into a chronological narrative which marries event and theology and harmonizes the two with scriptural prophecy. The reflections in it of oral traditions – deliberate repetitions and symmetrical arrangements – and of the patterns of popular story-telling are very strong. In presenting his material in written form he had, it is true, some Greek models, and he must have been influenced by the literary doctrines of Aristotle's *Poetics*. All the same, he was trying to do something which had never been done before and his problems were not only those of an unpractised writer but also those of an amateur theologian trying to transmit a complex message which he himself had received from the far from lucid Peter. Hence he often does not attempt to solve the problems of comprehensibility and falls back on a constant use of a 'secrecy motive'. He stresses that the apostles and disciples did not always understand what Jesus was trying to do; he implies that the full meaning of his person and message was not understood during his ministry, though some followers grasped more than others, and indeed that not all of Jesus's teaching was intended for the public. Mark's gospel has thus been called a book of secret epiphanies, mysterious glimpses of a manifestation of divinity, rather than a coherent explanation of the phenomenon of Jesus Christ. The text was much altered and interpolated during the earliest period, for both good and bad reasons, and was a favourite source-book for primitive heresiarchs to justify their divergencies.

Matthew and Luke, quite independently, produced their own narratives. They evidently found Mark unsatisfactory, both in general and from the point of view of their own particular interests – Luke belonged to the school of Paul's gentile mission, and Matthew represented the rump of the Jewish Jerusalem Church after the murder of James and the departure of Peter. Each had Mark to work from, though probably in a carelessly copied form; and they also had another source, called by modern scholars 'Q', which may be the 'oracles' which Papias mentioned, but is really nothing more than an academic device to designate non-Marcan materials common to both Luke and Matthew. All these synoptic gospels, moreover, emerged from a miasma of oral tradition and counter-tradition; and it is possible that Mark's Greek gospel was itself derived from an earlier version of Matthew written in Hebrew – this would accord with the traditional view in the early Church that Matthew was the first of the synoptics, a view still held by some Roman Catholic scholars. The gospel attributed to John, on the other hand, has no demonstrable connection with the synoptics, though it also derives, naturally, from the same oral miasma. It is, however, more of a theological treatise than a historical narrative and shows strong connections both with the Pauline epistles and with the Jewish apocalyptic tradition. It has been edited, as its closing words make clear; and there is evidence of heavy tampering in the earliest manuscripts – obvious glosses, and so forth – as well as sheer muddle. Thus chapter 5 should follow chapter 6, and the final chapter, 21, is clearly an addition.

These imperfections add to the ordinary difficulties of evaluation. All four gospels, being literary documents some 1,900 years old, suffer from the problems created by handwritten transmissions. For most of the history of Christianity, scholars and theologians have had to work from corrupt late manuscripts (most of them without realizing the dangers). Few medieval writers made any effort, when copying, to find ancient models; this was primarily a Renaissance concern. Even so, Erasmus's Greek New Testament (1516) and Robert Etienne's (1551) came from Greek medieval manuscripts which contained innumerable accumulated errors. Earlier manuscripts emerged only gradually. In 1581 Theodore Beza found the sixth-century Graeco-Latin text known as the Codex Bezae; in 1628, a fifth-century codex, the Alexandrinus, containing the whole Bible, was transferred to western Europe; this was followed by an incomplete fifth-century codex, the Ephraemi Rescriptus, and, more important, by the nineteenth-century discoveries of two fourth-century codices, the Vaticanus and the Sinaiticus. This does not take us further back than the days of Jerome and Augustine, still leaving a huge 300-year gap. Unfortunately, most of the earliest manuscripts were not in codex form, that is, parchment bound in leather volumes, but were in highly perishable papyrus. Fragments survive only in the dry climate of Egypt: there, in recent years, ancient rubbish dumps have yielded portions from the third, and even a few from the second century. The earliest of all, only two inches square, but containing verses from the eighteenth chapter of John on both sides, has been dated to the early second century. No first-century fragment has yet been found. These early versions of New Testament texts can be supplemented by biblical quotations from the earliest manuscripts of the patristic writings, some dating from the second century, and from church lectionaries which, though late themselves, reflect very early texts. Altogether there are about 4,700 relevant manuscripts, and at least 100,000 quotations or allusions in the early fathers.

Analysing this mass of evidence in the search for the perfect text is probably self-defeating. Beyond a certain point, scholarship tends to raise as many problems as it solves; thus, even if substantial first-century fragments were discovered, it is feared they would enlarge, rather than reduce, the areas of uncertainty. Modern aids, such as computers, are of only limited assistance. Some alterations can be identified with reasonable certitude. Thus the end of Mark (16:9–20) is not authentic. Again, the very impressive story of the woman taken in adultery, which seems to float without anchor in the gospel of John, does not occur in any manuscript before the end of the fourth century. Scholars have discovered one or two flagrant examples of the early Church 'back-dating' theological concepts by tampering with New Testament passages. Thus, the Trinitarian texts in the first Epistle of John, which make explicit what other texts merely hint at, originally read simply: 'There are three which bear witness, the spirit and the water and the blood, and the three are one.' This was altered in the fourth century to read: 'There are three which bear witness on earth, the spirit and the water and the blood, and these three are one in Christ Jesus; and there are three who bear witness in heaven, the Father, the Word and the Spirit, and these three are one.'

Such manifest fabrications should not be regarded as deliberate fraud, done with intent to deceive, and to obfuscate the truth. They occur throughout the history of Christianity, up to the Renaissance and even beyond, and they spring from a concept of the nature of documentary proof which is alien to us. Thus, an earnest scribe, believing wholeheartedly that the doctrine of the Trinity was true, thought it merely an accident or oversight that it was not made explicit in 1 John, and therefore saw it as his duty to remedy the matter. He was merely doing constructive work in the cause of truth! Where these accretions occur late enough, they are easily identified and removed by modern scholars. The earlier they were inserted, the more difficult it is to detect them. And, of course, beyond a certain point, which occurs early in the second century, there is no longer any possibility of cleaning up the text. Moreover, even if we were to have the perfect and original texts of the gospels, they would not protect us from the efforts to create 'constructive truth' made by the evangelists themselves, and their oral sources. These are particularly obvious when the evangelists are engaged in aligning or shaping events in Jesus's life to fit Old Testament prophecies: there, the temptation to create, and so to falsify, is obvious, and we are on our guard. We are also fortunate to have, even within the canon, four gospel narratives drawn from a variety of sources, whose blatant conflicts again indicate dubious areas of truth. The most obvious concern Jesus's background: thus his Davidian descent, necessary for his role, is traced through Joseph, though this is incompatible with the theory or fact of the virgin birth. Again, there are important conflicts about Jesus's movements during his mission, especially over his visit or visits to Jerusalem, and the various accounts of the Last Supper cannot easily be reconciled.

None of this would matter very much if the central doctrine and teaching of Jesus emerged strongly, consistently and coherently from all the canonical sources. This, indeed, is what we should expect to happen, since the core of the gospel – the fact of his death and resurrection, and what he said in reference to them – was the first to assume the form of regular oral narrative. Yet even in these central areas there are major obscurities and apparent contradictions. And if we reduce our knowledge of Jesus to points where there is unanimity, plausibility and an absence of objections, we are left with a phenomenon almost devoid of significance. This 'residual' Jesus told stories, uttered various wise sayings, was executed in circumstances which are not clear, and was then commemorated in a ceremony by his followers. Such a version is incredible because it does not explain the rise of Christianity. And in order to explain Christianity we have to postulate an extraordinary Christ who did extraordinary things. We have to think back from a collective phenomenon to its agent. Men and women began frantically and frenetically to preach Jesus's gospel because they believed he had come back to them from the dead and given them the authority and the power to do so. Naturally, their evangelical efforts were imperfect, for, despite Jesus's instructions, they could not always remember his teachings accurately or coherently and they were not trained divines, or orators, or indeed educated people. But, even more important, the teaching he had given them was itself intrinsically difficult both to understand and convey. Both these factors left their mark on the gospels and explain their imperfections, for the gospels were a transcribed version of what the first and second generation of Christians believed and taught.

In short, we must dismiss any idea of Jesus being a simple figure. His actions and motives were complex and he taught something which was hard to grasp. The religious background from which he sprang was itself unusually complicated. The Hellenist world was moving towards monotheism but on a dualistic basis which postulated rival forces of good and evil. The Judaic world was also going through a religious crisis provoked by the political situation. All kinds of solutions were being proposed, but each was fatally anchored in some particularism of time or place or race. How could the intentions of God be conveyed so as to be understood by all men, and for all time? Equally, how could any solution contain elements meaningful for all types and temperaments of men, as well as all races and generations: the activist, the militant, the doctrinaire, the ascetic, the obedient, the passive, the angular, the scholar, and the simple-hearted? How could it impart both a sense of urgency and immediacy, and at the same time be valid for all eternity? How could it bring about, in men's minds, a confrontation with God which was both public and collective, and individual and intimate? How could it combine a code of ethics within a framework of strict justice and a promise of unprecedented generosity? These were only a few of the evangelical problems confronting Jesus. Moreover, he had to resolve them within a preordained series of historical events which could be adumbrated but not forecast and whose necessary enactment would terminate his mission.

The teaching of Jesus is therefore more a series of glimpses, or matrices, a collection of insights, rather than a code of doctrine. It invites comment, interpretation, elaboration and constructive argument, and is the starting point for rival, though compatible, lines of inquiry. It is not a summa theologica, or indeed ethica, but the basis from which an endless series of summae can be assembled. It inaugurates a religion of dialogue, exploration and experiment. Its radical elements are balanced by conservative qualifications, there is a constant mixture of legalism and antinomianism, and the emphasis repeatedly switches from rigour and militancy to acquiescence and the acceptance of suffering. Some of this variety reflects the genuine bewilderment of the disciples, and the confusion of the evangelical editors to whom their memories descended. But a great deal is essentially part of Jesus's universalist posture: the wonder is that the personality behind the mission is in no way fragmented but is always integrated and true to character. Jesus contrives to be all things to all men while remaining faithful to himself.

This complex and delicate operation was conducted against a politico-religious background full of perils and traps. Jesus had a new doctrine to deliver – salvation through love, sacrifice and faith – but to some extent he had to present it in the guise of a reformation of the old. He was preaching to Jews, introducing new concepts through traditional Jewish forms. He was anxious to carry the orthodox with him, without compromising his universalism. He confronted the establishment on their own territory, while including all the outcast elements in his mission; thus he had to carry on the process of disassociation from the Temple and the law while trying to avoid accusations of blasphemy. Then, too, there was the revelation of his own position. This had to be a gradual process. It was always to some extent ambiguous. He radiated authority – it was, from the very start, the most conspicuous thing about him. But of what kind? He was anxious to show that he was not a priest-general, performing a military role against a foreign oppressor. He was not the Messiah in *that* sense. On the other hand, he was not just the articulator of suffering and sacrifice: he had come to found a new kind of kingdom and to bring a message of joy and hope. How to convey that his triumph had to be achieved through his death? It was not an idea which appealed to the ancient world; or any world.

Then, too, there was the central paradox that the mission had to be vindicated by its failure. A great many people found Jesus impossible to accept or follow. He was repudiated by his family, at least for a time. His native district did not accept him. There were certain towns where his teaching made no impact. In some places he could not work miracles. In others they caused little stir or were soon forgotten. He made many enemies and at all times there were a large number of people who ridiculed his claims and simply brushed aside his religious ideas. He could assemble a crowd of supporters, but it was always just as easy to collect a mob against him. Once he began to operate openly in the Temple area he became a marked man for both Roman and Jewish authorities, and an object of suspicion. His refusal to make his claims explicit and unambiguous was resented, and not only by his enemies. His followers were never wholly in his confidence and some of them had mixed feelings from time to time about the whole enterprise. What had they involved themselves in? There is a hint that Judas's betrayal may have been motivated less by greed – an easy and unconvincing apostolic smear – than by shock at the sudden fear he might be serving an enemy of religion.

By the time of his trial and passion Jesus had succeeded in uniting an improbable, indeed unprecedented, coalition against him: the Roman authorities, the Sadducees, the Pharisees, even Herod Antipas. And in destroying him, this unnatural combination appears to have acted with a great measure of popular approval. What conclusions can we draw from this? The actual execution was carried out by Romans under Roman law. Crucifixion was the most degrading form of capital punishment, reserved for rebels, mutinous slaves and other unspeakable enemies of society; and it was also the most prolonged and painful, though Jesus escaped its full horrors by his unusually rapid death. Pilate, the Judean procurator, is presented in the canonical gospels as a reluctant executioner, the beginnings of an imaginative early Christian tradition which later transformed him into a believer and even into a saint. This charitable emphasis, it can be argued, was introduced after the final break between the early Christian community and the Jewish establishment, to impose the whole moral responsibility for Jesus's death on the Jews. Following up this line of argument, Jewish scholars and others have urged that the trial before the Sanhedrin never took place; that the passages which refer to it do not compare with what we know from other sources of the procedure and competence of this court; that Jesus had done nothing to break Jewish law, let alone invoke capital punishment; and that the episode is a fiction – Jesus had simply fallen foul of the Romans who regarded him as a political agitator.

Certainly, what we know of Pilate's career does not suggest he would be merciful, or hesitate to kill a Jewish troublemaker. Although the attitude of the imperial government towards Jews oscillated from time to time, in accordance with a number of political and economic factors, in general it was becoming steadily more oppressive. The honeymoon of Herod the Great's day was over. Immediately after Herod's death in 4 BC, perhaps in the very year of Jesus's birth, there had been disturbances in Galilee, and some 2,000 Jews had been crucified by Varus. Galilee was an area of mixed religious cults, where Judaism was active and becoming predominant by vigorous and aggressive proselytizing. In Jerusalem it was associated with violence and militancy, so to describe Jesus as 'the Nazarene' or 'the Galilean', as his critics did, was to mark him as a troublemaker. Pilate did not like troublemakers, particularly Jewish ones. He may have thought Jesus was a Zealot. Zealotry, initially a religious anti-tax movement, was on the increase. There had been a Zealot revolt in Judea as long ago as AD 6, and since then individual Zealot outrages had become common. Pilate had been sent to Judea in 26 with what might be termed a repressive mandate. He had been appointed by Tiberius on the recommendation of his anti-Jewish praefectorian prefect, Sejanus. It had been traditional policy to keep procurators in office only a bare three years, and then switch them to another post; Tiberius, an old soldier, introduced longer spells, on the cynical grounds, as he put it, that after a fly had sucked its fill at a wound it was better to let it stay there and keep other flies away. In fact, no procurator could make a success of Judea, and none did. Pilate soon made himself unpopular by bringing troops into Jerusalem to keep order during religious feasts and by omitting the customary precaution of masking the images of animals and deities on their standards and equipment. The Jews found this grossly offensive, and they were outraged by Pilate's seizure of Temple funds to finance improvements in the Jerusalem water-supply. He took a harsh line with awkward Jews, and surely executed Jesus without hesitation or scruple.

On the other hand, we know that Pilate's career in Judea finally came to an end in AD 36, following his violent suppression of another exotic religious movement. On this occasion, by contrast, the entire Jewish establishment in

Palestine and the diaspora protested to the imperial legate in Syria, and Pilate was recalled in disgrace. Why, then, the silence in Jesus's case? The acquiescence of the Jewish authorities, taken in conjunction with the quite explicit accusations of the gospel narratives, make it hard to reject the explanation that Jesus had effectively, and quite dramatically, broken with the Jewish faith, as least as conceived by the prevailing opinion in Jerusalem. That the Sadducees should regard Jesus as a nuisance, disturbing their relations with the Roman authorities (as well as a teacher of heterodoxy), was to be expected. What is much more significant is that the Pharisees should accept, and indeed promote, his extinction, and carry public opinion with them in so doing. Evidently what Jesus had claimed or preached was regarded as so outrageous by a predominant section of the Jewish community, and by thousands of ordinary pious Jews, that they were prepared to invoke the Roman power – normally abhorrent to them, especially in a religious matter – to rid Israel of his mission.

Such a breach with the Jewish consensus was perhaps inevitable. Jesus was a practising Jew from a conformist background, learned in his faith, and with a deep respect for the Jewish tradition. Many of his ideas had Jewish origins. If he sometimes brushed aside the law, he sometimes – on marriage, for instance – interpreted it strictly. He showed a higher respect for the Temple than its own custodians. Yet the core of his message could not be contained within a Jewish framework. He was, in effect, giving the Jews a completely new interpretation of God and, in delivering his message, claiming not merely divine authority, but divine status. It was not a conflict on ethics. There were many ethical tendencies within the Jewish spectrum, and on this aspect accommodation could have been reached. But Jesus linked his new ethics, and the link was causal and compulsory, with a new description of the mechanism of salvation. He was telling the Jews that their theory of how God made the universe work was wrong, and that he had a better. He was asking them to embark with him on a religious revolution. They had either to follow or repudiate him. For the Sadducees to follow was out of the question. They and Jesus had nothing in common; they did not even believe in life after death and there is no evidence he expected to draw them into his movement. Equally, though he shared some concepts with the Essenes, and only with the Essenes, their logic led away from universalism, and his towards it. With the Pharisees he could have a dialogue, but he was in effect asking them to abandon their profession as canon lawyers, accept a theory which enabled men to justify themselves without the law, and a doctrine of grace and faith which made legalism impossible. In the end, then, his real appeal was to ordinary, uninstructed Jewish lay opinion, the *Am Ha-Aretz*, the 'people of the land' or lost sheep, especially to the outcasts and the sinners for whom the law was too much. This was Jesus's constituency; but as events showed, it could be manipulated against him. The entry in Jerusalem on Palm Sunday was the high-water mark of his democratic appeal; after that, the unholy coalition formed against him, and the establishment prevailed.

One possibility, ended by the crucifixion, was that Jesus' movement would capture the Jewish religion; another, and perhaps a more real one, was that after his departure Judaism would capture Christianity. Judaism was a collection of tendencies, as well as embodying a great historical tradition. It was not over-centralized. It produced fanatics and outsiders, but then accommodated them within a framework of tolerance. Jesus's dynamism was too great, and his divergence too wide, to remain within this system of nonconformity. But it might have been a different matter for his movement, shorn of his leadership. Many such groupings in the past had been recuperated, and so fitted into the pattern of Judaic variety. Much of the strength of Judaism lay in its capacity to digest the heterodox; it had a strong stomach.

The Jesus movement was worth recapturing. After Jesus's arrest it had instantly disintegrated – a climax to the period of strain it was clearly undergoing in the last phase of the public ministry, and which had produced the defection of Judas. It virtually ceased to exist. Then came the rapid spread of the resurrection news, the appearance of Jesus, and the pentecostal event. The movement was in being again, but it was not exactly the same movement. Unfortunately, our knowledge of it is limited and distorted by the ineptitude of the early portion of the Acts of the Apostles. Luke, assuming he wrote this document, was not in Jerusalem at the time. He was not an eye-witness. He was a member of the mission to the Gentiles and a product of the diaspora movement. He was not in cultural or indeed doctrinal sympathy with the pentecostal apostles; in this situation he was an outsider and an ill-informed one. The evangelical speeches he produces are to some extent reconstructions, inspired by appropriate passages in the Septuagint, a diaspora document not in use among Jerusalem Jews. Even granted all this, however, Luke's account of the religion preached immediately after Pentecost does not bear much resemblance to Jesus's teaching. Its starting-point is the resurrection, but otherwise it is Christianity without Christ. Indeed, the word Christ had not yet come into use – that was a product of the later diaspora and gentile mission. What the apostles were preaching was a form of Jewish revivalism. It had strong apocalyptic overtones – very much part of the Jewish tradition – and it used the resurrection event to prove and heighten the urgency of the message. But what was the message? In all essentials it was: repent and be baptized – the revivalist doctrine preached by John the Baptist before Jesus's mission even began! Only disjointed fragments of Jesus's mechanism of salvation, his re-definition of the deity, and his own central role in the process survived. The Jerusalem apostles were in danger of slipping into the theological posture of Jewish baptists. Their Judaic instincts were still powerful and conservative. They were orientated wholly to Temple-worship. Luke's gospel tells us that after the apostles parted with Jesus at Bethany, 'they returned to Jerusalem with great joy, and spent all their time in the Temple praising God.' Again, after the first Pentecost campaign, we learn from Acts that 'With one mind, they kept up their daily attendance at the Temple.'

The inference is that the leaders of the movement in Jerusalem were much closer to Judaism than Jesus, and indeed had been all along. Alas, we know very little about them. The gospel of John says that the earliest disciples came from the circle of the Baptist, and this at a time when Jesus's early, simple teaching was strongly reflective of the Baptist's, at least according to Mark's account of it. Our authorities give a very confusing picture of Jesus's following, both during his ministry and afterwards, when the personnel seem to have changed radically. The synoptics agree that twelve men were constituted, in Mark's words, 'to be with him, and to send them to preach and to have authority to cast out demons'. Both John and Paul refer to the figure twelve. But were the twelve the same as the apostles? The synoptics and Acts provide lists, but only agree on the first eight. John gives only half. Most of them are just names, if we leave aside later traditions. 'The Twelve' seem to relate to the 'true people' of the twelve tribes; but apostle in Greek implies an expedition across the sea and must refer primarily to the gentile or diaspora mission. Luke, in the Acts, does not tell us what rights or duties or privileges were enjoyed by 'the twelve' or by 'the apostles'. Indeed, when he gets to Paul's work he forgets all about them, and thenceforth refers to him as 'the apostle'. Only with Peter can we trace any activity; with John it is barely possible, though we can assume it since he was martyred. And it is quite impossible with the rest. James, Jesus's brother, is an identifiable personality, indeed an important one. But he is not an 'apostle', nor one of 'the twelve'.

It is thus misleading to speak of an 'apostolic age', and equally misleading to speak of a primitive pentecostal Church and faith. The last point is important, because it implies Jesus left a norm, in terms of doctrine, message, and organization, from which the Church subsequently departed. There was never a norm. Jesus held his following together because he was, in effect, its only spokesman. After Pentecost, there were many; a Babel of voices. If the famous Petrine text in Matthew is genuine and means what it is alleged to mean, Peter was a very unsteady rock on which to found a Church. He did not exercise powers of leadership and seems to have allowed himself to be dispossessed by James and other members of Jesus's family, who had played no part in the original mission. Finally, Peter went on foreign mission and left the Jerusalem circle altogether.

The impression we get is that the Jerusalem Church was unstable, and had a tendency to drift back into Judaism completely. Indeed, it was not really a separate Church at all, but part of the Jewish cult. It had no sacrifices of its own, no holy places and times, no priests. It met for meals, like the Essene groups, and had readings, preaching, prayers and hymns; its ecclesiastical personality was expressed solely in verbal terms. Thus, we are told, it attracted a good many people. Many of them must have regarded it as little more than a pious and humble Jewish sect, keen on charity, sharing goods, revering an unjustly treated leader, and with an apocalyptic message. This view was also shared by some in authority. A number of priests became members. So did some of the Pharisees. How did this participation square with the execution of Jesus? That, it was now admitted in some quarters, had been a mistake; just as, later, the execution of James in 62 would be denounced subsequently as a blunder by one man acting *ultra vires*. Of course, there were Jewish establishment elements who were opposed to the Jesus movement all along, and attacked it whenever opportunity offered, as they attacked other religious 'troublemakers'. But with the penetration of the Jerusalem circle by priests and scribes, there were always influential people to speak on its behalf when the authorities tried to act. Thus, on at least two occasions, members were hauled before the religious courts but reprieved, or at most escaped with a scourging; they were unruly yet still Jews. But of course this protection and forbearance was bought at a price. It imposed limits both on doctrinal divergence and on missionary activism among the ordinary Jewish people. Thus the whole movement was in danger of being first contained, then reabsorbed.

It is at this point that the idea of a gentile mission became crucial. It had always been inherent in Jesus's work. His chosen district, as well as his native place, had been Galilee, not the obvious Judea: Galilee was only partly Jewish and it was very poor. His mission was to the poor and deprived, without distinction. And universalism was logically implied in his theology. Of course, the road to the Gentiles lay through the diaspora. Jesus met many diaspora Jews when they came on pilgrimage to attend great feasts at which he was active. But there is no evidence of his movement in the diaspora until after the Pentecostal drive. Then it followed naturally: the diaspora, among other things, was a proselytizing agency. But the very existence of a gentile mission, run by a movement which was already itself heterodox, and careless of many Jewish regulations, was incompatible with its accommodation with mainstream Judaism. Most Jerusalem Jews of substance disapproved of the gentile mission even when conducted by learned and respectable Pharisees. And, equally, there were diaspora Jews, especially Pharisees, who disapproved of the whole enterprise, were fiercely conformist and strongly opposed to any bending of the law for the benefit of converts and 'God fearers'. What they ultimately feared, of course, was the grave risk of Hellenization implicit in any gentile mission, a risk much increased when the mission was carried out by members of an unstable and nonconformist Jewish sect.

Indeed, it is impossible completely to separate the cultural and doctrinal points at issue. The teaching of Jesus had a much stronger appeal to Greek-speakers than the Judaism of the diaspora mission. It seems to have attracted converts almost from the start, especially in Antioch. Thus, if one wing of the Jesus movement was being penetrated by Pharisees, another was being penetrated by Greek-speaking Gentiles and diaspora liberals. There was soon, says Acts, 'disagreement between those of them who spoke Greek and those who spoke the language of the Jews'. The issue was money: the distribution of charity. Most of it came from the diaspora and Gentiles and went to the more orthodox Jews of the Jerusalem community. The Greek party set up a committee of seven to look into the matter. One of its members was Stephen; another was Nicolas of Antioch, described as 'a former convert to Judaism'. Almost immediately afterwards, a group of orthodox Pharisees from the diaspora synagogue in Jerusalem, denounced Stephen to the Sanhedrin, and he was stoned to death. There followed 'a time of violent persecution for the church in Jerusalem' which soon spread elsewhere. From the account of Stephen's teaching, it is evident that he and his Greek-speaking party were putting forth a much more radical doctrine as regards the Temple and the law and one much closer to Jesus in his final phase, than the group referred to as 'the apostles'. Indeed, 'the apostles' were not persecuted at this stage; they alone were not forced to scatter into the country districts. The object of the persecution was to purge the movement of its radical wing, end the Gentile mission, exclude the Greek element, or force it into conformity, and so complete the reabsorption of Jesus's followers. This process continued so long as there was a Jerusalem Church, that is, up to AD 70. Sometimes it was aimed at radicals, like Stephen. Sometimes it got out of hand and struck at men of the centre, like James. Its object was not to destroy the movement but to keep it within the broad circle of Judaism. And it came very near to success.

Into this struggle for the soul and personality of the new sect came the apostle Paul, 'the Jew of Tarsus' as he called himself. He was the first and greatest Christian personality; he has always been the most argued about, and the most often misunderstood. He has sometimes been accused of 'inventing' Christianity; and in addition, or alternatively, of perverting Christ's teaching and forcing them back into Jewish channels. This was the complaint of Nietzsche, to whom Paul was 'the eternal Jew *par excellence*' –

'Paul embodies the very opposite type to that of Jesus, the bringer of good news: he is a genius in hatred, in the vision of hate, in the ruthless logic of hate. What has not their nefarious evangelist sacrificed to his hatred! He sacrificed first and foremost his saviour, he crucified him on his cross. . . . A god who died for our sins: redemption by faith: resurrection after death – all these things are falsifications of true Christianity, for which that morbid crank must be made responsible.'

This is a favourite line of attack. Indeed, a frontal attack on Christianity itself is usually an attack on what is regarded as the Pauline element. Thus Alfred Rosenberg and the Nazi anti-Christian propagandists concentrated primarily on 'the evil rabbi Paul'. But the truth is that Paul did not invent Christianity, or pervert it: he rescued it from extinction.

Paul was the first pure Christian: the first fully to comprehend Jesus's system of theology, to grasp the magnitude of the changes it embodied, and the completeness of the break with the Judaic law. Herein lies the paradox.

For by birth Paul was a pure Jew, of the tribe of Benjamin. 'Circumcized on the eighth day,' he intones, 'of the people of Israel, of the tribe of Benjamin, a Hebrew born of Hebrews; as to law a Pharisee, as to zeal a persecutor of the church, as to righteousness under the law blameless.' From a tradition passed on by Jerome, we learn that his family came from northern Galilee, near the Lake of Genasseret, and was ultra-conservative. The Pharisaic background went back to his great-grandparents. The family had moved to Tarsus at the time of the Roman occupation, had become wealthy Roman citizens, but remained pillars of the conformist diaspora. Thus Paul's sister was taken to Jerusalem to be married, and his father sent Paul to the rabbinical high school there. He spoke Greek and Aramaic, and read the scriptures in Hebrew as well as in the Septuagint. As a young man Paul had assisted at the martyrdom of Stephen and had subsequently taken a leading part in the Pharisee drive in the diaspora against the Hellenizing Christian element. It is important to realize that Paul did not simply become a Christian. Many Jews might do this without any great change in ideas. Paul moved right across the religious conspectus, from narrow sectarianism to militant universalism, and from strict legalism to a complete repudiation of the law – the first Christian to do so: not even Jesus had gone so far Paul insists, repeatedly, that his change of view was instant and complete; it was in fact miraculous; he did not argue himself around but had the truth in all its plenitude revealed to him instantaneously by Jesus himself. Unless we accept Paul's view of how he became a follower of Christ, it is impossible to understand him. He believed in it as passionately and completely as did the disciples who had seen the risen Christ: in fact he drew no distinction between the two types of vision. It was his title to the rank of apostle and his claim to preach the authentic Christian message.

But Paul had more than a divine mandate for the gentile mission. He came from Tarsus, which has been termed 'the Athens of Asia Minor'. It was a trading emporium, a centre of cults of every kind, gnostic, exotic, oriental and Stoic. It was a focal-point of syncretism, a cultural and religious crossroads, a city familiar with weird religious processions outdoors and Hellenic debate within. Paul was a product of this diversity, and thus he can be presented as a Hellenist or a rabbi, a mystic or a chiliast, even as a gnostic. He was well-equipped to be the apostle of universalism, but behind the Janus-face and the varying tactics of the professional evangelist there was a terrific consistency of inner doctrine and purpose.

Indeed, when he arrived at the Jerusalem Council in AD 49 to present his case for complete freedom of action for his gentile mission, his teaching was assuming its mature form. It was based not merely on direct communication from God but illuminating experience in the field. And Paul and his companion could and did point vociferously to the success of their presentation. He had found a Church which believed in baptism, had a Last Supper rite, and a belief that Jesus's death and resurrection was a fulfilment of prophecy; but it was also inclined to hold that circumcision was linked to salvation and that a great deal of the Mosaic law was still valid – perhaps all of it. This was not a programme for gentile converts, even though it raised no difficulties for diaspora Jews. Gentiles regarded circumcision as distasteful; it was associated in their minds with the objectionable features of a nation Tacitus called 'enemies of the human race'. More important, however, was that Paul found he could not explain the nature of Jesus's doctrine without using concepts and terms comprehensible to those nurtured in the Graeco-Roman world. Jesus foresaw his passion but had not explained it. Paul had to explain it, to a Greek-speaking, Greek-thinking audience. The act of salvatior had to be wider than the mere messianism of the Jews, which sounded to Greeks like local politics, and bounded in time as well as geography. What was Judea to them? Paul found it hard to explain why Jesus was a Jew, let alone why he had to be a Jew. Thus the circumstances which led up to his crucifixion were irrelevant, and he omits them. The historical Jesus he simply identified with the pre-existent son of God, and he interprets the crucifixion as a divine action with salvationist intent, and of cosmic significance. And of course, the more Paul preached along these lines, the more clear it became to him that his Hellenized gospel was closer to the truth as he understood it than the restriction imposed by the narrowing vision of Jewish Christianity – if, indeed, it could be called Christianity at all. The Hellenic world could accept Jesus as a deity but Judaism placed a gulf of absolute difference between God and man. And there was nothing in Jewish literature which suggested the idea of an incarnated saviour of mankind who redeemed by virtue of his own sacrificial death.

Paul's gospel, as it evolved, could be seen to be alien to traditional Jewish thinking of any tendency, even though it contained Jewish elements. It can be summarized as follows. Jesus of Nazareth came from the line of David. He was born of a woman, but was established as Son of God, with full power, through his resurrection from the dead. He lived a short life in Palestine, embracing earthly poverty, and for our sins humbled himself in his death on the cross. God raised the crucified and buried one and exalted him to the highest throne at his own right hand: 'For our sake he made him to be sin who knew no sin, so that in him we might become the righteousness of God.' The atoning death of Jesus the Messiah, sacrificed for our sins, served as our expiation and ransomed humanity. His dying affects the redemption of the cosmos and humanity as a whole, for in his death the world has been crucified and has begun to pass away; Christ will shortly come again from heaven as the Son of Man. Here we have, in all essentials, the central doctrines of Christianity: the view of history, the salvation mechanism, the role and status of Christ Jesus. Everything in it had been implicit in the teachings of Christ. Paul made it explicit, clear and complete. It is a theological system, capable of infinite elaboration, no doubt, but complete in all essentials. It is cosmic and universalist; it is, in fact, Hellenized – Paul, the Jew, whose natural tongue was Aramaic and whose Greek was singular, had supplied the part of the

Hellenized processing machine, and thus made Judaic monotheism accessible to the entire Roman world.

But there was one key aspect of the saving mechanism which caused Paul problems, and his attempt to solve them drew him and his successors into an endless series of new difficulties. Christ's coming on earth set in motion the mechanism: that was clear. But when did it culminate? What was the time-scheme of Christianity? The whole of Jesus's work implied that the apocalypse was imminent; some of his sayings were quite explicit on the point. It is true that his teaching also contains the concept of an individual, interior relationship with God and of a personal salvation which makes the apocalypse superfluous and irrelevant: the soul has its individual drama with God in addition to the vast collective performance on the eschatological stage, with its terrifying scenery and sound effects, its *deus ex machina* descending for the Second Coming, the *parousia*. But this remained to be discovered and interpreted: one of the hidden matrices of Jesus's gospel. The *prima facie* view of the Jesus mission was that it was an immediate prelude to a Last Judgment. Hence the urgency of the pentecostal task, an urgency which Paul shared throughout his life, so that his final hope was to carry the good news, while there was still time, to Spain – for him, 'the ends of the earth'.

It was this sense of urgency which gave a twist to Paul's theology. To him it made the accumulated apparatus of Jewish legalism particularly intolerable. Before his conversion he had been, he thought, a righteous man, keeping the law. The blinding insight of truth showed him this was a complete illusion. He realized he had not begun to live until he saw God through Jesus Christ. And the relationship was absolutely direct. As he put it: 'I am convinced that neither death nor life, nor angels nor principalities, nor things present or future, nor powers, nor any created thing, will be able to separate us from the love of God which is in Christ Jesus our Lord.' Or again: 'If God is for us, who is against us?' So for him the coming of Christ automatically ended the old Jewish law. For him the law became a curse, for no man could fulfill its 613 commands and prohibitions completely; thus it made sinners of everyone. In some ways it was a direct incentive to sin. Paul did not preach license. On the contrary, he constantly urged that the commandments must be kept. He advocated activism, especially in charity. And he told his converts to work. As a budding rabbi he had been taught a trade: he was a tent-maker. This was a practical as well as symbolic sign of the great, central therapy of work: one Jewish concept he triumphantly transmitted to Christianity. But Paul knew it was madness to suppose that salvation lay through the law and such externals as circumcision. The law was formal; its observation was perforce based on a degree of hypocrisy; indeed, all the systems of its interpretation were necessarily an attempt to refashion something originally inspired by God in man's distorting image. Good works were important, indeed: 'God will repay each in accordance with his works.' But salvation came primarily through faith (which was a rebirth and an identification with the true righteousness of

God), so perfect that it can only be bestowed by God, who in doing so makes man righteous. The Jews had taken the false direction by believing that their works would establish their righteousness. They believed themselves chosen so long as they kept the law. However, the mark of election is not birth, but God's promise as enacted through the grace of faith. It applied to all, without respect of race, sex or status. Of course if all Israel became zealous for the conversion of the Gentiles, it would fulfil its role as the elect nation. But the prime object of the gentile mission was to set the machinery of God's election in motion. Paul noted that the scriptures adumbrated a system of predestination, and he quoted the case from Ezra: 'And thou didst set apart Jacob for thyself, but Esau thou didst hate.' The concept was made far more terrifying in the Qumran texts. But there is no mandate in Paul for the Calvinist insistence on the eternal predestination of the individual to salvation or damnation. Paul saw damnation as the shadow that was cast by election from grace; it ensures the purity of the gospel message; he did not put forward a theory about God's system of selection, but an explanation of what happens to a man when he hears the gospel – he chooses, and so he is chosen.

This tremendous attack on the whole Judaic concept of man's relationship with God, and its replacement by a new salvationist system, was summarized in Paul's great essay in determinist theology, the epistle to the Romans. What an extraordinary document to be received by a young congregation who had never met the apostle! No one has ever fully understood Romans. No one can remain undisturbed by it, either. It is the most thought-provoking of all the Christian documents. It has a habit of forcing men to reconsider their whole understanding of religion even when they have spent many years in theological inquiry. Thus Romans profoundly changed Augustine's thinking in the last years of his life. It was the detonator to Luther's explosion. It has been used again and again to demolish and reconstruct systems of theology, most recently by Schweitzer, Bultmann and Barth. Most theological revolutions begin with Romans, as indeed did Paul's own. Romans is an imperfect document, the work of a man not wholly satisfied with his case: that is its merit as a key. The circular form of the argument, its return again and again to the same starting points and conclusions, betray the anxiety of a man who still saw, and knew he saw, through a glass darkly. The imperfection of his vision was, indeed, implicit in the majesty of his conception of God, the distancing he achieves between God and man, and time and eternity. Paul was the beneficiary of a vision. We must accept his sincerity on this: it was clearly the most important event in his whole life. But, as a man who demanded the whole truth, he recognized that his vision had been incomplete. The difference between the theology of Jesus and Paul is not merely that one is implicit, the other explicit; it is that Jesus saw as a God, Paul thought as a man. But the process of trying to think through the theological problem made Paul into a very formidable figure. On the one hand he presents an insuperable obstacle to any humanist rescue-operation on Jesus – any presentation of him as the greatest and noblest of all human beings, stripped of his divine attributes. Paul insisted he was God: it is the only thing about him which really matters, otherwise the Pauline theology collapses, and with it Christianity. But equally, Paul is an obstacle to those who wish to turn Christianity into a closed system. He believed in freedom. For him, Christianity was the only kind of freedom that matters, the liberation from the law, and the donation of life. He associated freedom with truth, for which he had an unlimited reverence. And in pursuing truth he established the right to think, and to think through to the ultimate conclusion. The process of inquiry, in fact, mirrored his salvationist theology: he accepted the bonds and obligations of love, but not the authority of scholarship and tradition. He established the right to think in the full Hellenistic sense and thus showed that the Christian faith has nothing to fear from the power of thought. Schweitzer called Paul 'the patron saint of thought in Christianity', and added: 'All those who think to serve the gospel of Christ by destroying the liberty of thinking must hide their faces from him.'

This detailed analysis of Paul's theology and personality has been necessary to illuminate the significance of the Jerusalem Council and its aftermath in the whole history of Christianity. Behind the controversy over circumcision and the attitude to gentile converts a whole range of the deepest issues was at stake. Nor did the suggested compromise of James and Peter work. It was based upon a ruling from Leviticus which provided for the entertainment of strangers and allowed a certain relaxation of the law. This was precisely the kind of misplaced casuistry which Paul thought ruinous to Jesus's message. Paul made no attempt to put it into operation; later generations, puzzled by its significance, reinterpreted it as a general moral command – thus it appears in the writings of Irenaeus, Tertullian, Jerome. But equally, Paul's opponents did not abide by the apostolic ruling. Both the Acts and Paul's own epistles make it plain that the struggle continued, and became more bitter. For Paul, it was literally a matter of life or death, and his own writings make no attempt to hide its gravity and acrimony. The Jerusalem Council revealed the existence of a 'centre party', led in somewhat pusillanimous manner by Peter and James. Afterwards, the centre crumbled and surrendered to the Judaistic wing of the Christian-Pharisees: hence Peter's shamefaced refusal of table-fellowship to Gentiles at Antioch and Paul's stern rebuke. Peter eventually broke with, or at any rate left, the Jewish-Christian Church of Jerusalem. He accepted Paul's theology – he may well have contributed to it with his own knowledge and insights – and joined him in the mission to the Gentiles. In all probability they died together as martyrs at Rome. But the rest of the Jerusalem Church maintained its connection with Judaism and became increasingly hostile to Paul's efforts. The attempt to divide the missionary work was doomed to failure. The missions to the Jews of the diaspora and to the Gentiles in Syria, Asia Minor and Greece, were bound to overlap. The centres were the same: the major cities like Antioch, Ephesus, Tarsus, Corinth, Athens, Thessalonica. Moreover, the first Christian missionaries were, in effect, taking over the work of the old Jewish diaspora mission, using the same contacts, buildings, helpers. How could they be separated? And how could two sets of evangelists, claiming the same authority and working in the same area, preach two gospels which were increasingly divergent? Paul complained repeatedly of attempts to pervert and appropriate his congregations, so lovingly brought into existence by his own titanic efforts. He reacted vigorously: his incessant journeys, the immense burden of his life-task, which he sometimes portrays as beyond his resources, almost unbearable, reflected his need to fight on two fronts: against ignorance on the one hand, malicious obstruction on the other. Of course he counter-attacked: Romans itself was a preliminary move, a manifesto, to announce his arrival in Rome and a projected attempt to evangelize the Christian-Jewish community there. Money seems to have been used on both sides to provide the maximum number of evangelists and to sustain welfare-efforts and their administrators.

The evidence suggests that, after his initial great successes, Paul lost ground steadily. The Jewish Christians had the enormous advantage that they could draw on the resources, in men and money, of the diaspora communities. Moreover, they could rightly claim that they were led by men who had known Jesus personally and received the truth from the source. They included members of Jesus's own family, who took an active part in the Pauline campaign. Who, then, was Paul to claim a monopoly of truth? His reply was to draw attention, again and again, to his personal vision. It was his only credential. This inevitably exposed him to vicious personal attacks, stressing his vanity and pretensions; he was guilty of 'the cult of personality'. Paul lamented the difficulty of his position, which forced him into a posture of pride, and to claims which sounded like boasting. In the late fifties he returned to Jerusalem for the last time in a vain effort to reach a settlement. The Jewish wing deliberately forced him to make a reluctant gesture of Temple-worship which led to his arrest and imprisonment. Paul could plead Roman citizenship to get out of the clutches of the Judaic religious courts, but the legal tangle in which he became involved – transportation to Rome under escort and then house arrest – ended only in his death during the Neronic persecution. Thus the Jerusalem Church effectively terminated his missionary career.

What ensured the survival of Christianity was not the triumph of Paul in the field but the destruction of Jerusalem, and with it the Jewish-Christian faith. One of the many collateral reasons why Paul was anxious to disassociate Christ's teaching from Judaism was that he wished to rescue it from Jewish irredentist politics. The Jewish political and military messiah meant nothing to Greeks and Romans. And to Paul Jesus had never been a messiah in this sense. That was not at all what Christianity was about. As a diaspora Jew, he had no quarrel with the Romans. On the contrary, he seems to have admired the Roman system and took advantage of it. His public claim to Roman citizenship was more than a physical escape from the justice of the law, now odious to him: it was a symbolic renunciation of Judaic status. Paul did not wish to see the Christian movement damaged and perhaps ruined by involvement with the (to him) irrelevant and hopeless quest for a Jewish state. Christ's kingdom was not of this world! In this respect Paul saw eye to eye with Josephus: would that the two might have met, for Paul could have found a convert. But Paul was defeated and the Jewish-Christian Church of Jerusalem moved closer to Judaism, and – being a radical movement – to Zealotry and nationalism. A Slavonic translation of an early, uncensored, version of Josephus's history suggests that the missing passages on Christianity emphasize the political aims of the Jewish-Christian resurrectionists in Judea. During the sixties the Jerusalem Church lost its Christian significance and the remains of its universalism as it became identified with the growing revolt against Rome. Zealots roamed the country districts. Religious terrorism increased in the towns. The crowded processions of the great feasts became the occasions for sudden murders which provoked riots and brutal retaliation. Law and order broke down and Rome was blamed for the economic distress which ensued. In Jerusalem a despairing proletariat turned against Rome, against a collaborationist sacerdotal aristocracy, and towards wonder-workers, patriotic brigands, and the sectaries. The final revolt and its repression lasted four years. It placed a great strain on the military and economic resources of the empire and Rome was correspondingly vengeful. The total of Jewish losses provided by Josephus add up to nearly one and a half million. The figure is unrealistic but it accurately mirrors the horrors of those years. There was a new, desperate diaspora. The Temple was destroyed and henceforth Judaism became the religion of the Talmud. The Jewish nation never recovered from the blow, though the final dispersion took place in the next century, when Jerusalem was razed and rebuilt as a Roman colonial city. The Jewish-Christian community was dispersed; most of its leaders were no doubt killed. Survivors fled to Asia Minor, the east, Egypt, especially to Alexandria.

Thus the centre of Christian gravity shifted to Rome; and the theological vacuum left by the extinction of the Jerusalem Church was filled by the Pauline system. A number of readjustments followed. Paul's Christ had not been anchored to the historical Jesus of the Jerusalem Church. This was remedied by Mark, who wrote the first biography of Jesus, presenting him as a deity. Luke, in his gospel and his Acts, completed the plastic surgery by giving the decapitated trunk of the Jerusalem Jesus a Pauline head. The change of balance and direction in the Church was eventually accepted by most Christian-Jewish communities in Africa and Asia. It is reflected in a number of documents, such as the gospel of Matthew, who neatly contrives to be both very Jewish and very Christian, and the gospel of John, which marks the triumph of Pauline theology. But other Christian-Jewish fragments declined to change and so became heretical. Such were the Ebionites, or poor ones, chiefly in Egypt. They saw themselves as the true, primitive Church; they had allowed themselves to be by-passed by events, lost their title to orthodoxy, and so came to be treated as false innovators – a familiar paradox in the history of religion. It is interesting that their writings and those of other Jewish-Christians in the fifties who had first introduced the idea of heresy in the portray Paul as antichrist and the first heretic. It was in fact the Jewish Christians in the fifties, who had first introduced the idea of heresy in the campaign against Paul and Hellenization; thus the arrow flew swiftly back to the archer. In Judaism itself, heresy was already a mature and powerful concept. Hence, following the collapse of Jewish Christianity, the orthodox Judaic authorities did not wait long to anathematize Christianity as such. Around 85, the judgment was incorporated in the synagogue liturgy: 'May the Nazarenes and the heretics be suddenly destroyed and removed from the book of life.' Heresy was another Judaic gift to the Christian Church, where it soon began to flourish mightily.

Yet what was Christian heresy? And, for that matter, what was the Church? Most of our knowledge of early Christian history comes from the writings of Bishop Eusebius of Caesarea in the fourth century. Eusebius was in many ways a conscientious historian, and he had access to multitudes of sources which have since disappeared. But he believed, and was therefore concerned to demonstrate by his presentation of the evidence, that a Christian Church, vested with the plenitude of Christ's teaching, and with divine authority to uphold it, had been ordained by Jesus right at the beginning, and had then been solidly established by the first generation of apostles. Moreover, it had triumphantly survived the attempts of various heretics to tamper with the truth it passed on intact from generation to generation.

This view is a reconstruction for ideological purposes. Eusebius represented the wing of the Church which had captured the main centres of power, had established a firm tradition of monarchical bishops, and had recently allied itself with the Roman state. He wanted to show that the Church he represented had always constituted the mainstream of Christianity, both in organization and faith. The truth is very different. We have already seen that the original legatee of Jesus's mission, the Jerusalem Church, did not hold steadfast to his teaching and was slipping back into Judaism before it was, in effect, extinguished, its remnants being eventually branded as heretics. The Christology of Paul, which later became the substance of the Christian universal faith, came from the diaspora, and was preached by an outsider whom many in the Jerusalem Church did not recognize as an apostle at all. Christianity began in confusion, controversy and schism and so it continued. A dominant orthodox Church, with a recognizable ecclesiastical structure, emerged only very gradually and represented a process of natural selection – a spiritual survival of the fittest. And, as with such struggles, it was not particularly edifying.

The Darwinian image is appropriate: the central and eastern Mediterranean in the first and second centuries AD swarmed with an infinite multitude of religious ideas, struggling to propagate themselves. Every religious movement was unstable and fissiparous; and these cults were not only splitting up and modulating but reassembling in new forms. A cult had to struggle not only to survive but to retain its identity. Jesus had produced certain insights and matrices which were rapidly propagated over a large geographical area. The followers of Jesus were divided right from the start on elements of faith and practice. And the further the missionaries moved from the base, the more likely it was that their teachings would diverge. Controlling them implied an ecclesiastical organization. In Jerusalem there were 'leaders' and 'pillars', vaguely defined officials modelled on Jewish practice. But they were ineffective. The Jerusalem Council was a failure. It outlined a consensus but could not make it work in practice. Paul could not be controlled. Nor, presumably, could others. Nor could the 'pillars' of the centre party maintain their authority even in Jerusalem. They slipped back into Judaism. Then came the catastrophe of 66–70, and the central organization of the Church, such as it was, disappeared.

It is true that the Christians now had a homogenous and extremely virile body of doctrine: the Pauline gospel or *kerygma*. It stood a good chance of surviving and spreading. But it had no organization behind it. Paul did not believe in such a thing. He believed in the Spirit, working through him and others. Why should man regulate when the Spirit would do it for him? And of course he did not want a fixed system with rules and prohibitions: 'If you are led by the Spirit you are not under the law.' The Church was an inversion of normal society. Its leaders exercised their authority through gifts of the Spirit, not through office. The two noblest gifts were prophecy and teaching. The apostles set the process in motion, then the Spirit took over and worked through many people: 'And God has appointed in the Church first apostles, then prophets, third teachers, then workers of miracles, then healers, helpers, administrators, speakers in various kinds of tongues.' Worship was still completely unorganized and subject to no special control. There was no specific organization to handle funds. And there was no distinction between a clerical class, and laity. There were, indeed, presbyters in the Judaic Christian Church, but not in Paul's new convert congregations. The atmosphere in short was that of a loosely organized revivalist movement. Many, from time to time, 'spoke with tongues'; all expected the *parousia* soon. Clerical control seemed needless and inappropriate. And the atmosphere in the Pauline churches was reproduced elsewhere, in a rapidly spreading movement.

Granted this, it was inevitable that the Church expanded not as a uniform movement but as a collection of heterodoxies. Or perhaps 'heterodoxies' is the wrong word, since it implies there was an orthodox version. The Pauline system did, indeed, become orthodox in time, but the other Christian versions which spread from Jerusalem were not deviations from it but evolved independently. From the start, then, there were numerous varieties of Christianity which had little in common, though they centred round belief in the resurrection. They were marked by two things: individual oral traditions, which eventually found written expression as 'gospels'; and, linked to this, claims to an apostolic succession. Each Church had its own 'Jesus story'; and each had been founded by one of the original band who had handed over the torch to a designated successor and so on. The most important element in all these early Churches was the genealogical tree of truth.

This was a Greek, rather than a Judaic, concept. Indeed, it was essentially a gnostic idea. No one has yet succeeded in defining 'gnosticism' adequately, or indeed demonstrating whether this movement preceded Christianity or grew from it. Certainly gnostic sects were spreading at the same time as Christian ones; both were part of the general religious osmosis. Gnostics had two central preoccupations: belief in a dual world of good and evil and belief in the existence of a secret code of truth, transmitted by word of mouth or by arcane writings. Gnosticism is a 'knowledge' religion – that is what the word means – which claims to have an inner explanation of life. Thus it was, and indeed still is, a spiritual parasite which used other religions as a 'carrier'. Christianity fitted into this role very well. It had a mysterious founder, Jesus, who had conveniently disappeared, leaving behind a collection of sayings and followers to transmit them; and of course in addition to the public sayings there were 'secret' ones, handed on from generation to generation by members of the sect. Thus gnostic groups seized on bits of Christianity, but tended to cut it off from its historical origins. They were Hellenizing it, as they Hellenized other oriental cults (often amalgamating the results). Their ethics varied to taste: sometimes they were ultra-puritan, sometimes orgiastic. Thus some groups seized on Paul's denunciation of the law to preach complete license. Paul fought hard against gnosticism, recognizing that it might cannibalize Christianity and destroy it. At Corinth he came across well-educated Christians who had reduced Jesus to myth. Among the Colossians he found Christians who worshipped intermediate spirits and angels. Gnosticism was hard to combat because it was hydra-headed and always changing. Of course all the sects had their own codes, and most hated each other. Some conflated the cosmogony of Plato with the story of Adam and Eve, and interpreted it in various ways: thus the Ophites worshipped serpents, arguing that the serpent had triumphed over God; so they cursed Jesus in their liturgy. Some accepted Christian redemption but ruled out Jesus as the redeemer: the Samaritans preferred Simon Magus, others Hercules.

The most dangerous gnostics were those who had, intellectually, thought their way quite inside Christianity, and then produced a variation which wrecked the system. The Basilides group in Egypt, and the Valentinians in Rome, though they differed on other things, both rejected the incarnation and denied Jesus had ever been man: his body was semblance or *dokesis*. The Docetists had wide appeal among the Greek cultures because they effectively cut off Christianity from its Judaic origins, something which responded to a popular demand, especially among the well-to-do. Indeed, those of Greek culture found it hard to understand why Christianity should wish or need to maintain the Jewish connection. They found the Septuagint a monstrous document: barbarous and obscure or, when comprehensible, repugnant. Why should Christians lumber themselves with it? This line was all the more insidious in that it merely carried Paul's logic a little further. There must have been times when Paul, for all his Jewishness, was tempted to drop the Septuagint himself. How much of it was authentic? Valentinus argued that a great deal had simply been inserted by Jewish elders and possessed no authority; and many other portions represented compromises with contemporary opinion, Moses being a prime culprit. As forms of Christianity spread and enveloped, or indeed produced, highly-educated men, the glaring blemishes of the scriptures were closely examined. By the early decades of the second century there were masses of Christian texts, too, which had no precise status and spoke with many tongues. Which were valid and which were not?

The problem attracted the attention of a brilliant and wealthy Greek convert from Pontus, Marcion, who had come to Rome in the 120s or 130s to take an active part in propagating the faith. He was from the school of Paul, indeed his greatest theological follower. He represents two important and permanent strains in Christianity: the cool, rationalist approach to the examination of the Church's documentary proofs, and a plain, unspectacular philosophy of love. He was, as it were, a preincarnation of a certain type of Renaissance scholar, an adumbration of Erasmus. Marcion had no doubt that Paul's essential teachings were sound and he knew they were closest to Jesus in date. His difficulty was how to square them either with the teachings of the Old Testament, or with post-Pauline Christian writings. Using historical and critical methods basically similar to those of modern scriptural scholars, he identified only seven Pauline epistles as authentic, rejecting all the later documents which were circulating in the apostle's name. Of the so-called evangelists he accepted only portions of Luke (in his gospel and Acts) as inspired, rejecting all the rest as later fabrications, rationalizations and muddle. This stripped the New Testament down to its bare Pauline bones: indeed, to Marcion, the teaching of Paul was, essentially, the gospel of Jesus. The Old Testament he rejected *in toto* since it seemed to him, as it has seemed to many Christians since, to be talking of a quite different God: monstrous, evil-creating, bloody, the patron of ruffians like David. His textual analysis and the process by which he arrived at the first 'canon', thus had a unity: the breach with Judaism, initiated by Paul, had to be complete, and Christian texts with Judaizing tendencies or compromises expurgated or scrapped.

No book of Marcion's has survived. He quarrelled with the Roman Christian authorities in AD 144 and went east. Later he was denounced as a heretic by Tertullian, earliest and noisiest of the Christian witch-hunters. This means his works have not survived, except in extracts quoted in books attacking him. Preservation of an ancient author required positive effort over a long period. Early Christian writings were produced in very small quantities on highly perishable papyrus. Unless they were constantly retranscribed they did not survive at all. There was no need of a censor, unless a heresiarch had followers over successive generations to keep his work alive. So we do not know the details of Marcion's system. His God was the Pauline God of love. He rejected fear as a force God would employ to compel obedience. This reliance on love alone as the mechanism underpinning ethics was the main burden of Tertullian's complaint against Marcion and his sympathizers. For them, he sneered, 'God is purely and simply good. He indeed forbids all sin, but only in word . . . for your fear he does not want . . . they have no fear of their God at all. They say it is only an evil being who will be feared, a good one will be loved. Foolish Man! Do you say that he whom you call *Lord* ought not to be feared, whilst the very title you give him indicates a power which *must* be feared?' Without fear, men would 'boil over into lust,' frequent games, circuses, theatres – all forbidden to Christians – and submit instantly to persecution.

Marcion's controversy with Tertullian gives us a glimpse, perhaps for the first time, of two basic types of Christian: the rational optimist who believes that the love-principle is sufficient, man having an essential desire to do good, and the pessimist, convinced of the essential corruptibility of human creatures and the need for the mechanism of damnation. Successful Christianity is essentially a coalition of views and spiritualities: it needs to contain both types even when they produce a certain conflict and friction. In this case it was unable to accommodate either, at any rate in Rome. Rome was universalist and Marcion's ruthless pruning of the Christian texts would have narrowed the limits of its appeal. And then, he did not believe in marriage, believing that procreation was an invention of the evil Old Testament God – or so Tertullian reported. Marcion was a flawed character: his biblical exegesis reveals a superlative mind, his doctrine of Pauline charity an admirable character, but his views on sex set him down as an eccentric. They were compatible with belief in an imminent *parousia* but by the 140s the Church had settled down to the long haul, and procreation had to be carried on. Marcion's departure was a heavy financial blow to the Rome Church and his money enabled him to attract a huge following in the east. But belief in celibacy necessarily proves fatal to a heretical movement.

Tertullian and Marcion never met: they were of quite different generations and Tertullian was attacking an attitude of mind rather than a real personality. Both had powerful intellects. Tertullian, in addition, was a master of prose, the prose of the rhetorician and the controversialist. He was at home in both Latin and Greek but he usually employed Latin – the first Christian theologian to do so. His influence, indeed, was enormous precisely because he created ecclesiastical latinity, hammered out its linguistic concepts and formulations and, thanks to his eloquence, endowed it with unforgettable and influential phrases: 'The blood of the martyrs is the seed of the church'; 'The unity of the heretics is schism'; 'I believe because it is absurd.' The last indicates the distance which separates him from the rationalist Marcion. Tertullian came from Carthage where, even in the closing decades of the second century, a distinctive regional Church had emerged: enthusiastic, immensely courageous, utterly defiant of the secular authorities, much persecuted, narrow-minded, intolerant, venomous and indeed violent in controversy. There is some evidence that Carthage and other areas of the African littoral were evangelized by Christian Zealots and Essenes and had a very early tradition of militancy and resistance to authority and persecution. Tertullian embodied this tradition. To him the Church was a precious elite of believers, to be defended against contamination from whatever quarter; the Devil, he thought, roamed the earth seeking to corrupt. Christians should limit their contacts with the state to the minimum: they should refuse to serve in the army, or the civil service, or even in state schools; they might not earn their living in any trade connected, even indirectly, with pagan religion. He particularly deplored the attempts of rationalists, like Marcion, to reconcile Christian teaching to Greek philosophy: 'What has Athens to do with Jerusalem? What has the Academy to do with the Church? What have heretics to do with Christians? Our instruction comes from the porch of Solomon, who had himself taught that the Lord should be sought in simplicity of heart. Away with all attempts to produce a Stoic, Platonic, and dialectic Christianity!'

In his contempt for intellectual inquiry, Tertullian appeared anti-Pauline. Yet in another sense he sprang from the Pauline tradition. He stressed the overwhelming power of faith, the precious gift of the elect. To him Christians were supermen because the spirit moved in them. This is Paul's conception of the Church: a community where the spirit worked through individuals, rather than an organized hierarchy where authority was exercised by office. Tertullian's burning faith made him a scourge of heretics and an avid propagandist for the Church – one of the best it ever had. Yet his alignment with orthodoxy, at any rate orthodoxy as conceived by a clerical establishment, was fundamentally against his nature. He thought direct communication with the deity not only possible but essential. And so did many other people. It was among the earliest traditions of the Church, and it had the full stamp of Pauline authority. But the idea of a free-lance, self-appointed proclaimer of truth was, in the end, incompatible with a regular priesthood, charged with the duty of protecting the canon.

The crisis came to a head in the second half of the second century but it had been building up for a long time. The nature of Christianity, carried rapidly forward by wandering evangelists, attracted charlatans. Some of the earliest Christian documents (and the earliest pious forgeries) were attempts to establish the *bona fides* of missionaries and warnings against fraud. Sophisticated pagans sneered at Christians for their gullibility. That sparkling Greek satirist Lucian, who took a contemptuous view of human credulity, was particularly critical of Christians because 'they take their beliefs from tradition, and do not insist on definite evidence. Any professional fraud can impose himself on them and make a lot of money very quickly.' Lucian gave as one example the Cynic philosopher Peregrinus who picked up Christianity in Palestine, 'and in no time made them all look like children – he was prophet, cult-leader, head of the synagogue, everything. He interpreted their holy books, and composed some himself. They revered him as a god, treated him as a lawgiver, and made him their leader – next, of course, after the man who introduced their cult into the world, and who was crucified in Palestine, whom they still worship.' Peregrinus may have been more sincere than Lucian gave him credit for: he eventually cremated himself on a funeral pyre at the close of the Olympic Games in 165. It was always difficult to distinguish between the truly inspired, the self-deluded, and the plain criminal. And, inconvenient as individual ecstatics and 'speakers with tongues' might be, there was always the more serious danger that they might fall under the spell of an outstanding charismatic and prophet who would constitute a counter-Church. Just as the varieties of gnosticism risked capturing the Church's personality and absorbing it into a disintegrating mess of sub-Hellenic cults, so the charismatics might submerge the Church's unitary voice under a Babel of 'prophecies'. The moment was judged to have come about 170 when Montanus, a successful charismatic who described himself as the Paraclete, was declared an enemy of the Church. Many of his closest followers were women, and they clearly played an outstanding role in his movement – as, indeed, they did in one or two of the Pauline congregations. Montanus was attacked by his enemies for breaking up marriages and then giving these inspired matrons who flocked to join him ecclesiastical offices. Montanism, or rather the efforts to combat it, played a conclusive role in persuading the orthodox to ban the ministry to women. Tertullian, while still an orthodox propagandist, snarled at this subversion of Church order: 'The impudence of the heretics' women! They dare to teach, to dispute, to carry out exorcisms, perform cures – perhaps they even baptize. . . . Of course, nowhere is promotion easier than in a camp of rebels: the mere fact of being there is meritorious!' In his tract *On Baptism and the Veiling of Virgins*, he emphatically denied that women could exercise any ministerial functions.

There were two lines of attack on the Montanists. On the one hand, they were accused of excessive austerity; thus Hippolytus, putting the orthodox case in his *Refutatio omnium haeresium*: 'They introduced novelties in the shape of special fasts and ceremonies, and diets of radishes which they adopted on the inspired advice of their womenfolk.' But Montanus was also attacked for handling large sums of money, for moving about in an ostentatious manner and for paying stipends to his chief followers. Some of the orthodox smears on him are manifest inventions. Eusebius repeats a tale that Montanus and his chief woman-prophet died as a result of a suicide pact, but he indicates that this is fiction. Many of the accusations levelled merely suggest that the Montanists were behaving like the Church, *were* in fact the Church in large areas – thus they raised money, paid their clergy and so forth. The best indication of the moral worthiness of the movement is that Tertullian, the scourge of heretics, eventually joined it. He could not continue to endorse an orthodoxy which denied any independent role to the Spirit and insisted that all communication with the deity should be through the regular ecclesiastical channels. So profound was his conviction of the reality of direct spiritual intervention that he accepted aspects of it he had hitherto regarded as quite repugnant; especially after he had witnessed their efficacy. Thus, as a Montanist, he wrote in *De Anima* at the end of his life: 'We have now among us a sister who has been granted gifts of revelations, which she experiences in church during the Sunday services through ecstatic vision in the Spirit.'

Tertullian's case gives us a precious, in some ways unique, glimpse into the workings of the early Church. Here was a great Church statesman, a man of impeccable rectitude and burning faith, embracing heresy. His adherence thus completely undermines the orthodox attacks on the morals and public behaviour of the Montanists, sets a stamp of ethical approval, at any rate, on the movement. The Montanists were evidently sincere, holy and probably humble and abstemious people. But that we know this is due to accident, or rather to the conscious decision of orthodox authority to preserve Tertullian as a personality and a theological writer. Normally he would have been allowed to sink into oblivion, or have survived as a caricatured fragment. But he was not only the first, but one of the most outstanding Latin theologians; the bulk of his work constitutes a tremendous affirmation of the Christian faith. It was exciting to read then, as indeed it still is now. Tertullian was too precious to be sacrificed to orthodox uniformity. Though the first Protestant, he was saved by his art. The Church continued to reproduce and use his works, or the bulk of them, and thus, incidentally, confirms the good faith of the Montanists.

As a rule, however, those who disputed with what later became, or already was, the orthodox tradition, have been buried under a mountain of ecclesiastical Billingsgate. *Odium theologicum* was not a Christian innovation. It was part of the Judaic heritage, along with the concept of heresy and the anathema. As we have seen, the bland, eirenic tone of the Acts, picturing the early Church as a collegiate body of fair-minded senators, moving peaceably to collective decisions, belies the reality we find in Paul. Harsh words among the brothers in Christ made their appearance early and thereafter there was a steady inflation in the exchange of abuse. In the second century, discussion with heretics yielded to polemic and the magnitude of the orthodox accusations and the scurrility of the abuse, usually corresponded to the success of the movement. With the growth of polemic, it became necessary to attack the morals as well as the doctrine of the divergent. In fact the theory soon developed that doctrinal error inevitably induced moral decay. Thus orthodox polemicists could invent and believe accusations in good faith.

Montanist officials were accused of gluttony and avarice simply because they received salaries. The orthodox Apollonius accused Alexander, whom he called a heretic, of highway robbery; he held disgusting feasts with the prophetess Priscella, and she was covetous. The indictment continues: 'Does a true prophet use make-up? Does he dye his eyebrows and eyelids? Does he love ornaments? Does he gamble? Play dice? Does he lend money at interest?' What was normal practice among all Christians – the practice of calling widows virgins, the payment of priests, the use of money to get persecuted brethren out of state prisons, were in heretic sects described as evil. The sects which attracted the largest followings were, as a rule, the most austere and God-fearing; but, being the most successful, they had to be the most bitterly assailed on moral grounds.

There is thus a sinister Goebbels' Law about early Christian controversy: the louder the abuse, the bigger the lie. In a circular letter to bishops in *c.* 324, Bishop Alexander of Alexandria wrote of Arians:

'Impelled by avarice and ambition, these knaves are constantly plotting to gain possession of the richest dioceses . . . they are driven insane by the devil who works in them . . . skilled deceivers . . . hatched a conspiracy . . . vile purposes . . . equipped dens of robbers . . . organized a gang to fight Christ . . . excite disorders against us . . . persuade people to persecute us . . . their immoral womenfolk . . . their younger women followers run around the street in an indecent fashion and discredit Christianity. . . .'

And so on. There was a constant and depressing inflation in the vocabulary of invective during the course of the first two centuries; thus the orthodox were told that among the Manichees 'no modesty, no sense of honour and no chastity whatever is to be found; their moral code is a mass of falsehoods, their religious beliefs are shaped by the devil, and their sacrifice is immorality itself.' Where their writings survive, we find that heretics, schismatics and critics of the orthodox used the same language. Thus the anti-Nestorian Bishop Cyril of Alexandria was described by Isidore of Pelusium as 'a man determined to pursue his private hatreds rather than seek the true faith of Jesus Christ'; and another critic, Bishop Theodoret of Cyrrhus, greeted Cyril's death with the words: 'The living are delighted. The dead, perhaps, are sorry, afraid they may be burdened with his company. . . . May the guild of undertakers lay a huge, heavy stone on his grave, lest he should come back again and show his faithless mind again. Let him take his new doctrines to Hell, and preach to the damned all day and night.' The mind boggles at the lists of offences with which distinguished ecclesiastics accused each other. The historian Sozomen relates that at the Council of Tyre, 335, Athanasius, the orthodox Bishop of Alexandria, was charged with breaking a mystical chalice, smashing an episcopal chair, false imprisonment, deposing a bishop unlawfully, placing him under military guard and torturing him, striking other bishops physically, obtaining his bishoprics by perjury, breaking and cutting off the arm of one of his opponents, burning his house, tying him to a column and whipping him, and putting him in a cell illegally – all this in addition to teaching false doctrine.

The venom employed in these endemic controversies reflects the fundamental instability of Christian belief during the early centuries, before a canon of New Testament writings had been established, credal formulations evolved to epitomize them, and a regular ecclesiastical structure built up to protect and propagate such agreed beliefs. Before the last half of the third century it is inaccurate to speak of a dominant strain of Christianity. So far as we can judge, by the end of the first century, and virtually throughout the second, the majority of Christians believed in varieties of Christian-gnosticism, or belonged to revivalist sects grouped round charismatics. Eusebius, seeking to push back the origins of uniformity and orthodoxy as close as possible to the generation of the apostles, constantly uses phrases – 'countless', 'very many', 'all', – when he deals with the orthodox Church, its size, its influence, its success, its champions and its heroic sacrifices, which is not borne out by evidence, even when he cites it. In particular, he exaggerates the volume of orthodox literature from the earliest times. His motive was to show that a massive quantity of books setting out the true faith was produced in the first two centuries, that they had wide circulation, were faithfully preserved and enjoyed a long life; they grew up and spread so vigorously that they smashed the heretics or drove them into tiny enclaves. But the books to which Eusebius refers have not survived and he does not seem to have read them, to judge by his references. Why should they survive up to the fourth century, then disappear? On the other side, the overwhelming bulk of heretic writings, including diatribes between rival heresies, have disappeared. But often their titles survive and these, in many cases, do not suggest polemics – the works of sects struggling for survival against orthodoxy – but the regular teaching of the established majority faith.

A very complex picture of orthodoxy and heterodoxy in the early period is revealed if we study the 'succession lists' of individual bishoprics. By the third century, lists of bishops, each of whom had consecrated his successor, and which went back to the original founding of the see by one or other of the apostles, had been collected or manufactured by most of the great cities of the empire and were reproduced by Eusebius. The idea was first developed by the gnostics who listed teachers, and *their* teachers, going back to Jesus, and transmitting the sacred knowledge. Thus Basilides, one of the gnostic heretics, appealed to Glaucias, described as Peter's interpreter, and so back to Peter and Christ; another gnostic, Valentinus, claimed he had been instructed by Theodas, a disciple of Paul; both the Carpocratians and the Nassenians appealed to Mariamne, to whom James, Jesus's brother, handed on the secrets. During the second century this gnostic device was adopted by orthodox Christianity. Indeed to some extent it was systematized, about 180, by an orthodox writer from the east, Hegesippus. His writings are lost, but according to Eusebius he travelled round collecting evidence about the succession in various Churches and then wrote a huge tome in which 'he presented the undistorted tradition of the apostolic preaching in the simplest possible form.' He identified intellectual continuity, preserved on a personal basis, with juristic and sacramental continuity. He thus linked the 'correct' tradition and succession with order and unanimity. Early teachers were identified and then transformed into a series of monarchical bishops. There was no conscious falsification, since by the second half of the second century it was assumed there had always been such bishops; all that was necessary was to prod people's memories to get the details. Then the list could be tidied up. Hence the longer and more impressive the list, the later its date of compilation and the less its accuracy. Eusebius, however, presents the lists as evidence that orthodoxy had a continuous tradition from the earliest times in all the great episcopal sees and that all heretical movements were subsequent aberrations from the mainline of Christianity.

Looking behind the lists, however, a different picture emerges. In Edessa, on the edge of the Syrian desert, the proofs of the early establishment of Christianity were forgeries, almost certainly manufactured under Bishop Kune, the first orthodox bishop, and actually a contemporary of Eusebius. Christianity seems to have been brought to the area by Marcionites, about 150, and later flourished in various non-orthodox forms, including the Manichean. Different texts of the New Testament, varying in important essentials, were in use. Thus orthodoxy did not arrive until the last decades of the third century.

Equally, the first Christian groups in Egypt were heterodox by later standards. They came into existence about the beginning of the first century and were Christian-gnostics. Their teaching, put in writing about this time, was the 'Gospel of the Egyptians', in Coptic, later declared heretical. Very recent discoveries in the Upper Nile Valley suggest that gnosticism was also the dominant form of Christianity in Upper Egypt at this time. And in Alexandria in Lower Egypt there was a Jewish-Christian community, using the 'gospel of the Hebrews', also later declared heretical. Orthodoxy was not established until the time of Bishop Demetrius, 189–231, who set up a number of other sees and manufactured a genealogical tree for his own Bishopric of Alexandria, which traces the foundation through ten mythical predecessors back to Mark, and so to Peter and Jesus. Orthodoxy was merely one of several forms of Christianity during the third century, and may not have become dominant until Eusebius's time.

Even in Antioch, where both Peter and Paul had been active, there seems to have been confusion until the end of the second century. Antioch harboured a multitude of esoteric religious cults. Gnosticism was powerful, and may have taken over Christianity after the departure of the apostles. Some early Christians there seem to have used a heretical text, called the gospel of Peter. The 'apostolic succession' may have been lost completely. When Eusebius's chief source for his episcopal lists, Julius Africanus, tried to compile one for Antioch he found only six names to cover the same spell of time as twelve in Rome and ten in Alexandria. Orthodoxy in Antioch really dates from the episcopate of Ignatius in the late second century who had to free himself as well as his diocese from the local gnostic tradition and who imported orthodox clergy from elsewhere to help the process. We have evidence that the same sort of process was repeated in western Asia Minor, in Thessalonica, and in Crete. Indeed, wherever evidence exists, it indicates that the process of achieving uniformity, thereby making orthodoxy meaningful, began only towards the end of the second century, and was far from complete by the end of the third.

A number of factors made this process possible. The first was the evolution of a canon of New Testament writings. Although oral tradition continued to be important right up till the end of the second century, most traditions had found written form by its early decades; they constituted an enormous mass of writing, only part of which has come down to us, covering a wide range of doctrine and assertion, much of it contradictory. The Church was bothered by this problem from an early date, as is evident from the work of Bishop Papias, and was originally inclined to adopt a rigorous policy, excluding anything which it did not believe to be demonstrably connected with one or other of the apostles. During this period, indeed, Christians were still aware of the way in which traditions were finding written form and were far more conscious of the element of fraud during the post-apostolic age than the later legislators of Church councils. But Marcion pushed this tendency too far: his exegetical methods, impressive though they were, would not merely have cut off Christianity from Judaism completely – thus distorting the character and intellectual background of Jesus's work – but would have reduced the New Testament virtually to the authentic Pauline corpus. The historical Jesus would have disappeared, Christianity would have been completely Hellenized and thus made far more vulnerable to gnostic penetration and disintegration. In the reaction from Marcion, the tendency was for the canon to become less exclusive. A fragment survives from the late second century (in an eighth-century Latin translation, first printed in 1740 by L. A. Muratori) listing the 'received' works, and indicating a major expansion since Papias's day. The instinct was to give a multi-focal vision of Jesus and his ideas and thus to broaden the appeal of his teaching and its interpretation. This meant accepting a large number of theological and ethical, and indeed historical-factual contradictions; on the other hand it preserved the universalist spirit of Christianity and was more faithful to the tradition of Jesus himself as a provider of innumerable matrices and insights than a homogenous theology like Paul's.

Expanding the canon was also a weapon against heresy. All the evidence suggests that heresiarchs did not create heresies: they merely articulated popular moods which already existed or in some cases fought for traditions which were being trampled by the march of orthodoxy. An inclusive canon allowed the Church to make a wider appeal to heretical populations or, to put it another way, to include under its umbrella of faith the followers of old and divergent traditions. At the same time, the process of selection and canonization allowed the orthodox leaders to demolish dangerous documents once their adherents had been captured. Thus in the third, fourth and fifth centuries, many written 'gospels', particularly those penetrated by gnosticism, were excluded and so disappeared. At the same time, dangerous elements within the canon could be to some extent de-fused by attaching more orthodox documents to their authors. Thus Paul, damaged by the championship of Marcion, was credited with the so-called 'pastoral epistles', which have the tone of the emerging orthodox church; and the gospel of John, much used by the Montanists and other heretics – and certainly a candidate for exclusion at one time – was saved by attributing to its supposed author three unobjectionable epistles. There was horse-trading between rival centres of Christianity and, increasingly, between East and West. Thus the West successfully insisted on the elimination of many Alexandrine documents, but it was unable to foist on the East a number of important Roman writings of the early second century. It almost failed with Revelation, about which most Greeks were sceptical even in the eighth century; some never accepted it. The epistle to the Hebrews, as most of the early fathers knew, was not by Paul. It was excluded from the Muratorian fragment and rejected by Tertullian and virtually everyone else in the West. The first notable Latin figure to accept it as canonical was the mid-fourth century Bishop of Poitiers, Hilary. But it was popular in the East and finally categorized as Pauline, as a result of a deal at the Council of Carthage in 419 – though we know that the most influential ecclesiastic present, Augustine, was quite sure it was not written by Paul. In general, the determining figure in the evolution of the canon was Eusebius, whose object was to associate as closely as possible the actual teaching and structure of the Church with its documentary credentials; after his death, useful documents he had considered doubtful were accepted as canonical, the process being virtually completed by 367, when Athanasius gave a list in his Easter Letter. By this time, the New Testament, roughly as we know it, had largely superseded the old Hebrew scriptures as the principal teaching instrument of the church. It was an instrument which had been fashioned by the Church, rather than vice versa.

Moreover, the very idea of a body of 'new scriptures', containing the essence of the Christian faith, assisted the forces which were creating an institutional Church. Paul had been writing in an age when the *parousia* was still thought to be imminent, though by the end of his life hope that it would come immediately was fading. During the next two generations, the .Christians had to face the problem of a receding eschatology and accept that the period of waiting for the apocalypse was 'normalcy'. For a time, the idea of a general resurrection and of individual expectations of heaven at death were presented side by side, without reconciliation; then the first gradually fell into the background. Ethics once more became complicated and subtle. Paul's simple eschatological call for repentance, the summons to 'watch', yielded to the idea of the 'Christian life' as expressed in the pastoral epistles and the epistle to the Hebrews, which were fathered on him. Thus the regulation of life once more tended to be portrayed as the condition of salvation and the great ethical commandment of the gospels assumed the status of a new law. But law implied obedience; and obedience implied authority. What was this authority? The Church. What constituted the Church? The men who ran it.

The same process of reasoning was at work in faith as well as ethics. Hebrews stressed the importance of faith and of its public confession by Christians. The first epistle of John introduced the idea of the confession as a defence against heresy and false knowledge. Hitherto, the confession produced a decision for or against faith; now it was a decision for or against particular groups in the Church. In short the confession had to be interpreted. The author of 1 John insisted that anyone who rejected his interpretation not only rejected part of the faith but *the* faith, because it was indivisible. We see here the rise of dogma. The sacred writings not only had to be classified as authorative or not, they had to be explained – and the explanation itself was authoritative. Who was in charge of the process? The Church. What was the Church? The men who ran it.

The idea of a clergy seems to have been a marriage between Greek and Judaic ideas. The Jerusalem elders of the Jewish-Christian Church possessed an element of authority; they were 'pillars'. The bishops and deacons of the Gentile Church originally had purely spiritual functions. They were charismatics – not organizers, fund-raisers or legislators. This was the situation portrayed in Paul's genuine epistles and also in Luke's Acts. But by the time the early Roman sources appear, early in the second century, the matrix of a clerical structure had been forged. The first epistle of Clement stressed the importance of 'decency and order' in the Church. And part of this order was a hierarchical structure. Women were to be subject to men, the young to the old, the 'multitude' to the presbyters, or alternatively to bishops and deacons selected for this purpose. A historical theory of episcopacy had already been evolved: 'Our apostles also knew, through our Lord Jesus Christ, that there would be contention over the name of bishop. For this reason, being possessed of complete foreknowledge, they appointed the above-mentioned men, and then made a decree that, when these men died, other reliable men should take over their office.' By the time Ignatius of Antioch wrote his letter, perhaps twenty years later, the hierarchical order had developed further, and clergy were divided into grades: the bishop, the council of the presbyters, and the deacons. Ignatius, who may well have written hymns and introduced antiphonal singing to the Church, used a musical image: only if all performed their parts as allotted, would the essential unity of the Church be preserved. By this stage, as we see from the pastoral epistles, the primitive democracy of the eschatological period had gone: the congregation had lost its freedom, the bishops taught authorized truth and office was seen as the instrument by which the apostolic tradition was to be preserved. The authority of the bishop was then buttressed, as we have seen, by the compilation of episcopal lists going back to the apostolic foundations. All such Churches produced their list, and no one Church alone had to bear the burden of proving that its teaching was the one originally given. Thus the Churches established intercommunion and mutual defence against heresy, on the basis of the monarchical episcopate and its apostolic genealogy.

With the episcopate established as the unifying principle in the Church, the way was open for fresh developments. The idea of succession, originally stressed to safeguard belief in the tradition, was detached from its setting and used to create a doctrine of spiritual office. Tertullian saw this in legal terms: the bishops were 'heirs' to spiritual property. And part of their property was that their authority was valid everywhere because they became special people by virtue of their office. How did they become heirs? The answer was shortly supplied by Hippolytus of Rome, writing early in the third century, with the notion of a special sanctifying power in episcopal consecration. This service, he argued, was the means by which bishops, like the apostles before them, were endowed with the threefold authority of the high priesthood, the teaching, and the office of 'watchman'. They could be ordained only by other bishops – thus for the first time a sacral differentiation was made in consecration rites.

The creation of an international Church, moving slowly from doctrinal diversity to the semblance of orthodoxy, based on an agreed canon and underpinned by the institution of the bishops, was essentially the work of the second century. This was pragmatical work, evolved in response to the collapse of the eschatological hope, and during a fierce and continuous battle against heresy; theory was made up to rationalize and justify change rather than to advance it. The character the Church – or rather the increasingly victorious trend within the Church – was acquiring was empirical and inclusive; it tended to reject one-sided ideological interpretations. Thus Marcion, the ultra-Pauline, and Tertullian, the defender of charismatics, found themselves outside. This policy paid, even at the sacrifice of splendid talents. It meant that the Church, operating on the principle of collective commonsense, was a haven for a very wide spectrum of opinion. In the West, diversity was disappearing fast; in the East, orthodoxy was becoming the largest single tradition by the early decades of the third century. The Church was now a great and numerous force in the empire, attracting men of wealth and high education. Inevitably, then, there occurred a change of emphasis from purely practical development in response to need, to the deliberate thinking out of policy.

This expressed itself in two ways: the attempt to turn Christianity into a philosophical and political system, and the development of controlling devices to prevent this intellectualization of the faith from destroying it. The twin process began to operate in the early and middle decades of the third century, with Origen epitomizing the first element and Cyprian the second. If Paul brought to the first generation of Christians the useful skills of a trained theologian, Origen was the first great philosopher to rethink the new religion from first principles. As his philosophical enemy, the anti-Christian Porphyry, summed it up, he 'introduced Greek ideas to foreign fables' – that is, gave a barbarous eastern religion the intellectual respectability of a philosophical defence. Origen was also a phenomenon. As Eusebius put it admiringly, 'even the facts from his cradle are worth mentioning'. Origen came from Alexandria, the second city of the empire and then its intellectual centre; his father's martyrdom left him an orphan at seventeen with six younger brothers. He was a hard-working prodigy, at eighteen head of the Catechetical School, and already trained as a literary scholar and teacher. But at this point, probably in 203, he became a religious fanatic and remained one for the next fifty years. He gave up his job and sold his books to concentrate on religion. He slept on the floor, ate no meat, drank no wine, had only one coat and no shoes. He almost certainly castrated himself, in obedience to the notorious text, Matthew 19:12, 'there are some who have made themselves eunuchs for the kingdom of heaven's sake.' Origen's learning was massive and it was of a highly original kind: he always went back to the sources and thought through the whole process himself. Thus he learnt Hebrew and, according to Eusebius, 'got into his possession the original writings extant among the Jews in the actual Hebrew character'. These included the discovery of lost texts; in the case of the psalms, Origen collected not only the four known texts but three others he unearthed, including 'one he found at Jericho in a jar'. The result was an enormous tome, the *Hexapla*, which probably existed only in one manuscript, now lost, setting out the seven alternative texts in parallel columns. He applied the same principles of original research to every aspect of Christianity and sacred literature. He seems to have worked all day and through most of the night, and was a compulsive writer. Even the hardy Jerome later complained: 'Has anyone read everything that Origen wrote?' His scriptural commentaries were so vast that none has been transmitted in full. Some have been lost, others survive as drastic paraphrases.

The effect of Origen's work was to create a new science, biblical theology, whereby every sentence in the scriptures was systematically explored for hidden meanings, different layers of meanings, allegory and so forth. And from the elements of this vast scriptural erudition he constructed, in his book *First Principles*, a Christian philosophy from which it was possible to interpret every aspect of the world. Hitherto, Christians had either dismissed philosophy as irrelevant or pagan, or had simply appropriated Plato and other writers, categorized them as incipient Christians, and fitted the Pauline superstructure on to their foundation. Origen waved aside this tradition, dismissed the Greek philosophers as false and constructed a new synthesis out of profane and sacred knowledge. Thus he offered to the world the first theory of knowledge conceived entirely from within Christian assumptions, pre-figuring both the encyclopedists like Isidore of Seville, and the systematic *summae* of the medieval schoolmen. With Origen, Christianity ceased to be an appendage of the classical world and became, intellectually, a universe of its own. It was also, if only as yet by implication, becoming a society of its own. Origen was the first theorist of clericalism, as well as other aspects of mature Christianity. His own relations with the Church were stormy. He could not get ordination from his own bishop of Alexandria; aroused clerical censure by preaching in Palestine as a layman; was ordained uncanonically, and thereafter was frequently attacked for propagating a false doctrine. He had no respect for the clergy as individuals, and in general gave a gloomy picture of their avarice and ambition. But this in no way undermines his exaltation of the dignity and power of ecclesiastical office. Indeed, one might say he can afford to castigate clergymen precisely because he believes their position as a caste is indestructible. Origen accepted an absolute distinction between clergy and laity. He gave it juridical flavour. He portrayed the Church, as part of his theory of universal knowledge, as a sacred sociological entity. The analogy was with a political state. Of course the Church had to have its own princes and kings. Of course they governed their congregations far better than corresponding state officials. Their position was infinitely higher and holier, since they administered spiritual things, but their status was similar to those of judges and secular rulers, and therefore the laity had to show them reverence and obedience even if they were inadequate or bad men.

Within the broad philosophical system elaborated by Origen there was room for an internal system of regulation and discipline. This was supplied by his younger contemporary, Cyprian of Carthage. If Origen adumbrated the concept of a Christian universe, Cyprian unveiled the machinery necessary to keep it together and make it work. These different interests reflect their backgrounds. Origen was an intellectual. Cyprian came from a wealthy family with a tradition of public service to the empire; within two years of his conversion he was made a bishop. He had to face the practical problems of persecution, survival and defence against attack. His solution was to gather together the developing threads of ecclesiastical order and authority and weave them into a tight system of absolute control. He reasoned as follows. The Church was a divine institution; the Bride of Christ; Mother Church, the mediatrix of all salvation. It was one, undivided and catholic. Only in association with her could catholics have life. Outside her holy fellowship there was nothing but error and darkness. The sacraments, episcopal ordination, the confession of faith, even the Bible itself, lost their meaning if used outside the true Church. The Church was also a human, visible community, found only in an organized form. The individual could not be saved by direct contact with God. The carefully graded hierarchy, without which the organized Church could not exist, was established by Christ and the apostles. The laity was allowed to be present at the election of the bishop but the actual choice was made by all the presbyters, especially by other neighbouring bishops. And bishops, under the Metropolitan, had the right of removal. Through the bishop 'all ecclesiastical measures whatsoever must be carried out'. Without the office of bishop there could be no Church; and without the Church, no salvation. The man who determined who was, or was not, a member of the Church, and therefore eligible for salvation, was the bishop. He interpreted the scriptures in the light of the Church's needs in any given situation; the only unambiguous instruction they contained being to remain faithful to the Church and obey its rules. With Cyprian, then, the freedom preached by Paul and based on the power of Christian truth was removed from the ordinary members of the Church; it was retained only by the bishops, through whom the Holy Spirit still worked, who were collectively delegated to represent the totality of Church members. They were given wide powers of discretion, subject always to the traditional and attested truth of the Church and the scriptures. They were rulers, operating and interpreting a law. With Bishop Cyprian, the analogy with secular government came to seem very close.

But of course it lacked one element: the 'emperor figure' or supreme priest. Cyprian was still thinking in terms of a collectivity of bishops, as, it might be argued, were the elders or pillars of the Jerusalem Church, more than a century and a half before. Yet since the bishops themselves based their authority on the tradition derived from apostolic descent, it was evident that some Churches, and therefore some bishops, carried more weight than others. Jerusalem was the mother-Church, where all the apostles had operated; but the Jerusalem congregation had ceased to exist by AD 70, and it never recovered its pristine status. The only other apostolic foundation was Rome, since both Peter and Paul were believed to have been martyred there. Peter's martyrdom was alluded to in John's gospel, 13:36 and 21:18–19, and both Clement's epistle to the Corinthians and Ignatius's Letter to the Romans indicate it took place in Rome. The claim was made explicit by Eusebius, who quoted Gaius (c. 200) and Dionysius Bishop of Corinth as his authorities; and there is a further statement in the *Chronicle* of Sulpicius Severus (d. 420). Eusebius and Dionysius agree that Paul was beheaded, Peter crucified. This belief that the two apostles were executed and buried in Rome was evidently very ancient. Tertullian accepted it as fact; by his day there was already a monument on the Vatican Hill, built about 160. Recent excavations make it clear that it was set up in Peter's honour and that those who did so thought he was buried there. Gaius mentioned this monument and also one to St Paul on the Ostia road, the present site of St-Paul's-Without-the-Walls. There was also a third joint monument on the Appian Way, where services were held on 29 June as early as the second century. Thus Rome's connection with the two greatest apostles was never disputed and it was exploited from the earliest times. Rome had the most impressive genealogy of all the earliest churches. Indeed, it had an *embarras de richesse*—not one apostle, but two. Peter, however, was the more valuable founder, as he was in some sense the chief apostle, Jesus's closest associate, and the beneficiary of the famous 'rock and keys' text in Matthew. There is no evidence that Rome exploited this text to assert its primacy before about 250 – and then, interestingly enough, in conflict with the aggressive episcopalian Cyprian – but what is clear is that in the second half of the second century, and no doubt in response to Marcion's Pauline heresy – the first heresy Rome itself had experienced – Paul was eliminated from any connection with the Rome episcopate and the office was firmly attached to Peter alone. In fact the first Roman bishop in any meaningful sense was probably Soter, 166–74, but by that time the concept of an episcopal tradition going back to Jesus had already been established, and Rome may also have been behind the process which made 'her' apostle, Peter, the founder of the Church of Antioch, and his assistant, Mark, the founder in Alexandria, thus turning into Roman ecclesiastical colonies the second and third cities in the empire.

Even before this stage, however, there is evidence that Rome was using its position as the imperial capital to influence the Church in other centres, and thus to build up a case-history of successful intervention. The first such instance of which we have record is Clement's Letter to the Corinthians, where Clement weighs in on the side of established order. There were other second-century cases, usually on what seemed like marginal issues: cultic practices, the date of Easter, and so forth. Rome was appealed to as the best apostolic authority, and responded eagerly. It had an early reputation for robustness in the faith: it was the first Church to undergo a systematic state persecution and to survive it triumphantly. It was also orthodox: that is, it was felt to have preserved intact the teaching of Peter and Paul. The danger-zone of heresy, of gnosticism, of credal instability and osmosis was the east, especially Syria, Asia Minor and Egypt. Rome was far removed from the infection. It seems to have excluded gnostic tendencies right from the start. It set the pace in defining the canon, eliminating the spurious and producing authorized texts. It had no experience of heresy until Marcion, and then it quickly forced him to operate in Asia; equally, it defeated the Montanist challenge – Montanism flourished in Asia long after it had been eliminated from Rome's Christian circles. The great antiheretical campaigners, Hegesippus, Justin Rhodo, Militiades, were Rome-oriented, most of them living and working there. Rome profited not only from its apostolic foundation but from its associations as the capital of the empire: it was the standard for faith, ritual, organization, textual accuracy and general Christian practice. It was the first Christian Church to eliminate minority tendencies, and present a homogenous front to the world. From there it was a natural development for Rome to probe into the affairs of other Churches, with a view to assisting the victory of the 'orthodox', that is Roman, element.

Moreover, Rome had an excellent excuse for such interference. From the earliest times, it had assisted small and struggling Churches with money. This was charity, but charity, increasingly, with a purpose. Money certainly accompanied Clement's letter to Corinth, where it helped to turn the minority into the majority party. Apollonius, writing against the Montanists, says that of course money played an important part in religious conflict – as in any other kind of struggle. From the, admittedly later, description by Eusebius of Constantine's use of cash to promote Christianity, we can deduce the variety of ways in which financial power influenced religious development. Money was used to get prominent Christian teachers out of state prisons; to ransom valuable men who had been sent to the Sardinian mines; to build up congregations out of freed slaves and the poor; to support welfare services and provide bail sureties, or even judicial bribes. The Rome congregation was rich, and became much richer during the second century. Thus towards the end of it we find Dionysius of Corinth writing in gratitude: 'From the start it has been your custom to treat all Christians with unfailing kindness, and to send contributions to many churches in every city ... thus you Romans have observed the ancestral Roman custom, which your revered Bishop Soter has not only maintained but enlarged, by generously providing the abundant supplies distributed among God's people.' A similar dispatch, from Dionysius of Alexandria, says that 'all of Syria' was in receipt of such aid, and adds that the donations were accompanied by letters – of advice and instruction, no doubt. With Roman money there went a gentle but persistent pressure to conform to Roman standards.

It is easy to project backwards into these developments – the extension of orthodoxy, the rise of the monarchical episcopate, the special role of Rome – the operation of a deliberate policy, pursued relentlessly from generation to generation with the object of creating a system of ecclesiastical law, a privileged clerical class and an authoritarian faith. This, indeed, was what was beginning to emerge by the third century. But the element of planning for this purpose is not reflected in the documents. They suggest, rather, a series of *ad hoc* responses to actual situations and then a tendency to use such responses as precedents or platforms on which to erect more ambitious structures. Throughout this period the Church as a whole was fighting for its very survival. And, within it, there was a continuous and multi-faceted struggle among rival philosophies and systems. The first battle was made inevitable by Christianity's unwillingness to remain a mere cult, and its claim to be the universal religion. The second was a reflection of its founder's clear desire to establish a religion of diversity as well as universality, to be 'all things to all men'. Jesus's ministry was conducted in an atmosphere of dissension, angry argument and party spirit; it ended in death by violence. The spirit of the early Church was well conveyed by Paul's epistles, which suggest doctrinal bitterness and unresolved controversy. There was no calm period in the history of the Church. In its first generation it was very nearly reabsorbed by Judaism. Then, for at least a century, there was a risk it would become an other-worldly religion, inflexibly ordering life by superhuman standards, or a complicated mystery cult for intellectual connoisseurs. There was no long-term future in either direction. The Church survived, and steadily penetrated all ranks of society over a huge area, by avoiding or absorbing extremes, by compromise, by developing an urbane temperament and erecting secular-type structures to preserve its unity and conduct its business. There was in consequence a loss of spirituality or, as Paul would have put it, of freedom. There was a gain in stability and collective strength. By the end of the third century Christianity was able to confront and outface the most powerful corporation in ancient history – the Roman empire.

PART TWO

From Martyrs to Inquisitors
(AD 250–450)

IN 313, from the great imperial city of Milan, Constantine and his co-emperor Licinius despatched a series of flowery letters to provincial governors. The two rulers thought it 'salutary and most proper' that 'complete toleration' should be given by the State to anyone who had 'given up his mind either to the cult of the Christians' or any other cult 'which he personally feels best for himself'. All previous anti-Christian decrees were revoked; Christian places of worship and other property seized from them were to be restored; and compensation provided where legally appropriate. The new policy was to be 'published everywhere and brought to the notice of all men'.

The so-called 'Edict of Milan', by which the Roman Empire reversed its policy of hostility to Christianity and accorded it full legal recognition was one of the decisive events in world history. Yet the story behind it is complicated and in some ways mysterious. Christian apologists at the time and later portrayed it as the consequence of Constantine's own conversion, itself brought about by the miraculous intervention of God before the Battle of the Milvian Bridge outside Rome, where Constantine defeated the usurper Maxentius. This was the story Constantine liked to tell himself, later in life. Bishop Eusebius, who informs us gloatingly that he was 'honoured with the Emperor's acquaintance and society', says he heard from Constantine's own lips that 'a most incredible sign appeared to him from heaven.' But there is a conflict of evidence about the exact time, place and details of this vision, and there is some doubt about the magnitude of Constantine's change of ideas. His father had been pro-Christian. He himself appears to have been a sun-worshipper, one of a number of late-pagan cults which had observances in common with the Christians. Thus the followers of Isis adored a madonna nursing her holy child; the cult of Attis and Cybele celebrated a day of blood and fasting, followed by the Hilaria resurrection-feast, a day of joy, on 25 March; the elitist Mithraics, many of whom were senior army officers, ate a sacred meal. Constantine was almost certainly a Mithraic, and his triumphal arch, built after his 'conversion', testifies to the Sun-god, or 'unconquered sun'. Many Christians did not make a clear distinction between this sun-cult and their own. They referred to Christ 'driving his chariot across the sky'; they held their services on Sunday, knelt towards the East and had their nativity-feast on 25 December, the birthday of the sun at the winter solstice. During the later pagan revival under the Emperor Julian many Christians found it easy to apostasize because of this confusion; the Bishop of Troy told Julian he had always prayed secretly to the sun. Constantine never abandoned sun-worship and kept the sun on his coins. He made Sunday into a day of rest, closing the lawcourts and forbidding all work except agricultural labour. In his new city of Constantinople, he set up a statue of the sun-god, bearing his own features, in the Forum; and another of the mother-Goddess Cybele, though she was presented in a posture of Christian prayer.

Constantine's motives were probably confused. He was an exceptionally superstitious man, and he no doubt shared the view, popular among professional soldiers, that all religious cults should be respected, to appease their respective gods. He clearly underwent a strange experience at some time in his military career, in which his Christian troops played a part. He was a slave to signs and omens and had the Christian Chi-Rho sign on his shields and standards long before Milan. Superstition guided his decision to build a new capital, the choice of its site, and many other of his major acts of state. He was not baptized until his last illness. This was by no means unusual, since few Christians then believed in a second forgiveness of sins; sinful or worldly men, especially those with public duties seen as incompatible with Christian virtue, often delayed baptism till they were about to depart. But Eusebius's account of Constantine's late baptism is ambiguous; and it may be that the Church refused him the sacrament because of his manner of life. Certainly it was not his piety which made him a Christian. As a young man, he had the imperial look about him. He was tall, soldierly, athletic, with strongly marked features, heavy eyebrows, a powerful chin. But there were early reports of his violent temper and his cruelty in anger. He was much criticized for condemning prisoners of war to mortal combat with wild beasts at Trier and Colmar and for wholesale massacres in north Africa. He had no respect for human life, and as emperor he executed his eldest son, his own second wife, his favourite sister's husband and 'many others' on doubtful charges. He was a puritan of sorts, passing laws forbidding concubinage, prostitution of inn servants, and the seduction of slaves, but his private life became monstrous as he aged. He grew fat, was known as 'the bull-neck'; he may even have suffered from goitre. His abilities had always lain in management, the operation of the mechanics of power; he was a professional arbitrator, a master of the eirenic phrase and the smoothly-worded compromise, but also overbearing, egotistical, self-righteous and ruthless. The public-relations side of his job took over in later years. He showed an increasing regard for flattery, fancy uniforms, personal display and elaborate titles. His nephew Julian said he made himself ridiculous by his appearance – weird, stiff eastern garments, jewels on his arms, a tiara on his head, perched crazily on top of a tinted wig.

Bishop Eusebius, his fulsome eulogist, said Constantine dressed thus solely to impress the masses; privately, he laughed at himself. But this contradicts much other evidence, including Eusebius's own. Vain and superstitious, Constantine may have embraced Christianity because it suited his personal interests, and his growing megalomania. There was a Caesaro-papalist flavour about his regime. Many of his ecclesiastical arrangements indicate that he wanted a state Church, with the clergy as civil servants. His own role was not wholly removed from that of the pagan God-emperor – as witness the colossal heads and statues of himself with which he littered his empire – though he preferred the idea of a priest-king. Eusebius says he was present when Constantine entertained a group of bishops and suddenly remarked: 'You are bishops whose jurisdiction is within the church. But I also am a bishop, ordained by God to oversee those outside the church.' Constantine does not seem to have acquired any knowledge of Pauline theology but, again according to Eusebius, he apparently imbibed some of Origen's more grandiose ideas and secularized them, seeing himself as the chief divine instrument. Thus, said Eusebius, he 'derived the source of imperial authority from above'; he was 'strong in the power of the sacred title'. Constantine was especially beloved of Christ and 'by bringing those whom he rules on earth to the only-begotten and saving Word, renders them fit subjects for Christ's kingdom'; he is 'interpreter of the word of God', a 'powerful voice declaring the laws of truth and godliness to all who dwell on earth', 'the appointed pilot of the mighty vessel whose crew it is his aim to save'. God, said the Bishop, was the author of kingship, and 'There is one king, and his Word and royal law is one; a law not subject to the ravages of time, but the living and self-subsisting word.' Clearly, according to this analysis, Constantine, as emperor, was an important agent of the salvation process, at least as vital to it as the apostles. So, evidently, the emperor himself thought. Thus he had a tomb prepared for himself within the new Church of the Apostles he built and gloriously endowed in Constantinople, 'anticipating', says Eusebius, 'that his body would share the title with the apostles themselves, and that he should after his death become the subject, with them, of the devotions performed in their honour in this church.' His coffin and tomb, in fact, were placed in the centre, with monuments to six apostles on each side, making him the thirteenth and chief; and he contrived to die on Whitsunday.

How could the Christian Church, apparently quite willingly, accommodate this weird megalomaniac in its theocratic system? Was there a conscious bargain? Which side benefited most from this unseemly marriage between Church and State? Or, to put it another way, did the empire surrender to Christianity, or did Christianity prostitute itself to the empire? It is characteristic of the complexities of early Christian history that we cannot give a definite answer to this question. It is not at all clear why the empire and Christianity came into conflict in the first place. The empire extended toleration to all sects provided they kept the peace. Jewish Christianity may have been penetrated by Zealotry and Jewish irredentism, but the gentile Christianity of the Pauline missions was non-political and non-racial. Its social implications were, in the long run, revolutionary, but it had no specific doctrines of social change. Jesus had told his hearers to pay taxes. Paul, in a memorable passage, advised the faithful, while waiting for the *parousia*, to obey duly-constituted authority. As early as the mid-second century, some

Christian writers saw an identity of interests between the burgeoning Christian movement, with its universalist aims, and the empire itself. Christians might not yield divine honours to the emperor, but in other respects they were loyal Romans. Tertullian claimed:

> 'We are for ever making intercession for the emperors. We pray for them a long life, a secure rule, a safe home, brave armies, a faithful senate, an honest people, a quiet world, and everything for which a man and a Caesar may pray. . . . We know that the great force which threatens the whole world, the end of the age itself with its menace of hideous sufferings, is delayed by the respite which the Roman Empire means for us . . . when we pray for its postponement we assist the continuance of Rome. . . . I have a right to say, Caesar is more ours than yours, appointed as he is by our God.'

By Tertullian's time (c. 200), as he pointed out, the Christians were numerous enough to overthrow the Empire, had their intentions been hostile: 'We are but of yesterday, and we fill everything you have – cities, tenements, forts, towns, exchanges, yes! and camps, tribes, palace, senate, forum. All we leave you with are the Temples!' Christians were, he urged, a docile as well as a loyal element in society.

And of course for the most part they were left alone. As a rule, the Christians, like the Jews, enjoyed complete freedom from persecution. The impression that they lived and worshipped underground is a complete fallacy, arising from the name (Catacombus) of one of their earliest cemeteries. They had their own churches, as the Jews had synagogues. They made no secret of their faith. From the earliest times, Tertullian says, they identified themselves: 'At every forward step and movement, at every going in and out, when we put on our clothes and shoes, when we bathe, when we sit at table, when we light the lamps, on couch, on seat, in all the ordinary actions of daily life, we trace upon the forehead the sign of the cross.' There seems to have been no attempt at concealment, strangers being invited to attend part of the Christian service, and to present themselves for instruction.

Yet there was from the start considerable prejudice, a form of anti-semitism which persisted even after Roman conformists had learnt to distinguish between Christians and Jews. Thus an anti-Christian writer c. 180 calls them 'people ignorant of learning, unlettered and unskilled in the meanest arts'. They were 'a gang of discredited and proscribed desperadoes', formed from 'the lowest dregs of the population, ignorant men and credulous women'. At their 'nocturnal gatherings, solemn feasts and barbarous meals, the bond of union is not a sacred rite but crime'. They were 'a secret tribe that lurks in darkness and shuns the light, silent in public, chattering in corners . . . and these vicious habits are spreading day by day. . . . These conspirators must be utterly destroyed and cursed.' In this atmosphere of ignorance and prejudice, Christians became objects of suspicion and the victims of wild rumour. The Christians automatically placed themselves outside the law by refusing divine honours to emperors. Under weak and vulnerable rulers, like Caligula, Nero and Domitian, they became scapegoats for failure or disaster. As Tertullian put it: 'If the Tiber reaches the walls, if the Nile failes to rise to the fields, if the sky doesn't move, or the earth does, if there is famine or plague, the cry is at once: "The Christians to the Lion!"' Prejudice was much stronger in the central and western Mediterranean than in the east, but certain rumours were current everywhere. The doctrine of the eucharist, under which 'flesh' and 'blood' were eaten, was understood to mean the practice of cannibalism. The 'kiss of peace' at Sunday services was also misinterpreted. Clement of Alexandria complained: 'There are those that do nothing but make the churches resound with a kiss, not having love itself within. This practice, the shameless use of the kiss, which ought to be mystic, has occasioned foul suspicions and evil reports.' There was a reference to incest.

The wilder Christians sects – later branded as heretics – naturally attracted more attention from critics and Roman officials. Writing from Bythinia in Asia Minor, a worried local governor, Pliny the Younger, asked for detailed instruction from the Emperor Trajan (98–117). Christianity, he reported, was spreading from the towns to the countryside. The temples were empty and it was becoming difficult to sell the meat from sacrificed animals. He was under local pressure to execute Christians. What was their crime? Should they be charged with incest and cannibalism, their reputed offences? If they remained contumacious then it was clear they had to be executed, but what if they recanted? Some admitted they had been Christians but denied their faith and cursed Christ. They made offerings to the emperor and the gods. But they also denied that Christians practised enormities. They did not eat murdered children: just food. And they had suspended their secret rites following an edict against religious societies. He had tortured two deaconesses, but found nothing but 'squalid superstition'. Severity undoubtedly brought people back to the temples. What should he do now? Trajan advised moderation. There should be no general inquisition. Anonymous informers should be ignored. Accusations from responsible folk should be properly investigated. No Christian should be punished if he made sacrifices.

This was the line usually followed by Roman governments. If they were strong and secure they were less inclined to yield to prejudice. Undisavowed Christianity remained a capital offence, but government did not, as a rule, force Christians into the choice between avowal and apostasy. It left them alone. One reason why the Church strove for uniformity, and so against heresy, was that non-orthodox practices tended to attract more attention and therefore hostility. 'Prophesying', the great offence of the Montanists, was strongly disapproved of by the State. It caused sudden and unpredictable crowd movements, panic and disruption of the economy. We hear of early bishops in the Balkans leading their flocks out of the towns, or away from the fields, in response to spirit instructions. Rome could be severe with such people. Marcus Aurelius, a reasonable man, justified persecuting Christians by arguing that it was dangerous to upset 'the unstable mind of man by superstitious fear of the divine'. And then he disliked the 'sheer spirit of opposition' of Christians. The more obdurate were, of course, members of Christian revivalist groups, 'speaking with tongues'. The great majority of the early martyrs were Christians of a type which the Church would later classify as heretic. The first stories of martyrs reflect not only Jewish martyrologies, as one might expect, but a form of literature echoing the defiant opposition of Greek rebels against Roman domination. The so-called 'Acts of the Pagan Martyrs', which survive in Egyptian papyrus fragments, glorify men able to defeat their Roman persecutors in intellectual dialogue – philosopher heroes smashing tyranny with words, even though they subsequently lost their heads. These became models for Christian nonconformists, openly challenging the might of the State. The Church took an increasingly severe view of provocative would-be martyrs. Ignatius, martyred at Rome around 117, begged his influential friends not to intervene and deprive him of suffering in the Lord; this attitude would have been regarded as heretical later in the century, when the saintly Polycarp, Bishop of Smyrna, set the pattern by doing nothing to provoke the authorities. The Church would not compromise on the matter of emperor-worship or the divinity of Christ, but otherwise it did not look for trouble.

There was no systematic persecution of Christians before the second half of the second century. The worst episodes were isolated incidents, as in the Rhone Valley in 177. Eusebius, who quotes from a contemporary letter, does not explain what set in motion this savage affair. The occasion was the annual summer gathering in the region for the payment of tribal taxes. Eusebius says that rumours were put about that Christians had been engaging in cannibal feasts and incest, the old tales; under pressure some of their household servants gave testimony to that effect. What followed was like a state-supervised riot. The letter speaks of 'the mighty rage of the heathen', 'the whole mass of the people', 'an infuriated mob'. Many Christians were tortured, in the stocks or in cells. Sanctus, a deacon from Vienne, had red-hot plates applied to his testicles – 'his poor body was one whole wound and bruise, having lost the outward form of a man'. Christians who were Roman citizens were beheaded. Others were forced through a gauntlet of whips into the amphitheatre and then, before an audience composed largely of un-romanized tribesmen, given to the beasts. Severed heads and limbs of Christians were displayed, guarded for six days, then burned, the ashes being thrown into the Rhone. But there were regular interrogations and trials before the Prefect, Rusticus. Some Christians 'were manifestly unready, untrained and still weak, unable to bear the strain . . . ten proved apostates'. This does not sound like an uncontrolled pogrom. One lady, Blandina, was the worst treated of all, 'tortured from dawn till evening, till her torturers were exhausted and . . . marvelled that the breath was still in her body'. She was then scourged, roasted in the 'frying pan', and finally put in a basket to be tossed to

death by wild bulls. Of course she was a mystic and a prophetess, probably a
Montanist. If one reason why the Church branded such people as heretics was
its fear of attracting persecution, then equally the State tended to strengthen
the orthodox elements in the Church by concentrating its savagery on the
antinomian elements among Christians.

By the middle of the third century, however, a much more critical period
had opened. Christians were now far more numerous, better organized, and
more homogenous in their views and practices. Once it had been possible to
dismiss them for their lower-class credulity. The pagan propagandist Celsus,
writing his *True Word c.* 180, claimed: 'Some do not even want to give or
receive a reason for what they believe, and simply say "Do not ask questions:
just believe", and "Thy faith will save thee". They say: "The wisdom of the
world is evil" and "Foolishness is a good thing".' Celsus illustrates a Christian
line of argument: 'Let no one wise, no one sensible, no one educated draw
near. For we think these things are evils. But as for anyone ignorant, educated
or stupid – anyone like a child – let him draw near.' This was of course a
caricature of genuine Christian attitudes which could be traced back to Jesus.
But as a portrait of the Church as a whole, it was ceasing to be true even when
Celsus wrote. The class and education barriers came down and Christianity
penetrated deep into circles which shaped secular policy and imperial culture.
The age of Origen, of a Christianity which had achieved intellectual maturity
in terms of the ancient world, made a direct and final confrontation with the
State inevitable. It was now a universalist alternative to the civil religion and a
far more dynamic (and better organized) one; it had either to be exterminated
or accepted.

The Decian persecution, around 250, marked the attempt to apply the first
policy, which was continued at intervals until Constantine switched to the
second sixty years later. State hostility was exercised universally, persistently,
and in due legal manner. There was no longer mass-hysteria, simply relentless
bureaucracy. Everyone had to obtain certificates proving he had made
sacrifice to the official gods. Some of these have been recovered from sites in
Egypt. Thus:

> 'To the commission appointed to supervise sacrifices at the village of
> Alexander's Isle. From Aurelius Diogenes, son of Satabus, of the village of
> Alexander's Isle, aged 72 years, with a scar on the right eyebrow. I have
> always sacrificed to the gods and now in your presence in accordance with
> the edict I have made sacrifice and poured a libation, and partaken of the
> sacred victuals. I request you to certify this below. Farewell: I, Aurelius
> Diogenes, have presented this petition.'

There is no doubt that this and later persecutions were extremely effective. The
blood of the martyrs, as Tertullian had claimed, might be the seed of the faith;
but the property of the Church was a temptation to compromise. By 250, for
instance, the Church in Rome was rich enough to support a bishop, forty-six

presbyters, seven deacons, seven sub-deacons, forty-two acolytes and fifty-two exorcists, readers and doorkeepers; it had a charity list of over 1,500. State inventories show that vast quantities of goods were seized, gold and silver plate, precious ornaments and vestments, supplies of food and clothing, books and cash. Christian clergy might be more willing to surrender their lives than the Church's valuables. Cyprian, writing from Africa, said there was mass apostasy, led by bishops; multitudes flocked to the magistrates to make their retractions, 'spontanously submitting to the commissions in charge of that dreadful deed'. There was a general collapse of morale: 'Many bishops, who ought to have been an encouragement and example to others, gave up their sacred ministry, deserted their people, left the district, tried to make money, took possession of estates by fraudulent means, and engaged in usury.' Some of the faithful made state sacrifices but also continued as Christians; in Spain, for instance, we hear of Christians acting as civic priests. The Church was never able to adopt a uniform policy towards persecution. Thus there were acute divisions about the degree of compromise to adopt, not only between regions, but within them. Old schisms between 'revivalist' and 'official' Christians instantly reappeared and became inextricably mingled with doctrinal questions. Spasmodic persecution of Christian 'extremists' tended to strengthen orthodoxy in the Church, as we have noted, but blanket persecution, especially over a long period, weakened it in many ways, especially by undermining its unity.

However, the systematic harassment of huge groups within the empire also weakened the State, not least in the army, where Christians were numerous. The Decian persecution had to be called off when there was trouble on the frontier. Later edicts, c. 300, were never fully applied in the West for this reason. Then, too, actions against Christians were increasingly unpopular. Whereas, in the first and second centuries, official hostility was a response to anti-Christian feeling among urban mobs, from 250 onwards the State usually had to act alone, indeed against public criticism. There is an air of desperation about the last great wave of persecutions, conducted by Maximinus in 308–12. In Damascus, said Eusebius, the authorities 'seized the market-place whores, and under the threat of torture forced them to state in writing that they were once Christians and give evidence of orgies practised in Christian churches.' This deliberate attempt to revive old slanders suggests they had lost their potency. On the contrary, the Christians had long been recognized as a virtuous and essentially inoffensive element in the community. They were, of course, different. As the so-called Epistle to Diognetus puts it:

'They live in their own countries, but simply as visitors . . . to them every foreign land is a fatherland, and every fatherland foreign. . . . They have a common table, but yet not common. They exist in the flesh, but they do not live for the flesh. They spend their existence on earth, but their citizenship is in heaven. They obey the established laws and in their own lives they try to surpass the laws. They love all men, and are persecuted by all. . . . They are poor, and make many rich. They lack everything, and in everything they abound. They are humiliated, and their humiliation becomes their glory. They are abused – and they bless. They are reviled, and are justified. They are insulted, and they repay insults with honour.'

It was the Christian spirit of mutual love and communal charity which most impressed pagans. Tertullian quotes them as saying: 'How these Christians love one another!' And he adds that the funds which financed their charities were essentially voluntary: 'Every man once a month brings some modest coin, or whenever he wishes and only if he does wish, and if he can – for nobody is compelled.' And the funds were spent 'not on banquets and drinking parties' but 'to feed the poor and bury them, for boys and girls who lack property and parents, and then for slaves grown old and shipwrecked mariners; and any who may be in the mines, on the penal islands, in prison . . . they become the pensioners of their confession.' The Christians had enormously expanded the old charitable trusts of the Jewish diaspora. They ran a miniature welfare state in an empire which for the most part lacked social services. The Emperor Julian, seeking to revive paganism in the fourth century, tried to introduce similar charitable funds for the poor. In a letter ordering imperial clergy to set these up, he noted: 'Why do we not observe that it is in their benevolence to strangers, their care for the graves of the dead, and the apparent holiness of their lives that they have done most to increase atheism?' (i.e. Christianity). He thought it 'disgraceful that, when no Jew ever has to beg, and the impious Galileans support not only their own poor, but ours as well, everyone can see that our people lack aid from us'. Julian noted bitterly the important role played by Christian women. He told leading citizens of Antioch: 'Each one of you allows his wife to carry out everything from his house to the Galileans. The wives feed the poor at your expense, and the Galileans get the credit.' Women played a much bigger part in the Christian charitable trusts than corresponding organizations in the Jewish diaspora; this was one reason why Christianity took over the old proselytizing role of Judaism, which now had ceased to expand. Christianity offered solid advantages to women. It treated them as equals in the eyes of God. It told husbands to treat their wives with as much consideration as Christ showed to his 'bride', the Church. And it gave them the protection of Jesus's unusually definite teaching on the sanctity of marriage. Women converts began the Christian penetration of the upper-classes and then brought their children up as Christians; sometimes they ended by converting their husbands.

But these factors alone would not have persuaded the State to reverse its policy and embrace its enemy. The truth is that during the large-scale anti-Christian operations of the second half of the third century, the State was obliged to recognize that its enemy had changed and had made itself a potential ally. In the long struggle to suppress internal division, to codify its doctrine and to expand its frontiers, Christianity had become in many striking ways a mirror-image of the empire itself. It was catholic, universal, ecumenical, orderly, international, multi-racial and increasingly legalistic. It was administered by a professional class of literates who in some ways functioned like bureaucrats and its bishops, like imperial governors, legates or prefects, had wide discretionary powers to interpret the law. It was becoming the *Doppelgänger* of the empire. In attacking and weakening it, the empire was debilitating itself. For Christianity had become a secular as well as a spiritual phenomenon: it was a huge force for stability, with its own traditions, property, interests and hierarchy. Unlike Judaism, it had no national aspirations incompatible with the empire's security; on the contrary, its ideology fitted neatly into the aims and needs of the universal state. Christianity had been carried towards the State by the momentum of its own success. Would it not be prudent for the State to recognize this welcome metamorphosis and contract, as it were, a *mariage de convenance* with the 'bride of Christ'? Thus it would relinquish a state religion which seemed increasingly forlorn and required public support just to stay alive and replace it by a young and dynamic partner, capable of development and adjustment to underpin the empire with its strength and enthusiasm. Here lay the very mundane logic of Constantine's edict of toleration: he perceived that Christianity already possessed many of the characteristics of an imperial state Church.

But the position adopted by Constantine, of general religious toleration, was not tenable for long. Perhaps there was no such thing as religious equipoise in the ancient world. The empire, as it became less liberal, had found it impossible not to persecute Christianity. Now, having accepted Christianity, it found it increasingly difficult not to persecute its enemies, internal and external. The same compulsive forces were at work on the Church. The manner in which it transformed itself from a suffering and victimized body, begging for toleration, into a coercive one, demanding monopoly, is worth studying in some detail.

The problem really centres round the existence of a separate and exclusive clerical class. As we have seen, such a phenomenon was virtually unknown to the Church in its earliest stages, but became entrenched in the third century. Constantine, having recognized Christianity, having in effect decided to make it a buttress of his State, felt he had no alternative but to acknowledge the existence of a clerical class and provide for it accordingly. Of course there was nothing new in this. The emperor had been the Pontifex Maximus of the gods, just as he now considered himself a bishop. The pagan priests were paid state officials, who met once a week in conclave as an act of government; the vestal virgins travelled through the streets in veiled state carriages, and sat in an imperial box at the games. Constantine began the transfer of privileges to Christian clergy almost from the start, exempting them from compulsory public office (which was onerous and expensive) in the towns, and in non-urban areas from the payment of district taxes. This implied class status, the secular underwriting the spiritual. Indeed Constantine was the first to use the words 'clerical' and 'clerics' in this sense – and a generation later, the anti-Christian Julian was already using such terms in a pejorative sense.

Of course the favour of the State enormously increased the value of clerical status, and the desirability of office, particularly higher ones. The council held at Sardica in the Balkans in 341, for instance, tried to prevent transfers of bishops from one see to another, as 'a bad custom and a wicked source of corruption'. It noted severely: 'We don't find bishops wanting to transfer from a large see to a smaller one: all are aflame with the fires of greed, and are slaves of ambition.' The historian Ammianus, a pagan but fair-minded as a rule towards Christianity, drew the connection between disputed episcopal elections and the revenues of the see. Thus after the election battle between Damasus and Ursinus for the bishopric of Rome in 366, Ammianus says that 137 bodies were found in a church – on the site of what is now St Maria Maggiore. Naturally, he adds, such things happened, since once in office, the bishops of Rome:

'are free from money worries, enriched by offerings from married women, riding in carriages, dressing splendidly, feasting luxuriantly – their banquets are better than imperial ones. But they might be really happy if, despising the vastness of the city, in which they can hide their faults, they lived like provincial bishops, with harsh abstinence in eating and drinking, plain apparell, eyes cast to the ground – proclaiming themselves pure and reverent men to the everlasting deity and his true worshippers'.

The Sardica canons also indicate that the rich and well-connected were making their way into the Church purely for material advancement. They lay down: 'If a rich man, or lawyer, or state official be offered a bishopric, he should not be ordained unless he has previously acted as a reader, deacon or priest, and so rises to the highest rank, the episcopate, by progressive promotion . . . ordination should only be conferred on those whose whole life has been under review for a long period, and whose worth has been proved.' This canon proved totally ineffective, to judge by the number of famous clerics who broke it, or had it broken on their behalf. It was common for the State or private interest groups to push their nominees into key Church posts, irrespective of their status. St Ambrose was baptized, went through the various clerical ranks and was consecrated bishop of Milan all within eight days. Among laymen ordained direct to the presbyterate were St Augustine, St Jerome, Origen and Paulinus of Nola. Fabian was a layman when made Pope in 236; Eusebius was only a catechumen when made bishop of Caesarea in 314; other laymen-bishops were Philogonius of Antioch in 319, Nectarius of Constantinople in 381 and Synesius of Ptolemais in 410. Eusebius, it should be added, was enthroned by the military, as were Martin of Tours and Philiaster of Brescia. Gregory of Nazianzus says it was common in the fourth century for bishops to be selected 'from the army, the navy, the plough, the forge'. Jerome complained: 'One who was yesterday a catechumen is today a bishop; another moves overnight from the amphitheatre to the church; a man who spent the evening in the circus stands next morning at the altar, and another who was recently a patron of the stage is now the dedicator of virgins.' Direct bribery was also common. John Chrysostom, Bishop of Constantinople, found six cases of episcopal simony at the synod he held at Ephesus in 401. They came clean: 'We have given bribes – the thing is admitted – so we would be made bishops and exempt from civil duties.' They asked to be confirmed or, if this were impossible, to have their money back. They were evidently small men: 'Some of us have handed over furniture belonging to our wives.' They got their bribes back and, after Chrysostom's fall, their bishoprics too, keeping their wives all the time.

Almost from the start, the State tried to limit the exploitation of clerical privilege or, rather, use it for secular purposes. As early as 320, and again in 326, Constantine tried to prevent tax-evasion by the rich by edicts which banned decurions, their descendants and other wealthy groups from becoming clergy; the priesthood was to be open only to 'those with small fortunes who are not liable to compulsory municipal services.' The merit of the rule, in Constantine's eyes, was that he, as emperor, could dispense exceptions to the rule. He wanted a system in which the clergy was mainly recruited from uninfluential groups, plus men of his own choosing from the upper ranks. Thus the State was already acting in a discriminatory fashion. It continued to do so in an increasing number of ways. Ammianus notes that Constantius II allowed the clergy to use the imperial transport system free when travelling on official journeys. This was a discriminatory ruling in favour of orthodox bishops: Ammianus says they bankrupted the service by travelling in hordes to endless synods, ensuring that orthodoxy was always in the majority. And were clergy judged heterodox to enjoy fiscal privileges? Here again, Constantine forged a useful weapon for himself. He ruled against most schismatics and heretics at the behest of orthodox clergy; but in the case of the Novatianists, for instance, he ordered that 'they shall firmly possess, without disquietude, their own church buildings and places for burial', and other properties 'acquired in any manner whatsoever' – and their priests were accordingly exempt. Constantine justified this on the grounds that they differed from the Catholics on disciplinary rather than doctrinal grounds. His real reasons were doubtless very different; and the extension or withdrawal of fiscal privilege clearly gave him and his successors a powerful voice in the Church's internal affairs.

Julian recognized that the strength of the orthodox Church rested to a great extent on imperial discrimination in its favour. According to Ammianus, he tried to atomize the Church by ending the system:

'He ordered the priests of the different Christian sects, and their supporters, to be admitted to the palace, and politely expressed his wish that, their quarrels being over, each might follow his own beliefs without hindrance or fear. He thought that freedom to argue their beliefs would simply deepen their differences, so that he would never be faced by a united common people. He found from experience that no wild beasts are as hostile to men, as Christians are to each other.'

By Julian's day, however, official Christianity was entrenched enough to survive such tactics; it was continually extending its legal privileges and thwarting State efforts to curb them. It had become rich, indeed very rich. As an illegal organization, it had been forbidden, in theory at least, to own property until the edict of toleration. In fact it had acquired a great deal: by purchase, gift and inheritance. With toleration, however, and the removal of all legal restrictions by an edict of 321, endowments multiplied. It became common for wealthy men and widows to leave one-third of their property to the Church; rank and file Christians were taught to treat 'Christ's bride' as an additional child in their wills. There were abuses, too. Julian, an infallible expert on the darker side of Christianity, wrote that he would 'no longer allow "clerics" to sit as judges and draw up wills and take the inheritance of other men, and assign everything to themselves.' In the second half of the fourth century, for the first time, we get hints of public complaints against the wealth of Christian clergy and the splendour of its buildings. Some Christian writers took note: 'Our walls glitter with gold', wrote Jerome, 'and gold gleams upon our ceilings and the capitals of our pillars; yet Christ is dying at our doors in the person of his poor, naked and hungry.' But others were dying too: rich men and women with wills to make and wealth to bequeath. For the first time, also, we get efforts by the State to prevent too great a proportion of the collective wealth, especially real property, falling into the dead hand of the Church. There was a batch of laws in the 360s dealing with the individual and collective wealth of the Church, some passed under Julian, some under his Christian successors, which indicated that the State, irrespective of its religious complexion, thought that clerical manipulation of the tax-laws, and the Church's progressive tendency to absorb wealth, had to be brought under control. In 360, clerical land was in some cases subjected to taxation and clerics themselves were declared non-exempt for tax on their private incomes. In 362 decurions who escaped compulsory public services by taking clerical rank were ordered to be dismissed and two years later they were obliged, on ordination, to transfer their property, and so their duties, to a member of their family; four years later still, clergy were forbidden to benefit from legacies made by widows or female wards, or to solicit for the same. Jerome, in his comments on this last law, was divided by his outrage at the discrimination (as he saw it) against the clergy and his grief at the skill with which they evaded it: 'Pagan priests, actors, jockeys and prostitutes can inherit property: clergymen and monks alone are forbidden by law, a law enacted not by persecutors but by Christian emperors . . . but though the law is strict and detailed, greed marches on heedless: by the fiction of trusteeship, we defy the laws.'

The association between clerical wealth and the idea of a privileged clerical caste, between property and doctrinal orthodoxy, and between an authoritarian Church and a possessing Church, is very marked in the first centuries of Christianity. It was, for instance, from the orthodox elements in second-century Alexandria, as they struggled successfully to impose their brand of Christianity on the hitherto dominant gnostic and Jewish-Christian sects, that we get the first defence of worldly means to spiritual ends. Clement of Alexandria explained away Jesus's absolute command to the rich young man to sell all he had, adding: 'A man must say goodbye to the injurious things he has, not to those which can actually contribute to his advantage if he knows the right use for them; and advantage comes from those that are managed with wisdom, moderation and piety . . . outward things are not necessarily injurious.' Significantly, too, Clement also put forward the first philosophical and theological defence of the clerical power to remit sin.

The argument over the existence of this power, and its extent, went right to the heart of the interconnected debates over the function and status of the clergy, the organization of the Church, and its relations with the State and society. Indeed, it was one of the great determining factors in Christian history. Baptism, all agreed, involved a complete remission of sin by the power of the spirit. But thereafter? The earliest Christians had thought in terms of a short period between baptism and the *parousia*. But with a receding, indeed disappearing, eschatology, the problem of sins committed after baptism, perhaps during a whole lifetime, became acute. Some, like Constantine, delayed baptism until they were on their deathbeds; on the other hand we have evidence of infant baptism from the second century. How could the baptized Christian be cleansed from sin? Did the Church have the power to do it? Certainly the idea of penance as an institution was unknown to Paul. There were hints of it in the pastoral epistles, and the famous 'binding and loosing' text in Matthew (interpolated or not) could be used in this sense. Clement, as noted, thought the Church could restore the lapsed to full communion, and penance had begun to take institutional form by the time of Tertullian. Indeed, it was essentially on this issue, holding as it did the key to many others, that he left the orthodox Church.

Tertullian was a puritan and, like most puritans, took an elitist view of the Church. Its appeal and nature were universal, but the process of selection, or election, was strict. Once baptized, a Christian must abstain from serious sin or lose his election; indeed, the fact of a serious post-baptismal sin proved he never had it. This was God's clear will; there was nothing the Church could do about it, though it had powers of forgiveness in minor matters. The breaking point for Tertullian came, he tells us, when a 'senior bishop' (probably Calixtus of Rome), decided that the Church had the power to grant remission after baptism, even of such serious sins as adultery or even apostasy. It was this claim on behalf of the clergy – to him inconceivable – which made the former scourge of the heretics into, as it were, the first protestant. And, once he denied clerical rights in this respect, he was led, progressively, to question clerical claims to separate status in the Church. In his orthodox days, Tertullian had attacked the Montanist-type heretics because 'they endow even the laity with the functions of the priesthood.' Now, having denied the penitential power, he became a Montanist himself, and asked, in *De Exhortatione Castitatis*:

'Are not we laymen priests also? . . . The difference between the order and the people is due to the authority of the church and the consecration of their rank by the reservation of a special branch for the order. But where there is no bench of clergy you offer and baptize and are your own sole priest. For where there are three, there is a church, though they be laymen . . . you have the rights of a priest in your own person when necessity arises.'

So he attacked bishops who showed what he termed 'mildness' in forgiving the sinful and lapsed. He appealed to 'the priesthood of all believers' against the 'usurped' rights of particular office-holders, unspiritual 'lordship', the 'tyranny' of the clerics. Even a woman, if she spoke with the spirit, had more authority in this sense than the greatest bishop. He represented an empty office, she the living spirit. The division was clear cut, between a Church of saints, who administered themselves, and a huge rabble of saints and sinners who had to be administered by a professional clergy. How could such a Church be squared with the clear teaching of St Paul? Tertullian read Romans, as Luther was to do. The spirit in Tertullian's view does not relax its rigour; it judges without partiality or leniency and will never forgive one in mortal sin.

On the other hand, it was easy to see why the bishops, the clergy, the orthodox Church, favoured 'mildness'. It was conducive to the universal mission and conducive, too, to the emergence and consolidation of a clerical caste. The power of the keys would be kept more firmly in their hands if latitude, to be determined by their personal and collective judgment, were allowed. And the power to decide whether a sinner were readmitted or not was necessarily based not on spiritual authority, or direct illumination, but on status, the possession of office. A bishop could remit sins, or not, only as an authorized, appointed, and officially ordained person. Soon the privilege, dependent on office, could be extended to all ordained clergy. Then the cleavage between clergy and laity became complete, and the Church was divided between rulers and ruled.

Tertullian saw the implications of the issue very clearly. And it is no accident that it came to a head in his native territory of North Africa, around Carthage. Nor is it simply coincidence that the debate on penitence and forgiveness erupted most ferociously over the readmittance of the lapsed. The great imperial persecutions of the second half of the third century not only inflicted enormous damage on the Church; in some ways they permanently damaged Christianity. Christian communities were split down the middle on the degree to which they should resist state coercion; or rather they were split three ways. Some, from bishops down, stood their ground, refused all compromise and were killed. Some fled into hiding or exile (this was official Church teaching, in so far as there was one). Some remained, and in varying degrees collaborated. And of course such collaboration involved, often enough, the surrender of Church property. When the persecution was lifted, the runaways returned, the dead were counted and the personal records of all were publicly examined; the arguments and recriminations were bitter. Nearly everyone left alive had something to hide or justify; those without stain were dead. Augustine, in his *Contra Cresconium*, gives us a rare glimpse of the mutual recriminations of that period, in the first decade of the fourth century, when he quotes one Purpurius of Limata under interrogation in a Church court, angrily lashing back at his accusers:

'Do you think I am frightened of you like the rest? What have *you* done? You were forced by the curator and the soldiers to give up the sacred books. How did you come to be set free by them, unless you surrendered something, or ordered it to be surrendered? They did not let you go by chance. Yes, I did kill, and I intend to kill those who act against me. So do not now provoke me to say anything more. You know that I interfere with nobody's affairs.'

This was in Carthage. And of course, after the Edict of Milan, many in Carthage and the territories of the old Punic empire, with its anti-Roman tradition, its continuing separatism and sense of independence, its own Punic, or Berber, language and culture, viewed with repugnance the idea of their Church making common cause with the imperial authorities, their recent persecutors. In a way, the Carthaginian church, founded in the second century, had become the repository of Punic resistance to Roman ideas. It had always had a strong, almost orthodox, Jewish element. It was strict, puritanical, strongly opposed to any compromise with the world and its pagan ideas. It denied the idea of duties to the State. It had its own sense of brotherhood and a readiness to model conduct – including the acceptance of martyrdom – on the examples of the Maccabees. In a sense it looked forward to Luther; in a more concrete sense it looked back to the Dead Sea Scrolls, for men in the Essene tradition had been among its founders. The original Essene insistence on absolute ritual purity found a new expression in the refusal of African Christians to re-admit anyone who had compromised his faith in the time of persecution. And of course this particularly applied to the clergy. He who administered baptism must be undefiled and uncompromised. And a bishop, who ordained priests, had to be above all possible reproach. Unless he were, his baptisms and ordinations were wholly ineffective, indeed, positively evil, for an ecclesiastical organization composed of such men constituted an anti-church, directed by the devil, and casting a hideous shadow over the true Church of the faithful. We have here, in short, a recapitulation of the struggles of the Essenes against the false priests of the defiled Temple.

This was the background to the so-called Donatist heresy. Most Carthaginians believed that Church orders were subjective, that is, invalidated by personal unworthiness. A few thought them objective, that is, universally and always efficacious provided the ordination were valid and this view was increasingly held by orthodox elements outside North Africa. The conflict was bound to produce a disputed episcopal succession sooner or later; and in 311 it did. Some eighty Numidian bishops declared invalid the ordination of Caecilian, Bishop of Carthage, on the grounds that the ceremony had been conducted by a *traditor* bishop who had handed over holy books to be burned by the official persecutors. They elected another bishop in Caecilian's place and in due course the succession went to Donatus. But, as Caecilian pointed out, many of the eighty bishops had themselves been *traditores*. He refused to resign. Both sides appealed to Constantine, now the protector of the Church. After much inquiry and hesitation, the emperor opted for Caecilian. That, for the Donatists, completed the persecution syndrome. They now regarded the alliance with the Constantinian state with horror. One of their slogans was: 'The servants of God are those who are hated by the world.' They asked: 'What has the Emperor to do with the church?' Efforts by Caecilian and his supporters to occupy their benefices were resisted by organized force, usually successfully. Donatists were able to play not merely on the rigorist religious sentiment of their congregations but on local Punic nationalism and anti-Roman, anti-imperial sentiment. We have a little vignette of Donatus, no doubt malicious, from Optatus, Bishop of Milevis: 'When people visited him from any part of Africa, he did not ask the usual questions about the weather, peace and war, and the harvest, but always: "How goes my party in your part of the world?"'

Thus religious politics were superimposed on the politics of geography, race and economics. Constantine kept the Caecilian or imperialist Church party in being but he did not attempt, or perhaps was not able, to do much more. Orthodox catholicism was confined to wealthy landowners and to the Romanized urban bourgeoisie of the coastal cities and towns; it was the religion of respectability, conformity and acceptance of the world. The Donatist Church rejected the world in a political and economic sense, expressing the aspirations of the native poor of the inland plains and hill districts. About 347, the Caecilians resorted to State violence. A government commissioner, Count Macarius, imposed an imperial peace of sorts by force and fear. Many Donatists were killed, and were instantly revered as martyrs. The fierce and traditional orthodoxy of the African church, fortified by pagan persecution, was branded overnight as heresy – a heresy identified and attacked by the same power which had formerly persecuted in the name of a pagan State. The issue at stake was not just the protest of a particularist sect but the survival of a provincial tradition of Christianity in a universal and (to Africans) parasitic empire. Constantine invited the problem by aligning the empire with the universal Catholic Church; his successors had to cope with it. If they persecuted they aroused a resistance movement; if, like Julian, they withdrew the support of the legions from the orthodox party, the Donatists moved forward and threatened the State's interests, as well as the Church's.

From 'the Time of Macarius' as they called it, the Donatists memorized a bitter folklore of martyrs, injustice and outrage. The original issues were forgotten as class, race and nationality closed ranks. The Donatists were a fully organized church, with over 500 bishops, most of them, of course, of small sees. They were basically orthodox in their ritual and teaching; as they saw themselves, ultra-orthodox. Their priests consciously re-created the attitudes of Zealots, and went around in parties armed with clubs, which they called 'Israels', to chastise backsliding, pro-Roman clergy. When they seized an 'orthodox' church, they purified it, as the Essenes might have done, with buckets of whitewash. And they had their private armies, the 'circumcellions'. Much mystery surrounds the composition, motives and significance of these bands. They could be portrayed as desperate, landless men, virtually brigands, who lived in and around Donatist cemeteries, guarding the shrines of the martyrs and issuing forth from time to time to avenge them. But they can also be seen as seasonal labourers, working mainly in the vast olive plantations of the inland plains and hills, wild, semi-civilized Berbers, traditionally and grossly exploited by Roman landowners, most of them absentees. There were, indeed, huge latifundia in North Africa, owned by Roman millionaires, who did not even set eyes on their estates until they took refuge in Carthage after the fall of Rome in 410. Some of these wealthy men, heiresses and widows had already become orthodox Catholics by the mid-fourth century; in addition there were many large-scale local landowners identified with the Caecilian party and, of course, with imperial authority.

Judaic Zealotry had always shown a tendency to attack the rich in the name of religion. Had not the hated Sadducees also aligned themselves with the Roman State, thus defiling the true faith and assisting the grasping oppressor? Josephus accused the Zealots of the 66–70 war of 'thirsting after the blood of valiant men and men of good families'. The conjunction of religious and economic forces in the case of the circumcellions was fundamentally the same; it was yet one more episode in a continuing phenomenon – one which was later to include, for instance, the fourteenth-century peasants' revolt in England. Donatism was a movement of poor men led by puritan clergy. Their shock-troops, the circumcellions, were millenarians who saw the idea of a revived eschatology as an occasion for settling scores on earth first. They called themselves the 'Captains of the Saints'. Their phases of violent activity usually coincided with periods of economic depression. They protected peasants in debt by terrorizing creditors and landlords. They also extended their umbrella to slaves, who thus became a powerful element in the Donatist Church. In an empire where the carrying of lethal weapons was, strictly speaking, illegal except for privileged categories of people, the circumcellions wielded the huge staves they used for knocking the olive-harvest off the trees. Outside the cities their threats usually sufficed. If not, they burnt crops and houses and seized and destroyed the documents attached to slaves. To Augustine, the hammer of the Donatists, the ideologue of the Christian empire, they were agents of anarchy and social horror, 'crazy herds of abandoned men'. He noted that they feasted their martyrs with drunken rioting, which he attributed to the survival of pagan traditions. No doubt there were pagan survivals in the country areas and the hills; but so there were in the towns also. And Catholics, as well as Donatists, liked these riotous saints' days. Augustine's real fear sprang from his hatred of religious dissent in alliance with social revolution. 'What master was there', he asked,'who was not compelled to live in dread of his own slave, if the slave had put himself under the protection of the Donatists?' And he was able, no doubt with exaggeration but also with some justice, to show the Donatists creating private empires in defiance of law. There was the case of the Bishop of Timgad, who left behind him one of the largest cathedrals ever built in Africa. Augustine says he travelled around 'with intolerable power, accompanied by bodyguards, not because he feared anyone but to inspire fear in others. He oppressed widows, evicted minors, distributed other people's patrimonies, broke up marriages, saw to the sale of innocent persons' properties, and took a share of the proceeds while the owners wept.' Of course this portrait can be interpreted in two ways: of a man perpetrating injustices, or seeking to correct them.

Religious struggle, indeed, throws an illuminating light on social and economic tensions in the fourth-century Roman empire. One characteristic of the Donatist church was the ability and willingness of its bishops and priests to use Punic as well as Latin. They had vernacular services; there may even have been vernacular translations of the scriptures. The political and economic posture was anti-Roman, and the cultural stand, to some extent, was anti-Latin. The surviving writings on the Donatist controversy cast, as it were, a periodic searchlight on the North African theatre; elsewhere, we know much less but we sometimes get hints of similar patterns of conflict and stress. It was a feature of the Montanists, for instance, that they spoke the local, often tribal, language or patois of the areas where they operated; they did so, for instance, in Phrygia. It was one reason for their undoubted successes. How far nonconformist Christianity worked in conjunction with local tribalism and nationalism is hard to determine and harder still to prove it was deliberate and systematic. But the probability is that almost from earliest times Christian groups over widely scattered parts of the empire had become identified or had identified themselves with local aspirations and grievances. This would help to explain the earlier persecutions, always conducted purely at local level. It would also help to explain the anxiety of orthodox Christianity to disengage itself from this kind of religious adventurism – the Montanists being an outstanding example but not the only one. From the second century the Catholic Church, as it increasingly called itself, stressed its universality, its linguistic and cultural uniformity, its geographical and racial transcendance – in short, its identity of aims with the empire. These are the themes of most Catholic propagandists of the Roman school, especially in the third century. In due course, the orthodox Church received its reward: imperial recognition, beneficence and support against its enemies. For, and this is the key point, were not the enemies of the Catholic Church the enemies of empire even before the alliance was forged? From the antinomian perspective of Julian we again get an insight into the truth. In a letter defending his religious policy of withdrawing state military support from the orthodox brand of Christianity, he points out passionately that this had ended bloodshed. 'Many whole communities of so-called heretics', he claims, 'were actually butchered, as at Samosata, and Cyzicus in Paphlagonia, Bithynia and Galatia, and among many other tribes villages were sacked and destroyed; whereas in my time exile has been ended and property restored.' We have here a picture of the Catholic Church and the Roman State operating jointly over a wide area for diverse but compatible motives, to impose order, uniformity and central control. And of course one reason why Julian's own policy, idealistic though it might be, failed to work and was abandoned and reversed, was that diversity of religious belief was incompatible with the purely secular needs of the imperial administration.

Thus, while there is no real evidence that primitive Christianity at any stage in its formation constituted a revolutionary social force, conscious or unconscious, what it did do was to breed a multitude of divergent sects springing from, and aggravating, local particularism, as well as a dominant strain which identified itself with the empire, the possessing classes, and the *status quo*. So Christianity produced and reflected forces which were both holding the empire together and trying to tear it apart. In Rome and Constantinople, Christians were orthodox and imperial. In North Africa they were predominantly schismatic and nationalist. And over large parts of the empire Christian elements formed a multiplicity of troublesome groups, each trying to thrust its own levers into the cracks in the imperial structure. And these dissenting groups often overlapped. At one time in a single Phrygian town there were churches run by Montanists, Novatianists, Encratites and Apotactites or Saccophori, all of them forbidden sects. Scattered throughout the imperial territories there were varieties of Christian Enthusiasts, priest-deserters or *vacantivi*, *catenati* or long-haired, chained ascetics, fanatic robber monks and great numbers of heretical groups. By the 390s, Filastrius, the elderly Bishop of Brescia, who had spent his entire life collecting information about heresy, had compiled a list of 156 distinct ones – all, it would seem, still flourishing. Heresy held particular attractions for dispossessed tribesmen, or tribes within the frontiers which had been subjected to collective punishments, for bands of military deserters, or fugitives from barbarian raids who lived by robbery. And, to both the imperial authorities and the orthodox Church, the most frightening aspect of heresy, particularly of the Montanist or Donatist type, was the speed with which it could spread, leaping like a prairie fire from one local tuft of grievance to the next. Rome had tolerated the old tribal religions, provided they did not involve human sacrifice, because they were essentially as conservative as her own; all underwrote hierarchical human structures. Christian heresy, on the other hand, was almost by definition anti-authoritarian and it linked in unholy communion men whose notions were otherwise merely tribal, or even criminal, by supplying them with transcendental and dangerous concepts.

For all these reasons the imperial State found itself obliged – it was not unwilling – to become the enforcement agency of Christian orthodoxy. By the time of Theodosius, in the fifth century, there were over 100 active statutes against heresy and heretics. The first general statute, dating from the 380s, shows the essentially secular nature of the State's concern: it is attacking heresy now as it once attacked Christianity as a whole because it provoked disorder. Thus sanctions are laid down against 'those who contend about religion . . . to provoke any agitation against the regulation of Our Tranquility, as authors of sedition and as disturbers of the peace of the church. . . . There shall be no opportunity for any man to go out to the public and to argue about religion, or to discuss it or to give any counsel.'

This law was very severe indeed, as it appears to forbid religious debate of any sort outside, presumably, the authorized channels. But in some ways it was merely a logical culmination of a train of events set in motion by Constantine's decision to seek alliance with orthodox Christianity. Indeed, to a great extent Constantine himself may have been aware of the logic at the time of his Milan Edict. His policy was, and remained, that of toleration as between Christianity and paganism; he stuck to this and he boasted of it – he had, he said, 'left them their Temples'. But his attitude to divergency within Christianity was not the same; in fact, one of his main reasons for tolerating Christianity may have been that it gave himself and the State the opportunity to control the Church's policy on orthodoxy and the treatment of heterodoxy. Of course Constantine was not concerned with doctrinal truth. So far as was possible he wanted the Church to be universalist and inclusive. He wrote threateningly to Bishop Athanasius in *c.* 328: 'As you know my wishes, pray admit freely any who wish to enter the church. If I hear you have stopped anyone claiming membership I will immediately send an official to depose you and send you into exile.' He knew that Athanasius, though orthodox, was a violent man, who regularly flogged his junior clergy and imprisoned or expelled bishops. That was not the sort of Church Constantine wanted: his Church must reflect the empire at its best – harmony, serenity, multiplicity in unity. Equally, he disliked doctrinal argument, for which he had no sympathy or understanding. His initial reaction to the Arian dispute was that it was about a trifle – 'a point of discussion . . . suggested by the contentious spirit fostered by misused leisure . . . merely an intellectual exercise.' He thought the matter 'too sublime and abstruse' to be settled with certainty, or, if settled, above the heads of most people. The issue was 'small and very insignificant'. He urged both sides to be 'sparing of words' and to 'exhibit an equal degree of forbearance and receive the advice which your fellow-servant righteously gives.'

It was in this spirit that Constantine (and the great majority of his successors) approached his role in Church politics. He was to be a mediator, a role he was good at and enjoyed. From Eusebius's descriptions of Constantine presiding at the Council of Nicea in 325 and at other great ecclesiastical gatherings we see the emperor in his element, arranging elaborate ceremony, dramatic entrances and processions and splendid services. He brought his skill in public relations to the management of Church affairs. It was a far cry from the days of the 'pillars' and the Council of Jerusalem. Constantine, in fact, may be said to have created the *décor* and ritual of Christian conciliar practice. He tried also to set the tone of debate: eirenic, conciliatory, urbane. It was he who insisted, as a formula for compromise, the insertion of the phrase 'consubstantial with the father' in the credal agreement. 'He advised all present to agree to it,' says Eusebius, 'and to subscribe its articles and assent to them, with the insertion of the single word "consubstantial" which, moreover, he interpreted himself.' Constantine, in accordance with the interests of the State, was anxious to avoid a row if possible and, if one occurred, to look for an honourable solution. Thus, although at Nicea he arranged for an overwhelming majority of the bishops to condemn certain specific beliefs of Arius and his followers, he later showed himself very eager to have Arius restored, on the basis of a confession of faith; again, in 321, to avoid a wrangle with the Donatists over the church he had built at Constantine (Cirta), which they occupied and the orthodox claimed, he gave the latter the State customs house as a substitute. Constantine, in brief, put order and stability, the rule of law, before any other religious consideration. But when dissent in his view challenged the rule of law he acted quite ruthlessly. In 316 he thought it necessary to persecute the Donatists, and did so; one Donatist sermon complained that 'local judges were imperatively ordered to act and put the secular power in motion; buildings were surrounded by troops; our wealthy followers were threatened with proscription, the sacraments were defiled, a mob of heathen were unleashed on us, and our sacred buildings became the scene of profane feasts.' Again, in 333, in the first instance of censorship being employed in defence of Christian interests, he ordered savage action against Arian writings: 'If any treatise composed by Arius is discovered, let it be consigned to the flames . . . in order that no memorial of him whatever be left . . . [and] if anyone shall be caught concealing a book by Arius, and does not instantly bring it out and burn it, the penalty shall be death; the criminal shall suffer punishment immediately after conviction.'

Such ferocity betrays an element of exasperation. Indeed, one might say that the attitude of the emperors towards their religious responsibilities tended to follow a regular pattern: they began in a spirit of self-confident ecumenicalism and ended in blind rage and repression. They always underestimated the tenacity with which clerics clung to minute distinctions, and the depth of their *odium theologicum*. In the end, the emperor always felt he had to back one party, to give it official status and destroy the other simply to keep the peace; but the choice was not always well-judged and the peace was not therefore kept. The empire did not, in the end, solve the Donatist problem which convulsed North Africa, nor the dispute over free will, which flickered over all the Mediterranean, nor the huge series of Christological controversies which fascinated the East and Egypt throughout the fourth and fifth centuries. The empire embraced Christianity with a view to renewing its strength by acquiring a dynamic State religion. In effect, however, it exchanged a State ritual, which was harmless because it was dead, for a religious philosophy which defied easy definition because it was alive and was therefore a risk to the administrative setting in which it found itself. Christianity, by its nature, always ends by damaging its secular patrons.

Generations of emperors grappled with the problem of the Christian deity and how to give it a final and universally accepted definition which would end the argument. But it was, by its very nature, insoluble. In the first century the world was waiting for a monotheistic, universalist religion. Christianity supplied it. But then: was Christianity truly monotheistic? In the last resort, what distinguished it from Judaism was belief in the divinity of Christ. If Jesus were a mere messiah then the two religious systems were reconcilable, as indeed the Jewish Christians had argued. But insistence that Jesus was the son of God placed the movement right outside even the furthest confines of Judaic thought and not only separated the systems but brought them into mortal enmity. This situation was in time brought about by the victory of Pauline theology. The divinity of Christ gave Christianity its tremendous initial impact and assisted its universality. But it left Christian theologians with a dilemma: how to explain the divinity of Christ while maintaining the singularity of God. Were there not two Gods? Or, if the concept of the Spirit were introduced as a separate manifestation of divinity, three?

The point became an irritant at a very early stage of Christian history. One possible solution was to regard Christ as a manifestation of a monolithic God and therefore not a man at all. This was the line followed, in general, by the gnostics. Thus Valentinus wrote: 'Jesus ate and drank in a peculiar manner, not evacuating his food. So much power of continence was in him that in him his food was not corrupted, since he himself had no corruptibility.' This weird theory invalidated most of the gospels, devalued the resurrection and made nonsense of the eucharist. The Docetists, who also belonged to this school, faced the issue squarely: as Christ's human body was phantasm, his sufferings and death were mere appearance: 'If he suffered, he was not God. If he was God, he did not suffer.' Christianity thus presented lost much of its attraction.

There were attempts to meet this objection by more sophisticated definitions. The Monarchianists, while emphasizing the unity of God, suggested that the Father himself descended into the Virgin Mary and became Jesus Christ, a formulation also known as Patripassionism. The Sabellianists put it a slightly different way: Father, Son and Holy Ghost were one and the same being, that is the body, the soul and the spirit of one substance – one God in three temporary manifestations. These were intellectually digestible concepts but they were still incompatible with the historical Jesus who was now an integral part of the canonical scriptures.

A second line of solution was to stress the manhood of Christ. This, of course, had been preferred all along by the Judaizing elements in Christianity and was the essence of the heresy maintained by the Ebionites, the displaced rump of the Jerusalem Church. The objection, of course, was that it was then difficult to differentiate Christianity from Judaism and impossible to retain Pauline theology or (among other canonical texts) the gospel of St John. The half-way stage along this line was to deny Christ's pre-existence as God and this is more or less what Arius, the most important of the Christological Trinitarian heresiarchs, tried to do. As he put it himself: 'We are persecuted because we say that the Son had a beginning, but God is without beginning . . . and this we say because he is neither part of God nor derived from any substance.' According to the historian Socrates, writing c. 440, his actual formulation was as follows: 'If the Father begat the Son, he that was begotten had a beginning of existence; hence it is clear that there was a time when the Son was not. It follows then of necessity that he had his existence from the non-existent.'

The intrinsic difficulty of the problem lay in the lack of room for manoeuvre for a middle course. A right-thinking theologian, anxious to remain orthodox, tended to smash his ship on Charybdis while trying to avoid Scylla. Thus Apollinaris, Bishop of Laodicea (d. 392), in his efforts to demonstrate his anti-Arianism, emphasized the divinity of the Lord at the expense of his manhood and ended by creating a heresy of his own which denied that Christ had a human mind. Nestorius, Bishop of Constantinople 428–31, reacting from Apollinarianism, reasserted the manhood of Christ to the extent of questioning the divinity of the infant Jesus and thus denying Mary her title of *theotokos* or 'God-bearer'. He, too, found himself a reluctant heresiarch. In turn, Eutyches, a learned monk from Constantinople, in his anti-Nestorian fervour, swung too far in the direction of Apollinarianism and came to grief over Constantine's compulsory word 'consubstantial'. Summoned to recant before a council in 448, he gave up in despair: 'Hitherto I have always avoided the phrase "consubstantial after the flesh" [as tending to confusion]. But I will use it now, since your holiness demands it.'

What room for manoeuvre there was consisted in verbal manipulations behind which lay nebulous concepts. 'Consubstantial after the flesh' was, indeed, such a device. But a clever formula might, in solving an old problem, raise an entirely new one and a compromise meaningful and satisfactory to one generation of fathers was often interpreted in rival ways by the next. The Church's collective memory was an imperfect instrument. By the third century, for instance, it had forgotten the origins of the old Jewish-Christian Ebionites and assumed they were the followers of a heresiarch called Ebion; not only was he denounced by orthodox writers but sentences from his works were produced for refutation. All kinds of subsequent constructions were placed upon the Nicene formula, and the motives of those who approved it. Then there were language difficulties. Greek lent itself to complexity of religious discussion. This was one important reason why the great Christological rows were all of eastern origins and were mere imports in Latin-speaking areas. Our word 'essence' can be used in a general or a particular sense. The Greeks had two, *hypostasis* and *ousia*, each of which could be used in either sense. Some of the leading fourth-century Greek theologians began to employ *ousia* in the general sense and *hypostasis* in the particularist – 'person' or 'character'. But the Latin for both words is *substantia* – which in fact is the exact equivalent of *hypostasis*. The Latin *essentia*, the equivalent of *ousia*, never gained currency. The Latins did, however, have the word *persona*, which they employed for the particularist sense. The Greek equivalent of this, *prosopon*, was not used by orthodox theologians because it had been discredited by the Sabellians. The upshot was that it proved comparatively easy to devise a definition in the Latin West; much more difficult to produce one for the Greek East, and almost impossible to create a translatable formula which both East and West could accept in good faith. It was difficult for non-theologians, especially in the West, to keep up. Augustine tells the story of the Italian general who engaged him in a debate on the Trinity under the impression that *homousios* was an Eastern bishop. But in some ways it was even more difficult for the educated since they tended to invest words with portentous imagery. Thus Nestorius was appalled by the implications of the word *theotokos*, or God-bearer, as applied to the Virgin Mary. To him it implied Mary was a goddess. He went adrift on this one word; as the historian Socrates said, 'He was frightened by that word *theotokos*, as though it were a terrible ghost.'

It can be said that Rome, speaking for Latin theologians generally, and taking a simpler and less sophisticated view of the affair, consistently supported a definition which accorded Christ full godhead and avoided charges of polytheism by use of the word *persona*. Rome, indeed, was more interested in blocking the evasions and misconstructions of heretics than in evolving an absolutely comprehensive and irrefragable formula of its own. Its position was put out most fully in the Tome of Leo, Bishop of Rome 440-61, and sent East as an authoritative statement representing not only the view of the oldest apostolic Church but the united opinion of the Latin West. The Greeks regarded the Latins as amateurs in theology and in general as barbarous and ill-educated persons. Nevertheless, they were so divided among themselves that Roman and Latin support ensured the eventual triumph of the 'orthodox', anti-Arian faction at the Council of Chalcedon, 451. Christ was 'one substance with us as regarded his manhood; like us in all respects apart from sin; as regards his Godhead, begotten of the Father before the ages, but yet as regards his manhood begotten, for us men and for our salvation, of Mary the Virgin, the Godbearer; one and the same Christ, Son, Lord, Only begotten, recognized in two natures without confusion, without change, without division, without separation.'

This complicated formula has been held to mark the end of the controversy so far as the mainstream of Christianity is concerned. In fact it did nothing of the sort. It enormously strengthened the antagonism between East and West, in which the Trinitarian debate became not so much the cause of conflict as its most convenient and hallowed battlefield, and in the East it produced merely the illusion of ecumenical agreement. But the terminology of the debate changed, with those who refused to accept Chalcydon being grouped under the term 'monophysite'. Right from the first, it can be argued, the tendency in Christian Asia and in Egypt was to insist rigorously on a monotheist interpretation of Christianity. Jewish Christianity with, in effect, its denial of Jesus's divine nature, never successfully progressed beyond Asia Minor into Europe but traces of it remained important in the composition of Christianity all along the North African coast, in Syria, in the Middle Eastern desert, and right up the Nile. But as the Trinitarian doctrine evolved in the orthodox Church, the emphasis changed from an insistence on One God, to an insistence on One God Christ, with a single, divine nature, not two. This appeared to preserve the centrality of Christ along with the monotheistic principle, yet at the same time it differentiated Christianity decisively from Judaism, which rejected Christ altogether. Among the less sophisticated, especially the desert tribes, there was still lingering fear of the old gods dispossessed by Christianity. They were now believed to take the form of demons – this was to some extent official Catholic doctrine – who intervened constantly in the world, inflicting evils ranging from minor discomforts to earthquakes. Only a Christ who was fully divine could provide adequate protection against such creatures.

The Chalcedon formula was not therefore widely accepted south and east of Antioch. An underground episcopate was created and its monophysite elements can be traced today in the history of a number of schismatic or separated churches – the Copts of Egypt, the Armenians, the Ethiopians and the Syrian Jacobites. The Trinitarian and Christological divisions in the East remained unresolved, just as further west in Africa the Donatist schism was never finally healed. Orthodox Christianity appeared triumphant but its strength was undermined by popular feeling which remained heterodox, especially in tribal areas. In a great arc around the eastern and southern Mediterranean littoral, glittering Romanized cities, with their wealthy bourgeoisie, their huge orthodox basilicas and their ecclesiastical apparatus of complacent conformity, testified to the apparent solidity of the Christian world. Further inland, however, and often in the great cities themselves, Christianity as imposed by Chalcedon lacked a popular basis. This source of weakness was never eliminated; indeed it increased and ultimately the whole structure was swept away in a few decades by the Arab tribes and their clear Moslem doctrine of One God. Errors of Christian statesmanship thus delivered Asia and Africa to the Moslem alternative. The speed with which it was adopted and the unavailing efforts of Christianity to win back lost ground, indicate the strength of the Moslem popular appeal which banished all dubeity about the one-ness and nature of the divine.

Why was it that the arguments about the nature of Christ and the Trinity evoked so much more passion in the Greek-speaking East than in the Latinized West? It is not easy to reconstruct the religious sociology of the fourth and fifth-century Mediterranean world. To some extent there had been elements of mass emotional appeal in Christianity right from the start. This is apparent from the description of Pentecost in Luke's Acts. And from an early stage internal Christian disputes had been conducted to some extent with a mass public in mind. Lucian describes a revivalist-style meeting held by Alexander, one of the leading sectarians, designed to whip up frenzy against orthodox Christians. It was held at night, with massed torches, and began with a ritual casting-out of Christians, whom Alexander denounced as spies. He would shout: 'Out with the Christians!' and his cheer-leaders were taught to reply: 'Out with the Epicureans!' Mass-meetings and slogan-shouting were characteristic of the Montanist movement, and later of the Donatist church in North Africa. The huge basilicas Donatist bishops built for their flocks served as echoing auditoria at which the congregations could be worked up into a frenzy by popular orators, sometimes as a preparation to issuing into the streets as an armed mob to impose the Donatist will on the orthodox or on the Roman authorities. The use of money to manipulate crowds of slaves and poor people in a specific doctrinal direction had been one of the earliest features of Christianity. The tendency became more marked under the later empire, with the emergence of trade and craft guilds, in effect hereditary and compulsory unions, which bound sections of the community into tightly organized groups, each with its own series of economic and social interests, and each bribable, or persuadable. These craft-guilds had long played a leading role in municipal politics. By the fourth century they operated in the religious sphere, influencing or even determining the outcome of the episcopal elections, where these were still open to the whole population of Christians, and ready to be marshalled on the popular side in any religious dispute. No wonder Donatus used to inquire about his 'party' in distant towns! Direct bribery in a religious cause was by no means unknown. At a time when the free distribution of bread had become part of the system of government in many cities and towns, the fact that the Donatists controlled the main public bakery in Hippo was regarded as a prime source of their strength.

In the West, the mob could not easily be stirred by what we would term the more abstruse aspects of theology. The same had been true of the East as late as the third century. Origen had lamented that in Alexandria, then perhaps the most populous Christian city on earth, there was an immense gap between Christian intellectuals on the one hand and the city masses who knew nothing 'except Jesus Christ and Him crucified'. The change seems to have come about through the development of a primitive monastic movement in Egypt and Syria. Monasticism in its general sense we will analyze later. For the present, what concerns us is the existence in the East, in the third century and far more so in the fourth and fifth, of large numbers of monks living in the vicinity of towns like Alexandria. The great majority came from the lower social groups and were mainly illiterate. As such, however, they formed a link between the Church authorities and the masses and thus an instrument in the hands of a clever episcopate. The great bishops of Alexandria, Athanasius and still more Cyril, were the first to use the monks for the purpose of popularizing doctrinal positions. The monks were Coptic-speaking like the Egyptian masses and they translated into household terms, and popularized as slogans, the complex formulations of the theological experts. In this way what Origen had desired was brought about, though he might have shuddered to see the result.

The monks were often formed, or formed themselves, into black-robed squads for the execution of the Church's business, first to smash up pagan temples, later to rampage through the streets and basilicas in time of doctrinal controversy. Monasticism attracted misfits, bankrupts, criminals, homosexuals, fugitives, as well as the pious; it was also a career for raw peasant youths who could be drilled into well-disciplined monkish regiments to be deployed as an unscrupulous bishop might think fit. They were taken in bands to Church councils to bully hostile delegates and try to influence the outcome. The secular authorities fought to keep the monks out of the cities and towns by banishing them to their desert holes. But some monks had urban tasks. There were thousands of Alexandrian monks who worked, allegedly, as sick-attendants at the city's infirmaries, leprosies and so forth. They were liable to riot at a nod from the bishop. An imperial edict of 416 tried to confine their numbers to 500, the rest being expelled, and to forbid them to interfere in municipal affairs or court-business; it was not easily enforced. And the work and the example of the Alexandrine monks gradually spread through Eastern Christendom to create the phenomenon of the 'religious mob'. Alexandrine bishops who had raised mobs to smash Arians and Nestorians were soon imitated by their rivals in Antioch, and the habit of mobs intervening in religious politics spread to Constantinople where the two banishments of Bishop John Chrysostom, for instance, reflect the workings of mob theology. A fanatical religious mob could be used to blackmail a council of frightened ecclesiastics or even to overturn an imperial decision which impinged on Church affairs. Thus the bishops of Alexandria, who controlled the seamen's union of the port, threatened from time to time to starve the imperial capital, Constantinople, of its Egyptian grain supplies. But a bishop who created a theological mob was liable to find himself in the role of *apprenti sorcier*. Popular enthusiasm for a certain doctrinal line became a menace when compromise had to be reached to preserve the unity of the Church – one reason why it proved so difficult. Bishops who returned to their cities having accepted an unpopular formulation were liable to be thrown out or worse. Bishop Proterius of Alexandria so infuriated his flock by accepting the decision of Chalcedon that in the end they literally tore him to pieces. The phenomenon was not unknown in Rome: Pope Virgilius, 537–55 who travelled to a council at Constantinople and accepted an eastern formulation, was saved from repudiation only by his death on the voyage home.

In general, however, mob theology was an eastern growth. It was not confined to the cities. We hear of 'great mobs of rustics' taking part in torchlight processions to hail 'victories' at councils. And rustics swarmed into Edessa to take part in the terrifying demonstrations which were organized against Bishop Ibas when he returned to the city in 449, having compromised on the 'two natures'. We have a record of some of the slogans that were shouted: 'To the gallows with the Iscariot', 'Ibas has corrupted the true doctrine of Cyril', 'Long live the Archbishop Dioscurus', 'The Christ-hater to the arena', 'Down with the Judophile', 'The works of Nestorius were found with Ibas', and 'Where has the church property gone?' Mingled with the theology, then, we get acccusations of moral turpitude and overtones of anti-semitism. Among the wilder eastern mobs it was customary to classify the 'two nature' theory with Judaism. All kinds of powerful forces – localism, regionalism, patriotism, racism, class and commercial interest – were at work behind the theological facade. But it was religion which crystallized them and gave them open, even permissible expression.

Thus Christianity had become a crude form of populist democracy and this was made possible by its universalism. Christians were taught that the games and the circus were wicked and to be avoided as serious sins. In the East at least, theology was a form of sport. Gregory of Nazianzus, Bishop of Constantinople, used to claim of its citizens: 'If you ask a baker the price of a loaf, he will reply: "The Father is greater and the Son inferior". And if you ask if your bath is ready, the servant will tell you: "The Son was made out of nothing".' But it was a sport which transcended class barriers. Or, to put it more soberly, by the fourth century Christianity had completely penetrated all classes. Historical writers of this period do not treat any belief as characteristic of the masses, the vulgar, the uneducated. Where doctrinal divisions arose, they cut across the social pyramid. Now this was in marked contrast to paganism. Any religion tends to be a combination of intellectual theorizing among the élite, and popular belief (or superstition). Roman paganism did not hang together and therefore was ultimately a failure because the intellectual élite could not transmit their theoretical justifications to the masses; and the reason why they failed was that they could not, in practice, share the beliefs of the masses. Cicero's defence of the gods was that of a sceptic, a man of the world, a political conservative; it meant nothing to the man in the street. Thanks to St Paul, the central mystical and miraculous belief of Christianity, the resurrection of Christ, could be presented to the sophisticates and thanks to Origen it could be woven into a complete philosophical system and so become part of the normal intellectual furniture of the upper classes. Christian intellectuals, in turn, starting from the same foundation of belief as the masses, could transmit their formulations downwards. Within Christianity there was by about 350 no way of defining a clear separation between an upper-class culture and a lower-class culture. There was, rather, a balance, and a highly delicate one; it could not be maintained without frequent crises, involving the reconciliation between belief and reason; and sometimes these led to heresy. Christianity, by abolishing the internal frontiers between the learned and the vulgar, obliged cultured people to accept a number of uncritical and unsophisticated beliefs in miracles, relics, ghosts and so forth; and for the mob it meant treating theological controversy as a subject for popular enthusiasm, or rather fanaticism.

If, however, the cultural unity of Christianity tended to find release for its tension in doctrinal warfare and heresy, the Church always presented a united front to paganism, which was slowly demolished in the course of the fourth and early fifth centuries. But here again there was another important difference between East and West. Constantine's conversion coincided with a further effort to de-centralize the empire, this time marked by the creation of a new imperial capital in the East. Constantinople contained buildings for pagan cults but it was from the start essentially a Christian town and the court there soon acquired a flavour of episcopacy. There Christianity was the religion of the establishment *ab initio,* and elsewhere in the East, where Constantine's writ ran strongly, there was little resistance from official paganism. It was a different matter in the West, especially in Rome, where paganism and upper-class culture were deeply entwined and where the state gods were identified with the city's heroic past. Rome formed, as it were, a natural urban theatre for paganism and many of the cults were spectacular. Christianity, at this stage at least, could not match the huge mass celeb-rations which marked the funeral feast of Attis on 24 March: the *taurobolium* or blood-bath, the howling crowds of flagellating penitents, the castration rites. There were tableaux and miracle-plays, and wild dances, accompanied, according to hostile Christian observers, by obscene acts and songs. For the cult of the Syrian Atargatis there were musical processions in which fanatics danced, slashed their arms and whipped themselves with knotted scourges. The colour and in some cases the majesty of these ceremonies appealed to the same instincts which kept the Roman games going. And, at a higher social level, the meetings of the pagan Pontifical College in chapter, the solemn and very ancient state rituals, conducted in the superb surroundings of the temples whose history went back in some cases nearly a thousand years, had a powerful appeal, which was nostalgic, patriotic and aesthetic.

Not surprisingly, then, the assault on paganism was directed chiefly at its externals, above all at its fabric. Constantine himself began the depredations by removing gold and silver treasures from some temples and in the East he actually pulled several down to make way for Christian basilicas. But to some degree he kept his word about toleration, since one pagan writer admits that in his reign 'though the temples were poor, you could see the rites being carried out'. Constantius II passed the first major anti-pagan law in 341 and next year ordered that 'all superstitions must be completely eradicated'. Temples were allowed to stand only outside city walls, where they were to be used merely for 'plays, the circus and contests' being 'the long-established amusements of the Roman people'. By mid-century the temples were ordered to be closed 'in all places and cities' in order to 'deny abandoned men the opportunity to sin'; temple sacrifices were forbidden and anyone performing them liable to death and confiscation of property. By this time there is evidence that the court was under constant pressure from leading Christians to change a policy of qualified toleration to one of outright suppression. The Christian convert senator, Firmicus Maternus, wrote a book addressed to the Imperial House (c. 345) in which he demanded: 'These practices must be completely excised, destroyed and reformed. . . . Away with the Temple treasures! Let the fire of your mind and the flame of your smelting-works roast these gods!' There was a mass of legislation dealing with paganism in the later part of the fourth century, and the first two decades of the fifth. Much of it was contradictory or purely local. Thus in 399 some country districts were ordered to destroy the temples after closing them; others to preserve them intact; others still to remove idols and put the buildings to public uses.

Evidently some of these laws were only partly enforced, or not at all, depending on the allegiance of the officials concerned. But where the State was slow, the Church was increasingly swift. The pagan apologist Libanius, writing in 390, complained bitterly to the Emperor Theodosius about the behaviour of Christian monks:

'You did not order the temples to be closed, but the men in black – they eat like elephants and keep the servants busy with their drinking – attack the temples with stones, poles and iron crowbars, or even their bare hands and feet. Then the roofs are knocked in and the walls levelled to the ground, the statues are overturned and the altars demolished. The temple priests must suffer in silence or die. These outrages occur in the towns; it is worse in the country.'

He said that in rural areas, pagan shrines were seized by the Church, declared 'sacred' and the attached land appropriated by monks – a charge confirmed by the pagan historian Zosimus. The pagan priests lost their privileges in 396, and further laws attached their tax-incomes to the army and transferred the remaining property to the State. Little attempt was made by the authorities to protect pagan institutions from militant Christians, though very occasionally the pagans retaliated themselves. Sozomen recounts an incident at Aulon when Marcellus, the violently iconoclastic Bishop of Apamea, led a band of soldiers and gladiators in an attack on the local temple. 'He kept out of range of the arrows, for his gout prevented him from fighting, pursuing or fleeing. While the soldiers were attacking the temple, some of the pagans discovered he was alone, seized him, and burned him alive.'

In 391 another militant bishop, Theophilus of Alexandria, led a massed attack on the Serapeum, or Temple of Serapis, in Alexandria, said to be the largest place of worship in the world. This complex contained an immense wooden statue of the god, which threatened earthquakes if anyone touched it. According to Theodoret's *Ecclesiastical History*, 'The bishop looked on these tales as the drivel of drunken hags, and sneering at the lifeless monster's vast bulk, told a man with an axe to strike it . . . Serapis's head was cut off, and out ran a multitude of mice. It was broken into small pieces and burnt, but the head was carried through the town, in mockery of those who worshipped it.' Also brought to light were a number of weird priestly tricks, such as hollow statues of wood or brass, with hidden apertures from which priests had whispered oracles or maledictions. These seem to have born a striking resemblance to the various frauds, such as the Boxley Rood, later brought to light during the first great wave of iconoclasm at the Reformation. The destruction of the pagan temples indeed adumbrated many of the attitudes on both sides produced by the puritan campaign against sixteenth-century Christian 'idolatry'.

The weakness of paganism, in fact, was its dependence on external show and, among its upper-class defenders, on a purely aesthetic approach to religious practice. Third-century pagan intellectuals, such as Plotinus and his biographer Porphyry were unable, like the earlier critic Celsus, to attack Christianity as a barbarous superstition, unworthy of educated men. They wrote on the defensive, conceding much of the Christian case. The inability of pagan thinkers to supply a credible alternative to what was now the dominant religious group in the empire completely undermined Julian's attempt to reimpose paganism by state power in the 360s. The attempt ended with his early death in battle, a misfortune seen naturally as a judgment on his cause and we cannot know how successful perseverance might have proved. Julian's method, in effect, was to graft Christian practices on to paganism, while presenting the Christians as intolerant, brutish and destructive. He compiled a catechism, introduced pagan charities and constructed an ecclesiastical hierarchy on Christian lines, with a system of discipline and canon law. He deliberately promoted pagans to high office and discriminated against Christians, excluding them completely from the teaching profession. He thought that by withdrawing State backing from official Christianity he would encourage dissent, especially in the East, and he turned a benevolent eye on the Jews, promising to help them rebuild the Temple of Jerusalem. During a tour of the East he publicly exhorted local authorities to hold mass-sacrifices in the pagan manner and everywhere the temples were reopened and repaired. But there was little enthusiasm. On the contrary, in some areas there were complaints that the sacrifices had led to meat shortages. And then, Julian was superstitious. He believed he reincarnated the soul of Alexander of Macedon, that it was his destiny to re-create the Alexandrine empire, and that the newly-honoured pagan gods would ensure he fulfilled it. He thus made the error of identifying religious truth with military victory. The Roman aristocracy, though predominantly pagan, had ceased to do this. On the whole they thought a pagan revival might raise more problems than it solved. Their interest in the matter was antiquarian and aesthetic.

In any case, in these and other respects, Christianity was changing to meet public opinion. In the second century the Church had acquired the elements of ecclesiastical organization; in the third it created an intellectual and philosophical structure; and in the fourth, especially in the latter half of the century, it built up a dramatic and impressive public persona: it began to think and act like a state Church. This policy was shaped by the need to outface paganism – almost consciously so, after the failure of the Julian revival, during the pontificate of Bishop Damasus of Rome, 366–84. His aim seems to have been quite specific: to present Christianity as the true and ancient religion of the empire and Rome as its citadel. Thus he instituted a great annual ceremony in honour of Peter and Paul, making the point that Christianity was already very old and had been associated with Rome and the triumphs of the empire for over three centuries. The two saints, he argued, not only gave Rome primacy over the East, since it was their adopted city, but they were also more powerful protectors of the city than the old gods. Christianity was now a religion with a glorious past as well as an unlimited future. Damasus lived well and entertained sumptuously. In *c.* 378 he held a synod, 'at the sublime and holy Apostolic See' – the first time the phrase was used – which demanded state intervention to ensure that western bishops were subject to Rome. It also ruled that the Bishop of Rome should not be compelled to appear in court: 'Our brother Damasus should not be put in a position inferior to those to whom he is officially equal, but whom he excels in the prerogative of the Apostolic See . . .' Damasus seems to have been a wholly unspiritual man. His enemies called him the man who tickled ladies' ears – most of his important converts were society women. He was singleminded in his efforts to win over the rich to Christianity, no easy task for in his day more than half the senate were still pagan. Forgeries circulated to boost Christian credentials: thus a correspondence between St Paul and Seneca was produced. Christianity attempted to gain a footing in all the great families of the late empire, in both Rome and Constantinople. Prominent ecclesiastics became 'clients' of noble houses, with vast estates and influence at court. Such dynasties tended to take sides in doctrinal arguments or disputes about personalities and appointments. Wealthy widows of successful generals were ranged on both sides in the violent controversies which marked the career of John Chrysostom in Constantinople. A leading noble house could protect a fashionable cleric who otherwise might be classified as a heretic and it could get him a valuable bishopric – by this time bishops, at any rate in the Roman area, were entitled to a quarter of the total revenues of the see. There was also a role for wealthy, well-born, or merely clever laymen adopted by a leading Christian family: they produced much of the ecclesiastical literature of the time and, as we have seen, could easily be pushed into a bishopric if needs required. The palatial town houses of the rich served as centres for such circles: if a family took a strong ascetic line, these houses resembled lay monasteries, which later became a feature of Constantinople.

Worldliness was reflected in episcopal dress, which combined both the dignity of senatorial garb and the new exoticism introduced by Constantine. Bishops, in fact, dressed like wealthy noblemen of the late empire; it was resistance to change which eventually gave this uniform its distinctively clerical connotation. Some outstanding bishops loathed this compromise with Mammon. Gregory of Nazianzus resigned the bishopric of Constantinople when criticized for his austerities and preached an ironic and angry sermon:

'I was not aware we ought to rival consuls, governors and famous generals, who have no opportunity of spending their incomes – or that our stomachs ought to hunger for the bread of the poor, and expend their necessities on luxuries, belching forth over the altars. I did not know that we ought to ride on fine horses, or drive in magnificent carriages, with processions in front of us, with everyone cheering and making way for us as though we were wild beasts. I am sorry for these deprivations. At least they are over. Forgive me for doing wrong. Elect another who will please the majority.'

John Chrysostom was thrown out of the city for taking the same line. He banned episcopal entertainments altogether, eating alone, and sparingly. He would not put up visiting bishops, especially since he thought they ought to be in their own dioceses, instead of collecting large fees for preaching in the metropolis. His own sermons were frantically outspoken, especially when he became excited, flaying the court, the rich, and especially wealthy widows (some of whom supported him). This category of womankind seems to have been a peculiar object of criticism among austere clergy. Jerome, John's contemporary, writes angrily of:

'their huge litters, with red cloaks and fat bodies, a file of eunuchs walking in front; they have not so much lost husbands as seek them. They fill their houses with guests and flatterers. The clergy, who ought to inspire awe with their teaching and authority, kiss these ladies on the forehead and, putting forth their hands as though to bless, take money for their visits . . . after a vast supper, these ladies dream of the Apostles.'

Jerome wrote of priests 'who gain admission to aristocratic houses and deceive silly women . . . who seek ordination simply to see women more freely. They think of nothing but their clothes, use scent, and smooth out the creases in their boots. They curl their hair with tongs, their fingers glitter with rings . . . bridegrooms rather than clergy.'

Jerome had seen all this: he had been Damasus's secretary and therefore he knew there was another side to the coin. If Christianity was to become the universalist faith as its founder had plainly intended, must it not identify itself, to some extent, with the world? And was it not right to do this worthily and elegantly? This was the Damasus line of reasoning. Hence he spent a great deal of effort and money integrating Christianity with imperial culture. Since the time of Constantine, Christian basilicas, which had originally been private houses, had been built on an enlarged scale. Damasus developed the classic late-Roman type, capable of holding thousands, and covered within with gold and coloured mosaic. He employed leading architects and sculptors, beginning a tradition of papal patronage which was to last more than a millenium. He paid professional calligraphers to produce magnificent copies of the scriptures and create church almanacs, giving Easter tables, episcopal lists and so forth. He completed the Latinization of the western church which, even in Rome, had originally been Greek-speaking. Latin versions of the gospels had existed for some time; there was also a third-century North African translation of the entire scriptures. Damasus employed Jerome to make a fresh translation and the result, known as the Vulgate, became the standard until the Reformation.

Damasus also Latinized the mass, which had been conducted in Greek until his time. And he seems to have expanded it in accordance with existing Greek practice. The basic framework of the mass had already existed in the mid-second century, when it was described by Justin Martyr. It consisted of readings from the memoirs of the apostles and the Old Testament; a sermon; a prayer followed by the kiss of peace, and the distribution of the blessed bread and water. This Sunday eucharist had become an absolute obligation by Justin's time and the words of the central prayer became formalized in the next generation or two. Some of the congregational responses were also very ancient. The effect of the process of change introduced by Damasus was to change an essentially simple ceremony into a much lengthier and more formal one, involving an element of grandeur. The scriptural extracts were made longer and standardized, and prayers inserted at fixed intervals. This was how the West acquired the kyrie, the sanctus, the gloria and the creed, most of which were translated into Latin. Some of the ceremonial aspects were taken over from pagan rites, others from court practice, which became far more elaborate after the transfer to Constantinople. The impetus in making the liturgy longer, more impressive, less spontaneous and so more hieratic was essentially Greek but was seized on eagerly by Rome from the time of Damasus onwards. The object was partly to replace the magnificence of pagan ritual in the public mind, partly also to win the struggle against Arianism, which for a great part of the fourth century was dominant in the East, by emphasizing the awe of Catholic sacrifice. Thus from the late fourth century there was a spectacular explosion of colour in the vestments and hangings, the use of gold and silver vessels and elaborate marble piscinae, silver canopies over the altar, a multitude of wax candles (a mark of respect in Roman domestic practice), and elaborate censing with incense. This was accompanied by a deliberate smartening up of the proceedings on the altar and in procession to and from it, and by an even more deliberate mystification, especially in the East, of the more sensitive parts of the mass. At the end of the fourth century John Chrysostom spoke of the Lord's Table as 'a place of terror and shuddering', not to be seen by profane eyes, and it became customary to screen it with curtains. Again, from this period, or shortly after, we find the practice of erecting a screen or iconostasis, whose effect was to hide all the operations on the altar from the congregation as a whole, and to deepen the chasm between clergy and laity.

These changes were evidently introduced with considerable misgivings, and against a background of constant criticism. But they were popular: part of the process by which the Church was taking over society. To what extent should the Church employ all the resources of human ingenuity in the praise of God? The Church's tradition of music, for instance, was very ancient, indeed pre-Christian. It was a speciality of Essene-type sects, like the Therapeutics of Alexandria, described by Philo, who had elaborate hymns, written down with notation marks, and choirs of men and women, using harmony and antiphony. Paul twice refers to church-singing, which seems to have been taken over straight from the synagogue-Essene practice – as the use of the untranslated Hebrew word *Alleluia* indicates. Only a few Christian hymns survive from the pre-Constantine period, and only in one case have we a real indication of the music. Celsus, the pagan critic, admitted that it was beautiful, and said he envied the Christians their hymns. Antiphonal singing, with two choirs, spread from the Middle East across the Mediterranean in the fourth century, and was very likely introduced to Rome by Damascus. By the sixth century Roman chanting had become a model for other Western churches, and was later ascribed to Gregory the Great. But the use of music plainly aroused controversy from very early times. The Christians rejected ritual dances, though they were acceptable to the Jewish tradition, were used by gnostic sects (and survive in Ethiopia). Clement of Alexandria warned against such erotic dance tunes, even if they had an ostensible religious purpose; and also against the over-use of chromatic intervals, when they tended to obscure the meaning of the words. Augustine admitted this was wrong, but otherwise he thought the use of church music lawful and indeed essential – the argument was to recur, with great bitterness, in the sixteenth century. There were also two, or more, views on the use of images. Here again, Clement of Alexandria took a severe line, and not surprisingly was backed by

Tertullian, who thought all holy statues and pictures should be banned. In fact they made their appearance, with increasing frequency and elaboration, before the end of the second century; and after the conversion of Constantine all the barriers were broken down.

By the end of the fourth century, in fact, the Church had not only become the predominant religion in the Roman empire, with a tendency to be regarded as the official one, indeed as the only one. It had also acquired many of the external characteristics appropriate to its new status: official rank and privilege, integration with the social and economic hierarchy, splendid and elaborate ceremonial designed to attract the masses and emphasize the separateness of the priestly caste. It had arrived. It was well launched on its universalist career. It had, as it were, responded to Constantine's gesture, and met the empire half way. The empire had become Christian. The Church had become imperial. Or had it? Let us look at the Church at the turn of the fourth and fifth centuries, as represented by three great churchmen.

In Ambrose, Bishop of Milan, 373–97, we get the first close-up glimpse of the Christian as an establishment figure and member of the ruling order: the prototype of the medieval prince-bishop. Oddly enough, we almost certainly know what he looked like, too, for the mosaic of him in Sant'Ambrogio is early fifth-century, and seemingly taken from life. It shows Ambrose as St Augustine must have known him: a small, frail man, with a high forehead, long melancholy face, and huge eyes. Augustine was struck by the fact, when they first met, that Ambrose read to himself, a habit unknown to the classical world: 'His eyes scanned the page, and his mind penetrated its meaning, but his voice and tongue were silent.' There were other impressive things about Ambrose. His father came from the highest social class. As Praetorian Prefect of Gaul he ruled a huge chunk of western Europe and was one of the half-dozen most important civilians in the empire. Ambrose's election to the episcopal throne of Milan, a city which by then played a more important role in the administration of the West than Rome itself, appears to have been in some sense an act of state, since he was transformed from a prominent layman, not yet baptized, into a bishop within eight days. His biographer, Paulinus, says this was due to popular acclamation. But this is a simplification. The West was orthodox, the East, for the time being – roughly 360–80 – Arian, and it seems likely that the authorities were anxious to balance the existence of an Arian court circle in the West by appointing a staunchly Trinitarian bishop; and this of course would have been popular too. Ambrose played a pontifical role in the politics of his time. He seems to have thought that the bishops exercised collegiate power in the church, but that the influence of individual sees must depend on the importance of the city with which they were identified. 'What is said to Peter,' he wrote, 'is said to the Apostles' – thus brushing aside any special pleading for Rome. And again: 'All we bishops have in the blessed Apostle Peter received the keys of the kingdom of heaven.' 'Christ gave to his Apostles the power of remitting sins, which has been transmitted by the Apostles to the sacerdotal office.' 'We are not usurping a power but obeying a command.' 'Power' was a word constantly on Ambrose's lips: in his mind, the degree of power the Church exercised reflected its spiritual authority and claims, which ultimately must be limitless. Thus: 'We priests have our own way of rising to empire. Our infirmity is our own way to the throne. For when I am weak, then am I powerful.'

The degree of power exercised by Ambrose during the quarter century he ruled the church in Milan was something to which no churchman had hitherto aspired. He influenced the policy of successive western emperors, Gratian, Valentinian II, Theodosius. He won a public debate against the pagans, and prevented the restoration of the pagan Altar of Victory in the Senate House, despite the wishes of the Roman aristocracy. He excommunicated Theodosius for carrying out a mass-reprisal against the citizens of Thessalonica, who had murdered a barbarian army commander, and required the emperor to accept public penance before being readmitted to communion. His ascendancy over Theodosius explains the severity of the legal code enacted against pagans: this ensured that the most beautiful and ancient temples, and their treasures, would be preserved, but that otherwise temple-smashing would go unpunished.

Ambrose was thus instrumental in hastening the process which aligned imperial authority completely behind the orthodox Catholic Church, and also the Church completely behind imperial policy. It is a matter of fine judgment, therefore, whether Ambrose was a case of the ruling class penetrating Christianity, or vice versa. Perhaps the truth is both. He carried through the logic of the Constantinian conversion. In his day it began to be commonly assumed that non-membership of the Church was, in effect, an act of disloyalty to the emperor. State exile of dissenters went back as far as 314. In the time of Ambrose it became systematic, as a necessary characteristic of an orthodox empire. Those guilty of religious error became automatically enemies of society, to be excluded from it or reduced to second-class status. Who was the judge of error? The Church, naturally. Therein lay power. And, since religion concerned the higher things of the spirit, it was to take precedence over more material considerations. Therein lay superior power.

We see the workings of Ambrose's mind and method in his attitude to the Jews. They were now a 'problem' within the Christian empire, as they had been a problem in the pagan one – a large and conspicuous element which would not accept the Christian norms. And they were increasingly unpopular among Christians. Jews had assisted the authorities during the period of imperial persecution of Christians; they had collaborated with Julian in his pagan revival. Under Theodosius, when Christian uniformity became the official policy of the empire, Christian mob-attacks on synagogues became common. Any such unlicensed violence was contrary to public policy; moreover the Jews were regarded as a valuable and respectable element in society, notable for their general support of authority. In 388 the Jewish synagogue at Callinicum on the Euphrates was burnt down at the instigation of the local bishop. Theodosius decided to make this a test-case, and ordered it rebuilt at Christian expense. Ambrose hotly opposed the decision. His dictum was: 'The palace concerns the emperor, the churches the bishop.' Was this not a matter of Christian principle? No such depredations had hitherto been punished. To humiliate the bishop and the Christian community would damage the Church's prestige. He wrote to Theodosius: 'Which is more important, the parade of discipline or the cause of religion? The maintenance of civil law is secondary to religious interest.' He preached a sermon on these lines in the emperor's presence, and Theodosius lamely withdrew his orders. The incident was a prelude to the emperor's humiliation over the Thessalonica massacre. Indeed, it marked an important stage in the construction of a society in which only orthodox Christianity exercised full civil rights.

Ambrose, however, was well aware that those rights could only be secured and maintained by the exploitation of the potentialities of Christianity. He brought to his task as bishop the skills of a great administrator, evolving by trial and error a pastoral theology and canon law which supplied the answers to all the questions the Christian life raised. Perhaps no man played a greater part, in practice, in constructing the apparatus of practical belief which surrounded the European during the millenium when Christianity was the environment of society. At Milan, in the great new basilica he completed in 386, the prototype of the medieval cathedral came into existence, with daily mass, prayers at morning and evening and sometimes at other times in the day, and special ceremonies to commemorate the saints, according to a strict calendar. To combat the Arians in the city, Ambrose deliberately dramatized the cathedral services, introducing splendid vestments and antiphonal singing of psalms and metrical hymns. He employed professional choristers, but also trained his congregation. He wrote: 'From the singing of men, women, virgins and children there is a harmonious volume of sound, like the waves of the ocean.' He thought this celestial harmony drove out demons. It certainly angered the Arians, since Ambrose got his people to roar out the praise of the Trinity. He was, in fact, facing the Arians with their own weapons since Arius had himself been a writer of propaganda hymns – popular monotheist ditties for trades-guilds, marching-songs for soldiers, vast numbers of whom became Arians, and theological sea-shanties for merchant seamen. Ambrose was not the earliest hymn-writer in the West; some earlier though unimpressive efforts by Hilary of Poitiers survive. But Ambrose had the knack of producing verse which was memorable and adaptable to music, iambic diameters in four-line stanzas of eight syllables to the line. Four are still in use.

It was Ambrose, in his fight to defeat the popular challenge of Arianism, who first systematically developed the cult of relics. Milan was poorly provided in this respect: it had no tutelary martyrs. Rome had the unbeatable combination of St Peter and St Paul; Constantinople acquired Andrew, Luke and Timothy; and during the last fifty or sixty years amazing discoveries had been made at Jerusalem – the body of St Stephen, the head of John the Baptist, the chair of St James, the chains of St Paul, the column used in the scourging of Christ and, since 326, the cross itself. Ambrose, who took a fanatical interest in all the details of martyrology and relic-mongering, says that when the cross was discovered by Constantine's mother, Helena, it still had the *titulus* attached to it; and she found the nails, too, having one fashioned into a bit for her son's horse, and another put into his diadem. During the closing decades of the fourth century there was a wave of discoveries, forgeries, thefts and sales of saintly treasures. Pagans did their best to ridicule the practice. The writer Faustus accused the Christians of simply substituting martyrs for pagan idols, and reviving the idea of prodigies under another name. Some Christian writers were also disturbed. Vigilantius, a presbyter, called the cult 'a heathen observance introduced into the churches under a cloak of religion . . . the work of idolators'. He particularly deplored the placing of relics in costly caskets to be kissed, the prayers of intercession, the building of churches in the honour of particular martyrs, and the practice of holding vigils, lighting tapers and lamps, and attributing miracles to such shrines. The government, too, showed some alarm. It was angered by monks who stole the remains of holy men, and hawked portions of them for money. Theodosius laid down: 'No person shall transfer a buried body to another place; no person shall sell the relics of a martyr; no person shall traffic in them.'

But the government permitted the building of churches over the grave of a saint, and it was this that lay at the bottom of the whole theory and practice of relic-worship. Once that was conceded, the rest automatically followed, whatever the law said. The world was terrified of demons – now joined by the dethroned pagan gods, and the devils of the heretics – and the bones and other attachments of sanctified just men were the best possible protection against the evil swarms. Any church well endowed with such treasures radiated a powerful circle of protection; and its bishop was a man to have on your side. So Ambrose pushed the relic-system for all it was worth. At the dedication of his new basilica, he providentially discovered the skeletons of SS Gervasius and Protasius, 'of extraordinary stature, such as ancient times produced'. The episode was accompanied by the curing of a blind man, and other miraculous events, trumpeted abroad by Ambrosian flack-men, and embroidered upon by later generations – in the sixth century Gregory of Tours said that during the translation mass a panel fell from the ceiling, grazing the martyrs' heads, from which blood flowed. At the time, the Arians scoffed, but were soon dismayed by the popular success of Ambrose's find. It was followed by the unearthing of the bodies of SS Agricola and Vitalis, and SS Nazarius and Celsus. In the case of Nazarius, the 'martyr's blood was as fresh as if it had been shed that day, and his decapitated head was entire, with its hair and beard as if it had just been washed', according to Ambrose's biographer. A demon interrupted the sermon in which Ambrose celebrated this event, but the bishop rebuked and silenced him. Cloths dipped in the miraculous blood were sent all over Italy and Gaul.*

It is clear from Ambrose's writing that he was wholly sincere in his cult of relics. They were, to him, necessary counterparts to the monstrous cohorts of wicked spirits who roamed the earth, tempting man to forfeit his future in the next world, and making his life unpleasant and dangerous in this. But in addition to the saints, there were also the good angels: ninety-nine to each human being, in his opinion. Ambrose was a superstitious and credulous man, with a weird cosmology. He distinguished between paradise and the superior Kingdom of Heaven, already inhabited by Constantine and (after his death) Theodosius. He thought, in fact, there were seven heavens. Then there was Hades, where people waited for the last judgment, and purgatory, a place of second baptism or furnace of fire, where the precious metal in a soul was tested to rid it of the base alloy. Finally there was Hell, divided into three regions, of increasing horror.

With Ambrose we see the eschatology of the ancient world on the eve of its transformation into the medieval stereotype. But he was also medieval, and prelatical, in his curious blend of gross superstition and worldly wisdom tempered by genuine piety. Ambrose, like most Christian leaders, had reconciled himself to the vanished *parousia*. So life had to be lived out in this world, but of course with the next in view. He was feeling his way to a pastoral *via media*, in which the quest for perfection would be balanced by common sense, and the aspirations of the spirit reconciled with the clayey longings of the flesh in which it was imprisoned. Thus, on the subject of money, he thought that private property was objectively an evil; on the other hand: 'Just as riches are an impediment to virtue in the wicked, so in the good they are an aid to virtue.' He condemned commerce: an honest trade, he thought, was a contradiction in terms. So it served a merchant right if he were shipwrecked, since he was driven to put to sea by avarice. No doubt Ambrose would have taken a different view had he been bishop of Alexandria. As it was, being bishop of a great food-producing area, he thought the best form of property was inherited land: to cultivate, improve and extract profit from an inherited estate was not only legitimate but praiseworthy; thus he formulated one of the central religio-economic doctrines of the Middle Ages. Was not agriculture, he argued in *De Officiis*, the only form of making money which gave no offence? Millions of Christians would agree.

As for the clergy, Ambrose advised them to make regular charitable

---

* Relics were worn as charms, enclosed in little jewels hung from the owner's neck. The practice may well have derived, as St Jerome suggested, from the phylacteries worn by the pharisees and scribes. Gregory the Great had a cross containing filings from St Lawrence's gridiron and St Peter's chains; St Hugh of Lincoln carried 'innumerable relics of saints of both sexes', mixed up in a little casket like a snuff-box, and he had a tooth of St Benedict set into his ring. Bishops often wore relics from their cathedrals round their necks, a practice condemned by Aquinas and denounced by a council as 'detestable presumption', but which nonetheless persisted. See J. Sumption, *Pilgrimage, An Image of Medieval Religion* (London, 1975), chapter 2, 'The Cult of Relics'.

donations rather than dispossess themselves of their property – an opinion for which thousands of wealthy medieval prelates were to be profoundly grateful. He evidently followed this advice himself, despite the assertions of his biographer, Paulinus. Ambrose seems to have assumed that the clergy, at least of the higher grades, should normally be drawn from the wealthy and ruling orders, or at least conform to their social behaviour; he admitted he did not like presbyters or bishops who were unable to speak correct Latin, or who had provincial accents. Thus another aspect of the medieval pattern falls into place: a clerical career open to the talents but structured to the possessing class. Ambrose dressed appropriately, as a senator, in chasuble and alb. He dealt with many aspects of clerical behaviour. In his day the Church was tending to adopt the tonsure from some of the pagan sects. But opinion was divided. Some ascetics wore their hair long: Hilarion had it cut only once a year, on Easter Sunday. But then so did some less reputable figures, like Maximus the Cynic, Bishop of Constantinople, who was criticized for his long curly hair, much admired by the wealthy ladies of the capital, and which turned out to be a wig. Jerome said that hair should be just long enough to cover the skin; Ambrose characteristically ruled that it should be longer in winter than in summer. He occupied himself with many detailed aspects of administration: the rank, selection and payment of exorcists, who were attached to churches to expel demons, and who were classified just below the subdeacon; and the activities of Church courts, which were rapidly expanding their business in response to the increasing complexity and importance of canon law. And Ambrose was also the first bishop to deal at length with the question of sex.

Sex had seemed of no importance to the earliest Christians. Believing, as most of them did, in an imminent *parousia,* it seemed needless to devise rules for the correct means of perpetuating the species. Jesus himself had taken a strict line, compared to some Jewish exegetes, on the issue of marriage: that was the only positive element of basic Christian teaching on sex. It was virtually ignored by Paul; and the New Testament generally had no theory of sex and of the family. The Old Testament made no virtue of celibacy; on the other hand the New Testament did, at least by implication. In Jewish history, authority seemed to descend in the normal family way; in Christian history, however, the genealogical tree of authority propagated itself by spiritual transmission. And there was clearly a celibate tradition in Christian ministry going back through Paul to Jesus himself, to John, to the Essenes and the minority cult of celibacy in Judaism. The earliest Christian documents, written with the *parousia* in mind, seemed to stress celibacy as a virtue; so that when the *parousia* receded, and propagation was again seen as necessary, or at any rate unavoidable, the Church confusedly adopted an uneasy coexistence in which celibacy was praised but matrimony tolerated. The formula was reinforced in the fourth century when the Trinitarian controversy, and the triumph of orthodoxy, hugely increased the cult of the Virgin Mary, the *theotokos*. If, therefore, celibacy were superior, and marriage inferior, though licit, did this not imply that sex was intrinsically evil and even in the context of marriage a form of licensed sin?

The Church, then, did not have a doctrine of sex so much as a series of arguable suppositions; and the attempt to work them out consumed much clerical time and nervous energy. Ambrose wrote a great deal on the subject. He was clear that a full married life was incompatible with a career in the Church. Certainly, two marriages constituted an impediment to ordination. He did not like married bishops: he feared the creation of a priestly caste, with hereditary bishops. Married men ordained as bishops should cease to cohabit and beget children. He thought that this was how Adam and Eve had lived in Paradise. From his writing, it does not seem probable that Ambrose was a highly sexed man. But his judgments seem to have been influenced less by his personal habits and desires than by his pastoral experience. He acted as spiritual adviser to a large number of ladies, virtually all of them from the upper classes, and most with a long history of marital misfortunes. Their tales led Ambrose to take a pessimistic view of the marital state, at any rate as a promoter of felicity. His writings abound with lapidary comments. 'Even a good marriage is slavery. What, then, must a bad one be?' For a woman, marriage was 'a bondage, indignity, a burden, a yoke'. On the other hand, his experience of the Empress-Mother Justina, an Arian who wanted to steal one of his Milanese basilicas for the Arian Goths in the army, led him to reflect sourly: 'Every man is persecuted by some woman or another.' He advised his female penitents to fast, if possible to avoid food altogether for a week or more at a time; it was economical, it preserved beauty and health and stimulated the appetite – and it made chastity or continence easier.

But the best course for a woman was virginity. A virgin could redeem the sin of her parents in conceiving her. Ambrose's sermons on these lines angered parents. But he denied that virginity was responsible for a supposed falling birth-rate: history, he said, proved the world has suffered more from the ravages of ill-advised marriages than from virginity. 'Marriage is honourable but celibacy is more honourable; that which is good need not be avoided, but that which is better should be chosen.' There were contradictions here which Ambrose left unresolved. But on some aspects of virginity he was clear. A virgin was married to Christ. For her, the ceremony of taking the veil should be like a marriage-feast. Thereafter she should conceal herself. Ambrose took an old-fashioned line on this, acting as a bridge between the pagan vestal and the early medieval closed convent. Virgins should not even go to church often: churches were dangerous places, because frequented. 'Even to speak what is good is generally a fault in a virgin.' The true virgin should remain perpetually silent. Ambrose was strict rather than severe. A virgin suspected of sexual intercourse, he ruled, should not be medically examined by force, except in certain special cases, and then only on the authority and under the supervision of a bishop. If found guilty, she should not be executed (Ambrose did not believe in capital punishment but in redemptive justice), and certainly not tortured to death. Head-shaving and penance for life would suffice. A virgin threatened with rape or imprisonment in a brothel would be justified in committing suicide.

Ambrose connected in his mind the spiritual and sexual purity of the virgin with cleanliness. His virgins were spotless: his Virgin Mary, who to some extent became the medieval stereotype, wore white, silver and pale blue, the 'cleanest' of colours. It was quite a different matter with Jerome, his younger contemporary. He was not, like Ambrose, well adjusted to life. As secretary to Bishop Damasus, he seems at one time to have considered himself as a possible successor. But he had the temperament of the scholar, not the administrator. He was a wild man of God, not an urbane prelate. Jerome found sex an enormous difficulty. He was quite convinced it was evil: 'Marriage is only one degree less sinful than fornication'. He found women attractive, and especially virtuous women. This was why he left fashionable Church life in Rome, writing, on board the ship which was to carry him to Palestine: 'The only woman who took my fancy was one whom I had not seen at table. But when I began to revere, respect and venerate her, as her conspicuous chastity deserved, all my former virtues deserted me on the spot.' By this he appears to mean that his behaviour aroused hostile and malicious comment. In Jerusalem he founded and entered a monastery from which, for the rest of his life, he conducted a vast correspondence with scholars and saintly ladies all over the empire. One of his letters (to Augustine) took nine years to arrive; most have disappeared forever. Enough survive to reveal him as a wonderfully vivid and outspoken controversialist. His image made him the favourite of all the saints among Christian painters: Jerome and his lion (a sixth-century addition) were painted more often than any other figure outside the Holy Family. Indeed, his description, in a letter to a society virgin, of his struggles to avoid temptation in his monastery ('I often imagined myself among bevies of girls: my face was pale with hunger, my lips chilled, but my mind burned with desire, the fires of lust leapt up before me though my flesh was almost dead') one of the most frequently quoted of all patristic passages, enabled medieval artists devoutly to introduce the naked form into their paintings. Paradoxically, though, no passage did more to bring home to Christians the corruption and wickedness of sexual desire. To Jerome, sex was dirty in a literal or concrete sense; he writes often of his favourite virgins that they were 'squalid with dirt'. Dirt, to him, both epitomized the sexual act and the therapeutic process by which the virgin concealed her charms. The virgin he most esteemed in Rome, Paula, came to Jerusalem with her daughter (the product of an earlier avocation) to care for Jerome's old age. Both ladies dressed in rags and rarely washed or combed their hair.

We see in Jerome the disjunction between normal existence and an evolving idea of Christian virtue which really bore little relation to the teaching of Jesus and Paul, but was itself a reaction to the growing worldliness which flowed from the agreement with Constantine. The harsh Christianity of Jerome was, or seemed, a necessary corrective to the urbanity of Damasus or even of Ambrose. It made Jerome an unhappy and a bitter man. He wrote with particular venom against the heterodox. He claimed with relish to have 'destroyed in a single night' the sceptical Livinius who doubted the efficacy of the relic-cult; and of the Roman monk Jovinian, who had criticized what he regarded as the excessive cult of celibacy, Jerome sneered: 'After being condemned by the authority of the Roman church, and amid feasts of pheasant and pork, he did not so much breath out, as belch out, his spirit'. Other opponents were subjected to similar personal attacks, and Jerome could be equally sharp, even abusive, with his supposed allies. He had a donnish love of savage controversy, and seems to have quarrelled with most of his friends and acquaintances sooner or later. Palladius, whose *Lausiac History* is one of our chief sources for the period, said Jerome had a notoriously bad temper, and quotes the prophecy of another scholar, Posidonius: 'The noble Paula, who looks after him, will die first and be freed from his bad temper, I think. Then no holy man will live here, but his envy will include his own brother.' Jerome was the first Christian, of whom we have intimate knowledge, whose interpretation of his faith was quite incompatible with the realization of his nature – the result being profound misery. As Ambrose is the prototype of the medieval prelate, Jerome is the precursor of the agonized Christian intellectual, whose flesh is in irreconcilable conflict with the spirit, and whose enforced continence is bought at the cost of human charity.

The mental world of Jerome was a dark one: it was lit by flashes which seem more a reflection of hell-fire than glimpses of eternal light; nor is the picture produced by Ambrose's writings substantially different, despite his urbanities and his cult of common sense. Both derived from Christianity a pessimistic view of the human condition. It is difficult to judge where they found a scriptural mandate for this judgment. The epistles of Paul stress the joy occasioned by the 'good news' of divine redemption. The characteristics of the earliest Christian communities seem to have been eagerness balanced by serenity. When Origen turned Christianity from a theory of redemption into a philosophical system, he seized on the positive and expectant aspects of faith. Arguing with Celsus the pagan, he rejected the idea of a blind destiny or providence working itself out through the aeons, leaving behind limitless generations of suffering humanity, unchanged and unchangeable. He saw, instead, the Christian God as an agent whereby mankind was encouraged to improve, indeed perfect, itself: a continuous process of inching upwards to the light. He became a universalist in the double sense: the Christian message was addressed to all humanity, and ultimately all would be accommodated in the majestic forgiveness and beneficence of God, having progressively purged themselves of evil. Thus even the devil and the fallen angels would finally recover paradise.

It is notable that the post-Constantine Church repudiated Origen, or at least his optimism. As with Tertullian, his writings were so valuable, and in Origen's case so central to Christian understanding, that his works were never condemned as heretical, and so allowed to disappear *in toto* – though very few survive in their original form. But Jerome, once his admirer – 'the greatest teacher since the Apostles' – came to regard him not only as heretical in effect, but in intention. The object of Origen all along, he concluded, had been to pervert men's judgments and cause them to loose their souls, and he had written passages of undoubted orthodoxy simply to throw the unwary reader off his guard. Towards the end of the fourth century this view was widely held, not only among theologians but by laymen such as the Emperor Theodosius. Why the change in intellectual climate?

It is difficult to avoid the conclusion that the retreat from Origenist optimism reflected profound changes in the social and cultural structure of the empire itself, particularly in the West. The Constantinian revival had not been sustained; it had left the empire more fragmented, politically, militarily and administratively; the problems of currency and inflation in the West remained unsolved. The Church had brought no great accession of strength; in some ways it had added to the empire's burdens and divisions. Christianization had also accelerated the downwards drift in the social origin of the empire's cultural impulses. Christian culture was a unity, but despite the efforts of Christian intellectuals, it was a unity which took its colouring from the base. The culture of the fourth- and fifth-century empire was artisanal. The old self-confident republican elitism was gone. Higher education and secular literature remained almost entirely in pagan hands. But it was a paganism not only in decay but under constant attack. The murder of the pagan teacher Hypatia at Alexandria in 415 was only one example of the pressures and perils which faced non-Christian intellectuals. Many, like the poet Cyrus of Panopolis, became converts to escape vindictive treatment. The Christians do not seem to have been willing or able to present a cultural alternative at this level. They allowed the great classical universities to decline, then closed them down: Alexandria in 517, the school of Athens in 529. Some pagan analysts, like the historian Zosimus, were quite convinced that Christianity was wrecking the empire. What did the Christians have to say to this? Nothing. When they came to write secular history, as Procopius and Agathias did in Justinian's time, they left religion out of it, so dominated were they still by pagan theory.

The story might have been different. There were elements in Christianity at the beginning of the fifth century striving to create a distinctive Christian higher culture on Origenist lines. Their frustration and destruction was very largely the work of one man, in whom tendencies implicit in the work of Ambrose and Jerome were carried a decisive stage further. Augustine was the dark genius of imperial Christianity, the ideologue of the Church-State alliance, and the fabricator of the medieval mentality. Next to Paul, who supplied the basic theology, he did more to shape Christianity than any other human being.

Yet he is a difficult man to assess, partly because, like Paul, his ideas were steadily changing under the impact of events, cogitation and controversy. He admitted: 'I am the sort of man who writes because he has made progress, and who makes progress by writing.' The events of his own lifetime were spectacular and sombrely provocative of thought. He was born at Souk Arras in Algeria in 354, in a middle-class family; became a professor of rhetoric at Carthage; pursued his public career in Rome and then in Ambrose's Milan, where he became a Christian; was raised to the Bishopric of Hippo (near Bône), where he led the struggle against the Donatists; witnessed, from Africa, the sack of Rome in 410; spent ten years fighting the Pelagians; and then in his old age saw the Vandals overrun North Africa. Augustine wrote an enormous amount, much of it influenced by the events of his own day and his personal experiences. And a great deal of this writing survived in its original form. For a thousand years Augustine was the most popular of the Fathers; medieval European libraries contained over 500 complete manuscripts of his *City of God*, and there were, for instance, twenty-four printed editions between 1467–95. Above all, Augustine wrote about himself: he issued his so-called *Confessions* in 397, two years after he became a bishop. He was a tremendous egoist: it is characteristic of him that his spiritual autobiography should have been written in the form of a gigantic address to God.

Yet it is arguable that Augustine's references to himself hide more than they reveal. His *Confessions* is one of the few works of classical literature still read today because it centres around a personal relationship, between the young, sinful Augustine and his pious Christian mother, Monica (his father, Patrick, is virtually ignored), and because it describes the author's efforts to overcome the sexual impulse. These are transcendental themes, fascinating in any age. But it is not clear that either had much actual bearing on Augustine's life and spiritual development. It is true that Augustine, aged seventeen, took a regular concubine, who bore him a son. But there is no evidence that he was ever a libertine. The arrangement was normal at the time; later, Pope Leo used to say that a young man's desertion of his concubine was the first step to godliness. Augustine seems to have been if anything undersexed, and to have had a very limited interest in worldliness. The notion that he turned from the pleasures of the classical culture to the austerities of Christianity is false. Augustine was always a person with a very strong and austere religious bent, which he plainly inherited from his mother. The question was, what precise direction would this religious impulse take? For most of Augustine's youth and early manhood he was a Manichee. The Manichees were not really Christians at all. Mani was a late third-century Mesopotamian ecstatic, who had combined Montanism with eastern elements into a new synthetic religion. He had been executed by the Persians in 276, but his cult had spread east to China, where it was very influential, and west into the Mediterranean. It had reached Augustine's home territory about sixty years before his birth. Our knowledge of Manicheism, from recently discovered Coptic and Chinese sources, is still fragmentary. Like gnosticism, it was dualist. But it was characterized by intense pessimism about the potentialities of human nature and its inherent goodness, relieved only by confidence in the existence of a godly élite. Manichees were passionate, self-disciplined, righteous and obstinate. They demanded an exceptionally long catechumenate: Augustine became a 'hearer' aged twenty, and remained one for nine years – he never graduated to the 'elect'. Manichees were secretive and had their own personal networks of contacts. That was one chief reason why they were hated by all established regimes. Except for brief intervals, they were never tolerated by any government, whatever its racial, religious or ideological complexion. For over a millenium they were savagely persecuted by both Byzantine and Chinese emperors; and they inspired or influenced innumerable riotous heresies in the European Middle Ages. They were also, at times, secretively influential. Augustine himself went to Rome, and later Milan, on the Manichee 'net', a freemasonry which provided him with contacts and jobs. It is not absolutely clear why he became a Christian convert. One factor was his health – bouts of psychosomatic asthma which became serious enough to prevent him from pursuing a career demanding public oratory in the law courts and government service. Another was clearly the massive personality of Ambrose. It was the bishop himself who led Augustine into the deep, dark pool of the Milan cathedral baptistry and pushed him under, stark naked, three times, before clothing him in a white robe and handing him a candle. The service was solemn and portentous, preceded by the first lessons in the catechism, still regarded as secret, at least in part, and highly minatory in tone. Under Ambrose, Augustine felt he was joining a great and awesome organization, with enormous potential. But he carried with him the marks of his Manichee background: thirty years later, one of his opponents, Julian of Eclanum, claimed that his twisted views on sex were the direct result of his Manichee training.

Julian also called him *poenus,* 'the African'. And this, also, is a fair point. Augustine was the product of a Carthaginian environment as well as Manichee formation. Though an excellent Latinist, he lacked a wider culture. He knew almost no Greek, less even than Jerome. He found no difficulty in sorting out Trinitarian notions; he lifted the problem straight out of its Greek complexities, which he dismissed. Augustine's Christianity was Punic. As the hammer of the Donatists, he is assumed to have confronted its localism, or regionalism, with a wider international outlook. But this is only partly true. Augustine retained certain strong African characteristics, which merged with his Manichee strain: severity, lack of compromise, intolerance, courage, profound faith. He invented a kind of Christian nationalism which sprang from his Carthaginian roots. Thus Carthage was, in the end, to conquer Rome, as Troy, through Aeneas, had conquered Greece.

What Augustine absorbed in Ambrosian Milan, what he brought back to

Africa, and what he opposed to Donatist particularism, was the new sense of the universality of the Church which the Constantine revolution had made possible. In Milan, Augustine had seen the Church, through the person of a shrewd and magisterial prelate, helping to run an empire. His creative mind leapt ahead to draw conclusions and outline possibilities. In Milan the Church was already behaving like an international organization; it would soon be universal. It was already coextensive with the empire; it would ultimately be coextensive with humanity, and thus impervious to political change and the vicissitudes of fortune. This was God's plan. Augustine had a historical view of human development. There were six ages: man was now living in the last, between the first and second comings of Christ, when Christianity would gradually envelop the world, as preparation for the final and seventh age. Against the background of this concept, the Donatists seemed ridiculously petty. They had grasped the seriousness of Christianity. But, by worrying about what particular bishops had done at a particular time and in a particular place, they had lost sight of the enormous, objective scale of the faith, its application to all places, times, situations. 'The clouds roll with thunder,' Augustine wrote, 'that the House of the Lord shall be built throughout the earth; and these frogs sit in their marsh and croak – "We are the only Christians!"' Moreover, the Donatists had got the wrong notion of the world. Because of their obsession with their own limited local predicament and history, they saw the world as hostile and themselves as an alternative to society. But the world was there to be captured; and Christianity was not the anti-society – it was society. Led by the elect, its duty was to transform, absorb and perfect all existing bonds of human relations, all human activities and institutions, to regularize and codify and elevate every aspect of life. Here was the germ of the medieval idea of a total society, with the church permeating everything. Was she not the Mother of All? 'It is You,' he wrote, 'who make wives subject to their husbands . . . you set husbands over their wives; join sons to their parents by a freely-granted slavery, and set parents above their sons in a pious domination. You link brothers to each other by religious bonds tighter than blood. . . . You teach slaves to be loyal to their masters, masters to be more inclined to persuade than to punish. You link citizens to citizen, nation to nation, you bind all men together in remembrance of their first parents, not just by social bonds but by common kinship. You teach kings to rule for the benefit of their people, and warn the peoples to be subservient to their kings.'

But the idea of a total Christian society necessarily included the idea of a compulsory society. People could not choose to belong or not to belong. That included the Donatists. Augustine did not shrink from the logic of his position. Indeed, to the problem of coercing the Donatists he brought much of their own steely resolution and certitude, the fanaticism they themselves displayed, and the willingness to use violence in a spiritual cause. To internationalize Africa, he employed African methods – plus, of course, imperial military technology. When Augustine became a bishop in the mid-390s, the Donatist church was huge, flourishing, wealthy and deeply rooted. Even after a long bout of imperial persecution, inspired by Augustine, the Donatists were still able to produce nearly 300 bishops for the final attempt at compromise at Carthage in 411. Thereafter, in the course of the two decades before Vandals overran the littoral, the back of the Donatist church was broken by force. Its upper-class supporters joined the establishment. Many of its rank and file were driven into outlawry and brigandage. There were many cases of mass suicide.

Augustine watched the process dry-eyed. Of course the times were horrific. The late empire was a totalitarian state, in some ways an oriental despotism. Antinomial elements were punished with massive force. State torture, supposedly used only in serious cases such as treason, was in fact employed whenever the State willed. Jerome describes horrible tortures inflicted on a woman accused of adultery. A vestal virgin who broke her vows might be flogged, then buried alive. The state prisons were equipped with the *eculeus*, or rack; and a variety of devices including *unci*, for laceration, red-hot plates and whips loaded with lead. Ammianus gives many instances. And the State, to enforce uniformity, employed a large and venal force of secret policemen dressed as civilians, and informers, or *delators*. Much of the terminology of the late-imperial police system passed into the language of European enforcement, through the Latin phrases of the Inquisition. Augustine was the conduit from the ancient world. Why not? he would ask. If the State used such methods for its own miserable purposes, was not the Church entitled to do the same and more for its own far greater ones? He not only accepted, he became the theorist of, persecution; and his defences were later to be those on which all defences of the Inquisition rested.

We must not imagine that Augustine was necessarily a cruel man. Like many later inquisitors, he disliked unnecessary violence and refinements of torture. He thought heretics should be examined 'not by stretching them on the rack, not by scorching them with flames or furrowing their flesh with iron claws, but by beating them with rods'. He deplored, too, the dishonesty of using paid informers and *agents provocateurs*. But he insisted that the use of force in the pursuit of Christian unity, and indeed total religious conformity, was necessary, efficacious, and wholly justified. He admitted he had changed his mind on this point. He wrote to a Donatist friend that he had seen his own town, originally Donatist, 'brought over to the Catholic unity by fear of the imperial edicts'. That had convinced him. In fact heretics in their hearts welcomed persecution: they would say 'fear made us become earnest to examine the truth . . . the stimulus of fear startled us from our negligence'. And then, this was Christ's own way. Had not he, 'by great violence', 'coerced' Paul into Christianity? Was not this the meaning of the text from Luke, 14:23: 'Compel them to come in'? It was Augustine who first drew attention to this, and a number of other convenient texts, to be paraded through the centuries by the Christian apologists of force. He also had the inquisitorial emphasis:

'The necessity for harshness is greater in the investigation, than in the infliction, of punishment'; and again: '. . . it is generally necessary to use more rigour in making inquisition, so that when the crime has been brought to light, there may be scope for displaying clemency.' For the first time, too, he used the analogy with the State, indeed appealed to the orthodoxy of the State, in necessary and perpetual alliance with the Church in the extirpation of dissidents. The Church unearthed, the State castigated. The key word was *disciplina* – very frequent in his writings. If discipline were removed, there would be chaos: 'Take away the barriers created by the laws, and men's brazen capacity to do harm, their urge to self-indulgence, would rage to the full. No king in his kingdom, no general with his troops, no husband with his wife, no father with his son, could attempt to put a stop, by any threats or punishments, to the freedom and the sheer, sweet taste of sinning.'

Here, first articulated, is the appeal of the persecuting Church to all the authoritarian elements in society, indeed in human nature. Nor did Augustine operate solely at the intellectual level. He was a leading bishop, working actively with the State in the enforcement of imperial uniformity. We have a vignette of him at Carthage in 399, when imperial agents arrived to close down pagan shrines, preaching to excited mobs: 'Down with the Roman gods!' Perhaps more sinister is Augustine's contact with authoritarian elements in Spain, already a centre of Christian rigorism and orthodox violence. There, in 385, the Bishop of Avila, Priscillian, a notable ascetic and preacher, had been accused of gnosticism, Manicheism and moral depravity, had been indicted under the imperial law of witchcraft, tried at Bordeaux, and brought to the imperial court at Trier. There, under torture, he and his companions confessed they had studied obscene doctrines, held meetings with depraved women at night, and prayed naked. Despite the protests of a leading Gaulish bishop, Martin of Tours, they were executed – the first instance we have both of the slaughter of 'heretics' and of witch-hunting under Christian auspices. The episode aroused indignation, notably that of Ambrose, and provoked a reaction. But it did not end religious persecution in Spain; on the contrary, it was the beginning. Spain was already staging pogroms of Jews by the time Augustine became a bishop. And twenty years later we find him in correspondence with ferocious Spanish heresy-hunter, Paul Orosius, about the best means of winkling out heretics not only in Spain but at the other end of the Mediterranean in Palestine.

Augustine changed the approach of orthodoxy to divergence in two fundamental ways. The first, with which we have already dealt, was the justification of constructive persecution: the idea that a heretic should not be expelled but, on the contrary, be compelled to recant and conform, or be destroyed – 'Compel them to come in.' His second contribution was in some ways even more sinister because it implied constructive censorship. Augustine believed that it was the duty of the orthodox intellectual to identify incipient heresy, bring it to the surface and expose it, and so force those responsible either to abandon their line of inquiry altogether or accept heretical status.

These were the tactics Augustine employed against Pelagius and his followers. Augustine must have seen Pelagius briefly at the great confrontation in Carthage in 411, which Pelagius attended. But the men never met or conversed. They were roughly the same age and had gone to Rome – Pelagius from Britain – at almost the same time. But Pelagius had stayed there, a pious, well-educated layman, much in demand in high-born ascetic circles. He had many powerful supporters among the aristocracy and a number of rich, young and earnest followers. Basically, Pelagius was a reformer. Against the prevailing trend of his age, he looked back to Origen and the idea of Christianity as a great moral force changing and improving society, helping men to become more worthy, more socially useful and responsible. He thought the constricting force of the pagan social habits of the past could be removed. Christianity would become an active, ameliorative element not only among imperial citizens, but among the barbarians without, and the semi-barbarians within, its frontiers. Rich Christians should give away their money to the poor, set a good example, lead exemplary lives. Like Origen, he thought there was no such thing as a completely lost soul. The road to improvement was open to all. It was wrong to say: 'God's commands are too difficult to be carried out.' The fall of Rome, from which he fled, first to Africa, then to the more liberal East, had not dismayed him. It confirmed the need for reform, to create new structures. What mattered was the potentiality of man, his freedom to choose good, and the marvellous virtues with which God had endowed him, sometimes buried deep but waiting to be unearthed. Pelagius had a classical sense of the resources and authority of the human mind. Being a Latinized colonial, he had perhaps more faith in the qualities that had made the empire than its frightened fifth-century ruling class. After the sack of Rome he wrote, in 414, to a wealthy and pious woman, Demetrias, a message of hope and encouragement. Of course, he argued, man could save himself, in the next world as well as in this.

> 'We make the God of knowledge guilty of twofold ignorance – of not knowing what he has made, and not knowing what he has commanded. As if in forgetfulness of human frailty, which he made, he had laid upon men commandments which they could not bear . . . so that God seems to have been seeking not so much our salvation as our punishment. . . . No one knows better the measure of our strength than he who gave us our strength; and no one has a better understanding of what is within our power than he who endowed us with the very resources of our power. He has not willed to command anything impossible, for he is righteous; and he will not condemn a man for what he could not help, for he is holy.'

The Christian should have heroic fortitude like Job. And he should have compassion, should 'feel the pain of others as if it were his own, and be moved to tears by the grief of other men'.

With much of this the young Augustine might have not have disagreed. His earliest writings show an insistence on free will which was close to Pelagius's own. Later, as a militant bishop and persecutor, Augustine developed a grim determinism of his own. He took from Paul's espistle to the Romans a theory of grace and election which was not wholly unlike Calvin's. 'This is the predestination of the saints,' he wrote, 'the prescience and preparation of the benefits of God, whereby whoever are set free are most certainly set free. And where are the rest left by the just judgment of God, save in that mass of perdition, where were left the men of Tyre and the Sidonians, who were also capable of belief, had they but seen those wonderful works of Christ?' Every event was charged with a precise meaning as a deliberate act of God, of mercy for the elect, or judgment for the damned. A 'divine decree' had established 'an unshakeable number of the elect' who were 'permanently inscribed in the archive of the father'. What role had man's own efforts to play in this process? Very little. Deuteronomy warned, did it not: 'Say not in thy heart, My strength and the power of my hand has wrought this great wonder – but thou shalt remember the Lord thy God, for He it is who gives the strength to do great deeds.' Augustine was powerfully struck by a case he heard of – a man of eighty-four, of exemplary piety, who had lived a life of religious observance with his wife for a quarter of a century, and then had suddenly bought a dancing-girl for his pleasure, and so lost eternity. Was not this the hand of God, the fatal absence of grace, without which the human will was impotent?

Augustine's attention was first drawn to Pelagius by Jerome, who was still engaged in stamping out Origen's belief in the perfectibility of the soul, and who instantly recognized in Palagius a modern Origenist. Augustine saw in Pelagius a form of arrogance, a rebellion against an inscrutable Deity by an undue stress on man's powers. To Augustine, the duty of man was to obey God's will, as expressed through his Church. He wrote: 'Give what thou commandest, and command what thou wilt.' He noted, significantly, that Pelagius 'could not endure these words of mine'. And then, Jerome prompted him – a characteristic touch this – had not Pelagius, 'that corpulent dog, weighed down with Scotch porridge', denied original sin? To Augustine, original sin was important not so much for its own sake but because it influenced the theory of baptism, which to any African, involved in the Donatist affair, was a crucial test of orthodoxy. As a matter of fact it is hard to discover when, before Augustine, the Church had accepted original sin as a matter of faith. Tertullian had used the phrase (it was, indeed, a very African concept) but had specifically denied that children were born in sin. Since then, the practice of infant baptism had become common, and was tending to be general.

Once Augustine concentrated on the baptismal point, he seems to have become determined to drive Pelagius and his followers out of the Church, or enforce from them an abject submission. It is not even clear that Pelagius opposed infant baptism; as always with men branded as heretics, only snatches of his works survive, embedded in refutations of them. It was his disciple Caelestius who first appears to have raised the baptismal point, and he insisted, under pressure, that the issue was a matter simply for debate: 'On the subject of original sin and its transmission, I have already asserted that I have heard many persons of acknowledged position in the Catholic Church deny it altogether; and on the other hand many affirm it; it may fairly indeed be deemed a matter for inquiry, but not a heresy. I have always maintained that infants require baptism. What else does he want?' What Augustine wanted was what he had already obtained in the case of the Donatists, absolute condemnation followed by total submission – monitored by State enforcement. He did not want discussion. 'Far be it from the Christian rulers of the earthly commonwealth that they should harbour any doubt on the ancient Christian faith . . . certain and firmly-grounded on this faith they should, rather, impose on such men as you are fitting discipline and punishment.' And again: 'Those whose wounds are hidden should not for that reason be passed over in the doctor's treatment. . . . They are to be taught; and in my opinion this can be done with the greatest ease when the teaching of truth is aided by the fear of severity.'

Thus Augustine hunted Pelagius and his followers. He had them condemned twice in Africa. Pelagius, a reformer anxious to help the Church, desperately concerned lest his efforts should be frustrated by accusations of heresy, went to the East, to the much freer intellectual climate of Palestine, where debate was still possible. Meanwhile, he provided assurances and confessions of faith to any council or synod which asked for one, and to the Bishop of Rome. Rome was inclined to accept Pelagius at his word; he had the backing of powerful families, and there is evidence they were able to influence, for a time, the imperial enforcement authorities. But the will of the Africans prevailed. They brought pressure successfully, first on the Bishop of Rome, then on the emperor. Finally, they resorted to direct bribery: eighty fine Numidian stallions, bred on episcopal estates in Africa, were shipped to Italy and distributed among the various imperial cavalry commanders whose squadrons, in the last resort, imposed Augustine's theory of grace. To the imperial authorities, the Pelagians were represented as disturbers of the public peace, dangerous innovators, men anxious to dispossess the rich and redistribute property, no more acceptable to the orthodox of Church and State than the Donatists. Pelagian cells in Britain and Spain, Sicily, Rhodes and Palestine were identified and broken up.

Some Pelagians hit back at Augustine. One young follower, Julian of Eclanum, engaged in spirited controversy with the angry old bishop. From their exchanges, fragmentary alas, Augustine emerges in an unpleasant light, a clever man stooping low for the purpose of vulgar appeal, remorselessly exploiting popular prejudice, an anti-intellectual, a hater of classical culture, a mob orator, and a sex-obsessive. In the infinitive wisdom of God, he noted, the genitals were appropriately made the instruments for the transmission of original sin: '*Ecce unde!* That's the place! That's the place from which the first sin is passed on!' Adam had defied God – and for every man born, the shame at the uncontrollable stirring of the genitals was a reminder of, and a fitting punishment for, the original crime of disobedience. Did not every man, he asked his cringing congregation, feel shame at having a wet dream? Of course he did. By contrast, Julian's line seems a straightforward deployment of elementary classical reason:

> 'You ask me why I would not consent to the idea that there is a sin that is part of human nature. I answer: it is improbable. It is untrue. It is unjust and impious. It makes it seem as if the devil were the maker of men. It violates and destroys the freedom of the will . . . by saying that men are so incapable of virtue that in the very womb of their mothers they are filled with bygone sins . . . and, what is disgusting as it is blasphemous, this view of yours fastens, as its most conclusive proof, on the common decency with which we cover our genitals.'

Julian argued that sex was a kind of sixth sense, a form of neutral energy which might be used well or ill. 'Really?' replied Augustine, 'is that your experience? So you would not have married couples restrain that evil – I refer, of course, to your favourite good? So you would have them jump into bed whenever they like, whenever they felt stirred by desire? Far be it from them to postpone it till bedtime . . . if this is the sort of married life you lead, don't drag up your experience in debate.'

Augustine's own life ended in darkness. The Vandals broke into Africa in 429, and Augustine died next year in his episcopal city, already under siege. 'He lived to see cities overthrown and destroyed,' wrote his biographer, Possidius, 'churches denuded of priests and ministers, virgins and monks dispersed, some dying of torture, others by the sword, others captured and losing innocence of soul and body, and faith itself, in cruel slavery; he saw hymns and divine praises ceasing in the churches, the buildings themselves often burned down, the sacraments no longer wanted or, if wanted, priests to administer them hard to find. . . .' In the *City of God* Augustine had already contrasted the vulnerable earthly citadel with the imperishable kingdom of Christianity. Man should set his sights on the second; nothing was to be hoped for on earth. In his last, unfinished, work, he examined theodicy and the whole problem of evil. It was nonsense to suppose, he wrote, as the Pelagians did, that God was equitable in a human sense. His justice was as inscrutable as any other aspect of his nature. Human ideas of equity were like 'dew in the desert'. Human suffering, deserved or not, occurred because God was angry. 'This life, for mortals, is the wrath of God. The world is a small-scale Hell'. 'This is the Catholic view: a view that can show a just God in so many pains and in such agonies of tiny babies.' Man must simply learn to accept suffering and injustice. There was nothing he could do about either. Whereas Pelagius had portrayed the Christian as a grown-up man, a son no longer leaning on the

Father, but capable of carrying out his commands by free will – *emancipatus a deo*, as he put it – Augustine saw the human race as helpless children. He constantly used the image of the suckling baby. Humanity was utterly dependent on God. The race was prostrate, and there was no possibility that it might raise itself by its own merits. That was the sin of pride – Satan's sin. Mankind's posture must be that of total humility. Its only hope lay in God's grace.

Augustine thus bridges the gap between the humanistic optimism of the classical world and the despondent passivity of the Middle Ages. The mentality he expressed was to become the dominant outlook of Christianity, and so to encompass the whole of European society for many centuries. The defeat of the Pelagians was to be an important landmark in this process. To what extent Augustine's own Manichean pessimism was responsible for this dark coloration of Christian thought is hard to measure; certainly, if we contrast his philosophy with Paul's, it can be seen that Augustine, not Pelagius, was the heresiarch – the greatest of all, in terms of his influence. But Christian society in Augustine's age was already moving in this direction. By accepting the Constantinian State, the Church had embarked on the process of coming to terms with a world from which it had hitherto stood apart. It had postponed the construction of the perfect society until after the *parousia*. Augustine provided an ideology for this change of course, but he did not himself set it. In 398 a curious series of episodes took place in Constantinople. Following a high tide and a series of earth tremors, an official in the imperial army claimed that God had revealed to him that the city would be destroyed. In the second century, a man who spread such superstitions would have been prosecuted: this was precisely why the State had acted against Montanist bishops and 'speakers with tongues'. In 398 there was a very different sequence of events. The official told his bishop, who preached an alarmist sermon. At sunset, a red cloud was seen approaching the city; men thought they could smell sulphur, and many rushed to the churches demanding baptism. The next week there were more alarms, culminating in a general exodus from the city, led by the emperor in person. For several hours Constantinople was deserted, while its terrified inhabitants camped in the fields five miles away. Such human stampedes were to become a feature of medieval Europe. The incident at Constantinople in 398 was an indication that the classical era was over, and that men were now inhabiting a different mental universe.

PART THREE

Mitred Lords and Crowned Ikons (450–1054)

ON 23 DECEMBER, in the year 800, a lengthy meeting took place in the Secret Council Chamber of the Lateran Palace in Rome. Among those present were Charlemagne, the Frankish leader, the Pope, Leo III, Frankish, Lombard and Roman ecclesiastics and generals, and two French monks from Tours, Witto and Fridugis, who represented their abbot, the Yorkshireman Alcuin. There were two points at issue. First, should the Pope, who had been bitterly criticized, accused of a variety of crimes and vices, and very nearly assassinated by his enemies, be allowed to continue in office? And second, should western Christianity continue to recognize the imperial overlordship of the emperor in Constantinople? On the first matter, Pope Leo humiliated himself in front of Charles the Frank, swore a series of oaths that he was guiltless of the accusations against him, and was finally allowed to have 'justified himself'.

The second item on the agenda was more momentous. Since the disappearance of the last 'western' emperor in 478, the Christian West had acknowledged the emperor in Constantinople as the sole international authority. But his power, if legitimate, was in practice now virtually non-existent west of the Adriatic. Italy, Gaul and Germany, and Rome itself, were in the possession of the Frankish armies. Was it not an axiom of common sense, as well as a proposition endorsed repeatedly by the Scriptures, that a sovereign should rule as well as reign? Was not the great Charles the effective master of the West? And then, the throne in Constantinople was vacant. Three years before, its tenant had been arrested by his ferocious mother and blinded, and had died of his wounds. Not everyone recognized the 'empress'; certainly not the Franks, whose own ancient system of laws forbade an inheritance passing to a woman if there were male claimants. There was, therefore, a strong case for Charles to be accorded some form of imperial dignity. He was undoubtedly the greatest monarch in the West, perhaps in the entire world. As Abbot Alcuin, who was in effect his chief adviser, had pointed out, the English had evolved a system under which the most powerful and successful of their many kings was given the title of *bretwalda*, and exacted homage and obedience from the others. This argument, which presented the imperial idea in Germanic terms which Charles could grasp, was again put forward by Alcuin's two delegates at the council. And it appears to have proved conclusive. Charles agreed to become western emperor, and ceremonies of homage seem to have been carried out on that day.

Two days later, in the great basilica of St Peter's, Charles and his generals celebrated Christmas, and the Pope insisted on performing a Roman ritual under which he placed a crown on Charles's head, and then prostrated himself in an act of emperor-worship, the crowd of Romans present calling out a monotonous series of ritual acclamations. Charles was taken aback by this weird, eastern enactment, which was completely alien to anyone coming from north of the Alps, with a Germanic background. And it seemed suspicious to him that the crown, which he had won by his own achievements, should be presented to him by the Bishop of Rome, as though it were in his gift. Charles said afterwards that, if he had known what was to happen, he would have refused to attend mass in St Peter's that day. When he appointed his own eldest son the successor-emperor some years later, he insisted on placing the crown himself. The disagreement on the coronation ceremony reflected ambiguities about its precise significance which were to echo through European history for centuries. And historians still argue about how exactly the coronation of Charlemagne came about, and what it meant to those concerned. What cannot be denied is that it was one of the key events in the evolution of western society and Christian civilization. Let us now trace the long series of interconnected events which led to it, and its vast and ramifying consequences.

Between the death of Augustine in embattled Hippo and the coronation of Charlemagne there is an interval of nearly four centuries. These are the formative centuries in the history of medieval Europe and also of the Christian Church as a world-society. The conversion of Constantine had aligned the Roman empire with the Christian Church in a working partnership. But the empire, as the earlier institution, had changed the less of the two; in some ways it had barely changed at all – it had replaced one State religion by another. The Church, by contrast, had changed a great deal. It had adapted itself to its State and imperial function; it had assumed worldly ways and attitudes, and accepted a range of secular responsibilities; and in the emperor it had acquired a protector and governor whom it might influence but could not directly control.

Hence the Church, by marrying the imperial Roman State, was necessarily influenced by changes which overcame that State in the fifth and sixth centuries. In effect the empire split into two. In the East, the government succeeded in maintaining a trading system and a strong gold-based currency; hence it could afford to pay regular armies, and so maintained its frontiers. The process of integration of Church and State, begun by Constantine, continued until the two became inseparable: the Byzantine empire became, in effect, a form of theocracy, with the emperor performing priestly and semi-divine functions, and the Orthodox Church constituting a department of State in charge of spiritual affairs. This conjunction endured for a thousand years, until the remains of the empire were overrun by the Ottoman Turks in the mid fifteenth century.

The western sector of the empire, after the closing decades of the fourth century, lacked a coordinated economic system which could be policed, and so taxed, by a central government. Unable to collect taxes, the authorities could not maintain a currency and pay the legions. There was, in effect, a vacuum of government. After 476, no further western emperors were elected; and except for a period in the mid sixth century, when Constantinople succeeded in re-establishing its authority in Italy, Spain and North Africa, the old imperial system of government was inoperative in the West. Byzantium had a powerful navy. Until the Arab-Moslem conquests of the late seventh century, the Byzantine empire had naval superiority throughout the Mediterranean, when it chose to exert it. This meant it controlled the Adriatic, and from Ravenna on the east coast of Italy it maintained a residual connection with the West. The Pope, as Bishop of Rome, ruled what was a duchy of the empire, and paid taxes accordingly. The West as a whole became an area of tribal settlement, in which semi-barbarous kingdoms existed behind fluctuating frontiers. In these circumstances, the western Church found itself the residual legatee of Roman culture and civilization, and the only channel by which it could be transmitted to the new societies and institutions of Europe. It thus faced a greater challenge and opportunity than at the time of Constantine's conversion. It had the chance to recreate the secular framework of society *ab initio*, and in its own Christian image. It was the only organized international body left with ideas, theories, a sophisticated hierarchy and advanced cultural technologies, in an empty world which possessed little but tribalism. Moreover, the Church, in the writings of St Augustine, possessed an outline – albeit a pessimistic one – of how a Christianized, earthly society should work.

During these four centuries, then, the Church acted as a 'carrier' of civilization rather as, in its formative period, the Hellenistic religious-culture machine had 'carried' Christian Judaism into a Roman, universalist context. The great merit of the Latin Church – the chief reason for its success – was that it was not anchored in any particular racial, geographical, social or political context. It bore the marks of its development but it was still genuinely universalist, the church of St Paul: 'all things to all men'. It is important, however, to appreciate the elements of continuity, as well as those of discontinuity, between the Roman world of St Augustine, and the Christian-barbarian world which succeeded it.

The great tribal confederations did not so much break up the western empire as occupy an area which had already lost its unifying institutional force. There was no sudden catastrophe; indeed, no series of catastrophes. The process was economic, rather than military and political. Skilled tribal tradesmen – carpenters, gardeners, smiths and so forth – had been emigrating into the empire for centuries, in search of money-wages, or higher wages. And they had joined the Roman army, as individuals and as units. This movement of peoples was accepted, even institutionalized. It seems to have increased in the fifth century, and taken on some of the aspects of a tribal migration into settled Roman territory. But those involved had had long contact with Roman civilization. Some of their leaders were Roman allies. Most of them were Christians in the sense that they were Arians; for the great Christian missionary Ulfilas, a Goth who had carried the new faith back to his people in the middle of the fourth century, had been an Arian. Both the Vandals, who settled in North Africa, and the various Gothic tribal groupings – Visigoths in Spain and southern Gaul, Ostrogoths in Italy – were Arians. This fact quickly became the chief differentiation between the 'barbarians' and the Romans, who accepted the Trinitarian doctrine worked out by Augustine.

The tribesmen were also hungry Arians. Most of them were after food rather than booty. There was no food in Rome when Alaric took it in 410: most of the surplus food supplies came from North Africa. Where the tribes could buy or obtain food peacefully they seldom resorted to violence. Equally, they were anxious to get land. In Gaul, for instance, a number of Gallo-Roman landowners moved out; but in some cases they were paid for their property, and the deeds were transferred in a regular manner. The total number of tribesmen moving in was comparatively small, and in general they took over existing tenurial complexities. Thus, Gothic placenames in southern Gaul are personal rather than topographical, indicating a high degree of cultural continuity. Indeed, the settlers accepted the local languages: the basic distinctions between French, Italian and Spanish had already begun to emerge long before the 'era of the barbarians'. Gothic and Vandal tribesmen were unable and probably unwilling to resist the drift towards Romanization; Latin or romance languages became the mother-tongue for second and succeeding generations.

Hence the environment in which the Church now found itself was not, on the whole, hostile. The Arians did not as a rule persecute; they were tolerant to orthodox Christians, as well as to the Jews and other sects. Between the Church and the 'barbarians' there was a certain *rapport*. In many cases, the Romanized towns may have regarded the Goths as saviours from the exactions of imperial tax-collectors based on Ravenna; and the Goths respected many aspects of Roman civilization. In the cities and towns the bishops provided the natural element of stability and local leadership. They were identified with conservation of the worthwhile past, continuity in administration, and the Roman tradition of peace and order. These were attractive characteristics in Gothic eyes too. Of course there was some fighting; a number of Catholic Roman cities were even destroyed: Aquileia was one tragic example. But most survived, with the Catholic bishop as their chief inhabitant and decision-maker. He organized the defences, ran the market economy, presided over justice, negotiated with other cities and rulers. Who were these bishops? They were, of course, chiefly members of the old Roman ruling class. Aristocratic, landowning and official Roman families had been infiltrating the upper echelons of the church since the fourth century – perhaps even before. The movement accelerated in the fifth century: the sub-Roman or post-Roman episcopate in Italy and Gaul was essentially upper-class. Thus Augustine's friend, Paulinus, came from a rich Bordeaux family; he had been a consul, then Governor of Campania at the age of twenty-five; he sold his patrimony in Aquitania and later became Bishop of Nola, playing a leading role in resisting Alaric. Another example was Eucherius, consecrated Bishop of Lyons in 434; he had been a senator. Again, Sidonius Apollinaris, Bishop of Clermont from 470, was rich, a large landowner, the son-in-law of an emperor, a man who had been a city prefect and President of the Senate. By means of the episcopate, the Roman world projected into its barbarian successor elements of administrative continuity, and a rallying force which kept part of the city-civilization together. In some cases, the bishops organized 'civilized' resistance against the 'invaders'. Far more often, however, they negotiated with them; and in time came to act as their advisers. The Arians, at any rate among the Goths and Vandals, were never able to develop an episcopate of comparable prestige and resolution. This was one reason why orthodox Christianity in the West was eventually able to de-Arianize the tribes, a process which began in the fifth century and continued for the next two hundred years. Almost simultaneously, orthodox Christianity began to penetrate the wholly pagan tribes further north – the Franks in north France, the Burgundians in eastern France. The Christianization of the Franks dates from the opening decades of the sixth century, at a time when the Goths were still largely Arian. The monarchical bishop, loosely tied to an international system which gave authority, but able to act with decision and flexibility within the clearly defined area of his jurisdiction, an impressive, quasi-imperial official who conducted himself with much pomp and who spanned the spiritual and secular worlds, was the ideal institution for this transition of cultures and societies.

Thus the Church saved the cities – or, rather, those which remained or became bishoprics. This was particularly true of cities which were also, in accordance with Roman practice, tribal centres. Over a huge area of western Europe, the functioning of the episcopate ensured urban continuity. Often, the change in the siting of the episcopal residence was the factor which determined the growth of a town, or its decline or eclipse (this was how Maastricht and Liège were created). City and town cathedrals were at this time, and for long after, virtually the only churches in the diocese. The bishop was the first, and almost always the most influential, magistrate of the city. Only he carried out ceremonies of baptism: early baptistries were always in cathedrals. Cathedrals also possessed relics, which acted as magnets. In the West, the fashion for pilgrimages began in the Merovingian age, in the early sixth century, and it tended dramatically to increase the importance of episcopal towns, as cult-objects or stages. It was the rule for fifth- and sixth-century cathedrals to be built on the ramparts of towns, usually as an integral part of the fortifications. The bishops certainly had a great deal to do with the local militia, and often commanded it; in fact in some towns – Angers is one example – the bishop was officially listed as *defensor civitatis*. Where a

Christian cult became associated with a particular town, the likelihood was that the town would expand. Christian 'villages' grew up around the tombs of 'saints' buried on the outskirts, beyond the original walls. Soon monasteries were built. The two groupings became the nucleus of 'burgs', which led to a progressive expansion of the towns, and the building of new enclosing walls. This happened at Paris, Tours, Reims, Metz, Rouen, Le Mans, Poitiers, Châlons and many other places. In some cases, monasteries themselves became the isolated nucleus of a new urban centre. In a variety of ways, the episcopate preserved and strengthened the towns, which in turn enhanced the power and influence of the episcopate and thus of the religion of which it formed the vertebrae.

The greatest of the bishops, of course, was the Bishop of Rome. Rome was also the greatest of cities. In the early fifth century it had eight bridges over the Tiber, fourteen aqueducts, 4,000 statues, 1,797 private palaces, 46,602 *insulae* or apartment blocks, and twenty-four churches. It had more than a score of fine public libraries, as well as dozens of private ones. This great city, though in economic decline, survived the disappearance of central Roman administration without disaster. There was no 'sack' by the barbarians. The late fifth-century poet Rutilius Namatianus, addressed the Romans: 'What was once a world, you have left one city.' It was still intact in his day, as it was around 500, when the African monk Fulgentius, later Bishop of Ruspe, visited it and wrote: 'How wonderful must be the heavenly Jerusalem if this earthly city can survive so greatly.' The damage to the structure of Rome occurred in the mid sixth century, when it was repeatedly besieged and plundered during the attempts of the Emperor Justinian to re-attach Italy to the Byzantine empire. The ruin of the ancient buildings was completed in 664, when the Emperor Constans II made the last imperial visit: he stripped it not only of its remaining metal statues, but of the metal parts of the buildings, bronze and lead tiles and roofs, which kept out the rain, and the metal clamps and ties which held the massive walls together – all these were pulled out to be melted down into armaments. The destruction of classical Rome was the act of the Byzantines, not the barbarians. Nevertheless, it was delayed sufficiently for Rome to survive into the new era, and establish itself as the leading Christian city, the cynosure of the western, Latin world.

Thus if, in a general sense, we find the Christian bishops bridging the gap between the Roman world and the emerging world of the Dark Ages, there was a particular role for the Bishop of Rome. It was, for instance, Leo I who negotiated with Attila in 452, and arranged his retreat into central Europe. From generation to generation, the Bishops of Rome steadily established their dominance in the city itself and its neighbourhood, and so in turn their influence throughout Italy. They had certain practical advantages: large estates, which were carefully administered, and which allowed them to carry on, as and when politic and necessary, the free distribution of food which had been a prime function of the late empire. They had had, since the fourth century, an administrative machine, consisting of a chancery modelled on Roman imperial lines, a library and a depository of records. The Bishop of Rome, in fact, had the elements of a comparatively sophisticated government. Administrative personnel were also available. Leading Roman families, such as the Anicii and Symmachi, had survived; this social stratum, with its traditions of authority and decision-making, provided bishops not only for Rome itself but for many other Italian sees, which were thus confirmed as appendages of the city. Just as the Roman upper class had once been associated with state paganism, so now it was tied to Christianity. Leading families claimed proprietory rights over early saints: thus the Anicii adopted the early fifth-century St Malania, and the Turcii adopted St Marius, though on the grounds that one of their ancestors had sentenced him to death. In many cases rich families invested their future in the Church by transferring their lands to Church foundations, which were then run by their descendants – the family estates would be more secure in consequence, and escape taxation. Such families, of course, attempted to control the papacy; as did the East, stretching out long tentacles from Constantinople. The papacy, for its part, fought hard both to preserve its independence in a hard world, and to extend its doctrinal and canonical authority over a scattered Church.

We get occasional glimpses of these Dark Age Bishops of Rome. Gelasius I who was in office 492–6, reflects the importance of administration and sheer bureaucratic persistence in the pursuit of power. He had been secretary to his two predecessors; was very much a machine-man, springing from the chancery; and even as Pope 'he would pen documents in his own hand'. This last remark we owe to Dionysius Exiguus, whom Gelasius promoted to a key position in the papal see, charged with creating order out of chaos. It was Dionysius who invented the method of dating we still use in the West, that is from the birth of Christ; and who calculated an accurate date for Easter. He and Gelasius sorted out the Church's long lists of saints and martyrs, eliminating spurious claims – many of them advanced by leading Roman families who were threats to the Pope's authority – and drawing up an authoritative calendar. They also classified all the decrees of western synods, adding to them important decisions from the East, in Latin translations, and thus consolidating the teaching of both the eastern and western Church into one body of canon law. The fact that the bishopric of Rome had an accurate and authoritative list of saints, and scientific dating and calendarizing, and had a reference system, with authorities, for all questions which impinged on Church doctrine, practice and discipline, was an immeasurable advantage in dealing with bishoprics all over the West; they increasingly looked to Rome not just because they venerated St Peter and his shrine, but because Rome knew the answers. Where else was there to look?

The bureaucracy served material as well as ecclesiastical purposes. Gelasius had a full register not only of Church documents but of the lands and revenues of his see. He carried into the dangerous centuries the methods and expertise of efficient Roman estate administration. This tradition was built upon by his more careful successors. At the close of the sixth century, for instance, we have another glimpse of a Bishop of Rome, Gregory I. Later ages called him 'the Great', but he does not seem to have been popular in his own lifetime, or for long after. He was a hard and practical man, brought up to believe in efficient administration. He was almost certainly from the Anicii family. His grandfather, Felix III, had been Gelasius's predecessor; his father, Giordanus, was a wealthy lawyer in charge of the administration of the episcopal property. Gregory was born about 540, and became Prefect of the City when he was thirty-three; later he invested part of his patrimony in a family monastery, grouped round his parents' house on the Coelian Hill. He took over as Pope, probably because he was the best man available (he was already in deacon's orders), in 589, a time of terrible disasters for Rome. The Byzantine effort to recover Italy had finally been abandoned. The Lombards now held the north, and the Bishops of Rome were already looking to the Franks as possible protectors. Rome and its bishopric had suffered grievously during Justinian's wars and afterwards. In the late fifth century, papal revenues from the province of Picenum were 2,160 *solidi*; by 556, they had sunk to 500 or less. More recently there had been a Lombard siege and, in the year of Gregory's accession, flood and plague.

Like Gelasius, Gregory had been secretary to his predecessor. He was a man of undoubted spiritual strength, but his essential talent and interest lay in administration. Like Gelasius he was hard. A successful pope had to be in that period; indeed, Gregory's successor, Sabinian, was hated for refusing to hand out free grain from the papal stores – the mob hooted and pelted his funeral procession. No contemporary wrote a pious life of Gregory. There is nothing about him in the series of biographical annals of the Popes kept at the time. Instead we have a ninth-century account compiled by John the Deacon, who used older sources and traditions. From near-contemporary frescoes, later destroyed, he discovered that Gregory was of medium height, with a large bald head, light-brown eyes, and long, thin, arched eyebrows; he had an aquiline nose, red thick lips, a swarthy complexion, often flushed in later life. Rather like St Paul, he lacked personal dignity or impressiveness, and he called himself 'an ape forced to play the lion'. He also lamented his poor health, his weak digestion, his gout and his bouts of malaria, which he dosed with retsina wine from Alexandria. Like many frail clerics, however, he had a strong will, and much practical common sense. He might have been born to rule in the Dark Ages, when the Church could not afford frills and had to concentrate on essentials. He surrounded himself with hard-working monks. The future, he thought, lay with the 'emerging nations' north of the Alps. The job of the Bishop of Rome was to bring them into Christianity, to integrate them with the ecclesiastical system. It was no use lamenting the empire. 'The eagle', he wrote, 'has gone bald and lost his feathers. . . . Where is the senate, where are the old people of Rome? Gone.' It was no use speculating on doctrinal niceties. As one of his immediate successors put it, the debate over Christ's 'will' – the fashionable Constantinople topic of the moment – was for grammarians, not active churchmen; philosophy was for 'croaking frogs'. Gregory preached a basic evangelical religion, shorn of classical complexity and elegance; and he sent his monks to teach it to wild, coarse Germanic-speaking warriors with long hair and the future in their strong arms.

Meanwhile he himself concentrated on creating a papal patrimony for the ecclesiastical administration of Italy. He developed and expanded the systematic charity which had always been a feature of the Christian Church. But he also raised funds to repair the aqueducts. We find him employing his considerable energies on such matters as horse-breeding, the slaughter of cattle, the administration of legacies, the accuracy of accounts, the level of rents and the price of leases. He took a direct part in the running of estates scattered throughout Italy, and in North Africa, Sardinia and Sicily. He obliged his peasants to pay a tax on marriage, death-duties, and a land-tax payable three times a year. All papal administrators had to be clergy, or at least tonsured. Gregory did not exactly create this system, but he enormously enlarged and strengthened it. He found the Roman clergy already with a distinctive caste structure and dress. They had a white fringed saddlecloth or *mappula*, and wore flat black slippers, *campagi*, and *udones* or white stockings – all inherited from the imperial senate and magistrature. Here, then, we have the clergy taking over from imperial Rome in appearance as well as function. The Roman clergy were already organized in colleges, according to grade. Gregory extended this to the regions and provinces, to the lay lawyers and *defensors* who ran papal towns and estates. The senior notary became the Chancellor of the Lateran, and he drew up the standard formulae for papal correspondence; thus in Gregory's day the papal *scrinium* was already a mighty bureaucratic engine. Cardinal-priests and cardinal-deacons were about to emerge and form the higher ranks of the Roman clergy. In all essentials, the administrative matrix of the medieval papacy was in existence.

We have seen, then, that in the episcopacy, led by the senior bishop of Rome, Christianity possessed an effective institution whereby to transmit ideas and procedures from the Roman world to the new, evolving society of barbarian Europe. What, more precisely, were these ideas and procedures? The most important of them centred around the concept and application of law. Legalism had always been the great strength of the Romans; and it was a strength that did not diminish – in some ways it increased – as their relative military power declined. During the fourth century, the Church had become increasingly involved in the law-making process. Much of the first great collection of laws, the mid-fifth century Theodosian Code, was of the Church's making. There was, of course, no distinction between secular and ecclesiastical law; in administering and transmitting the one, the Church automatically made known the other. In 539, the imperial law was again codified; commentaries, or *digesta* or *pandecta*, were added in 533, plus new laws thereafter called *novellae*, the whole making up the Corpus Juris Civilis, or Justinian civil law, to which the papacy's own digests of canon law were added. The early Dark Age Church thus had an enormous and highly sophisticated body of written law, to transmit to the barbarian world as and when this was possible or appropriate, and to develop for its own administrative purposes.

Of more direct and immediate importance, however, was the tradition of codification which the imperial codes had created, and which the Church could now apply to new purposes. As pagan societies, all the tribal confederations possessed vast and ancient bodies of customary law, not written but memorized, and slowly and occasionally altered in the light of changing needs. When the Church came into contact with these barbarian societies, and induced them to accept baptism or, in the case of Arians, full communion with Rome, its bishops almost immediately set up arrangements to link Christian legal customs with existing pagan law codes. This was necessary, in the first instance, to ensure that the Church was protected in its missionary activities – bishops and priests had to be given high *wergilds,* for example. These arrangements took the form of putting the customary law in written shape, under chapters, and adding specific, *ad hoc* provisions for Christian purposes. The mission-bishops went over the customs with the elders of the tribal courts, wrote them down in some kind of order, read them aloud to the king, and then rewrote them with his emendations and corrections.

The process often followed swiftly on conversion. Thus, in England, the mission despatched by Gregory the Great landed in Kent in 597; between then and 616, when Æthelbert, the Kentish king and English *bretwalda*, died a code of ninety laws had been written down and promulgated. Although Christian matters are referred to, there is little specifically Christian in the details of the code; and it is in Old English – by far the earliest body of written law in any Germanic language which has survived. We are, in short, at an early stage in the development. Very likely other such Germanic codes appeared then, and before, drawn up under the guidance of the Church, and basically pre-Christian in content. But later Latin superseded the Germanic tongues in most cases – except in England – and the Christian element steadily grew in importance. Already in the sixth century, the Church had produced a codification of many Frankish customary laws. The Lex Salica as it came to be known, comes to us in a ninth-century format, with an eighth-century preface; but it was originally conceived as a collection of customs designed for study and consultation by the clergy in their missionary activities, and thus written in Latin. Gradually, as repeatedly amended and revised, it became the chief body of written law available to all Frankish society. Again, in Italy, the Church made a collection of customs in 643 in the reign of King Rothari, and known as Rothari's Edict. It was written in Latin, not Lombardic, and consists of 388 chapters or titles, with an introduction and a list of Lombard kings. The introduction states that the king had decided to correct the law as he knew it, amend it, add to it, and, where necessary, subtract from it. This whole last sentence, significantly, was taken from Justinian's seventh novella. In this code, in fact, there are not only Roman elements but a formal foundation in Roman law. Rothari was an Arian; but his court had clearly been infiltrated by Catholic clergy, and his code indicates that his political and legal thinking was moving on a moral level which was plainly the result of Christian influence.

In these legal codes, and the whole complex business of cultural interchange which lay behind them, we see the Church exerting its influence at the most formative and sensitive point in the whole body politic of the new Germanic societies – their basic customary law. In transforming memorized to written law, the missionary clerics almost imperceptibly begin to Christianize it, and so to Christianize the societies which obeyed it. Here, for the first time, Christianity is not being superimposed on society, but is meshing itself with its customs, and at a stage when they are undergoing rapid development. Of course in some respects there is a strong community of interests. Both the Church and the Germanic races exalted the family – on this point Christianity had far more in common with the Franks than with Roman society. The law-codes, therefore, reflect the bond. In other fields there was divergence: Germanic society was deeply attached to the blood-feud, whose ravages and ramifications coloured the whole of social and public behaviour; the Church was equally anxious to stamp it out, by a system of fines settled and exacted by law. In the early written law-codes we see how compromises on this and other points were reached, with the Church slowly pushing lay society in the direction of settlements in court, rather than in combat.

The Church also possessed a peculiar law-making instrument of its own: the episcopal synod, or council. This was made available to the new kingdoms at a surprisingly early stage. The first Frankish Church council we hear of took place at Orleans in 511, and it is not clear to what extent the secular element took part. But these councils dealt with the general welfare of the population, as well as purely Church matters. Orleans put the onus of providing relief for the poor squarely on the bishops. A council at Tours in 567 extended responsibility for the poor to the whole community, to be financed by the tithe or tenth. At Macon, in 585, everyone was instructed to pay their tenths into the bishop's chest; it thus became a kind of income-tax, part of which went to the poor. What is more, at this meeting we first hear of poor-houses or 'hospitals', which were attached to the cathedral or episcopal buildings. Here we see the Church moving right to the centre of the stage, performing a new and executive function of government, presumably under the instructions of the king, who must have presided at such legislative gatherings. We know a little more about similar councils held in Visigothic Spain, which became a central feature of government after King Reccared, in 587, changed from Arianism to Catholicism. He began the practice of summoning to Toledo, his chief city, gatherings of bishops and other ecclesiastics, who were joined by all the chief nobles and officials of the court, the king usually taking the chair. Clerics formed the majority of those present, but topics debated and determined covered the whole range of business, secular as well as clerical, and lay-lords affixed their seals and signatures to the decisions, alongside the bishops. These councils were, in fact, state parliaments. Hence, from a very early stage, we see the Church becoming not merely part of the governing corpus of the European kingdoms, but shaping the pattern of their law-making processes. Moreover, it is the Church which sponsors and makes possible any innovation. In these primitive, conservative, post-pagan societies, it was Christianity which stood for progress and the future.

If the Church was identified with the future in the minds of the barbarians, it also established itself as the custodian and interpreter of their past. The tribes had their memorized verse-histories, as they had their memorized customary laws; again, in the process of reducing them to written form, Church scribes inevitably gave them a Christian colouring, if often a rather superficial one. More important, however, was that the Church possessed from the start a monopoly of the writing of history. This was absolutely central to its success in making so deep an impression on Dark Age society. For Christianity was essentially a 'religion of the book' – that is, a historical religion. It taught that certain things had happened, and that certain things were going to happen. The first was a matter of record, in the shape of the Scriptures; the second a matter of prophecy, drawn from a variety of sources, not least the authority of the Church itself. The correct teaching and interpretation of history was thus central to the Church's evangelizing mission. It was in some ways well equipped to carry it out, for it could draw from a double tradition – the historical style of writing of the Old Testament, and the more sophisticated historiography of Rome. Using these techniques, Christian writers drew upon the collective ancestral memories of their tribal confederations to construct historical accounts of their national origins in which Christianization was seen to play the determining part, marking the point at which the people, or folk, passed from primitive and barbarous (and morally reprehensible) existence to civilization and the opportunities of salvation. Tribal history was thus readjusted not only to fit Christian assumptions in the present life, but to give added point to the Christian mechanic of redemption.

A good example of this 'constructive' history written with a view to influencing the present is the history of the Franks, dating from the second half of the sixth century, written by Gregory, who became Bishop of Tours in 573. Gregory was a Gallo-Roman aristocrat from the south, typical indeed of those who 'carried' elements of Roman civilization to the tribes through the episcopal institution. The Franks had been converted directly to Catholicism and were therefore seen as natural allies of orthodoxy (against Arianism) and, indeed, from the last decades of the sixth century, of the papacy itself. Gregory had no written texts to work on, and only mythical versions of Frankish origins. He regarded the Franks as the saviours of Gaul, and thus felt at liberty to present their early history as a purposeful tale of advance towards Christianity and unity, which he saw as closely connected; to do this he predated the conversion of Clovis, the first Frankish Christian king (which in fact took place *c*.503) to show that his conquests were the result of Christianization. He says that while Clovis was at Tours he received a legate from the Emperor Anastasius, who bestowed on the king the title of consul – 'and from that day he was hailed as consul of Augustus'. Here is an example of a Christian writer retrospectively bestowing on a barbarian royal line their official legitimacy and, indeed, a form of imperial pedigree, the Church and Christianization being the transmitting instrument.

At a somewhat later date, the history of the Lombards was written by Paul the Deacon, who was born at Pavia in 775 and spent some time both at the Lombard court and at Charlemagne's. Paul traces Lombard history from the time when the tribe first set out from the Baltic to the death of King Liutprand in 744. The theme is not the victory of the Lombards, but the victory of Catholicism, and he invited his Lombard readers to see themselves in a Roman mirror. Tribes did not have written history. This was, as it were, the consequence and reward of civility: the business of reading and writing history was itself Roman; for a Lombard to conceive of himself in a historical context was to be Roman; and to be Catholic was to be Roman. These histories assumed and emphasized a triple process of identification – Christianity with Rome, Rome with civilization. Into this framework patriotic rejoicings in the heroic deeds of tribal ancestors could easily be fitted. So these Christianized tribal histories were very popular, pushing aside pagan poetry as the chief source of popular self-knowledge; they survive in many manuscripts. They include one masterpiece: Bede's *History of the English Church and Nation*, written a generation or two before Paul the Deacon's Lombard history. Bede was too great a historian to readjust the past in Christian terms. Thus his book is not a national history; it is a straightforward account of how Christianity came to England, and the progress of the English Church thereafter. But the effect is much the same. Indeed in some ways it is even more successful in stressing the importance of the Christianizing process, for Bede shows that, from the moment of conversion, the history of the English people and of the English Church among them are virtually the same thing. The same conclusion is implicit in the *Res Gestae Saxoniae*, the story of the Ottonian dukes of Saxony and Franconia, written by a monk of Corvei, Widukind. The work was dedicated to Matilda, daughter of Otto I, and abbess of Quidlinburg in the Harz Mountains, the seat of Ottonian power; and it was written in the light of Otto's coronation as the first Saxon emperor. Here, then, is Saxon tribal history presented as a success-story for Christianity.

These basic tribal histories were only one element, though for long the most important, in the comprehensive grip which Christianity established on the whole vision of the past. Christian monks also wrote lives of the saints, taken from eastern models, which in time were used as prototypes of lives of Frankish, Lombard, Saxon and English saints and notable bishops; and from the early ninth century we get the first secular biographies, notably Einhard's fine life of Charlemagne: the model here was Suetonius, but the atmosphere and moral assumptions are Christian, and there is no firm dividing-line between the life of a great king and hagiography. At about the same time we get continuations of the basic histories such as, in Burgundy, the *Chronicle* of Fredegarius, and in the Paris region the *Historiae Francorum*. These, in time, gave place to monastic and royal annals. Annals were originally drawn up by abbeys and monastic cathedrals to calculate the date of Easter – lunar calendars in fact. Then events of importance were entered for each year, and gradually grew more detailed and continuous. The royal annals in France, and the Anglo-Saxon chronicles in England developed into quasi-official records of events, compiled by monks in houses patronized by the government; and these documents were soon joined by the records of actual government business, deposited in the record-rooms of abbeys and cathedrals, modelled, in a small way, on the papal archives kept since the fourth century, which themselves were based on Roman imperial practice. In France some forty diplomas, the permanent records of grants to church communities and lay individuals, survive from Merovingian times – that is, for the period 500–750. In Charlemagne's time, such documents were systematically collected and filed, together with cartularies, that is the king's ordinances springing from the discussion of public business, and with royal correspondence. In 791 Charlemagne himself ordered that all correspondence between himself, and his predecessors, and the papal court should be collected together; it was bound into a huge volume, called the *Codex Carolinus*. All this work, of course, was carried out by clerics. At every stage in the writing, collecting, transmission and preservation of Dark Age history – and its documentation and editing – the Church was the active and monitoring force. Dark Age man saw his past, as he saw his future, though exclusively Christian eyes. To him, there was no other way of looking at history except as the working out of God's purposes.

Thus the Church gave barbarian society institutions, law and history: but these themselves would not be enough to explain the extraordinary degree of penetration achieved by Christianity in the period AD 400–800. There had to be an economic element too – a means whereby the Church made a positive and fundamental contribution to the well-being of society, and a contribution which only the Church could make. It had to do this, in any event, to justify its existence, for the Church was a very expensive institution and absorbed an increasing share of the gross product for its own intrinsic purposes. The tribal confederations which filled the vacuum of Roman power in the West were subsistence societies; they moved because they were starving. To succeed among them, the Church had to be a carrier of superior economic techniques.

We have already seen how hard the early popes worked as estate administrators. Their assumption seems to have reflected St Ambrose's ruling: trade and commerce were necessarily evil, but farming an estate was honourable in the eyes of God. The Church did not engage in trade, at any rate on a big scale; but it was, from the fourth century at least, a landed proprietor. All over the West, bishops ran large estates; and practical-minded popes like Gelasius and Gregory I set the example. They provided an element of continuity between the best kind of Roman imperial estate management and the domanial 'high farming' of the Middle Ages, especially, for example, in Gaul, where agricultural units changed very little in many cases. In barbarian eyes, churchmen were 'modern' farmers, who kept accounts, planned ahead, invested. The Church also had a key legal instrument, the Roman-style land deed, which embodied the concept of freehold. In primitive Germanic societies there seems to have been no such thing as freehold. When the Church was first received at Frankish courts, it insisted that land made over to it for churches and so forth be conveyed in perpetual possession and the transaction embodied in the type of written deed to which it was accustomed. Laymen, naturally, were impressed and envious, since written freehold had immeasurable advantages over any other form of tenure. The result was a phenomenon we have already come across in the fourth-century empire – lay magnates transferring their lands to church-tenure as a form of family investment, to escape taxation. Bede, writing in the third decade of the eighth century, drew attention to this trend, which he rightly saw as damaging to the Church as well as to the State. More dynamic, from an economic point of view, was the development, on the example of the Church, of quasi-freehold tenures among the laity, especially in marginal and reclaimed land. Then, too, land actually farmed by the Church grew enormously in extent; throughout western and central Europe the Church established itself as the largest landowner.

This development could not have taken place, or certainly could not have endured, if clerics had not proved themselves to be better than average farmers and land administrators. For this the development of monasticism was largely responsible; and the key figure, here also, is Gregory the Great. It was he who first perceived the economic importance of the right kind of monastic rule and organization. For it must be remembered that there was no intrinsic reason why monks should be associated with farming. On the contrary: the first Christian monks of whom we hear, in the third century, were ascetics who took refuge in the desert in order to starve themselves into sanctity; they were almost certainly repeating an earlier, pre-Christian pattern. A great many primitive biographies of the earliest monks survive, but most of them are pure fiction. This is certainly true of the life of St Barlaam, who probably never existed; and the life of Joasaph is based on Buddha. The prototype monk, by Christian calculation, was St Paul of Thebes. He may have existed; and it is clear the first monks settled in the Egyptian deserts, not far from the Nile. St Jerome, who wrote a largely imaginary life of Paul, says he lived for a hundred and thirteen years near Thebes, wore palm-leaves and was fed for sixty years

by a crow, which brought him half a loaf of bread each day. When he died in
347 two lions dug his grave and then greeted his successor, St Anthony. St
Anthony, too, was a historical person, though a shadowy one; we are told he
spent over ninety years as a solitary, having given away his possessions in
youth, never learnt to read or write, never changed his clothes or washed his
face, and died in 356 aged a hundred and five.

From about this time we get primitive monkish communities in the desert.
Anthony's disciple, Ammon, persuaded over 5,000 to join him in the desert of
Nitre, south-east of Alexandria. These monks were nearly all lower-class
illiterates. They were bankrupts fleeing from taxes, conscripts from military
service, brigands from justice, slaves who had broken their bonds. Some
hoped to achieve a reputation for sanctity (and possibly even wealth) by
eccentric behaviour: they had more in common with Hindu fakirs than monks
as we understand them. Thus Makarios of Alexandria claimed he had not spat
on the ground since his baptism. For seven years he ate only raw vegetables;
had a bread-fast for three years; never slept for twenty nights; exposed himself
for seven months to swamp-mosquitoes; and fasted for forty days, remaining
in one corner of his cell without speaking or moving, and eating only raw
cabbage on Sundays. He lived to be a hundred, having lost his teeth, and with
only a few hairs to mark his beard. Makarios had many exotic or miraculous
adventures with animals. So did all the successful eccentrics. St Gregory and
St Malo saved the damned by pulling them out of hell. St Malo also changed a
stone into a chalice of rock-crystal so he could celebrate mass. St Martila and
St Frontus used St Peter's staff to raise the dead, and St Hubert was converted
by a ten-point stag he was pursuing – between its antlers was a cross. St Gildas
commanded a dangerous monster to die, which it obligingly did; a similar tale
was told of St Hilarion, at whose command a boa-constrictor roasted itself in
the flames.

Sorting fact from fiction is not easy. The first cenobites, that is, monks living
in communities, appear to have been gathered by Pachomius, who had a
monastery of a hundred at Tabenna, on the big end in the Nile. Jerome gives
a circumstantial account of their life. He says: 'Monks of the same trade are
housed together under a superior, that is, weavers, mat-makers, tailors,
carpenters, fullers and shoemakers . . . every week an account of their work is
made to the abbot.' We have other fourth century accounts of basket-weaving
monks; none of farmers. Early in the fourth-century Hilarion introduced the
monastic movement to Syria: but there, too, monks were either anchorites or
solitaries, or lived in large, ill-organized communities, off charity or worse.
The accent was on conspicuous self-torture or deprivation. Hilarion himself
ate only half a measure of lentils a day, later only bread, salt and water; later
still, wild herbs and roots, and after the age of sixty-four he never touched
bread again. Syrian monks were particularly ingenious in devising torments.
One carried such a heavy load of iron to frustrate his tendency to wander that
he had to move on hands and knees. Another devised a cell which forced him

to live doubled up. A third spent ten years in a cage shaped like a wheel. Dendrite-monks perched in trees; Grazier-monks lived in the forests and ate like wild animals; some went completely naked, except for a loin-cloth of thorns. A number of these weird figures are quite well authenticated. Thus we can say with reasonable certitude that Simon Stylites was an illiterate, born on the Syrian border *c*.389. He was dismissed from a monastery for excessive asceticism and went to live in a cistern, where he had himself walled up with no food during Lent. His chain, with a stone attached, prevented him from walking more than a few yards – witnesses testified that the gap between the skin and chain was infested with worms. Near Antioch he lived on a column, first ten feet high, later raised to sixty. His platform was two yards square and there he prostrated himself 1,244 times a day and in Lent was, in addition, chained to a stake. He had a ladder for special occasions, but normally communicated by basket. He died in 459, having spent thirty-seven years on his column, from which he preached regularly and administered cures, so it was claimed, for infertility. The emperor dispatched 600 men to retrieve his body from the Bedouin, and a church was built over his grave, about 476–90, with the remains of his column in its central court: it can still be seen as a ruin today.

Such monks achieved notoriety, or even celebrity, as individual ascetics; or they made nuisances of themselves in a variety of ways and were hounded by the authorities. Or they acted as episcopal claques and bully-boys in Church elections and councils, as we have seen. Or they congregated in large establishments on the fringes of the desert, selling artifacts to travellers and visitors. They had no economic purpose. Indeed, they were one of the spiritual luxuries a rich society could, or at any rate did, afford. Even when eastern monasticism was placed on a more organized basis by Basil, Bishop of Caesarea, from about 360, it was still essentially parasitic. His collections of written rules, the first we possess, with their emphasis on commonsense and moderation (though monks were not allowed to comb their hair), were widely adopted and spread throughout the eastern empire. By the eighth to ninth centuries 100,000 monks were said to be living under St Basil's rule. These monasteries ran schools in some cases, and thus had an educative role. But they rarely farmed. Monks were gathered together in big city houses; or in groups of houses in the remote countryside, as at Mount Athos. They lived on charity, though they performed few social functions, and were mostly desperately poor. Indeed, like the earliest monks, they were recruited from the poorest classes, and included many illiterates; the majority, in fact, never became priests or took any orders. This was not a pattern of organization which would induce wealthy laymen to transfer lands, thus setting up family estates under clerical tenure. Nor, when the monks owned land, was it conducive to efficient farming or administration.

The Byzantine empire could afford such a phenomenon; the impoverished West could not. Thus eastern monasticism never really developed from its earliest forms. By the time the empire collapsed, in the fifteenth century, it was too set in its ways; and so Orthodox monks even today retain the essential characteristics they possessed in the age of St Basil. The possibility is that similar patterns would have endured in the West, if the Roman imperial structure had held firm. Monasticism came to the West along the Mediterranean trading routes, to Marseilles and then up the Rhone Valley into Gaul. The inspiration seems to have been Athanasius's popular life of St Anthony, which reached Gaul in 336 and was widely copied. The earliest western monks were ascetics and eccentrics, like their eastern model. But they tended to be much more actively involved in the life of their society. The most famous of them all, St Martin of Tours, who died in 397, followed the eastern type of cenobitic settlement: he and his eighty companions lived in caves in the river-cliffs at Marmoutier and he himself, though formerly an army officer, was described as plebeian in appearance, small, badly dressed and uncombed. On the other hand, unlike the easterners, he seems to have been a rural missionary, preaching against paganism, working evangelical miracles, and attacking shrines with a pickaxe. He protested strongly against the executions of the Spanish Priscillians, and seems to have played a part in ecclesiastical politics at a high level. At any rate we are told that when he entered the presence of the Emperor Valentinian, and the latter refused to stand up in respect to the holy man, 'his throne became covered in fire, and the emperor was burnt in the part of the body that sat on it.'

The Life of St Martin, by a wealthy Bordelais, Sulpicius Severus, was the first example in the West of aretology, or panegyric of the virtues, and proved a highly influential treatise. Along with Martin's name and miracles it popularized the monastic cult; in France alone there are nearly 3,900 parishes bearing his name in one form or another – Martinge, Martigny, Martignac, Martincourt, Martineau, Martinet, Dammartin, and so forth. The growth of the Martin legends coincided with the introduction of what may be termed regular monastic theory in France by John Cassian, a Scythian from the Dobrudja, who established two monasteries, one for men and one for women, in the Marseilles area. Cassian was a scholar, a younger contemporary of Augustine, who steered a cautious middle course between Pelagianism and the Augustinian determinism, visited a number of eastern monasteries to gain experience, and set down his reflections on the monastic life in a series of Institutions and Conferences. Of course he was an ascetic: we hear of him and his friends dining with one Abbot Serenus and each consuming three olives, five grains of dried vetches, two prunes and a fig – plus salt. But he was anxious to escape from the aimless and undirected self-deprivation which characterized eastern monasticism. He gave the monks an aim: to convert and to educate.

In passing northwards through Gaul, therefore, the Egyptian style of monasticism acquired, in the course of the fifth century, a cultural purpose, and it was in this transformed state that it attracted the interest of upper-class

Christian ascetics in the areas of Celtic dominance – Brittany, Wales, Ireland and Scotland. Ireland had been Christianized from Wales, probably by a Romanized Briton called St Patrick, in the fifth century, and a 'normal' ecclesiastical system with bishops and dioceses had been established in rudimentary form. But from about 540 we hear of the first Irish monks. Ireland had trading contacts with the Loire Valley, sending shoes in exchange for wine and oil, and this, presumably, is how the Irish first acquired the monastic idea. It took root very quickly for a number of economic and social reasons, becoming, instead of a marginal Christian activity, the dominant religious form. Ireland had never had any towns; indeed it scarcely possessed villages. It was to a great extent still a nomadic and tribal society. Sixth-century monasticism, too, had a mobile element, tending to move between fixed points of reference, the sea forming the chief means of communication. In each tribe a leading family could found an abbey, plus a series of dependent houses, and retain certain rights in them. Abbots were nearly always members of the ruling clan or tribal family; and monastic holdings, embracing lands, fishing-rights and other forms of subsistence-living, covered huge areas. The monastic quest for remoteness and solitude, exported from Egypt via Gaul, thus fitted perfectly into the geography and life-style of a precarious economy on the rim of Europe. The earliest Irish monastic settlements, brought to light by an aerial survey in 1969, were small, primitive, scattered and numerous: more like shrines than abbeys. This, indeed, is what they were: religious markers covering the area of tribal activity. Thus a shrine like Skellig Michael, which consists of six stone beehive cells and a small oratory, set on a 700-foot pyramid of rock seven miles into the Atlantic off south-west Ireland, was in a tribal fishery. Irish monasticism was wholly integrated with local society: in fact it was the Church in Ireland.

Egyptian monasticism had been, to some extent, a revolt against ecclesiastical organization, and the episcopal system in particular. St Martin and his followers showed the same disposition. They believed that episcopacy and orders were among the weapons with which the devil attacked religious men. Irish monks shared this belief. The Irish Church was never consciously in rebellion against orthodoxy. It is remarkable that it Christianized the people without a single case of martyrdom, and without any recorded instance of heresy or internal persecution; there was no violence whatever. Bishops were retained: there were certain functions, such as blessing the baptismal chrism, and ordination, which only they could perform. But they were functionaries, not leaders. They were expected to be humble and obey the abbot, who of course represented tribal leadership. Not that the abbot behaved like a grand personage. One reason why the early monks disliked the episcopal system was that it was identified with the external trappings of worldly society. It was considered wrong, even sinful, for a cleric, even an abbot or a bishop, to ride a horse. By doing so he elevated himself above the common man, and denied the principle of humility. St Martin occasionally used a donkey, for long journeys: that was permissible, for Christ had done the same. Nor should an abbot dine in state with secular chieftains, or otherwise integrate himself with a vainglorious world. He and his monks should live as close to the subsistence level as possible, consistent with good health; and they should preach the gospel on foot, 'after the manner of the apostles'.

Irish monasticism was thus an insidious challenge to the early Dark Age Church and its hold on society. Like the Montanist-type sects, it advocated a return to primitive Christian purity, but unlike them it could not be attacked on grounds of doctrinal error. As with the eastern monks, it was antinomial, in the sense that it evaded the normal hierarchical system of the Church. But, unlike the easterners, it was not passive and stationary. On the contrary, the Irish monks had a tremendous cultural dynamic. They were enormously learned in the scriptures, and wonderfully gifted in the arts. They combined exquisite Latin scholarship with a native cultural tradition which went back to the La Tène civilization of the first century. Their rudimentary dry-stone houses were unpretentious without, but treasure-houses within. They had a great deal to teach western Europe. And, above all, they were nomadic. In the western part of the British Isles, in fact in western Europe as a whole, sixth- and seventh-century communications were maritime. The Celtic monks were all sailors; they travelled by water and they lived on fish. The semi-mythical St Brendan, who founded the monastery of Clonfert in Galway, and died about 580. was supposed to have undertaken a remarkable series of voyages, the story of which was translated into French, Norman, Provençal, German, Italian and Norwegian. Monks were often buried at sea: the Welsh monk Gildas, the British equivalent of Gregory of Tours, though a far less gifted historian, asked, when he died, to be laid in a boat and pushed out to sea. What is more, clan relationships spanned the seas. Thus St Columba's mission from Ulster to the Western Isles of Scotland, where he founded the great monastery of Iona, was almost certainly a product of clan politics. And from western Scotland the Celtic monks penetrated east and south; during the course of a century they moved in a great arc round the north-western fringes of the British Isles, reaching the English kingdom of Northumbria in the early sixth century, where Aidan from Iona was invited by the Northumbrian court to found a sister-house at Lindisfarne in 634.

Meanwhile the Irish had moved far east. St Columbanus, born c.540, was like Columba an Irish tribal leader, head of a family monastery. He was a big man, with big ideas, a good knowledge of Latin – he had read Virgil, Pliny, Sallust, Horace, Ovid and Juvenal as well as the Fathers – and even a little Greek; and a burning passion to spread his own austere brand of Christianity. In 575 he landed in Brittany with a shipload of monks. They wore long white habits, nothing else, carried curved staffs and their liturgical books packed in waterproof leather bags; and around their necks they had water-bottles and pouches containing holy relics and consecrated wafers.

This was one of the most remarkable expeditions in history. By the time

Columbanus died in 615, he, his entourage and their immediate followers had spread Celtic monasticism across a huge area of France, Italy and the Alps, and had founded about forty monasteries, including Rebais, Jumièges, St Gall, Bobbio, Fontenelle, Chelles, Marmoutier, Corbier, St Omer, St Bertin, Remiremont, Hautvilliers, Montierender, St Valéry-sur-Somme, Solignac, Fontaine and Luxeuil, many of them to become among the glories of the Middle Ages. Columbanus was disgusted with the Europe he found. Travelling east through Gaul he noted that 'virtue is more or less non-existent'. The last vestiges of ancient civilization, he thought, had disappeared. He found himself fighting loose morals, rather than ignorance, and teaching discipline instead of grammar. The rule he drew up for his new establishments was very severe, and corporal punishment harsh and frequent.

This was all very well: Columbanus's success indicates the appeal of his mission. But his activities, for the first time, brought the nature of Celtic monasticism firmly to the attention of the Church authorities – to western bishops in general, and to the Bishop of Rome in particular. The Irish monks were not heretical. But they were plainly unorthodox. They did not look right, to begin with. They had the wrong tonsure. Rome, as was natural, had 'the tonsure of St Peter', that is, a shaven crown. Easterners had the tonsure of St Paul, totally shaven; and if they wished to take up an appointment in the West they had to wait until their rim grew before being invested. But the Celts looked like nothing on earth: they had their hair long at the back and, on the shaven front part, a half-circle of hair from one ear to the other, leaving a band across the forehead. More serious was their refusal to celebrate Easter according to the calculations made by Rome. There were a number of divergent calendar systems in the Mediterranean area; the one used by the Celts corresponded with none of them. The issue was more important than it may seem to us. Getting the right date for Easter was the most obvious instance of the problem of calculating time – man's effort to orient himself in relation to events. There had been liturgical rows about Easter going back to the second century, perhaps even to the distant conflicts between gentile and Jewish Christians. In western Europe, the newly Christianized barbarian societies had adjusted their sense of the annual routine, from the court downwards, to fit the Christian year. Divergence over the most important and awesome event in the yearly round was not merely indecorous but sinister. And how could the Church claim unity if it could not even agree on the date of the resurrection, the core of its belief?

Behind these discrepancies, which reflected not so much deliberate defiance on the part of the Celts as a drifting apart on details during a period when contact with Rome and Gaul had been lost, there was a much more fundamental difference about the nature of the Church. In a sense, the parallel was with the Donatists. Was the Church to embrace and reflect society, in the process of transforming it, as Augustine had taught, and as Rome and the Gaulish episcopate still assumed? Or was it an alternative to society? Celtic monasticism, so well adjusted to its native economic and social framework, seemed to pose impossible standards in areas of settled culture. Even in Northumbria, Aidan had appeared to reject integration: invited, as the leading ecclesiastic, to dine at court, 'his practice was to go with one or two clerks, and having taken a small meal, make haste to be gone with them, either to read or write'. Then there was the issue of the use of horses, a practical symbol of conflicting ideas – which ultimately involved the whole question of the wealth, status, and attitude of the Church in the world – wherever the Celts and Rome came in contact. In immediate terms, Columbanus would not brook supervision or interference by local bishops in monastic houses founded by him in their dioceses. Summoned to defend himself at an episcopal conference held at Chalons in 603, he declined, was declared contumacious, and expelled from Gaul. He went to Italy where he founded more monasteries without resolving the issue.

The Celtic penetration of Europe was of great importance culturally, as we shall see; in ecclesiastical terms it threatened to undermine the Church's oldest and central institution, the episcopate, which was already being integrated with the barbarian societies, and to produce a different kind of Church, in which the monastic ideal would become normative. This would allow a cleavage to develop between clerical and secular society and so make impossible the realization of the Augustinian dream. Of course such a challenge had always been implicit in the notion of the monastic life – it was the old withdrawal principle, going back to the Essenes. Celtic monasticism presented it, however, in a new and attractive form.

The response of Rome was to take over, to discipline and so to contain the monastic movement. The process took several generations, but it was set in decisive motion by Gregory I, a younger contemporary of Columbanus, who was Bishop of Rome when the Celts were most active in eastern Gaul. It is not clear why Rome had so far refused to sponsor a definite type of monasticism, and had allowed the movement to develop without any guidance. The answer is no doubt that Italy was in too disturbed a state for most of the middle decades of the sixth century. It was, in fact, the accident of the troubles which followed the collapse of Justinian's restored empire in Italy, and the Lombard invasions, which gave Gregory a monastic policy. Benedict of Nursia, according to Gregory's later account, was born about 480, of wealthy parents, and educated at Rome. First at Subiaco, later at Monte Cassino, he alienated some of the family property to establish a monastery following a rule he devised himself. He died in 547; about thirty years later, when the Lombards swept through Italy, some of the Monte Cassino monks escaped to Rome with the autograph copy of their rule in Benedict's hand. They handed it to Gregory, who was enormously impressed. He not only wrote Benedict's biography, which became famous, but did everything in his very considerable power to push the Benedictine rule as the norm for monasticism in the West.

The great merit of Benedict's system is common sense. It steered a skilful middle way between severity and decency. Monks were to have separate beds, except the younger ones, who were to be 'dispersed among the seniors'. They were to be properly and warmly clad, with two tunics and cowls each; and they were issued with a mattress, a woollen blanket, under-blanket and pillow, shoes, stockings, girdle, knife, pen and writing tablets, needle and handkerchiefs. Otherwise no property was to be held individually, 'neither a book, nor tablets, nor a pen . . . nothing at all'; and beds were to be searched frequently for private possessions. Monks were to be adequately but simply fed: two cooked dishes a day, a pound of bread, a pint of wine, and fruit and vegetables in season, but no meat, at any rate of four-footed beasts. On the other hand monks who were ill were to have a special diet; they must be kept healthy. 'Before all things, and above all things, care must be taken of the sick'. 'All guests are to be received as Christ himself', for which a special separate kitchen (also used by the abbot) was to be provided. The monks were to spend their time in manual labour and sacred reading, when not attending divine services. They were to 'practise silence at all times, especially during the night'. Grumbling was the 'greatest sin', and 'idleness is the enemy of the soul'. Infractions of the rules were to be met by withdrawal of communion; the abbot and the older and wiser brothers were to try to reconcile the excommunicated; but 'the punishment of the lash' was to be used if necessary, and 'the surgeon's knife' (expulsion) in the last resort; boys were to be 'punished with extra fasts or coerced with severe blows'.

We possess the Benedictine rule in virtually its original state. In the time of Charlemagne, the then Abbot of Monte Cassino, Theodemar, had a copy made direct from Benedict's holograph, and sent to him at Aix; there a fine copy was made, which still survives. It is perhaps unique in antique texts, a copy separated from the original by a single intermediary. It is written in Vulgar Latin – the vernacular of the day in central Italy – for comparatively simple men. It does not envisage the monastery as a great centre of learning, or indeed of anything else except piety and hard work. But one can see exactly why it appealed to the practical-minded Gregory. It is wholly lacking in eccentricity. It does not expect heroic virtue. It is full of provisions for exceptions, changes and relaxations in its rules; yet at the same time it insists that rules must be kept, once made. The monk must live to a timetable, and he must be doing something all the time, even if this only takes the form of eating and sleeping to enable him to labour afresh. 'Idleness is the enemy of the soul': that is the keynote, echoing Paul's advice to the earliest Christians as they awaited the *parousia*. And then the rule exuded the universality which had always been the object of Catholic Christianity, of Rome, and above all of Gregory himself as a missionary pope who wanted to convert the world and society. The rule is classless and timeless; it is not grounded in any particular culture or geographical region, and it will fit into any society which allows it to operate.

Gregory's endorsement of the Benedictine rule, and the vigorous efforts he and his successors made to secure its general adoption, thus flung into the business of Christianizing the convert societies of Europe and evangelizing the pagan an immensely powerful and flexible institution. The new monks were neither wholly withdrawn from society nor wholly integrated with it; they canalized the ascetic urge while enabling it to perform useful services to man and Church; their rule was compatible with papal leadership and the episcopal structure. Above all, and this especially appealed to the efficient estate manager in Gregory, they had a decisive economic contribution to make.

We must not imagine that the Benedictine rule immediately and generally became the norm. It was already well known in the seventh century but it did not become the exclusive rule until the ninth–tenth. Individual abbots usually devised their own rule when setting up a new house. Thus Augustine, sent to Kent by Gregory to evangelize the pagan English in 597, laid down his own regulations for his house at Canterbury. An abbot or founding bishop might like to draw from a variety of traditions. In Whitby, founded by Bishop Wilfrid, Rome and Irish traditions were mingled. Royal founders, too, were often eclectic. Benedict Biscop, founder of Wearmouth and Jarrow in conjunction with the kings of Northumbria, 674–81, wrote: 'You cannot suppose that it was my untaught heart which dictated this rule to you. I learnt it from seventeen monasteries, which I saw during my travels, and most approved of. . . .' But he added that he thought Benedict's rule had special authority, and from the mid-seventh century it provided the basic framework for the overwhelming majority of new monastic foundations, particularly those lavishly endowed by kings and landed magnates.

Thus a great and increasing part of the arable land of Europe passed into the hands of highly disciplined men committed to a doctrine of hard work. They were literate. They knew how to keep accounts. Above all, perhaps, they worked to a daily timetable and an accurate annual calendar – something quite alien to the farmers and landowners they replaced. Thus their cultivation of the land was organized, systematic, persistent. And, as owners, they escaped the accidents of deaths, minorities, administration by hapless widows, enforced sales, or transfer of ownership by crime, treason and folly. They brought continuity of exploitation. They produced surpluses and invested them in the form of drainage, clearances, livestock and seed. Of course earlier monastic patterns had occasionally produced economic drive. In the Vosges, for instance, where Columbanus founded a monastery at Annegray, his monks began the process of forest clearance. But Celtic monasticism was rather a cultural than an agricultural instrument. The transformation took place when the Benedictine or Benedictine-type rule was grafted on to earlier forms. Thus the foundation at Fontenelle on the banks of the lower Seine, near Rouen, originally an offshoot of the Celtic Columbanus movement, became a major agricultural colony after adopting a regular discipline in the mid-seventh century. In less than three generations it had converted an area of brushwood and swamp into prime arable land, and had become very wealthy. In west, north-west and central Europe, the clearance of forest and the draining of swamp were the prime economic facts of the entire Dark Ages. In a sense they determined the whole future history of Europe: they were the foundation of its world primacy. The operation was so huge, and took place over so long a period – nearly a millenium – that no one element in society can claim exclusive credit: it was a collective effort. But it was the monasteries which led the movement and for long sustained it. Among the greatest clearers were the abbeys of Jumièges, Saint Riquier, Saint Bertin, Corbier, Stavelot, Plum, Murbach, Luxeuil, Moissac, St Benoit-sur-Loire, all Merovingian foundations, and destined to remain among Europe's leading abbeys until the age of the French revolution. The continuity and permanence of these foundations, the merging of the individual life-span in the eternal collectivity, was particularly well adapted to to the slow transformation of forest, scrub and marsh into arable and pasture. But great abbots supplied the dynamism of individualist ambition: they were, like Gregory himself, drawn from the ruling class, administrators by blood, whose masterful gifts allowed them to play a role in the making of Europe comparable to the captains of industry in the nineteenth century.

Some records survive of their efforts. From the late eighth and early ninth centuries comes the *Polyptyque of Abbot Irminon* as it is called. A polyptyque was an ecclesiastical land survey or inventory, in this case dealing with the Parisian Abbey of St Germain-des-Prés, which had wide estates in the area now covered by the Paris suburban belt. Within the compass of this single document, the abbot amassed a staggering amount of information about the twenty-four manors it covers; everything, down to the last egg and the odd piece of spare roof-timber, is carefully listed. The polyptyque indicates how the optimum use was made of the total labour force on the acres available. In many cases the Church found that most efficient returns could be secured by settling manors with *coloni*, peasant tenant-farmers. In this way the Church led the move away from slavery, and hopelessly unproductive slave-farming. It had never opposed slavery root and branch, while always urging that manumission was meritorious. What the monastery showed was that slavery was economically unnecessary – indeed, undesirable. Of course close supervision was needed: the St Germain records show that the closer the estate lay to Paris the more effectively it was worked. So branch houses were set up further afield; and often these in turn expanded into major houses and so began a new cycle of growth. The monks also moved into fresh areas where the vine could be cultivated. The Church needed wine to celebrate mass, and the liturgy gave it a decisively higher status than beer, so the monks pushed the vineyards north and east, and the Franks got wine as part of their Roman (and Christian) inheritance. The monks were innovators in other ways. We find them pioneering the systematic and large-scale use of hedges, banks and ditches. And they founded towns – Laval, for instance, created by the monks of Marmoutier – and developed markets for their surplus produce.

The great Gaulish abbeys were mostly of the sixth and seventh centuries; east of the Rhine, monasticism followed in the wake of conversion and Carolingian expansion, especially in the eighth to ninth centuries, where huge monastic foundations were established in the heart of Europe, where they still flourish in one way or another today. Parallel to this monastic development, often working in conjunction with it, was the expansion of the episcopal estates which had been founded in the fourth and fifth centuries. In many provinces the bishop was the real master, running it from his episcopal town. Bishops were the equals, almost the superiors, of the greatest landed magnates, next on the rung to kings and emperors. The abbots were only a little way behind them. Of course in some areas, especially England, it was hard to distinguish between the two, since cathedrals were usually monastic foundations, and the monks formed the chapter. Together, bishoprics and abbacies constituted the core of the agricultural economy of Europe. Bishops and abbots were the innovatory élite of society. But the situation did not last. The Church estates reached their peak in the mid ninth century, and thereafter tended to contract. The ravagers from Scandinavia proved too powerful and persistent either for the declining Carolingian state or the rising House of Wessex. They could not protect Church estates, and bishops and abbots could not protect themselves. The heavily armoured and professional lay soldier-lord moved in. In many cases the Viking attacks broke up large-scale monastic estates; and in the tenth century lay seigneuries were founded on what had once been episcopal lands. In Maine, for instance, the Bishop of Le Mans was replaced as the leading territorial magnate by the Viscounts, later to flower into the House of Plantagenet. Both bishops and abbots built up their wealth again; but more often on the basis of tithes and quit-rents, rather than domanial farming. Nevertheless, the monks still continued to play a pioneering role in agriculture. We have evidence from the cartularies of a number of abbeys – St Aubin d'Angers, La Trinité de Vendôme, St Vincent du Mans, Marmoutier, to give examples from only one part of France – that the monks were still hard at it clearing the forests in the eleventh century, after the worst period of the Viking attacks was over.

From the end of the eleventh century, in fact, there was a second great wave of monastic enterprise in agriculture, with the establishment of the Cistercian type of Benedictine house. The Cistercians claimed to be the only true followers of St Benedict, in the stark and true simplicity of primitive monasticism. It is significant that they interpreted this return to an idealized past in economic terms. Population was rising rapidly in the eleventh century, very rapidly in the twelfth; land was becoming scarce. Kings and great magnates who had once made over to the Church huge chunks of marginal and underdeveloped land were no longer able to do so. If generous, they endowed new foundations with bits and pieces rather than unitary estates. Wealth was increasing fast and there were, for example, more foundations in the period 1060–1120 than ever before. But new monastic resources were made up of small parcels, often widely dispersed, and items of money income. The lord who founded the priory of St Mont in Gascony, for instance, endowed it with the profits of forty-seven churches, one hamlet, seven manors, four small parcels of land, one vineyard, six arable lots, one wood, one stretch of fishing rights and various small rents and tolls. This produced an income, but gave the monks no real economic role. The Cistercians would have nothing to do with such arrangements. They would take only agricultural property, and they demanded full possession. Moreover, they would not make up their income by saying masses and performing other sacramental functions for the laity; on the contrary, their rules stipulated that they were to place their houses far away from towns, castles and other sources of temptation.

Thus perhaps by accident, perhaps by conscious design, they took on a frontier role, pushing the areas of cultivation and pasturage well beyond anything hitherto attempted in Europe. In an expanding society it was the marginal lands which alone offered opportunities for development; and the Cistercians became the agricultural apostles of Europe's internal colonization. Other individuals were engaged on this task; but the Cistercians worked on a vast scale, and with terrific organization and panache. Most of them were aristocrats, the younger sons of magnates. They saw themselves as a small, pure élite. Their discipline was ferocious. They developed a great driving-force, became outstanding managers, and so prospered enormously. Their twelfth-century expansion is an economic phenomenon almost without parallel in history. The first house was founded in 1108; twenty years later there were seven. By 1152 there were 328, and by the end of the century 525. By this means, in just a century, a huge addition was made to the available resources of Europe, chiefly in Spain and Portugal (which included the world's biggest monastery, Alcobaca), Hungary, Poland, Sweden, Austria, Wales, northern England and the Scottish border. One monastery, Goldenkron in Bohemia, covered nearly 1,000 square miles, and its agricultural exploitation involved the creation of seventy villages. But the Cistercians might also destroy villages if their spiritual and economic purposes required it. They uprooted three villages, for instance, to create the Abbey of Revesby in Lincolnshire in 1142: the peasants broke the solitude and were not needed to work on the abbey lands. The Cistercians were completely ruthless. Like the Israel *kibbutzim*, which they resembled in some ways, they were not allowed either to spend money on themselves, or to decorate their churches with expensive ornaments, so they saved money and invested their surpluses. They had a strong chain of authority from top to bottom: a triennial general chapter, frequent visitations and, by papal favour, complete freedom from local authority, lay or ecclesiastical. They ran their own affairs completely, and could if they chose operate as a national, even international, economic units. A monastery which got into economic difficulties could be rapidly re-financed by a sister-house; or it could be wound up quickly, the losses cut, and the force of monks moved to an area where returns were greater. An abbey could also tap liquid capital from central funds when a bargain offered. At Fountains, for instance, we find a steady process of consolidating the estates by buying up intervening plots of land the moment neighbouring landowners got into difficulties.

Cistercian regulations were plainly designed for farming purposes laying down procedure in considerable detail: 'Pigstyes may be two or even three leagues from a grange; but pigs, though allowed to wander by day, must be kept in styes at night.' Above all, regulations dealt with, and for over a century completely solved, the labour problem. We have seen how the early Benedictines prospered by replacing slave labour by a peasant tenantry. By the twelfth century, even by the eleventh, the use of labour services, which the peasant supplied, was becoming an increasingly inefficient method of working big domains. The Cistercians cut them out altogether. Instead, they took advantage of the population increase, and the huge numbers of landless and workless young men from twelve upwards, to create a secondary order of lay brothers. These youths and men were illiterate and if they remained so could not aspire to full monastic status. But in other respects they were monks, and had the same food and clothing as the 'real' monks; they were also, if they behaved themselves, given a full assurance of salvation – something which all monasteries offered but extended as a rule only to comparatively well-born literates. These *conversi*, as they were called, were recruited in great numbers, sometimes outnumbering the full Cistercians by three or four to one. They provided the abbey estates with a large, highly disciplined labour force, which had no wives and families to keep, and which need be paid no wages. They were, in effect, willing and highly motivated slaves, the perfect labour formula for the cultivation of large, well defined units of undeveloped land. Hence the enormous success of the order as frontier colonists.

Western monasticism, unlike its counterpart in the East, was an upper-class movement. Or rather, it tended to reflect the natural hierarchy in society. Abbots and priors were drawn from the families of tribal chieftains or, later, large landowners; the monks, who had to be literate, came essentially from the landowning class. The sons of illiterate peasants, in minor orders or no orders at all, performed the menial tasks. Apart from its spiritual preoccupations, an abbey tended to operate like a large seigneurial household, only in a rather more orderly and efficient fashion, the object of which was to extract the maximum economic benefit from the land. But the abbey, being a literate institution, unlike the seigneurial household, soon acquired and developed an additional social function, as a carrier of culture. It had no such role in the Byzantine empire, with its secular schools and universities; or only to a very limited degree. Nor, certainly, did St Benedict or even Gregory I see monks as cultural conservators or harbingers. Yet this is what they became, providing the main channel through which the learning and arts of the ancient world reached Dark Age Europe, and mingled with its own native cultures.

The Christian Church of the Roman empire, it should be stressed, was not a cultural institution. On the contrary, it was still trying hard to demonstrate its cultural respectability a century after Constantine's conversion. Whole branches of arts and letters remained exclusively in pagan hands until the break-up of the western empire. The Church had no schools or centres of learning of its own. The universities and public academies were run by the State and were usually in pagan hands. Even in the East, where paganism was eliminated much more speedily, education remained the concern of the State. When new universities replaced the pagan academies, their essential purpose was to train the civil service. They did not teach theology at all. In the East the Orthodox Church was never able to establish a monopoly of education.

It was a different matter in the West. During the course of the fifth and sixth centuries, the public system of education disappeared. This presented the Church with a unique opportunity to capture society by its roots. It had the chance not merely to establish a stranglehold on education, but to recreate the whole process and content and purpose of education in a Christian setting. In a way, Augustine had foreseen and prepared for this. Lacking Greek, he had sketched the outline of a Latin-Christian system of knowledge in which every aspect of human creativity and intellectual endeavour was related to Christian belief. He produced the matrix which continued to be elaborated throughout the Middle Ages. But how was this knowledge to be transmitted? It is curious that during the fifth century, when Roman institutions were crumbling, no attempt appears to have been made to create Christian schools. The first such suggestion was made in 536, when Cassiodorus, a prominent Catholic layman who was secretary to the Ostrogothic king, Theodoric, asked Pope Agapetus to found a Christian university in Rome: 'Seeing that the schools were swarming with students with a great longing for secular letters', he urged the pope 'to collect subscriptions and to have Christian rather than secular schools in the city of Rome, with professors, just as there had been for so long in Alexandria'. The project was started but collapsed in the Gothic-Byzantine wars, which finally put paid to the state system of education, and indeed to what remained of Roman civilization in Italy. By the time Gregory the Great came to the papal throne, the West had descended to an altogether lower level of culture.

Yet something had been saved. Boethius, another sixth-century Catholic layman and minister at the Gothic court, had contrived – before he was executed in a Gothic-Arian persecution – to translate into Latin the complete works of Plato and Aristotle. His manuscripts were copied, and re-copied, and slowly proliferated. Cassiodorus himself, during the darkest days, created a Christian institution at Squillace in Calabria, at which learned laymen or monks copied manuscripts of standard texts. Developing the ideas of Augustine, he prepared an encyclopaedic course of study, both secular and divine, for Christian ascetics. Thus, for the first time, a great portion of available knowledge was assembled for a Christian purpose and in a monastic

context. In the next two generations, the Cassiodoran system was taken up in
Seville, under Bishop Leander, a friend of Gregory the Great, and his
successor, Bishop Isidore. Seville had already become a gathering place for
scholarly Christian refugees, and with the conversion of the Arian court it
became possible to build up a centre of Christian culture. Over a period of
twenty years Isidore and his helpers compiled a vast survey of human
knowledge, arranged etymologically and incorporating the works and
transmissions of Boethius and Cassiodorus, and much else. His object was
partly to assist the Visigothic kings, partly to instruct his own priests and
monks. Amost by accident he founded a civilization, or at any rate an
educational system. His work, made public in 636, first describes the seven
liberal arts, grammar, rhetoric, dialectic, arithmetic, geometry, music and
astronomy; then their dependent arts, medicine, law and chronology; then it
moves on to the Bible and its interpretation, and the Church's canons and
offices. The central part deals with God, the bonds that hold God to man, the
relations of man with the State, and man's anatomy. Finally he moves on to
animals and inanimate nature. We have here a *summa* of human knowledge in
which Christian doctrine and teaching, and the role of the Church, is placed
right at the centre of the intellectual universe, and radiates to its most remote
corners. Isidore completes the Augustinian revolution: the Church now
embraces every aspect of society and contains the answers to all questions.

Isidore's *Etymologies*, edited in twenty books by Braulio, Bishop of
Saragossa, became the basis for all teaching in the West for about 800 years.
They determined educational method, as well as content, from the primary to
the university level. Everything taught thereafter was no more than an
elaboration of what he wrote: it was impossible for the medieval mind to
break out of his system. This, of course, lay in the nature of his work, which
was essentially a salvaging operation: his team of research assistants
ransacked literature then available which has long since totally disappeared.
Isidore was a huge conduit to the ancient world – the only link, really, until
independent access to ancient texts was established, first through Arab
transmitters in the twelfth century, then direct to the East in the fifteenth.

In the seventh and eighth centuries, the monks were the only agents through
which the Isidorian corpus could be dispersed throughout barbarian Europe.
They were the only bodies of literate men who had the time and resources to
act as professional transcribers. Transcription of manuscripts was first
practised by monks at Tours, under Martin, in the late fourth century. But
most monastic *scriptoria* were based on the model set up by Cassiodorus at
Squillace in the mid sixth century. The dominant material in the West was
parchment – the most durable, but also the most expensive and difficult to
work. Moreover, its raw materials could be obtained anywhere – from
sheepskin, calf or goat – unlike papyrus, which came from Egypt, or paper,
shipped from the East but not generally available before the twelfth century.
And it could be washed, scraped and used again. The method used was to take

four sheets folded together, that is eight leaves of sixteen pages, recto-verso, which formed a *quaternio* or copy-book. One of these was then distributed to each of a number of scribes, who had to transcribe the copy-book on the same number of pages. There might be as many as twenty in a *scriptorium*. Each sat on a bench or stool, with his feet on a footstool, and wrote on his knees; a desk in front held the book he was copying, and a side-table his quills, ink, knife, eraser, compasses and ruler. Scribes worked in absolute silence (dictating of original work and letters was done in another room), but they communicated with posterity by marginal graffiti: 'Christ, favour my work'; 'Only three fingers are writing: the whole body is in agony'; 'This work is slow and difficult'; 'Now it is night and dinner-time'; 'The scribe has the right to the best wine.' The Irish were great margin-writers. Thus, in a ninth-century Irish manuscript of Cassiodorus on the psalms, we find: 'Pleasant is the glint of the, sun today on these margins. It flickers so.'

During the seventh and throughout the eighth centuries, the *scriptoria* reached a high stage of activity, especially at Canterbury, Ripon, Wearmouth, Jarrow, York and Lindisfarne in England; at Bangor, Burrow and Kells in Ireland; at Autun, Luxeuil, Corbie, St Medard-de-Soissons in Gaul, and, further east and south, at Echtenach, St Gall, Bobbio and Noantola. The work was very slow. It was said that Columba of Iona was such a fast copyist that he completed the *Book of Durrow* in twelve days, at the rate of twenty to thirty pages a day. In fact he cannot have been responsible for this manuscript, which dates from a century after his time. A first-class bible would take a monastic *scriptorium* a whole year to produce. When the copying was done, the head copyist assembled all the copy-books, put them in order, re-read and collated them, and then handed over the assembled codex to be bound in skin. Thus several shorter works were often bound together in one volume. Production was small, in our terms. Corbie produced well over fifty codices, but this was exceptional. We hear of libraries which contained thirty-three, eighteen, fifty volumes, and so on. In the eighth century a library with a hundred books was outstanding. But they grew steadily: by the ninth century the library of St Rémy at Reims, enjoying royal patronage, had six hundred volumes. And many of these books were made to last. A small seventh-century St John's Gospel, from Wearmouth or Jarrow, which was once probably Bede's own copy and is now at Stonyhurst, survives in superb condition in its original binding of red African goatskin.

The monks were cultural carriers, not creators. The most learned and enterprising of them – Bede of Jarrow is a good example – interested themselves in biblical translations and commentaries, in chronology, and in the writing of history. Other monastic centres of historiography arose in the ninth century. Thus the abbey of St Denis, near Paris, became closely associated with the French crown and the history of the men that had worn it. One of its monks, Hincmar, author of a partly fictitious account of the abbey's relationship to the crown, was promoted Archbishop of Reims, where he made the Abbey of St Bertin the leading centre for the writing of French, especially royal, history and records. Such work might stretch the capacities of a fine mind. Hincmar, from 861–82, turned the terse and bare *Annals of St Bertin* into a full and colourful account; and, like Bede before him, used all the resources of the Church to get information which was scattered over the realm of Francis. But there was no real attempt to turn even history into a speculative, creative, or interpretive art; its writing was firmly limited by biblical and classical conventions, and by certain outstanding Latin models. The leading abbeys were the universities of the Dark Ages. But the curriculum was limited and the intellectual purpose humble. John Cassian, who did so much to determine the cultural perspectives of western monasticism, had argued that the era of creative exploration of Christian doctrine was over; all that remained to be done was a tidying-up process. There could be no question of another Jerome or Augustine. This conviction arose partly from the feeling that the work had already been done; partly, also, from an immense sense of inferiority towards the classical world which had now vanished. Eighth- and ninth-century monks believed that under the Romans mankind had possessed virtually the sum of ascertainable human knowledge, nearly all of which had since been lost; the most that they could do was to transmit faithfully what had been preserved. Augustine, writing on the brink of catastrophe, had allotted an essentially humble and unenquiring role for the human mind in the total Christian society. In destroying Pelagianism he had snapped the tradition of speculating on first principles, and banned the practice of critical re-examination of accepted conclusions. 'Rome has spoken; the debate is over' – those were his very words. The impact of his teaching was to apply the phrase in a much wider context than he had, perhaps, intended. His message to the Dark Ages was seen as: 'The ancient world and the Fathers have spoken: the debate is over'; and by debate was understood the whole process of acquiring knowledge by thought and experiment. It was not for monks, however able, to challenge the conclusions of the past: merely to transmit and where necessary translate them.

It can be argued that, in the long run, civilization has benefited from the intellectual self-abasement of these centuries. Much of the ancient world survived because of the intense reverence of a handful of men for the literary relics of the past. Monks put the preservation of the surviving texts above their own lives, and regarded their reproduction as infinitely more important than their own creative labours. Thus a *Mediceus* of Virgil, dating from the end of the fifth century, and probably once in the possession of Cassiodorus, was preserved in various monastic houses, found its way to Bobbio, and is now in the Laurentian Library in Florence. The monks argued that the more copies they succeeded in making, the more likely it was that one at least would survive; and they were right. In the eighth century, the *scriptorium* of St Martin's of Tours transcribed a fifth-century Livy; the copy survived, the original is lost. Right at the end of his life, Bede was urging his scribe to 'write faster'. There was a sense of gloomy urgency about the task, for men believed that, however horrible the period since Rome's decline had been, things would get worse, not better; and there was much evidence to support their belief. One chief reason why King Alfred, at the end of the ninth century, wanted all the essential Latin texts translated into English was that he believed the coming hard times would wipe out Latin scholarship and that, even if the originals were not destroyed, no one would be able to read them.

Hence, in the eighth and ninth centuries virtually all the ancient texts were re-copied, often many times, and so saved. Much of this work was carried out in the big German monasteries – Lorsch, Cologne, Witzburg, Reichenau, St Gall, and so forth. Outstanding was Fulda, the centre of historiography east of the Rhine, to which we owe, for instance, vital texts of Tacitus, Suetonius, Ammianus, Vetruvius and Servius, through whom medieval men learnt their Virgil. Fulda had huge resources, and recruited a large number of conspicuously able men. One of its ninth-century monks, Hrabanus Maurus, later Archbishop of Mainz, put together an encyclopaedia of received knowledge, modelled on Isidore of Seville; and one of Hrabanus's pupils, Servatus Lupus, later Abbot of Ferrières, became the nearest approach to the modern idea of a scholar before the twelfth century John of Salisbury. Yet the work of both these Fulda monks is essentially derivative. Hrabanus's encyclopaedia contains no original thinking; Servatus's chief contribution was to compile a corpus of barbarian laws for the Duke of Friuli. These works were useful but uncreative. Moreover, we must not think that the monks were primarily concerned with transmitting the classics. No Greek secular works were preserved in the original. Even the Greek fathers were studied, and copied, in Latin translations. Profane literature in Latin occupied only a fraction of the time available. The work of the *scriptoria* was overwhelmingly centred on the Fathers, chiefly Ambrose, Augustine, Jerome, Gregory the Great, and later Bede; on bibles and lives of the saints; and on liturgical works – that is, sacramentals, lectionaries and gospelaries, missals (sacramentary plus the lectionary), antiphonaries or song-books, and hymnals. There was also a mass output of psalters, ordines, martyrologies, pontifications – that is books dealing with the bishop's functions – and penitentials. Perhaps only one in a hundred manuscripts prepared during these centuries had a function or interest which was not directly Christian.

Moreover, the Christian element impregnated not merely the written word but every other aspect of culture. The idea of secular art virtually disappeared, along with secular education. As with the law, we find a certain blending of pagan-barbarian and pagan-classical elements into new homogenous styles which were Christian in purpose and flavour, the agents of the transformation being in all cases monks. This process can be seen most clearly at work in late seventh-century Northumbria. The merging of Roman and Celtic monastic attitudes we have already noted was paralleled in culture. Benedict Biscop, the key figure, was a Northumbrian nobleman who had travelled to Rome, and quite consciously (with the encouragement of the court) founded his twin-monastery to raise cultural as well as religious standards. At Rome he had seen the products of the Byzantine-imperial *ateliers*, which produced, for home consumption as well as for export, a wide range of luxury articles: elaborate gospels with gold letters on purple grounds, ivory episcopal chairs, silk vestments and hangings, and precious reliquaries. Benedict brought from Gaul masons who knew how to 'build in the Roman manner', and glaziers who could work with coloured glass; and from Rome he borrowed John, Archcantor of St Peter's, to teaching chanting and reading aloud to his English monks. In addition to books, he imported relics, vestments, chalices and ikons. Within a generation, Northumbria was producing not only the works of Bede but reproductive craftsmanship of the highest order: one of its manuscripts, the Wearmouth-Jarrow *Codex Amiatinus*, was inspired by a copy of Cassiodorus's great Bible but rendered in the local vernacular style; it was taken by Abbot Ceolfrid to Rome in 716 and presented to the Pope as a spectacular example of English skill. Now in the Laurentian Library in Florence, it is one of the glories of the Dark Ages. Nearby at Lindisfarne, the craftsmanship was essentially Celtic. There was a first-rate jeweller's shop, producing patterns and employing techniques based on a 600-year-old pagan tradition. These Celtic-pagan forms and colours were translated into manus-cript illumination, especially in the great Lindisfarne Gospels, where the magnificent initial letter on folio 149r, surrounded by its 10,600 dots, is a two-dimensional rendering of a piece of jewellery, which might once, as it were, have been fashioned for a pagan Celtic princess. Indeed, two great con-temporary Irish artifacts, the Ardagh Chalice and the Tara Brooch, both correspond closely with the forms of the *Lindisfarne Gospels*. The pagan work of abstract imagery again surfaces in a Christian context in the seventh-century *Book of Durrow*, where the colouring is limited and primitive, and in the ninth-century *Book of Kells*, where Roman-Byzantine influence has added polychromatic brilliance to the basic Celtic-pagan skeleton. Perhaps most spectacular of all was the development of the entirely new Celtic-Christian idiom of the stone cross. The stone-art of Ireland went right back to the La Tène period of the first century AD. The Christian device of the cross gave pagan technology the opportunity to develop a unique art-world of its own, with a multitude of periods and schools, and an increasing elaboration of the message conveyed. Eventually what we have in these high stone crosses is a theology in stone, imparting a number of elaborate Mediterranean religious concepts in a purely Celtic artistic vernacular. The crosses stood at the wayside, throughout the western parts of the British Isles, wherever tracks converged and men gathered – lifted fingers both admonitory and benign, mute witnesses to Christianity which spoke powerfully to the eyes.

The stone crosses of the Celtic world symbolize the intense and complete identification between art and Christianity which was so striking and powerful a feature of these centuries. Christianity was not just a carrier of culture;

through the agency of the monks it in effect became culture. At the height of the Wearmouth-Jarrow epoch, there were over 700 monks in the two houses, all literate, each with a disciplined skill: this must have represented an enormously high proportion of the total literacy and talent of a small semi-barbarian kingdom. Again, a very large percentage of the available economic resources of Northumbria must have been invested in this enterprise. Monasticism, in fact, proved highly effective in persuading these emergent western societies to devote a dramatic part of their wealth and skills to cultural purposes. If the monks performed prodigies in raising the total amount of land used for crops and pasture, as we have seen, they also ensured that agricultural surpluses, or at any rate a large part of them, were diverted to art and literacy, and not squandered in consumption. They thus raised Europe from the trough of the post-Roman world in two distinct but complementary ways. Moreover, because of the international character of their organization, they ensured that the transmission and diffusion of this culture was accomplished as rapidly as possible. Here again, Christianity impinged directly. Monastic houses were essentially the product of intense local religious enthusiasm. Where this was greatest, the adoption of a high level of cultural activity came most quickly. And it was from these culturally dynamic centres that the monks fanned out, driven by their urge to proselytize.

Thus the British Isles were able to play a part out of all proportion to their economic or population resources. Ireland began 'exporting' scholars to the Continent (as well as to Britain) at a very early stage. It was an Irishman, Dicuil, perhaps an Iona monk, who produced the earliest geographical survey written on Frankish territory, the *Liber de Mensura Orbis Terrae*, which included a description of the elephant sent to Charlemagne in 804 by Harun-al-Rashid, and notes on Iceland and the Faroes, which Dicuil seems to have visited. There was an Irish circle at Liège in the mid ninth century, led by Sedulius Scottus, or Scottigena, who even knew some Greek – a monopoly of the Irish in western Europe at this time – and whose writings range from political theory to a large group of Latin poems, some delightfully humorous. There was a similar circle at Laon and Reims in the ninth century, under 'John the Irishman' or Johannes Scotus Erigena, whose knowledge of Latin and Greek was outstanding for the period, and whose *On the Division of the Universe* is an ambitious attempt to construct a philosophical and theological theory of the creation and the origins of the universe. And along with the Irish, the English monks were the great cultural transmitters of the eighth and ninth centuries. We get an early example in Wilfrid, a bishop who wholly identified his office and his religion with cultural grandeur, and who was active as a missionary on the Frisian 'Coast; and, still more so, with Boniface, whose English mission to Germany carried Christianity into northern and central Europe and founded such cultural centres as Fulda, Boniface's favourite monastery. Perhaps the most important of the cultural lines in transition was the chain which stretched from Wearmouth-Jarrow (itself, as we have seen, linked to Rome, and through Rome to Byzantium) to the archiepiscopal school of York in the eighth century, and from York to the Frankish territories. Here the agent, in this last stage, was the greatest cultural transmitter of all, Alcuin, described by Charlemagne's biographer, Einhard, as 'the king's master, nicknamed Albino, a deacon, but a Saxon of Britain by birth, and the most learned man of his day'. We have already seen him at work at Charlemagne's coronation; we shall meet him again. Alcuin, first as head of the palace school, later as the Abbot of St Martin's, Tours, France's most revered monastery, became Charlemagne's chief cultural and religious adviser – the two roles were inseparable.

Indeed in the mind of a man like Alcuin the desire to spread the faith, to understand it fully through literacy and knowledge of the scriptures and the ancillary disciplines, and to adorn and celebrate it through art, was all part of the same Christian vision, whose intensity and brightness were the products of personal conviction. The level of culture was directly related to the degree of faith. It was Alcuin who filled Charlemagne's mind with the missionary fervour of Augustine's *De Civitate Dei*, and it was Alcuin who showed him a copy of Gregory the Great's letter to King Æthelbert of Kent on the subject of conversion by race. In 789 Alcuin caused the king to issue the *Admonitio Generalis*, a magisterial statement of Church policy, based on earlier Frankish capitularies and Roman canonical collections, and dealing with almost everything. It has, as it were, a Roman imperial vision of a Christian society living at peace within itself, united under its king and fearing nothing but injustice – an Augustinian vision, we could say. Article 62 reads: 'Let peace, concord and unanimity reign among all Christian people, and the bishops, abbots, counts and our other servants, great and small; for without peace we cannot please God.' What is perhaps even more remarkable, however, is the central role which culture played in this vision. Article 72 dealt with the establishment and maintainance of monastic and cathedral schools, and the transcription and correction of biblical and liturgical texts. It is clear from this and other documents that Charlemagne, inspired by Alcuin, saw a cultural renaissance, directed by the Church, as the chief means by which the perfect Christian society would be brought into existence. The Church had given the rulers of the western barbarians an awareness of their classical heritage, and an anxiety to preserve and transmit it almost as strong as among the men of the late empire and after, like Cassiodorus and Boethius. But of course the inheritance was now seen entirely in a Christian context. And because the cultural urge was Christianized, it was linked to Christian policy and objectives. Charlemagne built and endowed schools because he needed a trained clergy to convert the Frisians, Saxons, Slavs and Avars, and live among them; and because he needed more priests for the Frankish world which was already nominally Christian. And, in teaching the faith, accurate and standardized texts were needed in huge quantities. There was thus a call for trained manpower to overhaul the texts and copy them exactly and economically. Material was brought from Lombardy, but more from England. Alcuin used the resources of the English monasteries and cathedral schools which, with their direct links with Rome, had become clearing-houses for manuscripts. 'Reliable' versions from Rome reached Canterbury, Jarrow, York and Malmesbury, and were there copied for the use of English missionaries abroad, and for export to Frankish centres. The point about the *Codex Amiatinus* which Ceolfrid took to Rome was not only its beauty but its accuracy. Other important English manuscripts were sent to monastic libraries in Corbie, Tours, St Denis, Utrecht, Echternach, Mainz, Lorsch, Amorbach, Wirzburg, Salzburg, Reichenau and of course Fulda. There they were recopied. Along with biblical and devotional texts went a small number of manuscripts of secular books, which had been recommended by Cassiodorus as useful to spiritual purposes, and also his advice on the careful copying of manuscripts, the technique for spotting possible emendations, and rules for spelling, binding and keeping of books. This last work was embodied in a circular to all religious houses, written presumably by Alcuin and despatched by Charlemagne's chancery, urging on them the need to cultivate letters as the proper introduction to the scriptures. Another general letter sent out by Alcuin and Charlemagne noted that the king had set up a task-force to 'correct with all possible care' the entire Bible 'degraded through the ignorance of copyists'. Alcuin was in charge of this effort: and it was the great codex embodying the results which, as we have seen, was handed to his master in Rome on Christmas Day 800. In a way, the revised and amended Bible of Alcuin sums up, not unfairly, the limitations of Dark Age Christian culture – a conscientious, and in the circumstances heroic, effort to recover as much as possible, and as accurately as possible, the understanding of the past; but an almost total absence of the desire to reach out for new frontiers.

These Dark Age scholars believed that God had imposed definite limits on what knowledge man might acquire in this world without sin. In accepting these limits they were motivated by fear, as well as by respect for the past. They were, indeed, fearful and superstitious men. The Christian Church of Alcuin in the late eighth century was still, in certain basic essentials, recognisably the same as the Church of Paul's letters to the Corinthians, around AD 50–60. But in certain other respects it was very different. If Christianity had been 'imperialized' in the fourth century, it was to some extent 'barbarianized' in the West, during the three centuries beginning about 500. Nothing exactly new was created; but certain elements already present in 'imperial Christianity' were enormously inflated and so transformed. Of these by far the most important was the cult of relics. The popularization of this cult by Ambrose in fourth century Milan was a decisive event in Christian history. Relics rapidly became, and for some 800 years remained, the most important single element in Christian devotion. They were the Christian's only practical defence against inexplicable suffering, and the constant and malignant activities of devils. Saints were believed to communicate with the world through contact with their earthly remains. Thus relics radiated a kind of energy, rather like a nuclear pile, and were correspondingly dangerous as well as useful. Important relics were approached with terror, and frequently revenged themselves on the profane and the sceptical. They conveyed a sense of supernatural power constantly humming through the world, which could be switched on through access to the right liturgical and sacramental channels.

It had been acknowledged at least since imperial times that 'the age of miracles' was over, in the sense that Christian leaders could no longer spread the gospel, like the apostles, with the aid of supernatural power – at any rate as a rule. From the time of the Montanists onwards, the Church had eliminated those who claimed to be able to work miracles and speak with tongues. An alternative theory had been evolved. As Gregory I put it: 'Now, my brethren, seeing that ye work no such signs, is it that ye believe not?' and answered: 'Not so. For holy church worketh daily now in the spirit, whatsoever the Apostles then wrought in the body . . . And indeed these miracles are the greater for being spiritual: all the greater, as uplifting not the bodies but the souls of men.' Nevertheless, it was allowed that, in certain exceptional cases, miracles did occur, always associated with saints, when alive, or with their relics after death. Everyone accepted this, in theory and in practice. Bede, for instance, was an educated man who knew how to use evidence and who did not rule out natural explanations – the sudden rise and fall of storms at sea, and so on. For him miracles occurred for a moral and didactic purpose. In his life of St Cuthbert, one of the most influential biographies of the Dark and Middle Ages, he described how the creatures of the air and sea – indeed, the air and sea themselves – obeyed the saint. Man, says Bede, had originally exercised such dominion over his environment, but had lost it through the first sin; but it was possible for individuals to recover it by showing exceptional virtue. Bede demonstrated that groups of miracles performed by holy men highlighted and furthered the conversion of England. He never describes a miracle just to astonish: it must further God's work. And he always 'checked' his sources, insisting that anecdotes must come from dependable persons. Describing the visions of Hell of Fursey, an Irish saint who lived among the East Angles in the 630s, Bede writes:

'An aged brother is still living in our monastery who relates that a most truthful and pious man told him he had seen Fursey himself in the kingdom of the East Angles, and had heard these visions from his own mouth. He added that, though it was during a time of severe winter weather, and a hard frost, and though Fursey sat wearing only a thin garment when he told his story, yet he sweated as though it were the middle of summer, because of the great terror and joy his memories aroused.'

With an absolute belief in miracles worked by saints, the possession of relics became for ordinary people the most important aspect of religion. It was the one level of religious activity in which the laity and the clergy were on an equal footing. Relics served a variety of practical purposes. They were virtually indispensable for the saying of mass, being attached to the altar. They played a vital part in the judicial system, for swearings and judicial combats. Kings carried them into battle: the power and excitement of the relic cult, and its direct influence on military success, was one reason why the barbarian leaders were prepared to embrace Christianity. William I went into action at Hastings wearing round his neck a string of relics given to him by the Pope, as the champion of orthodoxy and reform; a generation later, the discovery of the Holy Lance gave a powerful impetus to the First Crusade. Pilgrimages to the sites of important relics, common since the fourth century, became the chief motive for travel for over a thousand years, and determined the communications-structure and often the shape of the international economy. It was not just that towns expanded around relics: so did regional, national and even international fairs, which were timed to coincide with the annual parade of key relics. A major factor in the prosperity of northern France, for instance, was the great fair which originated as a joint procession of the relics of St Denis and Notre Dame.

Relics were much more valuable than any precious metal. They were in fact the most important focus for the highest metallic art of the Dark Ages. A good example is the Holy Image of St Foy at Conques. Foy was supposedly a young girl of twelve, martyred during the last persecution by Rome of 303. Some of her remains were brought to the abbey in 866, and rapidly produced miracles, pilgrims and precious donations. In *c.* 985 the relics were encased in a gold statue, to which were later attached donations in the form of emeralds, agates, pearls, onyx, sapphires, amethysts, crystals and old Roman cameos; her skull, wrapped in silver, was hidden in a cavity in the statue's back. The tenth century produced a large number of these luxurious reliquaries, such as the golden foot-shaped box, made in the jewel-workshop at Trier, which housed St Andrew's sandal; or a two-foot high reliquary of the Blessed Virgin, of wood covered in gold leaf, made in Essen for the abbess-granddaughter of the Emperor Otto I, and probably the oldest free-standing figure of the Virgin in existence. Most of these wonderful artifacts have disappeared, looted and melted down in the sixteenth century. Thus at Rochester there was once a set of folding chairs, made in silver, and presented by the mother of King Harold; and an ivory horn presented by William the Conqueror. Reading Abbey had a beautiful statue of Our Lady, of which a Bohemian visitor wrote in the fifteenth century: 'I have never seen its equal, nor shall I ever see one to compare with it if I go to the ends of the earth.'

A huge proportion of society's liquid assets were tied up in relics and their precious settings. It was one way of keeping money safely. For an abbey or episcopal church, a good relic collection – or even one outstanding item – attracted pilgrims and thus wealth. Kings amassed collections as big as those of major churches, to enhance their prestige and authority. They took their best relics with them wherever they went, thus ensuring they were always

within the ambit of spiritual power. The primitive candle-clock which Bishop
Asser says King Alfred invented was used to provide a perpetual light before
his travelling relic-collection. These collections had to be comprehensive to
impress the public. Like modern national art collections, there were certain
'musts' – and there had to be a cross-section of local saints. It is a pity we do
not know more about the big Dark Age collections. From later centuries,
however, detailed inventories survive. We have a full catalogue of the
collection formed by the newly founded Reading Abbey, between the 1120s
and the 1190s. It was composed of 242 items, and included Our Lord's shoe,
his swaddling clothes, blood and water from his side, bread from the Feeding
of the Five Thousand and the Last Supper, Veronica's veil and shroud, Our
Lady's hair, bed and belt, the rods of Moses and Aaron, and various relics of
St John the Baptist. This group was not as impressive as it might seem: the
relics, of course, were only tiny fragments; all of those listed could easily be
bought in Constantinople in the twelfth century, and most were almost
certainly fakes. Hairs of Our Lady were particularly common. Reading's
English relics were presumably genuine. It kept up to date – another
important point – and had a splendid list of bits of St Thomas à Becket, and
relics of Bernard of Clairvaux, St Malachy of Armagh, the popular boy-saints
William of Norwich and Robert of Bury, both supposedly murdered by Jews
in 'anti-Christian' rituals, and – this was a rarity – the head, jawbone,
vestments, rib and hair of St Brigid, recently 'discovered' at Downpatrick in
1185. Reading's prize possession, however, was the hand of St James, which
its benefactress, the Empress Matilda, had stolen from the German imperial
chapel, and which had once been an imperial possession in Constantinople.
Almost as good was the 'head' of St Philip (that is, a bone encased in a gold
head), which was later added by King John. This was part of the loot of the
Fourth Crusade, which sacked Constantinople and was a potent source of
primary relics.

   The trouble with relics was that, being valuable, they could not be separated
from crime. There were various acute phases of relic-forgery: in Syria and
Egypt during the post-Constantine age; in eighth-century Germany during
the Carolingian relic-inflation, when Italian travelling salesmen peddled vast
quantities to the Franks; and in the early thirteenth century, when the looting
of Byzantium brought quantities of 'genuine' relics, plus even larger numbers
of recently forged ones, to western Europe. But there were frauds on a huge
scale and at all periods. In 761 Pope Paul I protested in a decree that 'many of
the cemeteries of Christ's holy martyrs and confessors, of great antiquity, sited
outside the walls of Rome have fallen into a state of neglect and now through
the devastations of the impious Lombards are in ruins; for these men most
sacriligiously desecrated them, digging up the graves of the martyrs and
removing the bodies of the saints as plunder.' This was an old tale: Gregory I
found some Greek monks had been digging up ordinary bodies at Rome by
night, and when arrested and questioned they said they were taking the bones

back to Constantinople to pass them off as relics of saints. At least the monks were honest enough to insist on Roman bones.

Successive popes made efforts to check the worst abuses: on important relics it was necessary for the Pope's personal signet to be stamped, as a guarantee of authenticity. But the popes had a huge vested interest in the trade. Rome was constantly 'finding' bodies, rather like St Ambrose. Thus in the ninth century it discovered the corpse of St Cecilia, following a miraculous vision of Pope Paschal. In many cases, the flesh of these discoveries was found intact, or almost so. This, in Rome's view, was a sign of sanctity. But Constantinople believed the opposite: the refusal of the flesh to rot was a certain sign of heresy; it might remain thus for 1,000 years, or until the person was properly absolved. But of course this violent disagreement on a central aspect of the cult did not, in practice, make any difference, since all that Constantinople shipped westwards were bones and scraps of clothing. As for Rome's own 'discoveries', these went north and west to powerful sovereigns, in exchange for diplomatic or military support. In 826, the Emperor Louis the Pious exerted tremendous pressure on the Pope to hand over the body of St Sebastian, which was taken in triumph to Soissons; there were popular riots in Rome when the Pope gave in. Again, in 834, the Roman mob howled when the Pope sold the relics of St Alexander and St Justin to a delegation from Freising, who handed over to him, in return, 'a noble and weighty pile of precious things'. Ten years after this, Sergius II sold to Abbot Varcuard of Prum the relics of St Chrysantius and St Darius. There were plenty more where they came from.

High dignitaries of Church and State not only bought and sold relics but countenanced open theft and piracy. There were professional relic-thiefs, such as Alfred, Canon of Durham, who piously visited Jarrow every year until he succeeded in pinching the body of Bede, which he placed alongside St Cuthbert's at Durham. Durham, in turn, was robbed of relics by its own bishops – Æthelric and Æthelwine, bishops in turn, transferred some of the cathedral treasures to their native abbey of Peterborough. Kings, bishops and abbots might employ professional criminals, or they might venture into crime themselves, using whatever power was available or necessary. Men did not make a distinction between political and military force, and the spiritual force generated by holy bones. An ambitious man like King Cnut, for instance, took risks in this field, just as he staked his kingdoms and his life in battle: the potential rewards were worth it. In 1020, Abbot Æthelstan of Romsey, instigated by the Bishop of Dorchester and with the consent of Cnut, sent a naval expedition to Sohan to steal the body of St Felix: there was nearly a naval battle with the monks of Ely. Three years later, Archbishop Æthelnoth, with Cnut's help, opened the sarcophagus of St Ælfeah in St Paul's, using crowbars, while the king's housecarles stood guard against the angry citizens. Cnut hurried half-clad from his bath to take part in the raid, and himself took the tiller of the boat which carried the corpse, on a plank, across the Thames, to travel under armed escort to reinterment in Canterbury. Cnut also abetted the theft of St Mildred, pinched from Thanet and taken, again, to Canterbury. These incidents were not pranks or escapades, but high acts of State, concerned with power, privilege, authority, jurisdiction and the hopes and fears of primitive rulers.

During the twelfth century we get the first doubts cast on certain aspects of the system. About 1120, Guibert, Abbot of Nogent, wrote his *Relics of the Saints*, which argued that many of the saint-cults were spurious – he instanced a young squire who became the object of a cult solely because he happened to die on Good Friday. A generation later, Pope Alexander III made the whole business of canonization a papal monopoly. Guibert also pointed to elements in the system which were clearly fraudulent. Churches in both Constantinople and Angeli claimed to have the head of St John the Baptist. Was he two-headed then? Ely and St Albans each claimed all the bones of St Dunstan; and so did Odense in Denmark. A rich bishop or abbot might easily be duped. Bishop Odo of Bayeux was swindled by the monks of Corbeil who pretended to sell him the body of St Exupéry but in fact handed over the corpse of a peasant. How could it be explained that duplicate relics, or wholly fraudulent ones, seemed able to exert spiritual power? By this time, of course, the system was in decline. In the thirteenth century the eucharist became the centre of popular devotion, and saints had to be new and spectacular – like St Thomas – to inspire important cults.

In the meantime, however, the relic cult had changed the face of Europe. The most important relic of all was the body of St Peter, which Christian opinion had believed, at least since the mid second century, was buried on the site of the Vatican church called after him. Possession of the body was regarded as final 'proof' that Peter was the first Bishop of Rome. The following chronology was constructed: in AD 34 Peter became Bishop of Antioch; in 40 moved his see to Rome; in 59 consecrated Linus and Cletus his successors. No one challenged these assertions. Peter was supposed to have founded an episcopal line which had never been broken since. Moreover, Paul's body was also in Rome. These relics made Rome a doubly apostolic foundation, the only one apart from Jerusalem, which was not a force in Church politics. Leo the Great, Pope from 440 to 461, made the point that Peter and Paul, the most potent of the apostles, had replaced Romulus and Remus as the city's protectors. Rome thus inherited, in Christianized form, something of the invincibility of the imperial city. But clearly Christ had intended Rome to play a special international role too, in his Church. Hence the famous text of Matthew 16:18. Rome was exerting its authority over other churches as early as the second century, as we have seen. The Petrine text did not, however, play any part before c. 250; it was first invoked in the controversy over baptism with Carthage. But from the time of Pope Gelasius, Ambrose's contemporary, and the dawn of the age of the relic-cult in the late fourth century, it became a key text, frequently invoked in conjunction with

Peter's 'presence' in the city. It was from this time that collections of canons, and synodal and conciliar decisions, began to appear. Where there was any doubt, it was natural that the Petrine city should be appealed to, and should give a ruling which everyone should regard as authoritative. For centuries this development of unity centred on Rome was a spontaneous devotion to St Peter, rather than the result of papal activity, which was minimal. Monasteries and bishoprics were founded, saints canonized, regulations laid down, and local councils met under the chairmanship of kings, all without reference to Rome. Appointments of bishops and abbots were decided on the spot. Rome, when informed, simply confirmed what had been done. Yet there was a residual element of authoritarianism, always present in theory and sometimes in practice. This was a combination of the special role of St Peter and Rome's original legacy as the founding-capital of the empire. All the Popes who found it desirable, or possible, to exert their authority did so on a Petrine basis. Gelasius II, Pope from 492 to 496, claimed that the 'see of blessed Peter has the right to loose what has been bound by the decisions of any bishops whatsoever'. Petrine collections of canons and conciliar decrees were thus more authoritative than any other. Then, too, the metropolitan system, early established in the East, was slow to take hold in the West. Individual bishops in Gaul or Spain would write to the Bishop of Rome, rather than their metropolitan, for a verdict or advice. From the time of Damasus on, popes treated such requests on the lines of the old imperial 'rescripts', modelling their technique and style on the imperial chancery. Papal letters began to take the form of decretals, the Popes assuming they had a juridical power based on their historical foundation. Moreover, Rome transformed the metropolitan system into a part of her imperial legacy. The English metropolitan church of Canterbury had been founded directly from Rome, as a result of Gregory I's efforts, and had always had a special relationship with the papacy. The Pope invested the Archbishop of Canterbury with a *pallium*, or fur tippet, which emperors had originally placed round the shoulders of legates on their appointment. From the seventh century the practice began to spread to other metropolitans, and to be accompanied by a confession of faith, which an archbishop had to make to the Pope as a testimony of his orthodoxy, Rome being the custodian of credal perfection.

From the last decades of the fourth century, Rome had become a centre of pilgrimage, gradually ousting Jerusalem from this role. As a result, Roman liturgical practices, rather than the very different ones of Jerusalem, tended increasingly to become standard, at any rate in the West. In 416, indeed, Innocent I argued that, as Rome had brought the gospel to all the Latin provinces – an assertion which was not quite true – they should automatically adopt the Roman liturgy. This did not happen, at any rate until the time of Charlemagne, who adopted Roman practice throughout his dominions as a matter of state policy. Many powerful figures in the early Church had, in fact, argued against liturgical uniformity. There was, for instance, the Ambrosian rite in Milan; and even Augustine, who believed strongly in unity, centrality and authoritarianism in Church matters, put the case for regional rites. But the popes set high standards in music and spectacle, and it was natural for those who came to Rome to wish to imitate its usages in their home churches.

Moreover, had not anything Roman the sanction of St Peter? It would be hard to exaggerate the manner in which, to the minds of the Dark Ages, his continuing presence and power dominated the city. From the time of Damasus it became the object of every Christian, if possible, to make the journey to Rome. The popes encouraged these pilgrimages. Damasus first began the official cataloguing of the martyrs in the catacombs, and this and other efforts to systematize the pilgrimage were continued under his successors. Oil from lamps in the catacombs was collected in small *ampullae*; these shrines were visited in order, either clockwise or anti-clockwise, and the bottles labelled accordingly – some sixth-century labels survive. From the seventh century we have guide books, two of which survive; they are surprisingly detailed and accurate. The papacy set up hostels for pilgrims, but various 'nations' provided their own as well; thus the English had a series called, in their own language, the borough – later the *borgo*.

Gregory the Great's writings, amongst the most widely read throughout this period, popularized the superstitious element of the Petrine presence and miracles. He wrote to the empress: 'The bodies of the apostles Peter and Paul glitter with such great miracles and awe that no one can go to pray there without considerable fear.' He related two anecdotes of workmen dying after being too near the bodies. As with the tomb of Tutankhamen, proximity might prove fatal. The place was dark, mysterious, with queer noises and exhalations; pilgrims could not actually get at the underground sepulchre, but lowered handkerchiefs or gold keys from above, and then pulled them up transformed into holy and potent relics. Everyone believed that St Peter was *there*, in a physical sense. He dominated all the activities of his see. His remains guarded his rights, and struck down those who tried to usurp them. In a way he was more real than the Pope, who was merely his vicar. A pilgrimage was not a symbolical business: it was an actual visit to St Peter. When Abbot Ceolfrid of Jarrow took the splendid bible the monks had illuminated to Rome, it was dedicated, said Bede, not to the Pope, but to St Peter's body. Peter not only radiated power from his tomb, he took an active part in Church affairs if necessary. Thus when Pope Leo the Great presented his 'Tome' to the Council of Chalcedon as an authoritative statement of Christological and Trinitarian doctrine, he declared it to be directly inspired by Peter; indeed, one seventh-century theologian, John Moschius, believed that the tome had received its final corrections in Peter's own miraculous hand. In Bede's graphic description of the Synod of Whitby in 664, which met to settle the date of Easter, he shows that the King of Northumbria opted for Rome, as opposed to Iona, because he believed that St Peter literally held the keys of entrance to Heaven, and so was much more powerful than St Columba. Peter was not a stationary relic but an active, executive presence, who took decisions. St Boniface, setting out on his German mission, swore an oath 'to you, St Peter, and to your vicar'. And Peter might show displeasure, and punish. In 710, the Pope, as the imperial official in Rome, accused the Archbishop of Ravenna of rebellion and ordered his eyes to be put out. The sentence was presented as coming direct from St Peter, who imposed it because the archbishop had disobeyed his vicar. The belief was, in fact, that while Peter's relics did their work from his tomb, his earthly *persona* was entrusted to the current Pope, who acted vicariously.

The above evidence suggests that it was only in the eighth century that the full importance of St Peter's connection with Rome began to be fully understood and proclaimed. As Peter's reputation and continuing power swelled, what more natural than that men should believe that previous ages had acknowledged it, not merely in theory but in a highly practical manner? The issue gradually came to the fore in the course of the eighth century as a result of a number of factors which were changing the relationship of Rome to the political world outside. The first was a fiscal breach with the Byzantine empire which occurred in the years after 726. The Bishop of Rome, as a Byzantine duke and the ruler of part of the imperial territories in Italy, had owed taxes to Constantinople since at least the second half of the fifth century. Their collection had been resented, especially since the fearful ravaging of Italy by Justinian's forces in their long and ultimately futile effort to restablish imperial power. When Byzantine tax assessments were raised in 726, the Pope simply refused to pay, and never thereafter did so. This left the papacy without a formal political and defensive relationship with any major power. Having renounced Byzantium, and unwilling to trust the Lombards, the Popes looked increasingly to the rising power of the Franks beyond the Alps. The Franks had been converted directly to Catholic Christianity, like the English. As a result of English missionary efforts culminating in the great drives of St Boniface, Christianity was spreading rapidly across the Rhine and Frankish power was expanding accordingly. Why should not this great emergent Catholic power supply the protection which Byzantium was no longer capable of providing? The transfer of alliance from Byzantium to the Franks implied, however, that the papacy was an independent power, free to move from one jurisdiction to another. Hence the theory developed that the central Italian lands controlled by Rome were of special significance, being the core of a renewed Roman empire, over which the Pope exercised control. This appeared to solve a historical problem which had long proved puzzling. Why had Constantine transferred his capital to New Rome so soon after his conversion? The answer could only be that he wished, as a testimony to his new faith, to transfer Old Rome and its dependencies to St Peter, as an outright gift. Some time in the eighth century this explanation found written expression in the shape of a 'letter' from Constantine to Pope Sylvester I, dated 30 March 315. Like many other Christian forgeries, this was very likely a sincere attempt by clerks in the papal chancery to document a transaction which they had convinced themselves had actually taken place. The letter listed the emperor's gifts to the Bishop of Rome as vicar of St Peter: preeminence over all the patriarchal sees, including Constantinople (this was a mistake, as Constantinople did not exist in 315) and all other churches; the imperial palace of the Lateran and the imperial insignia of Rome; and all imperial powers in Rome, Italy and the western provinces. Constantine was described as depositing the document on the body of St Peter, as his personal gift to him.

The *Donation of Constantine* appeared to place at the disposal of the Pope, acting as the vicar of St Peter, the whole of the western provinces of the empire. At a stroke it proffered the keystone needed to complete the arch of the total Christian society. In the West the Church had imposed Christian characteristics on the law, it had achieved a dominant role in the agrarian economy, and it had established a monopoly of education and culture. Now it had the chance to integrate the basic system of government with Christian teaching and practice by making the ruler a functionary of Christian theology.

The theory was already there. The idea of Melchisedech, the priest-king, was present in the Old Testament. Paul, in his effort to separate Christianity from Jewish Zealotry, and to show that it was in no sense a threat to the Roman empire, had written passage after passage insisting that established authority had divine sanction: 'There is no power but of God: the powers that be are ordained of God.' The prince, he insisted, 'is the minister of God to thee for good. But if thou do that which is evil, be afraid; for he beareth not the sword in vain; for he is the minister of God, a revenger to exact wrath upon him that doeth evil.' Paul's idea of the ruler as an ecclesiastical figure fitted easily, as perhaps it was meant to do, with the pagan convention of the divine or semi-divine emperor, the supreme pontiff. When the emperor shifted his religious allegiance, Christian ideologues were only too anxious that he should conserve his regal pontificalism, so that he could bring the full weight of the State behind the extirpation of heresy and schism, and the maintenance of Catholic orthodoxy. So Augustine argued that when an emperor ordered what was good, Christ himself gave the order. He said that emperors were invested with this sacred power to perform quasi-episcopal functions. As we have seen, Bishop Eusebius thought Constantine had been right to regard himself as a bishop. By the beginning of the fifth century, this Christian Caesaro-papalism was the official doctrine of the empire: Honorius and his imperial brother Arcadius issued edicts equating heresy with treason, and vice versa; and in the next century the Justinian code established the emperor as judge of dogma and the worthiness of priests, his authority over the Church stretching to all matters save the actual spiritual content of the priestly functions. At the Council of Constantinople (448), Theodosius was hailed by the bishops as Pontiff-Emperor; at Chalcedon (451), Marcian was called 'Priest and King'. Eastern patriarchs and metropolitans quickly fell into this pattern as subordinates. But Rome, too, accepted the idea of the priest-emperor. Leo I, though a champion of the sacerdotal dignity, told Marcian that he prayed that God 'may confer on you, besides the regal crown, the priestly rod also'. In Rome, as well as in Constantinople, the imperial dignity was treated as of divine origin and institution. Honouring the emperor was a form of religious service. When the Theodosian Code was promulgated at Rome in 438, the senators chanted out 'Through you we hold our honours, through you our property, through you everything' a total of twenty-eight times; there were fifteen other similar repeated acclamations, making a grand total of 352 rhythmically chanted praises – thus forming a model for later Christian litanies addressed to God, Jesus and the Virgin Mary. The regal pontiff in Constantinople was surrounded by an elaborate apparatus of worship. From a tenth-century description by Liutprand, Bishop of Cremona, we gather that the emperor was levitated up and down on a throne worked by hidden machinery, to increase his impressiveness, and beside the throne were mechanical lions, which roared and thumped their tails when a visitor approached.

Some of the imperial ceremonial was adopted by the papacy. At the Lateran there was a blend of the trappings and symbolism from the eastern court with forms taken over earlier from the Roman senate and magistracy. Music played an important role, and organs – the first in the West – were imported from Constantinople to enhance it. The papal functionaries were strictly graded; an elaborate series of antechambers led to the papal throneroom; the Pope himself was greeted with a profound *proskynesis* at the foot of his throne; and in the late seventh century we first hear of a tall, white papal headpiece, called the *phrygium* or *camelaucon*, which later evolved into the tiara; it was said to have been presented to Sylvester by Constantine in lieu of a temporal crown, which would have obscured his tonsure. Liturgical manuals which have survived, such as the *Ordo Romanus*, describing the formal stations when the Pope celebrated mass at a particular Roman church on a particular day, present us with a fully articulated ceremonial, carefully executed, centering on the glorification of the papal person, in accordance with Byzantine court practice, rather than on the mass itself. As the split with Byzantium widened, the papacy buttressed its claims to the independent acquisition of power by stressing its divine connections. From 727 Byzantium itself was split by the issue of iconoclasm, which became the official policy of Constantinople. Pope Gregory II condemned iconoclasm, and in 729 the political links between Rome and the empire were effectively severed; under John VII, frescoes appeared in the church of Santa Maria Antica showing the pope receiving the symbols of the papacy not from the emperor, but from the Blessed Virgin herself, robed and crowned as an empress.

Yet while the papacy might defy Byzantium, which seemed increasingly distant and feeble, and assume the trappings of sovereignty itself, it lacked the physical means to act like a sovereign power. It needed protection, and from the early eighth century it looked increasingly to the emergent power north of the Alps to provide it. The desire of the papacy for close alliance with the chief secular authority in western Europe coincided with a comparable urge, on the part of barbarian kings, to obtain the highest Christian sanction for their authority. Under paganism, these royal lines had claimed descent from mythical gods. Then came Christianization; and when, and if, the line failed, because of a lack of heirs, or defeat in battle, or poverty, the new royal house which succeeded needed the introduction of a religious ceremony as an initiation into the powers of kingship. Sacramental grace was poured into the new king as a substitute for the royal blood he lacked.

Some primitive form of Christian service to mark the accession of kings no doubt developed in the West as early as the sixth century; and it is possible that a king, in Spain, received a Christian coronation anointing as early as 672. But in the eighth century events transformed the situation. By the 740s, the Merovingian kings of the Franks had lost their power in all but name. They had parted with their estates and thus could no longer afford to reward followers with land. Effective power was in the hands of the hereditary Mayors of the Palace. The head of the house, Pepin, asked the Pope's opinion whether a king who could not effectively discharge his duties was in truth a king at all. The Pope replied, with abundant biblical quotations, that a king must rule in order to reign. Immediately this reply was received, Pepin and the court ecclesiastics acted. The last of the Merovingians, and his son, had their long kingly locks cut off, were tonsured, and imprisoned in a monastery. Pepin was anointed as king, in 751, by Archbishop Boniface, as the Pope's special envoy with *plenitudo potestatis*; and three years later the Pope himself travelled north to repeat the ceremony. It is not absolutely clear how those concerned saw the function of the anointing. It may be that it served to absolve Pepin from the vow of fidelity to the fallen monarch. What is certain, however, is that king and Pope both regarded Christian sacramental intervention as in some way ending the magic of the old line and transferring it to the new.

The Pope had now become a king-maker. The rapid expansion of the Frankish dominions in the second half of the eighth century, and the development of papal theory based on the forged *Donation of Constantine*, suggested that the Pope could now assume the role of emperor-maker. Perhaps 'maker' is too strong a word. The Pope was more a sacramental functionary than a determining agent. With the eclipse of Byzantine power in Italy, the papacy had emerged, under Paul I, as the recognized residual legatee of imperial authority in the centre, a position it was to occupy until 1870. But the papacy itself was a prey to violent local faction. When Paul died in 768, a local duke, Toto of Nepi, seized the Lateran and carried out a coup in conjunction with his three brothers, one of whom, Constantine, was proclaimed Pope. The *primicerius*, Christopher, who resisted the coup, was blinded and mutilated in the square in front of the Lateran, dying a few days later of his injuries. Under threats from Duke Toto, Bishop George of

Palestrina, the vice-chamberlain, reluctantly invested Christopher, a layman, with clerical orders. But two rival popes were made in quick succession, and the coup collapsed in a welter of blood and barbarity. One of the brothers was blinded, and their chief clerical supporter blinded and his tongue slit in addition; Constantine was dragged from his palace, placed side-saddle on a horse with weights attached to his feet, locked up in a monastery, had his eyes put out, and was flung, prostrated, at the feet of one of his rival popes, Stephen iii, who told him that all his ordinations were invalid. As a result, a decree was published declaring that 'under sanction of anathema no layman or person of any other status shall presume to attend a papal election in arms; but the election shall be in the hands of the known priests and leaders of the church and of all the clergy'. The object was to remove the papacy from local politics. In fact the papacy was already drifting, like all else in the West, into the orbit of the Carolingian State. Charlemagne himself came to Rome, for the first time, in 774. Under his powerful shadow, the Pope, Hadrian i, was able to give the city, for the first time under the papacy, a settled internal government. During his pontificate of twenty-three years, the papal estates were reorganized, and dignity and decorum restored to the office. He became a personal friend not only of Alcuin, Charlemagne's chief adviser, but of the king himself; so that when Hadrian died in 795, Charles 'wept as if he had lost a deeply-loved son or brother'. But Hadrian was never more than a superior bishop, in Charlemagne's eyes, to be treated as a state ecclesiastical functionary. And when the papacy again got into difficulties, in 799, when Leo iii was kidnapped, and barely escaped blinding, it was natural for Charlemagne to intervene and sit in judgment. So we come back to the famous and ambiguous coronation of Christmas Day, 800, with which we began this part of the book. It was the logical culmination of a number of tendencies – the growth of Frankish power in the West, the elimination of Byzantium, the ecclesiastical ascendancy of Rome and its claims to be the residual legatee of the empire in the West; and last but not least the development of sacramental kingship.

The ambiguity, however, lay in the Pope's role, as Charlemagne instantly recognized, when the nature of the ceremony caught him by surprise. Was the Pope donating him the empire, or merely acknowledging his *de facto* possession of it by imposing the sacramental seal and thus making it *de jure*? Or to put it another way, did Charlemagne by receiving the crown from the Pope's hands in some way acknowledge papal superiority to his own imperial status? Leo iii had decorated the Lateran with a huge wall-painting of Christ, flanked on one side by Constantine and Sylvester, and on the other by Charlemagne and Leo. This evaded the issue. In the eighth century, theory tended to reflect the fact that the Pope was in need of Frankish protection, and therefore inferior. Royal ecclesiastics drew a distinction between the eastern emperor, who had always been crowned by the Church since 457, but was not anointed, and the western king, who was. The western Church had taken the anointing straight from the Old Testament; when Samuel performed the anointing, 'the spirit of the Lord came upon David'. Thus the king became *Christus domini*, the Lord's Anointed. He was supreme on earth. Charlemagne was told in 755, by one of his bishops: 'Always remember, my king, that you are the deputy of God, your king. You are set to guard and rule all his members, and you must render an account on the Day of Judgment. The bishop is in a secondary place, being simply the Vicar of Christ.' Writing to Charlemagne in 799, Alcuin put it another way:

'There have so far been three positions in the world of the highest rank: the Pope, who rules the see of St Peter, the prince of the apostles, as his vicar . . . the imperial dignity and secular power of the second Rome [Byzantium] . . . and the royal dignity, in which the dispensation of our Lord Jesus Christ has placed you as the ruler of the Christian people, in power more excellent than the other two, in wisdom more distinguished, in the dignity of your rule more sublime. On you alone depends the whole safety of the churches of Christ.'

Obviously, when the coronation of 800 amalgamated the second and third roles, Charlemagne's authority was confirmed and enhanced: his ruling duties embraced the entire Christian people. Alcuin saw Charlemagne as *sacerdos* as well as *rex* – like Melchisadech. He was head of the Church as well as the State. He told him: 'You endeavour to purge and protect the churches of Christ from the doctrines of false brethren within, as much as from destruction by pagans without. The divine power has armed your majesty with these two swords in the right hand and in the left hand.' Again, such a Melchisadech-figure naturally appointed bishops and other Church dignitaries – the theory was elaborated to protect the otherwise defenceless Church against the lay nobility. The point was underlined, for instance, by Thietmar, Bishop of Merseburg early in the eleventh century: 'Our kings and emperors, vicars of the supreme ruler in this our pilgrimage, alone arrange the appointment of bishops, and it is right that they should have authority before other men over their pastors; for it would be wrong if those pastors whom Christ made princes after his own likeness should be under the dominion of any except those who are set above other men by the glory of benediction and coronation.' The anointed king-emperor was thus raised above any other type of secular ruler; and the theory was completed by a description of the complementary roles of priest and king. 'Both priest and king in their office,' as a late eleventh-century Anglo-Norman writer put it, 'bear the image of Christ and God; the priest of the inferior office and nature, namely the human; the king of the superior, the divine.'

With the coronation of Charlemagne, therefore, the Christian take-over of human society in the West became, in theory at least, complete. Both the papacy and the strong-minded ecclesiastical element at the Carolingian court saw the new power-structure they had brought into existence not only as a restoration of the Roman empire in all its glory, but as a reconstruction from within of society in all its aspects, to produce a model of the Christian kingdom on earth. Charlemagne was to realize the Augustinian vision. He supplied much of the drive himself. He was a very intelligent, and in many ways clear-minded man. He grasped the intimate connection between effective government, culture and Christianity. But of the three, the last undoubtedly had priority in his mind. Charlemagne was, above all, a religious man. He fully accepted the Augustinian mission the Church placed on his shoulders. Einhard shows his efforts to educate himself, to improve his knowledge and practice of the Christian life: '. . . he tried to write, and usually placed tablets and sheets of parchment under his pillows so that at odd moments when he was resting he could practise tracing letters. But he took up writing too late, and the results were not very good . . . He gave much attention to correct reading and psalmody; for he was an expert, although he never read in public, and sang only in unison or to himself.' His aim, especially in the last decades of his life, was enormously to expand the literate manpower of his empire, to create a clergy capable not only of evangelizing the new Christians he had brought under his rule, but of deepening the knowledge of Christianity everywhere. He accepted Alcuin's definition of the king as a kind of lightning-conductor between heaven and earth: 'The goodness of the king is the prosperity of his nation, the victory of his army, the calmness of the atmosphere, the fertility of the earth, the blessing of sons, the health of the people.' Bishops, abbots, priests and monks were the king's chief agents. Royal officials were selected from among the higher clergy, and Charlemagne and his successors expanded and developed the use of Church councils as legislative and executive organs. Almost everything came under their purview. Thus a council at Frankfurt in 794, and another at Arles in 813, dealt with weights and measures, and other commercial matters. The council of Paris, in 829, attacked the practice of lords forcing their dependents to sell corn and wine at fixed prices, and enacted a good deal of similar legislation to protect the weak against the strong. Aachen, in 816, decreed the erection of houses for destitute travellers, widows and poor girls, and made provision for isolation hospitals and leper-colonies. Successive councils decreed and enforced the compulsory payment of tithes, so that a financially viable parish system came into being.

Through the Church, the Carolingian age legislated in enormous detail on every aspect of conduct, especially on economic, family and sexual relationships. A huge, determined and continuous effort was made to bring the actual behaviour of individuals into line with Christian teaching. Bishops set up courts, which increasingly covered the whole field of marriage and inheritance. They went on visitations to ensure that the law was obeyed. A great deal of legislation covered the discipline and conduct of clergy, in an attempt to ensure that, at the parish level where it really mattered, the right teaching was given and enforced. For the first time we hear of the sermon as a regulatory instrument. It was, of course, a form of theocracy. Clerical supervision of morals, which was to remain legally binding in some countries until well into the nineteenth century, was first firmly established at this time.

The system was grossly unsatisfactory in many ways. From this period we must date the extraordinary muddle of Christian marriage laws, which in some ways still plague us to this day. The Carolingian State was also timid over slavery. None of its legislation impugned or attacked the status of slavery or even questioned whether this condition was compatible with Christian principles. It merely dealt with the treatment of slaves, their manumission and their marriage – and on the last point it backed the owner, since the Council of Châlons, 813, decreed that marriages of slaves owned by different masters were invalid, unless the owners agreed. There were, too, hideous blemishes on this Christian society. Legislation codified a good many earlier Spanish and Roman anti-Jewish decrees, which, among other things, prohibited Jews from holding public offices or owning Christian slaves, obliged them to keep to their homes on Christian feasts, and punished with excommunication any Christian who ate a meal with a Jewish family; marriage between Christians and Jews was dismissed as fornication. The Christian society which the Carolingians and other contemporary Christian rulers tried to shape was in many ways incorrigibly crude; its racial, if not its pagan, origins could not be erased. Despite the charisma of things Roman, in northern Christendom at least, the Church was Germanized, rather than society Romanized. The law was Germanic rather than Roman; Church organization, in the dioceses, tended to correspond to the German folk-system; where kingdoms were feudalized, the Church was feudalized too. In England, the king addressed his archbishops, bishops and abbots as he did his earls and thegns; the prelates were his servants, in effect, and their benefices and estates in his gift and control, as well as under his protection – it was significant, for instance, that he could grant the rank of bishop without the office or benefice. If society was a theocracy in one sense, it was also a royal tyranny in another.

It was a very harsh age, and in some ways society had to set its sights low. We have an insight into the Church's view of secular sanctity in a little life by Odo, second Abbot of Cluny, of St Gerald of Aurillac, who died at the end of the first decade of the tenth century. Gerald was a count, a major landowner and a soldier; he was prevented from renouncing secular life by public opinion, backed by the Church itself. It is not exactly clear why he was generally regarded as a saint. Odo himself felt this difficulty. He was critical of those who 'extol him indiscreetly, saying that Gerald was powerful and rich, yet lived well, and is certainly a saint'. Yet he admits he cannot find much evidence of miracles or successful prophecies. He goes on, rather lamely the modern reader may think: 'There is much evidence for the wonderful things which Gerald did. For it is well known that he preserved those things which were given him by his parents and by kings . . . that he increased his property without injuring anyone . . . that he was exalted in power but nevertheless remained poor in spirit.' Gerald, at least as Odo presents him, was a conservative figure, somewhat harsh and severe in his views. He was furious when he discovered that people were using the water in which he washed to effect cures: 'he said that if a serf did it he should be maimed, and if a free man, he should be reduced to servitude . . . people took his threats of mutilation seriously, knowing that he would not yield in the matter of punishment.' So far as one can gather, Gerald did nothing more than treat his dependents justly, by the very imperfect standards of the times; that, in the tenth century, was sufficiently rare to promote a reputation for sanctity. It is a chilling little tale.

Of course, the expectations of Dark Age man were not high. The Carolingian age itself was a comparatively brief episode of order between repeated breakdowns in society. The profound pessimism which Christians drew from Augustine's writings itself seemed to mirror the uncertainties of life as they knew it. There grew up at this time a strong sense of the pointlessness of earthly life, which persisted long after horizons had widened – indeed, until the Renaissance. We find it particularly in endowment charters and documents justifying gifts of property to the church. In 1126, for instance, Stephen, Count of Boulogne, made over lands to Furness Abbey, 'seeing that the bonds of this our age are breaking and falling daily into decay, seeing, again, how all the transitory pomp of this world, with the flowers and rosy chaplets and palms of flourishing kings, emperors, dukes and all rich men do wither from day to day; how, again, death casts them all into one mingled mass and hurries them swiftly to the grave . . .' And so forth. Otto, Bishop of Bamberg, asked why he founded monasteries when there were already so many, replied: 'This whole world is a place of exile; and so long as we live in this life we are pilgrims of the Lord. Therefore we need spiritual stables and inns, and such resting-places as monasteries afford to pilgrims. Moreover, the end of all things is at hand, and the whole world is seated in wickedness; wherefore it is good to multiply monasteries for the sake of those who would flee from the world and save their souls.'

Despite these limitations, however, the attempt to create a totally Christian society was neither ignoble nor wholly unsuccessful. There is something enormously impressive, almost heroic, about the work of such men as Charlemagne and Alfred. The Christian theory of kingship had allotted them a giant's role: they did their best to rise to it. Augustinian theory saw Christian mankind and its institutions as a whole, fully integrated, almost organic. During this period a conscious effort was made to realize the conception, and genuine progress was made. Never before or since has any human society come closer to operating as a unity, wholly committed to a perfectionist programme of conduct. Never again was Christianity to attempt so comprehensively to realize itself as a human institution, as well as a divine one. And of course the experiment had profound and lasting consequences. It laid the foundations for the complementary concepts of Christendom and Europe. It projected, in broad outline, the directions which European institutions and culture would take. And it determined in embryo many of the aspects of the world we live in now. We are right to regard the total Christianity of the Carolingian age as one of the great formative phases of human history.

Yet as an ideal it contained the elements of its own destruction. It led, irresistibly, to the dissolution of the ancient Christian inheritance of the fourth century. For the vertical unity of the Carolingian society, however desirable, was incompatible with the geographical unity of the Christian Church. Both the Carolingian empire, and the Ottonian Germanic empire which succeeded it in the tenth century, were totally at enmity with the theory of the Byzantine State and its Church. Byzantine rulers might be brought, *in extremis*, to recognize western emperors as a matter of practical politics; but full-hearted recognition in the deepest sense was impossible, for to do so would have wrecked the Byzantine theory of government, indeed its basic cosmology. Byzantium saw itself as coterminous not only with Christianity but with civilization – with moral and cultural legitimacy in effect. The *Book of Ceremonies* used at the imperial court, which was a manual of political theory built on etiquette, presupposed the existence of a hierarchy of subordinate states revolving in obedient concord round the throne of the supreme autocrat in Constantinople; his authority, in its rhythm and order, reproduced the harmonious movement of the universe laid down by the Creator. The Byzantines termed this the *oikoumene*. The emperor was God's vice-regent on earth, and the empire the prefiguration of the heavenly kingdom. The imperial, supra-national community was the God-appointed custodian of the one Orthodox faith, until the last days and the coming of anti-Christ, which would precede the *parousia*. Byzantine State philosophy was a neat compound of Rome, Hellenism and Christianity. It preempted the empire of Christmas Day 800 because it specifically assumed that the Byzantines had inherited everything that mattered in Rome even if, for the moment, they did not possess the city: they called themselves *Rhomaioi*, and claimed exclusively the inheritance of the Roman imperial tradition. Thus a reconciliatory theory based on the idea of two empires would not wash with them. It might make logical or geographical sense for the Popes to speak of 'Romans' and 'Greeks', but to the Byzantines this was to deny both faith and history. Liutprand of Cremona says that that in 968 when papal legates came to Constantinople with a letter addressed to 'the Emperor of the Greeks', in which the Pope referred to Otto I as 'the august emperor of the Romans', the Byzantines were outraged: 'The audacity of it, to call the universal emperor of the Romans, the one and only Nicephorus, the great, the august, "Emperor of the Greeks", and to style a poor, barbaric creature "Emperor of the Romans"! O sky! O earth! O sea! What shall we do with these scoundrels and criminals?'

The rise of the Franks had, moreover, been accompanied by a steady erosion of Byzantine military power, and therefore political and ecclesiastical influence, in the whole Mediterranean era. In the seventh century, the doctrinal errors which had led to the Monophysite schism finally came home to roost: the whole enormous area where Monophysite belief was dominant succumbed with great speed to the new Islamic version, which not only engulfed these territories but swept along the coast of North Africa and into Spain. By 700, Christianity had lost more than half its territory, including the oldest patriarchal churches, Alexandria, Antioch and Jerusalem. There was virtually no contact or intercommunion across the new Islamic line: when the first crusaders made contact with Antioch Christians at the end of the eleventh century, they did not even know the succession of the Popes after 681. The loss of the old patriarchates in some ways brought Constantinople and Rome closer together. Byzantium still controlled part of Italy, from Ravenna, and the emperor's writ ran as far as Marseilles. Rome was to a considerable extent under eastern influence: between 654 and 752 only five out of seventeen popes were of Roman origin – three were Greek, five Syrian, three from Greek-speaking Sicily, and one from somewhere in Italy. The Greek emperor visited Rome as its lawful ruler in 663; in 680, papal legates at a council in Constantinople agreed in condemning the teachings of four patriarchs and one pope; in 710 the Pope himself paid an amicable visit to Constantinople. But this was the limit of the ecumenical mood. Outside Rome, very few western Christians spoke Greek; there was deep-rooted prejudice against Greek liturgical customs. Thus when, in 668, the Pope made the Greek Theodore of Tarsus Archbishop of Canterbury, he sent an African, Hadrian, with him, to ensure that Theodore 'introduced no Greek customs contrary to the true faith into England'. The big changes came in the first half of the eighth century. Byzantine power was in rapid retreat from Italy and all the western Mediterranean theatre – the Moslems pressing north, the Lombards south. The Popes stopped paying imperial taxes, flatly declined to follow Constantinople on the iconoclasm issue, and, from the 750s, turned north to the Frankish house of Pepin for protection. Pope Zacharias, who died in 752, was the last of the Greek Popes.

Moreover, the creation of the Frankish connection, while ensuring the Pope's security against the Lombards, local despots, and indeed Byzantium, robbed Rome of much of its freedom of action. The determined and clear-minded ecclesiastics who advised Charlemagne were bent on imposing unity on the West; it was part of their dream of a total Christian society. The king, for his part, saw the Church, and the Roman connection, as an instrument of State power and a cohesive force in an empire which was expanding rapidly. Universal agreement on ritual and doctrine was therefore essential. Right at the beginning of Charlemagne's reign, in 769, Roman-style baptism, prayers and mass received the force of law; Roman practice was insisted on in regard to the manner of chanting, the administration of sacraments, and dress – down to the wearing of sandals. And, once Roman forms were adopted in Carolingian territories, the Popes lost the right to change them. A council was held at Nicea in 787 to heal the iconoclastic split; the Pope sent legates, who agreed to the compromise. But there were no representatives from the western Church. Charlemagne denounced the outcome of the council, which he saw as an affront to his dignity, and the status of the western Church. He and his court priests produced the *Libri Carolini*, a violently anti-Greek diatribe, which presented the council findings as 'stupid, arrogant, erroneous, criminal, schismatic and lacking in sense or eloquence . . . one filthy pond of Hell'. Charlemagne's own copy survives: it includes exclamations of his approval ('*mire!*') which he ordered to be noted in the margins. The Franks not only denounced the council – which proved, not surprisingly, the last universal gathering of the Church – but drew attention to an emergent doctrinal difference between Latins and Greeks. This was the insertion, in the creed, of the Augustinian formulation *filioque*, emphasizing the full godhead of Christ by insisting that the Holy Spirit proceeded from the Son as well as the Father. They brought this into the creed, which they now made standard and compulsory at all masses in Frankish territories. The papacy advised strongly against inserting *filioque*, since it knew the formulation could not be accepted in Constantinople. But it was overruled, and in the ninth century began to insist that it was essential to a true and complete statement of doctrine. When, in 1014, Rome finally inserted the creed in its own mass, at the insistence of the German emperor Henry II, *filioque* was included. By this time Rome was convinced that it had introduced the phrase itself and that it was of immemorial antiquity. In 1054, when the final breach with the East came, the papal legates were so ignorant of the true story that they accused the Greeks of having deliberately omitted the *filioque* from their creed centuries before.

In the meantime, however, further conflicts had developed in Europe. The seventh-century Islamic conquests had closed the world south and east of the Mediterranean to both Rome and Constantinople. But both retained the universalist urge; indeed both had begun to look north for converts long before Moslem troops reached the Straits of Gibraltar. The creation of the Frankish empire in the eighth century, penetrating into central Europe for political and military reasons, with a strong proselytizing urge and its own distinctive and hotly defended ecclesiology, brought western missionaries up against Greek ones, who had been pushing north into the Balkans. Thus the ninth century became an age of intense missionary rivalry. The presence of two Christian Churches in the area of central Europe, each seeking to convert kings and nations and so enlarge its sphere of influence, helps to illuminate the obscure subject of why pagan societies chose to become Christian. In general, we possess remarkably little information on this subject. The first Frankish converts seem to have been guided by military considerations, rather like Constantine himself: a Christian army was more likely to win a battle. Another factor was the failure of Germanic pagan societies to produce a satisfying explanation of what happened after death, in contrast to the certitude of salvation which Christianity provided. A famous passage in Bede's *History of the English Church and Nation* suggests how powerfully the

Christian missionaries could rely on this point. But rulers who were contemplating leading their tribe or nation into Christianity had to consult not only their own feelings but take into consideration the likely impact of the new religion on their society in all its aspects. The Christianity brought to the Franks in the early decades of the sixth century, and to the English at the end of it, was a comparatively simple affair; moreover, Gregory the Great, in his instructions to Augustine of Canterbury, had stressed that his teaching should remain flexible and should be married, where possible, to existing customs. By the ninth century, however, the idea of a total Christian society had taken shape: the faith not only had answers, but definitive and compulsory answers, to questions on almost every aspect of human behaviour and arrangements. A pagan society embracing Christianity was accepting a completely new way of life. Moreover, in large parts of central Europe and the Balkans, such societies were offered the choice between two increasingly different brands of Christian practice, each attended by different cultural and geopolitical consequences.

Fortunately, we have a unique glimpse of the dilemma, as it appeared to a barbarian monarch, thanks to the survival of two documents. In the 850s, the emergent state of Bulgaria, which feared both Carolingian and Byzantine imperialism, had seemed set on a pro-Frankish course, and in the early 860s it looked as though its king, Boris I, would accept Christianity from Frankish hands. In 864 a powerful military and naval demonstration by the Byzantines led him to change his mind; and he became an Orthodox Christian in 865. Orthodox clergy moved into his territories in huge numbers, and this rapid introduction of new customs provoked a revolt of the Old Bulgar aristocracy, which Boris put down with some savagery. In consequence, Boris wrote to the Patriarch of Constantinople, Photus, asking for an autonomous Church – that is, a patriarchate equivalent to the five which already existed. Photus's reply, which survives, was long but unsatisfactory; and in 866, Boris made a move to Rome, sending the Pope a letter asking for replies to a hundred and six questions. The Pope, Nicholas I, was delighted, despatched two bishops, and answered all the queries. His reply, which we possess, is one of the most fascinating documents of the entire Dark Ages.

Boris did not raise any theological issues. He was concerned with behaviour, not belief. His questions reflect the tensions created in Bulgarian society by the reception of Christianity, and in particular by the rigorous ritualism of the Orthodox Greeks. Were the Byzantines right to forbid the Bulgars to take baths on Wednesdays and Fridays? To take communion without wearing their belts? To eat the meat of animals killed by eunuchs? Was it true that no layman could conduct public prayers for rain, or make a sign of the cross over a table before a meal? And that lay-folk must stand in church with arms folded over their breast? ('No, no, no,' said the Pope.) Were the Greek clergy right to refuse to accept the repentance of some of the pagan rebels? ('Of course not,' said the Pope.) On the question of Byzantine ecclesiastical claims, the Pope denied that Constantinople was the second in rank of the patriarchates; it was not, he said, an apostolic foundation at all, its importance being purely political. Their claim that only their empire could produce holy chrism was dismissed with contempt. On the other hand, the Pope declined Boris's request to make Bulgaria a patriarchate; he must be content with an archbishop for the time being.

Boris's queries bring us closer to the realities of the Christian impact on Dark Age pagan society, especially on daily life, than any other document that has survived. How many times in the year should one fast? When should one breakfast on non-fasting days? Is sex permissible on Sundays? Should one take communion every day in Lent? What animals and birds might a Christian eat? Should women cover their heads in church? Can you work on Sundays and feastdays? What should one do when a military campaign coincides with Lent? Or when news of an enemy attack interrupts prayers? How can soldiers on campaign perform their religious duties? Was Christian charity compatible with punishing murderers, thieves and adulterers? Could torture be used? Might criminals claim asylum in church? How should one treat disobedience or cowardice in the army? What about frontier guards who let fugitives escape – was there an alternative to the death sentence? What should an officer do about a soldier whose weapons and horse did not pass muster before battle? Did criminal law contradict Christian ethics? (The Pope took the general line of tempering justice with mercy.) How should one treat inveterate worshippers of idols? Should they be forced to accept Christianity? (The Pope advised gentle persuasion.) How should one conclude an alliance with a friendly nation? What happens if a Christian State breaks a solemn treaty? Could a Christian country make a treaty with a pagan one? (The Pope was a little hesistant: international treaties depended on the customs of the country concerned; in case of difficulty, ask the Church's advice; alliance with a pagan country was permissible, provided attempts were made to convert it.)

Boris also wanted to know what Nicholas thought of Bulgarian customs the Greeks had banned. Was it all right to use a horse's tail as a banner; to seek auguries, cast spells, have ceremonial songs and dances before battle, and take oaths upon a sword? ('Alas, no,' said the Pope.) Could miraculous stones cure, or neck-amulets protect against sickness? (Certainly not.) Was the cult of ancestors permissible? (No: Bulgars must not pray for dead parents if they had died as pagans.) Among customs approved by Nicholas were the eating of birds and animals slain without shedding blood; the practice of the ruler eating alone, at a raised table (the Pope thought this bad manners rather than sinful), and various dress-customs: Nicholas saw no objection to wearing trousers.

The struggle for the soul of Bulgaria envenomed relations between Rome and Constantinople. First the Greek, then, in turn, Latin clergy were expelled. Patriarch Photius called the Latin missionaries 'impious and execrable men from the darkness of the West'; they were like thunderbolts, violent hailstones, or wild boars trampling up the Lord's vineyard. Among other false practices they were trying to impose on the hapless Bulgarians were fasting on

Sundays, a shorter Lent, a celibate clergy, and the weird theory that only bishops could confirm! This was unacceptable: 'Even the smallest neglect of tradition causes complete contempt for dogma.' And, of course, teaching of *filoque* was downright heresy. The two sides met in council, to no avail. The dispute became jurisdictional, based on provincial frontiers which had once been part of the Roman system of government, and now had no meaning. The papacy accused the Greeks of resorting to large-scale bribery among the Bulgarians. This may well have been true. To the Bulgars, Byzantium seemed much richer and more powerful than Rome; it was also nearer. These factors in combination determined the Bulgarian allegiance, and with it went, in time, virtually the whole of the Slav world.

Nevertheless, the Orthodox penetration of south-east and eastern Europe was not merely a matter of proximity. On one issue, the use of the vernacular for Christian services and sacred writings, the Greeks were far more flexible than the Latins. In central Europe and the northern Balkans, Latin missionaries were in the field before the Greeks, and had early recognized the importance of being able to operate in the vulgar Slav tongue. During the first half of the ninth century, Frankish priests translated a few Christian texts from Latin into Slavonic, and transcribed them into Latin characters (the Slavs had no alphabet). These included formularies for baptism and confession, the creed and the Lord's prayer. Missionaries, in fact, were keen on using the vernacular – as they were to be in a wider world in the sixteenth and seventeenth centuries. The papacy was, at first, ambivalent. Hadrian II issued a bull in 867–8 authorizing the use of the Slavonic liturgy. John VIII imposed a temporary ban on Slavonic in 880, but agreed, in a letter to the Moravians: 'It is certainly not against faith and doctrine to sing the mass in the Slavonic language, or to read the Holy Gospel or the Divine Lessons in the New and Old Testaments well translated and interpreted, or to chant the other offices of the hours, for he who made the three principal languages, Hebrew, Greek and Latin, also created all the others for his own praise and glory.' Nevertheless, this was in fact the last papal pronouncement in favour of the vernacular. The Frankish governments, in their almost ideological quest for unity and standardization, were strong Latinists; they argued passionately that, while Hebrew and Greek might be permissible for divine service in the East, Latin alone was the liturgical and scriptural language of the West. This argument, urged by Rome's political masters, also appealed strongly to the authoritarian element which was always present in papal thinking, and after John VIII all the Popes banned the use of local tongues. Thus the western Church locked itself into the world of Latin, from which it was only to emerge in the twentieth century. Once again, as with *filioque*, it was the Frankish ideologues, rather than the papacy itself, who made compromise impossible.

The same school of thought existed on the Byzantine side. The Greeks were, in a cultural sense, far more arrogant than the Latins. Probably a majority of them strongly opposed the vernacular liturgy and scripture. Writers like Anna

Comnena and Archbishop Theophylact of Ochrid felt it necessary to apologize to their readers for mentioning even proper names of 'barbarian' origin. Latin itself was termed (by the liberal Emperor Michael III) 'a barbarian and Scythian tongue'. In the thirteenth century, the Metropolitan of Athens, Michael Choniates, said Latins would take longer to appreciate 'the harmony and grace of the Greek language than asses to enjoy the lyre, or dung-beetles to savour perfume'. The existence of polemical literature indicates that, at this time and long afterwards, the issue was controversial, with conservatives sticking to the 'three languages' theory, and denouncing a Slavonic liturgy as heretical.

The government, however, was much more inclined to be pragmatic. And it could quote St Paul: 'For if the trumpet give an uncertain sound, who shall prepare himself for the battle? So likewise ye, except ye utter by the tongue words easy to be understood, how shall it be known what is spoken, for ye shall speak into the air? . . . For if I pray in an unknown tongue my spirit prayeth but my understanding is unfruitful . . .' And so on. The problem, indeed, had arisen before, in the case of the Goths; and St John Chrysostom, the most revered of the eastern patriarchs, had given a notably liberal ruling, and rejoiced that the Goths chanted the litanies in their own language: 'The teaching of fishermen and tentmakers shines in the language of barbarians more brightly than the sun.'

Moreover, the Byzantine government had a tradition of multilingual diplomacy, and employed a large number of high-born linguists in its civil service. In the 860s, Michael III selected for its Slav mission two brothers, Methodius, a provincial governor, and Constantine (who called himself Cyril after he became a monk), a state philosophy teacher. They were born in Thessalonica, the sons of a staff-officer, and had previously been on diplomatic assignments. When Michael decided to switch them to missionary work, in 862, he said to them: 'You are both natives of Thessalonica, and all Thessalonicans speak pure Slav.' He admitted that previous attempts to create a viable Slavonic alphabet had failed, for a variety of technical reasons. Constantine-Cyril, who was an accomplished linguist and bibliophile, appears to have invented a form of written Slav in less than a year, so that when the brothers left on mission in 863 they were able to take with them selections from the gospels already translated; and in due course Constantine translated into Slavonic, according to his contemporary biographer, 'the whole ecclesiastical office, matins, the hours, vespers, compline and the mass'. He appears to have adapted the alphabet from his local dialect of southern Macedonia, then intelligible much further north.

The oldest Slavonic manuscripts are in two scripts: what are termed Glagolitic and Cyrillic. Scholars now agree that it was Glagolitic that Constantine invented; Cyrillic, called after him, was developed later, by Methodius's disciples, probably in Bulgaria, in the attempt to adapt Greek uncial writing of the ninth century to the phonetic peculiarities of Slavonic speech. Glagolitic is more complicated, and may have been developed from Greek minuscule script, plus adaptations from Semitic and perhaps Coptic. It was a highly distinct and original creation, entitling Constantine to rank among the great philologists. Cyrillic, except for half a dozen letters, is little more than an adaptation of the Greek alphabet; it thus had the merit of simplicity, and close connection with the script possessing the most prestige and widest range. Even today, the church-books of the Orthodox Slavs, Bulgarians, Serbs and Russians are printed in a slightly simplified form of Cyrillic, and of course their modern alphabets are based on it. (The Rumanians, too, used it until the late seventeenth century.) At the same time, the translations made by the brothers laid the foundations of a new literary language, known to modern scholars as Old Church Slavonic. After Greek and Latin, it became the third international language of Europe, the common literary idiom of Russians, Bulgarians, Serbs and Rumanians.

Byzantium triumphed over Rome in most of the Slav world because it showed itself willing to compromise over the cultural issue. But the point must be made again: the source of western intolerance was Frankish, rather than papal, at least in origin. In the 860s both Pope Nicholas I and his successor Hadrian II were anxious to give backing to the mission of Constantine and Methodius, to remove it from Byzantine tutelage, and place it under Roman ecclesiastical jurisdiction. The brothers were invited to Rome; there, Constantine-Cyril died (he is buried in San Clemente) but Methodius was issued with a bull (868) authorizing the use of the Slavonic liturgy, and given authority, in the Pope's name, over a huge area of central Europe. Papal policy was to use the mission to establish control of central Europe at the expense both of the Franks and the Greeks. The strategy was deliberately foiled by the Frankish clergy; in 870 they had Methodius arrested, condemned by a synod for Greek-style 'irregularities', and imprisoned. It took the Pope more than three years to secure his release. The mission was finally driven back into the arms of Byzantium by the revival, by Frankish clergy, of the *filioque* issue. For Methodius as, on the other side, for the Franks, this was the heretical breaking-point, and he had no alternative but to relinquish his Rome connection and identify himself with the Greek Church. The Franks settled the matter by forcing the papacy to renounce the idea of a Slavonic liturgy.

The truth is that there was a price to be paid for the Frankish experiment in creating a Christian social structure and culture. It gave to the western Church a wonderful sense of unity and coherence; it gave to western society great dynamism, which lies at the source of the European impact on the world. But it involved a degree of doctrinal, liturgical and, at bottom, cultural and racial intolerance, which made an ecumenical Church impossible. Unity in depth was bought at the expense of unity in breadth. The Christian penetration of every aspect of life in the West meant a highly organized, disciplined and particularist ecclesiastical structure, which could not afford to compromise with eastern deviations. Moreover, the imperiousness of the Carolingian

Church gradually coloured the attitudes of the papacy and governed the Roman posture long after the Carolingian empire itself had disappeared. In the tenth and eleventh centuries, Rome used arguments in its confrontations with Constantinople which had been initiated by the Frankish court in the eighth and ninth centuries, and which it had then resisted or sought to tone down.

It is useful, at this stage, to trace the dispute to its bitter end. Perhaps a final breach was inevitable once the Popes had committed themselves to the creation of an empire in the West. Either the western empire had to absorb the eastern, or vice versa; certainly, two Christian empires, essentially rivals to the same legacy, meant, if both survived, two brands of Christianity. Thus the coronation of 800, which made the total Christian society of the West conceivable, was also fatal to the unity of Christendom, a decisive milestone on the road to schism. In 1054, papal legates went to Constantinople for talks, the object being joint action against a common enemy, the Normans of southern Italy. The episode merely served to bring all the various strands of conflict together into one envenomed mass, from the Greek use of leavened bread for communion to their practice of fasting on Saturdays. Paradoxically, the reopening of the Mediterranean to Christian traffic, which was a feature of the mid eleventh century, served to sharpen the antagonism · it brought East and West into closer contact, and so made both aware of the innumerable differences which had grown up in the previous three centuries. One difference became only too apparent in 1054: the papacy, from being conciliatory, was now wholly insistent on discipline, obedience and uniformity.

The 1054 meeting also revealed a shift in papal tactics, which then remained constant for the next 400 years. By the mid eleventh century, the papacy was becoming increasingly aware of the dangers presented by the existence of a western empire. It wished to be on good terms with the Greek empire, as a potential counterpoise. Hence in 1054, the papacy, in effect, put forward a package proposal: papal support for the Greek empire, in return for the submission of the Greek Church to the Pope. The Pope wrote in warm terms to the emperor, calling him *serenissimus* (whereas the western emperor, Henry III was merely *carissimus*); the letter he addressed to the patriarch, by contrast, was severe and punitive: Rome was the mother, and her spouse was God; Constantinople was a naughty and corrupt daughter; any Church which dissented from Rome was a 'confabulation of heretics, a conventical of schismatics, and a synagogue of Satan'. This dual approach did no good. Nevertheless, it remained essentially Rome's line until the Turkish conquest of the mid fifteenth century made the dispute obsolete. For Rome it was the only possible tactic. A compromise with the patriarch was ruled out. For one thing, the Greeks did not think the barbarous Latins capable of serious theological discussion. This obstacle could have been overcome: in the fourteenth century, Greek intellectuals translated the classics of medieval Latin theology, and thereafter eastern churchmen were prepared to debate on equal terms.

But this was never conceded by the papacy. The Latins, with their authoritarian tradition, did not want discussion: the Popes had already pronounced. They thought that to admit any issues were still open was to abandon their case. As Pascal II wrote to the Emperor Alexius in 1112: 'The cause of diversity of faith and custom between the Greeks and Latins cannot be removed unless the members are united under one head. How can questions be discussed between antagonistic bodies when one refuses to obey the other?' The other alternative was conquest. In theory, at any rate, Rome might have directed the crusades against Byzantium, and given them the mission of extirpating heresy and schism, rather than liberating Jerusalem. But by the eleventh century, when such a proposal might have been militarily possible, Rome was wary of adding to the power of any of the sources of secular authority in the West. Who would have been the beneficiary of an eastern conquest? The Hohenstaufen, the Angevins or the Capets. Rome feared them all.

Hence the Popes clung to their policy of seeking to split the emperor from the patriarch. It never had any real hope of success. However anxious the eastern emperor might be to get western help and finance in return for ecclesiastical submission, he could not deliver his Church. In his empire there was a large and well-informed segment of lay theological opinion which was stronger than him and the patriarch put together, and totally opposed to yielding to Rome. In 1274, at the Council of Lyons, the Emperor Michael Paleologos, *in extremis*, submitted to Gregory X and accepted *filioque*. The Pope's vicar in Sicily, Charles of Anjou, who was hoping to lead an attack on Constantinople, was so furious at the news that he bit the top off his sceptre. But the reaction from the Byzantine clergy and people was far more violent. The emperor savagely tried to enforce compliance with his surrender. The public orator was flogged and exiled. One leading theologian was ordered to be scourged daily by his own brother until he submitted. Four of the emperor's relatives were imprisoned and blinded; another died in prison; monks had their tongues torn out. Even today the monks of Mount Athos maintain (falsely, as it happens) that Michael visited the place, plundered three recalcitrant monasteries and massacred their monks, burying many of them alive. All was in vain; when Michael died he was buried as a heretic in unconsecrated ground, and orthodoxy was restored in 1283, when *filioque* was again repudiated. Nevertheless, the papacy still persisted in its policy. The Pope got another submission from the eastern emperor at Florence, in 1439. Once more the Greeks agreed to include the wretched word, and admit that 'Filioque has been lawfully and reasonably added to the Creed.' The submission was finally proclaimed, to an apathetic congregation in St Sophia, in 1452. On this occasion the papal promise of aid against the Turks was as insincere as the Greek acceptance of Rome's doctrinal position. Six months later the city had fallen, and the eastern empire no longer existed.

The great African Church radiating from Carthage was ultimately lost because of fatal divisions over the sacramental powers of bishops. Syria and the East, and much else, were lost because no compromise proved possible, or rather durable, over the definition of the Trinity and the nature of Christ. Byzantium came to grief, and European Christianity remained divided, because East and West could not agree on an institutional means to resolve their comparatively trivial points of difference. Christ had founded a universalist Church which would be all things to all men. But it was also a Church with an intense vision, which bred adamantine certitudes. The more the vision was realized, the stronger the certitudes became, the less likely it would be that universality would be based on unity. The Augustinian idea of an authoritarian, compulsory and total Church was incompatible with the ecumenical spirit. Hence the attempt to give it substance in Carolingian times led inevitably to the split with the East. We shall now see how the Augustinian drive within the western Church proved too powerful for its unifying bonds, and how it smashed the Christian society into fragments.

PART FOUR

The Total Society and its Enemies (1054–1500)

'ANTIQUITY RELATES that laymen show a spirit of hostility towards the clergy,' wrote Pope Boniface VIII in 1296, 'and it is clearly proved by the experience of the present time.' Having uttered this melancholy reflection, in his bull *Clericis laicos*, Boniface went on to make a number of pronouncements calculated to ensure that the warfare continued. Clerics were not to pay taxes; those who did so, and secular officials who collected the money from them, were to be excommunicated. Universities who defended the practice of clerical taxation were to be placed under interdict; and those under sentence of excommunication or interdict were not be absolved, except at the moment of death, without the express authority of the papacy. Four years after this bellicose pronouncement, he issued a further one, *Unam Sanctam*, which attempted to define the claims of his caste. Christianity, he wrote, provides for two swords, the spiritual and the temporal:

'Both are in the power of the church, the spiritual sword and the material. But the latter is to be used for the church, the former by her; the former by the priest, the latter by kings and captains but at the will and by the permission of the priest. The one sword, therefore, should be under the other, and temporal authority subject to spiritual. . . . If, therefore, the earthly power err, it shall be judged by the spiritual power. . . . But if the spiritual power err, it can only be judged by God, not by man. . . . For this authority, though given to a man and exercised by a man, is not human, but rather divine. . . . Furthermore, we declare, state, define and pronounce that it is altogether necessary to salvation for every human creature to be subject to the Roman pontiff.'

One of the great tragedies of human history – and the central tragedy of Christianity – is the break-up of the harmonious world-order which had evolved, in the Dark Ages, on a Christian basis. Men had agreed, or at least had appeared to agree, on an all-enveloping theory of society which not only aligned virtue with law and practice, but allotted to everyone in it precise, Christian-orientated tasks. There need be no arguments or divisions because everyone endorsed the principles on which the system was run. They had to. Membership of the society, and acceptance of its rules, was ensured by baptism, which was compulsory and irrevocable. The unbaptized, that is the Jews, were not members of the society at all; their lives were spared but otherwise they had no rights. Those who, in effect, renounced their baptism by infidelity or heresy, were killed. For the remainder, there was total agreement and total commitment. The points on which men argued were slender, compared to the huge areas of complete acquiescence which embraced almost every aspect of their lives.

Yet these slender points of difference were important, and they tended to enlarge themselves. There were flaws in the theory of society, reflected in its imagery. If society was a body, what made up its directing head? Was it Christ, who thus personally directed both arms, one – the secular rulers – wielding the temporal sword, the other – the Church – handling the spiritual one? But if Christ directed, who was his earthly vicar?

There was no real agreement on this issue. The popes had been claiming to be vicars of St Peter since very early times. Later, they tended to raise this claim, and call themselves vicars of Christ. But kings, too, and *a fortiori* emperors, claimed a divine vicariate derived from their coronation; sometimes it was of God the Father, sometimes of Christ; when it was the former, the Christ-vicariate, being in some way inferior, was relegated to the Church. Now none of this should have mattered in the slightest. Since the vicarial direction, in all cases, was coming from the same source – Heaven – and since, presumably, there was no disagreement between the Father and the Son and St Peter, it should have made no difference who was vicar of whom. The direction would be the same, and all would obey. Alas, experience showed that this did not always happen. So Christian theory had an answer to this point. There could be wicked emperors, kings, popes, bishops. They represented the work of the Devil, who might well contrive, from time to time, to get one of his own elected to such offices. But this would soon become manifest; God would then arrange that they would be detected, judged and deprived. But such a process implied a court. Whose court? Therein lay the difficulty. In the Dark Ages and Middle Ages everyone of any importance had his own court, where he judged subordinates. A man could not really be described as free unless he had his court. Indeed, he could not be fully free unless his court was supreme. As the German emperor Henry III put it, rather crudely, in the mid-eleventh century: 'For those who govern laws are not governed by laws, since the law, as they commonly say, has a nose of wax, and the King has an iron hand, and a long one, and he can bend the law in whatever way it pleases him.' Who had the supreme court – king and emperor, or pope? Who could judge and depose whom? It was the same as asking who was the head of the body: the argument was circular. And since it could not be resolved by argument it was, in practice, determined by the balance of force.

Until the latter part of the eleventh century, the balance lay heavily with the secular arm. Charlemagne had sat in judgment on the Pope, Leo III, and confirmed him in office after trial. In a letter to Leo, which has survived, he treats him, quite unambiguously, as merely the chief of his bishops. And bishops were royal functionaries. They helped to run the government; they sat as judges; they collected taxes; they acted as royal emissaries to distant parts of the domains; they took up station in royal fleets and armies, where they had definite roles to perform; and, perhaps most important of all, they helped the king or emperor to legislate. They were enormously well endowed in land to enable them to discharge these tasks. As such they buttressed the throne; they held lands and castles in trust to ensure the well-being of monarch and commonwealth. Naturally, then, the king, or emperor, appointed them; and he did so at a ceremony which emphasized their dependence on him. Indeed, he controlled and supervised the Church. More than half of the Carolingian legislation deals with church matters, ranging from the shape of bishop's beards to the fate of the bastard children of clergy.

This system persisted long after the Carolingian empire fell into decay, and long after the imperial title, in 963, was vested in the new Salian line from Saxony. The German emperors, like their Frankish predecessors, ran their territories through state bishops, archbishops and abbots, whom they appointed and judged. The system was essentially the same in Spain, England and France. The ruler was, in effect, the head of the Church. The ambiguity appeared to have been resolved in his favour. Of course, he did not actually confer the sacraments. But in every other respect he was pontiff, a priest. That was one of the meanings of his coronation. The kings and bishops we see enthroned in the Beauvais Tapestry, from the late eleventh century, are almost interchangeable. For ceremonial occasions they dressed alike. In 1022, the Emperor Henry II presented the Abbey of Monte Cassino with a gospel codex; one of the illustrations shows him sitting in judgment: he is wearing a tippet, like the popes and the patriarchs – the same garment which Rome despatched to archbishops in the West, as a symbol of their authority.

The order of the royal coronations was strikingly similar to that used for the consecration of a bishop. Both began with a ritual procession of the elect to the church, preceded by relics; there was an identical formal interrogation to ensure the orthodoxy of the bishop/king. There then followed the unction of the head, breast, shoulders, both upper arms and hand (in the case of the king) and of head and arms (in the case of the bishop). Both were then invested with ring and staff, the king getting, in addition, the sword of state, pallium, bracelets and sceptre. Both ceremonies concluded with the kiss of peace and high mass. Vestments and sandals worn were almost exactly the same; and the ring received by the Salian emperors, for instance, is variously described as 'episcopal' or 'pontifical'. The emperor was like a bishop, only he had many more duties; the ceremony was expanded accordingly. A famous and influential eleventh-century sermon, usually attributed to the reformist Peter Damian, describes the regal coronation as the Church's fifth sacrament, the episcopal consecration as the fourth.

The king, then, was an ecclesiastic – the kingship was a clerical office. He might hold others. From Henry II onwards the Salians served as canons in various cathedral churches – Henry II at Bamberg, Magdeberg and Strasburg, Conrad II at Worms, Neuhausen and Eichstatt, Henry III at Cologne, Basel, Freising; and Henry V at Lièges; Henry IV was a canon of Spier and a suffragan of Echternach. These offices were performed by deputies as a rule, but if the emperor were present he did the duties himself. Indeed, the ecclesiastical function of the ruler was not just symbolic but actual, particularly as an ecclesiastical judge. Wipo, chaplain to Conrad II, writes in his biography of his master: 'Although he was ignorant of letters, nevertheless he prudently gave instruction to every cleric, not only lovingly and courteously in public, but also with fitting discipline in secret.' He presided over synods, either by himself or jointly, on one occasion, with the Pope. He punished bishops and bestowed privileges on religious establishments. His son, Henry III, showed himself zealous in reforming the Church and seems to have set no limit to his powers in ecclesiastical matters. As 'head of the Church', he presided in 1046 at Sutri over a synod which deposed two popes, secured the abdication of a third, and elected yet another. Three years later he, and the outstanding reforming pope, Leo IX, presided jointly over the innovatory Council of Mainz and again at the Council of Constance, where he is described as 'ascending the steps of the altar together' with Leo.

Yet within a few decades the harmony which ruled Church and State, based on papal acceptance of the wider and superior status of the monarch, had been completely shattered. It was never restored. The pontifical king, Henry IV, found himself challenged by a regal pontiff, in the shape of Pope Gregory VII. The dispute began in the 1070s when Henry, who had succeeded as a minor, began to redress the erosion of the power which had taken place during his minority, and in particular to assert his full right to appoint bishops in imperial Italy. The Pope hotly denied his power to invest bishops with ring and staff, and the dispute quickly became a confrontation over the whole range of Church and State authority, culminating in the excommunication of Henry, his election of an anti-pope, open warfare, the king's submission at Canossa, and then a long, inconclusive period of attrition.

How did this come about? Why did the papacy abruptly attempt to reverse a situation which had at least the merit of tradition and feasibility? There can be little doubt that Gregory VII was the aggressor, in that Henry IV was merely doing what all his predecessors had done. Henry seems to have been a pious and earnest man – Ebo, the biographer of Otto, Bishop of Bamberg, says that Henry used his psalter so much that it became 'wrinkled and almost unreadable'. But this was irrelevant: or, rather, it could be said that a pious emperor might be storing up trouble for his successors. The efforts of Conrad II, and especially Henry III, to improve standards in the Church, in Rome and elsewhere – their conscientious discharge of their pontifical duties – did a great deal to create a reformed body of clergy which promptly denied Henry IV the right to exercise such duties. The mid-eleventh century was a springtime for Europe. The worst phase of the Viking raids from the north, and the Saracens from the south, was over; western Christendom was no longer a sandwich about to be devoured between barbarous and infidel fangs, but an expanding society. The production of food was growing; so was population, and trade;

new ideas were circulating in the Mediterranean. There was an increase in books and in learning, and also in literacy, which meant an expansion of the clergy. Old records, and claims, were being re-examined, and forgotten texts brought back into use. Many documents in the papal archives were incompatible with the idea of a pontifical king, and the Pope as a mere sacerdotal functionary of the empire. The *Donation of Constantine* had been joined by a succession of elaborate forgeries, especially the so-called 'pseudo-Isidorian decretals', which served to enhance clerical claims in all directions. And there were perfectly genuine papal pronouncements, by Gelasius, Gregory the Great, Nicholas I, and so forth, which could be cited as precedents for almost anything the papacy chose to advance.

There had also been a real shift in the relative positions of power. During the tenth and eleventh centuries, the power of the crown *vis-à-vis* other elements in society – lay and ecclesiastical magnates – slowly declined throughout western Europe. The process was very marked in tenth century France, and in eleventh century Germany and Italy. Power rested essentially on the amount of land the crown held in relation to subjects. The ratio dropped everywhere. It dropped, for instance, in England, until it was violently arrested and reversed by William I's conquest, which gave him one fifth of all the land in the country. Elsewhere, the crown continued to lose ground. Thus kings, for instance, had less control over local officials, who established their rights as hereditary. Kings could not always protect the Church. They were too poor to reward military services, or to endow Church foundations. In fact, they often had to raid Church revenues to survive; and they tended to enforce hospitality from bishops and abbeys on their progresses without making expensive presents in return – they seemed, and were, an increasing burden. Thus in France, Germany and Italy, bishops were increasingly made by dukes and other local potentates, rather than kings. This made simony inevitable and widespread.

The emperors were strong enough in the 1040s to restore order in Rome, and make the launching of a reform movement possible. It soon rocketed right out of their control. Perhaps this was inevitable. The quality of the higher clergy could not be improved unless its personnel were more clearly distinguished from the brutal and materialist secular magnates. In 1057, Cardinal Humbert, the leading light of the Roman reformers, asserted in his *Adversus Simoniacos Libri Tres*, that bishops were elected by the clergy, and on request by the people, and that they were consecrated by the bishops of the province on the authority of the metropolitan: no mention of royal appointment or consent. Again, the papal election decree of 1059 made the choice depend firstly on the cardinal-bishops, then on the other cardinals; the participation of clergy and people was reduced to ratification. The idea was to differentiate sharply between clergy and laymen and, among clergy, between the various grades; above all, to make clergy independent of secular control. If the emperor replied: yes, but bishops perform secular tasks, as part of the

State, the answer was St Paul's 'No one in God's service involves himself in secular business.' But if the emperor again replied: in that case, why should bishops enjoy fiefs like secular magnates, the answer was that their lands had been freely given to the Church, and had thus become God's property. A bishop was bound to protect his patrimony – as St Anselm put it: 'I would not dare to appear before the judgment seat of God with the rights of my see diminished.' The Church, in short, was insisting that it wanted the rights and privileges of the material world, without submitting to its criteria or assuming its burdens. Gregory VII brought the issue right out into the open by flatly denying the emperor's power to appoint or invest bishops, however important their temporal possessions might be to the running of the empire. He dismissed the idea of the emperor as a priest-king. There was, he insisted, an ancient and absolute distinction between clerics and lay people. And he denied the right of 'emperors, kings and other lay persons, whether men or women' to presume 'contrary to the statutes of the holy fathers' to appoint to bishoprics and abbacies. Such actions were void, and the perpetrators excommunicate.

The papal policy made the traditional empire unworkable. If the emperor could not dispose of bishoprics and abbacies, and their resources, in the pursuit of administrative order, authority would in practice fall into the hands of the imperial princes, and the realm would dissolve. Gregory was unmoved by this argument; or rather, he accepted the consequence and drew some radical conclusions from it. The State without the Church was nothing. Just as the spirit animated the body, so the Church ultimately determined the motions of the State. Indeed, the State, in carrying out its temporary functions, was merely exercising the authority delegated to it by the Church. Having dismissed the idea of a pontifical king he replaced it by the regal pontiff, thus turning the old imperial theory of government upside down. He looked right back into the past for inspiration. Above all he turned to the era of Constantine. It is fascinating to observe how, during the Gregorian reform period, pictorial comments on the *Donation of Constantine* appear in Italian mosaics and wall-decorations carried out under papal orders or inspiration. Some of these frescoes have disappeared, but we know them from sixteenth-century drawings. Thus the Secret Council Chamber of the Lateran Palace – the very room where Charlemagne once sat in judgment over a wily but frightened Leo III – was now covered with paintings of various popes, Gregory included, shown seated in triumph, with their feet resting on the prostrate bodies of their vanquished secular enemies.

As a matter of fact, Gregory was not entirely happy with the *Donation*: it was presented as the gift of Constantine, and therefore was capable of an imperialist interpretation. In his view, the primacy, and all that followed from it, came from Christ himself. Some time in the late 1070s, he caused to be inserted in his letter-book a statement of papal claims which he seems to have dictated to his secretary. It amounted to a theory of papal world-government. It is significant that it began with a statement that the Pope could be judged by no one. He was, in fact, the only truly free man because, while his own jurisdiction was universal and unqualified, the only court in which he was obliged to sue was that of Heaven. From this proposition world theocracy inevitably followed. The Roman Church, continued Gregory, has never erred and never can err. It was founded by Christ alone. The Pope, and only the Pope, can depose and restore bishops, make new laws, create new bishoprics and divide old ones, translate bishops, call general councils, revise his own judgments, use the imperial insignia, depose emperors and absolve subjects from their allegiance. All princes should kiss his feet, and his legates took precedence over bishops. Appeals to the papal court automatically inhibited judgments from any other court. Finally, a duly ordained pope was made a saint *ex officio* by the merits of St Peter. Gregory was a colossal innovator in terms of papal theory but in this one respect he was old-fashioned: he still believed in the almost physical presence of St Peter brooding over the papal fortunes. Thus, when he excommunicated Henry IV he wrote: 'Blessed Peter . . . it is your good pleasure that the Christian people, who have been committed to you, should specially obey me, because you have given me your authority.' Papal claims had a natural tendency to inflate themselves, and soon the Petrine vicariate, on which Gregory insisted so hotly, did not seem impressive enough. By the 1150s, the popes had stolen the old imperial title of Vicar of Christ; and by the 1200s, Innocent III was insisting: 'We are the successors of the Prince of the Apostles, but we are not his vicar, nor the vicar or any man or apostle, but the Vicar of Jesus Christ himself.'

The aggressive presentation of the new papal theory of world government amounted to a physical assault on the office of the emperor, and of the politico-religious structure on which it was based. The structure was a flimsy affair; it was crumbling anyway. It could not, and in the end did not, withstand a determined papal war of destruction. There did not exist any real ground for compromise. Either the Pope was the emperor's chief bishop; or the emperor was the Pope's nominee and puppet. The first arrangement was workable; had, in fact, worked. The second was not: a puppet-emperor could not acquire the financial and military means to maintain the imperial system of government. It was a war of attrition one or other institution, as an effective instrument, had to go.

Uncommitted contemporaries watched the contest with dismay. It fitted into pessimistic theories of the universe, based on the traditions of Jewish prophecy, which circulated in various forms, and were incorporated into works of historical analysis. Around the mid-twelfth century, for instance, the most learned German of the day, Otto, Bishop of Freising, wrote a huge chronicle of world history, *The Two Cities*. As the name implies, the thought behind the book was Augustinian, and Otto accepted Augustine's view that history was a series of phases, reflecting God's plan for man's destiny, culminating in an apocalypse and the final judgment. Otto thought the long period between Constantine and the reign of Henry III had been one of godliness and harmony because empire and papacy had been able to work together. Then Gregory VII and Henry IV had destroyed the unitary structure; heresy and schism had followed; and Otto detected other portents of impending dissolution. Obviously the power of evil was increasing, the world was in its death-throes, and the last trump would soon sound: 'We are here,' he wrote, 'set down as it were at the end of time.'

Otto, however, was open to conviction. In 1152, his young nephew, Frederick Barbarossa, head of the house of Staufen, became emperor. A few years later he and his advisers confided to Otto their grand design for the reinvigoration of the Germanic empire, based on the creation of a new series of territorial fiefs directly administered by imperial agents, which would give the emperor the economic and political power to make him completely independent of papal support. As a result, Frederick and his court persuaded Otto to revise his gloomy prognostication. He not only altered the text of his *Chronicle* but, more important, set to work to write a biography of Frederick, the *Gesta Frederici Imperatoris*, in which he described the beginning of a new renaissance in the life of mankind, made possible by the glorious emergence of the Staufen family. In total contrast to his *Chronicle*, he wrote in his preface: 'I consider those who write at this time as in a certain manner blessed, because after the turbulence of the past, there has dawned the unheard calm of peace'.

The progress of Otto of Freising's historical and political thought indicates the importance men attached to the idea of harmony in the regulation of the Christian world. Nor is this surprising. If there was something wrong in the top direction of the total Christian society, how could the organism as a whole function? Must not breakdown impinge on every aspect of human life? That would be the prelude to total dissolution, the end of the world. But Otto was foolishly optimistic in assuming a new royal house could reconstruct world order on a permanent basis. The Staufen were immensely gifted. But they were human, and therefore vulnerable. Their flesh and blood was no match for the impersonal institution of the papacy. Accident, death, minorities: these fatal weaknesses of medieval secular power did not hold the same terrors for the elderly tiara-men. It is no accident that the contest began as the result of an imperial minority; or that the papacy pursued a personal vendetta against members of the Staufen clan, on at least two occasions stooping to plans for assassination. Frederick Barbarossa died by drowning, his even more magisterial son, Henry VI, of that relentless Mediterranean killer, dysentery. The popes were not always willing to wait for God to strike. Unspeakable ferocity was throughout the hallmark of these death-struggles between popes and emperors. In 1197 the Pope engaged in a conspiracy to murder Henry VI, in conjunction with his estranged wife Constance of Sicily; the plot was detected and some of its agents arrested: Henry forced Constance to watch their deaths – Jordanus of Sicily had a red-hot crown placed on his head and fixed to his skull with nails; others were burnt at the stake, flayed alive or covered in tar and ignited.

But Henry VI himself died the same year; and the minority of his son, Frederick II, coincided with the pontificate of Innocent III, the most formidable of all the medieval lawyer-popes. He took the final steps in the subtle evolutionary process which stretched back to late Roman times, and progressed through Gelasius I, Nicholas I and Gregory VII. After Innocent III, the triumphalist pontification of Boniface VIII and others were mere hyperbole. Innocent III placed the papacy in the centre of the world's motions. He quoted Nicholas I: 'The world is an *ecclesia*.' The Pope had not merely a right but an obligation to examine the person chosen as king of the Romans and emperor-elect. The Roman Church enunciated the fundamental law for the whole of Christendom. He, not the emperor, was Melchisadech, who 'with the Lord at his right hand doth crush kings in the day of his wrath'. Italy, by divine dispensation, was pre-eminent over all other regions. The authority of the central government of Rome extended over all the *societas Christiana*, whose subordinate rulers, in their conflicts with one another, must submit to the judgments of the Pope. The universal Church, he wrote in his *Deliberatio*, exercised plenary powers in all aspects of government, since temporal matters were of necessity subservient to the spiritual: 'By me kings reign and princes decree justice.' In the realization of these goals, the papacy was entitled to use all the spiritual weapons at its command, especially excommunication and interdict, and to employ all the resources of spiritual privilege. Thus the world tended to be divided not into good and bad men, but into papalists and anti-papalists. Markward of Anweiler, loyally trying to uphold Staufen claims in Italy and Sicily during the minority of his royal master, was excommunicated by Innocent as follows:

'We excommunicate, anathematize, curse and damn him, as oathbreaker, blasphemer, incendiary, as faithless and as a criminal and usurper, in the name of God the almighty Father, and of the Son, and of the Holy Ghost, by the authority of the blessed apostles Peter and Paul, and by our own. We order that henceforth anyone who gives him help or favour, or supplies him and his troops with food, clothing, ships, arms or anything else which he can benefit from, shall be bound by the same sentence; any cleric, moreover, of whatever order or dignity, who shall presume to say the divine service for him, may know he has incurred the penalty due to one of his rank and order.'

Such sentences could still inspire terror. In the thirteenth century, medieval men, fighting for the great prizes, often oscillated unpredictably between gross, barbarous impiety and violence, and the most craven superstition. We have a picture of the wretched Emperor Otto IV, created as a papal puppet, then a renegade and papal victim, dying of dysentery; in his horror of Hell flames, he caused his weak and emaciated body to be 'vigorously scourged'; but he still clung, gibbering, to the imperial insignia which were also potent relics, radiating spiritual forces – the crucifix-standard presented to Henry II, the crown, the Holy Lance, which had a nail of the True Cross embedded in it, and which had been mended with a silver band by Henry IV, and the gold-encased tooth of John the Baptist. But the net effect of the excommunications and counter-excommunications, the hurling of spiritual power into the mundane battle, was to produce a certain confusion in the participants, especially the minor agents or the innocent, who did not know which to fear most – an armed imperialist or a cursing papalist cleric. And then, legitimate spiritual power so often appeared to fail. Thus the anti-imperialist troops of Milan, mysteriously beaten at Cortenuovo by the excommunicate troops of Frederick II, 'raised their heels against God' in consequence; they turned the crucifixes upside down in their churches, hurled sewage on the altars, threw out the clergy, and gorged themselves on meat throughout Lent.

In an increasing number of ways, the contest appeared to be subversive of the whole natural and moral order. Thus, to devalue the emperor, Innocent III built up the power of the German princes, especially the ecclesiastical ones; they ceased to be one of the chief supports of the central authority and looked, instead, to the selfish advancement of their principalities. Again, other monarchs and powers were brought into papal coalitions, the humbling of the imperial authority being considered to justify any arrangement, however artificial. But then, the theory of papal plenary power meant that all moral or written laws were suspended, inoperative, in the Pope's case, since he was subject only to heavenly judgment. Thus Gregory IX, who became Pope in 1227, and persecuted heretics, antinomians and deviants with relentless ferocity, said that the moral law did not apply to his anti-imperial campaign: his conduct towards Frederick II could not be judged as immoral or unethical, his methods being unrelated to the standards of conduct common to mankind since they were subject only to God's estimation of their acceptibility. To emphasize the point, in 1239 he produced the relics of the two unassailable guardians of the papal city: 'the heads of the apostles Peter and Paul' were carried 'in solemn procession' through Rome, and in front of a huge crowd Gregory removed his tiara and placed it on the head of St Peter.* The Pope was acting on Peter's instructions – and how could Peter do wrong?

A few years later, in 1246, Gregory's successor, Innocent IV, was almost certainly a party to the attempted murder of the Lord's Anointed, Frederick II; the plot misfired – the conspirators were blinded, mutilated and burned alive – but there was no let-up in the papal campaign. Observers, participants indeed, saw it as an eschatological conflict, as in the apocalyptic books of the Old Testament; Antichrist was loose on the earth; here was no question of nuance, of political tactic, of give or take, compromise and manoeuvre, but a

---

* Although Peter was supposed to be buried beneath the high altar of St Peter's, his head, together with St Paul's, encased in magnificent reliquaries, were kept in the Lateran basilica, along with the Ark of the Covenant, the Tablets of Moses, the Rod of Aaron, an urn of manna, the Virgin's tunic, John the Baptist's hair shirt, the five loaves and two fishes from the Feeding of the Five Thousand and the dining-table used at the Last Supper. The nearby chapel of St Lawrence in the Lateran Palace boasted the foreskin and umbilical cord of Christ, preserved in a gold and jewelled crucifix filled with oil.

final conflict between absolute good and absolute evil. In credal terms, Frederick was strictly orthodox, though his wide reading, knowledge of the world – especially the East and Islam – had bred in him a spirit of speculative tolerance. But papal propaganda, concocted not by hack clerical scribes but by the popes personally, presented the head of the earthly society as incarnate wickedness. Frederick, the Pope claimed, had turned a holy altar in an Apulian church into a public latrine, he had used churches as brothels and had practiced sodomy openly; blasphemed by calling Christ, Moses and Mohammed 'three impostors'; denied the Virgin Birth; and said of the Eucharist: 'How long will this hocus-pocus continue?' He was 'a beast filled with blasphemous words . . . with the feet of a bear, the mouth of an outraged lion, the rest of the body shaped like a panther . . . the creator of lies, oblivious of modesty, untouched by the blush of shame . . . a wolf in sheep's clothing . . . a scorpion with a sting in its tail . . . A dragon formed to deceive us . . . the hammer of the earth.' He wanted to turn the whole world into a desert, and rejoiced when he was called Antichrist. He denied the faith, and his aim was to smash up Christian doctrine. He was 'the master of cruelty . . . the corrupter of the whole world . . . a poisonous serpent . . . the fourth beast in the book of Daniel, whose teeth are of iron and whose nails are of brass'.

From the twelfth century we can date the beginnings of anti-papal literature, inspired by the deepening gulf between the claim to spiritual (and therefore material) power, and the spiritual poverty of so many of its own actions. If the Church had a monopoly of education, it had never really possessed a monopoly of literature. Or, to put it another way, the secular element in society found expression even if the hand was strictly a cleric's. A long line of thought and half-memory stretched back to the imperial Roman concept of earthly authority before the total impress of Christianity was received. In a way, reversion to imperial Rome was one line of escape from an all-enclosing, compulsory Christian society. In the tenth century, shortly after the revival of the imperial title by Otto I at Rome in 962, a nun from the royal monastery of Gandersheim, Hrotswitha, produced a number of ideological verse-histories, and six 'dramas' in metrical prose, supposedly to provide a Christian alternative to Terence, which included *Gallicanus*, set in the court of Constantine. In the latter part of the twelfth century, we have an imperial Staufen propaganda play, the *Ludus de Antichristo*, written for Frederick Barbarossa – Otto of Freising may have had a hand in it – which is not merely pro-German (and anti-French and anti-Greek accordingly) but distinctly anti-papal. Reflecting on the way in which the papacy switched from one emperor to an anti-emperor and back again, under Innocent III, the poet Walther von der Vogelweide denounced papal duplicity: 'Two tongues fit badly into one mouth.'

Frederick II fought back against the ferocious assaults of Gregory IX and Innocent IV with his own propaganda: a materialist papacy, a 'temporal' Church was against reason, contrary to nature. Writing of the German ecclesiastical princes, he denounced priests 'who grasp the spear instead of the crozier . . . one calls himself duke, another margrave, and another count. One of them organizes phalanxes, another cohorts, another incites men to war. . . . Such today are the pastors of Israel: not priests of the church of Christ, but rapacious wolves, wild beasts, who devour Christian folk.' As for the Pope: 'From him in whom all men hope to find consolation of body and soul comes evil example, deceit and wrongdoing.' In Frederick's propaganda we find, for the first time, the assertion that the monstrous growth of papal power made a fundamental reform of the Church necessary. He appealed to the cardinals (1239) as 'successors of the apostles', on an equality with the Pope, to demand 'equal participation in whatever he who presides over the see of Peter proposes as law or promulgates officially'.

Frederick thus anticipated the attempts to revert to the conciliar system as a counterweight to the regal pontiff. He also argued, especially in his letters to other princes, that the papal claims were not directed at the emperor alone but were an assault on the whole concept of secular authority and the freehold monarch. Excommunicated, he wrote to the kings of Europe, warning them that the papacy threatened them all: 'Has not the King of England seen his father, King John, held in excommunication until both he and his kingdom were made tributary?' The clergy were 'insatiable leeches'. Innocent III had used the barons against King John, then deserted them and helped to crush them. 'Disguised in sheep's clothing, these ravenous wolves send legates hither and thither to excommunicate, to suspend, to punish – not as sowers of seed, that is the word of God, but to extort money, to harvest and reap that which they did not sow.' He appealed to the idea of primitive Christianity: 'No man can erect a church other than on the foundation laid down by the Lord Jesus himself'; and he warned the princes to unite: 'Look to your own house when your neighbour's has been set on fire.' To Richard of Cornwall, his brother-in-law, he wrote: 'True, it begins with Us [the empire], but it will end with all the other kings and princes . . . kings, therefore, defend the justice of your own cause in ours.' Frederick's arguments directly foreshadowed the development of secularist theory in the next century by Marsilio of Padua, in which, as he argued in his *Defensor Pacis*, the ambitions of the papacy had become the prime cause of war and the dissolvent of Christian social unity: 'The singular cause which in the past has produced civil discord in princedoms and communities, and which will soon spread to other states unless checked, is the belief, the desire and the effort by means of which the Roman bishop and his clerical associates, in particular, aim to seize each secular sovereignty and so gain possession of its temporal wealth.'

But Frederick II was before his time in his almost desperate efforts to erect defences, ecclesiastical and secular, against the papal exploitation of spiritual power to conjure up divisive forces within society. The papal victory over the Staufen was total. Frederick II died still at liberty, but thereafter the 'viper's brood' as the popes called it, was exterminated. His son Manfred had been defeated and killed at the battle of Benevento, 1266, and buried without religious ceremony; on the orders of the Pope, Clement IV, what he referred to as 'the putrid corpse of that pestilential man' was dug up again, and reburied outside the borders of the Sicilian kingdom, now a papal fief. Conradin, the last emperor, aged sixteen, fell into the Pope's hand two years later, and (according to one account) Clement remarked, when ordering his death: 'Vita Conradini, mors Caroli [Charles of Anjou, the papal agent]. Vita Caroli, mors Conradini.' The boy was executed in Naples. The end of the Staufen was pitiless. Manfred's daughter Beatrice was kept in prison for eighteen years; his three bastard sons never emerged – one was still alive in 1309, having been in papal custody forty-five years. Of Frederick's children and grandchildren, ten died by papal violence or in papal dungeons.

We must not imagine that the battle between Church and State took place only at the highest level. The popes fought the Staufen not merely as rival claimants to supreme rule, but as the heads of a caste. The clerical challenge to the layman ran right down through society. It is no accident that Gregory VII spoke, and wrote, of laymen with peculiar bitterness. Of course there had been tension between the clerical and secular elements in Christianity since very early times. The exaltation of the clerical caste had always been connected with the development of authority in Church discipline, and orthodoxy in dogma. Montanism, in the second century, had been a protest against all three, and Tertullian, in embracing it in the third, became the first articulate Christian anti-clerical. In Dark Age Europe the antagonism appears to have subsided almost completely. The clergy were playing a salient role in the reconstruction of society, as we have seen; their attitudes were integrated with those of society, economically, legally, constitutionally. Yet signs of strain were beginning to appear. One of the healthiest characteristics of Carolingian society was the attempt, using the resources of the Church, to produce the educated layman – Charlemagne himself trying to set the example. Not long after his death we hear of complaints from monasteries that it was not their job to educate men unless they intended to be monks. But monastic and cathedral schools were virtually the only ones available. The failure of lay education to develop at the same pace as clerical was, perhaps, the prime cause of the cleavage. What increasingly differentiated clerics and laity was the use of Latin. In the East, where similar clerical-secular tensions never developed, the social, and the liturgical, languages were the same, and developed together. In the West they diverged. By the eighth century, nobody learned Latin as his vernacular language; but no learned, devotional or liturgical work was written in any other. Latin became the clerical language. Thus proof of ability to speak or write it became the usual test of a claim to clerical status (and privilege). It became the mark of civilization, and so the badge of arrogance. In the eyes of the self-conscious clericalist, the laity were either labouring louts or armed thugs. It was galling for clergy who could read Augustine to find their affairs ordered, at the highest level, by Conrad II, an illiterate. Of course by 'illiterate' they meant having no knowledge of Latin. Thus, Henry I of England, who knew Latin, was known as 'beauclerc' – a fine priest. Behind the clericalist movement was a terrific amount of cultural snobbery and also, in a more realistic way, a sense of superiority: clerics carried out the whole administrative side of government, running chanceries and exchequers and keeping accounts and records of every kind.

The last point, in one respect, is the most important of all: the Church had the literate manpower and the techniques to produce more sophisticated forms of government than any available to the secular world. In the Dark Ages these had been placed at the disposal of the barbarian tribal states: the Church, for instance, gave them written legal codes. But all the time the Church retained its old traditions of separate canonical legislation, dating back to the fourth century. The papacy had the oldest legal and administrative machine in western Europe. The essence of the Carolingian renaissance, and of the Ottonian empire which followed it, had been the identity of aim of Church and State, expressed in legal codes, and conciliar legislation, which dealt with both. Within this system the Church had always enjoyed a privileged position. Indeed, the laws had first been put in writing to provide specifically for the protection of clerks and their property. In England, for instance, clerks had never been thrown completely on the tender mercies of the secular courts. Though every kind of charge could be brought against them in the ordinary courts, special penalties were provided for clerical offenders; and, when accused of capital crimes, they were always judged by a bishop. Bishops often presided in the shire-courts; not until after the Norman Conquest were bishops and archdeacons forbidden to hear cases in the (lower) hundred courts. Moreover, royal legislation made ecclesiastical offences into secular offences; and canon law, as well as secular law, was admitted in the shire courts. Thus in Anglo-Saxon England the clergy were already, in a legal sense, a privileged class; the same was true, with variations, elsewhere in Europe.

This system of privilege, however, was still under royal, that is secular, control. The effect of the mid-eleventh-century church reforms, and of the Gregorian revolution which followed, was to drive a wedge into the joint legal system, and split it into two distinct streams of law. In the 1050s, the papal administration underwent a formidable expansion. A primitive Parkinson's Law began to operate. More clerks were available to do the Pope's bidding: work, therefore, expanded to occupy the time available. More clerics were learned in canon law: compilations of canon law were made, therefore, and sent all over the Christian world; they were used locally, and appeals made to Rome; and canon law was added to by an increased use of clerical legislative machinery. As canon law expanded, and became more subtle and sophisticated, and as it evolved into a uniform international system, with the papacy as its supreme court of appeal, it was bound to diverge more and more from the national secular system. Different systems meant different courts; and if clerical courts tried ecclesiastical offences, should they not also deal with clerics who committed any offence whatever? The clerical affirmative was delivered with all the more conviction in that canon law was, in their eyes, clearly a superior system; it went back to Roman times, was, indeed, based on Roman principles of jurisprudence. Here the cultural snobbery came in again. One reason why Gregory VII treated the *Donation of Constantine* with reserve was that it was incorporated in a secular document, and it was a principle of the canonist reformers that the Church could not entertain any legal proposition that was based on secular documentation alone: there must be confirmation in clerical archives.

There was, also, a sense of exhilaration among the clerical revolutionaries. They were bringing mankind out of the dark past, into a brave new world of administrative efficiency. Away with government by illiterates and barbarous folk-laws! This was a view shared by many, especially, of course, clerics. The growth of an efficient papal court and chancery not only made the exercise of papal-clerical authority easier, it also attracted litigants and business. From the late eleventh century, every index of papal and central church activity began to show a sharp increase. 'Big' government and papal claims went hand in hand: the demand for power expanded *pari passu* with the administrative capacity to exercise it. In England, for instance, there had been no legislative councils until 1070 (except one in 786); in the period 1070–1312 there were between twenty and thirty. The West had played little part in the early general councils; then, between 1123–1311 there were seven. Papal correspondence increased accordingly (making allowance for a higher survival rate the later the period), from an average of one a year under Benedict IX, 1033–46, to thirty-five up to 1130, 179 under Alexander III, 1159–81, 280 by the turn of the thirteenth century and 3646 by the beginning of the fourteenth. Virtually all this business was legal. Of course, the twelfth century was an age of legal discovery and expansion generally. Every other kind of court, especially the royal court, was expanding fast. But canon law, radiating from Rome, set the pace and kept the lead by far.

The run-up to the canonical explosion took about seventy years, from 1070–1140; then, in a mere decade, it suddenly became a universal fact of life. We saw how the notions of Christianity penetrated deep into every crevice of society in the Carolingian period; now, a papally-controlled legal system suddenly moved into the forefront of every individual's experience. It began to settle vast areas of ordinary life in great and expensive legal detail: the administration of the sacraments and all other aspects of the strictly religious side of existence; the rights, duties, payments and obligations of the humblest parish priest and his congregation; the dress, education, ordination, status, crimes, punishments of clerics; charity, alms, usury, wills, graveyards, churches, prayers, masses for the dead, burials, marriage, inheritance, legitimacy, sex and morals. Until the 1040s, the popes had only a vague idea of what was going on at the highest level in places like England, north Germany or Spain; a hundred years later, in 1144, we find Lucius II writing to the bishops of Hereford and Worcester ordering them jointly to settle a disput about a parish church in the diocese of Lichfield.

The legal revolution enormously strengthened the hands of the papacy because to be able to dispense justice effectively was, to medieval man, a chief sign of power. The growth of papal law was both a cause of the papacy's claim to total sovereignty, and the means whereby successive emperors were humbled or smashed. On the other hand, it gradually turned the papacy, and so the Church as a whole, into a totally different kind of institution. It became not so much a divine society, as a legal one; and a legal society increasingly divorced from the total society surrounding it. Its verbal integuments were no longer the scriptures, but canon law. About 1140 appeared the great *Concordia Discordantium Canonum*, known as the *Decreta*, compiled by Gratian. This was, in a sense, the last of a long line of more primitive canonical collections; it provided a systematic exposition of a vast corpus of ancient church law and did it so thoroughly that further efforts to codify the past were superfluous. It distinguished between necessary law, as laid down in scripture; and convenient law, formulated by the Church in the interests of discipline and the cure of souls. The first was immutable, the second might be relaxed, in a variety of ways and for many different purposes; and this dispensory power was an inherent function of the papal office.

The theory of Gratian, and the practice of the papal court, was thus the culmination of a long process, beginning in the second century, whereby the Church interposed itself between the code of conduct divinely ordained in the scriptures, and the obligations and prescriptions actually enforced on Christianity. The tendency, therefore, was to replace pastoral theology with legal interpretation and administration, as the chief preoccupation of the Church. From the time of Gregory VII onwards, all the outstanding popes were lawyers; the papal court, or *curia*, became primarily a legal organization, with over a hundred experts employed there by the thirteenth century, plus other lawyers who looked after the interests of kings, princes and leading ecclesiastics. Most of the popes' advisers were canonists. As Roger Bacon bitterly remarked, for every theologian in Innocent IV's entourage there were twenty lawyers. Popes tended to get bogged down in legal business. St Bernard, a papalist and a clericalist, but a man who kept the prime pastoral function of the Church constantly before his eyes, thought the papacy's concern with the legal nexus was obsessive: 'Why do you sit from morning until evening,' he wrote to Eugenius III in 1150, 'listening to litigants? What fruit is there in these things? They can only create cobwebs.' His warnings were ignored. The litigious habit gradually permeated the whole Church. Ecclesiastical institutions tended to see their relationship with the lay world, and with each other, primarily in legal terms. The most bitterly fought and enduring cases were inter-clerical battles. One such medieval *Jarndyce* v. *Jarndyce* between the monks of St Augustine, Canterbury, and their archbishop, was hotly contested for fifteen years, successive popes being obliged to write seventy letters. Innocent III, exasperated, wrote: 'I blush to hear of this mouldy business.' But when had the law not generated mould?

St Bernard's cobwebs continued to spread. For, when he asked what fruit there was in legalism, the answer, of course, was money and power. A successful court – and the papal court was the outstanding legal success of the Middle Ages – generated income, and the need of great and small to solicit its verdicts. The Pope's legal relations with a king, a duke or an archbishop, might involve a dozen or more cases going on at one time, some momentous, many trivial, all of which had to be weighed by both sides in considering total policy. Much of the Pope's practical ability to get his way sprang from the power of his court to deliver. So it was impossible for the Pope to avoid the details. And to think chiefly in legal, was to think chiefly in secular, terms. The popes became progressively more entangled in legal-diplomatic considerations, and in the effort to hold together their estates in central Italy as a secure base for their ramifying international activities. In short, they became like any other rulers. The Gregorian reform, which sought to improve moral standards in the Church by disengaging the clergy from their role as supporters of the State, ended, by a kind of helpless logic, in thrusting the Church far more deeply and completely into the secular world. Indeed, the Church became a secular world of its own.

As such – as a separate, rival institution – it was bound to come into conflict with the State at every level. Of course clerics and seculars were both Christians and shared not only major assumptions but most minor ones. But they were locked in a conflict of laws, and this could be brutally aggravated by a conflict of personalities. The outstanding case was Henry II's tragic dispute with Thomas à Becket. Henry was only twenty-nine when he appointed Becket, his chancellor, to be chief ecclesiastical officer of his kingdom in 1162. He hoped that this combination of duties would help to smooth out difficulties which inevitably arose from the conflict of the two legal systems. After all, 'when business was over the King and he would sport together like boys of the same age; in hall or in church they sat together; together they went riding . . .' In fact this contemporary description fails to note that Becket was sixteen years older than the king, and already set in his ways. He was probably a bad influence over the young monarch: an obstinate insistence on the unequivocal acknowledgment of rights, and a fondness for extravagant gestures, marked Henry's policies when Becket was his chief adviser. In the 1160s, Henry, maturing, gradually adopted a much more conciliatory attitude to the world, and sought to woo opponents rather than shout them down, or smash them. He changed, and became a master of *realpolitik*. Becket remained the same: an obstinate and at times hysterical man, with an actor's passion for noisy drama.

It was against this personal background that Henry's England felt the first full impact of the papal revolution. In the Conqueror's time, wrote Eadmer, 'all things, spiritual and temporal alike, waited upon the nod of the King'; a council of bishops could not 'lay down any ordinance or prohibition unless

they were agreeable to the King's wishes, and had first been approved by him';
and a bishop could not, without the king's agreement, 'take action against or
excommunicate one of his barons or officials for incest or adultery or any
other cardinal offence or even when guilt was notorious, lay upon him any
penalty of ecclesiastical discipline.' That was still the world of the Dark Ages.
Under William II, and Henry I, there had been a growing sense of antagonism
between king and senior clerics; and during the disturbed period of Stephen's
reign a progressive encroachment by the Church on royal legal territory. On
the other hand, there is plenty of evidence that compromise was possible. The
papal curia was not a monolithic organization; the curia was often divided
itself, or sometimes imposed a restraining collective leadership on an
impetuous pontiff. John of Salisbury, noting that Eugenius III's decisions were
often subsequently revoked, explains this by saying 'he was too ready to rely
upon his personal opinion in imposing sentences'. At a local level, ecclesiastical authorities had their own motives for trying to avoid a showdown.
Becket's predecessor, Archbishop Theodore, for instance, disliked appeals to
Rome unless litigants 'are in the grip of some necessity from which they cannot
free themselves by their own efforts'. He thought that 'the transgressions of
malicious persons are best punished by those who have intimate knowledge of
the merits of the parties concerned'; he rebuked the Bishop of Chichester for
appealing to Canterbury: 'That disputes within your jurisdiction find their
way to us is a sign of weakness or negligence.'

Everything depended, in fact, on whether the people concerned placed the
creation of a harmonious society above the logical pursuit of rights. This was
particularly true in the case of criminous clerks, over which the king and
Becket came to grief. Everyone in positions of authority in society had an
interest in the preservation of law and order – the Church, perhaps, most of
all, since it was most vulnerable to a general increase in lawlessness, of the kind
which confronted Henry II in the first few years of his reign. The clerical
profession, if so it can be called, had expanded enormously in the previous
century. Perhaps one in fifty people could make some claim to be considered in
orders. And of these about one in six could expect to get into trouble with the
law. Many were not clergy in any but a legal sense. Often they took minor
orders to get an education, and then entered the service of lay masters; they
never intended to be ordained priest. Many clerks in secular service lived like
laymen, and then married. And the parish priests, ·even, often lived like
peasants – 'their houses and hovels', as Giraldus Cambrensis put it, 'filled with
bossy mistresses, creaking cradles, newborn babes and squawking brats'.
Parsons often did week-work for the local lord, in exchange for their crofts;
they usually had a double share in the communal holding, and maintained the
parish boar, bull, ram and stallion.

At this level, a good deal of crime among clerics was inevitable. Why should
they have the right to trial by a separate and much less severe legal system? It
was a fact that the Church had been much more successful in asserting the

rights claimed by the reformers, than in imposing the higher standards and discipline on the clergy. Indeed, the more ardent for the first, the more they tended to ignore the latter. Becket was a case in point. As archbishop he took no interest in pastoral work, and never showed much enthusiasm for the creation of a godly clergy. Efforts to force clerks to wear clerical dress, or to forswear marriage and concubines, were unsuccessful. The church courts worked badly in many ways, especially in serious cases, owing to what Archbishop Theodore called 'the subtlety of the laws and the canons'. Henry II reluctantly allowed the Church to deal, for instance, with the case of Archdeacon Osbert of York, accused of poisoning his archbishop. He regretted it both in principle and in practice. After a year of delays and argument, no verdict was reached and the case was appealed to Rome. The archdeacon was eventually deprived and unfrocked, but otherwise un-punished and twenty years later he was still claiming the judgement was improper. So far as we can judge he was almost certainly guilty.

The Becket episode really began when Henry arrived back in England in 1163 and was told that more than a hundred murders had been committed by clerks since his coronation on 1157. There were, too, vast numbers of cases of clerical theft and robbery with violence. Henry might have had more sympathy with Becket's absolutist claims if Becket had shown better sense in running the church courts. But often their verdicts seemed intolerable to a king dedicated to stamping out lawlessness. A canon of Bedford had killed a knight and then, in open court, furiously abused the judge, a local sheriff: the offence was doubly capital, yet Becket merely had the man banished. Again, a Worcestershire clerk had seduced a girl, then murdered her father; Becket had the clerk branded. This was open to four objections: it was inadequate; it was a sentence unknown to canon law; it was, indeed, a usurpation of royal authority; and it flatly contradicted Becket's own argument that clerks should not suffer mutilation, normal in royal courts, 'lest in man the image of God be deformed'. At a conference with the king to discuss the whole problem of bringing justice to bear on clerical offenders, Becket argued that degredation, deprivation of orders and loss of privileged status was enough. He put the case for a separate caste: 'The clergy, by reason of their orders and distinctive office, have Christ alone as King. ... And since they are not under secular kings, but under their own king, the King of Heaven, they should be ruled by their own law; and if they are transgressors they should be punished by their own law, which had its own means of coercion.' When the conflict became open, Becket took up a still more 'Gregorian' position: 'Christian kings ought to submit their administration to ecclesiastics, not impose it upon them. ... Christian princes should be obedient to the dictates of the church, rather than prefer their own authority, and princes should bow their heads to bishops rather than judge them.'

Most of the English bishops disapproved of Becket's attitude, and of his tactics throughout the dispute. Becket's own election had been improper; the forms had been observed, but he had in fact been forced on the Church in 1162 by pressure from the royal justiciar, Richard de Lucy. There was a feeling that, because of the nature of his appointment, Becket was anxious to impress the monks of his own chapter that he was independent of the royal will. Running through the vast number of clerical letters which surround the Becket drama there is a perceptible mood of resentment among many of his nominal allies, at his posturings and intransigence. His murder was the most celebrated state crime of the entire Middle Ages; it brought him almost instant canonization; and his shrine became, after Rome itself and St James's at Compostella, the most celebrated in Europe. Until the Reformation, St Thomas was the most frequently portrayed of all English saints, at home and abroad, and more English boys were called after him than any other namesake. Yet he did no service to Christianity. Henry II often used words he later regretted: he cannot have intended his angry words to his knights to be taken seriously. As John of Salisbury, a friend of Becket's points out, he had used a similar expression on at least one earlier occasion, in 1166: 'They were all traitors who could not summon up the zeal and loyalty to rid him of the harassment of one man.' As a matter of fact, the expression 'one man' is significant; Henry felt he was fighting not so much the system as one outrageous individual who prevented any sincere attempt to work it on a basis of compromise. By the time the climax of the dispute came, Becket was virtually isolated: martyrdom was a spectacular, and theatrical, way out from the impasse into which he had driven himself. The actions of the four knights were a series of confused blunders. Their object in going to Canterbury was not clear: it was Becket who forced them to decide between killing him, or returning to court looking like fools. One of Becket's biographical eulogists, Edward Grim, virtually conceded this point: 'He who had long yearned for martyrdom now saw that the occasion to embrace it had arrived.' Another, William FitzStephen, adds: 'Had he so wished, the Archbishop might easily have turned aside and saved himself by flight, for both time and place offered an opportunity to escape without being discovered.'

Becket's episcopal colleagues must have viewed his canonization, and the wild and immediate popularity of his relics, with a good deal of cynicism. One such, well-disposed to Becket personally, was John aux Bellesmains, Bishop of Poitiers. John regarded the archbishop as 'always a follower of his own will and opinion . . . it was a great misfortune and an immense hurt and danger to the Church that he had ever been made a ruler of it.' He himself had opposed Henry II's Constitutions of Clarendon as going too far in upholding royal rights; and he had successfully protected a clerk, accused of treason, from trial in a royal court; yet he remained on excellent terms with Henry (as well as the curia), was promoted Archbishop of Lyons, and lived in harmony with Church and State until his eighties, long enough to receive a respectful visit from Innocent III. In the eyes of men like John, the real danger of Becket was not just that he antagonized decent kings like Henry, who were perfectly well disposed to the Church, but that Becket-style gestures, rewarded with the martyr's palm, tended to create a climate of clerical opinion which forced other prelates to insist on church rights more than they thought prudent.

It says a lot for the practical sagacity of Henry and Pope Alexander III that the cleavage in society opened by the murder was so soon healed. In practical terms Becket achieved nothing by his death. Alexander endorsed Henry's choices for vacant bishoprics – faithful royal supporters, variously denounced by Becket as 'archdiabolus' 'that offspring of fornication', and 'that notorious schismatic'. At Canterbury, Henry got the sort of man he wanted, Richard, Prior of Dover, who gave first place to the reform of the clergy and cooperation with the State. Alexander warmly supported Henry's policy of conquering Ireland, and threatened excommunication to anyone who declined to aid 'this catholic and most Christian king'. On the question of appeals to Rome, it was evident that Henry did not oppose them in principle; he merely wished to control them. When Cardinal Vivian, papal legate, arrived in England in 1176, 'without the King's license', Henry, according to the chronicler Roger of Howden, sent two bishops to warn him that 'unless he was ready to abide by the will of the King he would not be allowed to proceed further'. The cardinal swore 'that he would do nothing on his legation hostile to [Henry] or to his kingdom'; Henry then treated him with great honour, and the next legate took good care to obtain the king's permission to land in advance. Henry liked upright and spiritual-minded churchmen; he disliked those whom, he said, 'embraced the world with both arms'. He often promoted men who might have been expected to give him trouble, such as Baldwin of Ford, whom he first made Bishop of Worcester, then Canterbury. Henry II was one of those medieval sovereigns, by no means uncommon, who genuinely wanted to make the Christian society work; who thought that an active, vigorous, even militant church and higher clergy were necessary for the material, as well as the spiritual, well-being of the commonwealth. Such rulers, in the Carolingian tradition, were willing to work with the Church even after it had robbed them of much of their theoretical status and power as anointed servants of the Lord. But of course none of them, however well disposed, could conceivably have accepted the line of thinking illustrated by Boniface VIII's bulls cited at the beginning of this section. The result was that, after the twelfth century, it was rare even for the more serious-minded and hard-working monarchs to devote much of their energies to reforming the Church and improving its pastoral performance – objects which had been central to the policies even of mediocre Dark Age Christian monarchs. On the contrary, the ruler's interest now centred on blocking and controlling the Church, and diverting as much as possible of its resources in money and personnel to secular purposes.

This might not have mattered so much if the bishops had preserved their status. In western and northern Europe they conserved much of their wealth, but in other respects they became the principal victims of the papal contest with secular power. Ever since the emergence of the monarchical bishop in the second century, episcopacy had been the key institution of Christianity. The quality and drive of the clergy, and therefore the level of Christian conduct, depended above all on able, holy and vigorous bishops. Without good bishops, the papacy could not in practice have any real influence on society. After the capitulation of King John of England to the papacy for instance, Innocent III, in theory at least, had virtual charge of the English church. But he did, or could do, virtually nothing to promote reform. He possessed neither the machinery nor the administrative manpower for detailed supervision. So his advice to his legates was nearly always to do what the king wanted. Again, in theory, by the beginning of the thirteenth century the papacy had won the battle to appoint bishops. The object of the campaign had been to improve the quality of episcopal personnel. In fact if anything the quality went down. In practice, local rulers and the Pope engaged in a carve-up of appointments. Both were motivated by considerations other than provision of the best kind of man. Kings did not particularly like having clergy as ministers of state, since they could not be brought to book in royal courts for peculation, treason, and so forth; on the other hand, they could not afford to pay laymen, and clerical ministers could be rewarded with bishoprics and other benefices. The financial argument nearly always won. Hence about half the bishoprics went to royal officials, courtiers and so forth. The Pope, too, needed to reward his clerks and supporters. His share of the jobs varied, but might be as much as a third. The division of the episcopal spoils was not conducted by any formal system, but in man-to-man bargains between the papacy and the royal representative.

Royal appointments could be very bad. The Black Prince got his illiterate friend Robert Stretton the bishopric of Coventry and Lichfield, despite the fact that his profession of canonical obedience had to be read out on his behalf; the Pope and the Archbishop of Canterbury made a fuss, but had to give way in the end. On the other hand, some papal appointments were just as bad, or worse. In 1246, with the object of 'liberating' the Church from the Hohenstaufen, Innocent IV forbade any episcopal elections on the Lower Rhine without permission of the Holy See. The next year he appointed to Liège Henry, brother of the Count of Gueldre, who was only nineteen and illiterate. He was sent to Liège purely for the papacy's political and military purposes. As bishop, he was an imperial elector, and one of his first acts was to help elect the Count of Holland as the anti-Staufen king of Germany. He was allowed to remain in minor orders 'in order to engage more freely in the affairs of the church in Germany' – that is, lead troops in battle. He was also given dispensations to grant tithes to papal supporters, to keep benefices vacant and appropriate the proceeds to raise troops. He had expert clerks and a full-time deputy to carry out the essential work of the diocese while, for twenty-five years, he carried out his political and military duties. From his episcopal registers, he appears a model diocesan. In fact he was a scoundrel, and eventually, when the Staufen were smashed, he lost his usefulness: in

1273, Gregory X accused him of sleeping with abbesses and nuns, fathering fourteen bastards in twenty-two months, and providing all of them with benefices. Disgraced, he reverted to his natural bent, and became a brigand.

Such men were exceptions. The trouble with most bishops, under the royal-papal carve-up, was that they were worldly and mediocre. Often they were absentees, on royal or papal business. But even if they were not officials, they were rarely active diocesans. This was not always their fault. Bishops were expected to move in great state. An episcopal visitation thus became a serious financial burden for the inferior clergy. Odo Rigaud, the Archbishop of Rouen 1247–76, was an exemplary prelate by the standards of his time. But he travelled with a mounted retinue of eighty, and in 1251 this led to a joint protest to the Pope from all the bishops of Normandy. William of Longchamp, Bishop of Ely, was another notorious offender on this score, though the chief complaint about him was the number of his hounds and hawks (hawks had a specially expensive diet). The visitations could be carried out by vicars-general or archdeacons; but they were liable to offend just as grievously. Innocent III was told the Archdeacon of Richmond took with him ninety-seven horses, twenty-one hounds and three hawks. Hubert Walter, Archbishop of Canterbury, laid down a maximum scale: an archbishop could not have more than fifty men and horses; bishops thirty; archdeacons seven – and no hounds or hawks for any of them. The scale was never adhered to. Things were just as bad 200 years later. When Archbishop Kempe of York was criticized for visiting his diocese for only two or three weeks at a time, at intervals of ten to twelve years – this was in the mid fifteenth century – he replied that he tried to enter one archdeaconry, which none of his predecessors had visited for 150 years, but was told it was too poor – would he accept a composition instead?

As a matter of fact, it is not at all clear that medieval man wanted a really devoted episcopate. The Carolingian idea that Church and State should combine to enforce Christian morals lingered on; attempts to bring it to life were not popular with any element in society. Strictly speaking, the bishop had the right to carry out episcopal visitations among the laity as well as the clergy. He could enter the house of a lord and hold court there about the owner's morals; or subject an entire village to a sexual and financial inquisition. Robert Grosseteste, the devoted and courageous mid thirteenth-century Bishop of Lincoln – perhaps the most admirable of all the medieval diocesans – actually took the Christian society, and his duties to it, seriously. In 1246–8, he carried out a thorough visitation. Among the questions he put to local panels was: 'Whether any layman is notoriously proud or envious or avaricious or liable to the sin of slothful depression, or rancorous or gluttonous or lecherous.' This seems to have been the most thoroughgoing effort to raise and enforce moral standards of which we have record; and so unusual as to seem intolerable. The reaction of the secular authorities was characteristic. In 1249 the bishop was summoned to appear in person before the king, to 'show cause for his forcing unwilling men and women, under pain of excommunication, to come before him to give evidence on oath to the grievous prejudice of the crown'. The king complained that such gatherings interrupted the lawful activities of his subjects and prevented them from performing their duties. The bishop got no support from the Pope, who deplored his moral enthusiasm, and once had a dream in which Grosseteste upbraided him and 'smote him a tremendous blow with his staff'.

Most bishops would not soil their hands with lay visitations. For the enforcement of the moral law they developed the office of rural dean. He dealt with local cases of fornication, slander, non-payment of tithes, perjury, breach of faith, usury, witchcraft, heresy, proving of wills and blasphemy. The deans hated doing these jobs, which were unpaid. They hired apparitors or summoners to deliver episcopal warnings. These men were paid by results, but often engaged in blackmail and were generally hated. The bishops therefore turned to the churchwardens. In any case, it was really only the poor and humble who were in practice forced to conform to the Christian ideal, or rather punished when they did not. Powerful men would not have their morals controlled by bishops, let alone rural deans. When, around 1310, the Dean of Crewkerne served an episcopal admonition on Sir Alan Ploknet, he found himself seized by the throat and forced to eat the bishop's letter, seal and all. The same principle applied to disciplining the clergy. The actual working clergy, living on stipends, were poor, and could be brought to book without too much trouble. Senior clergy, or pluralists – the two were often synonymous – who were more likely than most to break canon law or set a bad example, could fight the bishops in the courts. As the bishops had to pay the costs of such actions, which might well go to Rome, they left offenders alone. Thus the development of canon law, in theory designed to improve the morals of the clergy, in fact made improvement more difficult.

The devaluation of the bishop was, for the clergy as a whole, perhaps the most baleful consequence of the reform programme of the papacy. From the late eleventh century onwards they lost their power and independence in such matters as the liturgy, canonization, inspection of abbeys and convents, and definitions of law and doctrine. They were merely lines of communication to the Pope. Hence men who aspired to change and improve society, to carry through a Christian revolution, no longer, on the whole, sought bishoprics. These went, instead, to the younger sons of great territorial magnates, and to successful civil servants. They kept their wealth and their nominal status. Many of the 500 bishops of the Latin church could claim to occupy thrones which went back to the second century, or at any rate were older than any secular royal house. Thus the episcopate had to be treated as one of the key institutions of western society. When attempts were made to reform the Church in the fifteenth century, beginning with the papacy, it was natural to turn to the bishops, and to a revival of the conciliar system, to do the job. But they proved incapable of performing it. Crown and papacy, between them, had destroyed the once-powerful tradition of episcopal initiative and leadership. At the fifteenth-century councils, the bishops tended to vote either by nationalities, in response to royal instructions, or in the supposed Roman interest. The idea of acting independently as an international college had been lost. The spring had broken in an institution which had had its origins in New Testament times.

The destruction of episcopal independence obviously enhanced papal authority within the Church; but the main beneficiary was the State. The Ambrosian bishop was a real check to royal power, as well as the Pope's. With the bishop reduced to a dignified functionary, the Pope was left on a lonely eminence, face to face with the secular world. Indeed, it could be said that papal policy had created this secular spirit, and turned it into an enemy. The Christian society of the ninth century, say, had been an entity. There was then no such thing as a 'clerical world' and a 'secular world'. The Gregorian reforms had brought the idea of the secular state into existence by stripping the ruler of his sacerdotal functions. For a time this enhanced the Church's power, or appeared to. The superiority of the priestly element in society was emphasized, and the lay element was demoted along with the monarchy. There was a tendency to equate the clergy with 'the Church'. In the long run this was fatal to the whole concept of the Christian society. The lay element was initially put on the defensive but it eventually responded by developing its own modes of thought outside the assumptions of the Christian-clerical world. These modes were alien to Christianity, and ultimately hostile to it. Again, the idea of a militant clerical caste, with all the advantages of superior learning and sophisticated legal and administrative techniques, initially carried all before it. It was the first great trades union. But the secular world learnt from its methods. In the twelfth century, royal justice was a generation or two behind canon law, but it soon caught up. The old empire was destroyed, but kings took its place. They learnt to manipulate papal legal and administrative techniques, and copy them. The militancy of the clerical interest produced, in the end, the response of the secular interest, represented by the crown. Thus anti-clericalism was born.

Take the case of England. It had always had a peculiar, and fond, relationship with the papacy. The English thought they owed their faith and civilization to Gregory the Great's mission, and were grateful. The award of the pallium to English archbishops was regarded as a signal favour. Many English churches were called after SS Peter and Paul, a tribute to Rome; and from very early times there was an English church, St Mary's in the eternal city, supported by a special English tax, 'Peter's Pence'. No other country paid such a tax. It was originally a free-will gift by English kings, then in the tenth century became an obligation, provided by the people. The first sour note crept in under Gregory VII, when he wrote to William I pointing out that the tax was in arrears. William conceded that it had to be paid, but thereafter the English treated it as a burden. Far more was collected than was actually transferred to Rome, the crown taking its cut. In the twelfth century it was standardized at 299 silver marks annually, but it was paid sporadically, when the opportunity arose, was often withheld, to annoy the Pope, and in general was treated as a diplomatic manoeuvring device. When, in the mid fourteenth century, the papacy peremptorily demanded its payment, Edward III appealed to Parliament, which promptly declared the tax illegal and unconstitutional, and it was never paid again.

Provided a crown, and the royal line which held it, was itself secure, it had little to fear from an out-and-out war with the papacy. The Pope could impose an interdict, but it was hard to make it work. When Innocent III quarrelled with King John, some English bishops remained at their posts; the Cistercians, claiming exemption, 'rang their bells, shouted their chants and celebrated the divine office with open door'. John carried on with his normal ecclesiastical duties, and continued to pay his charities – 3 marks to the Templars, £15 to the canons of Trentham, and so on. The interdict went on for six years, and the king seems to have received general support. It is true that the excommunication of John in 1209 embittered things. But the main loser was the English Church. The sums from ecclesiastical lands paid into the exchequer rose from £400 in 1209 to £24,000 in 1211, and these do not include Cistercian losses, which came to over £16,000. In all John got over £100,000, which went to finance successful campaigns in Wales, Scotland and Ireland. If John had not, over quite separate issues, antagonized a large section of the baronage, his submission to the Pope would have been quite unnecessary. Indeed, in general, a king who handled his domestic front prudently could always fight the papacy to a stalemate, even at its zenith under Innocent III.

Thus, though papal claims expanded, what the popes actually gained scarcely justified the increasing odium which their demands aroused. This was particularly true of papal provisions to foreign benefices. In England, for instance, between 1216–72, there were six direct papal provisions to bishoprics; under Edward II, thirteen out of twenty-eight; and after 1342 it became the norm – John Trilleck, made Bishop of Hereford in 1344, was the last English bishop not appointed by papal provision until the Reformation. But this did not mean the Pope's power was increasing. On the contrary. The system was simply employed as the crown wished. There was a regular formula – for example for the institution of the Bishop of Norwich in 1446:

'Since the Lord Pope has recently provided to the church of Norwich ...
Walter Lyhert, the elect of Norwich, bachelor in theology, and has
appointed him bishop and pastor in that place, as we are informed by the
bulls of the Lord Pope, directed to us. ... And whereas the bishop has
renounced before us openly and expressly all words and every word
contained in the bulls, which are prejudicial to us and to our crown, and has
submitted himself humbly to our grace; wishing to act in this matter
graciously with him, we have taken the fealty of the bishop, and we have

restored to him the temporalities of the bishopric. . . .'

In this case, as in virtually all others, the king nominated and the Pope provided, but the bishop was nevertheless forced to renounce everything prejudicial in the provision. Again, clergy going to Rome were forced to take a standard oath, of which that sworn by the Abbot of St Augustine's, Canterbury in 1468 is typical: '. . . that you shall sue, or procure to be sued, in the court of Rome, or in any other place beyond the sea, nothing that may be hurtful or prejudicial to the king our sovereign lord, or his crown, or any of his subjects; nor do anything or attempt anything that is or may be contrary to the laws of this land.' There was a mass of very severe statutes to back up the royal position that any decisions of the Pope, or anything done on his behalf in the English church, must first be filtered through the royal machinery. In all except doctrine, the king was the effective head of the English church long before Henry VIII assumed it by parliamentary statute.

This was the position in virtually all western countries. In some it is difficult to identify any period in which the papacy made successful inroads into royal control of the national church. In Spain, for instance, the crown had had the whip hand since Visigothic times. The sixth century councils, the earliest examples of Church-State cooperation in Christian-barbarian Europe, show the Church acting virtually as a department of the State, and as essentially subordinate to it. It was the kings, not the bishops, who governed Spain and with it the Spanish church. The position did not change in any essential throughout the Middle Ages. Thus, an examination of the synods and councils held in Castile and Aragon in the thirteenth century, at a time when we might expect to find the papacy on top, in fact shows an almost total subservience of the clergy to state and royal policy. The Church was protected, even cosseted, by the State: but it was a captive Church. In the fifteenth century, and still more in the sixteenth, the grip of the crown was tightened, as it was elsewhere in Europe, by formal concordats and agreements, which spelt out the respective rights of crown and papacy in such a way as to make it clear that the state interest remained paramount. The fact that Spanish-Habsburg diplomatic and political policy might be, as a rule, in general alignment with papal aims, or that the Spanish crown might be in full agreement with papal doctrinal positions, and enforce them in its territories, does not alter the absolute determination of the Spanish State to control the ecclesiastical scene – to the total exclusion of independent papal action. The Spanish Inquisition was essentially an organ of royal power, one of whose functions was to 'protect' the Spanish Church from influence by outside agencies, including the papacy. Hence the domination of the Church by the crown was perhaps more comprehensive in Spain during the sixteenth century than in any other Europe state, including those with a Protestant, Erastian system.

France, too, ceased to be an effective field for papal penetration, once the monarchy began to establish itself as the dominant force, from the beginning of the thirteenth century. The popes repeatedly used French power to smash the Staufen. It could be said that they thus replaced a potential master with an actual one. The papacy, which had helped to create the western empire as a protective force in the eighth century, destroyed it in the thirteenth without making any long-term arrangements to provide an alternative source of assistance. Yet the papacy still needed protection; and, *faut de mieux*, it had to look to one or other of the emergent nation-states. The choice was usually France until, in the sixteenth century, it shifted to Spain and Austria. And the French kings, like the more exigent emperors before them, tended to treat the Pope as their chief bishop, rather than as an independent power. Thus, as the thirteenth century progressed, there was a yawning gap between the inflation of the papal claims, and the deflation of its real authority. In 1298, for instance, Boniface VIII was asked to arbitrate between Edward I of England and Philip the Fair of France over their Gascon disputes. Proctors were appointed, and the Pope issued a series of bulls; but at the last minute, under pressure from France, he was obliged to admit that he acted, as he put it, 'simply as a private person, as Lord Benedict Gaetani'.

The career of Lord Benedict Gaetani, indeed, may be said to have led to the calling of the papal bluff. Before him, there was still a certain mysterious potency to the papal claims, a lingering possibility that they might be established. After him, it was evident that the institution had reached its maximum development as a physical force in European politics, and could only decline. Boniface published *Clericis laicos* in France in 1296, and in England the following year. Edward I retaliated by ordering judges to withdraw the protection of the courts from clergymen who declined to pay taxes, and at the same time he instructed sheriffs to seize and hold church lands. In France, Philip the Fair banned the export of currency. Thus the secular world responded with material measures to the spiritual threats of the clerical: it was a reminder that clergy needed royal justice as much as kings needed clerical absolution, and that the papacy could no more survive without French and English bullion shipped to Rome, than the crowns of England and France could govern without taxing the clergy. Boniface did not heed these warnings, and the contest with France came to a head. The Pope issued a series of bulls in France – *Ausculta fili*, addressed directly to the king; *Super Petri solio,* threatening excommunication; *Salvator mundi*, withdrawing all previous papal grants and favours; and *Ante promotionem*, ordering all French prelates to come to Rome for a council to preserve the liberties of the Church. In 1302, Philip got unanimous support for his anti-papal policy from the French Estates-General. In April 1303, Boniface issued an ultimatum threatening excommunication and an interdict by September. In June, Philip had Boniface charged at the court of the Louvre with illegal election, simony, immorality, violence, irreligion and heresy, and the court gave the crown authority for the Pope to be seized. William of Nogaret, who had pressed the charges on Philip's behalf, arrested the Pope at Anagni on 7 September, the day before the ultimatum expired, using men drawn from the Pope's enemies in Rome and its neighbourhood. Boniface was soon released, but died in October. It was the end of the papal afflatus. The papacy had discovered, again, that secular power, however inferior, was necessary to the protection of the Holy See. Two years later, the papacy moved from the disorders of Rome to the tranquility and comfort of Avignon, under the umbrella of French power. There followed the 'Babylonian captivity', the Great Schism, the conciliar epoch and, in due course, the restoration of an independent papacy. But in the meantime the national, secular state had emerged, and the total Christian society had ceased to exist.

It may be asked: after the decisive defeat of papal pretensions by the secular monarchs, why did the clerical system, radiating from the papacy, continue to survive for so long? The answer is not simple. Of course, the system was inherently strong and ramifying. It was the only international system in Europe, with a centralized direction and a tentacle in every village. Its roots were very deep, and it dominated a huge area of human behaviour. By Boniface's time, the canonical system had already reached its full development – only details remained to be added – and it would have been exceedingly hard to dig out. It handled a lot of matters which the secular law and authority did not touch. The machinery to replace it was not then available, and would have had to be improvised. For this, and for a variety of other reasons, the kings were against change. So long as the papacy was prepared, in practice, to do a deal with them, they were content to leave the theoretical debate unresolved and unargued. On the whole, it was simpler and cheaper to deal direct with the papacy, than with an uncontrolled national clergy. On clerical taxation, which was what the kings cared about most, pope and king agreed to share the spoils, as they had over the appointment of bishops; and they came to the same agreement about lesser benefices. Of course the crown, increasingly, got the lion's share; but this would probably have happened anyway. The maintenance of the papal-dominated system of canon law enabled such transactions to be conducted with dignity and legality, in outward appearance at least. There was nothing Christian, or indeed religious, about such arrangements. It was in every respect morally and socially inferior to the Carolingian ideal of clerics and laymen, each in their allotted roles, working together to build an Augustinian earthly city on scriptural precepts. With the new system, in effect, the leading clerics and laymen conspired together to milk the Church largely for worldly purposes. All the possessing classes benefited, in one way or another. So long as the various crowns found it desirable to uphold the institutions and doctrines of the Church, and defend its property and privileges, there was not much possibility of change. In due course, and in certain areas, rulers were persuaded by reformers that it was their religious duty to amend matters; that was a different story.

Nevertheless, though the system endured, it lost its appeal to the popular imagination. In the Dark Ages, the Church had stood for everything that was progressive, enlightened and humane in Europe; it had made, as we have seen, an enormous material contribution to the resurrection of civilization from the ashes and the raising of standards. It had created a continent in (with all its imperfections) a benign image. In the eleventh century, even in the twelfth, the Church – by which we now mean essentially the clergy – still preserved its identification with ameliorative change. At certain levels, the Gregorian reforms were undoubtedly popular. Many different categories of people, for a variety of reasons, welcomed an alternative power to the crown or (more usually) a clerical counterpoise to the local secular lord. Then, between 1150 and 1250, a fundamental change took place. Royal justice improved and manorial courts slipped into the background. Clerical sources of income came to be seen as exactions, and clerical privileges as abuses. The Church, as a hierarchical institution, ceased to be regarded with affection and respect; as a powerful phenomenon, it continued to inspire awe and fear, but the obedience it received was tinged with a growing element of hostility.

Above all, the official Church began to be associated with financial exactions. We have hints of this even in the late twelfth century. Then, in the opening decades of the thirteenth, we have the first real evidence, at the lowest level, of resistance of payment of tithes; and, in more educated circles, of downright anti-clericalism. One such episode occurred in 1238, during the visit of a papal legate to Oxford. It began amicably, with the student-clerks paying what was intended to be a courtesy-call at the legate's lodging. But there was a linguistic misunderstanding, and they were rudely refused admittance by the legate's Italian butler. Immediately, the atmosphere changed and latent hostility came to the surface. The students pushed their way in. A poor Irish chaplain, who happened to be begging at the back door, had a basin of scalding water flung in his face by the legate's brother. General fighting broke out, the clerks shouting: 'Where is that usurer, that simoniac, robber of revenues and insatiate of money who, perverting our king and subverting our kingdom, plunders us to fill strangers' coffers?' The legate had to flee for his life, and there were long and complicated legal consequences.

This kind of incident was unusual in the thirteenth century. The big change came in the next hundred years. Even around 1300 hardly anyone questioned either the spiritual supremacy of the Pope, or the validity of his legislative acts and appointments. By 1400 the papal *plenitudo potestatis*, and the whole medieval ecclesiastical system was being openly and repeatedly challenged. Of course the intensity and the subject matter of criticism varied from place to place. England, for instance, came of age linguistically and culturally in the fourteenth century, and an emergent xenophobia, force-fed by the war with France, identified the papacy and thus the Church as an international institution with the French cause. It was a commonplace to say: 'The Pope is French, but Jesus Christ is English.' On the other hand, the fourteenth century identification of the papacy with France did not make it any more popular with Frenchmen; on the contrary. The papacy never really recovered from the move to Avignon. It lost the magic of the imperial connection. Much more important, it was no longer associated with the radiating power of the dead apostle Peter. It is true that, by the fourteenth century, the cult of relics was very much on the decline – by the time the popes moved back to Rome it was virtually dead – or perhaps one should say that relics no longer inspired total belief and real fear, but rather appealed to the residual superstition of all. On the other hand, the popes in Rome were a metaphysical fact, on top of everything else; in Avignon, they were simply an institution.

In 1300, 200,000 people had come to Rome for the jubilee; Christians did not come to Avignon except on business. It worked far more efficiently than the old Roman *curia*. It was more centralized. Avignon generated more missionary activity than Rome, and a great deal more diplomacy. It was a brilliant court, with up to thirty cardinals in residence, each with his palace. But it was totally without a spiritual atmosphere. The English parliament officially termed it 'the sinful city of Avignon'. Its concerns were power, law and money. Petrarch wrote:

'Here reign the successors of the poor fishermen of Galilee. They have quite forgotten their origins . . . Babylon, the home of all vices and misery . . . there is no piety, no charity, no faith, no reverence, no fear of God, nothing holy, nothing just, nothing sacred. All you have ever heard or read of perfidy, deceit, hardness of pride, shamelessness and unrestrained debauch – in short every example of impiety and evil the world has to show you are collected here. . . . Here one loses all good things, first liberty, then successively repose, happiness, faith, hope and charity.'

During the Avignon regime, the central machinery of the Church turned itself primarily into a money-raising organization. In France alone, there were twenty-three papal collectors, and their staffs, distributed through the thirteen archbishoprics; and in the Vatican Library today there survive twenty-two huge manuscript volumes containing petitions and letters concerning appointments settled by papal provisions, the principal source of papal wealth.

The sources are really too fragmentary to make accurate estimates of what the Church as a whole, and the papacy in particular, received. In England, the clergy, with one per cent of the population, disposed of about twenty-five per cent of the gross national product. This was about average. In some parts of France and Germany the Church was wealthier and owned one-third to a half of all real estate. The papacy creamed off about ten per cent of the Church's income, in the form of annates; and it received huge sums direct from the public. In the popular mind, the Church was thought to be even wealthier than it actually was. In 1376, for instance, a House of Commons petition stated that sums received from the English clergy by the papacy in the form of annates amounted to five times the revenues of the English crown. This was manifestly absurd. What is clear is that by the beginning of the fifteenth century, the image of the Church was financial rather than spiritual. Adam of Usk, a case-hardened ecclesiastical lawyer from Wales, was nevertheless shocked by his first visit to Rome in *c*. 1415: 'At Rome everything is bought and sold. Benefices are given not for desert, but to the highest bidder. Everyone with money keeps it in the merchant's bank, to further his advancement. . . . As, therefore, under the old dispensation, miracles ceased when the priests were corrupted by venality, so I fear it will come to pass under the new; the danger standeth daily knocking at the very doors of the church.'

On the whole, this type of criticism tended to come from the clergy. Laymen did not care how clerics got their appointments, provided they were decent men who attended to their duties. But there were certain exactions which affected all classes, and were deeply and increasingly resented. Most of these became obtrusive, and so came to be regarded as abuses, in the thirteenth and fourteenth centuries. Perhaps the worst was the mortuary, a clerical by-product of the feudal heriot or death-duty. It may have been voluntary in origin, as so many of the payments to the Church were; or it may have been based on the presumption that the dead man had failed to pay all his tithes, so his second-best possession should go to the Church as compensation. It had no foundation in secular law. Indeed, it varied enormously. One common form was for the dead man's family to hand over his bed, or bedding, to the parish priest. This was causing resentment even by the beginning of the thirteenth century. Innocent III wrote to his French legates in 1204: 'Warn the clergy that they use no burdensome exaction and dishonourable importunity with regard to the bedding which is brought with the corpses to their churches; on the other hand, take care to induce the laity by diligent warning to maintain in these matters that laudable custom.' Why was it laudable? It would be hard to think of anything more calculated to scandalize than such a compulsory exaction from a bereaved family. What made it so odious was that it was applied to the very poor. The Abbot of Schwanheim could claim a heriot 'from any who had only so much land on his domain as he could set a three-legged stool upon'. On the Continent, certain abbeys could claim up to one-third of the goods of the dead man. There was nothing like this in England. But the Vicar of Morstow claimed 'the best day-garment of each parishioner that dieth in the said parish'; and the Rector of Silverton 'the second-best possession or best'. Sometimes clerical landowners got a double death-duty, as lord and as rector; thus the Abbot of Gloucester Abbey got his tenants' 'best-beast as lord, and another as rector'. Mortuaries were taken on a wife's death, as well as a husband's; and if a husband died away from home, his estate was sometimes charged in two parishes. Sometimes, in one parish, both the rector and the vicar claimed.

Mortuaries were so much hated, and led to so much trouble, that secular authorities tried to ban them. But by the latter part of the medieval period the Church, as an organization, had become totally insensitive to this type of appeal; and it was imbued with the philosophy of canon law which tended to insist that to abandon a customary right might actually be sinful. Pierre

Albert, Grand-Prior of Cluny, defending them at the Council of Basle, 1431–43, could not produce any intrinsic, scriptural or natural law justification, and fell back entirely on custom: 'And so this custom began as a lion-cub, which cometh forth at first as an abortion, and is afterwards quickened by his mother's licking . . . this is quickened by an unbroken course of time and by consent, whether tacit or by the mere rendering and payment of the thing.' In fact, mortuaries were often refused; then the clergy might have taken them by force. This led to riots, as we know from reports to the authorities. Or a man might make transfers of property before death; but these were often invalidated by law (the Church had charge of wills). In Zurich, a man had to be able to walk without staff, crutches or help seven feet from his house to make a valid transfer. The most usual method of enforcement, however, was simply to refuse burial until the goods were handed over. Pierre Albert admitted this could be called simony, but added: 'In these cases, let the corpse first be buried, and then let an action be brought against the heirs'. The big-wigs of the Church were anxious to defend the custom not least because it was an important part of the income of the underpaid working clergy, who had no access to the pluralities system. As one sixteenth-century lawyer put it: 'Curates loved mortuaries better than their lives'; and 'therefore in many places there arose great division and grudge between [clergy and laity].' The abuse continued, even increased, right up to the Reformation. In 1515 Parliament petitioned Henry VIII that priests 'daily refuse to fetch and receive the corpses of such deceased persons . . . but if some best jewel, garment, cloth or other best thing as aforesaid be given them'. Following a major scandal, 21 Henry VIII *c*.6(1529) regulated mortuaries, and abolished them altogether for people dying with less than ten marks in movable goods; but trouble did not end until it was scrapped completely – 'There were few things within this realm that caused more variance', wrote an Elizabethan, 'among the people, than they did when [mortuaries] were suffered.'

Mortuaries led to rows with the clergy at every level of society. On the whole, townsmen were more likely to give trouble than peasants. It was the refusal of a Londoner to hand over his child's burial-robe, as mortuary, which led to the notorious 'murder in the Lollard's Tower' in 1515, a real harbinger of the English Reformation. Yet townsmen in the later Middle Ages were not exactly anti-Church, as such. They supported an enormous number of clergy – about twenty times as many, per head of population, as today. Most of these were paid by voluntary contributions or out of endowments. A survey of urban wills shows that wealthier townsmen, at least, left a huge percentage of their property for religious purposes or charities. And the sums they contributed to the building or rebuilding of their parish churches, in the fourteenth and fifteenth centuries, were enormous. The great majority of extant English medieval churches, for instance, were rebuilt in the Perpendicular style, from about 1320 onwards – usually the naves, in contrast to the chancels, which were the responsibility of the rector. Nor did they spend their money simply on the stone fabric: parishioners installed glorious tie-beams, arch-beams, waggon-beams, coffered ceilings, angel-and-hammer beams, chancel and parclose screens, carved oak pulpits, lecterns, font-covers and pews, and reredoses and effigies of alabaster; and they presented pattens, chalices, vestments, altar-cloths, bells, crucifixes, lamps and censers in prodigious quantities, to judge only from those that have survived. It would be true to say that laymen in the towns and large villages spent more on building and adorning churches, in the later part of the Middle Ages, than the clergy. But the money was spent essentially on aspects of religion directly related to their own lives, and within a stone's throw of their houses and workshops: on the parish church or, even more, on thousands of chantry chapels and religious guilds to which they belonged (Norwich alone had 164 guilds in 1389). It could be called a selfish form of religion; indeed, the whole trend of Christianity in these centuries – led by the clergy as a caste – was in the direction of the pursuit of eternal self-interest. Clergy used their privileges, and laity used their money (when they had it) to buy the mechanical means to salvation. The idea of the anonymous Christian community, so very powerful in earlier times, was pushed into the background.

One outstanding example of this tendency was the construction, maintenance and functioning of the medieval cathedrals. There are a good many common illusions about these institutions. In the first place, they were not built by the clergy, or by the community, but by professional workmen, on a strict cash basis. This is made quite clear by surviving fabric-rolls and other documents. Where clergymen played a part, it was a matter of note: thus the Gloucester Chartulary records: 'In 1242 was completed the new vault over the nave of the church, not by the extraneous aid of professional workmen, as before, but by the vigorous hands of the monks who resided on the spot.' During the construction of the new choir at Lincoln, 1191–1200, the work of the lay master-mason, Geoffrey de Noiers, the Bishop, Hugh the Burgundian, 'oftentimes bore the hod-load of hewn stone or of building lime'. But these were exceptional cases. The bishop or chapter, or both, promoted the building scheme, and a member of the chapter was appointed *custos operis* or warden, but his duties were purely administrative. Elyas de Derham, who had been a master-mason, designer and Keeper of the Works for Henry III at Winchester, was later made canon of Salisbury and put in charge of the cathedral building there – the only case of a cathedral being built as a piece, in the space of one lifetime (twenty-five years); but even so, the *cementarius*, or master-mason, during most of the construction period was a professional layman, one Robertus. The master-mason was, in effect, the designer, builder and controller. Master Robert built St Albans, in the period following 1077; Master Andrew the nave of Old St Paul's, from 1127; William of Sens the choir of Canterbury, from 1174; William Ramsey worked on Canterbury and Lichfield in the second quarter of the fourteenth century; William of

Colchester built the central tower of York, from 1410, and Thomas Mapilton worked on Westminster Abbey, 1423–34, and so on. Sometimes master-carpenters played key roles – the outstanding example being William Hurley, who built the famous Octagon at Ely in the 1320s. But the master-masons, who can be identified in about 300 cases, were almost always the men who mattered. They were grand figures. They travelled in style with a retinue, as we know from their expenses, and were sometimes granted manors, or exempted from jury-service or other irksome duties. It was not uncommon for them to own stone-quarries, and to serve as consultant-architects to a number of cathedrals and important ecclesiastical (and secular) fabrics. Such great figures, summoned from afar, might arouse local resentment: when Henry IV lent his royal master-mason to York about 1410, the locals 'conspired together to kill him and his assistant' – the assistant was actually slain.

Building was purely a secular operation. Especially at Exeter and York, the fabric-rolls furnish details over long periods (though there are important gaps). In England, except during the Norman period, when Saxon labour was conscripted (for instance at Durham), the workmen were all professionals, and had to join lodges. In many parts of central Europe and Spain conscript labour was used; and in England, too, craftsmen were conscripted, but only for work on royal foundations, and fortresses. There is no evidence that compulsion was applied to non-royal ecclesiastical buildings. And of course there was no question of voluntary unskilled labour – the guilds would not have allowed it. The cathedral chapters, or the monks, had to pay the going rates. It was not a labour of love. Indeed, constant and strenuous efforts were made to lay down rules and hours of work, and enforce them. This is attested by the survival – especially at Ely, Winchester and Gloucester – of thousands of 'banker-marks' on individual stones, which allowed masons to be identified and their work counted and checked. The 1370 fabric roll of York notes: 'All their times and hours shall be revealed by a bill, ordained therefore'; they were to be at work 'as early as they may see skilfully by daylight and they shall stand there truly working all day, as long as they may see skilfully for the work.' They got an hour at noon for a meal, and 'all their times and hours shall be revealed by a bell ordained therefore'; a slacker was 'chastised by abaiting of his payment'. This brief was laid down in 1344 after a report to the chapter revealed negligence, idleness and indiscipline, in which everyone from the master-mason and master-carpenter down was involved. The master admitted he had lost control; the men were unruly and insubordinate; there had been strikes among the labourers; timber, stone, lime and cement had been stolen; and much expensive damage had been caused by carelessness and incompetence.

The major cost items were wages, and the purchase and transportation of stone and timber. All this had to be paid for at market-prices. True, the crown sometimes helped by allowing bulk goods to travel without paying tolls. William I, a generous benefactor of the Church, gave Bishop Walkeleyn of

Winchester permission to cut as much timber in the Forest of Hempage as his men could remove in four days and nights; he was furious when the bishop brought 'an innumerable troop' and denuded a large part of the forest. Such generosity became almost unknown in the later Middle Ages. Royal cash and resources went exclusively to foundations in the king's name – another example of the growing religious self-centredness. To build cathedrals meant raising enormous quantities of hard cash. Wealthy court bishops, like Stapleton of Exeter, or Wykeham of Winchester, provided large sums themselves. But most of the money was raised by the sale of spiritual privileges. The thirteenth century choir-arm of St Paul's was financed by forty-day indulgences, sold all over the country, and even in Wales. The 1349–50 fabric roll of Exeter itemized a payment of eight shillings for a scribe to write out 800 indulgences for sale to contributors to the building fund. Money could also be raised by financial penances; the system was critically examined in a book published in 1450 by Thomas Gascoigne, the fiercely orthodox but reformist Chancellor of Oxford. He says that in the desperate efforts to raise funds for York, largest and most expensive of all the English cathedrals, parishes were being 'farmed out' to professional fund-raisers, who were taking a large cut of the proceeds. There were also straightforward begging-missions, run by *quaestores*, much used by York, and also open to abuse; and there were guilds of benefactors formed to raise regular sums – the members being compensated by privileges, exemptions, and so forth. The privileges, right to issue indulgences, and other spiritual knick-knacks had to be obtained in Rome (or Avignon) and likewise paid for. So the wheels of the Church went round. Nothing was for nothing. Even so, money to build often ran out; it is the chief reason why the cathedrals took so long to complete: a century for the nave of Old St Paul's, 150 years for the nave of Westminster Abbey; major construction was going on at York from 1220–1475, over 250 years, and at Lichfield from 1195–1350.

Anyway, what were cathedrals for? Originally they had been the only church of the diocese, or at any rate the only one where all the sacraments could be administered. Then they tended to become, in addition, shrines for valuable (and money-raising) relics. Thomas Becket posthumously paid for much of the rebuilding of Canterbury in the later Middle Ages. The body of Edward II, brutally murdered, and in the eyes of many martyred, paid for the marvellous perpendicular choir at Gloucester Abbey. Among the most popular were Cuthbert at Durham, Etheldreda at Ely, William of Perth at Rochester, Swithun at Winchester and Wulfstan and Oswald at Worcester. A cathedral without a well-known saint was missing an important source of revenue; and for this reason efforts were made to secure from Rome the canonization of people buried within the fabric; but Rome had to be cajoled, and paid. Even so, there were shrines of many unofficial saints whose status had never been regularized by Rome – Bishop Button at Wells, for instance, who cured toothache, and in York Archibishop Richard Scrope, executed as a rebel. Almost any royal or princely person who came to a tragic end was liable to be venerated, irrespective of his actual merits: thus Thomas, Earl of Lancaster, executed by Edward II in 1322, attracted an enthusiastic cult in St Paul's until the king angrily had his remains removed.

These shrines were nearly always in the choir or sanctuary, which were barred from the rest of the cathedral by massive iron gates. They were only opened at stated times, when the public was admitted in groups on payment of a fee. Otherwise they never got beyond the nave. Indeed, it is hard to see the cathedrals as serving Christians as a whole. They were built essentially for the clergy and the upper classes, and to some extent for well-to-do townsmen. The choir-arm was a chapel reserved exclusively for the canons in a secular cathedral, or the convent in a monastic one. The laity had no part in the services, and indeed when they stood in the nave (which had no benches or chairs), the high altar would be obscured by the screen or *pulpitum*. Sometimes no nave was built at all, as at Beauvais. Usually, it formed a vast vestibule for the choir, used for professional purposes. It was not intended for lay worship except where, as in a few cathedrals, building it had involved knocking down a parish church. Then an altar would be set up and function. But most naves were big, empty and dirty places, not elaborately decorated like the 'clerical' part of the building. Often they were used for trade. In 1554, under 'Bloody' Mary, the City of London corporation forbade anyone to use the nave of St Paul's as a short cut to carry casks of beer, or loads of fruit and fish, from the river to the markets.

In some cases the public could get into the transepts. More often these and other parts of the cathedral were filled up by chantry chapels, paid for from the wills of wealthy people for the saying of daily masses for their souls, and to which only the donors' families were admitted. Chapels gradually occupied all the empty space, together with extra altars for the saying of masses for the dead – these, too, had to be paid for. From the fourteenth century, in fact, the cathedrals became an accumulation of chapels and altars under one roof for the endless round of soul-masses for lay and ecclesiastical benefactors. Even by the beginning of the thirteenth century, before commemorative masses became popular, Durham had accumulated over 7,000 a year; later they were reckoned in tens of thousands. From the thirteenth century, too, dates the practice of burying wealthy laymen and ecclesiastics within the fabric. Hitherto it had been rare, except for founders; even the early kings and queens of Kent were buried outside in the grounds of St Augustine's, Canterbury. Then, in 740, the papacy decreed that archbishops might be buried within their cathedral, and thereafter the rule was broadened until from about 1250 it was a matter of cash – thus the rich and well-born cluttered up the interior. Over this ocular assertion of the fact that money might count in the next world, as well as in this, soared the dramatic battlements of the edifice, the needs of stone architecture – stone progressively replaced timber – to a large extent dictating shape, while size became, as it were, an arrogant assertion of the power and distinctiveness of the clerical class, and of their lay benefactors whose bones were housed below. Vaingloriousness led to length in England (the nave of St Paul's was 585 feet long; Winchester 526), and height in France (beginning with Notre Dame, *c.* 1165, at 110 feet, then leaping up with each successive cathedral in the Île de France – Chartres 114, Reims 125, Amiens 140, and culminating in Beauvais, 154). When, in the sixteenth century, relics were discredited and masses for the dead forbidden in northern Europe, the cathedrals lost much of their purpose; the radical reformers were puzzled what to do with them. No wonder; an analysis of the building, growth and functioning of the cathedrals explains many of the reasons why the Reformation occurred.

'Mechanical Christianity' as we may call it, was accordingly conducted, in the towns, primarily for the 'respectable' citizen, and more particularly for the well-to-do benefactor. What about the country? The overwhelming majority of parish churches, as such documents as *Domesday Book* indicate, were privately owned and expected to make a profit. Whether the peasantry were well served by priests depended very largely on the fertility of the soil and the general level of prosperity. Priests tended to concentrate in the towns or the wealthier country districts. In theory, every adult was expected to know the basic elements of the faith. An early Carolingian decree laid down: 'Let all men be compelled to learn the Creed and the Lord's Prayer, or profession of faith.' The sanctions for males were 'to be beaten or abstain from all drink except water', and for females 'stripes or fasting'. These orders could not be carried out, since the trained clergy were lacking or unwilling to live in country districts. Most country priests were ignorant men themselves, though in theory they had to be literate. This is a ground of bitter complaint by visiting and other dignitaries in every country throughout the Middle Ages. In 1222, out of seventeen priests serving livings held by the dean and chapter at Salisbury, five could not construe the first sentence of the first collect of the canon. Such examples are endless. Guillaume le Maire, Bishop of Angers in the early fourteenth century, complained that his priests included 'innumerable contemptible persons of abject life, utterly unworthy in learning and morals ... from whose execrable lives and pernicious ignorance infinite scandals arise, the church sacraments are despised by the laity, and in many districts the layfolk hold the priests as viler and more despicable than Jews.' This was a problem of poverty and education. The bishops might well complain: why did they not do anything? Selection and training of clergy was the bishop's responsibility; yet not one built a seminary throughout the Middle Ages – there was no such thing until the sixteenth century. Nor did any bishop, so far as we know, institute diocesan funds to raise the stipends of the poorer priests and so improve their 'abject life' – though such equalization funds had been used in the earliest Church.

The truth is that the Church tended to be hostile to the peasants. There were very few peasant saints. Medieval clerical writers emphasize the bestiality, violence and avarice of the peasant. We get few genuine glimpses of peasant life in the documents; most clerical critics dealt with popular stereotypes. Clericalism was increasingly an urban phenomenon in the later Middle Ages. It was rare to see a priest in the country districts. Joan of Arc came from a pious family; but it is interesting to observe in her deposition how infrequently the clergy impinged on her life. What the Church and peasant had most in common was devotion to relics. In the villages they were used for oath-taking and all kinds of purposes. And the peasants valued the church for its efforts to avert natural disasters.* Parish priests exorcized and cursed storms, and they tried to drive away swarms of locusts by excommunications and processions. In a monastic formulary dating from 1526–31, we find a service for banishing caterpillars and 'palmer worms' from the diocese of Troyes, on condition the peasants paid their tithes. Documents often refer to the excommunication (and hanging) of animals for antisocial offences. In 1531, a French canon lawyer, Chassenée, defended the practice in his *De Excommunicatione Animalium Insectorum*. He claimed it had often worked, citing eels expelled from lakes, sparrows from churches, and so on. Caterpillars and similar pests would laugh if proceeded against in a secular court; therefore they should be struck 'with the pain of anathema, which they fear more, as creatures obedient to the God who made them'. However, he added, the law should be observed, and an advocate appointed to plead their defence. In some cases, pieces of waste ground, to which they were sentenced to remove themselves, were provided.

Above all, however, what the peasant wanted from the Church was some hope of salvation. This was the overwhelming reason why Christianity replaced paganism: it had a very clear-cut theory of what happened after death, and of how eternal happiness could be gained. The appeal was to all classes: it was the one thing which enabled the Church to hold society together. Yet this aspect of Christianity, too, was subtly changed over the centuries, and balanced in favour of the possessing classes: indeed, it became the central feature of mechanical religion. As we have seen, baptism was originally regarded as the prelude to an imminent *parousia*. Only gradually, as the *parousia* receded, did the Church have to grapple with the problem of sin after baptism, and the second (or third and subsequent) repentance.

---

* Peasants also benefited from feast-days, which grew more numerous throughout the Middle Ages. Alfred's law-code, *c*. 890, listed twelve days at Christmas, fourteen at Easter, a week in mid August, and three other days. These were 'to be given to all free men but not to slaves or unfree labourers'. By the twelfth century all agricultural workers were included, and got thirty–forty free days; manorial records show that the system was gradually enforced, though certain days were more holy than others, and more holy for some people than for others. The tendency was for the number of days to increase – first vigils were demanded, then octaves; and after the Black Death, when labour became scarcer, 'servants', who hitherto had not been paid on most or all of the holy-days, now had to be paid for some and eventually for almost all. The system was enormously complicated and bore little or no relation to the needs of agriculture: so much for the theory that Christian feasts merely reproduced immemorial pagan ones. See Barbara Harvey, 'Works and *Festa Ferianda* in Medieval England', *Journal of Ecclesiastical History* (1972). The idea of workers' holy-days persisted after the Reformation and re-emerged in the form of the 'Grand National Holiday', on which the Quaker William Benbow, in 1832, based the first theory of the General Strike. See Patrick Renshaw, *The General Strike* (London, 1975).

Moreover, it is fair to say that the problem was never satisfactorily resolved. It was agreed that a post-baptismal sin had to be confessed in some form. Ambrose thought it might be done publicly, to a priest, or privately to oneself. If confession took place to a priest, he would try to intercede with God; but the confessors (here Ambrose quoted Origen) had no power to do anything except pray and advise. The Church's actual formularies were framed only for public confession, and penance. But an exception was introduced in the case of adulteresses, who might risk their lives if they confessed publicly; and these exceptions, or concessions, multiplied. In 459, Leo I forbade reading confessions in public; he said it sufficed to confess to God, and then to a priest or bishop, who would pray for the sinner. By the time of Gregory the Great it was accepted that confession was necessary for the remission of sin, and that it was in sacerdotal hands; but it was apparently accompanied by a public ceremony. Auricular confession, in its mature form, was probably a by-product of the conversion of the Germanic tribes; it was established much more slowly in southern Europe. Of course most people preferred it to public humiliation; the chief brake on its expansion was the shortage of priests. The Council of Châlons, 813, laid down that confessions in private to God or to a priest were equally effective; and delayed, or death-bed, confessions were popular – as baptism had once been. Auricular confession as a standard, and as a sacrament, developed *pari passu* with papal and clericalist theory in the late eleventh and twelfth centuries, and was clearly connected with them. The first formulation of the sacramental basis was by the Paris schoolmen, especially by Peter Lombard, who relied on a forged Augustinian tract (Augustine did not in fact deal with the problem). Pseudo-Isidorian forgeries played a major role in the evolution of the related 'Power of the Keys' theory. The salient forgery was in the *Capitularies of Benedict the Levite*, a supposed document of Clement I, reciting his ordination as Bishop of Rome, in which Peter formally transmitted to him the power of the keys; Peter was made to say that bishops were the keys of the Church since they have the power to open and close the gates of Heaven. Hence, in the twelfth century, confession to a priest in private was the only form still used in the West, except in certain monasteries where the earlier tradition of public confession lingered on for a time. The Council of Paris, 1198, published the first synodical code of instructions for confessors; and at the Lateran Council in 1216 Innocent III made auricular confession compulsory for all adult Christians. There remained an unresolved argument throughout the Middle Ages whether confession was a human or divine institution; then, in the sixteenth century, the denial of the Reformers that it was a sacrament at all hardened opinion among the papalists, and the Council of Trent declared it divine.

Innocent III's insistence on confession to a priest, in private, undoubtedly sprang from his resolve to fight deviation and heresy by all means available. It enabled the Church to be far more flexible in its tactics, and to adapt them to particular problems, places and men. And, whereas public confession was a form of rude democracy, the carefully selected confessor underpinned the hierarchy of society. Confessing a king, a duke or an archbishop was a highly skilled clerical trade, as many manuals survive to testify – they give us, among other things, revealing insights into medieval political theory. The development of the 'private confessor' was yet one more indication that, in the eyes of the Church, Christians were not necessarily equal even in spiritual matters.

The principle tended to be extended to penance also; or, more particularly, to the methods of performing it. The Christian promise of salvation, so hugely attractive to the Mediterranean world and, later, to the northern barbarians, was balanced by a horrifying theory of the alternative for sinners. The existence of Hell, as some of the early Fathers had argued, helped to justify Heaven; at any rate, it seemed to unsophisticated minds to make salvation seem more credible. There was never absolute agreement about how many would be saved. Origen had thought it possible all might, in the end, be redeemed; but this opinion was condemned by a sixth-century council and the tendency in the Dark Ages was to reduce the possibilities sharply. By the thirteenth century, official opinion had stabilized: 'few', thought Aquinas, would be saved, and 'very many' damned; most later medieval preachers put the saved as one in 1,000 or even one in 10,000. Hence, with the development of Hell-theory and the paucity of the saved, the difficulty of obtaining full remission for sin naturally increased. Dark Age penances were almost incredibly arduous. Like secular crimes, they were based on the principle of compensation – not to the victim, however, but to God. And how could an outraged God be compensated in full? The only way to do it was to inflate the idea of self-denial. Thus most early penances centred on endless periods of fasting. Wulfstan of York refers to one man who was sentenced to fast, barefoot, on Monday, Wednesday and Saturday, for the rest of his life, to wear only a woollen garment, and to have only three haircuts a year. Fasting was often accompanied by compulsory pilgrimages, or visits to large numbers of shrines. Thus parricide – quite a common crime in the Dark Ages – was punished by exile: the penitent, bound in chains, had to go on pilgrimage until the chains were so worn that they fell off.

There were many practical problems connected with penance. Custom varied enormously. Written penitentiaries disagreed wildly, and rival experts heaped abuse on each other. Peter Damian was particularly violent in his criticism of confessors who took sodomy lightly; he thought the eighth-century penitentiary of Archbishop Egbert of York, standard in England, composed of 'theatrical ravings', 'the incantations of the devil', and 'a monster created by man, with the head of a horse and hooves of a goat'. Then, too, many penances were almost impossible to perform. The more sincere the repentance, the more seriously the penitent would take the task imposed on him; often a man might spend the rest of his life in terror at failure. And what if he died before the penance was over? The Church only slowly adopted the theory of purgatory to meet this difficulty.

The harsh, even cruel, Dark Age practice of inordinate penance not only gave credibility to the idea of salvation; in a way, it gave credibility to the whole of Christian society. The brutal scourging of a naked king or archbishop was exciting evidence of spiritual equality before God, and man. But once the clerical experts found mechanical means to erode the full penitential rigours, a yawning hole began to appear in the fabric of Christian conviction. Such means were all too easily discovered: the real evil of canon law was that it constantly chipped away – rather like modern tax-lawyers – at the egalitarian provisions in Christianity. It rebuilt hierarchies and pyramids on democratic spiritual foundations, and introduced the cash nexus into the supposed world to come. The canon lawyer was always engaged in a struggle with Death the Leveller, and always beat him – at least to the satisfaction of the papal curia.

It is in the seventh century that we first hear of men undertaking to perform the penances of others, in return for payment. This was forbidden; indeed, at first the Church opposed any form of commutation. The first loop-hole allowed was vicarious penance without pay. A man might perform another's penance from motives of love (or fear; or hope of future favour). Thus we find an early case where a powerful man got through a seven-year fasting penance in three days with the help of 840 followers. And once vicarial penance in any form was admitted, it proved impossible to keep money out of it. Was not alms-giving a form of penance? There, it was argued, the payment was to God, or to God's servants to perform God's purposes, and could not, therefore, be reprehensible. The Church at first opposed penitential alms-giving, too, as an easy way to Heaven for the rich man. But it soon found justificatory texts: 'The ransom of a man's life are his riches' (Proverbs, 13:8); and 'Make unto yourselves friends of the mammon of unrighteousness, that when ye fail, they may receive you into everlasting habitations.' This last passage was particularly useful; it might almost have been framed by an ingenious canon lawyer for his professional purposes. Thus the penitential system was quite quickly transformed into a means whereby the wealth of the sinful rich could be diverted into ecclesiastical endowments. An early case was that of the Anglo-Saxon Wulfin, who slew six priests; he went on a penitential trip to Rome, and was there told to endow a foundation for seven monks to pray for him for ever. Another case, from the tenth century, was Eadwulf, King Edgar's Chancellor. He loved his little son so much that he had him sleep between himself and his wife; one night, both were drunk and the son was suffocated. Eadwulf proposed to walk to Rome as a barefoot pilgrim; but he was told to repair a church instead.

The idea of ecclesiastical foundations as atonement for grievous sin became a striking feature of the tenth, eleventh and twelfth centuries. It explains why so many abbeys and priories were endowed by wicked men. Thus a period of pillage and lawlessness might also be characterized by a luxuriant crop of new monasteries, like the England of Stephen's reign. The Cistercians were outstanding beneficiaries of this syndrome. A robber-baron might also, it is true, have to perform a physical penance himself; but we hear less and less of such after the twelfth century. The mechanical process had taken over. And, of course, its forms proliferated. In 1095, Urban II, propagating the First Crusade, laid it down that a crusade to the Holy Land was a substitute for any other penance, and entailed complete remission of sin. This, of course, involved an actual and hazardous crusade, and the privilege, or indulgence, was hedged about with careful qualifications and terrific penalties if a man reneged. Throughout the twelfth century, crusading was the only source of indulgences, except in rare individual cases. But of course it was always these rare individual cases (that is, the rich, the well placed, the smart cleric) which shipwrecked the principle. Early in the thirteenth century, Innocent III extended crusader indulgences to those who helped merely with money and advice. Fifty years later, Innocent IV awarded indulgences without any conditions of crusader service, naturally only in special circumstances. By the end of the thirteenth century, indulgences were being granted to secular princes for political reasons. Soon after, individuals were allowed to buy plenary indulgences from their confessors on their death-beds; this meant they could enter Heaven immediately, provided they died in a state of grace, immediately after full confession. In the first six months of 1344, Clement VI granted this privilege to two hundred people in England alone; it cost them less than ten shillings each. The Pope justified this by saying: 'A pontiff should make his subjects happy.' By this time, the idea had already been extended to boost the pilgrimage trade to Rome. Boniface VIII gave a plenary indulgence to all confessed sinners who, in the course of the jubilee year 1300, and every hundredth year in future, visited the churches of the Holy Apostles in Rome. In 1343, Clement VI reduced the period to every fifty years, remarking: 'One drop of Christ's blood would have sufficed for the redemption of the whole human race. Out of the abundant superfluity of Christ's sacrifice, there has come a treasure which is not to be hidden in a napkin or buried in a field, but to be used. This treasure has been committed by God to his vicars on earth.' The period was reduced to a third of a century in 1389, to a quarter in 1470, and, from about 1400, extended to many local churches on special occasions.

At this point the dam burst, and indulgences were sold on almost any ecclesiastical occasion for quite trivial sums; or, indeed, given away by indulgent or emotional popes. We have an eye-witness account of an occasion in 1476, when Sixtus IV, on the spur of the moment, gave plenaries to the Franciscan nuns of Foligno every time they confessed their sins. This, of course, was to destroy the idea of physical penance absolutely, and for ever. The cardinals who were with the Pope clamoured for the privilege too; and he generously awarded it. By this time, inflation was bringing the system into disrepute. It had already completely devalued the Roman jubilees. It is significant that rich men continued to endow expensive chantries, thus ensuring that prayers and masses were said perpetually for their souls, although the easy availability of plenary indulgences should have made such largesse unnecessary. Here, of course, the class-wealth factor came in again. Indulgences lost their value once they became generally available to the poor; a man's road to salvation became more sure if he paid for hundreds, or thousands of masses, or better still if he invested his wealth to enable faithful monks to pray for him as long as the world should last. Thus the mechanical system of religion projected into eternity all the materialist divisions of the transient world.

Yet it would be wrong to categorize the medieval centuries as a slow descent into purely automatic forms of religious life. Christianity retained an astonishing dynamic, and great powers of spontaneous expression; the theological wisdom of Christ, in providing a whole series of matrices for future experiment, was demonstrated again and again as new varieties of Christian action came into existence, flourished and declined. But as always there was tension between such innovations and the existing order; indeed, as the claims of the clerical caste expanded, and as canon law, which underwrote them, became more magisterial, containing the religious impulse within the ecclesiastical system became progressively more difficult. Certainly the Church tried, creating new institutions to give orthodox vent to every form of religious experience. The traditional way had been through the monastic life, the retreat from the world. We have seen how the Benedictine system had changed this impulse into a vast and highly productive social instrument, which became one of the pillars of the Dark Age culture and economy: monasticism and the Church were almost coextensive. So successful was the Benedictine rule that all other forms of monasticism were absorbed into it; by 1050 it was the norm.

Thereafter, however, and in conjunction with the expansion of the clerical class, literacy, population, wealth, towns and social complexity, new forms of the regular religious life came into existence. The Cistercians, as we have seen, were in part a return to primitive Benedictine severity, in part a development of monastic economic techniques. About the same time emerged the regular canons of St Augustine, who operated in the new suburbs which had grown up around the walled cities of the Dark Ages: they lived in small, modest houses, on endowments a third the size of a Benedictine – it cost £3 a year to maintain an Austin canon, £10 at least for a Benedictine. They ran urban schools, leper-houses, hospitals, infirmaries and burial grounds. They served as confessors, chaplains and routine preachers; they baptized and said masses for the dead. They were ubiquitous and masters of all clerical trades, and flourished in enormous numbers; by the thirteenth century there were probably more Augustinian houses, albeit most of them small, than those of any other order. Early in the thirteenth century they were joined by the two chief orders of friars, the Franciscans and the Dominicans. Both took vows of poverty and both, especially the Franciscans, claimed to live off what they could beg. But the Dominicans, like the Austin canons, were middle class (sometimes upper class) and highly literate; their main function was to provide efficient and orthodox preachers, who could be rapidly deployed in an area infected with heresy. The Franciscans were the only religious order recruited predominantly from the lower classes, and for a long time they had a high proportion of laymen (and illiterates). The friars were essentially urban; they were most prolific in southern France, Spain and Italy; but there were friaries wherever towns existed. By the beginning of the fourteenth century, the Dominicans had 600 houses, with a total of 12,000 friars, and the Franciscans 1,400 houses and 28,000 friars.

Altogether, by this date, there were eight chief types of religious order, and about a score of sub-types. Most of them had corresponding organizations for women. About one-fifth of all the wealth of society passed through their hands. Much of it, of course, went back into society. They performed a wide variety of services, many of them free. And collectively they provided pious Christians with the chance to pursue almost every kind of religious life. They should have been an essential element in the strength of Christianity as the established, compulsory religion, and in the reputation of the clergy as a privileged class. In fact by the fourteenth century they were neither. On the contrary: at best they were a negative quantity, at worst an embarrassment, even a scandal. Why?

In theory, discipline in all the religious houses, even the least rigorous, was very strict. The gospel of work was paramount; the time of the inmates was provided for in great detail; and there was ample provision for inspection and visitation. If anything, most rules were neurotically oppressive. There was a convention that monks, even in private, should not do anything to offend the sensitive tastes of the angels, believed to be very elegant beings. Hugh of St Victor, in his *Rules for Novices*, forbids listening with the mouth open, moving the tongue round the lips while working, gesturing, raising the eyebrows while speaking, rolling eyeballs, tossing the head, shaking the hair, smoothing garments, moving the feet unnecessarily, twisting the neck, pulling faces, grinning, wrinkling the nostrils and 'all contortions of the lips which disfigure the comeliness of a man's face and the decency of discipline'. Again, for nuns, their bodily posture, for almost any activity, was laid down in detail. Both monks and nuns were scourged for comparatively minor faults, especially for murmuring at correction. For the Brigittine nuns of Syon in Middlesex, corporal punishment was mandatory for any fault, however venial, which a nun failed to report herself, and which was later noted. Five lashes was the norm, 'but if the default be of the more grievous kind, or she or they show any token of rebellion, the discipliners shall not cease till the abbess chargeth them to cease'. From Syon, too, we have a table of signs for both the sisters and brothers (who lived in separate establishments) which indicates that the rules of silence were enforced. But when the rules multiplied, spirit tended to fly out of the cloister; medieval man was superbly gifted at imposing rules on himself and then defeating their purpose. Giraldus Cambrensis noted, *c.* 1180, that the Canterbury monks were 'so profuse in their gesticulations of fingers and hands and arms, and in the whisperings whereby they avoided open speech, wherein all showed a most unedifying levity and license', that they looked like 'a company of actors and buffoons'. He thought it would have been better 'to speak modestly in plain human speech than to use such a dumb garrulity of frivolous signs and hissings'.

This is but a tiny example of the contempt which familiarity with the sacred inevitably breeds, and which is inseparable from the religious life. But the root causes of the monastic failure went deeper, and were economic and social. In northern and central Europe, where the Benedictines were strongest and wealthiest, and where the monks' economic role was most important, they were fully integrated into the tenurial system. The abbot was, and had to behave as, a pillar of feudal society. The big abbeys were nearly always on royal progress-routes, and had to entertain the kings and their courts; later, parliaments or estates-general. Abbots nearly always came from the higher social classes. By the twelfth century they already had their separate establishments, staff and buildings (especially kitchen), from which they dispensed large-scale hospitality to the rich. They were, in fact, in charge of something which was a combination of a luxury hotel and a cultural centre. Of course this role was not, initially, of their choosing. But use by governments of Benedictine abbeys (especially royal foundations) for state purposes goes back to a very early date. Nor did the reformed papacy make any attempt to change the system; on the contrary, the papacy developed its own forms of exploitation, chiefly by forcing the abbots-elect to come to Rome for confirmation. Thomas of Walsingham complains of 'horrible expenses', 'lavish presents' and 'greasing the palm of the examiners' – that is, papal officials who scrutinized the abbot's credentials. Many detailed lists of curial exactions survive. The new Abbot of St Albans in 1302, John IV, paid 'to the Lord Pope, for a private visitation, 3,000 florins, or 1,250 marks sterling; for a public visitation 1,008 marks sterling. . . , Item, by the hand of Corsini in the matter of obtaining the bulls, and for writing the bulls for the first time, 63 gros tournois; to Master Blondino, who corrected the annulled letter, 2 florins; to the scribe, for the second time, 60 gros tournois; to Master P., that they might be sooner enregistered, 4 gros tournois; for three supplicatory letters, 65 gros tournois; to the clerks who sealed the bulls, 12 florins and 2 gros tournois. . . .' And so on. The total came to over £1,700; and just over seven years later John died, and his successor had to produce another £1,000, plus the first-fruits. In due course, St Albans took out an insurance-policy with Rome, paying twenty marks a year instead; and in the fifteenth century they composed with a capital sum. However, the exactions of Rome did not prevent newly elected heads of houses from celebrating themselves. All the higher clergy (especially bishops) had monstrous installation feasts in the later Middle Ages. When the Prior of Canterbury was installed in 1309, there were 6,000 guests, who consumed 53 quarters of wheat, 58 of malt, 11 tuns of wine, 36 oxen, 100 hogs, 200 piglets, 200 sheep, 1,000 geese, 793 capons, hens and pullets, 24 swans, 600 rabbits, 16 shields of brawn, 9,600 eggs and so on, at a cost of £287.

From the twelfth century abbots were under fire for living like great territorial magnates. In particular, critics objected to their hunting, which was, above any other activity, the hallmark of upper-class status and behaviour. At the Fourth Lateran Council, in Canon 15, Innocent III laid down: 'We forbid hunting to the whole clergy. Therefore let them not presume to keep hounds or hawks.' This injunction, often repeated, was totally ineffective. Abbots argued that, if they had to entertain the great, they had to keep up the hunting. William Clown, Augustinian abbot of Leicester, was Edward III's favourite hunting companion (and the model for Chaucer's sporting monk); Edward visited him once a year in what is now the Quorn country where he ran a superlative pack of greyhounds for harrying. When criticized, Clown replied that he owed it to his house to keep in with the mighty. Abbot Littlington of Westminster also kept greyhounds, and in 1368 offered the waxen image of a falcon at the altar for the recovery of his best hawk. Bishops charged with visiting monastic houses made little attempt to correct this abuse. Indeed, if the abbey was in good country, they took the opportunity to hunt themselves. Some bishops and abbots conscientiously refrained from hunting; virtually all, as members of the possessing class, upheld the hunting laws, paradigms of the social system, in all their severity. In 1376, for instance, we find Thomas Hatfield, Bishop of Durham, on behalf of his friend Sir Philip Neville, ordering all clergy in his diocese to pronounce sentences of excommunication against those who had stolen Sir Philip's favourite hawk; and two years later he excommunicated the 'sons of iniquity, name unknown,' who 'to the grievous peril of their souls . . . have stealthily abstracted from our forest of Weardale certain birds called Merlin-hawks in the vulgar tongue'. If the bishops would not enforce the canons, who would?

By the thirteenth century, Benedictine abbeys had virtually ceased to be spiritual institutions. They had become collegiate sinecures reserved very largely for members of the upper classes. The abbot and his expenses took up about half the revenue; sometimes much more – at St Gallen in 1275 he took 900 marks out of 1042. New endowments had contracted sharply in the twelfth century. The abbeys, by and large, had now lost their pioneering economic role, and their incomes remained static. Hence there was a contraction in the numbers of monks. Christ Church, Canterbury, which had 120 monks in 1120, had less than 80 in 1207. The big German abbeys fell even more steeply, Fulda from 200 in the tenth century to 20–30 in the thirteenth and fourteenth; St Gallen and Reichenau from 100 to 10, or less. At the last, Benedict XII complained that 'none are received as monks unless they are of noble birth on both sides of the family'. Of course such aspirants brought 'dowries' with them. A place in a 'good' Benedictine monastery became very hard to get. For anyone outside the nobility it needed contacts, push and money. Full Benedictine monks were hardly ever working-class, and rarely middle-class, in the later Middle Ages. Numbers were kept low deliberately.

Besides Canterbury, at least three other Benedictine houses had over 100 monks in the early twelfth century; by around 1500, Canterbury was still the largest with 70, but the six next largest had 60 or less – three under 50. Evesham, which had 67 in 1086, fell to 38 in 1416, and had 33 at the Dissolution.

These monks had their own rooms, offices and servants. They lived like university dons or estate administrators. They hardly ever did manual work, and by the thirteenth century they found it increasingly difficult to keep up the full routine of services: there were not enough monks, and they had more mundane things to do. Attempts at reform, sometimes vigorous, came to grief on the fact that the Benedictine monastery had changed completely as an economic and social (and therefore spiritual) institution. There is a very full account of Mont St Michel, part of a survey of monastic property undertaken by Benedict XII in 1338. By this time the monks had moved out of highly concentrated domanial farming and were merely administering properties as rentiers. They might be busy, but they had lost their role. Of the ninety monks, fifty were scattered, usually in twos, to look after twenty-two priory estates. They lived like celibate country gentry, though comparatively cheaply, costing £40 a year each. The bulk of the monastic income, totalling £9,000 a year, went on the splendour and hospitality of the main house – including £1,700 on food, £500 on clothing, £460 on repairs, £500 on taxes, £300 on lawsuits and £120 on fuel. The largest single item was wine: £2,200.

By this time, the Benedictine ideal had disappeared almost entirely. Monks had private rooms, the dormitories having been partitioned. They took their meals in their rooms, the food being brought from the kitchens by the abbey servants. They entertained. They were paid stipends. Rules about silence and diet had virtually disappeared. They took holidays with pay at one of the abbot's country houses; or they went to stay with families and friends. Most of them were unenterprising, upper-class parasites. It was almost impossible to reform them effectively. As Benedict XII had noted, 'because of the power of their relatives, these monks cannot be restrained from unlawful acts, nor can they be compelled to observe the rules of the order'. In fact some very determined people did try and impose reforms. In 1421 Henry V proposed to end separate establishments for abbots, all excessive display, bright or rich clothes, long holidays, meat-eating and extravagant meals, private rooms for eating and sleeping, and all contact with women; and he laid down strict limits on money payments and visits to relatives and friends. Nothing came of this reform. The bishops lacked the power to impose radical changes, and were scared of getting involved in expensive lawsuits. The abbots had long since lost the authority needed to effect internal reform. We have a revealing glimpse of what happened at Thornton, in 1440, following a visitation by the reforming Bishop of Lincoln, Williams Alnwick: 'A discussion was held in chapter among them all concerning defaults that should be reformed ... but when some complained of certain things they were immediately met by others with terrible retorts, and the abbot said, clasping his hands, "Woe to me! What shall I do? I am undone"; and had he not been hindered and kept back by force, he would have rushed away from the chapter-house like a madman.'

Nunneries presented an even bigger problem in some ways. Many of them were very strict. But the most lax were also the most aristocratic. Widows and virgins from the upper classes were put there for a variety of non-religious reasons, and did not see why they should sacrifice any of the comforts to which they were accustomed. This could not be prevented, in practice, provided the endowment would stand it; more serious, from the authorities' point of view, was the habit of well-born nuns of breaking bounds. English bishops, for instance, spent over two hundred years trying in vain to keep nuns within their cloisters; they were still hard at it when Henry VIII dissolved the lot. Celibate upper-class women, living communally, and with too little to occupy them, tended to become eccentric and very difficult to control. There is a note of exasperation in the letter the great William of Wykeham addressed to the Abbess of Romsey in 1387: '. . . we strictly forbid you all and several . . . that ye presume henceforth to bring to church no birds, hounds, rabbits or other frivolous things that promote indiscipline . . . through hunting dogs and other hounds abiding within your monastic precincts, the alms that should be given the poor are devoured and the church and cloisters . . . foully defiled . . . and through their inordinate noises divine service is frequently troubled . . . we strictly command and enjoin you, Lady Abbess, to remove the dogs altogether.'

Nuns, however, often defied bishops, even bishops backed up by the secular authorities. When a bishop of Lincoln deposited a papal disciplinary bull at one of the nunneries in his diocese, the nuns ran after him to the gate, threw it at his head, and said they would never observe it. Johann Busch, the great Augustinian reformer, who held a commission from the Council of Basle to tackle recalcitrant nuns and monks, left a graphic description of his battle with the nuns of Wennigsen, near Hanover, in the mid fifteenth century. He says they had abandoned poverty, chastity and obedience, apparently with the connivance of the Bishop of Minden; but when, accompanied by armed local officials, he read out his disciplinary charge to them 'the nuns laid forthwith with one accord flat on the choir pavement, with arms and legs outstretched in the form of a cross and chanted at the top of their voices, from beginning to end, the antiphon *In the Midst of Life We are in Death*.' The object of this performance of part of the burial service was to invoke an evil death on the intruders. Busch had to use physical violence before the nuns submitted; and he came across similar opposition to reform in seven out of twenty-four nunneries in this diocese.

Of the new types of religious organization developed in the central Middle Ages, few were making a positive contribution to Christian standards and morale by the fifteenth century. The Cistercians had abandoned their pioneering agricultural role by the end of the thirteenth century. Their numbers declined; those that remained were mostly administrators and rent-collectors. The barriers they had erected against the luxuries which inevitably crept into the lives of monks who belonged to a well-endowed order were progressively dismantled. Wine was administered first to the sick; then to all on special feast-days; then on Sundays; then on Tuesdays and Thursday as well; then daily; then the ration was increased to a pint. And so on. The Cistercians were even more aristocratic than the Benedictines. Such 'country' orders were disliked by middle-class townsmen. But then the townsmen grew to view the urban orders, too, with suspicion. The Franciscans, in theory at least, clung to their vows of poverty. But the laymen in their ranks were soon eliminated. In 1239, the last lay general, Brother Elias, was deposed, accused of promoting laymen to positions of authority; three years later a new constitution was adopted which made the order a bastion of clericalism. The Dominicans, for their part, took over the routine conduct of the Church's anti-heretical machinery, especially the inquisition. They also invaded the universities, which in the thirteenth century replaced monasteries as the centres of western culture. The Franciscans followed suit. Soon the two were bitter rivals for dominance of the university scene, supplying between ten and fifteen per cent of the total university population at Paris and Oxford, for instance. They changed the universities from training-grounds for lawyers and financial administrators into centres of theology and philosophy. Both the orders were prepared to finance the university careers of clever recruits. Hence many scholars found it convenient to abandon the clerical rat-race for benefices, and join the friars – the scientist Roger Bacon, and the theologian Alexander of Hales being cases in point. In the thirteenth and fourteenth centuries most of the great university names were friars – Albertus Magnus, Aquinas and Eckhart among the Dominicans, Bonaventura, Duns Scotus and William of Ockham among the Franciscans. None of this was relevant to the original purpose of the founders. But it cost a great deal of money. Hence both orders, but especially the Franciscans, acquired reputations for sharp-dealing. Friars were supposed to be quite unscrupulous in matters of wills and legacies and in persuading the gullible sons of the rich to join them. One might say that the late-medieval layman tended to regard monks as idle and friars as con-men.

There were exceptions. The Brigittine nuns retained a high reputation. The Carthusians, one of the strictest enclosed orders, were rarely criticized for laxity. It is significant that such groups were the only ones to resist dissolution during the Protestant Reformation. The rest settled, often gratefully, for liberty and pensions. The truth is, the system of regular clergy had grown almost beyond reform, except of the most drastic nature. Far too many men and women took vows for non-spiritual reasons, or without forethought of the consequences. And vows, once taken, were extraordinarily difficult to get out of, unless one had high contacts or great wealth. Thus a high proportion of the late medieval regulars were reluctant saints whose chief object was to make their lives as comfortable as possible. One cannot reform men (or women) into piety against their will. Without the voluntary principle, the monastic movement was bound to become an embarrassment to Christianity. And then there were far too many houses, some too poor, others too rich. Rationalizing them would have involved prodigies of litigation; only the papacy could have done it without using force. The popes should have dissolved the main orders in the fourteenth century and reallocated their resources to new purposes. Instead, they milked them financially – always a temptation. They did point the way, however. Early in the fourteenth century the papacy, at the behest of the French crown, dissolved the Knights Templars. The lesson was not forgotten. During the Hundred Years' War the English crown seized the so-called alien priories – offshoots in England of French abbeys – on patriotic grounds. Legal devices were also developed within the Church for winding up groups of ecclesiastical foundations to form new and more promising ones. Cardinal Wolsey, for instance, was an adept at this type of canonical operation; and one of the legal experts he employed on it was Thomas Cromwell, who provided similar services, though on a much more extensive scale, to Henry VIII. Thus monastic dissolutions during the sixteenth-century Reformation evolved from established procedures within the Church, and were later employed by Catholic monarchs (in Austria for instance) in the eighteenth century. The monastic system, and its urban adaptations, had played an enormously important role from the sixth to the twelfth centuries; but it never recovered its pristine spirit until after radical reformation, which in some Catholic countries was delayed until the nineteenth century; and even then it survived only on a much reduced scale, as a small minority movement within the more conservative Christian communities. As a major element in western society and economy it had had its day, like, for instance, domaine farming and chain-mail armour.

What must strike the historian as curious is that neither western nor eastern Christianity developed missionary orders. Until the sixteenth century, Christian enthusiasm, which took so many other forms, was never institutionally directed into this channel. Christianity remained a universalist religion. But its proselytizing spirit expressed itself throughout the Middle Ages in various forms of violence. The crusades were not missionary ventures but wars of conquest and primitive experiments in colonization; and the only specific Christian institutions they produced, the three knightly orders, were military.

This stress on violence was particularly marked in the West. Eastern Christians tended to follow the teachings of St Basil, who regarded war as shameful. This was in the original Christian tradition: violence was abhorrent to the early Christians, who preferred death to resistance; and Paul, attempting to interpret Christ, did not even try to construct a case for the legitimate use of force. Again, it was St Augustine who gave western Christianity the fatal twist in this direction. As always, in his deep pessimism, he was concerned to take society as he found it and attempt to reconcile its vices with Christian endeavour. Men fought; had always fought; therefore war had a place in the Christian pattern of behaviour, to be determined by the moral theologians. In Augustine's view, war might always be waged, provided it was done so by the command of God. This formulation of the problem was doubly dangerous. Not only did it allow the existence of the 'just' war, which became a commonplace of Christian moral theology; but it discredited the pacifist, whose refusal to fight a war defined as 'just' by the ecclesiastical authorities became a defiance of divine commands. Thus the modern imprisonment of the conscientous objector is deeply rooted in standard Christian dogma. So is the anomaly of two Christian states each fighting a 'just' war against each other. What made the Augustinian teaching even more corrupting was the association in his mind between 'war by divine command' and the related effort to convert the heathen and destroy the heretic – his 'compel them to come in' syndrome. Not only could violence be justified: it was particularly meritorious when directed against those who held other religious beliefs (or none).

The Dark Age church merely developed Augustine's teaching. Leo IV said that anyone dying in battle for the defence of the Church would receive a heavenly reward; John VIII thought that such a person would even rank as a martyr. Nicholas I added that even those under sentence of excommunication, or other church punishment, could bear arms if they did so against the infidel. There was, it is true, a pacifist movement within the Church as well. But this, paradoxically, was canalized to reinforce the idea of sanctified violence. The motive behind it was to protect innocent peasants from the aimless brutality of competing lords. The bishops of Aquitaine, meeting in 898, said it was the duty of the Church to guarantee immunity for such poor folk. In 1000, William the Great, Duke of Guienne, summed a peace council at Poitiers, which threatened excommunication for anyone who sought to resolve disputes by force of arms. Various oaths were taken by landowners at public assemblies, while the priests and congregations shouted 'Peace, peace, peace'. Leagues of peace were organized, and every male of fifteen or over asked to swear to take up arms against peace-breakers. But mobs of peasants interpreted the campaign as a license to smash castles, and after one such incident were massacred, 700 clerics with them. Throughout the eleventh century the Church tried to keep the peace movement alive, but the popes eventually surrendered to the temptation to divert what they regarded as the incorrigible bellicosity of western society into crusades against the infidel.

The idea of Catholic Christians exercising mass-violence against the infidel hardly squared with scripture. Nor did it make much sense in practical terms. The success of Islam sprang essentially from the failure of Christian theologians to solve the problem of the Trinity and Christ's nature. In Arab territories, Christianity had penetrated heathenism, but usually in Mono-physite form – and neither eastern nor western Catholicism could find a compromise with the Monophysites in the sixth and seventh centuries. The Arabs, driven by drought, would almost certainly have used force to expand anyway. As it was, Mohammed, a Monophysite, conflated the theological and economic problems to evolve a form of Monophysite religion which was simple, remarkably impervious to heresy, and included the doctrine of the sword to accommodate the Arab's practical needs. It appealed strongly to a huge element within the Christian community. The first big Islamic victory, at the River Yarmuk in 636, was achieved because 12,000 Christian Arabs went over to the enemy. The Christian Monophysites – Copts, Jacobites and so forth – nearly always preferred Moslems to Catholics. Five centuries after the Islamic conquest, the Jacobite Patriarch of Antioch, Michael the Syrian, faithfully produced the tradition of his people when he wrote: 'The God of Vengeance, who alone is the Almighty . . . raised from the south the children of Ishmael to deliver us by them from the hands of the Romans.' And at the time a Nestorian chronicler wrote: 'The hearts of the Christians rejoiced at the domination of the Arabs – may God strengthen it and prosper it.' The Monophysite Moslems and the Monophysite Christians never fused theologically. But, unlike the Jews, they did not remain racially and culturally distinct. The religious pattern froze: the Arab Moslems tolerated all Children of the Book, but would not allow their rivals to expand. Christians were in the majority only in Alexandria and certain Syrian cities. Generally, they preferred Arab-Moslem to Greek-Christian rule, though there were periods of difficulty and persecution. There was never, at any stage, a mass-demand from the Christians under Moslem rule to be 'liberated'.

Three factors combined together to produce the militant crusades. The first was the development of small-scale 'holy wars' against Moslems in the Spanish theatre. In 1063, Ramiro I, King of Aragon, was murdered by a Moslem; and Alexander II promised an indulgence for all who fought for the cross to revenge the atrocity; the idea was developed in 1073 by Gregory VII who helped an international army to assemble for Spanish campaigning, guaranteeing canonically that any Christian knight could keep the lands he conquered, provided he acknowledged that the Spanish kingdom belonged to the see of St Peter. Papal expansionism, linked to the colonial appetite for acquiring land, thus supplied strong political and economic motives. There was, secondly, a Frankish tradition, dating from around 800, that the Carolingian monarchs had a right and a duty to protect the Holy Places in Jerusalem, and the western pilgrims who went there. This was acknowledged by the Moslem caliphs, who until the late eleventh century preferred Frankish interference to what they regarded as the far more dangerous penetration by Byzantium. From the tenth century, western pilgrimages grew in frequency and size. They were highly organized by the Cluniac monks, who built abbeys to provide hospitality on the way. There were three well-marked land-routes through the Balkans and Asia, as well as the more expensive sea-route; and elaborate hospices in Jerusalem itself. Powerful lords were allowed by the

Moslems to bring armed escorts; other pilgrims joined them; so western Christians moved in large, armed contingents – in 1064–6, for instance, 7,000 Germans, many armed, travelled together to Jerusalem. There was not all that much physical difference between a big pilgrimage and a crusade.

What really created the crusade, however, was the almost unconscious decision, at the end of the eleventh century, to marry the Spanish idea of conquering land from the infidel with the practice of the mass, armed pilgrimage to the Holy Land. And this sprang from the third factor – the vast increase in western population in the eleventh and twelfth centuries, and the consequent land hunger. Cistercian pioneer-farming at the frontiers was one solution. Crusading was another – the first great wave of the European colonial migrations. It was, in fact, deeply rooted in Christian cosmology. The Ptolemaic conception of a circumambient ocean had been accepted by the Fathers and reconciled with the bible in Isidore's encyclopaedia. The three continents were allocated to the sons of Noah after the Flood – Shem stood for the Jews, Japhet for the Gentiles, and Ham for the Africans, or blacks. Alcuin's commentary on Genesis reads: '"How was the world divided by the sons and grandsons of Noah?" "Shem is considered to have acquired Asia, Ham Africa and Japhet Europe."' The passage then went on to prove from the scriptures that Japhet-Europe was by its name and nature divinely appointed to be expansionist. Within a generation of Alcuin, early in the ninth century, we first hear of 'Christendom', an entity judged to be co-extensive with Europe, but with special privileges and rights, including the right to expand. Phrases like the 'defence of Christendom' against the Saracens were used (ninth century) and in the eleventh century Gregory VII referred to the 'boundaries of Christendom' and the Church being 'mistress of the whole of Christendom'.

The idea that Europe was a Christian entity, which had acquired certain inherent rights over the rest of the world by virtue of its faith, and its duty to spread it, married perfectly with the need to find some outlet both for its addiction to violence and its surplus population. The famous sermon at Clermont with which Pope Urban II preached the First Crusade in 1095 survives in a variety of conflicting texts. William of Malmesbury's text, for instance, should not be regarded as Urban's actual words, but more an expression of the mood which generated the crusading movement. It contains some striking phrases, the real adumbration of European expansion and colonialism: 'Can anyone tolerate that we [Europeans] do not even share equally with the Moslems the inhabited earth? They have made Asia, which is a third of the world, their homeland. ... They have also forcibly held Africa, the second portion of the world, for over 200 years. There remains Europe, the third continent. How small a portion of it is inhabited by us Christians.' Of course, he added, 'in one sense the whole world is exile for the Christian' but in another 'the whole world is his country'. In any case, he concluded, 'in this land' – meaning Christian Europe – 'you can scarcely feed the inhabitants. That is why you use up its goods and excite endless wars among yourselves.'

The crusades were thus to some extent a weird half-way house between the tribal movements of the fourth and fifth centuries and the mass trans-atlantic migration of the poor in the nineteenth. According to Anna Comnena, the Byzantine court was alarmed to hear that 'all the West and all the barbarian tribes from beyond the Adriatic as far as the Pillars of Hercules were moving in a body through Europe towards Asia, bringing whole families with them.' This was not true. But the numbers were large, particularly in the first two generations of the crusading movement. Peter the Hermit led a mob of 20,000 men, women and children, including, one presumes, many families carrying all their worldly goods with them. Most of these people were very poor; they had been unable to obtain land on any lease, or agricultural work during an acute and prolonged labour surplus; they intended to settle. So, of course, did the most determined of the knights. Most of them had no money or lands. Godfrey de Bouillon, Duke of Lower Lorraine, who emerged as the leader of the First Crusade, claimed descent from Charlemagne, but he held his duchy as an office not a fief, and may have been in danger of dismissal: hence his crusade. Apart from Raymond of Toulouse, all the crusaders who settled in the Holy Land were poor men; the rich, like Stephen of Blois, or the Counts of Flanders and Boulogne, returned to Europe as quickly as they honourably could.

From the start, then, the crusades were marked by depredations and violence which were as much racial as religious in origin. Mass-gatherings of Christians for any purpose invariably constituted a danger to Jewish communities in European cities. Local rulers nearly always tried to protect them, for their own selfish financial reasons; but they were powerless to control the vast crusading bands. To Christian crusaders, in particular, the Jews were hateful: they were believed to have helped the Roman pagans to persecute the early Christians, and they had assisted the Islamic conquests.* Men like Godfrey de Bouillon terrorized Jewish communities into providing considerable sums to finance crusading transport; the mobs, in 1096, turned to outright massacre—12 Jews were murdered at Speier, 500 at Worms, 1,000 at Mainz, 22 at Metz, and so forth. Some groups dispersed after attacking the Jews. But the great majority pressed on through the Balkans and Anatolia. They do not seem to have discriminated between Christians and Moslems.

---

*The theory of anti-semitism began to emerge in the second century, when theologians first foretold that Antichrist would be a Jew from the tribe of Dan. At the same time, the body of ritual developed during the diaspora prevented Jews from mixing with gentiles and thus increased the mystery. In Christian literature and art, Satan was given Jewish features; it was believed Jews held secret tournament as soldiers of Antichrist, during which they committed ritual murders. Money-lending came later. It was open to Jews under the negative provisions of the canon law, but the Jewish money-lender was a comparatively brief phenomenon; after the twelfth century Jews operated only on a small scale, chiefly as pawnbrokers. At the Lateran Council in 1215 they were barred from owning land and all military and civil functions. There were innumerable anti-semitic dramas, ceremonies and games. We know about one Holy Week ceremony in eleventh-century Toulouse, called 'Striking the Jew', because a leading member of the community was so badly beaten during it that he was taken out of the cathedral dying. See D. A. Bullogh, 'Games People Played: drama and ritual as propaganda in Medieval Europe', *Transactions of the Royal Historical Society* (1974).

Thus, in the villages attacked around Nicea by Peter the Hermit's band, non-Latin Christians were slaughtered in great numbers, and it was said their babies were roasted on spits. When cities fell, even to regular crusader forces, it was customary to kill some at least of the non-Latin inhabitants, irrespective of their religion. Dark-skinned people, or even those who simply wore conspicuously different garments, were at risk. The fall of Jerusalem was followed by a prolonged and hideous massacre of Moslems and Jews, men, women and children. This episode had a crucial effect in hardening Islamic attitudes to the crusaders. Unfortunately, it was not the only one. When Caesarea was taken in 1101, the troops were given permission to sack it as they pleased, and all the Moslem inhabitants were killed in the Great Mosque; there was a similar massacre at Beirut. Such episodes punctuated the crusades from start to finish. In 1168, during the Frankish campaign in Egypt, there were systematic massacres; those killed included many Christian Copts, and the effect was to unite Egyptians of all religions (and races) against the crusaders.

Of course, the crusading animus was chiefly directed against the Moslems – in 1182 there were even raids on the Moslem Red Sea pilgrim routes, in which, to the horror of Islam, a crowed pilgrim ship was sunk with all aboard. But from the start the crusaders learnt to hate the Byzantines almost as much, and in 1204 they finally attacked and took Constantinople, 'to the honour of God, the Pope and the empire'. The soldiers were told they could pillage for three days. In St Sophia, the hangings were torn down, and the great silver iconostasis was wrenched into pieces and pocketed. A prostitute was put upon the Patriarch's throne and sang a rude French song. Sacred books and ikons were trampled under foot, nuns were raped and the soldiers drank the altar wine out of the chalices. The last of the great international crusades, in 1365, spent itself on a pointless sacking of the predominantly Christian city of Alexandria: native Christians were killed as well as Jews and Moslems, and even the Latin traders had their houses and stores looted. The racialism of the crusaders vented itself particularly against any sign of alien culture. When Tripoli fell to them, in 1109, the Genoese sailors destroyed the Banu Ammar library, the finest in the Moslem world. In general, the effect of the crusades was to undermine the intellectual content of Islam, to destroy the chances of peaceful adjustment to Christianity, and to make the Moslems far less tolerant: crusading fossilized Islam into a fanatic posture.

They also did incalculable damage to the eastern churches, whether Orthodox or Monophysite. One of the first acts of the crusaders after the taking of Jerusalem was to expel the Orthodox and members of other non-Latin Christian sects, and Orthodox priests were tortured to force them to reveal the fragments of the True Cross. No attempt was made to reach an accommodation with Christians who did not acknowledge Rome fully. They lost their churches and their property, they were displaced from their bishoprics and patriarchates, and at best they were tolerated; even the

Maronite Christians, who were in communion with Rome, were treated as second-class citizens in the states the Latins created in the twelfth century. All the Christians clergy of any importance were recruited direct from the West. Even among the Latins, native birth was a bar to clerical promotion, chiefly because none except elementary schools were established, and schools run by non-Latin sects were not acknowledged. The only exception was William, Bishop of Tyre, the historian. He got a bishopric despite the fact he was born in Outremer, as the crusader states were called; but this was because he had studied in France and Italy for twenty years.

Above all, no attempt was made to convert the Moslems. The Latin Christians governed a conquered population like a colonialist élite. In one sense, the experiment disproves the theory that medieval Christianity was ruined by clericalism. For the Latin states, which were projections of the total Christian society across the seas, were run by laymen. There were, at any one time, about 300 Latin clerks there, but though well-endowed they had little power and were completely under the control of the lay lords. The great mistakes were all made by laymen. But the attitude of the Church did not help to establish a viable Latin society out in the East. Laymen were far more willing than clerics to adopt eastern customs and dress, to learn the language, and to integrate themselves with the natives. It was the popes who forbade Christian knights to marry Moslems, even if the children were brought up Latin Christians. This was fatal in the end. The chief reason why the crusaders failed to expand in the twelfth century, and had their kingdom reduced to an insignificant rump in the thirteenth, was that there were too few of them. In the first decade of the crusades, 1095–1105, about 100,000 people of all ages, classes and sexes went to the Holy Land; ten years later nearly all of them were dead. They left very few children. There is some evidence that childbirth was less risky in Outremer than in western Europe. But Frankish children did not live long, and the death-rate among males was particularly heavy. Many Frankish couples seem to have proved completely sterile. Thus Frankish settler-families tended to die out after a generation or two. In the twelfth century there was a second, then a third, wave of settlers. These, too, were decimated. There was no continuous process of reinforcing emigration, as the West learned to develop in the seventeenth century when populating America. Most of the intending emigrants were too poor. They could just about afford the land-route, where they could live off charity, but it was never made secure. The sea-route, run by Venice, Genoa and other Italian city-states, was too expensive for most. Those going by sea had to sleep on their chests, which also served as their coffins if they died. Each had a space six feet by two, marked in chalk. The conditions were horrific; even so, few could afford the fare. Why did not the maritime states develop cheaper forms of mass-transport? The answer is that they preferred to engage in highly lucrative trading, thus adumbrating the colonial merchant adventurer companies which developed in the late sixteenth century. They made huge profits shipping arms to the

Moslems: in the thirteenth and fourteenth centuries weapons were the Christians's chief exports to their ideological enemies. They also ran the Egyptian slave-trade on behalf of the Moslems. By comparison, ferrying Christian emigrants to make the colonies viable brought a poor yield. Of course the Church itself, out of its huge resources, should have financed emigration. But the idea does not seem to have occurred to it, any more than the idea of creating missionary orders, to achieve by the word what the knights were manifestly failing to achieve by the sword. The whole crusading movement was dogged by intellectual bankruptcy. Among the Outremer barons and their docile clergy there was nothing which could conceivably be called an intellectual élite. Nor had they any economic contribution to make. They made no attempt to introduce a Cistercian-style pioneer farming order. Most of the land continued to be farmed by Moslems, whose surpluses were then milked by the Latin baronage. Thus Outremer was chronically short of cash; it ran at a huge deficit, which had to be supplied by the West. This evoked growing criticism. Matthew Paris, for instance, claimed that the Hospitallers alone possessed 19,000 manors in Europe. This was untrue, but it is clear that it took a large landed investment in the West to keep even one knight in action in the Holy Land. Despite their wealth, the two main military orders could never maintain more than 600 knights together. A roughly similar number of knights was provided by Outremer's feudal levy of the barons. These 1,200 knights (at maximum) were backed up by a total, at any one time, of about 10,000 sergeants. None of these men could be replaced at short notice. There were no reserves. The crusaders built huge castles, which were exceedingly difficult to take when fully manned and supplied. But if they manned the castles, they could not field an army. If they fielded an army, the castles had to be stripped; and if the army was heavily defeated, there was nothing to replace it, the castles fell, and the Latin kingdoms became untenable. This, in the end, is more or less what happened.

After the twelfth century, the crusading idea lost its appeal in the West. Population was no longer rising at the same rate, and the surplus, in France, tended to drift instead to the towns; in Germany, led by the Teutonic knights who had transferred their activities to Prussia and Poland, it pushed to the east. After about 1310 population actually fell, and from the mid fourteenth century there was an acute labour shortage in Europe. Population did not begin to expand again significantly until the sixteenth century, when emigration was resumed, but in a westerly direction. But the decline of the crusade was due to more than demographic factors. By the end of the twelfth century some Europeans, at least, rejected the crude popular theology of the crusading movement. Wolframe von Eschenbach, the lay author of *Parsifal*, also produced, about 1210, the *Willehalm*, which deals with crusading but differs markedly in tone from the *Rolandslied*, from the mid twelfth century, which accepted the crusading ethic uncritically and happily rejoiced at heathen being slaughtered like cattle. In the *Willehalm*, the hero's wife is a converted Saracen, and argues that the infidel are God's children, urging: 'Hear the counsel of a simple woman and spare God's handiwork.' Here the emphasis is anti-Augustinian. The author stresses that everyone has a soul to be saved, and that the Church has a universalist mission; the poem is universalist in another sense – perhaps everyone can be saved, who knows? Much of the theology is close to Pelagianism, the layman's heresy *par excellence*. It is curious how the old fifth-century battles continue to be refought throughout Christian history. In the later Middle Ages, the western crusading effort was as much literary as military. To Raymond Lull, for instance, a crusade was a missionary enterprise; a belief he tried to practise, being stoned to death at Bougie in North Africa in 1315. Lull came from Majorca, an early harbinger of the Iberian maritime crusade against heathenism all over the globe. By this time, of course, the papacy had long since devalued the crusading ideal by adapting it for internal political and financial purposes. The legal mechanism of crusading was too tempting to escape abuse. A man who took the cross enjoyed the protection of the courts. He might evade his debts and taxes. On the other hand, careful investigations were made after a crusade had been preached to ensure that people had fulfilled their vows. Reneging was punished canonically. The papacy was quick to use the procedure against the Hohenstaufen. Frederick II was first excommunicated for not going on crusade, then for going without the Pope's permission; and he was denounced as an infidel for showing that, with the Saracens, more could be obtained by negotiation than by force. Later the weapon was turned against Henry III of England, who could not fulfil his vow to go on crusade by midsummer 1256: Alexander IV commuted it, but Henry in return had to provide troops for the Pope's anti-Hohenstaufen campaign in Italy, and pay in addition 135,541 marks, with excommunication and interdict in default. England could not pay and the result was a constitutional crisis and the famous Oxford Parliament of 1259, the episode forming an important landmark in the progressive breakdown of Rome's relations with England.

It is, in fact, a misleading over-simplification to see the crusade simply as a confrontation between Christian Europe and the Moslem East. The central problem of the institutional church was always how to control the manifestations of religious enthusiasm, and divert them into orthodox and constructive channels. The problem was enormously intensified when large numbers of people were involved. At what point did mass-piety become unmanageable, and therefore heresy? It was a matter of fine judgment, a dilemma as old as the Montanists. A crusade was in essence nothing more than a mob of armed and fanatical Christians. Once its numbers rose to over about 10,000 it could no longer be controlled, only guided. It might be used to attack the Moslems, or unleashed against Jews, or heretics; or it might become heretical and antinomian itself, and smash the structures of established society. This fear was always at the back of the minds of the clerical and secular authorities. In the Dark Ages, the West had been comparatively free of heresy. The Church was cocooned within the authoritarian tradition of Augustine. But occasionally strange figures popped up: nearly always lay-folk, spontaneously reenacting the Montanist tradition. Gregory of Tours tells of a freelance preacher from Bourges, who called himself Christ, collected an army of followers and amassed booty in the name of God. He and his men finally presented themselves to the Bishop of Le Puy, stark naked, leaping and somersaulting. The leader was killed on the spot, his female companion, Mary, tortured until she revealed 'their diabolical devices'. This type of incident became more common with the development of long-distance pilgrimages. Pilgrims brought back weird religious ideas and cults from the East, where dualist or gnostic heresies had always flourished, and indeed ante-dated Christianity. And then, the man from Bourges was an example of the low-born charismatic leader who often led mass pilgrimages, which in the eleventh century developed into popular crusades: Peter the Hermit was an archetype. The phenomenon took on huge and dangerous dimensions in the eleventh century, with the rapid growth of population, the increase in travel and the spread of ideas, and the impact of the Gregorian reforms. Gregory's vision of a pure, undefiled church aroused more expectations than it could fulfil. The clergy, in particular, simply could not produce the results, in terms of piety and pastoral enthusiasm, which Gregory had seemed to promise. Hence, as with the original Montanists, Christian activists tended to turn against the clergy, and take the religious reform, or revival, into their own hands.

Here was a mortal threat to the Church. We mistakenly think of medieval institutional Christianity as an immensely solid and stable structure. But in some ways it was much more vulnerable than the civil power, itself a fragile vessel. Like civil government, the regular routine of organized Christianity could easily collapse; the two often disintegrated together, under pressure. The Christian system was complex and disorganized with comparative ease; an accidental conjunction of two or more of a huge number of forces could bring about de-Christianization over quite a large area very suddenly. Thus St Bernard of Clairvaux on a preaching tour of southern France in 1145 reported that a number of heresies were common and that in large areas Catholicism, as he understood it, had disappeared. Naturally, where antinomian mobs were liable to sweep away church institutions, established authority was anxious to get them out of Christendom – preferably to the East, whence few would return. These mass crusades or armed pilgrimages were usually led by unauthorized *prophetae* or Montanists, and were a form of popular millenari-anism, highly unorthodox but to some extent controlled or canalized by authority. Sometimes they attacked the Jews, regarded as devils like the Moslems, but more accessible. But if no Jews or Moslems were available, they nearly always, sooner or later, turned on the Christian clergy. Hence the anxiety to despatch them to Jerusalem.

Yet returned crusaders undoubtedly brought back heresy with them. The dualism of the Balkan Bogomils, which had links stretching right back to the gnostics, reached Italy and the Rhineland in the early twelfth century, and thence spread to France. Once long-distance movement became routine, the spread of a variety of heresies was inevitable, and crusades provided means of communication among precisely the sort of people who took religious ideas seriously and were emotionally prone. Dualism was always attractive because it explained the role of devils, who were everywhere. It was also easy to portray the visible Church as evil because of the evident failure of its theodicy, that is the vindication of divine justice in respect of the existence of suffering. The Bogomils denied that Christ had established an organized Church; therefore Catholic teaching on images, saints, infant baptism and virgin birth, plus many other matters, was false. These ideas spread very rapidly in the West in the mid twelfth century; and once belief in the Church's system of confession, repentence, penance and redemption was undermined – no great problem – the only spiritual warrants were the outward signs of chastity, poverty, ascetism and humility, which the official Church, as a rule, clearly did not possess. These the heretics supplied.

'Cathar' was first applied to heretics in northern Europe about 1160. They were also called Publicans, Paterines (in Italy), Bougres or Bulgars in France, or Arians, Manichaeans or Marcionites. Around Albi the Cathars were termed Albigensians. The confusion over names reveals a confusion over ideas. But basically all these heresies were the same. They aimed to substitute a perfect élite for the corrupt clergy. Where they were numerous enough, as in southern France, they organized churches and bishoprics, and constituted an alternative Church. Very few of the sect were 'perfected' – perhaps 1,000 to 1,500 in the whole of Languedoc in *c*. 1200. The majority were 'believers', who married, led normal lives, and 'received the consolamentum' only on their deathbeds, thus dying 'in the hands of the Good Men'.

The Cathars were well-organized and orderly people. They elected bishops, collected funds and distributed them; led admirable lives. Unlike most charismatics, they could not be broken up by a sharp cavalry charge. They got on well with the local authorities. The only effective evangelizing against them came from equally poor groups, like the Poor of Lyons, founded by a former Lyonnais merchant, Waldo, around 1173-6. These men were strictly orthodox in their beliefs, but they took apostolic poverty literally and were outside the Church's organizational structure. The clergy thus regarded the Waldensians as a threat. As Walter Map put it, when he saw some in Rome in 1179: 'They go about two by two, barefoot, clad in woollen garments, owning nothing, holding all things in common like the Apostles . . . if we admit them, we shall be driven out.' They were excommunicated three years later. There was, indeed, no shortage of men prepared to defend orthodoxy. But they set standards which exposed the existing structures and personnel of the church, and thus formed a remedy more serious than the disease. Innocent III, despite his many limitations, did grasp the essence of this problem very clearly, and was the only pope to make a systematic attempt to solve it. His creation of the Franciscan and Dominican orders – the first to beat the heretics at their own game of apostolic poverty, the second to preach orthodox concepts in popular terms – sought to harness volcanic Christian forces to institutional objectives. But the dilemma could not be solved by a once-and-for-all operation. It was permanent; it was endemic in Christianity. If the Franciscans, for instance, were allowed to pursue their idealism, they got out of control; if they were controlled, they promptly lost their idealism and became corrupt. Within two generations, the whole friar experiment was a failure; within three it was a liability.

There remained the Augustinian solution: force. It was, in a way, a recapitulation of the fourth and fifth centuries. The Church was terrified by the rapid disintegration of Christianity in southern France. There was no question of peaceful coexistence of orthodoxy and heresy: orthodox bishops could not function and there was imminent danger that the collapse would soon be extended to other areas. It is notable that where there was strong, centralized royal power, to back up the organized Church, heresy was weak or even non-existent (as, for instance, in England at this time). Heresy took root in areas where the ultimate source of secular authority was obscure, and where secular power was divided or remote. Thus the Church, in its fear, tended to appeal to secular power outside the infected area. Suppressing a heresy became a crusade, promising tangible benefits, and bringing into play differences of language and culture, the forces of racism and the spur of greed for land. The Albigensian crusades, organized from 1208 onwards, the precursors of many other 'internal' papal crusades, were preached by upper-class Cistercians, the great disciplinarians of peasants. Heretics were either rabble or, if not, forfeited their privileged class status. Conversely, a crusade was an opportunity to rise in the social scale, for younger sons, would-be knights, and any kind of professional soldier with genteel aspirations. These crusaders got a plenary indulgence for forty days service, plus a moratorium on their debts and any interest payable; if they had lands, they could tax both their vassals and clergy. The Church reserved to itself the right to redistribute among the more faithful crusaders the confiscated lands of the defeated heretics. Thus the crusade attracted the most disreputable elements in northern France, and the result was horror. In 1209, Arnold Aimery exulted to the Pope that the capture of Beziers had been 'miraculous'; and that the crusaders had killed 15,000, 'showing mercy neither to order, nor age nor sex'. Prisoners were mutilated, blinded, dragged at the hooves of horses and used for target practice. Such outrages provoked despairing resistance and so prolonged the conflict. It was a watershed in Christian history. Of course it aroused much criticism even at the time. Peter Cantor asked:

'How doth the church presume to examine by this foreign judgment the hearts of men? Or how is it that the Cathari are given no legitimate respite for deliberation but are burned immediately? . . . Certain honest matrons, refusing to consent to the lust of priests . . . were written in the book of death and accused as Cathari . . . while certain rich Cathari had their purses squeezed and were let go. One man alone, because he was poor and pale, and confessed the faith of Christ faithfully on all points, and put that forward as his hope, was burned, since he said to the assembled bishops that he would refuse to submit to the ordeal of hot iron unless they could first prove to him that he could do this without tempting the Lord and committing mortal sin.'

A few years later, Innocent III abolished the ordeal on precisely these grounds. More generally, it was the type of criticism voiced by Cantor which led to the organization of a regular inquisition system, which would be effective yet less open to the abuses developed under the haphazard methods hitherto employed. Ever since the eleventh century, secular rulers had been burning those who obstinately refused to fit in with established Christian arrangements; the Church had opposed capital punishment, successive councils decreeing confiscation of property, excommunication, imprisonment or whipping, branding and exile. But in the 1180s, the Church began to panic at the spread of heresy, and thereafter it took the lead from the State, though it maintained the legal fiction that convicted and unrepentant heretics were merely 'deprived of the protection of the Church', which was (as they termed it) 'relaxed', the civil power then being free to burn them without committing mortal sin. Relaxation was accompanied by a formal plea for mercy; in fact this was meaningless, and the individual civil officer (sheriffs and so forth) had no choice but to burn, since otherwise he was denounced as a 'defender of heretics', and plunged into the perils of the system himself.

The codification of legislation against heresy took place over half a century, roughly 1180–1230, when it culminated in the creation of a permanent tribunal, staffed by Dominican friars, who worked from a fixed base in conjunction with the episcopate, and were endowed with generous authority. The permanent system was designed as a reform; in fact it incorporated all the abuses of earlier practice and added new ones. It had a certain vicious logic. Since a heretic was denied burial in consecrated ground, the corpses of those posthumously convicted (a very frequent occurrence) had to be disinterred, dragged through the streets and burnt on the refuse pit. The houses in which they lived had to be knocked down and turned into sewers or rubbish-dumps. Convictions of thought-crimes being difficult to secure, the Inquisition used procedures banned in other courts, and so contravened town charters, written and customary laws, and virtually every aspect of established jurisprudence. The names of hostile witnesses were withheld, anonymous informers were used, the accusations of personal enemies were allowed, the accused were denied the right of defence, or of defending counsel; and there was no appeal. The object, quite simply, was to produce convictions at any cost; only thus, it was thought, could heresy be quenched. Hence depositors were not named; all a suspect could do was to produce a list of his enemies, and he was allowed to bring forward witnesses to testify that such enemies existed, but for no other purpose. On the other hand, the prosecution could use the evidence of criminals, heretics, children and accomplices, usually forbidden in other courts.

Once an area became infected by heresy, and the system moved in, large numbers of people became entangled in its toils. Children of heretics could not inherit, as the stain was vicarial; grandchildren could not hold ecclesiastical benefices unless they successfully denounced someone. Everyone from the age of fourteen (girls from twelve) were required to take public oaths every two years to remain good Catholics and denounce heretics. Failure to confess or receive communion at least three times a year aroused automatic suspicion; possession of the scriptures in any language, or of breviaries, hour-books and psalters in the vernacular, was forbidden. Torture was not employed regularly until near the end of the thirteenth century (except by secular officials without reference to the Inquisition) but suspects could be held in prison and summoned again and again until they yielded, the object of the operation being to obtain admissions or denunciations. When torture was adopted it was subjected to canonical restraints – if it produced nothing on the first occasion it was forbidden to repeat it. But such regulations were open to glosses; Francis Pegna, the leading Inquisition commentator, wrote:

'But if, having been tortured reasonably (*decenter*), he will not confess the truth, set other sorts of torments before him, saying that he must pass through all these unless he will confess the truth. If even this fails, a second or third day may be appointed to him, either *in terrorem* or even in truth, for the continuation (not repetition) of torture; for tortures may not be repeated unless fresh evidence emerges against him; then, indeed, they may, for against continuation there is no prohibition.'

Pegna said that pregnant women might not be tortured, for fear of abortions: 'we must wait until she is delivered of her child'; and children below the age of puberty, and old folk, were to be less severely tortured. The methods used were, on the whole, less horrific than those employed by various secular governments – though it should be added that English common lawyers, for instance, flatly denied that torture was legal, except in case of refusal to plead.

Once a victim was accused, escape from some kind of punishment was virtually impossible: the system would not allow it. But comparatively few were executed: less than ten per cent of those liable. Life-imprisonment was usual for those 'converted' by fear of death; this could be shortened by denunciations. Acts of sympathy or favour for heretics were punished by imprisonment or pilgrimage; there were also fines or floggings, and penance in some form was required of all those who came into contact with the infected, even though unknowingly and innocently. The smallest punishment was to wear yellow cloth crosses – an unpopular penalty since it prevented a man from getting employment; on the other hand, to cease to wear it was treated as a relapse into heresy. A spell in prison was virtually inevitable. Of course there was a shortage of prison-space, since solitary confinement was the rule. Once the Inquisition moved into an area, the bishop's prison was soon full; then the king's; then old buildings had to be converted, or new ones built. Food was the prisoner's own responsibility, though the bishop was supposed to provide bread and water in the case of poverty. The secular authorities did not like these crowded prisons, being terrified of gaol fever and plague, and thus burned many more people than the Church authorized. The system was saved from utter horror only by the usual medieval frailties: corruption, inertia, and sheer administrative incompetence.

Where the system was employed against an entire community, as in Languedoc, it evoked resistance. There were riots, murders, the destruction of records. Many countries would not admit the Inquisition at all. In Spain, however, it became a state instrument, almost a national institution, like bullfighting, a mystery to foreigners but popular among the natives. It is surprising how often admirable, if eccentric, individuals were burned, not only without public protest but with general approval. Thus the fourteenth-century breakaway movement of Franciscans, the *fraticelli*, who opposed clerical property and reasserted the apostolic practices of their founder, were hunted and burned all over Europe but especially in their native Umbria and the Mark of Ancona; the crowds who watched them destroyed were apathetic or inclined to believe antinomianism was rightly punished. In the Middle Ages, the ruthless and confident exercise of authority could nearly always swing a majority behind it. And the victims of the flames usually died screaming in pain and terror, thus appearing to confirm the justice of the proceedings.

The total Christian society of the Middle Ages was based on an intense belief in the supernatural. It tended to live on its nerves. Lacking any kind of system for determining the truth scientifically and objectively, society was often bewildered. Today's heterodoxy might become tomorrow's orthodoxy; and vice versa. The enthusiasm of faith so easily toppled over into hysteria, and so became violently destructive. Inside every saint there appeared a heretic struggling to get out; and the converse. One man's Christ was another man's Antichrist. The official Church was conventional, orderly, hierarchical, committed to defend Society as it existed, with all its disparities and grievances. But there was also, as it were, an anti-Church, rebellious, egalitarian, revolutionary, which rejected society and its values and threatened to smash it to bits. It had its own tradition of revolutionary prophecy, inherited from the Jews, and continued into Christianity through the Book of Revelation, which acquired its place in the canon because it was believed to have been written by St John. Millenarianism had been, in the earliest days, almost the official political theory of the Church. But the eschatological moment had receded, and when Christianity became the state religion of the empire, millenarianism was frowned upon. Augustine, the ideologist of the official church, presented Revelation in his *City of God* as a mere spiritual allegory; the millenium had already begun with Christ and had been realized in the shape of the Church itself. But this did not end the argument, as he had hoped. Christians continued to believe in the millenium, the coming of Antichrist, cosmic battles, giant dragons, total upheavals of society – and endless series of signs which would presage these events. For better or for worse, the notion of the apocalypse was part of the canon, linked to bedrock articles of Christian belief it was too late to suppress. Moreover, the eschatological corpus was gradually added to by various sibylline texts: they had no canonical status but they were popular, and much used by preachers, writers and theologians. All stressed the coming battle between Christ and Antichrist. The idea could be reinterpreted to fit almost any political situation, and identified with kings and emperors, even popes, whether good or bad. All the signs could be made to fit.

This tradition confronted the official Church with an almost insoluble problem. If it played things quietly, the millenarians would demand reform. But if the Church tried to initiate reform, as under Gregory VII, this also was calculated to stir up the latent millenarian forces. The tradition of lay preaching had never been completely buried; laymen responded joyfully to efforts to improve the priesthood and tried to take the movement into their own hands. Much of the heterodox effervescence of the twelfth century was the indirect result of the Gregorian campaign. There were areas in the lower Rhineland, for instance, where forms of unorthodox revivalism coexisted with the official Church more or less throughout the Middle Ages. It is a mistake to believe everyone had his or her place in society. On the contrary: between the orderly guilds of the towns and the feudal hierarchy of the countryside there was an immense chaos teeming with the displaced, the dispossessed, the chronic sick or crippled, beggars, lepers, runaway serfs. Perhaps a third of the population did not fit into official categories, but formed the raw materials of huge crowds which formed and dispersed mysteriously and rapidly. Runaway monks or priests who had fallen out with the Church existed in plenty to provide leadership and half-knowledge. Once such a mob was on the march it was difficult to stop. In 1251, for instance, in response to the failure of the Fourth Crusade, a renegade Hungarian monk called Jakob preached an anti-clerical crusade and taught that the murderer of a priest gained merit. He gathered an army of thousands and rampaged through northern French towns. He was able to occupy places like Paris, Orleans and Amiens virtually without opposition, and loot the convents of the friars; in Tours he rounded up the Dominicans and Franciscans and had them whipped through the streets. Then he was murdered and his mob dispersed as quickly as it had collected. Almost any notable event could produce such outbreaks – the preaching of a crusade, a bad harvest, famine, industrial distress, defeat in battle, the failure of a promised miracle to occur. The authorities could do very little once a mass-movement got started. Then they had to wait until the mob's excesses produced a popular reaction, at any rate among the bourgeoisie, or until a regular army could be collected. Hence the Inquisition served as an early-warning device; it probed and checked and winkled out trouble-makers before they could collect and unleash a mob. If it failed, then there might be no alternative but to launch an internal crusade. Thus hateful devices like the Inquisition, or the crusade against 'heretics', were seen by many – not just the rich, but anyone who liked stability—as indispensable defences against social breakdown and mass terrorism.

The Church and the secular establishment could not, however, tackle such phenomena at the root by destroying their basis of credulity. Was not the Church itself based on credulity? Kill belief, and where was the total Christian society? In any case, popes and kings could not escape from the intellectual environment they shared with every wild-eyed fanatic and millenarian fakir. Prophecy, on which such movements were based, was not only scripturally orthodox but scientifically respectable. Prophetical analysts were among the most learned men of their day, part of a tradition of wisdom which stretched from the Magi to Newton, and included virtually all the intellectuals in western society until the mid seventeenth century. It is no accident that the most influential of all the medieval inventors of prophetic systems, Joachim of Flora (died 1202), was also the most learned, systematic and 'scientific'. He was not a rebel but a fashionable Calabrian abbot, patronized by three popes, whose conversation delighted Richard the Lionheart on his way to the Third Crusade. He brought together all the various prophetic sources, pagan, Christian, biblical and astronomical, and examined them far more carefully than anyone else had done before, deducing from them his own future projections. The method was basically the same as Marxist historical determinism and had the same mesmeric fascination. Joachim calculated that Antichrist would arise within the Church and hold high office – a new and riveting idea. On the basis of historical analysis and projection, he deduced that the 'last age' would be enacted within history (not, that is, after the Four Last Things) and would be marked by universal peace, in which the institutions necessary for a turbulent world would wither away. For Marxists the parallels are disturbingly close.

Men read Joachim with the same care and excitement with which they read the more imaginative historians like Otto of Freising. They thought that God intended the future to be discoverable and that it was the duty of society to prepare for it. Roger Bacon, perhaps the best true scientist of the Middle Ages, wrote to the Pope (*c*. 1267):

'If only the church would examine the prophecies of the bible, the sayings of the saints, the sentences of the Sibyl and Merlin and other pagan prophets, and would add thereto astrological considerations and experimental knowledge, it would without doubt be able to provide usefully against the coming of Antichrist. . . . For not all prophecies are irrevocable and many things are said in the prophets about the coming of antichrist which will come to pass only through the negligence of Christians. They would be changed if Christians would strenuously inquire when he will come, and seek all the knowledge which he will use when he comes.'*

This passage, representing the higher conventional wisdom of the thirteenth century, implies a degree of possible control over the universe, present and future, which fits in with the theory of limitless papal monarchy, then nearing its zenith. It springs from the same assumptions as the wild triumphalism of Boniface VIII, quoted at the beginning of this section. But neither the papacy nor the Church as a whole had a firm grip on the total Christian society even in the thirteenth century. Thereafter what grip it had slackened. From about this time, the unified Christian society began to dissolve, and forms of heterodoxy became endemic, their detection and punishment being part of the routine operations of the Church and State. Every form of religious manifestation filled the authorities with disquiet; none could be trusted not to slip out of control. And for much of the time there was not one pope, to act as invigilator and monitor, but two; sometimes three. Joan of Arc, for instance, was not a victim of English nationalism: only eight of the 131 judges, assessors and other clergy connected with her trial were Englishmen. She was, rather, the casualty of a French civil war which had a wide theological dimension. One of the things which aroused suspicion about her was that she headed her letters 'Jhesus Maria' – evidence of a Jesus-cult which did not have the sanction of Pope Martin v but of the anti-Pope Calixtus. We are not surprised to learn that one of the judges who originally condemned her, Jean le Fèvre, was also a judge at her rehabilitation; or that Thomas de Courcelles, who advised that she be tortured during her interrogation, was promoted to be Dean of Notre Dame the year she was cleared and lived to preach the funeral panygyric on her hero-Dauphin, Charles VII.

Because the Christian society was total it had to be compulsory; and because it was compulsory it had no alternative but to declare war on its dissentients. Thus in the later Middle Ages it was weighed down by the multiplicity of its enemies. If Joachim was an 'acceptable' prophet, he was soon saddled with a mass of interpretations and commentaries which became the small-change of rustic millenarians and village charismatics. It was a feature of medieval prophecy that 'sleeping' kings or emperors would awake, and either restore harmony or rampage, depending on whether you believed the Pope was the vicar of Christ or Antichrist himself. Men claiming to be

---

* Prophecy influenced the Italian expedition of Charles VIII, who saw himself as a 'second Charlemagne'. Luther identified his protector, Frederick of Saxony, as 'the good Third Frederick'. Charles v was seen as 'the good King who will chastise the church'. Columbus compiled a collection of prophesies about the restoration of the Age of Gold, a common humanist preoccupation. New geographical discoveries, and inventions like printing, were quickly fitted into the old prophetic systems. See Marjorie Reeves, *The Influence of Prophecy in the Later Middle Ages: a Study in Joachimism* (Oxford, 1969).

Arthur or Charlemagne or the first Latin emperor of Constantinople, or the Emperor Frederick II, appeared, raised a following, were hunted down, then hanged or burned. Disproof by events seems to have done nothing to shake men's belief in prophecy; crucial years came and went – 1260, 1290, 1305, 1335, 1350, 1360, 1400, 1415, 1500, 1535; nothing happened as foretold, but still men believed. Many of these pretenders produced elaborate social manifestos, with an egalitarian or distributive object. Most began, or ended, in anti-clericalism.

Religious hysteria expressed itself in almost every imaginable form of outrageous behaviour. Self-flagellation, for instance, had been a feature of certain sophisticated pagan sects absorbed into Christianity in the fourth century. We hear of it breaking out in eleventh-century Italy, then, on a huge scale, in the second half of the thirteenth century, after which it spread all over Europe and became endemic. The flagellants marched in procession, led by priests, with banners and candles, and moved from town to town, parading before the parish church, and lashing themselves for hours on end. The German flagellants, with their rituals, hymns and uniforms, were particularly ferocious: they used leather scourges with iron spikes; if a woman or a priest appeared, the ritual was spoiled and had to be started again; it culminated in the reading of a 'heavenly letter', after which spectators dipped pieces of cloth in the blood and treasured them as relics. The Church was ambivalent towards flagellants. In 1384 Clement VI had encouraged public flagellation in Avignon: hundreds of both sexes took part. And the pillar of Spanish orthodoxy, the Dominican anti-Semite and rabble-rouser, Saint Vincent Ferrer, led a party of flagellants through Spain, France and Italy, following the instructions of a vision in 1396. Thus there was orthodox flagellation, heretical flagellation, and apparently secret flagellation too. Generally speaking, if both sexes took part, it was permitted. Nearly all unofficial male flagellant movements ended in anti-clericalism, heresy or violence. Then the Inquisition was called in, and executions followed.

Christianity also had its orthodox tradition of apostolic poverty, and its theory that the world, in its pristine state, was egalitarian and just, before the irruption of sin produced the rule of the strong and the degradation of the weak. In the later Middle Ages, many millenarian movements launched themselves on crazy careers from these propositions. They took two main forms, some combining both. The first group, usually termed 'Free Spirits', were antinomians, of a type St Paul had had to deal with in Greece. They believed themselves to be perfect and above moral norms. The Abbot of St Victor, a fourteenth-century orthodox mystic, wrote of them indignantly: 'They committed rapes and adulteries and other acts which gave bodily pleasure; and to the women with whom they sinned, and the simple people they deceived, they promised that such sins would not be punished.' Some taught that women were created to be used by the brothers of the Holy Spirit; a matron, by having intercourse with one of the brethren, could regain her lost virginity; this was linked to their belief that they had rediscovered the precise way in which Adam and Eve had made love. They were often arrested for attempting to seduce respectable middle-class wives; or for eating in taverns and then refusing to pay. 'They believe that all things are common,' noted the Bishop of Strasbourg in 1317, 'whence they conclude that theft is lawful to them.' These men were often executed, sometimes with hideous cruelty. But many free spirits were not fraudulent or antisocial. In Flanders and the Rhine valley, the orthodox Brethren of the Free Spirit formed one of the largest and most admirable religious movements of the later Middle Ages, running schools and hospitals for the poor, and engaging in a variety of welfare work. Female free spirits, of Beguines, though not exactly nuns since they did not live in convents, worked among the poor in the Rhineland cities – at one time there were 2,000 of them just in Cologne – and were models of piety and orthodoxy. Rome did not like these patterns of religious behaviour, since they did not fit into established categories. So the bishops and the Inquisition kept a close watch, and frequently acted to break up groups of brethren or beguines who looked like toppling over into heterodoxy.

The second broad category combined millenarian egality with an overt assault on clericalism and the established Church. The belief that the millenium was imminent was the signal for an attack on the rich – they were to be dragged to the ground in an earthly apocalypse before being committed to eternal flames in the next world. Such ideas were expressed in the sermons of John Ball during the Peasants' Revolt in England; they recur constantly in France and Germany during the fourteenth, fifteenth and sixteenth centuries. In Bohemia, the only part of Latin Christendom where heterodoxy successfully established itself before the sixteenth century, egalitarians formed the radical wing of the Hussites after 1419; they had communal chests and kibbutz-type communities. These movements were the obverse side of the Augustinian coin: they were the 'alternative society' to the total Christian society of which Augustine had been the ideologist and which had been successfully brought into existence in the West during the Carolingian period. But, of course, so the argument ran, the orthodox Christian society had in every respect betrayed its origins and accepted the norms of the world; it was thus the society not of Christ, but of Antichrist, and to overthrow it would be the prelude to the parousia.

As Latin Christianity began to crack up under the growing weight of the enemies it harboured, the possibility of these alternative societies establishing themselves, if only briefly, became far stronger. There were egalitarian outbreaks in Germany in the 1470s, and again in 1502, 1513 and 1517. While Luther was conducting his theological debate with Rome, and while various brands of Protestantism were establishing themselves as official Christian religions, mirroring social needs as Catholicism had done since the fourth century, efforts to overthrow society completely, and replace it by a new social-Christian dispensation, were vigorously pursued by religious fringemen. These men and their movements tell us a great deal about Christianity and its distortions. Their inspiration was often early Christian; sometimes pre-Christian. They spoke with the authentic voice of the Montanists or the Donatists, whom orthodox Christianity and the Roman empire had joined forces to persecute; indeed, they echoed the moral rigorism of the Essenes, likewise victims of a combination of official priests and the established secular order. They were an indisputable part of the Christian tradition, shaped by one of the matrices which Christ had implanted in human minds in the first century. But they lacked the balance of the whole Christian vision. Outraged by the wickedness of official Christian society, anxious to replace it, they ended simply by trying to smash it, even caricature it. They embraced violence, denied culture, devalued human life and adopted purely arbitrary – and volatile – systems of morality. One such case was Thomas Muntzer, born in Thuringia (an area where illicit flagellation was rife) around 1488, a well-educated priest who read Greek and Hebrew. His beliefs were a combination of Hussite radicalism, Free Spirit libertinism, and orthodox eschatology. To him, Lutheranism was simply a betrayal of the attempt to reform the Church, just another compromise with godless Mammon. In July 1524 he preached before John, Duke of Saxony, and other German nobles perhaps the most remarkable sermon of the whole Reformation era, to a text from the Book of Daniel, the keystone of the millenarian arch. 'Deliver us from evil' he interpreted as 'deliver us from the anti-Christian government of the godless'. Society, he told his princely congregation, was being pulverized between Church and State in the hateful earthly kingdom of feudal-papal Christendom. But the royal priesthood of the common man would smash it – and the princes should join the covenanted people in overthrowing Antichrist.

Here we have the crowned ikons of the Dark Ages, the anointed priest-kings, replaced by the sovereign people. While Gregory VII, Innocent III or Boniface VIII had seen the contest for world power as between pope and emperor, or pope and king, there was now a new candidate for the post of Vicar of Christ – the proletariat. The bid for power was made as arrogantly as Gregory VII's had been; and accompanied by a heedless acceptance of violence as necessary and divinely commanded. Muntzer had the mark of the Zealot who had brought Jerusalem down in ruins. Indeed, he signed his letters with the Sword of Gideon and the phrase 'Thomas Muntzer the Hammer'. He was a biblical warrior-priest. 'Let not the sword of the saint get cold' was his motto; and his heraldic sign was a red cross and a naked sword – an early example of the use of an inflammatory political emblem. Luther was the mere propagandist of the ruling classes, 'the spiritless, soft-living flesh in Wittenberg', Dr Liar, the Dragon, the Archeathen. The rich were robbers; property was theft; 'the people will become free and God alone means to be Lord over them'. Muntzer saw the class-war being won only by a tremendous and bloody convulsion, a sort of premonitory apocalypse before the true one when, as Joachim had prophesied, human institutions would wither away and the *parousia* would mark the beginning of eternal and perfect government. Violence was thus necessary to his eschatology. It is a case, once again, of abuse of the text 'compel them to come in' – the text graven on every inquisitor's heart. Exactly like Augustine, Muntzer used the parable of the wheat and the tares to justify destruction and persecution: 'The living God is sharpening his scythe in me,' he said ominously, 'so that later I can cut down the red poppies and the blue cornflowers.' When either the Augustinian or the millenarian takes over, the patient, reasonable man, the reformist, the Pelagian-minded liberal, learns to tremble.

Muntzer detonated a peasants' revolt, as had so many millenarians in the past; but he was executed before he could found his post-apocalyptic society. A decade later, in 1534, millenarians seized the German town of Munster, which they held until the following summer. This was by no means the first time Christian fanatics had seized a city in the West; there are many examples, especially in northern France and Flanders, from the twelfth century onwards. But Munster is the first case in which we have a proper documentation, and thus know what it was like to live under a medieval egalitarian terror. The episode began on 25 February 1534, when the religious radicals captured the municipal council and their leader, John Mathijs, announced a Christian popular dictatorship. The 'godless' were identified: one, a critical blacksmith, was killed by Mathijs on the spot, the rest expelled – 'Get out, you Godless ones, and never come back.' At the same time a number of radical refugees were admitted, to form a police-force and bodyguard for the leadership. The entire population was then re-baptized, the city fortified, all food, money, gold and valuables impounded and communized, and housing reallocated on a basis of need. Mathijs was killed in a sortie, and his replacement, John Beukels, the actor-son of an unmarried female serf, reconstructed the regime on a more formal basis. He ran naked through the town, lapsed into prayer, and then announced a new constitution: himself as messianic king, or 'John of Leyden', assisted by twelve elders or judges, as a committee of public safety. There was to be a new moral code. All books, except the Bible, were to be burnt. A long list of offences, including blasphemy, swearing, adultery, backbiting, complaining, and any form of disobedience, were to be punished by instant execution. There was to be control of labour, and compulsory polygamy. The regime was violently anti-women. A man sexually dependent on one wife, thought Beukels, was led about 'like a bear on a rope'; women 'have everywhere been getting the upper hand' and it was high time they submitted to men. Hence any women who resisted polygamy were to be executed; and unmarried women had to accept the first man to ask them. Beukels instituted competitions to see who could collect himself the most wives. His histrionic talents, and the fact that Munster contained a large number of skilled craftsmen, enabled him to conduct his court as 'king of righteousness' and 'ruler of the New Zion' with considerable style. He had clerical vestments remade into royal robes, and designed for himself a golden apple, or orb; a new gold coinage was issued, stamped 'The word has become flesh and dwells amongst us.' His harem of wives, all under twenty, and his courtiers, were all beautifully dressed; and the 'king' staged dramatic performances and universal banquets, at one of which he distributed communion and then personally carried out an execution, being inspired to do it. This gaudy terror was particularly hard on women, forty-nine of whom were killed for infringing the polygamy decree alone; and it was maintained by dividing the city into twelve sections, each controlled by a 'duke' and twenty-four guards, who carried out daily executions and quarterings. The 'king' hoped, by despatching apostolic missionaries armed with propaganda printed on his press, to raise a confederacy of Christian-communist towns. But after a few brief successes, the scheme was crushed; Munster itself was betrayed and retaken by the bishop, and Beukels was led about like a performing animal until January 1536, when he was publicly tortured to death with red-hot tongs.

The atrocities perpetrated by both millenarians and orthodox Christians on this occasion were roughly equal, each side being anxious to 'compel them to come in'. During the later stages of the Munster commune, the Christian element became minimal, indeed virtually disappeared; but then it was not prominent on the other side of the barricades either. Attempts to realize perfect Christian societies in this world, whether conducted by popes or revolutionaries, have tended to degenerate into red terrors, or white ones. Pontifical theocracies and dictatorships of the proletariat both employ compulsive procedures involving suspension of the rule of law, torture, judicial murder, the suppression of truth and the exaltation of falsehood. Thus the 'alternative society' often developed similar, and distressing, features to the one it sought to replace. Yet millenarians, seeking to escape from what they regarded as the debased enactment of the original Christian vision, were not discouraged, or warned, by past failures. They emerged again in England, in the aftermath of the overthrow of the Stuart tyranny, in the 1650s. The puritan divine, Richard Baxter, wrote:

'They made it their business to set up the light of nature, under the name of *Christ in Men*, and to dishonour and cry down the Church, the Scriptures, the present Ministry, and our Worship and Ordinances; and called men to hearken to Christ within them. But withal, they conjoined a Cursed Doctrine of *Libertinism*, which brought them to an abominable filthiness of Life. They taught ... that God regardeth not the Actions of the Outward Man, but of the Heart, and that to the Pure all things are Pure (even things forbidden). And so as allowed by God, they spoke most hideous Words of Blasphemy, and many of them committed whoredoms commonly. Insomuch that a Matron of great Note for Godliness and Sobriety, being perverted by them, turned so shameless a Whore, that she was Carted in the streets of London.'

These extremists were prophets or Ranters, who had much in common with the Joachimites or, for that matter, Tertullian. Such elements have always seized the opportunity of a crisis or breakdown in society to promote apocalyptic or extraordinary solutions, whether moral or politico-economic. The English Civil War was just such an occasion. As one orthodox critic put it (1651): 'It is no new work of Satan to sow Heresies, and breed Heretics, but they never came up so thick as in these latter times. They were wont to peep up by one and one, but now they sprout out by huddles and clusters (like locusts out of the bottomless pit) ... thronging upon us in swarmes, as the Caterpillars of Aegypt.' More recently, the specifically Christian element, always the first victim when millenarianism lurches into terror, had tended to recede into the background or disappear altogether. Yet millenarians, from Tertullian on, had nearly always been anti-clerical – a characteristic they share with modern non-Christian prophets and apocalyptics, like Marx, the Paris communards of 1870, Trotskyites, Maoists and other seekers for an illusory perfection in this world. The secular Daniels of the twentieth century have scriptural credentials and their lineage is Christian.

This analysis of medieval Christianity thus presents two types of social experiment in moulding society around moral principles – an orthodox experiment and the radical alternative it provoked. Both tend to fail because both, in different ways, are too ambitious; and in the process of trying to fend off failure each type of experiment is liable to betray its Christian principles. One of the great, but perhaps inevitable, tragedies of history was the transformation of the Gregorian reform into an institutional obsession with power; and one of the perpetual, but equally fated, tragedies of history is the progression from millenarianism to the total abandonment of moral values. But Christianity, fortunately, contains more than these two imperfect matrices; in the sixteenth and seventeenth centuries we see the emergence and the struggle for survival of a third force: Christian humanism.

PART FIVE

The Third Force
(1500–1648)

SOME TIME BETWEEN 1511 AND 1513, two of Europe's leading scholars paid a visit to the shrine of St Thomas à Becket at Canterbury. One was John Colet, Dean of St Paul's and founder of its new grammar school; the other was the Dutchman Erasmus, author of the leading spiritual handbook for Christian laymen, and of a much-admired satire on the Church, *In Praise of Folly*. In one of his later *Colloquies*, Erasmus left an account of their visit, and it would be hard to conceive of a more poignant little episode, on the eve of the Reformation, than this confrontation between the shrine of the martyred clerical triumphalist, and the two earnest apostles of the New Learning. Both the scholars were pious men, and their visit was reverent. But Erasmus's account makes it clear they were deeply shocked by what they saw. The riches which adorned the shrine were staggering. Erasmus found them incongruous, disproportionate, treasures 'before which Midas or Croesus would have seemed beggars'; thirty years later, Henry VIII's agents were to garner from it 4,994 ounces of gold, 4,425 of silver-gilt, 5,286 of plain silver and twenty-six cartloads of other treasure. Colet infuriated the verger who accompanied them by suggesting that St Thomas would prefer the whole lot be given to the poor. He added insult to injury by refusing to give a reverential kiss to a prize relic, the arm of St George, and by treating an old rag supposedly soaked in St Thomas's blood with 'a whistle of contempt'. Two miles from the town, outside the Harbledown almshouse, the Dean's impatience with 'mechanical Christianity' was further tested when a licensed beggar showered them with holy water and offered St Thomas's shoe to be kissed: 'Do these fools expect us to kiss the shoe of every good man who ever lived?' he asked furiously. 'Why not bring us their spittle or their dung to be kissed?' After this memorable encounter, the two men rode back to London.

By the time this visit took place, it was already clear that the old medieval Church, the total society dating from Carolingian times, was breaking up. A year or so before, Johann Geiler of Strasburg, one of the last great preachers of the Middle Ages, had predicted the dissolution in his final sermon before the Emperor Maximilian: 'Since neither pope, nor emperor, kings nor bishops, will reform our life, God will send a man for the purpose. I hope to see that day ... but I am too old. Many of you will see it; think, then, I pray you, of these words.' It was true that the papacy itself, the Church as an institution, had proved unwilling or incapable of directing the reforming process. But other agencies were relentlessly at work. The Christian universities, which had sprung from the total society, and underpinned it with their metaphysical systems, were in a state of change and uncertainty. The universalist method of St Thomas Aquinas, with its logical superstructure providing answers to every conceivable human query, had been elbowed aside by the Nominalists in the fourteenth century; they taught that many of the basic elements of Christianity could not be demonstrated by logic but must be accepted by blind faith; and in the fifteenth century scholars turned increasingly to re-examine the fundamental credentials of Christianity: the scriptures, the documents of the church, the writings of the early fathers. In the 1440s, Lorenzo di Valla, secretary to Pope Nicholas v, demonstrated that the *Donation of Constantine* and many other key texts were blatant forgeries. He developed and popularized new techniques for the critical evaluation of sacred literature. Political changes in the Mediterranean world at this time brought to the attention of European scholars a large number of ancient books, sacred and profane, Greek, Latin and Hebrew, which had not been systematically examined for centuries. Where their Byzantine and Jewish custodians had been content to preserve these texts, Italian Renaissance scholars, like Valla, Marsilio Ficino and Pico della Mirandola, treated them as keys to the future, collated them, and used them as standards of measurement for conventional western learning.

In this new school, there was no separation of, and no desire to separate, religious and secular learning. Ficino thought of Plato, whose basic works were now available in the original Greek, as belonging to a series of interpreters of the divine, beginning with Zoroaster and stretching on through Hermes Trismegistus and Pythagoras – an ancient wisdom anticipating and confirming Christianity. At the same time, the whole range of Hebrew scholarship, which had been preserved untouched in Spain for centuries, was made available to the West by Mirandola, who married Jewish cabalistic theosophy to neo-Platonic cosmology. His pupil, the Hebraist Johann Reuchlin, produced the first Hebrew-Christian grammar in 1506, and tried to prevent the systematic destruction of these emerging Jewish books by the Dominican Inquisition. Thus was the New Learning first brought into conflict with the established Church. But conflict was inevitable. Men were now able to study the Greek and Hebrew texts in the original, and compared them with the received version in Latin treated as sacrosanct in the West for centuries. Valla, working from the Greek New Testament, pointed out numerous errors in St Jerome's Vulgate – the first glimmerings of modern scriptural scholarship. And once men began to look at the texts with fresh eyes, they saw many things which made them uncomfortable or excited. The message of the New Learning was, indeed, this: through greater knowledge to a purer spiritual truth. Ficino, Pico and Reuchlin suggested that there was, as it were, a natural religion; that behind diverse philosophical and religious experiences there was a unity. Its essential truth was most perfectly expressed in Christianity. Over the centuries, accretions had obscured this truth: the new learning would rediscover it and purify it.

Thus the new intellectual movement was pressed into the service of reforming the Church, something which had baffled popes, councils, bishops and kings for more than a century. Ignorance was identified with sin; knowledge with reform. The principle could be expressed in many ways: by the exposure of fraudulent documents; by the establishment of wholly accurate and authentic texts; by the re-examination of these texts in the light of new knowledge to discover their full meaning; and – the meaning of the scriptures having been finally established – by the elimination from the Church's life and activities of all beliefs and practices which lacked biblical authority or the sanction of the early Church. The effect of this movement, if allowed to progress unchecked, was to place the well-being and future of the Church in the hands of its empirical scholars. Or perhaps, indeed, in the hands of a wider audience. The spread of the new knowledge virtually coincided with the technical development of printing. The coincidence ensured the acceleration of both. The earliest printed books in the West were produced at Mainz in 1454–7, at the time Valli was annotating the Greek New Testament. By 1500 there were seventy-three presses in Italy, fifty-one in Germany, thirty-nine in France, twenty-four in Spain, fifteen in the Low Countries and eight in Switzerland. The most important of the firms, run by Aldus Manutius in Venice, was almost entirely devoted to publishing the recovered Greek classics; despite its extraordinarily elegant standards, the work was pushed forward with great speed: in the twenty years 1494–1515, twenty-seven *editones principes* of Greek authors and works of reference were produced, and when Aldus died in 1515 not a single major Greek author remained unprinted. These works were printed in very considerable quantities, and at prices well below even low-quality manuscript copies of similar length. The rapid development of printing, with its tremendous concentration on works of seminal interest to religion and reform, posed an entirely new problem to the Church and State authorities which traditionally controlled the dissemination of knowledge. Censoring or preventing the circulation of printed books was essentially the same as controlling manuscripts; but the difference in speed and scale was absolutely crucial. It took at least a generation for the censors to tackle it, and they were never able to exercise the same degree of effective supervision as in the days before cheap printing.

Erasmus was born into this new arena of scholarship and communication in 1466. His background was quintessentially that of the old age. He was the bastard son of a priest, by a washerwoman. This was the common fate of a vast number of people at the time. It testified to the unwillingness of the Church to sanction clerical marriage and its inability to stamp out concubinage. Probably as many as half the men in orders had 'wives' and families. Behind all the New Learning and the theological debates, clerical celibacy was, in its own way, the biggest single issue at the Reformation. It was a great social problem and, other factors being equal, it tended to tip the balance in favour of reform. As a rule, the only hope for the child of a priest was to go into the Church himself, thus unwillingly or with no great enthusiasm, taking vows which he might subsequently regret: the evil tended to perpetuate itself. Many thousands of men (and women) were trapped in this predicament, grudging and awkward members of a privileged class, sentenced for life to a spiritual role for which they had no calling and – since no seminaries existed – no training. Erasmus was a case in point. After his birth his parents no longer lived together. In an autobiographical fragment, written when he was already world famous, he concealed his bastardy, indicating that it still rankled. His schooling was wretched. The Brethren of the Common Life, founded by Gerard Groote, were one of the more successful of the idealistic orders of the later Middle Ages. They were genuinely poor, they took their social work seriously; in some ways they adumbrated the Protestant reformers by their stress on the Bible and their distaste for elaborate forms of worship, such as polyphonic singing. But Erasmus was taught as one of 275 boys in one room, under a single master; and the curriculum was largely confined to thought-conditioning Latin rhymes and sayings, such as 'The prelates of the church are the salt of the earth.' He was eighteen when both his parents died, and he saw no alternative but to join the clergy as an Augustinian; he soon regretted it and spent the next thirty years disentangling himself from his legal clerical ties, knowing that at any moment his superiors could ruin his career as a scholar and writer by forcing him to live in strict conformity with the rules of his order. He was one of many thousands who, while members of the privileged clerical order, were emotionally committed to its destruction.

Erasmus was fortunate to become secretary to the Bishop of Cambrai, who sent him to the university at Paris. Here, too, was the old medieval world. The College de Montaigu was known to Parisians as 'the cleft between the buttocks of Mother Theology'. It was ancient, dilapidated, dank and filthy; the food was revolting, the dormitories stank of urine, and there were frequent beatings. Erasmus was already twenty-six and hated it; so did Rabelais, who wanted it burnt down. Two other of its *alumni*, however, Ignatius Loyola and Jean Calvin, admired its austerities and welcomed their time there: here we have one of the great cleavages of the sixteenth century, between the Humanists and the Puritans. Work at the university stressed the mechanical side of religion. Thus, at the University of Louvain, where Erasmus spent some time, teachers and students were in 1493 debating the topics: do four five-minute prayers on consecutive days stand a better chance of being answered than one twenty-minute prayer? Is a prayer of ten minutes, said on behalf of ten people, as efficacious as ten one-minute prayers? The debate lasted eight weeks, longer than it had taken Columbus to sail to America the previous year, 1492. Erasmus' intellectual break-through came in 1499, when he went to England and, at Oxford, heard Colet lecture on St Paul's Epistle to the Romans. Colet did not know Greek but he had been to Florence and absorbed the spirit of Valla, Ficino and the neo-Platonists. In his lectures he went behind the endless layers of commentaries to re-examine the text of Paul afresh and discover its actual meaning as an exposition of Christian faith. Thus not for the first, or the last, time, Paul's Epistle to the Romans brought about a spiritual revelation and a new approach to the Christian life. Erasmus determined to re-examine the scriptures himself, and to learn Greek in order to do it effectively. And to support himself and his studies he began to write books.

For nearly four decades, until his death in 1536, Erasmus's output covered a huge field, embracing the Christian life, the theory and practice of education, the state of Church and society, and the meaning of the scriptures, besides including scholarly editions of sacred and patristic texts. Of these by far the most important was his Greek edition of the New Testament, which made the original text (albeit in imperfect form) available to Latin Christians for the first time. Erasmus made himself into a scholar with high academic standards; he was also a popularizer and a journalist who understood the importance of communication. He wanted his books to be small, handy and cheap, and he was the first writer to grasp the full potentialities of printing. He worked at speed, often in the printing shop itself, writing and correcting his proofs on the spot. He was exhilarated by the smell of printer's ink, the incense of the Reformation. As a result, the diffusion of his works is astounding. His first success, the *Adages* (1500), was a collection of Latin quotations used to teach the language but also reflecting his philosophy; it was constantly reprinted and gradually expanded into a collection of over 4,000 short essays, which influenced society in the same way as the crude proverbs of his schooling had done. His *Enchiridion*, or layman's handbook, first published in 1503, was reprinted in 1509 and 1515, and then every year, and by his death, had been translated into Czech, German, English, French, Spanish, Italian and Portuguese. His *In Praise of Folly*, 1511, went into thirty-nine editions before 1536; some of these were very substantial – thus one Paris printer, hearing that the book might be suppressed, quickly ran off an edition of 24,000 copies. There were some years, it has been calculated, when between one-fifth and one-tenth of all books sold in Oxford, London and Paris were by Erasmus. In the 1530s, 300,000 copies of his Greek New Testament were circulating, and over 750,000 of his other works. He was a new phenomenon, a living world best-seller. He got so much correspondence that, when he was living in Antwerp, then the richest city in Europe, the postman used to stop at his house first, before going on to the City Hall.

Erasmus was made a political counsellor by the Emperor Charles v and offered a cardinal's hat by Pope Paul III. A number of leading European cities gave him their freedom and invited him to live there as an honoured citizen. Yet if Erasmus had sought to propound his views a generation later, he would certainly have been hounded by the Habsburgs and excommunicated by the papacy: indeed, in 1546, only a decade after his death, the Council of Trent declared his version of the New Testament anathema, and at a later session Pope Paul IV branded him as 'the leader of all heretics' and called for the burning of his collected works. By this time, too, Erasmus's unrestricted presence would have been regarded as unwelcome in most of reformed Europe. Erasmus, in fact, rode on the crest of the New Learning, which seemed to offer unlimited opportunities for spiritual and intellectual advancement, and which presaged a thoroughgoing reform of society, conducted from within by a universal and voluntary movement. This rosy prospect was obliterated in the middle decades of the century, and what in fact happened was quite different: a division of Christianity on a compulsory and state basis. Two armed camps came into existence: one, half-reformed, basing its claims exclusively on scripture; the other, unreformed, based exclusively on authority; and between them an unbridgeable chasm, filling with the victims of war and persecution. The outcome, in fact, was almost the complete antithesis of the Erasmian dream.

Herein lies one of the central historical tragedies, of Christianity, of Europe, and of the world. The Erasmian dream was not wholly utopian. All men agreed that faith was a unity. Most agreed that there must be a unitary system of knowledge. Society was universally regarded not only as a unity but an organic one. Why should not the first and second infuse the third in harmony? In a sense, the object of these Renaissance reformers was merely to bring the ideal of Carolingian society up to date – to use the new knowledge to correct its accumulated abuses and imperfections. There was, certainly, a consensus of virtually all men that reform was overdue. The astonishing success of Erasmus's works suggests there was also a wide consensus of educated men for the kind of suggestions he was putting forward. Let us now see what these suggestions were, how much they had in common with the programmes of the Protestant reformers, and where they differed.

Erasmus, like all the reformers without exception, began by ignoring the existence of a privileged clerical class. He regarded himself as a layman, and made no distinction between men in orders, like Colet, and lay friends like Sir Thomas More. This was a commonplace among the men of the New Learning, who were interested in the same things and guided by the same considerations irrespective of their status. With leading scholars like Sir John Cheke and Jacob Sturm, for instance, it is often not easy to be sure whether they were in orders or not. Erasmus's *Enchiridion*, though specifically addressed to laymen, is a general statement of his views which might, and indeed did, serve equally well for clerics. Intellectually, he was in the tradition of Tertullian and Pelagius, who regarded it as normal and desirable that educated laymen should play their full part in the direction of the Church and declined absolutely to endorse an exclusive role for the clergy.

The coming into existence of a Latin-speaking laity was closing the gap that had opened up in the eighth century and had been widened, on an ideological basis, by Gregory VII and his successors. This process had been going on for some time, especially in the big towns; and Erasmus was very much a product of the new urban civilization and spoke for its middle-class members – one might call him the first really articulate urbanite in the West since the fifth century. In the fifteenth century the practical difficulty of reforming the clergy effectively had virtually compelled laymen to invade spheres, particularly education, which clerics had formerly monopolized. The Church still claimed the right to control teaching but more and more schools were being endowed by laymen and run by them. When Colet founded St Paul's in 1510, Erasmus noted: 'Over the revenues and the entire management, he set neither priests, nor the bishop, nor the chapter as they call it, nor noblemen; but some married citizens of established reputation. And when asked the reason, he said that though there was nothing certain in human affairs, he yet found the least corruption in them.' Erasmus, like Colet, regarded the sober, hard-working, middle-ranking townsman as the Christian élite, and the best hope for reform. Nearly all reformers took this view. They dismissed any special clerical claims. Luther glossed Galatians 3:28: 'There is neither priest nor layman, canon nor vicar, rich nor poor, Benedictine, Carthusian, Friar Minor or Augustinian, for it is not a question of this or that status, degree or order.' Or as Nicholas Ridley said: 'St Peter calleth all men priests.' William Tyndale, a typical reformer of the 1520s, wrote: 'Thou that ministereth in the kitchen, and art but a kitchen page . . . knowest that God put thee in that office . . . if thou compare deed and deed, there is a difference between washing of dishes and preaching of the word of God; but as touching to please God, none at all . . .' As John Knox put it a little later: 'This is the point wherein, I say, all men are equal.' For purposes of worship, 'Ye be in your own houses bishops and kings.'

This downgrading of the clerical role was linked to the belief, which again Erasmus shared with all the reformers, that there could be no intermediaries between the Christian soul and the scriptures. All wanted the Bible to be as widely available as possible, and in vernacular translations. Access to the Bible, whether in the original or in any other tongue, had never been an issue in the East. In the West, the clergy had begun to assert an exclusive interpretive, indeed custodial, right to the Bible as early as the ninth century; and from about 1080 there had been frequent instances of the Pope, councils and bishops forbidding not only vernacular translations but any reading at all, by laymen, of the Bible taken as a whole. In some ways this was the most scandalous aspect of the medieval Latin Church. From the Waldensians onwards, attempts to scrutinize the Bible became proof presumptive of heresy – a man or woman might burn for it alone – and, conversely, the heterodox were increasingly convinced that the Bible was incompatible with papal and clerical claims. From the thirteenth century many vernacular versions of the New Testament, in several languages, began to circulate. From the end of the fourteenth century the availability of the Bible to the public became the central issue between the Church, and its critics, such as the Lollards and Hussites. No popular Bible was authorized by the authorities, except in Bohemia which in effect had broken away from Rome by

1420; on the other hand these vernacular versions were never effectively suppressed.

'With the introduction of printing, the efforts of the censors became hopeless. Germany led the way. By the time Luther produced his own New Testament in 1522, there were fourteen different printed versions in German and four in Dutch; none contained a censor's imprimatur or had been printed on a monastic press, but the attempt to forbid their circulation had been virtually abandoned. Erasmus not only welcomed this development but wished to extend the principle by bringing into existence a wholly literate laity with unrestricted access to all sacred writings: 'Let us consider who were the hearers of Christ himself. Were they not a promiscuous multitude? . . . Is Christ offended that such should read him as he chose for his hearers? In my opinion the husbandman should read him, with the smith and the mason, and even prostitutes, bawds and Turks. If Christ refused not his voice to these, neither do I refuse his books.' He thought it essential 'each should hear the Gospel in his native and intelligible tongue' instead of 'muttering their psalms and paternoster in Latin, not understanding their own words'.

For Erasmus, as for all reformers, the Bible then was at the centre of Christian understanding, when presented in its authentic form. And he was at one with them in rejecting mechanical Christianity virtually *in toto*: indulgences, pilgrimages, special privileges, masses for the dead, the whole business of winning salvation by 'merit' artificially acquired, usually by money. He wrote: 'Perhaps thou believest that all thy sins are washed away with a little paper, a sealed parchment, with the gift of a little money or some wax image, with a little pilgrimage. Thou art utterly deceived.' Who had done the deceiving? Chiefly the papacy. And no wonder: the papacy was corrupt and desperately in need of reform. His *In Praise of Folly* was the outcome of a visit to the Rome of the scandalous soldier-pope Julius II, who stormed fortresses in full armour. In Julius's Rome, wrote Erasmus, 'you can see a tired old man act with youthful energy and without regard to labour and expense simply in order to overturn laws, religion, peace and humane institutions.' No man could hope to reach Heaven by using the machinery of the Church: 'Without ceremonies, perhaps thou shalt not be a Christian; but they make thee not a Christian.'

Where, then, was the road to salvation? Erasmus agreed with the reformers that the Bible must be studied. He agreed with the practice of private devotion, especially prayer. Man saved himself through knowledge of God, obtained directly, not through the mediation of an institution. But it is at this point that his thought diverged from both the Lutherans and the later Calvinists. Erasmus, as a scholar and textual critic, had learnt to distrust theology, whose dogmatic conclusions were often based, as he had discovered, on faulty readings of the text. (This distrust was violently reciprocated by the theologians, who hotly disputed the right of text-scholars to pronounce on 'theological' problems, and who clung fiercely to their old texts, however corrupt.) In his own investigations, he had found himself obliged to eliminate the famous Trinitarian verse from 1 John 5:7, since it was not in the Greek manuscript. This led him to doubt the process of metaphysical reasoning and logic which allowed the schoolmen to produce exact certitudes in any theological situation. In his commentary on Hilary of Poitiers, he asks: 'Is it not possible to have fellowship with the Father, Son and Holy Spirit, without being able to explain philosophically the distinction between them, and between the nativity of the Son and the procession of the Holy Spirit?' This was indeed a reasonable but also an audacious question – so much, Erasmus was saying, for the disputes which led to Arianism, to the Monophysite schism and to Islam, and so much for the fatal word which had divided East and West since 1054 and had lost Byzantium to the Christian world. He went on to dismiss the importance of much theological speculation and definition, and to reassert, instead, the virtues which Jesus had outlined in the New Testament and which, to him, were the essence of Christianity: 'You will not be damned if you do not know whether the Spirit proceeding from the Father and the Son had one or two beginnings, but you will not escape damnation if you do not cultivate the fruits of the spirit: love, joy, peace, patience, kindness, goodness, long-suffering, mercy, faith, modesty, continence and chastity.'

What the Church needed, Erasmus argued, was a theology reduced to the absolute minimum. Christianity must be based on peace and unanimity, 'but these can scarcely stand unless we define as little as possible.' On many points 'everyone should be left to follow his own judgment, because there is great obscurity in these matters.' Men searching for the truth should be encouraged to return to the scriptural and patristic sources. Perhaps there was a case for a commission of learned men to draw up a formula of faith. But it must be brief, just 'the philosophy of Christ', which was concerned chiefly with moral virtues. 'All that is of faith,' he wrote, 'should be condensed into a very few articles, and the same should be done for all that concerns the Christian way of life.' Then theologians, if they wished, should be left to develop their own theories, and the faithful to believe or ignore them. On most of the contentious points, he freely admitted: 'I would not dare deprive a man of his life, if I were the judge, nor would I risk my own.'

Of course here again Erasmus was essentially striking at the clerical point of view, with its urge to define and its need for an authoritative answer to every conceivable question. He thought it was not God's desire or intention to illuminate the whole in this life. Such agnosticism was abhorrent to the Church shaped by St Augustine, and organized by Gregory VII and Innocent III, to whom the extension of definition and the reinforcement of authority was the only criterion of growth and progress. It was abhorrent to the papacy; but it was also uncongenial to the Protestant reformers. At bottom, Erasmus believed in a moral reform, pure and simple: if the moral spirit of the Church were transformed and illuminated, then all the problems of Christendom, institutional and even doctrinal, would solve themselves in turn; but the

Church, in St Paul's word, had to become a 'new man' again first. To Luther, a moral reform was equally urgent. But it would prove meaningless and transitory unless it were able to operate within the context of institutional change and drastic doctrinal corrections. Indeed, moral reform was not only useless but perhaps worse than useless unless we got the theological equations right. We had first to understand how man justified himself to God, and this was a theological problem. The need was not to simplify doctrine, but to get it right – and that meant not less definition, but more.

From this basic disagreement, the area of discord widened. If theological definition were not essential, might even be undesirable, it followed naturally that one should not attempt to impose uniformity or force consciences. Erasmus hated the witch-hunting atmosphere engendered by the Inquisition and the endless search for an illusory certainty even about details. 'Formerly heresy involved only deviation from the gospels, or the articles of faith, or something of similar authority. Nowadays they shout 'heresy!' at you for almost anything. Anything that does not please them, or that they do not understand, is heresy. To know Greek is heresy. To pronounce it correctly is heresy.' This could only lead to endless turmoil. But 'the works of the mind, and charity, demand universal peace.' Reformers should be less reckless in demanding change; those who wanted to burn people at the stake should be less intolerant. Both should extend charity to each other. Persecution was an offence against charity. And it was unproductive: 'Vigorous minds will not suffer compulsion. To exercise compulsion is typical of tyrants; to suffer it, typical of asses.' In cities where men differed on religion, both sides should keep to their quarters and everyone be left to his conscience until time brought the opportunity for agreement. In the meantime, open sedition should be put down, but manifest abuses corrected; and toleration should be extended until a universal council met and achieved reunification on a new basis of faith.

This eirenic formula was unwelcome to Rome at all times; initially it appealed to Luther and other rebels, but later it was seen as an impediment to the consolidation of their position, and an infringement of what they regarded as their undoubted right to enforce their doctrines and institutions on areas under their influence. This was linked to a further point of difference, perhaps the most important of all: Erasmus deplored Luther's invocation of the aid of the German princes in establishing reform. He had the progressive townsman's intense suspicion of princely power, and the idea of the ruler of each state settling the religion of his subjects on the basis of his own personal predilections was abhorrent. Erasmus associated princely or kingly rule with war and destruction:

'The eagle is the image of the king, neither beautiful, not musical, nor fit for food: but carnivorous, rapacious, a brigand, a destroyer, solitary, hated by all, a pest. . . .
Are not noble cities erected by the people and destroyed by princes? Does

not a state grow rich by the industry of its citizens, only to be plundered by the greed of its rulers? Are not good laws enacted by the representatives of the people and violated by kings? Does not the commonalty love people while monarchs plan war?'

Erasmus was a pacifist. He did not accept the doctrine of the 'just war'. As a boy of eight he had seen 200 prisoners of war broken on the wheel outside the gates of Utrecht on the orders of its bishop. His *Dulce bellum inexpertis* was the first book in European history devoted entirely to the cause of pacifism. He pondered various schemes for international bodies of wise men to arbitrate between the quarrelling rulers: he thought that a de-politicized papacy might, perhaps, perform this role. He addressed his great international audience of readers: 'I appeal to you all, who are considered to be Christians – conspire together in this way of thinking. Show how much the unity of the masses can do against the tyranny of the mighty.' If each state opted for its own brand of religion at the ruler's bidding, war, he thought, would be inevitable: 'the long war of words and writings will end in blows.' As he wrote to the Duke of Saxony: 'Tolerating the sects may appear a great evil to you, but it is still much better than a religious war. If the clergy once succeed in entangling the rulers, it will be a catastrophe for Germany and the church . . . ruin and misery everywhere, and destruction under the false pretext of religion.'

The last twenty years of Erasmus's life, during which he saw the religious war-clouds assemble, were a progression from optimism to fear. In 1516, he had published his Greek New Testament with a commentary which included most of the programme which progressive men agreed was essential for reform. The work was acclaimed everywhere and Pope Leo was enthusiastic. In February 1517 Erasmus wrote to his friend Wolfgang Capito: 'Now I almost wish I were young again, for this reason – I foresee the coming of a golden age: so clearly do we see the minds of princes, as if inspired, devoting all their energies to the pursuit of peace.' Again, two months later – not long before Luther sprang into prominence with his theses – he addressed the Pope: 'I congratulate this age of ours, which promises to be an age of gold if ever there was one.' He saluted Leo on 'the public and lasting concord of Christendom'.

Before the end of 1517, Erasmus had changed his mind: 'I fear a great revolution is about to take place in [Germany].' He saw no serious objections to Luther's original Wittenberg theses. He tried, behind the scenes, to protect Luther from the anger of the authorities, and urged moderation on both sides. But as early as 1518 he took the view that both would end by turning against learning, because they were obsessed by theology. To Luther himself he wrote: 'I try to stay neutral to help the revival of learning as best I can. And it seems to me that more is accomplished by a civil modesty than by impetuosity.' This advice was ignored. Luther, though initially deferential to the sage of Europe, at least publicly, saw him as 'a proud sceptic', a man of

little faith – 'human conditions prevail in him much more than divine.'
Erasmus privately dismissed Luther as 'a Goth', a man of the past, but also in
a sinister way the portent of a horrific future – 'the tree which bears the
poisonous fruit of nationalism.' He was furious to find himself accused of guilt
by association, and still more to discover that some thought him the author of
Luther's diatribes. Dragged unwillingly into the controversy, he was attacked
by the orthodox Edward Lee, later Archbishop of York; and he was acutely
embarrassed by the vulgar counter-attack on Lee published by his friends:
'You filth, if you do not beg forgiveness of Erasmus, I shall throw your name,
like a piece of shit, across the frontiers of posterity, that people may remember
your stench forever.' This was just the kind of theologians' Billingsgate he
loathed, and in which Luther and his opponents were now freely indulging.
Luther invited Christendom to 'wash your hands in the blood of these
cardinals, popes and other dregs of the Roman Sodom', while the papist
theologians of Louvain called for the execution of 'that pestilential fart of
Satan whose stench reaches to Heaven'.

Erasmus tried to keep out of this distasteful row, which went directly
contrary to his view of how reform should be carried out. But the wide
dissemination of Luther's deterministic views of salvation, with which he
totally disagreed, forced him to make his own position clear. His *Discussion of
the Free Will* (1524) rejected the idea of predestination, and stressed man's
capacity to use his own resources to work out his salvation – here was the voice
of Pelagius, the true wisdom of the classical world. When Luther published
a characteristically rude reply, Erasmus thought it time for a rebuke: 'How do
your scurrilous charges that I am an atheist, an Epicurean and a sceptic, help
your argument? . . . It upsets me dreadfully that your arrogant, insolent and
rebellious nature should have put the world in arms. . . . I would wish you a
better disposition, were you not so marvellously satisfied with the one you
have already. Wish me anything you will – except your temper.' To Luther, he
was now 'a snake', 'a piece of shit', the 'insane destroyer of the church', the
'inflamer of the base passions of young boys'; he told his circle he had seen
Erasmus walking 'arm in arm with the devil in Rome'.

As Luther consolidated his position, and the secular powers – as Erasmus
had feared – became involved, the old scholar kept his distance from the
reformers. In *Hyperaspistes*, 1526–7, he re-emphasized his plea for a minimum
theology: 'In sacred literature there are certain sanctuaries into which God
wills that we shall not penetrate further.' He held to what he called 'natural
religion'. He refused to break with Rome: 'I shall bear with this church until I
find a better one . . . he does not sail badly who steers a middle course between
two evils.' He concentrated on attacking persecution and the Inquisition; and
on pressing for peaceful coexistence. On the Emperor Charles v he urged
compromise: the eucharist in both kinds, married clergy, toleration laws. He
spent his last years in various free cities, such as Basle and Freiburg, which he
hoped would escape the coming religious devastation: 'I am a citizen of the

world, known to all, and to all a stranger.' He was grievously shocked by Henry VIII's execution of his friend Thomas More. What had happened to the gifted and enlightened young king he had known? And why had More been so foolish as to defy him on an arguable point? Was the world going mad? Among his last works was *On the Sweet Concord of the Church*, a plea for mutual toleration, radiant with meekness, goodwill and moderation. It was violently attacked by both sides.

Erasmus undoubtedly had a huge constituency in Europe. At one time there seemed a real chance that his approach to reform might win the consensus, and be carried through. He had admirers over a very wide spectrum of opinion. In 1518, for instance, the orthodox controversialist Johann Eck had written: 'With the exception of a few monks and would-be theologians, all learned men are followers of Erasmus.' The moderate reformer Oecolampadius wrote to him in 1522: 'We want neither the Catholic nor the Lutheran church. We want a third one.' As late as 1526, the imperial chancellor, Mercurio Gattarina, said he saw Christendom divided into three parts: Roman, Lutheran, and those who sought nothing but the glory of God and human welfare – this was the party of Erasmus and he was proud to belong to it. Erasmus himself referred to 'the third church'. But an eirenic mood was essential to its construction, and its chances crumbled as the gap between Rome and Germany widened, and the battlelines were drawn.

At the same time, it is incorrect to present the Lutheran movement as a catastrophe which prevented the carrying through of an Erasmian programme within a framework of Christian unity. The issues were much more complicated. Erasmus had a modern kind of mind: in some ways this was an advantage in that it attuned him to progressive opinion in the wealthier cities and gave him a truly international following. He saw reform as an international movement coming from within the Church, and led by the élite. But to be modern minded was in some ways a disadvantage for it tended to make Erasmus gloss over the realities of power and the way things could actually be done. Luther, 'the Goth', the crude, earthy, but clever son of a successful tin-miner, was much closer to the thoughts of ordinary men of all classes, as opposed to intellectuals; and he was much clearer in his own mind about what forces and emotions moved men to action in the early sixteenth century, and which institutions carried weight.

Broadly speaking, the rulers of the states favoured reforms of the Church, within limits, and according to their individual requirements. The papacy was opposed to reform because it was expensive in terms of revenues, and of the power that generates revenues. There was thus a clash of interests. But it could be resolved, and during the fourteenth and fifteenth centuries had been resolved, by the papacy continually handing over to the rulers, as we have seen, portions of its ecclesiastical sovereignty. The states were growing stronger in relation to the Church; and the papacy, to prevent itself from growing correspondingly weaker, was trying to build up its own states in central Italy as a power base. The process can be seen at work under Julius II, whom Luther, during a visit to Rome, denounced as 'a blood-sucker' and 'a cruelly violent animal'. Maybe he was; but in preferring the role of a military commander and a king to that of a pontiff, he was following a certain line of logic. Before his election he had sworn a capitulation, repeated afterwards, that he would call a council within two years to conduct reforms. But in a universal council which he did not control, Julius realized he would be forced to dismantle much of the papacy's money-raising machinery without getting anything in return. He preferred to do his own bilateral deals with princes with the object of restoring the papacy as a universal monarchy. Yet pressure from the French king, from the emperor, and from within the Church for a reforming council continued. In 1511, nine cardinals, the outstanding one being Carvajal, who had twice been papal legate in Germany, took the unusual (though not unprecedented) step of summoning a council themselves, after taking the advice of eminent jurists, and with the tacit support of Louis XII and the Emperor Maximilian. Julius responded vigorously by excommunicating and depriving the nine men, denouncing them as 'sons of darkness' and 'true schismatics', and promptly called a council of his own, the Fifth Lateran of 1512. This council, the last of the undivided Church, was a mere manoeuvre and contemporaries saw it as such; it was not designed to carry through reforms; indeed it concentrated on the arid topic, dear to old-fashioned theologians, of the exact status of the soul between the death of the body and the Last Judgment. But it was marked by the signature of a new concordat with France which gave the French monarchy virtually everything it asked for in terms of controlling the French Church, made it possible for the French crown to carry through its own reforms, if it wished, and thus relaxed pressure on the papacy from France. Julius, in fact, had saved himself by a bilateral deal, and at the expense of the Church as a whole.

But the deal was expensive, and added to the papacy's already pressing financial problems. Shortage of money tends to produce constitutional crises in all states: the papacy was no exception. Its revenue at this time was half a million ducats, less than half of Venice's. The most upright popes tended to be those most in debt. Honesty came dear: reform cost money. This was something reformers did not understand. Alexander VI, the worst of the popes, kept himself solvent; most of his immediate predecessors and successors were desperate. But it was universally assumed that the popes were very rich – we must never underestimate the powerful effect on history of ignorance of state secrets. In 1517, Archbishop Albert of Mainz, the twenty-seven-year-old brother of the Elector of Brandenberg, had purchased from Rome a number of very expensive dispensations to hold sees in plurality; and to pay for them, he engaged in another deal with Rome to proclaim throughout Germany an indulgence for the building of St Peter's. The archbishop had a permanent and lucrative exhibition of relics, some 9,000 items, which included whole bodies of saints, a bone of Isaac, manna from the wilderness, a bit of Moses's burning bush, a jar from Cana (with actual wine in it), a bit of the crown of thorns, and one of the stones that killed St Stephen. But the Elector of nearby Saxony, Frederick the Wise, also had his money-raising collection of relics, some 17,433 fragments of bones, and the entire body of one of the Holy Innocents. He regarded the archbishop's show, and his sale of indulgences, as a rival, and he wanted to stop the export of bullion. Hence he forbade the sale in his territories, and was furious when some of the subjects simply crossed the border to buy them. It was at this point that Luther, a thirty-four-year-old Augustinian monk, intervened by nailing his 'Ninety-five theses against Indulgences' to the church door of Wittenberg Castle. 'The pope,' he said, echoing the prevailing misconception, 'has wealth far beyond all other men – why does he not build St Peter's church with his own money instead of the money of poor Christians?' Thus from the first statement of his protest, Luther aligned himself with the interest of his secular ruler.

This is not to say Luther was insincere; on the contrary, the monk's burning sincerity was the strength of his appeal. His approach to reform, as Professor of Scripture at the university, was originally Erasmian, in that it was based on a rejection of medieval metaphysics and a return to the scriptural texts. As he put it, five months before he nailed his theses: 'Nobody will go to hear a lecture now unless the lecturer is teaching my theology, the theology of the Bible and St Augustine and all true theologians of the church. I am sure the church will never be reformed unless we get rid of canon law, scholastic theology, philosophy and logic as they are studied today. . . .' Yet the reference to Augustine is significant. It relates almost exclusively to the doctrine of predestination which Augustine developed from a reading of St Paul to the Romans, at the end of his life. Luther, too, had been reading Romans. The moment of conversion came to him while he was on the privy – 'the Holy Spirit endowed me with this art when I was on the [cloaca]', as he put it – when he first understood the meaning of the phrase 'the just shall live by faith'. To Luther this was the whole answer to the superstructure of sacramental and mechanical Christianity which the Church had erected. The scriptures said plainly that man was saved by faith, not by good works – the fact that he performed good works was merely an outward confirmation of his consciousness of being saved.

The concept was alien to Erasmus, as was the enthusiasm and absolute conviction with which Luther deployed it. Unlike Erasmus his mind recoiled from doubt and embraced certitude. Hence the importance he attached to theology, as the means to discover truth, and the need he felt to construct an alternative system to the Catholic faith. Here was the parting of the ways: the Erasmians believed in moral reform, the Lutherans (and later the Calvinists) in a new theory of Christianity. There was also a personal difference which is at least as important. Luther, unlike Erasmus, was an evangelist. He believed he had been given the truth and the mission to deliver it. This certitude

explains his huge dogged will, which seems to radiate from the powerful head
we observe in his portraits, and his ruthlessness, which made Erasmus
shudder. Luther was not so much an intellect as a great force – a great spiritual
force, in fact. Perhaps the most striking thing about him was his power of
prayer, a relic of his training in a good monastery. He liked to spend three
hours a day at prayer, with his hands clasped, at an open window. Some of his
sermons on prayer are astonishing simple and unaffected. 'I take on a great
thing when I pray,' he said, and the remark carried conviction. The stress on
private prayer as the true alternative to mechanical Christianity was the most
powerful single element in Luther's positive appeal to lay-folk of all classes,
and well outside Germany; and his concept of household daily prayers
underpinned the devotion to the family with which he associated his scornful
repudiation of clerical celibacy and which his own warm circle epitomized.
Luther evangelized by concentrating on a few comparatively simple messages
which he drove home with endless repetition and furious energy. From 1517
when he first began to write, he averaged a book every fortnight – over a
hundred volumes by his death. The initial thirty writings, 1517–20, reached a
third of a million copies – his major tracts went into scores of editions.

Of these, the three most important were all published in 1520, the year
before Luther's formal excommunication and the beginning of the Protestant
schism. The *Babylonish Captivity of the Church* contained the essential
Reformation critique of the Church and the positive, biblical programme. *On
the Liberty of a Christian Man* outlined the doctrine of justification by faith,
the heart of Lutheranism; and, finally, *To the Christian Nobility of the German
Nation* set out the means whereby the new religion could, and in fact was,
established. In calling on the German princes to reform the Church by virtue
of their office, Luther was taking a step Erasmus would have shrunk from; but
he was in a perfectly sound Christian constitutional tradition. The medieval
assumption was that society was fundamentally one. It was proper, indeed
their duty, for the clergy to rebuke the *regnum* of lay authority and call on
Christians to amend it. Equally, the converse was true, and the *regnum* might
be called on to amend the *sacerdotum*. Both were within society, that is the
Church. The clergy had manifestly and repeatedly failed to do their part in
removing abuses; recourse therefore must be had to the other power in the
Church. In calling on the princes to take up the work of reform, Luther did not
mean – nor did any one suppose he meant – that he was appealing from the
Christian Church to the secular State, but merely from the clerical to the civil
authority within Christendom.

Yet, as Erasmus would have argued, there was undoubtedly a monstrous
danger in the line Luther adopted and consistently pursued. By the second
decade of the sixteenth century the power of the State was visibly growing
through all Europe; to displace clerical authority and entrust the headship of
the Church, and the arbitration of doctrine, to secular rulers was massively to
enforce a process already fraught with peril to other elements in society. It

meant, too, a degree of dependence on the princes which implied a blind endorsement of the social order they represented – a social order as much in need of change and reform as the clerical one. These consequences became immediately apparent when, in 1524, the explosion detonated by the Lutheran protest became inextricably mingled with economic discontent and took the form of a peasants' revolt. This, of course, is what tended to happen in the total society. It was hard to separate a successful attack on one aspect of authority from a challenge to another. Thus, at the close of the fourteenth century, Wyclif and his movement had lost all their powerful secular allies when the peasants rose and terrified the whole of the established order. And once Wyclif had been damned by association with millenarian revolution, the Church was able to hunt down his followers at its leisure. The tendency of wild millenarians to take over, and so ruin, any reformist movement was one reason why the Church had stayed unreformed so long. Luther was determined to avoid this fate. He saw that he could only save his reformation by sacrificing the peasants. Thus he not merely disassociated himself from the millenarians and the radicals, but positively commanded the princes to crush them. In his fearsome tract *Against the Murdering, Thieving Hordes of Peasants*, he identified himself wholly with the conservative, established order, and the counter-revolution. He asked the princes 'to brandish their swords, to free, save, help and pity the poor people forced to join the peasants – but the wicked, smite, stab and slay all that you can.' 'These times are so extraordinary that a prince can win heaven more easily by bloodshed than by prayer.' 'I do not want to struggle for the gospel by violence and murder.' 'You cannot meet a rebel with reason: your best answer is to punch him in the face until he has a bloody nose.'

By this ruthless advocacy of an anti-peasant crusade, Luther escaped from the blind alley which led to the millenarian bloodbath at Munster and established his social bona fides as a conservative reformer with whom the princes could do business. Thereafter, Luther always marched closely in step with his secular backers. In 1529, the reforming princes delivered their 'protest' against the Catholic powers at the Diet of Speier; two years later the Protestant movement was placed on a military footing by the formation of the Schmalkaldic League, extended in 1539 to include a vast area of Germany. From this point, there was no real chance that the Lutheran movement would be exterminated; the papacy and its secular allies were faced with the choice of compromise or permanent schism.*

The overwhelming consensus among secular statesmen was that a compromise, and reconciliation, was possible; and that a universal council should be

---

* Protestantism owed its survival to the Turks. The Habsburgs put the defence of Hungary before the suppression of Protestants. The Protestants knew this and exploited the ebb and flow of Ottoman aggression to win concessions. 'The consolidation, expansion and legitimizing of Lutheranism in Germany by 1555 should be attributed to Ottoman imperialism more than to any other factor'. Stephen A. Fischer-Galati, *Ottoman Imperialism and German Protestantism, 1521–55* (Harvard, 1959).

summoned to bring it about. From the start of the controversy this remained the Emperor Charles v's policy. His salient object was the reunification of Germany, and he saw this could only be realized by the restoration of religious unity. For the French crown, however, the salient object was the continued division of Germany, and France's influence was consistently deployed to make a satisfactory council impossible. Clement VII and his successor Paul III were similarly determined to avoid a council which they realized must end in the destruction of papal power; and their procrastinations were successful. By 1539, Luther and his Church were secure, and he had lost interest in compromise; or, rather, he did not believe that the papacy could be brought to entertain one in any circumstances. The principals, as it were, had opted out of the dialogue. But there were many on both sides who still believed the gap could be bridged. In some ways Luther, as they appreciated, was more Catholic than many of his Roman Catholic opponents. At the beginning of the controversy, Johan Eck had chosen deliberately to argue with him on the issue of papal authority rather than on grace, the sacraments and the nature of the Church. Some pious laymen, such as his patron Frederick the Wise, said they could not see where he had been refuted on the basis of scripture. It was the same with Luther's doctrine of justification by faith. Quite independently of Luther, Cardinal Contarini had reached the same conclusions as early as 1511. There were other instances of Catholic theologians adopting this position as a result of reconsidering St Paul. One example was Cardinal Pole, who became Archbishop of Canterbury in the attempt by Queen Mary Tudor to restore Catholicism in England in the 1550s. Other eirenicists on the Catholic side included Pierre Favre of Savoy, the first Jesuit to go to Germany and one of Ignatius Loyola's earliest companions. He advocated a policy of love and friendship to heretics and the search of doctrinal harmony. On the Protestant side, Melanchthon and Bucer consistently looked for intermediary positions. Before Erasmus died, some of the Lutheran pastors appealed to him: 'We hope, man of greatness, that you will be the future Soloman, whose judgment will deprive every party of something, and thereby put an end to discord.' There were, indeed, a great many reformers who believed a split in the Church was tragic and avoidable, just as there were many Catholics who were deeply disturbed by the Church's merit-theology and its teaching about the use of the sacraments, and who were anxious to embrace the Lutheran correctives. As a result of these pressures on both sides, a series of colloquies were held 1539–41. They, if anything, provide the answer to the question: was the Reformation split avoidable?

The first meeting at Hagenau, 1540, failed because of inadequate preparation. There was a further meeting at Worms, where the discussion was transferred to a diet at Regensburg in March 1541; but in the meantime secret talks were held in the second half of December 1540. Among those taking part were Gropper, a Catholic eirenic and humanist, Granvella, the imperial chancellor, Bucer and Capito. Gropper had already begun a reform of the

Cologne diocese, on behalf of the archbishop, and he feared it would be jeopardized by Catholic and Lutheran extremists. He had already set out in his *Enchiridion Christianae Institutionis* (1538), a view of justification which was close to that of Contarini and which he hoped would reconcile the Catholic and Protestant positions. Both he and the chancellor were Erasmians. For the colloquy itself, Contarini was appointed papal legate. He came full of goodwill, convinced that justification was the heart of the matter, and that once this was resolved, others, such as papal authority and the sacraments, would fall into place. Like Luther, he had come to justification through Augustine, and did not see what the Catholic objection to it could be: 'I have truly come to the firm conclusion,' he wrote in 1523, 'that no one can justify himself by his works . . . one must turn to the divine grace which can be obtained through faith in Jesus Christ. . . . Since therefore the foundation of the Lutheran edifice is true, we must say nothing against it but we must accept it as true and Catholic, indeed as the foundation of the Christian religion.' (The Inquisition suppressed such passages in the Venetian edition of his works of 1584.) The colloquy was opened by Charles v in person, who expressed hope that unity could be rapidly restored in the face of the renewed Turkish pressure. Contarini said: 'How great will be the fruit of unity, and how profound the gratitude of all mankind.' Bucer replied: 'Both sides have failed. Some of us have over-emphasized unimportant points, and others have not adequately reformed obvious abuses. With God's will we shall ultimately find the truth.'

Against this friendly background, Contarini and Gropper produced their mediatory compromise (which had already been worked on) of double justification: that is, imputed and inherent justification, faith and love. The Christian man is just in a two-fold way, by faith and grace, and by doing the works of love; the former is more assured, man being imperfect. When this formula was accepted, Pole, who was present, commented: 'When I observed this union of opinion, I felt a delight such as no harmony of sounds could have inspired me with; not only because I see the approach of peace and concord, but because these articles are the foundation of the whole Christian faith.' Unfortunately, the colloquy then proceeded to break down on the question of the real presence in the eucharist. Contarini was caught off balance by his own ignorance of Protestant teaching. This is not surprising: Protestant teaching varied. All believed in the real presence in one sense or another. None accepted the technical formulation of transubstantiation, which had been devised by Aquinas in the thirteenth century. Bucer, Melanchthon, Calvin, Zwingli all tended to produce different formulae. Luther taught a real, corporal presence of Christ's body and blood, 'in, with and under' the elements. Zwingli denied the corporal eating and drinking. Calvin was half-way between the two. Luther's position was essentially that of St Augustine (as on justification); his objection to Aquinas's formulation was more methodological than substantial. In effect, he accepted the Catholic doctrine; as he put it, 'I would rather drink blood with the papists than mere wine with the Zwinglians.' But Luther was not present at Regensburg. He thought the effort to meet Rome half-way useless, and he boycotted the colloquies. Charles v would have been willing to accept a simple declaration that Christ was really and truly present, and leave the technical issue of transubstantiation to a General Council. The centre group of princes were willing to accept what had been agreed, and build on it. But extremists on both sides carried the day. Contarini left Regensburg disappointed and baffled.

Political factors – the French, the Bavarian dukes and the papacy on the one hand, Luther's Schmalkaldic League and the Elector of Saxony on the other – had had as much to do with the breakdown as theology. It was the last chance for a compromise. When the General Council finally met at Trent five years later, Contarini was dead, the moderates were scattered, the Catholic Church was a defiant and intransigent rump, no longer thinking of anything but fire and sword, and Charles v had virtually despaired of unity. Luther died during the first session, and the fact was scarcely noted except for savage expressions of regret that it was no longer possible to burn him.

By this time, too, the Protestant movement itself was split beyond redemption: there was no longer a united front with which Catholicism might negotiate. Of course Luther had not been the only reformer in the field, or even the first. Zwingli, who brought reform to Zurich in 1522, claimed to have preceded him, and he preached a more radical doctrine. Unlike Luther he had no reverence for the past; no 'feeling' of Catholicism, and the outward transformation at Zurich was more thorough: the 'Lord's Supper' which Zwingli established in 1525 had little resemblance to the medieval liturgy. At Strassburg, the leading reformer, Martin Bucer, tried to effect a reconciliation between Luther's and Zwingli's ideas; the effort failed, but in making it he produced a lengthy body of salvationist doctrine from which his pupil, Jean Calvin, extracted a clear and coherent alternative to the Lutheran brand of reformed Christianity. Lutheranism was essentially conservative in doctrine and structure, a form of state Catholicism, shorn of its mechanical aspects, stripped and simplified, but not essentially different from medieval Christianity. In Lutheran areas, the reorganization was carried out by the secular authorities, at Luther's request: there was a systematic visitation of all churches, from which a consistory was formed at Wittenburg in 1542: this was, in effect, a Church court of lawyers and divines appointed by the prince, which replaced the jurisdiction of the bishops and was gradually extended: ecclesiastical and secular administration was thus tidied up together. Calvinism, by contrast, was not a tidying-up operation, worked by and through the existing state machinery, but a radical experiment in theocracy, an attempt to reduce the medieval organism of the Church-State to its supposed primitive origins.

Calvin came from north-west France, the son of a clerical lawyer; his own formation, at Paris, Orléans, Bourges, was essentially legal and canonical. But (next to Erasmus) he was the best-read of the reformers, and it is perhaps significant that his first work was a commentary on Seneca's *De Clementia*, markedly élitist in tone and approving of the Stoic doctrine of predestined fate; Calvin is a case to illustrate the theory that a man's dogmatic beliefs tend to reflect his emotional predispositions and his family background. By 1533, when he was twenty-four, he had rejected Catholicism, and within three years he had used the work of Bucer and Luther to construct not merely a new *summa* of Christian dogma but an entire system of state and ecclesiastical government. His *Institutes of the Christian Religion* were continually revised until his death in 1564; but in all essentials they were complete by 1538, when he first began to apply them in Geneva. Calvin was immensely intelligent, determined and self-confident; he had, he said, 'received from God more ample enlightenment than others'. But the controlling factor in his system was excommunication, on which all the male members of his family were brought up to be experts. Thus he pounced on Luther's rediscovery of Augustinian predestination, and drove it to its ultimate conclusion. He began by doubling it: men were not only predestined to be saved, but to be damned. Satan and the devils acted on the command of God: 'They can neither conceive any evil nor, when they have conceived it, contrive to do it, nor having contrived it lift even a little finger to execute it, save in so far as God commands them.' God forewills all the tiniest events or actions from all eternity, whether good or evil, according to his plan; some he plans to save, by grace (for all men are evil and worthy of damnation), some he plans to damn. 'If we ask why God takes pity on some, and why he lets go of the others, there is no other answer but that it pleases him to do so.' 'Furthermore, their perdition proceeds from God's predestination in such a manner that the cause and matter of it will be found in them. . . . Man stumbles, then, even as God ordained that he should, but he stumbles on account of his depravity.'

This terrifying doctrine of election, or damnation, was made palatable by the fact that election was proved by communion with Christ – that is, in practice, by membership of a Calvinist congregation: 'Whoever finds himself in Jesus Christ and is a member of his body by faith, he is assured of his salvation.' So long as a man avoided excommunication, he was secure. Here is both the strength and weakness of Calvanism: if you do not accept the horrific argument of double predestination, it is abhorrent; if you do accept it, it is almost irresistible.

From this theological system followed the earthly organization. To keep the elect pure, and to detect and excommunicate those predestined to be damned, Calvinist society required a policing process. The elected councils of each city appointed elders, disciplinary officials who worked closely with the pastors; their duty was to enforce the moral code, 'to take care of the life of everyone and . . . to bear report to the company which will be deputed to apply brotherly correction'. They met with the pastors in consistories, and their excommunications were passed onto the magistrates for law-enforcement. Calvin was not able to impose his theocracy on Geneva in a 'perfect' form, since the leading citizens insisted that a magistrate preside at the consistories, and, in theory at least, the pastors were forbidden to exercise any civil jurisdiction. On the other hand, he succeeded in getting his opponents, dismissed as 'the libertines', expelled and in some cases tortured and executed; and the system, as he worked it, perhaps came closer to the idea of a total Christian society than anything Catholicism had been able to effect. A consistory of 1542, for instance, dealt with a woman who knelt on her husband's grave and said 'Requiescat in Pace', a goldsmith who made a chalice, a man who criticized 'Godly' French refugees in the city, a woman who tried to cure her husband by tying a walnut with a spider in it around his neck, a sixty-two-year-old woman who married a man of twenty-five, a barber who gave a tonsure to a priest, a man who criticized the city for executing people for their religious opinions, and so forth. As Bishop Grosseteste had wanted to do in thirteenth-century Lincoln, the pastors paid an annual visit to everyone's house to detect faults. They dealt with high prices, short measure, interest rates, the charges of doctors, tailors and other tradesmen, and they produced city codes and other by-laws. In a curious way, and on a smaller scale, the Calvinist consistories resembled the Carolingian councils – they were motivated by the same Augustinian concept of creating the city of God on earth.

By the mid sixteenth century, therefore, there were three varieties of state religion in the West: papal Catholicism, state Christianity (Lutheranism), and Calvinist theocracy. Each, at any rate in theory, was universalist in its aims: it foresaw a future, and to some extent worked for it, when its doctrines and institutions would be imposed on the whole of Christendom. Each was organically linked to the state where it existed. Each was a compulsory religion, claiming a monopoly of the Christian ministry where it held power. Luther, as a heresiarch, had begun by pleading for tolerance, for (this was a new expression) 'freedom of conscience'. He did not want to 'triumph by fire but by writings'. Among his propositions condemned by Rome was: 'To burn heretics is against the will of the spirit.' The secular power should 'busy itself with its own affairs, and let each one believe this or that as he can and as he chooses, and not use any force with anyone on this account'. He even, at first, urged the princes to be tolerant towards millenarians, anabaptists and others of the Munster type, 'because it is necessary that there be sects and the word of God must enter the lists and wage battle.' This early moderation did not survive Luther's increasing dependence on the princes. Once his teaching became established as a state religion, all other forms of Christianity had to be eliminated, at least in their open expression. By 1525, he had forbidden the mass, 'that this blasphemy may be suppressed by the proper authority', and this ban was soon extended to other forms of Protestantism: 'A secular prince should see to it that his subjects are not led to strife by rival preachers whence factions and disturbances might arise, but in any one place there should be only one kind of preaching.' By 1527 he had passed to positive, rather than defensive, intervention to ensure uniformity by organizing state ecclesiastical visitations, and in 1529 he went further still to deny 'freedom of conscience': 'Even if people do not believe, they should be driven to the sermon, because of the ten commandments, in order to learn at least the outward works of obedience.' Two years later he agreed that anabaptists and other Protestant extremists 'should be done to death by the civil authority'.

Calvin, by contrast, had never asserted that consciences should be free. How could the perfected society of the elect tolerate among it those who challenged its rules? The obvious answer to critics was to expel them from the city, following excommunication. If they attempted to remonstrate they were executed. But execution, Calvin found, was also useful to inspire terror and thus bring about compliance. One of his favourite ways of triumphing over an opponent was to make him burn his books publicly with his own hands – Valentin Gentilis saved his life by submitting to this indignity. He was particularly severe with any who rebelled against his own rule, or who used the New Learning to challenge the doctrine of the Trinity.

One such was the Basque Erasmian polymath Michael Servetus, who worked and wrote in many parts of Europe as a printer, geographer, astrologer, physician and surgeon. He had an encyclopaedic mind and a passion for novelty, whether scientific or religious. In 1546, he sent a number of his writings to Calvin, and asked for his opinion. Calvin wrote to a friend: 'Servetus has just sent me . . . a long volume of his ravings. If I consent, he will come here [Geneva], but I will not give my word; for should he come, if my authority is of any avail, I will not suffer him to get out alive.' In 1553, Servetus, who had become prior of a Catholic confraternity at Vienna, published his *Christianismi restitutio*, under the initials MSV, proving from scripture that Christ was man only. The Catholic Inquisition at Lyons was alerted to it by Guillaime de Trie, a Calvinist and friend of Calvin, who pointed out that MSV stood for Michael Servetus Villanovanus, and who supplied documents, including Servetus's letters to Calvin, to establish his guilt. It looks as though Calvin was a party to this plan to have Servetus burned by the Inquisition. In the event, he escaped from the Inquisition but fled to, of all places, Geneva, where he was promptly recognized in church and handed over to Calvin's consistory. He was condemned to death under the Justinian Code, which was still in use even in Protestant cities as the basis for the persecution of heretics. Against Calvin's advice, he was burned – Calvin wanted a simple execution. This judicial murder of a distinguished scholar aroused protests from some reformers, especially in Italy.* Camillo Renato

---

* One of those who protested, under a pseudonym, was David Joris: the true Church, he wrote, 'is not the one that persecutes but the one that is persecuted'. He died peacefully in Basle in 1556, but three years later his secret was discovered and the Basle Protestants employed all the rites prescribed by the Inquisition for posthumous judicial procedure. Felix Platter left an eye-witness account: 'In the Square of the Franciscans, stood a bier with the dug-up corpse. Faggots were heaped up in front of the Steinenthor, the usual place of executions; there the executioner placed the coffin, and after it was smashed up the dead man could be seen, dressed in a cheap cloak and a pointed velvet cap, trimmed with scarlet. The corpse was quite well preserved and still recognisable.'

denounced it in a long poem: 'A fiery stake has been erected where we sought to discover a heaven.' But the burning was approved in advance by most of the Swiss Protestant cantons and later defended by many Protestant intellectuals, such as the Professor of Greek at Lausanne, Theodore Beza: 'What greater, more abominable crime could one find among men [than heresy]? . . . it would seem impossible to find a torture big enough to fit the enormity of such a misdeed.' Four months after Servetus died, Calvin published his own *Declaratio orthodoxae fidei*: 'One should forget all mankind when His glory is in question. . . . God does not even allow whole towns and populations to be spared, but will have the walls razed and the memory of the inhabitants destroyed and all things ruined as a sign of His utter detestation, lest the contagion spread.'

If both Lutherans and Calvinists (as well as Catholics) actively persecuted antinomian extremists, they also opposed and hated each other. Calvinists thought of Lutherans as virtually unreformed, Romanists masquerading in godly garments. The Lutherans would never admit that Calvinism was a 'legal' religion. They classified Calvinists as anabaptists, and thought their denial of the real presence a scandalous breach of the Catholic faith. Some Lutherans, like Polycarp Leyser, thought Calvinist errors worse than Roman. Lutherans would not provide military assistance to protect Calvinism from Rome and its allies – one factor which limited the Reformation's gains. All three parties, Calvinists, Lutherans and Catholics, accused the others of having double standards – demanding tolerance when weak, persecuting when strong. The Catholic George Eder wrote in 1579: 'In districts dominated by Protestants, Catholics are never tolerated; they are publicly humiliated, driven from their homes and lands, and forced into exile with their wives and children. . . . But as soon as a Catholic member-state of the empire proceeds in the same way . . . everyone gets worked up, is indignant, and the Catholic prince is accused of breaking the peace of religion.' The Lutheran Daniel Jaconi (1615): 'As long as the Calvinists are not in power . . . they are pleasant and patient; they accept life in common with us. But as soon as they are masters of the situation they will not tolerate a single syllable of Lutheran doctrine.' George Stobaeus, prince-bishop of Lavant, to the Archduke Ferdinand of Austria (1598): 'Entrust the administration of a town or province to Catholics only; allow only Catholics to sit in the assemblies; publish a decree demanding that everyone should profess the Catholic faith in writing, and urging them in case of refusal to find themselves another country where they can live and believe as they like.'

In fact, from the start each of the three main groupings tried to use all the apparatus of the State, where they could control it, to impose a religious monopoly. In 1555, after years of inconclusive fighting, the system was institutionalized at the Peace of Augsburg, which 'froze' the religious pattern of three years earlier and in effect allowed each prince, or prince-bishop, in Germany to determine the religion practised by his subjects. The principle was later defined as *cuius regio, eius religio*. There was nothing particularly new in this concept, which might be described as a return to tribalism, since in tribal societies kings had traditionally determined the tribe's form of religion. And of course it embodied the assumption, still current, that religious beliefs could not be separated from any other fundamental colouring of society: you could no more have two rival religions than you could have two rival legal codes, or two currencies or two armies. Since men could not agree, the monarch had to decide. And anyway, was not this natural, indeed God-ordained? Did not a ruler, at his coronation, receive sacramental grace for this sort of purpose? Thus the pontifical monarch, unfrocked by Gregory VII and his successors, entered into his clerical kingdom again. Liberty of conscience was denied to the subject, but conceded to the prince. But this meant that in some cases subjects who had had Lutheranism imposed upon them by their prince, later had Calvinism imposed by his successor. Or a prince might undergo a 'conversion'. The Landgrave Maurice of Hesse-Cassel, converted to Calvinism in 1604, told a Lutheran minister: 'I have the right to wield episcopal power in my state. . . . My predecessors ruled religious matters according to the word of God. In my turn, I exercise the same right as they.' Equally, the son and heir of a Lutheran might turn Catholic when he inherited the throne, and compel his subjects to turn back to Rome.

In practice, of course, the princes had to some extent to defer to the wishes of their leading subjects. But where did the process of consultation stop? At what point up the social ladder was a man sufficiently important to have his religious opinions taken into consideration? This was a point on which the sixteenth century was becoming increasingly uncertain. Again, what if the ruling circles of a society profoundly disagreed? In most of the German principalities it was possible to reach a consensus. In Spain, the Catholic crown, through its instrument the Inquisition, exterminated Protestantism in the 1550s. In the Italian states, Protestantism made little headway among the aristocracy, and the question really did not arise, except in Venice. But in France, under a Catholic monarchy, the aristocracy became divided. Great families like the Guises and the Montmorencys were strongly Catholic, and controlled Lorraine. Cities like Paris, Bordeaux and Toulouse were also Catholic. But the Prince of Condé was a Calvinist Protestant, or Huguenot; so was Coligny, the High Admiral; and so were the Bourbons of Navarre. The Huguenots numbered about one-tenth to one-fifteenth of the total population, but they were in the majority in parts of the Orléanais, Normandy, Navarre, the Dauphiné and many towns. How, then, could the principle be applied to France? There was a fierce debate among the Protestants as to whether they were justified in taking up arms against the lawful ruler. Beza, writing to the King of Navarre, thought it was 'the lot of the Church of God' to 'endure blows and not to strike them'; but, he added, 'remember that it is an anvil which has broken many hammers'. One Huguenot lawyer, awaiting execution in 1559, argued that any monarch who forced his subjects to live against the will of God must be illegitimate. But who was to define 'the will of God'? Therein lay the whole argument. Calvin, consulted, ruled that resistance to persecution was permissible if led by the chief magistrate or prince of the blood. Hence the importance in France of such figures as Condé, Coligny and Navarre, who made possible a rebellion which Protestants could regard as theologically legitimate: the 2,000 Huguenot consistories in France became a civil and military organization, as well as a religious one. This new principle was made to apply elsewhere. In 1559 in Scotland the predominant section of the nobility, goaded on by Calvin's pupil, John Knox, raised arms against the Catholic administration. The English crown, after much hesitation, decided that this rebellion, too, was legitimate and lawful, and assisted it. Again, in the 1560s, the Spanish Netherlands rose against the persecuting Catholic Habsburgs, using in justification their ancient constitutional machinery, and in defence of their traditional laws, customs and charters. Their leader was a blood-prince, William the Silent, Prince of Orange, and when he was assassinated their 'governorship' was offered to the anointed Protestant Queen of England.

Thus the theories determining the religious division of Europe, though springing from the same root-concept – the priestly power of the prince – were increasingly divergent and conflicting. The result was a drift towards civil war within states, and international war between them. This was absurd, since the whole object of pursuing religious unity in states was to avoid civil strife. Hence in France, where unity was unobtainable, there was a movement towards an alternative idea, of a non-denominational state, whose task was to hold the ring, and enforce a degree of peaceful coexistence on the rival faiths. This was a political solution, and its advocates were termed *politiques*. But it had some support among the religiously committed. Philip Camerarius, the German Lutheran jurist, argued in his *Historical Meditations* (1591): 'If the prince supports one party and tramples on the other . . . seditions will inevitably occur. . . . So it is equally certain that civil wars will cease if the prince stands with sword drawn between the two parties, neither inclining to the right nor left unless for the purpose of beheading, without exception, all instigators of riot, sedition and faction.' But this implied that the State itself, and those who ran it, should be, in effect, neutral in religion, something almost inconceivable to sixteenth- and indeed seventeenth-century minds. Thus in France, after various experiments in peaceful coexistence interspersed by three religious wars, a settlement was reached in the 1590s, whereby the Huguenots became the beneficiaries of an edict of toleration, signed at Nantes, and their leader and king, Henri IV, embraced Catholicism. But the monarchy remained Catholic, and when Henri's great-grandson, Louis XIV, turned to a more militant brand of papalism, the edict was revoked and the system broke down.

Again, if the principle of peaceful coexistence were admitted, how far should it stretch? Lutheranism achieved a kind of international respectability in 1555, Calvinism became an official state religion (in Scotland) in 1562. What about the more radical reformers? Where should the line be drawn? Varieties of Protestantism proliferated instantly and wherever state persecution was relaxed. One reformer, a Venetian weaver, Marcantonio Varotto, rejoined the Catholic Church in disgust in 1568, explaining: 'I left Moravia because during the two months I spent there I saw so many faiths and sects . . . all drawing up catechisms, all desiring to be ministers, all pulling in different directions, all claiming to be the true church. In one small place, Austerlitz, there are 13 or 14 different sects.' George Eder's *Evangelical Inquisition* of 1573 enumerates forty sects; they included the Munzerites, the Adamists, who ran naked, the secretive Garden Brethren, the Open Witnesses, the Devillers (who believed the Devil would be saved on Judgment Day), the Libertines, who cohabited freely, the Weeping Brethren, the Silent Ones, who banned preaching, the Augustinians, who believed in the sleep of the soul, various Munsterites, Paulinists, who claimed to have the originals of Paul's Epistles, priest-murderers, Antichristians, who worshipped a mythical harlot, and Judaizers. Some were violently anti-social, some not even Christian. Virtually all states banned and hounded them all. Poland was the most liberal. In 1573, the Polish nobility promulgated the Warsaw Confederation on religious freedom:

'As there is wide disagreement in our state on matters related to the Christian religion, and in order to prevent any fatal outburst such as had been witnessed in other kingdoms, we, who differ on religion, bind ourselves for our own sake and that of our posterity in perpetuity, on our oath, faith, honour and conscience, to keep the peace among ourselves on the subject of differences of religion and the changes brought about in our churches; we bind ourselves not to shed blood; not to punish one another by confiscation of goods, loss of honour, imprisonment or exile; not to give any assistance on this point in any way to any authority or official, but on the contrary to unite ourselves against anyone who would shed blood for this reason, even if he pretended to act in virtue of a decree or decision at law.'

This was an astonishing declaration for its time. Moreover, it was successfully applied to a wide range of sectarian belief, at any rate for a generation – it broke down because nobles or princes could not in practice bind their successors; and the Counter-Reformation ensured that these were Catholic. But the declaration extended the right of choice to everyone. Then as a footnote, it added that peasants had to obey their lords.

The assumption that it was right peasants should accept the religion of their lords, just as subjects followed their princes, reminds us that we are dealing with a society where individual freedom was still a very scarce commodity. Below a certain level, no one was expected to have political or religious opinions. The effect of the Reformation – and to some extent a cause of it – was a pushing down of this threshold of individual responsibility to enfranchise new categories – especially the well-to-do, educated townsmen. How far the poorer townsmen influenced events, and exercised choice, is hard to say. Most, like their social superiors in the towns, aligned themselves with the reforming movement – there was no conflict of interest on this point. An analysis of the 290-odd Protestants martyred during the Marian persecution in England, 1553–8, shows that, apart from clergy, most were middle-class or lower-middle-class artisans and trades-people, continuing a social pattern established by the Lollards in the early fifteenth century. This does not mean reformers were not to be found among the higher social classes: merely that the crown was less inclined to probe their opinions or enforce upon them a uniformity of religious belief which, in the case of the lower orders, it regarded as essential. Thus in England, under Elizabeth, peers were exempt from swearing the oath under the Protestant Act of Uniformity, 1559, which meant they could continue as Catholics without suffering the financial penalties inflicted on lesser folk. Moreover, it was generally assumed that peasants on the estates of Catholic peers would follow their masters and remain Catholic, as in fact the majority did. Thus even in Anglican England, small pockets of Catholicism remained throughout the period when Protestant uniformity was enforced by law.

It is, then, extraordinarily difficult to determine how far the religious changes were the result of popular pressure, and how far they were carried through against the popular will. The religious crisis of the sixteenth century was essentially an argument among the upper educated classes. The rest of society were largely spectators and followers (and victims). Whenever the crown moved decisively, as it did in England, the rest of society tended to follow without much protest. During the decade 1530–40, chiefly through the will of the monarch, Henry VIII, the old medieval Church was effectively destroyed in England. This involved huge changes in society at all levels, and the social strains thereby produced are reflected in the correspondence of Thomas Cromwell, who was charged with enforcing Henry's policy. He had a network of agents and informers throughout the country who kept him informed on who was critical of the changes, and on what grounds. Analysis of this evidence gives no suggestion of a 'Catholic', still less a 'papist' party of resistance. It might have been a different matter if the regular clergy, who constituted over a third of the Church's personnel, and controlled nearly half its resources, had resisted the royal programme. In fact, only a tiny minority did. Monastic dissolutions were accepted largely with indifference wherever they were carried out, in England, Scandinavia and Lutheran Germany. The parish clergy were likewise passive, as a rule. They were perhaps the only force capable of mobilizing conservative peasants against a reforming government. The only occasion on which they did so in England was in Yorkshire and Lincolnshire in 1536, the so-called 'Pilgrimage of Grace', where beneficed clergy provided the most important element in the local leadership. These clerics were motivated not by religious beliefs but by economic fears: they thought that reform would prevent them from holding small parishes in plurality, that the dissolved monks would be after their benefices, that the effect of the Act for First Fruits and Tenths would rob them of a year's income, and that episcopal visitations would be far more onerous under the Reform; they also credited vague rumours that the crown was planning to seize the parish silver-plate. Their rising was not so much an effort to force the crown to reverse its religious policy as a protest against economic grievances.

Indeed, when we look at Cromwell's reports, and are thus able to see the Reformation at a local level, we find not so much a religious or ideological conflict as a complicated morass of personal feuds and grudges, jealousies, rivalries of jurisdiction, provincial contests and sheer bloody-mindedness. Sometimes criticism was provoked by dislike of Henry himself, for the nation as a whole seems to have deplored his divorce and loathed Anne Boleyn, frequently described as 'a strong whore'. One Worcestershire suspect blamed Henry for the bad weather, and said it would never improve until 'he were knocked or patted on the head'. A Welsh priest 'wished to have the King upon a mountain in North Wales . . . called Snowdon Hill. . . . He would souse the King about the ears until he had his head soft enough.' A Londoner said: 'I set not a pudding by the King's broad seal, and all his charters be not worth a rush.' We get reports of reformers indulging in tremendous meat-eating during Lent, to annoy the Catholics; but often enough the Reformation dispute was stood on its head. Thus, in Salisbury, the 'proud stomach' of a reforming bishop infuriated the corporation and turned anti-clericalism, normally a chief engine of change into a conservative force. Equally, though the end of clerical celibacy was a lure successfully dangled by the reformers before many priests (a majority of the younger ones), some remained Romanists because they did not want to be forced to marry their concubines. Thus a Father Cornewell swore 'he had set his wench by the bishop's nose. . . . Let me see who dare meddle with her'; if only he would agree to marry her, he said, 'the bishop would be contented that [I] tilted up her tail in every bush.'

The remarks reported to Cromwell seem a long way from the subject-matter of the colloquy of Regensburg, taking place at the same time. A reforming London Dominican said the new scriptural faith was worth more than 'a whole shipload laden with friars' girdles and a dung-cart full of monks' cowls.' A pro-Henry lady thought the Scotch might bring the Pope back, but 'the clobbes of Essex shall drive them forth again, and a bush in Essex shall be worth a castle in Kent.' A London papist told Cromwell's informers that he 'cared not a fart for the Tower'. Many of these remarks were noted down in taverns. Thus we hear of four Coventry yeomen who met for a drinking session and eventually sallied forth to the market-place, where 'they all untrussed themselves, and did their easement at the Cross.' One tore down Henry's proclamations and statutes, nailed to the cross, 'and cast the same to the said Heynes, and bid him wipe his tail with them' – which he did. Next morning, hung-over, all four said they remembered nothing. Such protesters, and others who voiced their opinions, risked public whippings. We hear of one poor man who was sentenced, according to the court record, to have his ears 'cut off by the hard head' and to be tied 'to a cart's arse'. Generally speaking, however, protests at Church reforms were confined to words, usually under the influence of drink.

The Reformation, then, was not, by and large, a popular movement; nor was the resistance to it nor, when it came, the Counter-Reformation. Public opinion alone did not determine the issue in any state. The will of the ruler, or of the ruling circle, was the most important single factor. Yet, as the century progressed, the importance of public opinion was growing, and the unrestricted rights of the rulers were increasingly restrained. In England, for instance, neither Queen Mary nor her half-sister Queen Elizabeth was able to act in religious matters with the same freedom as their father. Mary's attempt to restore Catholicism in England was breaking down even before her death, largely because of anti-Roman feeling in London and the south-east. Elizabeth's power, and popularity, arose in great part from the fact that she sympathized with this feeling. But her parliaments were always more reformist than she was herself, and her religious settlement was more radical than she would have wished. Thus the common assumption in Rome and Madrid, and among English Catholic exiles, that the great majority of the English people favoured the Catholic cause, is surely mistaken. The only real figure we have suggests the opposite. In 1564 the bishops were asked by the Privy Council to report on the state of religious feeling in the country. The returns we have show that they found 431 magistrates were well-disposed towards the Anglican settlement, 264 were neutral, and 157 hostile. As the reign progressed, these figures must have shifted in favour of the regime and its religion. It is true that in the north the Catholic element was stronger, especially early in the reign. But during the 1569 rising only 7,000 out of a possible 60,000 young, able-bodied males responded to the appeal to rise on behalf of the old faith, and the rising itself was a fiasco. Even in the north, the south-east Lancashire towns, and York, for instance, tended to favour the Anglican settlement, and by the end of Elizabeth's reign the number of actual recusants even in Lancashire and Yorkshire, the most Catholic regions, was less than five per cent of the population. In France, the position was reversed, since the Huguenots were never able to pass the ten per cent mark, and in particular could not gain a substantial foothold in Paris. By becoming a Catholic, Henry IV was in effect bowing to public opinion, at any rate among the higher classes.

The will of the ruler, and the rising force of public opinion among the wealthier classes, were thus to some extent in equipoise during the second half of the sixteenth century. It is against this background that we must analyse the workings of the Counter-Reformation. Papal Catholicism had, however, one uncovenanted advantage. During the fifteenth century the tendency had been for the reform of the Church to fall into the hands of the monarchies, the only institutions willing and able to undertake it. The outstanding example was Spain, where the union of the crowns of Castile and Aragon, followed by the creation of the Spanish Inquisition under the secular control of the monarchy, gave it more power over the Church than any other secular government had possessed since the eleventh century. In the last decade of the fifteenth, and the first two of the sixteenth century, reform was entrusted to the vigorous and scholarly primate, Cardinal Ximenes, who possessed plenipotentiary powers over the Spanish Church (his first biographer lists his titles: 'Archbishop of Toledo, Cardinal of Sancta Balbina, Grand Chancellor of Castile, Reformer of Religious Orders, Inquisitor-General, Captain-General of All Africa, Conqueror of Oran, Confessor of Our Lady the Queen, Governor of Spain, Founder of the Great College of San Ildefonso, and University of Alcala, and other pious works.') His combination of ecclesiastical and secular power enabled him to carry through a thoroughgoing reformation of the religious orders, which involved shutting down many houses and amalgamating others, and to impose a higher degree of discipline on the clergy (especially bishops) than was possible anywhere else in Christendom. Nor was this all. Ximenes learnt Hebrew and Greek, and imported Erasmian scholarship. The new university he founded at Alcala repudiated the old scholastic methods still used at Salamanca and Valladolid, taught the grammatical and expository principles developed by Valla, and employed outstanding Greek and Hebrew scholars such as Antonio de Nebrija, who pledged himself as he put it, to root up *las barbari de los ombros de nuestra nacion*.* Nowhere else in the West had an all-powerful prelate identified himself with reform and renaissance, and though the experiment did not long survive Ximenes's death in 1517, it acted as a lightning-conductor to keep the anti-papal Reformation from Spain. Spain, in effect, had a national Church, with higher standards of discipline and pastoral care than could be found anywhere else. And in the Indies it had a new field of endeavour which attracted the evangelical and energetic elements among the clergy.

The Spanish crown, then, had no ecclestiastical demands to make on the papacy. It controlled its own Church, both at home and overseas, and could carry out such reforms as it judged necessary. The Inquisition was a popular instrument, directed against Jews and Moors. In the 1550s it was used effectively to root out Spain's very limited Protestant element. Moreover, in the 1550s, the Spanish Habsburgs lost direct responsibility for the empire.

---

* An unpublished contemporary life of Ximenes noted: 'Antonio de Nebrija dwelt at the printing-press at Alcala, and often when the Cardinal passed by the road to the College he went to the press and spent a short time talking with him in the street while Antonio was at the window. It was agreed between the Cardinal and his friend that for the rest of the day they would not leave off drinking wine.' Ximenes spent 50,000 gold ducats of his own money on his polyglot Bible; 600 sets were printed, of which about 150 survive (most were lost by shipwreck on their way to Italy). The Greek fount used was 'undoubtedly the finest Greek fount ever cut'. Victor Scholderer, *Greek Printing Types, 1465–1927* (London, 1927). For the polyglot Bible see Basil Hall, *The Great Polyglot Bible* (San Francisco, 1966), and 'The Trilingual College of San Ildefonso and the Making of the Complutensian Polyglot Bible', *Studies in Church History V* (Leyden, 1969).

Charles v, as emperor, had tried to uphold the Catholic cause in Germany while at the same time to bully the papacy into carrying out sufficient reforms to satisfy his German subjects. The effort had been unsuccessful on both counts, and had poisoned his last years as a ruler. When he abdicated, and divided his possessions, Philip II, as his Spanish heir, was freed from the incubus of empire, and the divisions of policy-ruling it entailed, and able to devote Spanish resources wholeheartedly to preserving the unity of papal Christendom, against the Turks on the one hand, and the Protestants on the other. Thus the Counter-Reformation acquired a single-minded secular champion, and one with vast means. The gold and silver of the New World was thrown into the struggle. Philip II was always short of money, and on occasions actually bankrupt. But he still disposed of funds which were more than three times as great as any other Christian state; he had the only really effective standing army in the West; and he controlled a narrow corridor which allowed him to move men and supplies from Spain and Italy to the Spanish Netherlands. Catholic military power thus divided Europe in two, a salient strategic fact which the militant Protestants were never able to circumvent; and Spanish fleets controlled the western Mediterranean, which ensured that the whole of Italy remained beyond the grasp of the reformers. At the same time, Spanish money was available to finance Catholic efforts to stem or reverse the Protestant advance wherever these could be organized.

The essence of the Counter-Reformation, therefore, was Spanish power. It was not a religious movement. It had no specific programme, other than the negative one of stamping out Protestant 'error'. It involved no substantial reform of the Church, and embodied no change of attitude on the part of the papacy. Between 1520–42, there was a distinct chance that a council would be summoned, probably in Germany, which would in effect impose changes on the papacy. Charles v did his best to bring it about. The only occasion on which he is recorded as having lost his temper arose from the delaying tactics of Paul III. These were successful, from the papacy's point of view. Up until about 1542, the evidence of secret consistories shows that many of the cardinals would have been willing to concede Protestant demands on a married clergy, on communion in both kinds, on vernacular translations of the scriptures, on justification by faith, on feast-days, fasts and on many other contentious points. A council held on these assumptions, and with a Protestant attendance, must have ended in a reduction of papal power. But no such council was held. After 1542 there was, in effect, a move to the right in Rome. The colloquies had failed. The Protestants were moving further apart, and it was increasingly evident that, whatever prospect there might be of compromise with the Lutherans, there could be none with the Calvinists. Contarini died, and those of his school fell under suspicion. The Inquisition was set up in Rome, under the fanatical Neapolitan papalist Cardinal Caraffa (later Pope Paul IV), whose watchwords were: 'No man is to abase himself by showing toleration towards any sort of heretic, least of all a Calvinist'; and 'Even if my own father were a heretic, I would gather the wood to burn him.' The new atmosphere in Rome was puritanical and intolerant, but not reformist. The Index of Forbidden Books was set up, and there were massive book-burnings; Jews were forced to wear the Yellow Star; Daniel of Volterra, 'the Trouserer', was employed to clothe the nudes of the Sistine Chapel; Protestants were burned and liberals silenced.

Against this background a council finally met, at Trent, in 1545. By this time few took it seriously. It had been delayed twenty-five years, during which time forms of Protestantism had spread over a large part of Europe. The dying Luther remarked: 'The remedy comes too late'. How could he negotiate and submit now? 'This might have been done a quarter of a century ago.' Its proceedings were 'twaddle'. Bucer, far more ecumenically minded, nevertheless dismissed it as 'a joke'. Catholics were scarcely less scathing. The Council began to assemble in March; but hardly anyone arrived on time. On the day appointed for the opening, it poured with rain and no one turned up for the ceremony. By April, only six bishops were actually in Trent. The opening, postponed from month to month, finally took place in December, with four cardinals, four archbishops, and only twenty-one bishops – including not a single ruling bishop from Germany. There seems to have been no sense of urgency or historical magnitude, no reforming spirit. A papal decree, ordering bishops actually to reside in their sees, a salient reforming issue, had been almost totally ignored, notably by most of the bishops present. Thus Cardinal Ippolito d'Este, Archbishop of Milan for twenty years (1520–50) never once visited the city. The 'host' bishop of Trent, Christoforo Madruzzo, was a symbol of the unreformed Church. He was handsome, well-born and well-connected, and always wore the red velvet dress of a secular prince – his scarlet biretta alone betrayed the fact he was a cleric. He had been given two parishes and a canonry in his teens, later three more canonries and a deanery, had been made a bishop at twenty-six and a cardinal at thirty. At the first banquet he gave to the council fathers, he served seventy-four different dishes and a famous Valtellina wine a hundred years old, while his private orchestra played. There were a good many ladies present. Madruzzo danced with them, and induced other clerics to do so; and, so few of the bishops having turned up, the ladies pushed their way into the chancel of the cathedral at the opening ceremony.

Nor did the council substantially improve. No preparatory work had been done. Seripando, the Augustinian General, characterized its first session as 'irresolution, ignorance, incredible stupidity'. Its first decision, to discuss reform and discipline simultaneously, was reversed by the Pope, who ordered it to concentrate on dogma; and he vetoed a statement on justification. The council muddled the issue of vernacular translations, and its decree enforcing episcopal residence was feeble; even while it was being debated, the Pope was issuing exemptions to cardinals, and licensed them to hold sees in plurality, one of the recipients being the notorious d'Este. An outbreak of typhus led to an angry and panicky debate in 1547, on the translation of the council to Bologna. When the motion was finally carried, some prelates had boats and horses waiting for them to get away. They barely listened to the last notes of the *Te Deum*, and one bishop did not even remove his vestments but galloped out of the city in full pontificals, to the jeers of the citizens. At subsequent sessions, which lasted until the 1560s, the Council of Trent improved both in attendance and decorum. But the atmosphere did not essentially alter. The objectives of Trent, as they developed, were seen to be not so much the reform of the Church as the strengthening of papal power. This was demonstrated by its first historian, the Venetian anti-papalist Fra Paolo Sarpi, whose three chief informants were all well-placed eye-witnesses. Even the reformist decrees were of limited scope, since they either applied only to Italy, or were not 'received' by the secular authorities in France, Spain and elsewhere. Reform of clerical standards was a very slow process indeed: in some respects it was not complete until the latter part of the nineteenth century. But there was a marked improvement of tone in the papacy itself during the decades after Trent. The Dominican Grand Inquisitor Michael Ghislieri, who became Pius v in 1565, created the new puritanical atmosphere, which involved the expulsion of prostitutes from Rome, the enforcement of strict clerical dress, and savage punishments for simony. The change was widely noted: 'Men in Rome have become a great deal better,' wrote Tiepolo, the Venetian ambassador, 'or at least have put on the appearance of being so.'

Where Trent did introduce an important change was in instructing bishops to create seminaries for the training of clergy. Charles Borromeo, Archbishop of Milan 1560–84, founded three in his diocese, and set about the creation of an educated and resident clergy by insisting on minimum standards before ordination and frequent visitations thereafter. This was something entirely new. Borromeo can be called the first modern Catholic bishop, as his predecessor Ambrose was the first medieval one. It is astonishing that no provision for training priests in their specific duties had ever existed before. This was the curse of the Church until Borromeo's system was widely imitated. Moreover, the creation of seminaries served to open up the whole question of Christian education. The Church had never looked at it systematically. There had been no need. It had exercised a complete monopoly. That monopoly had been undermined in the fifteenth century, when wealthy townsmen began to endow schools outside the clerical system. The layman entered the field decisively, at all educational levels, and the Renaissance fuelled the Reformation by presenting clericalism as an obstacle to learning and truth. Thus in the period 1520–50, to cite a small but significant instance, an almost infallible test of a scholar's religious views was the way he pronounced Greek: correct pronunciation was identified with reform. With each generation, there was an increasing tendency for the educated young people to turn against Rome. Then, too, Protestant societies devoted a far greater proportion of total resources to education, since a large slice of the endowments made available by the winding up of the monasteries had been allocated to grammar schools and universities. This Protestant challenge forced the Catholic world to take education seriously, and this meant a new type of cleric.

Yet the way in which the challenge was triumphantly met was largely an accident. The religious struggles of the sixteenth century inspired earnest Catholics to found new religious orders. Some successfully established themselves – the Capuchins (reformed Franciscans), the Theatines, the Somaschi, the Barnabites, the Oratorians; many proved abortive. There was a strongly held view in Rome that a multiplicity of orders was an embarrassment to the Church, and some even urged that all male religious be regrouped in one order, to re-establish the monopoly position the Benedictines had occupied in the latter part of the Dark Ages. Against this background Ignatius Loyola established his new order, the Society of Jesus, in the 1530s. He was a middle-aged Basque from a family of border-chieftains, and his dictated *Confessions* dismiss his earlier life in one sentence. Like many of the reformers, he was an ascetic and a puritan, and for a time lived as a hermit, growing his hair and nails long, and eating no meat. But he turned the reforming process on its head by translating the Lutheran doctrine of justification by faith into the principle of absolute obedience to the Church; this, for him, became the credal hinge, and the certain guarantee of salvation. Moreover, he developed a self-disciplinary technique, known as the 'Spritual Exercises', which took the place of the Lutheran 'conversion' and could be applied collectively. Loyola was thus a part of the new puritan-reformist movement but an aberration from it. For the Inquisition he was an object of intense suspicion, was twice gaoled by them, and for a number of years he remained on their records as a suspect person. He was also unclear about his aims. He began to collect companions from 1534, but his original idea was that they should work as stretcher-bearers and hospital porters in Jerusalem; then, for practical reasons, the field of operations was switched to Venice. In his long negotiations with the Inquisition and the papacy, however, Loyola revealed himself as an astute operator and organizer – as his successor put it, 'a man of great good sense and prudence in matters of business'. He insisted on an exceptionally long training for his men during which the principle of total obedience was absorbed. As Alfonso Rodriguez put it, the great consolation of the Jesuit – the equivalent of the Calvinist certainty of 'election' – is 'the assurance we have that in obeying we can commit no fault . . . you are certain you commit no fault as long as you obey, because God will only ask you if you have duly performed what orders you have received, and if you can give a clear account in that respect, you are absolved entirely. . . . God wipes it out of your account and charges it to the superior.' To illustrate the effectiveness of Jesuit discipline, Juan Polanco tells of the mortally ill novice who asked the Novice-Master for permission to die, 'something which caused great edification'. Paradoxically, this insistence on total subordination of the will did not deter the able; from the start, Loyola recruited men of unusual ability, mainly from the higher classes.

The creation of this remarkable human instrument gave the Tridentine papacy an opportunity to reinforce its educational policy. The only order which had hitherto specialized in ordinary education were the Flemish Brethren of the Common Life. The Jesuits were adept at training themselves. Why should they not train others in the faith? The alliance between the papacy and the Jesuits was consolidated during the first session of the Council of Trent, and the new order was given almost unlimited freedom to expand throughout Europe (and in the overseas Spanish and Portuguese missions) as propagandists and educators. By Loyola's death in 1556 they had over 1,000 members and 100 establishments. What in fact they did was to provide an educational service on demand. If a Catholic prince or prince-bishop wanted an orthodox school, college or university established and conducted efficiently, he applied to the Jesuits; he supplied the funds and buildings, they the trained personnel and techniques. They were, in effect, rather like a modern multi-national company selling expert services. And they brought to the business of international schooling a uniformity, discipline and organization that was quite new.

The Jesuits had originally intended to work among the poor and sick. In fact, the success of their educational mission cast their lot among the rich and the mighty: they became the specialists in upper-class schooling. Largely by chance, then, the Counter-Reformation forged itself a mighty instrument. For, granted that the determinaton of a state's religion was still to a large extent a matter for the prince to decide, and granted that this principle was qualified to the extent that the nobility and wealthier classes generally had an influence on his decision, what better way was there of ensuring orthodoxy than that the schooling of the well-born be in the hands of Catholic experts absolutely dedicated to the Tridentine faith? Jesuits provided education at all stages, from primary to university; and they complemented the service by allocating well-born men of the world to serve as private confessors to the great. Moreover, in a variety of ways, they sought to emphasize that the survival of Catholic orthodoxy was inextricably linked to that of the secular social order, based on privilege, hierarchy, grandeur and ceremony. The Jesuits did not practise austerities. They were allowed to use the shorter breviary. They moved in the world. At their schools and colleges, the pupils were encouraged to produce plays and public performances, at a time when such were closely linked to the rituals of royalty and lordship. Jesuit plays became famous: Lope de Vega and Calderon both learnt from them; and the European stage, especially in the fields of stage management and design, owes much to the Jesuit theatre. Their big city churches, designed to accommodate huge congregations for propagandist sermons (very like Calvinist edifices) were themselves theatres of the new Baroque arts, of which they became the leading patrons. They encouraged their princes to support artists such as El Greco and Caravaggio, who dedicated themselves to Counter-Reformation themes.* They fleshed out the miserable bones of the Tridentine reforms in such a way as to create a new universe, in which it seemed absolutely natural and inevitable that a man with a vested interest in the established order should be not only a Catholic, but a militant papalist.

The Jesuits opened a college at Padua, the most innovative of the Italian universities, as early as 1542, within three years of their establishment as an order. The same year, the Catholic bishops of southern Germany summoned them to operate' there. The Jesuits started their first secondary school at Messina in 1548, and this was quickly duplicated all over Catholic Europe. During the 1550s, they particularly concentrated on Germany, with an operational headquarters at Ingoldstadt University, and a German College in Rome (1552) to train Counter-Reformation clergy. Within a generation, pupils from the last occupied many of the key German prince-bishoprics. Jesuits moved into all areas where conflicting religions were struggling for the hearts and minds of the well-born. In 1580, we find the Prince of Parma, Governor of the Netherlands, writing to Philip II: 'Your Majesty desired me to build a citadel at Maastricht. I thought that a college of the Jesuits would be a fortress more likely to protect the inhabitants against the enemies of the Altar and the Throne. I have built it.'

The Jesuits were not only more effective than fortresses; they were cheaper. The Counter-Reformation made its most important gains not by battle but by capturing the loyalty and enthusiasm of well-placed individuals. Until the mid 1560s, Protestantism, both Lutheran and Calvinist, was gaining ground everywhere in Germany. In Graz, for instance, the population was almost entirely Protestant, and Protestant schools flourished in south German cities as well as in the north. Then, in 1573, the Archduke Charles of Austria founded a Jesuit school. Freedom of religion was granted by the Diet of Bruck in 1578; but three years later the duke expelled evangelical pastors and forbade Graz citizens to attend the Protestant city school. The old duke died in 1590, and Protestantism again flourished during his son's minority. When he attained his majority, however, the new Jesuit-trained duke announced: 'I would rather rule a country ruined than a country damned', and set about extirpating Protestantism by force. In 1598 he expelled all Protestant pastors and schoolmasters, and the next year he closed non-Catholic churches. The process was completed a generation later, in 1628, when 800 leading Protestant families were compelled to leave the country. The same forces were at work in Bavaria and, more spectacularly, in liberal Poland. There, Stephen Batory, elected king in 1574 on a platform of toleration, had allowed the Jesuits in as part of his policy of protecting both sides to the dispute. There

* El Greco's giantic *Burial of the Count de Orgaz* (Toledo) asserts the Counter-Reformation theory of the intercession of the Virgin and the saints on behalf of the individual; and his *Laocöon* is also a Counter-Reformation allegory. But Greco frequently got into trouble through the suspect theology of his paintings and his refusal to carry out clerical orders; so did Caravaggio, e.g. for his *Death of the Virgin* (Louvre). Later, Rome took over iconographical guidance directly. See Ellis Waterhouse, 'Some Painters and the Counter-Reformation before 1600', *TRHS* (1972).

were 360 in Poland by the time his successor, Sigismund III, a vehement
Catholic, was elected in 1587. Thereafter, Catholics alone were appointed to
office, and Catholic nobles were encouraged to evict Protestants from their
estates; the courts ruled that Protestants might not use parish churches, and
they were driven into the town halls; then, in 1607, the Protestant nobles were
provoked into revolt, and its suppression marked the end of reform. As the
papal nuncio reported: 'A short time ago, it might have been feared that
heresy would entirely supersede Catholicism in Poland. Now Catholicism is
bearing heresy to its grave.'

The Jesuits were instrumental in turning the tide in Austria, Bavaria, in the
prince-bishoprics of the Rhineland, and in Poland. Their city schools had a
marked success in deflecting the bourgeoisie from reform to orthodoxy. But of
course they worked chiefly through powerful individuals. Their last great
success came in the 1680s, when Louis XIV's Jesuit confessor, Le Tellier, finally
persuaded the monarch to smash the Edict of Nantes and (it was said) actually
drafted the revocation himself. But this influence was not exerted on the plane
of morals and piety. In the confessional, the Jesuits and their powerful
penitents had a lawyer-client relationship. The reason why they were popular
confessors, especially of the great, was that they tended to identify good
Christian behaviour with mere prudence, a kind of enlightened *realpolitik*
redeemed only by religious intention: as Escobar, one of their moral
theologians put it, 'Purity of intention may be justification for acts contrary to
the moral code and human law.' They adopted the role of defence-advocate,
trying to evade the moral law rather than interpret it; and they took the
'probabilist' line that penitents should be given the benefit in doubtful cases.
Casuistry was for them a form of charity, an attempt to make the moral law
human. But generosity tended to degenerate into laxism, as Jesuit confessors
adopted the *déformation professionnelle* of their worldly clients. Cardinal Noris,
an Inquisition expert, explained to Cosimo III of Florence (1692) why some
Jesuits opposed the strict morality of their General, Tirso Gonzales: 'As they
were confessors to so many great princes in Europe, so many princely prelates
in Germany, and so many high-ranking courtiers, they must not be so severe
as their General desires, because if they followed his teaching they would lose
their posts as confessors at all courts.'

It is clear, too, that Jesuit confessional activities covered the whole political
and military field. As Louis XIII's Jesuit confessor, Father Caussin, put it in a
letter to his General, Vitelleschi, whether an alliance with the infidel Turks was
right or not was, to the king's confessor, a matter of conscience, as well as
politics. In fact the Jesuits were at all stages, and in all countries, deeply
involved in the physical, as well as the moral, aspects of the Counter-
Reformation. They were active in the Catholic League in France, organized to
fight civil war against the Huguenots, and the legitimate King Henri IV; their
provincial, Odon Pigenat, was a member of the League's governing Conseil
des Seize and known to the Huguenots as 'the cruellest tiger in Paris'. Jesuits

organized subversion against Queen Elizabeth in England and Ireland, and against the regency government in Scotland. They played a leading role in the Thirty Years War, both in its opening, and the forced 'conversion' of Bohemia, and by preventing a compromise peace after the victories of the Swedish Protestant army under Gustavus Adolphus. In 1626, the papal nuncio in Vienna reported to Rome: '[The Jesuits] have the upper hand over everything, even over the leading ministers of state. . . . Their influence has always been considerable, but it has reached its zenith since Father Lamormaini has been confessor to the Emperor.' Gustavus Adolphus remarked: 'There are three Ls I should like to see hanged: the Jesuit Lamormaini, the Jesuit Laymann and the Jesuit Laurentius Forer.'

Above all, the Jesuits were widely identified with the view that the moral code could in some way be suspended when Catholic interests were at risk. The Jesuits not only advocated war as a legitimate instrument against heresy but defended the selective murder of Protestants, especially if they held important positions. It was an extension of their educational techniques: if a ruler could not be converted, let him be slain. Thus in 1599, Juan Mariani, offering Philip III advice on the question of the kingship, wrote of Protestant sovereigns: 'It is a glorious thing to exterminate the whole of this pestilential and pernicious race from the community of mankind. Limbs, too, are cut off when they are corrupt, that they may not infect the remainder of the body; and likewise this bestial cruelty in human shape must be separated from the state and cut off with the sword.'

The Jesuits were a striking case of a highly educated and strongly motivated élite allowing the stresses of religious conflict to confuse their moral values. They were not isolated. Indeed, the problem was general. It is a tragic but recurrent feature of Christianity that the eager pursuit of reform tends to produce a ruthlessness in dealing with obstacles to it which brings the whole moral superstructure crashing down in ruins. The Gregorian papacy, so zealous for virtue, fathered some of the worst crimes of the Middle Ages. So, in the sixteenth and seventeenth centuries, the desire to purge the Church of its errors and to recreate an apostolic society set off a chain of consequences which not only wrecked the unity of Christendom but induced its severed fragments to exercise unrivalled ferocity on each other. From the 1520s religious war was endemic in the West until 1648, with one brief respite in the first two decades of the seventeenth century. These wars, civil or international – usually both – were without redeeming features and were destructive of Christian faith itself, as well as human life and material civilization. They came, too, after a period when mankind had rediscovered the riches of the ancient world and was advancing rapidly in knowledge and techniques. The effect of religious conflict was not to halt this process completely but to retard and deform it. Reason was devalued. Dark and horrible forces were unleashed or resuscitated. The hopeful dawn Erasmus noted broadened into a tempestuous day where sensible and civilized men had to shout to make their voices heard above the winds of violence, cruelty and superstition.

The religious wars were based on the assumption that only a unitary society was tolerable, and that those who did not conform to the prevailing norms, and who could not be forced or terrified into doing so, should be treated as second-class citizens, expelled, or killed. They thus reinforced or brought back to life destructive forces which already existed in medieval society. South of the Pyrenees, for instance, the elimination of Protestant heretics was presented as a further chapter in the struggle against the Jews, which went back to Visigothic times. The triumphant Catholics of Castile had been systematically persecuting the Jews since the fourteenth century. Many had accepted Catholicism, and the *conversos*, always suspect, were a powerful element in Spanish society. In Spain, the Inquisition was part of the process whereby the Castilians penetrated and unified the whole of Spanish society: it was set up in 1478 to examine the credentials of the converts. The conquest of the Moors was virtually completed in 1492 with the fall of Granada; three months later the crown ordered all remaining Jews to leave the country, the culmination of twelve years of intensive anti-Semitic legislation. In fact, up to fifty per cent, perhaps 400,000, remained as forced converts, and solving the Jewish problem merely exacerbated the problem of the *conversos*. Christians with Jewish blood had been, and remained, powerful in finance, administration and medicine. By the end of the fifteenth century most of the noblest and richest families in Spain, including the royal family of Aragon, were 'tainted'. Nevertheless, racial legislation was introduced to 'purify' the upper regions of society. Statutes of *limpieza de sangre* were passed banning descendants of Moors and Jews (especially the latter) from universities and religious orders. The Inquisition effectively controlled their enforcement and progressively extended their scope. Torquemada, who set the system in motion, and his successor as head of the Inquisition, Diego Deza, both had Jewish blood. But the Inquisition could authenticate false genealogies, and the fact that virtually everyone of any importance was vulnerable merely increased its power – accurate genealogies, secretly circulated, were a form of subversive literature. It was the guardian of the Spanish race, and one of the reasons it was popular among the Castilian masses was that in general they alone had the *limpieza de sangre*. In a memorandum to Charles v, the historian Lorenzo Galindez de Carvajal pointed out that most of the members of his council were 'tainted'; among the exceptions was Dr Palacios Rubios, 'a man of pure blood because he is of labouring descent'.

The effect of the Inquisition under Torquemada was to confuse the theoretically separate matters of racial and religious purity. He issued instructions at Seville in 1484 that the 'children and grandchildren of those condemned [by the Inquisition] may not hold or possess public offices or posts or honours, or be promoted to hold orders, or be judges, majors, constables, magistrates, jurors, stewards, officials of weights and measures, merchants, notaries, public scriveners, lawyers, attorneys, secretaries, accountants, treasurers, physicians, surgeons, shopkeepers, brokers, changers, collectors, tax-farmers or holders of any other public office.' A new doctrine of original sin was thus introduced, all the more un-Christian since it could not be effaced by baptism; the saffron robes worn by the condemned (the great majority of whom were Jews) had to be hung up in churches as a perpetual reproach to their descendants – a law observed until the end of the eighteenth century. The *limpieza de sangre* system might have disappeared in the sixteenth century under the weight of its own contradictions and cruelties. In fact, the religious struggle not only prolonged its life but immeasurably increased the authority, power and durability of its control-mechanism, the Inquisition. By an almost magical process, Protestantism was simply identified with impure blood, that is with the Jewish taint. Archbishop Siliceo of Toledo expressed the common view in 1547: 'It is said, and it is considered true, that the principal heretics of Germany, who have destroyed all that nation . . . are descendants of Jews.' In fact no one had said this outside Spain; and Luther himself was notoriously anti-Semitic. But Spaniards of Jewish descent were duly identified by the Inquisition as Protestants, and burned, and these convictions were taken as proof of an unfounded assumption. By 1556 we find Philip II writing: 'All the heresies which have occurred in Germany and France have been sown by descendants of Jews, as we have seen and still see daily in Spain.' Protestantism was thus fitted into the hate-structure of the country, and doctrinal orthodoxy was reinforced by racism. The campaign was directed against foreigners as well as Spanish Jews and intellectuals; in fact after the mass-burning of Protestants in 1559–62, conducted at grandiose ceremonies in front of the king and other members of the royal family, most of the Protestants executed were foreigners, who were assumed to be actively plotting to subvert the State. Many of these were seamen and merchants, chiefly from France, England and the Low Countries; commercial rivalry was thus reinforced by doctrinal hatred, and sea-warfare took on a new ferocity.

The process tended to seal off Spain (and her colonies) from the rest of the world. The Spanish Erasmians were wiped out or driven into exile, one of the first victims being Ximenes's former secretary, Juan de Vergera. The great Spanish pedagogue Juan Luis Vives wrote: 'We live in such difficult times that it is dangerous either to speak or to be silent.' As one of Vives's correspondents, Rodrigo Manrique, put it (from exile): 'Our country is a land of pride and envy and, you may add, of barbarism; down there one cannot produce any culture without being suspected of heresy, error and Judaism. Thus silence has been imposed on the learned.' The Spanish Index of Prohibited Books was first published in 1551, and progressively updated and expanded. The 1559 list included sixteen of Erasmus's works, notably his *Enchiridion*, once a best-seller in Spain; and the Index of 1612 classified him among the *auctores damnati*, so that henceforth he could be quoted only as *quidam* ('someone'). The Spanish Index was quite independent of Rome's – it banned the orthodox historian Cardinal Baronius, who had been publicly praised by the Pope, as well as Thomas More, Cardinal Pole and Francis Borgia, General of the Jesuits. Indeed, the whole apparatus of repression was autarchic and nationalist, struck at the highest as well as the lowest, and was impervious to papal remonstrance. In 1559 the Inquisition arrested Barto-lomeo de Carranza, Archbishop of Toledo, and kept him in its underground cells at Valladolid despite papal intervention for seven years. In 1565, a papal legation including three future popes, Gregory XIII, Urban VII and Sixtus V, reported to Pius IV: 'Nobody dares to speak in favour of Carranza because of the Inquisition . . . and its authority would not allow it to admit that it had imprisoned Carranza unjustly. The most ardent defenders of justice here consider that it is better for an innocent man to be condemned than for the Inquisition to suffer disgrace.' Pius V finally got Carranza brought to Rome in 1566, where he was held in the fortress at St Angelo. The power of Spain prevented his clearance until 1576, just eighteen days before his death.

The Inquisition was not only supremely powerful (it constituted one of the governing councils of Spain); it proved durable, largely because it was self-financing from the confiscated property of the condemned. The fact that it needed the money for its operations meant that it had to secure convictions. Hence the use of torture. It is calculated that in the Toledo Tribunal, 1575–1610, about thirty-two per cent of those whose 'offences' made them liable to torture were in fact tortured; those thus brutalized, according to the records, included women aged seventy to ninety, and a girl of thirteen. After funds from confiscations ran out, the Inquisition raised money by selling posts as informers or 'familiars', who enjoyed privileges such as freedom from arrest; in 1641 they cost 1,500 ducats each. Even so, the Inquisition finally ran out of money in the late eighteenth century, and from that point it became moribund, though it was not effectively abolished until 1834. The last official Spanish execution for heresy was in 1826, when a schoolmaster was hanged for substituting 'Praise be to God' in place of 'Ave Maria' in school prayers. The *limpieza de sangre* statutes remained valid (though increasingly unen-forceable) until 1865.

While in Spain orthodox intolerance concentrated on Moors and Jews, and then on an amalgamation of Jews, Protestants, foreigners and those of 'impure blood', north of the Pyrenees Jews had ceased to be the main object of hatred in the thirteenth century, and attention had focussed on those heretics who fled into mountain areas to escape persecution. Almost imperceptibly, in these remote and backward areas, the heresy-hunt broadened out into the witch-hunt. Witches had not, on the whole, been hunted in the Dark Ages, since belief in their existence tended to be treated as pagan superstition: Charlemagne, in fact, passed laws against the hunting of witches. The position changed in the thirteenth century with the development of the Dominican Inquisition, which tended to create (often for financial reasons) a new category of victims when it ran out of an old one. Thus in the Alps witches were called Waudenses and in the Pyrenees Gazarii or Cathars. When the hunting of heretics and other antinomian groups became endemic in the late fourteenth and fifteenth centuries, witchhunting began to evolve its own theory and methodology, while at the same time it spread down from the mountain areas to embrace the whole of society.

The two leading German Dominican inquisitors, who specialized in witch-hunting, Heinrich Kramer and Jakob Sprender, compiled a huge dossier based on confessions extracted under torture; in 1484 they used this to persuade Innocent VIII to issue the bull *Summis desiderantes affectibus*, which gave them specially enlarged powers, and two years later they condensed their 'findings' into the great witch-encyclopaedia, the *Malleus Maleficarum*, which became a best-seller. The combination of bull and book internationalized their hunting techniques. Since their forms of questioning put words into the mouths of the victims, which they were compelled by torture to repeat, the patterns of the *Malleus* appeared to be confirmed by experience all over Christendom. In reality there is no reason to suppose that such a phenomenon as witchcraft ever existed. The myth was on a level with the supposed ritual murders of Christian children, of which the Jews were accused in the twelfth century. Witches simply replaced Jews as objects of fear and hatred, and torture supplied 'proof' of their existence and malevolence. Indeed, witch-hunting could not survive, or even become a powerful movement, without torture. The European craze really dates from about 1468, when the papacy first declared witchcraft a *crimen exceptum*, and made those accused subject to torture. Once torture was authorized, the confessions multiplied, the number of victims and accusations increased, and the movement generated its own momentum. Once torture was banned, the process was reversed, and the movement gradually died. Where torture was not used, as in England, cases were much rarer and the confessions less horrific.

The first big spate of witch-hunting was in the second half of the fifteenth century; then there was a period of relative calm, during which some governments took action against hunting. Charles V's imperial constitution of 1532 ordered punishments only for witches who did actual harm; merely being a witch was not enough to invoke the law. Erasmus and other Renaissance scholars were highly sceptical, and a new mood appeared to be setting in which would destroy the superstitious base on which the hunt had been created. This more enlightened attitude was rapidly reversed when religious war broke out and the persecution of heretics was intensified. Moreover, both Catholics and reformers tended to hunt witches, as they hunted anabaptists, to demonstrate their doctrinal purity and fervour. With the exception of Zwingli, the German reformers accepted the mythology of witchcraft. Luther thought that witches should be burnt for making a pact with the Devil even if they harmed no one, and he had four of them roasted at Wittenburg. The Protestants relied on Exodus 22:18: 'Thou shalt not suffer a witch to live.' As Calvin said: 'The Bible teaches us that there are witches and that they must be slain . . . this law of God is a universal law.' The Calvinists, in fact, were much fiercer against witches than the Lutherans. On the whole, Anglican Protestants were not keen witch-hunters, and during the whole period 1542–1736 many fewer than 1,000 were executed (by hanging) in England, against 4,400 in Calvinist Scotland during the ninety years beginning in 1590. The worst year in England was 1645, when the Calvinist Presbysterians were in power. Where English Calvinists could, they propagated witch-hunting. Bishop Jewel, who had lived in exile in Geneva, brought the craze with him on his return in 1559; and in the 1590s, the Calvinist William Perkins lectured on the subject at Emmanuel College, Cambridge, a Puritan institution where some of the Founding Fathers of New England were educated. Wherever Calvinism became strong, witches were systematically hunted.

Equally, on the other side of the religious barriers, it was the followers of Loyola, the puritanical Catholic, who now popularized the witch-hunt. This in itself is interesting, for the Jesuits were not necessarily intolerant. As a Spanish-dominated order, they might have been expected to show particular hostility to Jews. In fact they did not, because in Spain Puritanism was identified with Jewry-Protestantism. Loyola had been accused of Judaism as a student in 1527 simply because of his strict religious observances. He later said, defiantly, that he would consider it an honour to be descended from Jews: 'What? To be related to Christ Our Lord and to Our Lady the glorious Virgin Mary!' He and his first three successors as General of the Jesuits were all firmly opposed to the *limpieza* statutes and ecclesiastical anti-Semitism, and the Jesuits only gave way in the end because their attitude was ruining recruitment in Spain. In fact it was the moderate line the Jesuits took on the Jews which lay at the bottom of their ferocious 200-year struggle with the Dominican Inquisition. The rule seemed to be that, in a period of intense religious conflict, everyone needed to have an obsessional enemy, but no one could cope with more than one at a time. In Spain, orthodoxy hunted Jews but very rarely witches. The Jesuits were pro-Jewish (up to a point) but prominent witch-hunters. Burning of witches increased wherever they triumphantly carried the Counter-Reformation, especially in Germany, Poland and Franche-Comté; and in the Low Countries, where they were less successful, they intensified witch-hunting after a proclamation by Philip II in 1590, which declared witchcraft 'the scourge of the human race'. Jesuits were associated with the most savage campaign, conducted around Trier by Archbishop Johann von Schoneburg, and his suffragan, Bishop Binsfield. In the years 1587–93, the archbishop burned 368 witches in some twenty-two villages, leaving two of them with only one female inhabitant each. As with the Inquisition against heretics, officials who dragged their feet were liable to become victims: thus Schoneburg had the University Rector, Dietrich Flade, chief judge of the electoral court, arrested for leniency, tortured, strangled and burned. The hunters constantly alarmed the authorities by stories of vast and growing conspiracies of witches; once they were allowed to torture they produced not only scores of victims but hundreds of accusations – thus justifying their forecasts. Some hunters were paid by results: Balthasar Ross, minister to the Prince-Abbot of Fulda, made 5393 guilden out of 250 victims, 1602–5.

There seems to have been a fairly steady correlation between the intensity of the Protestant-Catholic struggle and the number of witches accused and burned. Just as there had been a lull in the early sixteenth century, ended by the Lutheran Reformation and its violent consequences, so there was another lull just before the outbreak of the Thirty Years War in 1618. Then, with the Catholic reconquest of Bohemia and parts of Germany, the witch-trials multiplied. This last great phase of witch-hunting was the product of Catholic-Protestant rivalry, since hunters on both sides often identified witchcraft with opposing beliefs; on the other hand, they drew on each other's theoretical writings and practical experiences. The Catholic witchcraft terror in Germany was remarkably like the Inquisition's 'Protestant-Jewish' terror in Spain, since it might strike at anyone. Philip Adolf von Ehrenberg, Bishop of Wurtzburg, burned over 900 during his reign 1623–31, including his own nephew, nineteen priests and a child of seven. In the Bavarian prince-bishopric of Eichstatt, 274 were burned in the year 1629 alone. In Bonn, the chancellor and his wife, and the wife of the archbishop's secretary, were executed. The worst hunt of all was at Bamberg, where the 'witch-bishop', Johann Georg II Fuchs von Dornheim burned 600 witches, 1623–33. His chancellor, accused of leniency, implicated under torture five burgomasters; one of them, arrested and tortured in turn, accused twenty-seven colleagues, but later managed to smuggle out a letter to his daughter: 'It is all falsehood and invention, so help me God. . . . They never cease to torture until one says something. . . . If God sends no means of bringing the truth to light, our whole kindred will be burned.' The hunt led a Jesuit, Friedrich Spee, who had acted as confessor to witches in the Wurzburg persecution, to circulate in manuscript an attack on hunting called *Cautio Criminalis*: 'Torture fills our Germany with witches and unheard-of wickedness, and not only Germany but any nation that attempts it. . . . If all of us have not confessed ourselves witches, that is only because we have not all been tortured.'

This revealing Catholic document fell into the hands of Protestants, who printed it in 1631. But exposures of Catholic enormities did not prevent Protestants from doing the same. Erasmian humanists like Johann Weyer had long since drawn the connection between torture and confessions. (His book was put on the Index). As Richard Scott, one of Weyer's admirers, put it in 1584: 'Note also how easily they may be brought to confess that which they never did, nor lieth in the power of man to do.' (Scott's book was burned by James I.) Many intellectuals shared the sceptical attitude of Montaigne: 'It is rating our conjectures highly to roast people alive for them'; and even in the worst affected areas the judicial authorities were eventually persuaded to discountenance torture. As Sir George Mackenzie, the Scottish Lord

Advocate, said: 'Most of all that ever were taken were tormented after this manner, and this usage was the ground of all their confession.' This had been apparent all along, to anyone with an open mind. But so long as men killed each other for their religious beliefs, witches were extensively hunted. Once the major fighting had stopped, with the Peace of Westphalia in 1648, reason had the chance to raise its head again, and the rapid diffusion of scientific ideas about the workings of nature undermined the theoretical basis of witch-hunting. Witchcraft ceased to be an international mania, but special local conditions produced brief outbursts, in Sweden in the 1660s, following the defection of Queen Christina to Rome, and in New England in the 1690s. The last legal execution of a witch was carried out in Protestant Switzerland in 1782; and there was an illegal burning in Catholic Poland eleven years later.

The identification of Protestants with Jews in Spain, and the persecution of old women in northern and central Europe, were only two of the ways in which the Christian schism of the sixteenth and seventeenth centuries, and the religious passion it generated, damaged the structure of European civilization and retarded the progress of reason. Here, then, we come to an important watershed in the history of Christianity. In Roman times, philosophers and intellectuals generally had tended to identify Christianity with obscurantism and superstition, an impression only gradually (and never completely) effaced in the fourth century. Thereafter, however, Christianity had appeared to associate itself wholly with Roman culture, and after the collapse of the secular Roman state in the West it had successfully grafted the civilization of the ancient world on to the dynamic barbarian societies of the West. Following this, and for many centuries, Christianity remained both the chief focus of culture and the driving force behind economic and institutional innovation. The strength of the total Christian society was essentially religious, and linked to the well-being and vigour of the Catholic Church. But then in the thirteenth and fourteenth centuries there came the first sign of a change: that is, a tendency for the more progressive and innovatory elements in society to operate not within the institutional framework of the Church but outside it – and eventually against it. The Church ceased to be in the van of progress, and quite rapidly became an obstacle to it. This switch-about came both in the economic and the intellectual field.

Let us look at the economy first. The Dark Age Church had been a perfect instrument for the relaunching of the economy of western Europe on an agricultural basis: it had the theory, and it had the institutional agencies. Its urban bishoprics also played a major part in founding the town economy, and its pilgrimage routes and relic-centres in developing communications and trade. But further than that it could not go. It did not develop a theology of trade or capitalism. It did not produce orders which made a contribution to commercial techniques in the way that the Benedictines and the Cistercians had developed agricultural techniques; indeed, even in agriculture, from the early fourteenth century it changed from a producer to a *rentier* role. The

Templars, by acting as bankers, were the only Christian order to make a commercial contribution, and they were suppressed and plundered by the papacy and the crown, acting in concert. During the crusades, which supplied a crucial forum for economic innovation, it was the secular merchants of the Italian maritime cities who took on the role of pioneers, right outside the institutional framework of the Church.

Those who practised the incipient capitalism of the later Middle Ages were not irreligious – often they were extremely pious – but they tended to conduct their religious life on their own terms, and outside the constraints and abuses of official Christianity. This blend of anti-clericalism, mild Puritanism, and devotion to commerce – soon to be associated with the 'Protestant ethic' of Calvinism – was commonplace in the bigger western cities by the fourteenth century. It is reflected, for instance, in the surviving correspondence of Francesco di Marco Datini, *c.* 1335–1410, who traded for thirty years at Avignon, and then at Prato near Florence. His ledgers were inscribed with the Ten Commandments, and many pages have at their head 'In the name of God and Profit'. This man was a sincere, and on the whole orthodox Catholic (though he joined a flagellant procession on one occasion). But, like Dean Colet, he did not want the money he left to the poor in his will to go through Church channels, and he therefore excluded clerics from its administration. This was very common at the close of the Middle Ages. A growing number of Christian charitable foundations were established beyond the reach of corrupt clerics; it was part of the reassertion of the laity which was the essential dynamic of the Reformation.

There is plenty of evidence, then, that the progressive elements in the commercial community were turning against the Church, as the epitome of clericalism, long before the Reformation, and long before Protestantism developed specific doctrines which have since been identified as the generating forces of the capitalist mentality and its work-concentration techniques. In putting forward the theory of the 'Protestant ethic', Max Weber and his followers argued that Protestant theology, with its heavy emphasis on justification by faith and predestination, generated 'a salvation panic' among believers. This, in turn, led to the methodical practice of good works (thus developing in economic terms habits of industry and capitalism). Good works were useless as a means of attaining salvation, since that was already determined, but they were indispensible as a sign of election, to get rid of the fear of damnation, and induce what Luther called 'the feeling of blessed assurance' – an inner conviction that you were saved. Weber thought that Calvinism was an anxiety-inducing ideology that drove its victims to seek self-control and confidence in methodical work and worldly success. But there is no evidence that Calvinism, or other powerful forms of Protestantism, induced anxiety. The anxiety was already there. It always had been. Origen, with his theory of universal salvation, had always represented a minority trend in Christianity. Vast numbers of Christians had feared Hell and its fires at all periods. These anxieties naturally tended to generate work. Anxious men assuaged their worries, in medieval society, by paying for masses to be said for them, or by buying indulgences. They had to work to get this salvation money. But profit thus generated was creamed off by the Church, and used in display buildings, masses and charitable foundations. It was not available for entrepreneurial investment. To this extent medieval society was not a saving society; or, rather, it banked its treasure in Heaven. It had a wealthy Church, rather than capitalist enterprises, to show for its industry. Again, medieval merchants were less inclined to bequeath large sums in cash to their heirs than their successors in the seventeenth and eighteenth centuries. Huge bequests went to purposes which Protestantism later ruled to be futile or anti-Christian. A comparatively small percentage change in such habits could effect, over a period, a major transformation in economic life.

This does not mean that passionate Protestants, especially Calvinists, were more likely to be successful in business. It has not been, and probably cannot be, demonstrated that, for instance, Englishmen who actually became Puritans and lived through the 'salvation panic' then became entrepreneurial businessmen or significantly changed their commercial habits as a result. The evidence from individual diaries, letters and memoirs suggests that the most significant expression of their new faith was in the cultural and political field rather than the economic. It is true that the Puritan spirit did tend to make good organizers; but, as such, it operated on both sides of the religious divide – Loyola and Borromeo were both brilliant organizers, as indeed had been the early Benedictines and Cistercians, quite independent of any particular salvationist theology.

Thus, though it is true that the commercial instinct tended to turn men against the Catholic Church, with its excessive clericalism, it did not necessarily turn them to Protestantism. There was nothing in Luther's teaching specifically favourable to commerce or industry. He condemned usury, as did most Catholic evangelists; both Lutheran and Catholic writers continued to attack usury in any form until well into the seventeenth century. The Calvinists, on the other hand, did not. Calvin argued that Deuteronomy 23:19 applied only to the Hebrews and was not intended to be universal: the sole guide was the law of charity. In 1564–5 Bartholomew Gernhard, pastor of St Andrew, Rudolstadt, was forced out of office for refusing communion to two men who had loaned money at interest; and in 1587 at Ratisbon five preachers were expelled for insisting on preaching against usury. The English Parliament, with Protestant majorities, approved lending at interest in 1545 and again in 1571; and in 1638, the Dutch Calvinist, Claude Saumaise, argued in *On Usury* that charging interest was now necessary to salvation. But all this proves is that theory and practice tended to be closer (though not all that much) in the Protestant world than in the Catholic. What cannot be shown is that Calvinism can be causally linked to capitalism (or economic progress generally) in any particular society. For instance, few if any countries were more completely Calvinist than Scotland between 1560 and 1700. Yet is is hard to demonstrate how the Reformation in any way favoured the rise of economic individualism in Scotland. On the contrary, the ethics of the 'Kirk Session', the institutional dynamic of Scottish Calvinism, was similar to the group discipline of the medieval guild and burgh, which militated against competition; and in fact ancient restrictions on free competition – the privileges of royal burghs, rights of merchant- and craft-guilds, single-staple ports, and so on – survived intact at least a century after the Scottish Reformation. Their defenders were the classes and communities most favourable to the new religion. Such bars to free enterprise lasted longer in Calvinist Scotland than almost anywhere else in Europe, and they were slowly removed after 1660 for reasons which had nothing to do with religion. Legislation passed by merchant-guilds, and by the Calvinist General Assembly, was often interchangeable in content, and even in its tone. What Calvinism did contribute was the foundations of a good educational system. In the eighteenth century this became the best and most liberal in Europe, but its fruition was a product of the relaxation of Calvinism; the Scottish culture and economy flourished, in fact, only when Calvinism with its all consuming demands began to relax its grip.

Here we begin to get at the heart of the matter. The progressive elements in the economy, which gradually became identified with the capitalist system, were distinguished not by their adherence to any particular doctrinal formulation but by their antipathy to highly institutionalized and highly clericalized Christianity of any kind. They were to be found in the later Middle Ages in the more advanced towns of Italy, south Germany, Flanders and the Rhineland, and in Iberian seaports like Seville and Lisbon. In the fourteenth and fifteenth century they were already in revolt against clericalism and 'mechanical' Christianity (or, if they were Jews, against the systematic operation of the race-laws and the Spanish Inquisition). The common characteristic of these entrepreneurs was their desire to be left alone by the religious enthusiasts and organizers, and to escape from the clericalist and canon law network. Their religion might be intense, but it was essentially private and personal. Thus it had a good deal in common with the type of religious piety advocated by Erasmus in his *Enchiridion*; indeed, the ideas of Erasmus, who had a similar urban background, both reflected and shaped the attitudes of the new economic élite. These well-to-do and hard-working men were educated. They wished to read the scriptures for themselves. They did not want their reading matter interfered with or censored. They disapproved of clerics, especially those in the orders, whom they thought dishonest or lazy, or both. They deplored the superstitious accretions of medieval Christianity, and preferred the simpler practices of the 'primitive' Church which they claimed to discern in the acts of the apostles and the epistles of St Paul. They believed in the worthiness, indeed sanctification, of lay life; they exalted the married state and thought laymen the spiritual equal of clerks.

This type of urban bourgeois had found it possible to come to terms with the pre-Reformation Church in roughly the same way as Erasmus himself. But after the 1520s the situation changed. Reformed Christianity seemed to offer a more viable alternative. Reformed Tridentine Catholicism, on the other hand, became less tolerable. Moreover, many of the urban centres where pre-sixteenth-century capitalism flourished were convulsed by the religious struggle, and life became intolerable for independent-minded businessmen who wished to keep their religion private. The sixteenth century thus witnessed a great series of displacements among the entrepreneurial class. Jews moved out of Seville and Lisbon, and to northern and central Europe. Merchants from Germany, the Rhineland and France moved to Lisbon and Seville. Italians moved northwards from Como, Locarno, Milan and Venice into the Rhineland. South Germans moved away from the Counter-Reformation into north Germany. From such Flanders towns as Liège, Brussels and Ghent, where Catholicism of the new Counter-Reformation variety was forcibly imposed by the Spanish *tercios*, there was a movement to Frankfurt, Hamburg, Bremen, the Rhineland and Switzerland; and a movement into the Protestant Netherlands, especially after the fall of Antwerp to the Spanish in 1585. Some of these emigrants were Catholics; among the Protestants many were Lutherans rather than Calvinists. They were seeking peace and toleration rather than a new doctrinal system.

It was from these emigrant business communities that the giants of the new capitalism were drawn. One such was the Calvinist Jan de Willem, who worked for Christian IV of Denmark. He and his brothers helped to create the Danish East India Company. They came from Amsterdam. King Christian also employed Gabriel and Celio Marcelis to farm tolls and mineral tithes, and advance loans on the proceeds, as contractors, munition merchants and timber exporters. Both were Flemish, refugees from the Counter-Reformation. Again, the great entrepreneur Louis de Geer, who controlled the iron and copper industries of Sweden, supplied the armies and fleets of Gustavus Adolphus, and performed similar services for other Protestant countries, as well as Venice, Portugal and Russia, was an Amsterdam Calvinist who came originally from Catholic Liège. Other displaced Calvinist families helped to found the Bank of Sweden in 1658. The state bankers of France, under both Henri IV and Richelieu, were Huguenots, the Rambouillets and the Tallemants, and the Calvinist financier from Catholic Brabant, Jan Hoeufft. Mazarin's chief financial adviser and Intendant des Finances, Barthelemy d'Herwarth, was a displaced Protestant. A Calvinist refugee from Antwerp, Hans de Witte, served as financial organizer to the Emperor Rudolph II and later to the Catholic generalissimo Albert von Wallenstein; at one point he controlled the empire's silver and tin, and supplied all its armies. The Spanish Habsburgs also used Protestants for such purposes – François Grenus, a Calvinist who had migrated from Switzerland to the Rhineland, while the Hamburg merchants employed by Spain to manage the sugar and spice trade were originally refugees from the Low Countries. Many of these capitalists were Calvinists, but their life-styles did not particularly reflect their religion. Some were Calvinist refugees from Lutheranism, or vice versa; or Calvinist followers of Arminius, who rejected fundamentalism. Some were Erasmian-type Catholics, or genuine religious independents.

Protestant states tended to be the chief beneficiaries of this international series of religious movements. They might have state religions but they tended to be more tolerant. They rarely persecuted systematically. They had no equivalent to the Inquisition. They were not clericalist. They permitted books to circulate more freely. They did not burden commerce with canon law. They accepted 'private' religion, and placed marriage and the family at the centre of it. They were thus more congenial to the capitalist community. As a result, Protestant societies appeared far more successful than Catholic ones as the capitalist system developed. The point was noted as early as 1804 by Charles de Viller in his *Essai sur l'esprit et l'influence de la réformation de Luther*. In the nineteenth century it became a commonplace to link economic success and industrialization with the Protestant creed, particularly when it was observed that, in Catholic countries like France, Belgium and Austria, the entrepreneurial lead was taken by members of the Protestant minority. Catholic leaders, and the Vatican in particular, grew very alarmed at Protestant propaganda which harped on this theme; it was one chief reason why the Vatican tended to damn all forms of 'modernism' and to detect Protestant heresy behind any kind of innovation.

Yet both the Protestant propagandists and the frightened Vatican were really missing the point. What inhibited the growth of the economic freedom necessary to allow capitalism to develop was not a particular theology but Christian institutionalism. Capitalism could not expand in a total Christian society, whether it were Catholic or Calvinist. The emigrant capitalists of the sixteenth and seventeenth centuries were fleeing not from particular dogmas but from the institutions which insisted that dogmas should control life. They took the Erasmian view that what Christianity needed was a change in morals, not in theology. Capitalism benefited from the observance of the Ten Commandments; but it regarded a society dominated by an expensive and arrogant institutional Church as a hostile environment. Capitalism, in its religious aspect, was a retreat from public to private Christianity. It was a movement·towards the freedom of the will and the individual, and against collective enforcement. The strength of clericalism varied greatly in Protestant countries, but it was everywhere weaker than in Catholic ones. Hence it was in Protestant societies that capitalism first took strong root. But as the institutional power of the Catholic church has declined, in the twentieth century, capitalism has spread into the once-clericalist states. The different theories of salvation are thus seen to be what they have always been – of marginal importance as an economic incentive. What is significant, and what, to the shrewd analyst was already ominous in the sixteenth and seventeenth centuries, was that the progressive economic forces in society were in conflict with its institutional religion. Clever businessmen were leaving areas where religious institutions were strong, and seeking cities and countries where they were weak. Such men often practised an intense personal and private Christian piety. Yet the long-term survival of Christianity appeared impossible without an institutional framework. If the economic forces of the future tended to find Christian institutions inimical, and therefore worked to destroy them, how long would it be before Christian faith itself was damaged by economic progress?

The period also witnessed the first breach between intellectuals and institutional Christianity. Here, again, we can trace the influence of Erasmus. All those, on both sides of the religious barrier, who worked for a compromise during the period of the colloquies, 1538–41 – Contarini, Pole, Melanchthon, Bucer – were essentially Erasmians, and Erasmian attitudes continued to find a response in all countries, and at all times, through the century of religious conflict. This 'third force' was never organized internationally, and often it worked, as it were, underground, especially during the periods of intense violence and persecution. But it was never entirely silent. It expressed itself in two chief ways. One was a straightforward protest against the horrors of religious war and the wickedness of burning men for their religious beliefs. The execution of Michael Servetus, for instance, evoked not only defences of persecution by Calvin and Beza but a vigorous and eloquent attack on the whole system of compulsion by Sebastian Castellio (1509–63). His protest was particularly courageous since, though a convert to Calvinism, he was suspect in both Geneva and Basle, and owed his livelihood as a teacher to Calvin's favour. His *De Haereticis an sint persequendi?* is less an argument than a collection of useful quotations from the Fathers and Protestant writers, and a series of vigorous assertions. 'I have carefully examined what a heretic means, and I cannot make it mean more than this; a heretic is a man with whom you disagree.' 'To kill a man is not to defend a doctrine; it is to kill a man.' 'The better a man knows the truth, the less he is inclined to condemn.' 'Who would not think Christ a moloch, or some such God, if he wanted men to be immolated to him, and burned alive?' The appeal was emotional, but effective – at any rate, Calvin and Beza tried to get him dismissed from Basle University, and their followers never ceased to hound him. But it met with a response chiefly in areas where both sides were strong and organized, and toleration was the only alternative to war. The best example was France, where civil war led to the Colloquy of Poissy in 1561, and the following year to the first of the toleration edicts. Castellio commented: 'I think that the aim and decisive cause of this illness – this insurrection and war which torment France – is the forcing of consciences.' He blamed both sides: 'Either the victim resists, and you murder his body, or he yields and speaks against his conscience, and you murder his soul.' But though sensible men in France were struggling towards some system of toleration, they were often in a small minority, at any rate among the educated and influential. Beza, on behalf of the Geneva Calvinists, denounced toleration in 1570 as 'a purely diabolical doctrine'. To support freedom of conscience was sinful. In 1588, at the States Assembly at Blois, the Bishop of Le Mans tried to maintain that 'heretics should be loved and brought back by instruction and good example', but the Assembly 'shouted with indignation' and 'was so angry that they made noises with their hands and feet and did not allow him to say a word'. When the Edict of Nantes was signed in 1598 it was promptly denounced by Pope Clement VIII as 'the worst thing in the world'.

Nevertheless, during the late sixteenth century, burnings for heresy as such began to decline. Most of the victims of the Reformation were killed aimlessly, in the course of religious warfare. Was there any way of ending the fighting, men asked, by finding a middle ground of belief? Here was the second of the two ways in which liberal opinion tried to exert itself. Among the Lutherans, the followers of Melanchthon broke away to form the 'Philippist' branch of the Church, which believed an arrangement with Rome was still possible. In Cologne, the Catholic humanist George Cassander put forward, in the 1560s, the idea of Fundamental Articles: 'In essentials, unity; in inessentials, liberty; in everything, charity.' Protestants used Catholic works, such as Thomas à Kempis' *Imitation of Christ*, and works by Melanchthon, Bucer and even Calvin circulated in Catholic countries; but in virtually every case the name of the author was suppressed and the books were edited.

Below the surface, we can detect a 'third force' at work. To some extent it was connected with the Renaissance discoveries of lost texts and especially the cabalistic and Hermetic philosophies. This led to the belief, quite common among sixteenth-century liberal intellectuals, that there was a complete and final system of knowledge to be discovered, which embraced all the arts and sciences, and revolved around Christianity. When, in due course, this system was completely unveiled, it would automatically solve all religious disputes and controversies. Hence it was important that men of goodwill and intelligence should work together. But it might also be dangerous, so there was a need for secrecy. One idea which constantly crops up is the 'invisible college' of learned men – an international network of scholars and humanists. Secret societies as such probably originated among fifteenth-century Italian intellectuals, and may have been brought to northern Europe by the Hermetic philosopher Giordano Bruno. He certainly formed a circle of like-minded men in Lutheran Germany.

In the Netherlands, the secret society or college took the form of the so-called Family of Love. Its members were eirenic Christians, who ostensibly conformed to the practice of whichever Christian sect was in power in the area where they lived, but privately subscribed to ecumenical doctrines and owed their true allegiance to the Christian unity of the Family itself. These men found themselves impotent to prevent the horrors of religious strife, or to still the doctrinal passions on both sides, and were forced back on their inner resources. Like the burgeoning capitalists, they believed in a private, Erasmian religion. They were, in fact, Stoics: the demands of reason were necessarily ineffective, so the educated must take refuge in private morality, while externally conforming and doing their best to serve the common weal. One such circle, in Antwerp, revolved around Philip II's typographer royal, Christopher Plantin, and included natural scientists, botanists, geographers, cartographers, antiquarians, linguists, Hebrew and oriental scholars, and many artists and engravers.

Some of these Christian humanists actively proselytized for the third force and travelled extensively, evangelists for a religion which was scholarly and pietist, rather than doctrinal. Giordano Bruno travelled from Germany to England, where he was in touch with Sir Philip Sidney, his sister, the Countess of Pembroke, and their intellectual circle. To men like Bruno and Sidney, there was no absolute distinction between Christian and secular knowledge, or between theology and the natural sciences. As Sidney put it, all forms of knowledge 'lead and draw us to as high a perfection as our degenerate souls, made worse by their clayey longings, can be capable of . . . all, one and other, having this scope – to know, and by knowledge to lift up the mind from the dungeon of the body to the enjoying of his own divine essence'. Just as Roger Bacon had advised the Pope to combine mystical prophetic exploration with biblical exegesis and scientific research, to discover religious truth, so many of the most enlightened scientists of the sixteenth century still believed that communication with the angels by cabalistic or Hermetic means could unravel the mysteries of the universe. Natural science had not yet emerged from within its metaphysical carapace. Hence many argued that religious peace was essential to scientific discovery and, equally, that such research was the key to unity and reconciliation. Dr John Dee, England's leading mathematician and a friend of Sidney and Bruno, wrote extensively on plans to reunite the Churches around an agreed body of learning, and the unity of Christendom was very much on his mind when he began a series of spiritualist experiments in the 1580s.

In 1583 Dee transferred his activities to the court of the Emperor Rudolf II at Prague, which, until the Counter-Reformation victory of the White Mountain, 1620, was a centre of 'third force' activity. Charles V and his imperial successors had tried hard to reunite Germany around an agreed religious settlement. Maximillian II refused to allow himself to be called either Papist or Lutheran; he was, he insisted, 'a Christian', and he refused the Catholic Last Sacrament as it was given to him in one species. His successor, Rudolf II, who patronized Dee, also refused the last rites, and cannot easily be called either Catholic or Protestant. He hated the internal squabbles of the Protestants, and what he saw as their doctrinal pettiness; on the other hand, he became increasingly alarmed by the militancy of the Counter-Revolution and the intransigence of the papacy. It was obviously in his political interests to devise some mediatory alternative. But this was also the drift of intellectual opinion at his court, a centre of the late Renaissance.

The third force had a philosophy and a theory of knowledge. There was a general belief in a divine scheme for Europe knowable only through revelation: popular wisdom was seen as superficial, and the pure evidence of the senses as fallible, so there was necessarily a need for properly illuminated guidance. With the blossoming of natural philosophy, it was felt that the mediation of the learned intellect has replaced prophets and mystics as the means by which God's truth would be revealed. Philosophy and science did not stand alone, either. Art has its rule. Rudolf's court was the centre of the Mannerist school, the artistic expression of the very dense symbolism, and the mixture of reason, mythology and metaphysics, which marks the writings of the Hermetics. Rudolf's court entertainments were organized by Giuseppe Archiboldo, whose grotesque 'composed heads' still strike us as mysterious and enigmatic. Just as artists like El Greco proclaimed Counter-Reformation doctrine, so others had an eirenic message, though often they were obliged to hide it in a maze of symbols and artifice. Sometimes we can get their point: thus Rudolf's favourite painter, Pieter Breughel the Elder, attacked the senseless folly of confessional strife between Catholics and Protestants in his allegorical *Combat between Carnival and Lent*, which hung in Rudolf's private gallery. But often their meaning, clear enough to their intelligent and learned contemporaries in the third force, is now unfathomable.

Those who ranked themselves as eirenic evangelists took risks on either side of the religious frontier. In Protestant countries they tended to be politically suspect. The Elizabethan authorities thought Bruno had come to England as a papal and Counter-Reformation agent, and he was watched. On the Catholic side there was a much more serious risk of the Inquisition and burning. One of those who took part in Dee's experiments in Prague was the Florentine humanist Francesco Pucci, who accepted Dee's idea of an 'imminent renovation' of Christianity, introduced by learned men, which would obliterate Protestant-Catholic factions. He wrote a book about it, the *Forma d'una republica catholica*, which spelt out many third force themes, including the idea of an enlightened, invisible 'college', and an ecumenical, universal form of Christianity. He had the temerity to wish to carry the good news to Italy. He only got as far as Salzburg, where he was arrested, transferred to Rome, judged and burned. The same fate befell Bruno himself. He went to Venice, where he felt himself reasonably safe. In fact he was 'delated' to the Inquisition. The charge against him was that he said (and the words seem plausible):

'The procedure which the church uses today is not that which the Apostles used, for they converted the people with preaching and the example of good life. But now, whoever does not wish to be a Catholic must endure punishment and pain, for force is used and not love. The world cannot go on like this, for there is nothing but ignorance and no religion which is good.

[He said] the Catholic religion pleased him more than any other, but this too has need of great reform. It is not good as it is now, but soon the world will see a general reform of itself, for it is impossible that such corruptions should endure. He hopes great things of the King of Navarre. . . .'

Great mystery still surrounds the Bruno case. Some of the documents turned up as recently as 1942, when they were dicovered in the effects of the librarian-pope, Pius XI; but the official *processo*, giving the precise reasons for his condemnation, has disappeared. What we do know is that Bruno was in Inquisition hands for eight years, recanted heresies twice, but finally denied that he had ever been a heretic and was burned alive in the Campo de'Fiori in Rome, 1600. Like all those who crossed and recrossed the religious borders, he was a particular object of Roman suspicion.* In some ways, the Counter-Reformation forces, especially the Jesuits, hated the third force people even more than the militant Protestants. Cabalistic and Hermetic knowledge had been prized in pre-Tridentine Italy: Cardinal Egidius of Viterbo, for instance, had been one of the greatest of the Christian cabalists. With the Council of Trent the atmosphere stiffened. Trent put many cabalistic books on the Index. Rome did not like a force and a system of knowledge which it did not wholly control. Orthodox suspicions grew when the third force went underground and began to form secret societies. These took many forms – the Spiritual Brotherhoods of Holland and Flanders, the Rosicrucians of Germany and, eventually, in a degenerate late seventeenth-century form, the various freemason movements. All incurred the relentless enmity of the papacy, and especially of the Jesuits, and thus tended to be driven increasingly into an anti-Catholic posture. But in the case of the Jesuits and the third force, the relationship was a love-hate one. The Jesuits also cultivated science and art, and tried to put them to religious purposes. They also studied the Hermetic and cabalistic texts. The vast work on Hermetic pseudo-Egyptology published in 1652 by Athanasius Kircher SJ was employed on the Jesuits' missions; and a colleague of Bruno's, Tommaso Campanella, arrested on similar charges and held in papal prisons for over twenty years, saved his life by writing Catholic missionary propaganda.

Both Campanella and Bruno believed in the idea of a vast, all-embracing general reform, which would be followed by a Christian utopia. At bottom the

* The harsh treatment of Galileo by the Roman Inquisition in 1633 was determined, at least in part, by Pope Urban VIII's belief that Galileo was somehow linked to Bruno's heresies, and that his *Dialogue of the Two Great World Systems*, setting out Copernican theory, was full of hidden Hermetic symbolism. Less foolhardy than Bruno, Galileo made a full submission: '. . . with sincere heart and unfeigned faith I abjure, curse and detest the aforesaid errors and heresies'; nor is it true that he then added *'Eppur si muove'*, which might have led to his death. What he did do was to note in the margin of his own copy of the *Dialogue*: 'In the matter of introducing novelties. And who can doubt that it will lead to the worst disorders when minds created free by God are compelled to submit slavishly to an outside will? When we are told to deny our senses and subject them to the whim of others? When people of whatsoever competence are made judges over experts and are granted authority to treat them as they please? These are the novelties which are apt to bring about the ruin of commonwealth and the subversion of the state.' See G. de Santillana, *The Crime of Galileo* (Chicago, 1955); and C. A. Ronan, *Galileo* (London, 1974).

notion was really a complicated and sophisticated version of the old millenium, to be brought about by a 'college' of learned men, rather than by fanatical armed peasants or 'saints'. And, like the millenarians, the members of the third force tended to identify this marvellous happening with a particular monarch. In this respect, indeed, Renaissance peoples differed very little from their medieval forebears: they still had the same theory of history. The third force needed a royal champion, the catalytic charismatic figure who would personally detonate the process that would bring the Golden Age into existence. Queen Elizabeth of England was certainly an Erasmian princess, learned, moderate in her religious views, and a protector of scholars like Dr Dee; but she was disqualified by her sex. After 1589, attention centred on the new king of France, Henri IV. As head of the house of Navarre, Henri was a Huguenot; as king of France he found it necessary to embrace Catholicism. But his policy was eirenic rather than sectarian, and it transcended the institutional frameworks of the big Christian religions. He disliked the Protestant militants almost as much as the fanatics of the Catholic League, and tended to be sceptical of the merits of organized religion. His follower, Montaigne, argued on the same lines in elegant essays. How could Catholics and Protestants be so sure they had the truth? Their arrogance was 'the nurse of false opinion'. We should admit our 'uncertainty, weakness and ignorance'. As for persecuting other people's views, no two opinions were exactly alike, 'any more than two faces'. Montaigne was a Catholic, but thought that both sides twisted religion cynically to suit their cause. 'There is no hostility that excels Christian hostility. How wonderful is our zeal when it is aiding our tendency to hatred, cruelty, ambition, avarice, lying, rebellion. . . . Our religion is made to extirpate vices: in fact, it protects them, fosters them, incites them.' The coronation of Henri IV persuaded many that a new age of Christian peace was dawning – it was the chief reason why Bruno thought it was at last safe to return to Italy. Henri did indeed impose religious toleration in France, but it was a long time before he could establish his authority effectively, and only towards the end of his life was he able to work towards a general European settlement. His minister, Sully, spoke of Henri's 'great design' for a peace treaty, and his earliest biographer, Perefixe, wrote that he was working towards a Christian commonwealth of Europe in his last years, to be based on the reconciliation of sensible, liberal Protestants and Catholics in France and elsewhere, and a resumption of the colloquies. His international coalition of states would almost certainly have been mainly Protestant in composition, and would have taken the form of an anti-Habsburg alliance; but this was inevitable, since it was the Habsburg-Papal-Jesuit axis which kept the Counter-Revolution going, with the object of a total extirpation of heresy, and so made peaceful coexistence impossible. Hence Henri, though a Catholic, was seen as Antichrist in Rome, and his assassination in 1610 as a divine deliverance.

After the death of Henri, the third force tended to look towards the young

Elector Palatine, Frederick v, the chief of the lay electors of the empire, as the ecumenical champion. He married Elizabeth, daughter of James I, and this was appropriate, since James saw himself as an ecumenical figure. In 1604 he told Parliament: 'I could wish from my heart that it would please God to make me one of the members of such a general Christian union in religion, as laying wilfulness aside on both hands, we might meet in the midst, which is the centre and perfection of all things.' The proposal was transmitted through the Venetian ambassador, Carlo Scaramelli, to the Papal legate in Paris, and so to Pope Clement VIII. The Pope's cynical response, scrawled on the back of the legate's letter, was: 'These are things which make me doubt that he believes anything.' The official reply was no more encouraging. James told the Venetian ambassador in 1606: 'Pope Clement VIII invited me to join the Roman church. I replied that if they would resolve the various difficulties in a general council, legitimately convened, I would submit myself to its decisions. What do you think he answered? Just look at the zeal of the Vicar of Christ! Why, he said: "The King of England need not speak of Councils. I won't hear of one. If he will not come in by any other means, things stand as they are."' There were, indeed, as Henri IV had already discovered, obstacles to an ecumenical agreement which could only be removed by force, that is, by a combination of enlightened Catholic and Protestant forces.

In the Jacobean period there appeared to be excellent hopes for the third force. It was a great time for free intellectual exchanges between scholars. The phrase 'the republic of letters' was coined, entirely in line with Erasmus's claim: 'I am a citizen of all states.' After half a century of darkness and killing, it seemed, for a few brief years, that the ideological barriers were coming down again, and that reason and knowledge would triumph over bigotry and ignorance. Bacon, who had his own vision of the 'great instauration' of learning and science, published his *Advancement of Learning* in 1605, and was already at work on his *Novum Organum* and *New Atlantis*, projects which placed the millenarian dream on a firm foundation of experimental science. As with Greece and Rome, he thought, a new civilization was coming into existence: 'Surely, when I set before me the condition of these times, in which learning hath made her third visitation, I cannot but be raised to this persuasion, that this third period of time will far surpass that of the Grecian and Roman learning – if only men will know their own strength and their own weakness both, and take, one from the other, light of invention, not fire of contradiction.' The times seemed propitious in other respects. England was no longer hag-ridden by the Spanish war and Jesuit subversion. In Holland, Arminius and his followers, such as Hugo Grotius, were triumphantly developing a new and liberal form of Calvinism. In Venice, the battling friar Paolo Sarpi had successfully persuaded the authorities to defy the Vatican, and keep the Counter-Reformation out of Venetian territory, which included the great Renaissance university of Padua. The English ambassador, Sir Henry Wotton, thought Sarpi's Venice might well embrace a form of Anglicanism. In

1616 Antonio de Dominis, Archbishop of Spalato, actually became an Anglican; and three years later he published in England Sarpi's *History of the Council of Trent*, which told the inside story of how the council was manipulated by the papacy; the book was dedicated to James I.

It is significant that Sarpi was in touch with Christian of Anhalt, chief adviser to the Elector Frederick at his court in Heidelberg. The idea seems to have been to create a liberal corridor running through central Europe, from England through Holland, Germany, Austria to Venice, which would cut the Counter-Reformation extremists in two, and ultimately with the help of France impose an eirenic religious settlement on Europe. The marriage between Elizabeth and Frederick was part of this plan, and it was to be followed by Frederick's establishment as the king of Bohemia and ultimately as emperor of a reunified, liberal Germany. These hopes were reflected in the publication of a number of Hermetic or Rosicrucian manifestos. Their theme was as follows: The Protestant Reformation has lost its strength, and the Catholic Counter-Reformation is driving in the wrong direction. A new reformation of the whole world is called for, and this third reformation will find its strength in Christian evangelism, with its emphasis on brotherly love, in the Hermetic and cabalist traditions, and in a turning towards the works of God in nature in a scientific spirit of exploration.

To the third force in England, the heroine, of course, was their princess, Elizabeth, who was seen as both an ecumenical talisman and a patroness of the sciences. Wotton wrote a poem to her, *On his Mistress the Queen of Bohemia*, and John Donne addressed her prophetically:

> Be thou a new star that to us portends
> Ends of great wonder; and be thou those ends.

Donne, Dean of St Paul's, was in many ways the outstanding figure of the English third force during this brief, illusory period. He had changed from Catholicism to Anglicanism without acquiring enmity to his old faith. Writing to his Catholic friend, Toby Matthew, he admitted men could go to heaven by different routes: 'Men go to China both by the Straits and by the Cape.' His library included many works of Catholic theology, most of them printed in Spain, and he made no bones about his ecumenicalism: 'I never fettered nor imprisoned the word Religion, not . . . immuring it in a Rome, or a Wittenberg or a Geneva; they are all virtual beams of one sun. . . . They are not so contrary as the North and South poles.' In 1619, when hopes were still high, James I sent Lord Doncaster on a peace-mission to the Palatinate and Bohemia, and Donne was senior member of the suite. At Heidelberg he preached a sermon to the Elector and the Princess Elizabeth, soon to be the 'Winter Queen' of Bohemia. The text has not survived; but we can imagine it, probably with truth, as an eloquent manifesto of the third force.

The ecumenical dream collapsed with the great Catholic victory at the White Mountain; Frederick was driven from Bohemia and his Palatinate, and his fine library was carted off to Rome; his princess spent a long exile in Holland, where scholarly remnants of the third force gathered round her. Among her later admirers, by an astonishing irony, was Descartes. Catholic, Jesuit-educated, he seems to have enrolled in the Duke of Bavaria's army in 1619 without being clear what the fighting was about, and fought on the winning side at the White Mountain without realizing that he was helping to crush a great intellectual movement. More than twenty years later he dedicated his *Principia* to Elizabeth; and in the long run Cartesian mechanics played a salient role in destroying religious institutionalism.

Meanwhile, however, the Renaissance third force, which had been about to emerge as what was later termed the Enlightenment, was thrust underground by war, persecution, witch-hunting, censorship, bigotry and priestcraft. The Counter-Reformation rolled across Germany, everywhere triumphant until Gustavus Adolphus intervened. The 1620s and 1630s were among the darkest decades in European history. James I was bitterly assailed for his failure to assist his son-in-law with Britain's force. The Venetian ambassador in London reported: 'The common prosperity depends on the success of the Palatine.' When James refused to intervene, Sarpi's friend Micanzio wrote bitterly: 'To stand looking on for doubtfulness of right and let him [the Habsburg] that is mighty grow still more mighty and be able to undermine all free states. . . . If from England there come not some helpful resolutions and that well accompanied with deed . . . the Spaniards are conquerors of Germany and have Italy at their discretion.' The liberal corridor was never constructed: Venice surrendered to the Counter-Reformation. In Holland, the Arminians were expelled or executed. In England, the attempt to erect a putative royal tyranny led to censorship, sectarian persecution and con-stitutional crisis. The opportunity for the third force to effect the religious reunification of Europe never recurred. The peace of exhaustion signed at Westphalia ended the doctrine of the prince's right to settle the religion of his subjects – and so the great age of Jesuit power – but it also froze the religious divisions of Europe, which henceforth became permanent. The seamless garment of Christendom had gone for ever.

Yet the third force remained, still waiting for the millenium of the intellectuals. At the end of 1640, Charles I of England bowed to the Long Parliament, the censorship was ended and London burst into a frenzy of political and religious excitement. Once more men thought that the 'great instauration' had come, and that Christendom was entering into the third and final reformation. The date deserves to be remembered: it was the last time men would place a renaissance of learning and a political revolution within an essentially Christian context. Milton believed the whole thing was plainly ordained by God: the ills of England, Scotland and Ireland were to be cured at the same time as a true reformation was set on foot to purge and reunite the Christian Church. Others thought the same. Among the third force survivors from the Palatinate circle was Samuel Hartlib who addressed to Parliament his *Description of the Famous Kingdome of Macaria*, a utopian scheme modelled on More and Bacon. The moment had arrived, he claimed; and he hoped the House of Commons 'will lay the corner stone of the world's happiness before the final recesse thereof'. Another Palatinate survivor, John Amos Comenius, reached liberated London in 1641 and published his *The Way of Light*, which brought the Hermetic programme up to date. He forecast 'an Art of Arts, a Science of Sciences, a Wisdom of Wisdom, a Light of Light'; this stupendous intellectual and religious breathrough was to be achieved through international cooperation, and the exchange of ideas and knowledge; there would be an invisible college, or sacred society, devoted to the common welfare of mankind.

Once again, the dawn proved illusory. The intellectual excitement generated in the heady months of the winter 1640–1 was dispelled by the Civil War, and the sectarian battles that followed it. After the 1640s, very few people believed any more in the possibility of a re-unification of Christendom and its recreation within a single Church. Indeed, the third force, and institutional religion, parted company completely. For the first time we get a disassociation between religious reform and scientific development. The Reformation and the Renaissance had been at one in thinking that the true way to God, and the secrets of knowledge, were to be rediscovered by examination of the mysteries and secrets of the past; it had been assumed that knowledge of the supernatural and the natural world was inextricably linked, that metaphysics began where physics ended, and that theology was indeed the Queen of the Sciences. These were bedrock Christian assumptions; assumptions, in fact, which even antedated Christianity, or rather had been absorbed by Christianity during the process of Hellenization which marked the triumph of Pauline doctrine.

During the twenty years 1640–60 we see the earliest challenge to the belief that knowledge was indivisible. We can observe it in the formative period in the history of the Royal Society. The Society, of course, was incorporated under Charles II at the Restoration; but its origins go back to the end of the Civil War. Indeed, it was none other than the materialization of the famous 'invisible college' so long demanded by the Christian Hermetics and third force propagandists. In origin it was undoubtedly part of a religious-scientific movement to purge Christianity and give it rebirth as part of a 'general instauration' of knowledge. We see this from what might be called the 'Palatine connection'. John Wallis, in his account of the first meetings in London in 1645, says that those taking part included 'Dr John Wilkins, afterwards Bishop of Chester, then chaplain to the Prince Elector Palatine in London', and 'Mr Theodore Haak, a German of the Palatinate, and then resident in London, who, I think, gave the first occasion and first suggested these meetings'. This group was undoubtedly the 'invisible college' referred to by Robert Boyle in letters dating from 1646–7. Later it met at Wadham College, Oxford, and moved to London in 1659, before finally attaining royal recognition, patronage and complete respectability. During its migrations and transmutations, however, the embryo Royal Society seems to have discarded its original religious context completely. Religious 'enthusiasm', attachment to a particular sect or credal confession – which might be politically acceptable one year, and illegal the next – were now seen as possible barriers to official approval, even fatal to the survival of the Society. The founder-members of the Royal Society were all sincere Christians, but they were coming to accept that institutional Christianity, with its feuds and intolerances, was an embarrassment and a barrier to scientific endeavour. Hence they decided to concentrate purely on science, and ruled that religious matters were not to be discussed at the Society's meetings. So for the first time we have a deliberate attempt to cut off science from religion, and to treat the two subjects as completely separate spheres of knowledge and lines of inquiry.

Fellows of the Royal Society, however, were not obliged to observe this dichotomy in their own studies; nor did most of them do so. Newton, the greatest of them, clung to the old connection in much of his work and interests. He was a magus, in exactly the same sense as Dr Dee, as well as a great empirical scientist. He was still searching for the one God, and the divine unity revealed in nature. He thought, for instance, that he had found his system of the universe adumbrated in Apollo's lyre, with its seven strings. The Renaissance type of thinking behind his scientific experiments led him to believe that ancient wisdom was concealed in myth, that the true philosophy behind mythology was discoverable, and that revelation was a scientific as well as a theological concept. He foresaw no future warfare between God and science; on the contrary, to him valid scientific research was, and must be, the confirmation of religious truth. Nevertheless, once religion and science were separated, as now they were, the possibility of their antagonism had to be considered. It cast a lengthening shadow as the Christian world emerged from religious warfare and began to construct a new theology on the basis of reason.

PART SIX

Faith, Reason and Unreason
(1648–1870)

THE TWO DECADES of the 1640s and 1650s form one of the great watersheds in the history of Christianity. Up to this point, the ideal of the total Christian society, embracing every aspect of man's existence, still seemed attainable; and masses of men were prepared to wage war, to massacre, hang and burn to realize it. Christendom was split, but each of the rival parties saw their system of belief ultimately becoming coextensive with humanity, and themselves bidden by divine command to hasten the process at whatever cost. They were still, in a sense, mesmerized by the Augustinian vision conceived over 1200 years before. With the 1650s we get a change: war and suffering are replaced by exhaustion and doubt, and the European mind seems to sicken of the unattainable objective, and focus on more mundane ends. There is a huge, long-delayed and grateful relaxation of the spirit, a dousing of angry embers.

Anthony Wood, writing his diary from an Oxford coign of vantage, gives a sardonic picture of the university moving back, in the years 1660–1, from republican commonwealth to parliamentary monarchy, from the dominance of Calvinism to Anglican conformity. A century before, the fires had burned fiercely outside St John's College. Now the atmosphere is low-key, a mere heightening of the customary struggle for places, fellowships and influence, the raucous exchange of abuse and insult, low japes and ribaldry. The age of the martyrs had ended, for a second time. Wood relates what happened when the triumphant Anglicans brought back vestments to the cathedral services. 'On the night of 21 January 1661, some varlets of Christ Church' took all the new surplices issued to the choristers, and threw them 'in a common privy house belonging to Peckwater Quadrangle, and there with long sticks [did] thrust them downe into the excrements. The next day, being discovered, they were taken up and washed; but so enraged were the deane and canons, that they publickly protested, if they knew the person or persons that had committed that act, they not onlie would lose their places and be expelled the Universitie but also have their eares cut off in the market place. The Presbyterians were wonderfully pleased at this action, laughed hartily among themselves, and some in my hearing have protested that if they knew the person that did this heroick act they would convey to him an encouraging gratuity.'

Of course the instinct to insist on doctrinal purity, and indeed to persecute, was by no means dead. The official English 1662 Prayer Book offered few concessions to Puritan scruples; the Act of Uniformity emphasized the importance of the monarchical bishop; and the 'Clarendon Code' made life difficult for anyone who refused to accept the statutory brand of Christianity. Difficult; but not impossible. Anglicanism had, in effect, abandoned the effort to include all, and had accepted the notion of a dissenting body in its midst. The search for unity had ended in failure, and a plural society came into being. The drift from fanaticism was slow, but it was steady and ultimately irresistible. A grudging but increasing respect began to be paid to private opinion in religious matters. It was no longer contended, even in theory, that the prince determined all. The Peace of Westphalia, 1648, really marked the end of *cuius regio, eius religio*. When, in the 1680s, James II tried to steer England back to his Catholic faith, he was obliged to depart and was replaced by a parliamentary sovereign.

The Glorious Revolution of 1688 plunged the Anglican Church into total ideological confusion, from which pure utilitarianism was the only possible egress. Seven bishops had defied James II, thus abandoning their doctrine of non-resistance to a king divinely appointed *de juro*. But five of them then refused to swear allegiance to a *de facto* monarch appointed by Parliament. Where was the consistency? Most Anglicans chose to be pragmatic; Archbishop Sharp of York dismissed the non-jurors with contempt: 'What an unaccountable Humour it is to make a Rent and Schism in the Church, upon a mere Point of State.' Thus there followed the first Toleration Act; and, thereafter, when the crown was settled, simply for constitutional convenience, on a reliably Protestant monarch, the idea of divine right, and of the pontifical king, was tacitly and totally abandoned. The 1660s had seen the first hint of divorce between religion and science; now religion and politics began to drift apart. In 1718 Parliament repealed the Schism Act and the Occasional Conformity Act; the Act for Quieting and Establishing Corporations allowed Dissenters to hold certain offices; and, from 1727, annual Indemnity Acts relieved the sectarians of most of their disabilities. It was, as a result, no longer possible to enforce by law the attendance of anyone at church on Sunday; so in England Christianity ceased to be a compulsory society. And, in the wake of the Dissenters, the Catholics slowly crept out into the open again.

Thus, at last, the Erasmian third force began to infuse society, and transform it from within. There were no spectacular victories – just a continual retreat from fire and sword. But with it, necessarily, there was a reconstruction of the intellectual and social basis of Christian belief. The idea of the total, compulsory society of faith had been a combination of the Augustinian system of Christian pessimism with the demands of the Dark Age agrarian economy of western Europe, as worked out by Gregory the Great, St Benedict, and their successors. The abandonment of compulsion and the emergence of a commercial economy rendered the old system obsolete, as Erasmus had foreseen, and made it necessary to evolve a new one, on the lines he had adumbrated. The century of religious warfare, witch-hunting and persecution merely imposed delay on its general acceptance: its roots were already firmly established in the Renaissance. What had seemed challenging, even dangerous, in the sixteenth century, began rapidly to acquire, after the watershed of 1640–60, the air of the prevailing wisdom. A case in point is Sir Walter Ralegh, reported to the Privy Council in the 1590s for challenging a clergyman, in a private conversation after dinner, to produce a rational definition of the word 'soul'. It was this sort of thing which led to the charge that he was an atheist. What Ralegh was trying to do, of course, was to reconcile religion with reason, not in the metaphysical terms of a schoolman like Aquinas, but in the real world of Renaissance knowledge and discovery. To Ralegh, the true evidence of God was in nature itself which, as he pointed out in his *History of the World,* spectacularly reinforced the revelation of the scriptures:

'By his own word, and by this Visible world, is God perceived of men, which is also the understood language of the Almighty, vouchsafed to all his creatures, whose Hieroglyphical Characters are the unnumbered stars, the sun and moon, written on these large volumes of the firmament: written also on the earth and the seas, by the letters of all those living creatures, and plants, which inhabit and reside therein'.

This splendid metaphor of the natural world, governed by laws ascertainable to reason, acting as a permanent if silent witness to God's Christian truth, established itself firmly in the minds of many western intellectuals by the end of the seventeenth century as the basis of a new system of apologetics. In England, such men were often members of the Royal Society. They did not bring their religious debates into science, but they were eager to select from science evidence for religion. Many were in orders, steering a sensible middle road between strict Calvinism and the High Church. In university circles, especially at Cambridge, they were characterized as neo-Platonists; within the Church, as Latitudinarians. Gilbert Burnet, one of them, sums up the Cambridge group thus:

'They declared against superstition on the one hand and enthusiasm on the other. They loved the constitution of the church and the liturgy, and could live well under them. But they did not think it unlawful to live under another form. They wished that things might have been carried out with more moderation. And they continued to keep a good correspondence with those who had differed from them in opinion, and allowed a great freedom in philosophy and in divinity.'

For these men, educated, urbane, up-to-date, constitutionalists in politics, religion was common sense. The days of persecution were over. All men would come to God in the natural way, if only the shouting and killing stopped, and the voice of reason was heard. Reason reinforced faith. The best ally of theology was natural philosophy. God could be seen in and through his creation. As John Smith put it: 'God made the universe and all the creatures contained therein as so many glasses wherein he might reflect his own glory ...

in this outward world we may read the lovely characters of Divine goodness, power and wisdom.' Joseph Glanvill, Rector of Bath, thought that 'the power and wisdom and goodness of the Creator is displayed in the admirable order and workmanship of the creation.' God's existence could thus be de-monstrated; they constructed a reasonable pattern of belief, then showed that scriptural revelation coincided with it – for instance Edward Stillingfleet, Bishop of Worcester, proved that Mosaic history conformed to the canons of reason. Like Erasmus, they thought that the essential beliefs were few and simple – reason was the corrective to Romanist superstition and the over-confident dogmatism of the Presbyterians. Like Erasmus, they were interested in morals, not theology. Tillotson, Archbishop of Canterbury, insisted 'the great design of Christianity was the reforming of men's natures.' There was a strong emphasis on ethics, duty, good works, but all to be conducted in a moderate spirit. Fanaticism in any shape or form was the enemy. Knowledge was the friend. Christian belief would be illuminated by the fresh insights of new discoveries, provided scientists were reverent. Robert Boyle and Isaac Newton agreed that nature showed God's order and beauty; and John Ray argued in the same manner from the evidence he found in the structure of plants and animals.

It was agreed that God had created the universe in a thoroughly scientific and rational manner, endowing it with immutable laws. What, then, did God do today? This was more difficult. Both Calvinists and Catholics thought God was constantly interfering, the former in pursuit of his predestined plans of salvation and damnation, the latter in response to prayer and the solicitations of the celestial court. But the Christian rationalists did not relish the idea of an active God: it led to superstition and 'enthusiasm'. They preferred the image of the clock: God made it, and wound it up; then left it to operate. Newton argued that God kept the mechanism in good repair, and prevented the occurrence of spatial catastrophe. Boyle thought God stopped the world from disintegrating. All agreed that scientific knowledge was a powerful agent against atheism; Boyle, in fact, endowed a lectureship for the defence of Christian truth, and its first holder, Richard Bentley, used Newtonian physics to confute those who argued there was no God.

The Augustinian system had stood for over a thousand years. How strong was its replacement? Let us look a little more closely at its most plausible and influential interpreter, John Locke. Locke was in many ways well suited to design a new ethical philosophy for an emergent capitalist system. He was born in 1632 in Somerset. Both his parents were middle-class Puritans, but he was young enough to have escaped the great age of 'conversion' and frenzy. His father was something of a lawyer, a JP, and a trader; his mother came from trade too. Locke was a senior student at Christ Church (1658), was associated with Robert Boyle in his chemical work, qualified as a physician, was elected to the Royal Society, and got into politics and public life as personal doctor to the Earl of Shaftesbury – he saved the Earl's life by using a silver tube to drain his infected liver. Locke shared Shaftesbury's work at the Department of Plantations and Trade, and later went into exile with him in Holland. He returned after the Glorious Revolution in 1688, and it was during the next six years or so that he published all his major works. He spent his last years (he died in 1704) living in a Tudor manor house near Epping Forest, as the guest of Lady Masham, wife of a parliamentary baronet; there he had over 5,000 books. He said that in his youth he read romances, and he certainly wrote some love-letters. But he was a very prosaic soul indeed, or at any rate became one. Cautious, money-loving, unadventurous, calculating, unemotional, sharp and legalistic, he was not interested in religious idealism at all. Ecstasy was not for him. He wanted, as it were, a solid, commercial contract with the Deity, a spiritual insurance-policy with no loopholes, a system which worked in practice, and would stand up to persistent probing by a hardheaded gentleman like himself.

Within these emotional limitations, Locke was an extremely powerful personality, and in some respects ideally fitted to construct a solid basis for belief. In Christianity, above all other religious systems, there is an absolute connection between faith and truth. The two are identified, and any interference with the truth is immoral. This was the message of St Paul, and it was something that Locke not only understood but totally identified himself with, even though he lacked Paul's passion. Locke thought traditional theology worthless because it was not primarily concerned with truth. He put the point nobly in his *Essay Concerning Human Understanding* (1691):

> 'He that would seriously set upon the search for truth ought, in the first place, to prepare his mind with a love of it. For he that loves it not, will not take much pains to get it; nor be much concerned when he misses it. There is nobody in the commonwealth of learning who does not profess himself a lover of truth; and there is not a rational creature that would not take it amiss to be thought otherwise of. And yet, for all this, one may truly say, there are very few lovers of truth for truth's sake, even among those who persuade themselves that they are so. How a man may know whether he be so in earnest is worth inquiry: and I think there is this one unerring mark of it, viz, the not entertaining any proposition with greater assurance than the proofs it is built upon will warrant. Whoever goes beyond this measure of assent, it is plain, receives not truth in the love of it; loves not truth for truth's sake, but for some other by-end.'

This was, indeed, a strict methodology. Locke was saying that Christianity ought to be subjected to the same rigorous tests as any scientific proposition; and this is what, on the whole, he attempted to do in *The Reasonableness of Christianity* (1695). He did not see the existence of God, or rather the need to demonstrate it. as the real problem – in Locke's day, hardly anyone at all denied God's existence altogether. He thought Newtonian physics made the existence of a creator inevitable. Purely material causes 'could never produce that order, harmony and beauty which are to be found in nature. And he adds: 'The visible marks of extraordinary wisdom and power appear so plainly in all the works of the creation that a rational creature who will but seriously reflect on them cannot miss the discovery of a deity.' However, to Locke the argument from design is not the clinching proof, which rests on causation. A mind, or at any rate the human mind, cannot be produced by a purely material cause. Hence the cause of our existence must be a 'cogitative being'. And, since this being must be adequate to produce all the perfections which can ever after exist, it must include infinite wisdom and power.

Locke found no difficulty in proving God exists by reason; but he thought it was the only doctrinal truth which could be so demonstrated. Reason could not prove the soul was immortal, for instance; all the rest of Christian belief thus rested on revelation. But the historical fact of revelation was itself reasonable. 'Reason is natural revelation, whereby the eternal Father of light and fountain of all knowledge communicates to mankind that portion of truth which he has laid within the reach of their natural faculties: revelation is natural reason enlarged by a new set of discoveries communicated by God immediately, which reason vouches the truth of by the testimony and proofs that it comes from God. So that he who takes away reason to make way for revelation puts out the light of both.' However, only reason provides knowledge – revelation nothing more than probable belief. If a truth is disclosed both by reason and revelation, reason therefore prevails: and if reason and a claim to revelation conflict, reason again prevails and the claim to revelation has to be rejected. For if we do not trust reason here, we cannot trust her anywhere, and this would make impossible the validation and interpretation of scriptural doctrines. On the other hand, revelation can provide truths which unaided reason cannot; and if revelation indicates a doctrine which reason itself would deem improbable (but no more), then revelation should be trusted.

Where, then, does this process of validation leave Christian belief? At what might be termed the irreducible Erasmian minimum. Locke distinguishes between essential and non-essential doctrine. In *The Reasonableness of Christianity*, he set out to identify the essential, and concluded that the only belief necessary and sufficient for salvation was that Jesus is the Messiah, and the Son of God. It might be argued that Acts and the Epistles require more: but Locke quoted St John's Gospel, generally believed to be later than them, as confirming the other gospels in requiring only the one central belief. It is Locke's demonstration that only this one dogma is necessary which confirms, at least to his satisfaction, that Christianity is a religion of reason and common sense, because the simplicity makes it workable. The fact that Jesus is the Son of God is 'a plain, intelligible proposition; and the all-merciful God seems here to have consulted the poor of this world and the bulk of mankind. These are articles that the labouring and illiterate man may comprehend. This is a religion suited to vulgar capacities and the state of mankind in this world destined to labour and travail. The writers and wranglers in religion fill it with niceties and dress it up with notions which they make necessary and fundamental parts of it, as if there were no way into the church but through the Academy or the Lyceum. The greatest part of mankind have not leisure for learning and logic and superfine distinctions in the schools.'

Here, indeed, was an argument Erasmus, who wanted the ploughboy to sing the psalms as he worked, would have relished. And of course it demolished at a stroke the opponents of the Latitudinarians on either side of the spectrum. Naturally, as an Anglican, Locke does not deny other doctrines. In his *Vindication* and *Second Vindication*, he defended himself against the charge that he was a Deist or a Unitarian. But he insisted that, once you departed from his definition of what was absolutely essential, you had to set up on your own, without the assistance of reason, as 'arbiter and dispenser' – and so you produced your own set of doctrines, typical of all systems 'set up by particular men or parties as the just measure of every man's faith'.

It was, Locke argued, precisely because men had departed from his minimum definition based on reason that Europe had sunk into confusion, division and religious war. As a younger man, he had used this as an argument for enforcement of uniformity. The exercise of private judgment in religious affairs leads to 'readiness for violence and cruelty' and 'grows into dangerous factions and tumults', especially 'among a people that are ready to conclude God dishonoured upon every small deviation from that way of his worship which either education or interest has made sacred to them, and that therefore they ought to vindicate the cause of God with swords in their hands.' But in the next thirty years he changed his mind completely. He would never grant toleration to Catholics, since he saw them as a political and military threat to the State which had nothing to do with religious truth; nor would he countenance atheists, since they assaulted society: 'The taking away of God, though but even in thought, dissolves all.' But across a wide spectrum of belief he found that, in practice, it was more sensible to allow people their heads. Persecution did not work – witness the Clarendon Code. It drove people, often valuable people, to emigrate, as he discovered from his experience at Plantations. During his exile he was much impressed by the Dutch Armenians. Indeed, Locke's life and philosophy illustrate the eventual power wielded by the liberal (and often persecuted) wings of all the three main groups, Catholic, Lutheran and Calvinist – it was the coalescing of their experience, common sense and brain-power which produced the Enlightenment.

Once Locke had abandoned compulsion, he fell naturally into an Erasmian attitude, to which he brought powerful commercial-type arguments characteristic of his own approach. 'I cannot be saved by a religion I distrust.' 'The care of each man's salvation belongs only to himself.' Persecution can only succeed with men of weak will; and then its effect is hypocrisy. A Church is a voluntary association, and its rules must be made 'by the members themselves, or by those whom the members have authorised thereunto'. The only sanction is expulsion. Enforced belief cannot be part of the civil contract of government, since no man can consent to abandon the care of his own salvation to another. Force means war, whereas 'moderate governments are everywhere quiet, everywhere safe.' Moreover, the points at issue are nearly always minor ones, properly considered: 'For the most part they are such frivolous things as these . . . which breed implacable enmity among Christian brethren who are all agreed in the substantial and truly fundamental part of religion.' Moreover, vice was a much greater evil than dissent – it was the elimination of immorality that should preoccupy the Church.

Here, exactly like Erasmus, Locke gets to the heart of the problem. What matters is not so much what a man believes, as what he does. Christianity is about morals, not dogma. What made Locke such an immediately influential thinker – not only in England, but throughout the civilized world – was that he avoided abstraction by employing the language and mentality of the commercial contract. Life, including religious life, was a series of bargains. If you got the moral arithmetic right, the result would be beneficial for all concerned, you, God, your neighbour. Just as reason and faith were identical, so, ultimately, was goodness and self-interest. Locke was concerned to show that Christianity made sense just as much in this world as in the next; and he could do this best by showing that Christian morals were essential to happiness. His religious system is thus essentially an ethical one. And his ethics are practical, having been worked out quite prosaically from his own experience. Locke was himself undoubtedly much influenced by that harsh and rigorous thinker, Thomas Hobbes. Hobbes was an atheist and had contrived to make his philosophy unacceptable to almost any category of opinion, religious or political. Thus the cautious Locke would not acknow-ledge him; nonetheless, Hobbes penetrated Locke's ethical thinking, and in Locke's unpublished manuscripts is a statement of personal ethics which perfectly reflects Hobbes's hedonism: 'I will make it my business to seek satisfaction and delight and avoid uneasiness and disquiet . . . But here I must have a care if I mistake not, for if I prefer a short pleasure to a lasting one, it is plain I cross my own happiness.' Again: 'Drinking, gaming and vicious delights will do me this mischief, not only by wasting my time but by a positive efficacy endanger my health, impair my parts, imprint bad habits, lessen my esteem and leave a constant lasting torment on my conscience.'

To Locke, then, morality was merely the long-term and prudent pursuit of happiness. The Christian, like a good merchant, forwent present pleasure to invest in more substantial, if delayed, rewards. He admitted that not all Christian commands could be demonstrated by reason: 'It is too hard a task for unassisted reason to establish morality in all its parts'; and even if it did, 'mankind might hearken to it, or reject it, as they pleased; or as it suited their interest, passions, principles or humours. They were under no obligation.' Therefore, says Locke: 'Such a law of morality Jesus Christ hath given us in the New Testament by revelation . . . Here morality has a sure standard that revelation vouches, and reason cannot gainsay nor question; but both together witness to come from God the great law-maker.' Why should men, motivated by love of pleasure and fear of pain, obey these commands of God? 'Because God, who has the power of eternal life and death, requires it of us.' The true basis of morality can only be 'the will and law of a God who sees men in the dark, has in his hands rewards and punishments, and power enough to call to account the proudest offender'. We kept the law because it was our interest to do so, in the long run. Conscience was no guide, being 'nothing but our own opinion or judgment'. Hence pagan philosophies, however admirable, were ineffective. Men guided their actions in practice according to whether 'they are likely to procure them happiness or misery from the hands of the Almighty.' Ethics would not work without Heaven and Hell; it was their existence which made Christianity uniquely effective as a religion:

> 'The [pagan] philosophers indeed showed the beauty of virtue . . . but leaving her unendowed, very few were willing to espouse her. The generality could not refuse her their esteem and commendation, but still turned their back on her, and foresook her as a match not for their turn. But now there being put into the scales on her side "an exceeding and immortal weight of glory", interest is come about to her, and virtue is now visibly the most enriching purchase and by much the best bargain.'

With the view of Heaven and Hell before their eyes, sensible men rejected short-term pleasures and vices, and invested in eternity. 'Upon this foundation and upon this only, morality stands firm and may defy all competition.' Thus Locke completed his religious system.

We may be shocked by Locke's brutal use of mercantile logic, and by his Stock Exchange terminology. There is no evidence that anyone was at the time. Granted the circumstances of his age, Locke argued with impressive skill. Seldom in its history has Christianity been presented more effectively to large numbers of people. He not only brought Christianity up to date, he made it the religion of the future, since capitalism, as a visible and embracing form of society, was only in its infancy; rational, utilitarian Christianity would grow with it. After the watershed of 1640–60, indeed, there had been a real risk that the reaction from the religious wars, and the enforced abandonment of many of the objects and assumptions on which they had been fought, would lead to a rapid displacement of the Christian faith itself. Locke's work, which crystallized and encapsulated a mood and provided it with a simple, clear argument, made it possible to dismiss the errors of the past and start afresh; and thereby it prolonged the life of Christianity, as the mass religion of the advanced societies, for more than two centuries.

But this very considerable achievement was bought at a price. Or, rather, several prices. Locke had cut dogma to the absolute minimum. In one way it was the absence of a heavy theological superstructure, with its inherent tendency to extend itself indefinitely, which made Locke's system so acceptable. But in another way it was a weakness. It could, so easily, lose its Christian character completely and topple over into mere deism. For some it did so. The risk, indeed, had existed before Locke. Lord Herbert of Cherbury, brother of the Anglican divine and poet, George Herbert, had reduced Christianity to five simple propositions; and this contraction was tightened by Charles Blount, who treated most of Revelation as superstition and Christ as little better than a pagan wonder-worker. Latitudinarian clergymen, of course, did not go so far. But the sermons of men like Tillotson stressed ethics and duties, and pleaded reason, while ignoring theology almost altogether. Quite early in the eighteenth century, thanks largely to Locke, what were essentially non-Christian forms of belief, attached, of course, to rationalized ethical systems, began to inch towards the area of toleration and res-pectability; and the process tended to go much faster in France (as we shall see shortly) where there was no roomy Anglican hotel to accommodate religious travellers.

Then again, Locke's system, as a working ethic for a modern society, was made absolutely dependent on rewards and punishments. Supposing belief in the rewards and punishments waned, as it was already doing in other departments of theology? The insistence on reason made this interpretation of eternity particularly vulnerable. The concept of Heaven could not easily be subjected to rational attack simply because theologians had never been able to define it in a concrete manner. On the other hand, because it lacked definition, it lacked real plausibility in the rewards-and-punishment mechanism. And then, supposing eternity itself were denied? Within a generation of Locke's death, this is precisely what some thinkers were doing, and getting away with it. David Hume was outstanding: he was not unique.

The real danger, however, came from the use of rational argument to undermine the effectiveness of Hell as a deterrent. The carefully imagined vision of Hell had been a very early Christian accretion, and it had always been regarded by the authorities as an essential element in maintaining Christian morality. Even those thinkers who were sceptical about the part played by physical punishment in Hell, or even about its existence, thought it right that the generality of believers should be encouraged to fear it. Origen, as we have already noted, thought it possible that all might ultimately be saved, but added (in *Contra Celsum*) that 'to go beyond this is not expedient for the sake of those who are with difficulty restrained, even by fear of eternal punishment, from plunging into any degree of wickedness, and into the floods of evil that result from sin'. The Church later ruled that Origen's scepticism was itself mistaken, the Council of Constantinople (553) insisting: 'Whoever says or thinks that the punishment of demons and the wicked will not be eternal, that it will have an end . . . let him be anathema.' From Augustine to the Reformation, only the ninth-century Irishman, John Scotus Erigena, pos-itively denied an eternal, or even material Hell, substituting the misery inflicted by the pangs of conscience; and he did not think his view should be taught pastorally. Among a few theologians there was the theory of double truth, which allowed a more qualified attitude in private but insisted on the full horrors for public consumption. Luther himself held that the doctrine of Hell should not be discussed with intellectuals, but only with persons of simple, deep piety. This was, or appeared, a confession of weakness; but the Lutheran Augsburg Confession (1530), article 17, requires orthodox belief in Hell: 'Christ . . . will give pious men eternal life and perpetual joy, but he will condemn impious men and devils to torture without end. They condemn the Anabaptists, who hold that there will be an end to the punishment of the damned and of devils.' The official Anglican position was broadly similar (though the Augsburg statement, article 42 of the 1552 collection, does not figure in the Elizabethan Thirty-Nine Articles).

In practice, then, the theologians had insisted on Hell, and done their utmost to bring it home to Christians by portraying it in the most vivid possible terms. Pastoral writers were much more specific about Hell than about Heaven; they wrote of it as though they had been there. The three most influential medieval teachers, Augustine, Peter Lombard and Aquinas, all insisted that the pains of Hell were physical as well as mental and spiritual, and that real fire played a part in them. The general theory was that Hell included any horrible pain that the human imagination could conceive of, plus an infinite variety of others. Hence writers felt at liberty to impress their public by inventing torments. Jerome said that Hell was like a huge winepress. Augustine said it was peopled by ferocious flesh-eating animals, which tore humans to bits slowly and painfully, and were themselves undamaged by the fires. St Stephanus Grandinotensis evaded the problem of imagination by saying that the pains of Hell were so unspeakable that if a human so much as conceived of them, he would instantly die of terror. Eadmer listed fourteen specific pains endured in Hell. Adam Scotus said that those who practised usury would be boiled in molten gold. Many writers refer to a continuous beating with red-hot brazen hammers. Richard Rolle, in *Stimulus Conscientiae*, argued that the damned tear and eat their own flesh, drink the gall of dragons and the venom of asps, and suck the heads of adders; their bedding and clothing consisted of 'horrible venomous vermin'. Another expert thought the damned would be nourished with green bread, washed down with a mere eggcupful of stinking water. German writers (and painters) were the most energetic in depicting the physical torments. They argued that a hundred million damned souls would be squeezed into every square mile of Hell, and would thus be treated 'like grapes in a press, bricks in a furnace, salt sediment in a barrel of pickled fish, and sheep in a slaughterhouse'. The French favoured more subtle psychological pains. Bridaine said that when the guilty asked, 'What is the time?' a voice answered, 'Eternity'. There were 'no clocks in Hell, but an eternal ticking'.

Most Christian writers stressed the pain of loss; and Aquinas, in addition, thought that the enjoyment occasioned by witnessing the sufferings of the damned was one of the pleasures of Heaven: *'Sancti de p.oenis impiorum gaudebunt.'* This displeasing notion was advanced and defended with great tenacity over several centuries, and was one of the points orthodox Calvinists and Catholics had in common. Scots preachers, in particular, thought the pains of Hell a matter for satisfaction. Thomas Boston thundered: 'God shall not pity them but laugh at their calamity. The righteous company in heaven shall rejoice in the execution of God's judgment, and shall sing while the smoke riseth up for ever.' Another Scots congregation was assured that the theological needs of the Atonement meant that the Son bore infinite pain 'from the vindictive anger of God . . . pure wrath, nothing but wrath: the Father loved to see Him die.' Some, at least, of Locke's contemporaries went so far as to argue that the damned may have been created in the first place to make heavenly bliss complete. Thus William King speculated in *De Origine Mali* (1702): 'The goodness as well as the happiness of the blessed will be confirmed and advanced by reflections naturally arising from this view of the misery which some shall undergo, which seems to be a good reason for the creation of those beings who shall be finally miserable, and for the continuation of them in their miserable existence.'

However, with the eighteenth century, this huge superstructure of imaginative awfulness tended to collapse under its own weight. Scientific knowledge made much of the mechanism of Hell-fire seem wildly implausible, and cast doubt on any effort to visualize God's punishments. 'Reasonable Christianity' needed Hell as the great deterrent, but it found the idea of a ferociously vindictive God unreasonable; Hell remained, but it had to be, as it were, cooled down a little. With sophisticated audiences, preachers tended to protect themselves from possible ridicule by avoiding the topic. Thus Alexander Pope used to tell the story of the dean, preaching at Whitehall, who said that if his congregation did not 'vouchsafe to give their lives a new turn, they must certainly go to a place which he did not think it fit to name in that courtly audience.' And certainly, some Latitudinarians at least found it unacceptably unethical that eternal punishment should be visited on those whose faults had necessarily been committed in time. It was true that 'eternal' was a scriptural threat; but Tillotson, preaching before Queen Anne, argued that God would not be breaking his word if he failed to carry out his promise of perpetual punishment, since vengeance, though justified in this case, was not compulsory. Eternal Hell-fire was for the lower classes, and to some extent for the middle ones. In *De Statu Mortuorum* (1720), Thomas Burnet argued strongly against eternal punishment, but insisted that only the traditional doctrine ought to be divulged to ordinary people. This would have been heresy north of the Tweed, or, for that matter, across the Channel. Catholics were taught that those who doubted Hell were themselves destined for it. A characteristic statement was Dom Sinsart in *Défence du dogme catholique sur l'éternité des peines* (1748): '. . . the system which limits the punishment in the after life has been conceived only by vicious and corrupt hearts . . . a good conscience has no motive for inventing quibbles about a matter which does not concern it. It is therefore to crime, stubborn crime, that this opinion owes its existence.' Many Anglicans held this view; but they were confronted with the problem of divines who rejected it, at least in private; and the effort to maintain a double standard gradually foundered. By mid century there was wide agreement that belief in Hell was less firm than hitherto, and that the damping down of Hell-fire was attended with perceptible social consequences. Preaching to Oxford University in 1741, William Dodwell lamented: 'It is but all too visible that since men have learned to wear off the Apprehension of Eternal Punishment, the Progress of Impiety and Immorality among us has been very considerable.' The authorities considered Hell to be the most effective deterrent against crime; as fear of it declined, therefore, judges and Parliament agreed that the statutory penalties must be increased. During the eighteenth century and well into the nineteenth, a series of Acts, extending capital punishment to cover over 300 offences, tried to repair the yawning gaps in Locke's system of ethical enforcement.

However, the chief defect of rational Christianity was that it made no appeal to the emotions. It offered no incentive other than enlightened self-interest. The element of sacrifice and abnegation was eliminated. Morality was presented simply as a shrewd bargain. As Tillotson put it, 'Now these two things must make our duty very easy: a considerable reward in hand, and not only the hopes but the assurance of a far greater recompense hereafter.' The whole thing could be worked out and calculated. Conscience had no role to play, since it was merely subjective opinion. Thus the element of personal responsibility was scrapped, and all a man needed to be saved was to stick to the rules. Now this was to sacrifice the whole point of the Reformation and to return, in effect, to the mechanical Christianity of canon law. And mechanical Christianity necessarily produced a corrupt Church, led by a secular-minded clergy. This is precisely what happened in the eighteenth century. In their anxiety to avoid fanaticism of any kind, the rational Christians tended to depersonalize religion, and to emphasize its forms and institutions at the expense of its spirit. In these circumstances, a state Church is bound to become corrupt. As in the Middle Ages, its bishops tended to be seen, and to see themselves, as government servants rather than sacramental ministers, and as financially, rather than spiritually, privileged. The process went furthest in Lutheran Germany, above all in Prussia, where the Church possessed virtually no independent rights, and the ruler had absolute powers over all forms of religious activity. The system evolved in the reigns of Frederick William I and Frederick the Great, and was finally codified in a law of the Prussian Landrecht of 1794. The pastor became a kind of civil servant, who registered births, collected statistics, appointed midwives, published official decrees from the pulpit, was the chairman of the local court, and an official recruiting-sergeant for the army. In England the situation was a good deal better, since in most cases clerical offices were freeholds. On the other hand, higher clerical patronage was entirely in the hands of the government, and the bishops became an important element in the ministerial control of Parliament.

It was, above all, Sir Robert Walpole who created the party bishop. He had a special expression for a prelate who could be brought to serve his ends: 'He is mortal.' In a letter to the Duke of Newcastle, 6 September 1723, he described how he made Edmund Gibson, whom he had promoted to be Bishop of London, the Whig government's adviser on ecclesiastical patronage:

> 'At first he was all *nolo episcopari*. Before we parted, I perceived upon second thoughts he began to relish it, and the next morning, *ex mero motu*, he came to me, talked comically, is a mortal man, wants to be ravished, and desired me expressly to write to my Lord Townshend to prevent the King's coming to any resolution about the disposal of the Clerks of the Closet's and Lord Almoner's places. We grow well acquainted. He must be pope, and would as willingly be *our* pope as anybody's.'

Bishops often decided the vote in the House of Lords; Walpole could usually count on twenty-four out of twenty-six of them. For government had the power of translation and salaries ranged from £450 a year for Bristol up to £7,000 for Canterbury. Thus bishops were made to earn their keep. Benjamin Hoadley was the son of a Norwich schoolmaster, and so crippled that he could only preach on his knees; but Whig subservience assured him of a steady rise. In the Lords he could be relied upon for even the most disagreeable tasks, such as attacking anti-corruption bills, and Walpole used him as a pamphleteer on secular as well as Church matters. He was kept so busy by the government that he never visited Bangor, though he was its bishop for six years; thereafter he was translated to Hereford, Salisbury and Winchester, the last worth £5,000 a year. He was the favourite object of abuse for clerical Tories: 'Deist Egyptian! A rebel against the Church! A vile republican! An apostate of his own order! The scorn and ridicule of the whole kingdom!'

Among the lesser clergy, stipends varied wildly. There were 5,500 livings worth less than £50 a year, of which 1,200 were less than £20; curates, of whom there were multitudes, could not expect to earn more than £30. Hence the upper classes were now reluctant to enter the Church. The Bishop of Killala pointed out that this limited the value of ecclesiastical patronage, and he urged: 'The only remedy to which is by giving extraordinary encouragements to persons of birth and interest whenever they seek preferment, which will encourage others of the same quality to come into the church and may thereby render ecclesiastical preferments of the same use to their Majesties with civil employments.' It was not just votes in the Lords: cathedral chapters often turned the scales in borough elections, and clergymen were widely used to organize local opinion. The Duke of Newcastle's election agent in Sussex was the Reverend James Baker; so keen was he to proselytize (on behalf of the Whigs, not Christianity) that he interrupted a cricket match at Lewes and was nearly mobbed by the spectators. Archbishop Secker of Canterbury maintained that 'the distinguishing mark of the present age' was 'an open and professed disregard of religion' reflected in 'dissoluteness and contempt of principle in the higher part of the world,' and 'profligate intemperance and fearlessness of committing crimes in the lower'. He claimed that 'Christianity is now railed at and ridiculed with very little reserve, and its teaching without any at all.' But who was Secker to talk? His was a purely political appointment; Horace Walpole says he had earlier been an atheist. His fellow-metropolitan John Gilbert, promoted to York the year before (1757), was no better advertisement for the bench. 'Gilbert,' wrote Walpole, 'was composed of that common mixture, ignorance, meanness and arrogance . . . On the news of [his] promotion, they rung the bells at York backwards, in detestation of him. He opened a great table there, and in six months they thought him the most Christian prelate that had ever sat in that see.' Walpole sums up the age neatly: 'There were no religious combustibles in the temper of the times. Popery and Protestantism seemed at a stand. The modes of Christianity were exhausted and could not furnish novelty enough to fix attention.'

In England the Establishment clergy virtually ceased to be a proselytizing or even an active force, though it remained a powerful social one. The many verbatim conversations recorded in James Boswell's diaries reveal the better sort of clergyman as learned, rather than pious. They were, in fact, encouraged to take a polite interest in the arts and sciences to fill the time. In 1785, for instance, William Paley, Archdeacon of Carlisle, gave a Charge entitled 'Amusements Suitable to the Clergy', based on the premise that 'the life of a clergyman . . . does not supply sufficient encouragements to the time and thoughts of an active mind.' He recommended natural history, botany, electrical experiments, the use of a microscope, chemistry, the measurement of mountains, meteorology and, above all, astronomy, 'the most proper of all recreations to a clergyman'. With these pursuits, 'there is no man of liberal education who need be at a loss to know what to do with his time.'

In Scotland, the collapse of fanaticism was long delayed, but then came (at least in the big cities) quite abruptly in the mid eighteenth-century. An index of it is the attitude to the theatre, once defined by the General Assembly of the Church of Scotland as 'the actual temple of the Devil, where he frequently appeared clothed in a corporeal substance and possessed the spectators, whom he held as his worshippers'. First, English players made their appearance. Then, in the 1740s, Edinburgh acquired a permanent theatre, disguised as a concert hall. In 1756, *The Tragedy of Douglas*, actually written by a clergyman, was put on, and it was attended by the leading moderate, the Reverend Alexander Carlyle. Carlyle was publicly rebuked by the General Assembly, and the unfortunate minister of Liberton, also present, was prosecuted by the Edinburgh Presbytery. He answered that 'he owned the charge, but pleaded by way of alleviation that he had gone to the playhouse only once and endeavoured to conceal himself in a corner to avoid giving offence.' But by 1784, when Mrs Siddons appeared in Edinburgh, the General

Assembly altered its timetable to give delegates the chance to go to a matinée. Clergymen led the Scottish Enlightenment, and Carlyle was able to claim in his *Autobiography*: 'Who has written the best histories, ancient and modern? It has been a clergyman of this church. Who has written the best system of rhetoric, and exemplified it by his own orations? A clergyman of this church. Who wrote a tragedy that has been deemed perfect? A clergyman of this church. Who was the most profound mathematician of the age he lived in? A clergyman of this church . . .' The claim was to secular, not spiritual, excellence.

On the Continent, Catholicism, the pattern set by France, made its way essentially to the same destination, though by a more devious and complicated route. After Westphalia, Spain ceased to count, and until 1815 France determined the course of Roman orthodoxy. Now the French Church was a peculiar case. It had not, like Spain, undergone a pre-Reformation renewal. On the other hand, it was Gallican, not papist. It had, by concordat, achieved a degree of independence which Henry VIII and England seized unilaterally. Thus the reform movement in France had never been buttressed by the salient force of xenophobia and nationalism, and that was the principal reason why it had never become the majority. Instead, the essential conflict was fought out in the seventeenth century within the French Catholic Church itself, with the puritanical Jansenists representing moral and doctrinal reform, the Jesuits and the crown standing for traditional Catholic authority, and an entirely secular third force pressing the claims of reason.

Jansenism needs to be examined in some detail because it serves to show, more explicitly than the Protestant movement in the sixteenth century, that reform was an evangelical rather than a progressive force, and explains why in the long run Locke's synthesis between basic Christianity and science was bound to break down. Cornelius Jansen, the Bishop of Ypres, was essentially à Catholic Lutheran – that is, he moved from Paul's Romans, through Augustine to the doctrine of justification by faith and predestination. For this reason, his *Augustinus*, published in 1640, was anathematized by orthodox theologians at the Sorbonne as early as 1649, and papal condemnations were constant, culminating in the notorious bull *Unigenitus* of 1713. Yet Jansenism remained a force, in one sense the only real force, in French Christianity. It had many assets. It was Gallican and anti-papal. It was, like Puritanism in England, a counter-monarchical force, associated with the constitutional lawyers of the *parlements*. It was zealous. Its centre was the pious foundation for women at Port-Royal, just outside Paris, and it was linked to such austere experiments as the Trappists. Above all, it opposed the attempt of the Jesuits to use canon law to transform Christianity into a mere court and state religion. These characteristics gave it a vicarious popular base, and ensured that even a monarch as powerful as Louis XIV, who grew to hate it as he aged, failed to eliminate its influence. But it was an élite, not a mass, religion; its appeal was not wide, but extremely deep, and it enslaved many highly intelligent men, as the Manicheans had done. Indeed, the link with Augustine was not fortuitous. The Jansenists were the Manichees of the pre-Enlightenment, the first harbingers of modern philosophies of pessimism.

Jansen himself regarded the human predicament as an unrelieved tragedy:

'From the moment of its origin, the human race bears the full burden of its condemnation; and its life, if it can be called such, is totally bad. Do we not arrive in a horrible state of ignorance? From the womb does not the child lie in impenetrable darkness? . . . Already guilty of a crime, and incapable of virtue, so enveloped and buried in obscurity that it is impossible to arouse him from the state of stupor of which he is unaware. And this torpor lasts for months and years. From this darkness come all the errors of human life . . . What love of vanity and evil, what gnawing care, worry, sufferings, fears, unhealthy joys, disputes, struggles, wars, pursuits, rages, hostilities, lies, flatteries, pains, thefts, rapes, perfidies, pride, ambitions, envies, homicides, parricides, cruelties, sadism, wickedness, lusts, boastings, impudences, impurities, fornications, adulteries, incests, infamies against the natures of both sexes, which are too shameful to mention – what sacrileges, heresies, blasphemies, perjuries, oppressions of the innocent, slanders, swindles, frauds, false witnesses, miscarriages of justice, violence, larcenies . . . Who can describe the yoke that weighs on the sons of Adam?'

Describing the yoke fell to the lot of Blaise Pascal, who found an uneasy relish in Jansen's huge and baleful pessimism. He was born in 1623, a hard, grasping Auvergnat, the son of a mathematician and government tax-collector. All the Pascals were fierce, aggressive, quarrelsome, arrogant, litigious and desperately clever. By the age of twenty-two, he had constructed a workable calculating machine; and he also experimented with vacuums and atmospheric pressure, and used gambling to work out theories of probability. He was the same generation as Locke but rejected the Royal Society type of attitude to religious experience. Why? Primarily because, while in Locke's England Zealotry was not only unfashionable but seen as dangerous and anti-social, in Pascal's France it was just coming into vogue among Catholics. His case suggests that even great minds are prisoners of their environment. For Pascal was a wonderful controversial writer, clear, profound, wise and savagely witty. Born a century later, he might have rivalled Voltaire in demolishing organized religion. As it was, he underwent the type of religious 'change' which transformed Englishmen of the previous generation, like Milton and Cromwell. In 1654, while reading the New Testament, he had a weird emotional experience; this was confirmed, two years later, when his little goddaughter, dying of a lacrymal fistula, was cured by an eccentric relic-collector, who touched her with a supposed thorn of Christ. Thus Pascal, who had the talents of a sensational journalist, became a propagandist on behalf of Jansenist Port-Royal, where his sister was a leading inmate. He used the batteries of rationalist ridicule to expose the verbosity and meaninglessness of the Thomists, who still flourished at the Sorbonne, and the immorality of the Jesuits and their system of casuistry. His *Provincial Letters* had to be printed secretly, under a pseudonym, but they sold 10,000 copies each, and were read by over a million. Bossuet, the orthodox Gallican court-preacher, said he would rather have written them than any other book.

Yet Pascal did not use rationalist techniques to advance the cause of reason; on the contrary. What he really disliked in the Jesuits was their lack of religion, as he understood it. He grew more angry, as he went on, at a system which tried to reconcile Catholicism with the hateful court of Louis XIV; it seemed to him worldliness and atheism masquerading as a faith. (In his last years he became convinced the Pope was wrong, and in heresy; but he did not press the point as he was wearying of controversy.) He wanted Christianity to preserve its original character – austere, harsh, almost scandalous in its rejection of earthly norms. In short, like Tertullian, he moved to a position where he saw Christian truth as transcending, even defying reason, and Christians rejoicing in its implausibility. René Descartes, an authentic member (though a late convert) of the old third force, had thought that truth was reached by a combination of careful doubting and clear reasoning. Pascal was concerned to point out that reason was human, not superhuman; it had its limitations and distortions. Cartesianism was an external enemy of the Church, just as casuistry was an internal one.

Now here Pascal touched on a very powerful line of argument, and a permanent one, calculated in all ages and in all societies to exercise a certain appeal. But he did not live to present it as a philosophical system. What he left behind was a 500-page volume of miscellaneous writing, which, after various vicissitudes, now forms MS 9,202 in the Bibliothèque Nationale. A selection of his *Pensées*, as they were called, appeared as early as 1670, and others, selected and edited by different hands, followed. The original manuscript was hopelessly confused, and raised intrinsic difficulties as to Pascal's meaning. It was not always clear, for instance, whether he was presenting his own or his opponents' arguments. Early editors shed darkness rather than light, and they irreversibly rearranged the manuscript, so that the editorial problems are now insuperable. Thus all except the most modern editions of Pascal give his thoughts in a distorted or misleading form, and commentaries by the most eminent names in French literature, Bossuet, Fénelon, Voltaire, Rousseau, Chateaubriand, Valéry and so forth, are often based on misconceptions which add to the disarray. We now know, for instance, that Pascal's supposed remark, 'the eternal silence of these infinite spaces terrifies me', was intended as a frightened comment from an atheist. There are many other pitfalls, equally fatal. Hence much of Pascal's influence bore no relation, or even a contrary relation, to what he actually thought, and one of the modern world's most provocative books proved only partly authentic. This was of considerable historical significance.

Pascal became, in effect, a secular monk, and he was undoubtedly concerned to emancipate his spirit from the flesh. He ate vegetables and drank water, swept his own room, took his plates to the kitchen and lived like a pauper; his method of sustaining meditation was to wear a spiked belt next to the flesh. But he was not an obscurantist. He suffered from fearful chronic rheumatism, and argued that this gave him peculiar insights. He was preoccupied with theodicy, and rightly recognized that suffering posed as many problems to rationalism as to religion. Illness, he thought, was 'an integral part of the mechanism of sanctity'. Christianity disintegrated 'without wretchedness, poverty and sickness', because it was, in a sense, an answer to them. Reason, too, claimed to shed more light that it actually could. 'Let me therefore be no longer reproached for lack of clarity, since I make a point of it; but let the truth of religion be recognized in its very obscurity, in the little understanding of it we have, and in our indifference about knowing it.' Man's suffering and ignorance were thus permanent facts:

> 'On seeing the blindness and misery of man, and the astonishing con-
> tradictions presented by his nature, and seeing the whole universe dumb,
> and man without light, abandoned to himself, and as it were lost in this
> corner of the universe, without knowing who has put him there, what he will
> become when he dies, I become fearful, like a man who, transported in his
> sleep to a deserted and frightful island, awakens without knowing where he
> is, and without having any possibility of leaving it; and I then marvel that
> one does not despair of so wretched a condition.'

Faced with this predicament, Pascal argued that Christianity provided a better answer than a solution which depended purely on reason. In all probability, it was a better bet. Pascal was not anti-reason. He saw it as neutral. A rational proof of God, or Christianity, would never displace the gift of faith. He saw a sinister tendency for man's reason to end in irrationality, just as his natural goodwill was corrupted by animosity. Human life was not necessarily progressing towards sweetness and light: man has a two-fold nature – the Fall, as well as divine grace, operates within him. More positively, the establishment and survival of Christianity was itself a challenge to rationalism (a point Tertullian, or for that matter St Paul, might have made), and in rare moments of inspiration we discover a reality which it is absurd to dissect by reason, and which shows Christ still operates in this world. Thus: 'Reason's final step is the recognition that there are an infinite number of things which are beyond it.' Or again: 'There is nothing more reasonable than the rejection of reason.' Finally: 'We come to know truth not only by reason, but still more so through our hearts.'

The phenomenon of Pascal, who echoed medieval mysticism and adum-brated nineteenth-century romanticism, dominated the forces of protest within French Catholicism, and so prevented the fusion of reform and reason which produced Locke's system in England, and allowed the Enlightenment there to develop peacefully within the framework of the Established Christian religion. Under continual official attack – the bull *Unigenitus* became the law of France in 1730 – Jansenism degenerated into a mere political party, lost its spiritual fervour, and eventually resurfaced as a lawyer's religion in 1789. Thus Catholicism remained unreformed, and the third force – the Enlightenment – emerged as varieties of deism or atheism operating outside Christianity, or even against it. Locke's arguments in favour of reason, and the methodology of empirical science, were eagerly applied but in a non-Christian context. Thus Montesquieu's *Esprit des Lois* and Diderot's *Encyclopedie* are essentially non-Christian monuments, something inconceivable in England (or Scotland, where Hume, though esteemed, was regarded as an aberration). The French Enlightenment emerged as the first European intellectual movement since the fourth century to develop outside the parameters of Christian belief.

The result was to subject the rational interpretation of phenomena to the test Locke had skilfully avoided, and which Pascal claimed it could not survive. French rationalism was even more self-confident than rational Anglicanism, and challenged wider targets. The *philosophes* ransacked the past to expose Christianity as the generator of evil – Raynal's *Philosophical and Political History of the Indies*, for instance, demonstrated how contact with Christianity destroyed societies. Voltaire wrote to Frederick the Great: 'Your Majesty will do the human race an eternal service in extirpating this infamous superstition, I do not say among the rabble, who are not worthy of being enlightened and who are apt for every yoke; I say among the well-bred, among those who wish to think.' Diderot and his friends conceived of enlightenment itself as an ethic, an alternative religion: 'It is not enough to know more than theologians do; we must show them that we are better, and that philosophy makes men more honourable than sufficient or efficacious grace.' For Diderot, man's self-fulfilment was a kind of vicarious atonement, and the love of humanity a substitute for the love of God: hence posterity, not God, was to judge man's present behaviour. 'Posterity is for the philosopher what the next world is for the religious man.' Or again: 'O, Posterity, holy and sacred support of the oppressed and unhappy, thou who art just, thou who art incorruptible, thou who wilt revenge the good man and unmask the hypocrite, consoling and certain ideal, do not abandon me.'

All this, of course, was to ask for trouble in the future. Locke would have argued that the common man was not interested in the verdict of posterity, whereas he might be persuaded to accept a system of rewards and punishments; Pascal would have asked why anyone should suppose posterity likely to deliver, in our terms, a rational judgment. Voltaire was careful never to entrench himself in such an exposed position. As a matter of fact, it is exceptionally difficult to determine what Voltaire's credal position really was. Some of his statements appear both definite and emphatic: 'I believe in God, not the god of the mystics and the theologians but the god of nature, the great geometrician, the architect of the universe, the prime mover, unalterable, transcendental, everlasting.' Voltaire lived to an immense age and wrote prodigiously at all times; but his real convictions are not necessarily reflected in anything he wrote on a particular occasion, or in a particular context, or at a particular time. It is an astonishing fact that, for quite different reasons, the inner convictions of both Pascal and Voltaire, the two most influential thinkers on the Continent after Erasmus, remain mysterious. Voltaire called himself both a deist and theist, and used the words as though identical. He contradicted himself constantly and without apology: 'There is not a single atheist in all Europe'; 'Only young and inexperienced preachers, who know nothing about the world, maintain that there can be no atheists.' Like George Bernard Shaw, he was a performer, often willing to allow style to take precedence over meaning. 'God is not for the big battalions but for those who fire the best' became, in another incarnation, 'God is always for the big battalions.' (The saying may not have been original with him.)

Where Voltaire was, it would seem, being most sincere, he edges off into doubt and qualification. He defined deist as 'pure adoration of a supreme being, free of all superstition'. Those who believed God created the world but did not endow it with a moral law should, he thought, be called *philosophes*. A deist who admitted God's law had, he argued, a real religion. And any belief beyond these two categories was an evil. He echoed Pascal's 'What is true on this side of the Pyrenees is false on the other', meaning that ethics were relative. (Like other eighteenth-century men he believed that they, with much else, depended on geography.) The more (apparently) sincere his intention, the closer he comes to God, or to a tone of resigned and reverent agnosticism. In the *Traité de metaphysique*: 'The opinion that there is a god presents difficulties; but there are absurdities in the contrary opinion.' Or: 'What is this being? Does he exist in immensity? Is space one of his attributes? Is he in a place or in all places or in no place? May I be for ever preserved from entering into these metaphysical subtleties! I should too much abuse my feeble reason if I tried fully to understand the being who, by his nature and mine, must be incomprehensible to me.' He was clear on one point: 'God cannot be proved, nor denied, by the mere force of our reason'; and his most serious work in this context, *Essai sur les moeurs*, touches the topic only once: 'To believe in absolutely no god . . . would be a frightful moral mistake, a mistake incompatible with good government.' A letter written as late as 1770, which has only recently turned up, reads: 'I do not believe that there is in the world a mayor or a *podesta*, having only 400 horses called men to govern, who does not realize that it is necessary to put a god into mouths to serve as a bit and a bridle.'

Voltaire, in short, was always careful to stress the social need for a deity, and so avoided falling into the Enlightenment trap. And he was too much of a historian to suppose that reason alone was likely to prove a reliable guide for mankind – he had no need of Pascal's admonitions – or that optimism was a sensible posture for a philosopher. What makes Voltaire a really great man, and an important figure in the history of Christianity, is that in this and other respects he swam against the prevailing tide of the Enlightenment. He found both the underlying notions behind Leibniz's *Theodicée* (1710), that everything was for the best in this world, and that in any event the Christian should resign himself and submit, quite misguided: the first fallacious, the second morally repugnant. He rejected Alexander Pope's *Essay on Man* (1733):

Safe in the hand of one disposing power,
Or in the natal, or the mortal hour . . .
One truth is clear,
Whatever is, is right.

He thought this was tempting Providence, and was delighted when Providence, tempted, produced the spectacular Lisbon earthquake of 1755. It was as though Voltaire had been waiting for this catastrophe to attack the received wisdom of the age, whether Christian or rationalist: 'My dear sir, nature is very cruel. One would find it hard to imagine how the laws of movement caused such frightful disasters in the *best of possible worlds* . . . I flatter myself that at least the reverend fathers Inquisitors have been crushed like the others. That ought to teach men not to persecute each other, for while a few holy scoundrels burn a few fanatics, the earth swallows up one and all.' Voltaire used the occasion of the earthquake, which aroused a European interest quite disproportionate to its magnitude, to rush out a didactic poem, which went through a score of editions in 1756:

Un jour tout sera bien, voilà notre espérance,
Tout est bien aujourd'hui, voilà l'illusion . . .

The poem was a challenge to the European intelligentsia, sceptical or Christian, to explain natural disasters in terms of moral assumptions. Pamphlets poured out by the hundred. Christian theodicy proved particularly feeble. Rousseau, trying to blend rationalism with emotion, was no better: men were responsible, he reasoned, since the casualties would have been less if men did not huddle together unnaturally in cities. Young Emmanuel Kant was another respondent. He was already moving towards a post-rational and romantic solution: insight is really more important than exact scientific knowledge, and moral experience carries us further than the truths revealed by phenomena: 'I have therefore found it necessary to deny knowledge in order to leave room for faith.' The lesson of the earthquake, Kant argued, was that in the world of phenomena man was subject to the necessities of natural law, but in the world of the spirit he is free – nature was subordinate to the realm of ends governed by purpose, and spirit was superior to matter. The process of reasoning thus ended in God. All this was beside the point for Voltaire, since he had, in fact, deliberately posed a non-question: the earthquake, horrible and inexplicable though it might be, was not the worst we had to fear: 'Men do themselves more harm on their little molehill than does nature. More men are slaughtered in their wars than are swallowed up in earthquakes.' He produced

Candide, which exposed the best of all possible worlds optimism as stupid fatalism, 'a cruel philosophy under a consoling name'. The true solution was 'to cultivate our garden', that is, oppose and remove evils, and use not just our reason but all our faculties to reform society and so to reduce the incidence of suffering. Here was a deist theodicy. In 1761 Voltaire punctured the prevailing optimism, in reality a form of complacency, the besetting sin of the eighteenth century, by pointing out that irrationality still flourished triumphantly, not least among the supposedly supine world of orthodox Christianity. His intervention in the Callas case made him the active conscience of the age, the prophet of justice and reason not in abstract but in concrete and personal form, on behalf of a judicially murdered Huguenot, demonstrably the victim of priestcraft and its legal and political (and social) accessories. What made Voltaire hate Pascal was not the latter's awareness of the limitation of reason, for he shared it, but the way in which Pascal was used to defend a Christianity still capable of monstrous cruelty. In 1766 there was a further outrage, when the young Chevalier de la Barre failed to doff his hat in respect while a Capuchin religious procession passed through the streets of Abbeville. (It was raining.) He was charged and convicted of blasphemy, and sentenced to 'the torture ordinary and extraordinary', his hands to be cut off, his tongue torn out with pincers, and to be burned alive. This atrocious case haunted Voltaire for the rest of his life, and indeed it was a reminder to the European intelligentsia that Catholic Europe, despite the apparent triumph of reason, was still basically unreformed.

Was the Church reformable? Or would it be necessary to smash it? The Treaty of Westphalia had been a catastrophe for the papacy. Thereafter, it was rarely consulted on international problems; it was unrepresented at great European peace congresses. The Catholic national Churches were virtually independent. Only Italy was ultramontane, a contradiction in terms. There was a general assumption that only a council was infallible in doctrine, and that it could overrule the Pope; normal authority in each country devolved on synods of bishops; but the Church was too comatose to put the theory to the test. The Popes were nonentities. The only exception, Benédict xiv (1740–58), was mildly progressive: 'I prefer to let the thunders of the Vatican rest. Christ would not call down fire from heaven . . . Let us take care not to mistake passion for zeal, for this mistake has caused the greatest evils to religion.' This was a Voltairian point. Progressive or no, however, the papacy seemed doomed to extinction, or complete impotence. It ceased to be able to protect its most avid defenders. In 1759, the Jesuits, accused of a variety of offences (true or false) ranging from plotting assassination to frauds in the colonies, were expelled from Portugal. In 1764 a royal decree dissolved them in France, and three years later they were suppressed in Spain and its dominions. In 1773, the European powers forced Clement xiv to dissolve the society by the bull *Dominus ac redemptor*. One of the few places where Jesuits still operated was Lutheran Prussia, where Frederick the Great found them useful for schooling his future officers and bureaucrats. In the 1770s, the papal position began to collapse in Counter-Reformation Germany, with the severing of many links to Rome, and the insistence on imperial permission before the publication of papal bulls. In 1781 the Emperor Joseph II ended religious persecution in the Austrian empire and passed an edict of toleration. Dissenters could worship in private; Lutherans, Calvinists and Greek Orthodox could even build churches (but with no steeples); anyone could practise law, medicine and hold office; education was secularized and made compulsory; and the censorship was abolished. Despite papal protests, the State engaged in a great shake-out of mechanical Christianity. Training of priests was placed under government control, 700 religious houses were shut down, only the utilitarian orders were allowed to survive, and 38,000 monks were turned loose; there was an imperial assault on pilgrimages, saints' days and superstition. In the Grand Duchy of Tuscany, Joseph's brother Leopold moved on a similar course, taxing clerical incomes, cutting off funds to Rome, abolishing Roman appeals and the nuncio's court, suppressing convents and transferring hospitals to lay hands, ending the Inquisition, papal *provisors* and curial control of the religious orders. Other, similar movement could be detected virtually all over Europe, in Protestant and Greek Orthodox as well as Catholic states. It was, in almost every case, reform from above, imposed by despotic or oligarchic governments which believed themselves in tune with the Enlightenment. It was often superficial, or ineffective or irrelevant; and, quite erroneously, it was assumed to mark the beginning of the final triumph of reason.

Oddly enough, the changes were least marked in France, supposedly the centre of Europe's enlightened forces. As in Britain, though for different reasons, the French State Church escaped the reforming visitation from above. Not that it was in a regenerate condition. What Horace Walpole said of England applied *a fortiori* to France: the modes of Christianity were exhausted. The century of Jansenist-Jesuit struggle had left no legacy except indifference. The Enlightenment had spread to the Church in some ways, especially among the higher clergy. Bishops, if they were energetic, busied themselves building roads or canals, and if they had intellectual pretensions set up as *philosophes*. Forms of deism were common. Louis XV, no prude, refused Paris to Cardinal Lomenie de Brienne: 'No, the Archbishop of Paris must at least believe in God.' Chamfort sneered: 'A vicar-general may permit himself a smile when religion is attacked, a bishop may laugh outright, and a cardinal may give his cordial assent.' In most other respects the Church was still the same organization as in the early sixteenth century. It was huge (130,000 clerics) and enormously rich, especially in the north: it owned thirty per cent of the land in Picardy, over sixty per cent in the Cambrésis. But differentials in income, bad enough in England, were nearly ten times worse in France, ranging from the statutory 300 livres minimum for a priest up to 400,000 for leading bishops, a ratio of 1:1300. Virtually all the bishops were nobles and most non-resident.

Seen from a local level, the Church was an extraordinary mixture of idleness and industry. In Angers, for instance, which had a population of 34,000 in 1789, there were seventy-two canons and over forty parochial clergy, plus a huge number of clerical hangers-on (most of them priests) at the cathedral, and at the parish and collegiate churches, sixty monks, forty friars and over three hundred nuns. One in sixty of the citizens was a priest, and this did not include tonsured clerks and students at the seminary. There were an enormous number and variety of ecclesiastical institutions, most of which rang bells at all hours of the day and night; houses facing on the main square were said to be 'almost uninhabitable' in consequence. Some clerics, as in England, were well-educated and dabbled in local antiquarianism. Some were modern-minded. The Benedictines of St Aubin installed plaster busts of Voltaire and Rousseau; and Fr Cotelle de la Blandinière, the local orthodox theologian and writer of the *Diocesian Handbook*, submitted his maiden speech at the Angers Academy to Voltaire for his approval. But much of the routine and atmosphere can only be described as medieval. Relics were exposed twice a week in the cathedral; and on the second Sunday after the Epiphany wine was still dispensed from a stone jar supposedly used at the marriage-feast at Cana. There were almost daily religious processions, a hazard or a humiliation for unbelievers, particularly since relics were carried in them – a piece of the True Cross, the head of St Loup, the bones of Saints Serene and Godebert, the arm of St Julian, a scrap of the Blessed Virgin's clothing and a lock of her hair, the blood of St Maurice and the tooth of St Decent – plus twelve portable waxworks, each with fifteen lifesize figures. When a medieval tomb was opened in the cathedral in 1757, word got around that a new saint had been discovered, and a frenzied mob tore the remains to pieces, making off with bits of bones and rags.

The religious houses of Angers presented a sorry, though not exactly a scandalous, picture. There were no reports of fornicating nuns; but the Benedictine sisters (the richest) were allowed to go out, unescorted and without veils, in their carriages. Unmarried noble ladies were almost exclusively the beneficiaries of this, and other, wealthy institutions; indeed it was officially admitted they existed 'to provide decent and honourable retreats for that numerous portion of the nation which is too well-bred to degrade itself by doing the humble tasks to which lack of income seems to condemn it' (1770). The monks, too, usually came from privileged backgrounds. The 'best' monastery, St Aubin, had an income of 50,000 livres a year. Of this 11,000 went on upkeep, taxes, and so on, 20,000 to the non-resident noble abbot, and the rest to fifteen monks. They led a gentlemanly existence with horses and carriages, 120 livres a year pocket-money, a month's holiday, card-parties and a concert on Sundays. They had given up the habit, and adopted comfortable shoes and silk stockings. It is true they did not eat 'red' meat (except at the so-called 'infirmary table', where the prior dined), but they had the best salt and fresh fish, hares, duck, teal, woodcocks and so forth. Many abbacies were now held *in commendam* by under-endowed (or well-connected) bishops. In Angers, four Benedictine houses provided four high ecclesiastics (non-resident) with supplementary stipends, and an easy life for fewer than fifty monks, out of a total income of over 200,000 livres; at St Nicholas, the abbot pocketed two-thirds of its revenue of 25,000 and spent his time entirely at Versailles. The Augustine canons were no better. Of the friars, recruited from the non-noble classes, the Capuchins were really poor. The rest led comfortable lives. One observer noted: 'There are more coffee-pots and tea-sets, snuff boxes and knick-knacks on their tables than books of theology.' The Cordeliers ate from silver, had a hundred and sixty linen sheets and twenty-four pipes of wine; the Dominicans had their own furniture, clothing allowance and private possessions, and their menu included capons, partridges, rabbits and pigs' trotters ('extraordinary expediture').

Among progressive-minded people it was agreed that reforms were necessary and overdue but no one foresaw a complete smash-up. There was a fundamental division in the Church between the cathedral chapters and religious, who were over-endowed, unemployed and mainly aristocratic, and the parish clergy, who were plebeian and poor. It was generally agreed, among *philosophes*, that the latter were worthy and hard-working too. Indeed, it was among the parish clergy that the clamour for reform was loudest. Everyone agreed the monks would have to go. Plans had been set on foot before the Estates-General met in 1789, and the eventual decree of 1790, which dispersed and sold up all but educational and charitable establishments, was carried through with virtually no protest and no resistance whatever. The *curés*, indeed, were seen as a reformist force; as one of them put it, they were 'to the Church of France what the Third Estate is to the nation.' Bowing to this pressure, in 1788, Necker changed the electoral rules in favour of the *curés*, and against the cathedral chapters and monks, and thus out of 296 clerical deputies, 208 were *curés*. An analysis of the *cahiers* of grievances brought to Versailles by the Estates-General shows that Catholicism was not, in itself, unpopular. There was a general assumption that it would continue as the state Church, with a predominant role in education and state ceremonial. Even the National Assembly was not, initially, anti-clerical; it included only three Jansenists and fifteen Protestants. It was, rather, Erastian and Gallican, and regarded the Church as a necessary part of the nation's moral machinery: otherwise, who would prevent the servants stealing the spoons? In November 1788, Louis XVI had discussed the possibility of an approaching crisis with his reforming minister, Malesherbes, and the relevancy of the English Civil War. Malesherbes remarked: 'Fortunately, religious quarrels are not involved.' The king agreed: '*L'atrocité ne sera pas la même.*'

In fact what happened was a combination of England's experience in the 1530s and the 1640s, a revolution directed not only against the crown and the possessing classes, but against the clergy as a whole, and against Christianity as such. Thus the idea of the modern secular State came into existence, and the concept of Christendom as a total, international society, already damaged by schism, finally dissolved. The process had its roots deep in the Enlightenment which in France (as we have seen) developed outside, rather than within, a Christian framework, and portrayed reason and religion pulling in opposite directions rather than (as in England) in harness. But if the roots were deep the flowering of anti-clericalism and atheism was to some extent accidental, one of the great muddles of history. The result was a confrontation between 'reason' and 'religion' which revealed the limitations and weaknesses of both, and raised a number of fundamental issues which have not yet been solved.

How did this happen? The *cahiers* of 1789 showed no general desire for fundamental changes in the Church; hardly one in fifty even wanted to end monastic vows. But the National Assembly was misled by two indicators. One was the popularity of the Paris anti-clerical theatre, which put on previously banned plays, including M-J. Chenier's *Charles* IX, showing a cardinal blessing the daggers of St Bartholomew. The other was the ease with which the first batch of Church reforms went through. The cancellation of annates in 1789 raised no papal protest, though it clearly breached the concordat. Tithes were abolished at the suggestion of the Duc de Chatelet (furious because the Bishop of Chartres had proposed to end hunting-rights). The appropriation and sale of Church lands was virtually unopposed. The bishops told the Pope: 'Our silence demonstrated how we were inaccessible, personally, to all the temporal interests whose possession had drawn on us hatred and envy.' The land was sold at high prices, usually to very respectable persons (including, it is thought, the king). The Assembly believed the sales would provide a wide number of people with a stake in the new regime, and they proposed to bind regime and state together by giving the clergy a civil constitution, which, among other things, would rationalize their salaries.

Here the deputies grievously miscalculated. What most of the parish clergy wanted was internal democracy within the Church, a system of convocation. Instead, they got a scheme which realigned parish and diocesan boundaries with the new civil ones, swept away cathedral chapters, colleges and benefices without cure of souls, and provided for bishops to be nominated by the electors of departments, and *curés* by the electors of districts. This was presbyterianism, a return to what was widely assumed to have been the practice of the Apostolic Age. Hardly any priests wanted the new system. Most were opposed, some strongly so; the bishops and higher clergy hated it. The Pope, too, was virtually obliged to oppose it, since all the elected bishops had to do was to write him a letter indicative of unity of faith. It was assumed that Pius VI could be blackmailed into compliance by using his property in Avignon (where the locals had revolted against papal rule) as a bargaining counter. In fact he wrote to the king informing him that the constitution was schismatic, and the king foolishly sat on the letter until the Assembly was too committed to draw back. The second blunder was the failure to consult the clergy before the constitution was framed, or to endeavour to sell it to them afterwards. Instead, the clergy were simply required to take an oath to observe it or face dismissal. Only seven out of a hundred and sixty bishops accepted it; the figures for parochial clergy are incomplete and somewhat confusing, but in general the constitution was accepted in the centre, the Île de France and the south-east, and rejected in Flanders, Artois, Alsace and Brittany. The non-juring areas remain, today, the most fervently Catholic in France. The divisions seem to have existed even in 1791, but the oath reinforced them. Even so, catastrophe might have been averted. Bishop Talleyrand, one of the seven juror bishops, duly consecrated eighty 'constitutional' bishops, most of whom were perfectly respectable and some of whom were outstanding; and the Assembly wanted the law to be interpreted liberally, so that non-juring clergy could administer to non-constitutionalist congregations.

Unfortunately, enforcement was entrusted to municipalities and local directories of Districts and Departments, many of whom were professional anti-clericals with scores to settle. Thus began the practice of treating non-juring clergy as suspects. Soon, fear of clericalism merged with fear of royal and aristocratic reaction, combined with foreign invasion. The new Assembly of October 1791 was crowded with anti-clericals and contained only twenty clergy, all jurors. It passed a decree declaring non-jurors 'suspects' and linking them with the swelling ranks of the militant emigrés. Then came war with Austria, which in effect made non-juring treason, and a provocative remark by Cardinal Maury, who told the emigrés at Mayence that the Pope needed 'their sabres to trim his pens'. Of course this was what the anti-clericals had suspected all along. In May 1792 came the first repressive decree, ordering the deportation of any non-juring priest denounced by twenty 'active' citizens. Many were locked up, and when the prison massacres of September 1792 took place, three bishops and two hundred and twenty priests were among the victims. There were a good many other killings. In what had been sleepy Angers, a new method of execution was devised, 'de-Christianization by immersion'. Clerics were bound together in pairs, packed into boats, and turned loose in the river. In December 1794, fifty-eight were disposed of in this fashion. A local anti-clerical wrote: 'Last night they were one and all swallowed by the river. What a revolutionary torrent is the Loire!' There was mounting terror until the fall of Robespierre, and stability was not restored until Napoleon established a quite different regime.

Thus for the first time a frontal attack was made on Christian institutions. Catholicism was tested to destruction and found to be, at least temporarily, highly vulnerable. But reason, which took its place, was also tested to destruction and found to be inadequate, even ridiculous. Of course all this had been foreseen by Voltaire, who guessed that reason in charge might cut an unimpressive figure unless linked closely to specific and justified reforms in society. (He admired the English approach.) As a matter of fact, by the 1790s, reason was no longer the guiding principle of the European intelligentsia. It was having to compete not only with the romantic movement, infused by

Kantian spirituality, but a swelling variety of fashionable superstitions. The situation was not unlike that of the first century, with paganism, gnosticism and scepticism, as well as Christianity, all jostling each other. In Germany, the most active form of eighteenth-century religious expression, Pietism, had yielded to Illuminism, which was connected to newly surfaced freemason and Rosicrucian movements – once, in the early seventeenth century, an expression of the third force. André Chenier described the *Illuminés* in his *De l'esprit de parti* (1791) as 'adapting a whole accumulation of ancient superstitions to the ideas of their sect, preaching liberty and equality like the Eleusian or Ephesian mysteries, translating natural law into an occult doctrine and a mythological jargon'. Such weird sects homed on Paris even before the Revolution. There was Mesmer, who arrived there in 1778, with his theory of animal magnetism as a healing force; he held séances at which social and intellectual leaders joined hands round a bucket of water. Lavater taught that character could be deduced from facial appearance; his rival measured skulls. The Rosicrucians presented apparitions and set up their boxes of tricks in the very room where Voltaire had once bandied rationalism with Frederick the Great. Joseph de Maistre was already working on his mystical theories of right-wing tyranny (*Considérations sur la France* appeared in 1796); there were gnostics in plenty, like Robespierre's friend Catherine Theot, and mystics like Saint-Martin, who described himself as 'official defender of Providence'.

Against this background, the new rulers of France set about the removal and replacement of Catholic Christianity. One eye-witness, Mercier, later recorded in his memoirs that if Robespierre had only appeared with an old Bible under his arm, and firmly told the French to become Protestant, he might have succeeded. But the Revolution was not reformist, it was millenarian. It was, in fact, the first modern millenarian revolt. It looked backwards to the Munster of the 1520s, and the Middle Ages, and forward to Karl Marx and Mao Tse-tung. It was also influenced by its own décor, a reflection of the classical revival: thus it had overtones of the Emperor Julian's pathetic attempts to revivify imperial paganism. Cadet de Vaux erected the first 'patriotic altar' in January 1790 at his country house; it had Roman axes and fasces, a pike crowned with a cap of Liberty, a shield with a portrait of Lafayette and verses by Voltaire; the arrangement was widely copied. Such altars were the foci of open-air ceremonies, where oaths of loyalty were sworn, the *Te Deum* sung, and communal banquets consumed. The designer and *régisseur* was J-P. David, who staged a huge ceremony in July 1791 to convey the remains of Voltaire to the Panthéon. This raised the issue of the role of religion in state ceremonies, and so in turn the question of civil marriage and secular education. Should not the Revolution, creating a new society, give it a new religion? Many of the revolutionaries were deists. They believed in nature; or, like Rousseau, in direct communication with God without intermediaries. Other elements in their belief were patriotism and the cult of *sensibilité* – hence Saint-Just's Temple of Friendship, where every adult was to record the names of his friends once a year, and explain to the magistrates why any had been dropped.

Unfortunately, the new cults could not be separated from de-Christianization and the guillotine, which served as it were to terminate awkward arguments in a thoroughly rationalistic manner. On 7 October 1793, a ceremony was held at Rheims in which a local blacksmith smashed the miraculous flask of holy oil used at the coronation. Many of the de-Christianizers were renegades, as in earlier millenarian movements – Fouché had been an Oratorian, Laplanche a Benedictine, Charles a canon of Chartres. Some were communists, like another former Oratorian, Joseph Lebon: 'If, when the Revolution is over, we still have the poor with us, our revolutionary efforts will have been in vain.' He said at his trial that he derived all his revolutionary maxims from the gospels, 'which, from beginning to end, preach against the rich and priests'. Some churches were wrecked. In Paris, the very poor provided the rank and file of the de-Christianizers; in the provinces it was often the troops of the line. Aristocratic tombs were smashed, and the royal mausoleum at St Denis demolished. (The shrunken and preserved heart of Louis XIV came to light, and was eventually eaten by mistake.) Some 30,000–40,000 of the non-juring priests became exiles; anything from 2,000–5,000 were executed. The 'constitutional' Church was wrecked when about 20,000 of the juring priests, most of them under pressure, agreed to be de-Christianized; forty-two bishops gave up their rank, though only twenty-three actually apostasized. Some priests married to save their lives, others voluntarily; but there were clerical marriages, performed by bishops, before the de-Christianization began. (Afterwards, when the Church returned to celibacy under Napoleon, thousands applied for absolution.) Formal separation of Church and State was decreed in 1795, the country became a Roman Republic in 1798, and Pope Pius VI became a French prisoner, dying at Valence in August 1799; the municipality recorded the death of 'Jean-Ange Bisaschi, exercising the profession of pontiff'.

But the alternative cults proved as unstable and ephemeral as the gnosticism they curiously resembled. And they had the air of travesty. David designed and organized funerals for republican martyrs, such as Marat; some women took an oath to bring up their children in the Marat cult, and give them no other scriptures but his works (mostly journalism). A feast was held for the 'translation' of his heart to a revolutionary clubroom, where it was hung from the roof in an urn. David also designed the celebration for the acceptance of the constitution in August 1793, held on the site of the Bastile, and based around a huge statue of Nature, spurting water from her breasts. A member of the Committee of Public Safety intoned: 'Sovereign of nations, savage or civilized – Oh, Nature! – this great people is worthy of thee. It is free. After traversing so many centuries of errors and servitudes, it had to return to the simplicity of thy ways to rediscover equality and liberty.' Then he drank from the fountain. For the Festival of Reason in Nôtre-Dame on 10 November, the Church itself was declared a Temple of Reason, and a stage mountain, crowned with a Temple of Philosophy, was built inside it. But there was no agreement on the forms of worship, or even on the subject, or object. At Poitiers, priests were forced to make humilitating abjurgations, and people dressed as popes and monks were whipped through the streets. (This ceremony, atheist in objective, was almost identical with anti-Catholic masquerades staged by Protestants in the mid sixteenth century.) Most of the ceremonies were deist. Occasionally, as an alternative to reason, such abstractions as law, truth, liberty or nature were worshipped. But God had a way of popping up behind these concepts; at Beauvais, reason, liberty and nature emerged as three goddesses, and at Auch, the celebrant asked: 'What is the cult of reason, if not the homage we render to the order established by the eternal wisdom?' Robespierre ended de-Christianization, and replaced reason with the Supreme Being; the creed he laid down included immortality of the soul, so it went beyond Locke's minimal Anglicanism. But without the savage excitement of de-Christianization, the ceremonies were tedious to the mob, and attracted only those solid bourgeois citizens who had a vested interest in them (like late-Roman paganism). The props were repainted and renamed. For a time, enthusiasts called their children Marat, Brutus, and so forth. Poupinel, who wrote republican hymns, urged: 'Let us use civic pomp to make people forget the old displays of superstition; in a word, provide more striking and attractive alternatives to the ceremonies that for so long have deceived the people, and the skeleton of sacerdotalism will disintegrate of its own accord.'

This was more easily said than done. Christianity, with its many insights and matrices, had found no difficulty at all in absorbing elements of pagan ceremonial, and transforming them. The Republicans, divided and self-conscious, floundered, and their ceremonies oscillated between parody and empty bombast, like the Red Square displays of Soviet Communism or the neo-gymnastics of Mao's China. It seems to have been assumed that public morale depended on religious or gnostic displays of one kind of another; the Erasmian emphasis on private belief and piety was dismissed as not enough. The Institut in two successive years set an essay-competition under the title: *'Quelles sont les institutions les plus propres à fonder la morale d'un peuple?'* A large number of cults were invented. There was the 'Culte des Adorateurs', compounded of ideas and images from Rousseau, Indian temples, Pompeii and the paintings of Greuze; its priests, elected annually, were to tend an eternal fire, burn incense at funerals and pour libations of milk, honey and wine. A variation had doctors and scientists serving instead of priests, with laboratory experiments replacing the mass. A third was an amalgam of the teachings of Moses, Christ, Confucius and Mohammad. There were social or communist secular cults. The most successful of all seems to have been *Théophilanthropie*, a form of deism close to Christianity (some of its members called themselves Christians), which had a manual, sixteen places of worship in Paris, and others in the provinces, and whose 'observances' were run by 'directors', most of them civil servants, schoolmasters and so forth. Former priests provided sermons. But a formal request to make it official was turned down by the Directory: Barras sneeringly told its advocate, La Revellière, that he should first get himself martyred, to launch the religion properly, and Carnot ended the discussion by saying that a successful religion needed absurdity and unintelligibility – and in these respects nothing could beat Christianity.

Beneath the public surface, the pattern of belief varied enormously, and often centred around individual Montanist-type figures, ranging from saints to pure charlatans. There was general agreement that some kind of religious mechanism was needed to keep people up to scratch. Some, like Madame de Stael, Necker's daughter, pushed the argument further. In *De la Littérature* (1800) she coined what later became a truism: 'Scientific progress makes moral progress a necessity.' Her own circle at Coppet swarmed with religious eccentrics, many from German pietist backgrounds. There was Madame de Krudener, 'converted' in 1804 at Riga, when an acquaintance raised his hat to her in the street and promptly dropped dead. She had been instructed by Councillor Jung-Stilling of Baden, who had calculated that the world would end in 1819, and Pastor Friedrich Fontaines, who gave her a detailed description of the Kingdom of Heaven; in turn, she later persuaded the Tsar Alexander I to found the notorious Holy Alliance. Another de Staël prophet was the poet Zacharias Werner, who had become a convert to what might be termed Catholic Sexuality. His mother had imagined she was the Blessed Virgin, and he Christ; and he himself believed in 'Christ and copulatory love' – 'man's soul in its ascent must pass during its earthly life through the purgatory of female bodies'. Thus he was a great grabber of servant-girls at inns and private houses, and at Weimar he shocked Goethe and broke up Frau Schopenhauer's tea-party by noisily trying to rape a maid in the kitchen. His pockets were full of crumpled mystic-erotic sonnets, variously addressed to current mistresses or God, 'the great hermaphrodite'. He wrote: 'Everything that love makes us do with a mistress, is done for the love of God.'

Such caricatures tended to make Christianity seem by comparison 'normal' and familiar (and rational). At the other end of the non-Christian spectrum, the rationalists had either been damaged by the association with terrorism or, at best, exposed as emotionally anaemic. Rivarol, in his *Discours sur l'homme intellectuel et moral* (1797), argued: 'The radical defect of philosophy is that it cannot speak to to the heart . . . Even if we consider religions as nothing more than organized superstitions, they would still be beneficial to the human race; for in the heart of man there is a religious fibre that nothing can extirpate.' This, of course, was the point on which Voltaire tended to agree even with the hated Pascal. And there was another Voltairian point: the State needed a religion, and a religion that worked, which actually made ordinary people conform to the daily rules of society. This Voltairian *aperçu* was the guiding principle behind Napoleon's reconciliation with the papacy and the Catholic Church, marked by the new concordat of 1801. He claimed he had himself lost his faith at the age of eleven, when he learned that Caesar and Cato, 'the most virtuous men of antiquity would burn in eternal flames for not having practised a religion of which they knew nothing.' At seventeen he wrote an essay approving Rousseau's contention that pure Christianity was a menace to the State. For him, Christianity was replaced by the cult of honour and the military ethic. Like others in the Directoire period, he leaned on patriotism, but eventually came to the conclusion that patriotism worked better when reinforced by religion, and that in France the religion had to be Catholicism – he saw no way of ending the guerilla war in the West otherwise. Thus he acted like Henri IV: if Paris was worth a mass, the Vendée was worth a concordat, which recognized officially that Catholicism was 'the religion of the great majority of French people'. The statement was true in the sense that, throughout this period, most French children had continued to be educated by the clergy; and Napoleon's decision to reopen the churches in 1802 was the most popular thing he ever did in France. His motives were entirely secular. 'The people must have a religion, and this religion must be under the control of the government.' Equality was unattainable, and belief in a future life helped the poor to accept their lot. Without a 'respectable' religion, people would turn to anything. 'Religion is a sort of innoculation . . . which by satisfying our love of the marvellous, makes us immune to fakes and sorcerers.' He was not sure what he believed in himself: he thought the soul was some kind of magnetic or electrical force. But he found that, in practice, foreign statesmen would not negotiate with him unless they thought he believed in God. So he set himself up as a sceptical Charlemagne, and went through an uneasy recreation of the papal coronation of 800, insisting (this time) on placing the crown on his head himself, with Pope Pius VII almost as a spectator.

Napoleon's coronation, which included an oath, wholly unacceptable to the papacy, to uphold 'freedom of religious worship', was seen at the time as a humiliation for the Pope. One of the Bourbon ministers remarked: 'The sale of offices by Alexander VI is less revolting that this apostasy by his weak successor.' In point of fact, the papacy was the one undoubted gainer of the whole Napoleonic period. In 1789 it was, as an institution, virtually on its last legs. The European crowns, and the states they represented, had been gaining ground at papal expense ever since the sixteenth century, and even in Italy. The papacy's one instrument of international control, the Jesuits, had been tamely surrendered, and in all Catholic states the churches had become virtually independent. The reason why the papacy had become so weak went back to the papal-Habsburg alliance of the sixteenth century. The popes had become accustomed to identifying their policies and interests with those of the great ruling Catholic families of Europe, and so had become in effect subservient to royalist states. This, of course, ran directly counter to the triumphalism of Hildebrand, Innocent III and Boniface VIII. Pius VII, no hero and no great intellect, halted and reversed the disastrous trend. He was one of those Italians who found the infusion of French revolutionary ideas welcome, at any rate up to a point. He had been Bishop of Imola when Napoleon invaded, and wrote 'Liberty and Equality' at the top of his letters. He urged in a sermon: 'Be good Christians, and you will be good democrats. The early Christians were full of the spirit of democracy.' Elected Pope in 1800, his decision to abandon legitimacy and negotiate a settlement with Napoleon allowed the papacy to emerge, once more, as an independent force in European affairs.

Now this occurred at precisely the moment when the failure of deism and rationalism in France had revealed the inherent, residual strength of Christianity, and indeed Catholic Christianity, as a mass religion, especially among the bourgeois, petit-bourgeois and peasants to whom the revolution had accorded political power. The point, and the conjunction, was brilliantly perceived by Châteaubriand, who published his *Génie du Christianisme* in 1802, just before the new concordat was celebrated with a *Te Deum* in Nôtre Dame. The horrible events of the past decade, he argued, had demonstrated the strength of Christian theodicy: Christians in their thousands had been able to face suffering and death, and transform these experiences, whereas to deists the killings and executions had merely served to call into question the existence of God. Where Napoleon made a Voltairian point, Châteaubriand made a Pascalian one. Christianity was not just a reinforcement of patriotism; it was – if not for all, then for a large and vocal minority – a continuous, living force, which responded to the permanent needs of the human spirit. Christianity not only spiritualized suffering but actually built on it. France, in particular, now had a lot of martyrs, whose blood refreshed the faith of those who remained. The stage was thus set for a Catholic revival, which the institution of the papacy could internationalize: 'If Rome understands her position truly, she never had before her such great hopes, such a brilliant destiny. We say hopes for we count tribulations in the number of things that the church of Jesus Christ desires.'

This proved to be an astute prediction, though for a number of additional reasons which Châteaubriand could not exactly foresee at the time. The Revolution and its consequences throughout Europe and the world did not assist the papacy directly, but it damaged forces and institutions which were inimical to it. It swept away institutions like the Inquisition, which embarrassed international Catholicism, but which the papacy was unwilling or powerless to reform or abolish itself. It terminated the ecclesiastical princedoms of Germany, which had interposed their own claims between the papacy and the German Catholic masses. It marked the end of the old legitimate monarchies, with their Gallican or national churches, whose 'enlightened' despots overruled Rome, whose bishops were greedy aristocrats and whose cardinals ensured that only the weak and the malleable should occupy the throne of St Peter. It opened up the crown colonies of Spain and

Portugal, hitherto royalist preserves, to papal penetration. Above all, it tended to establish a direct link between Catholic enthusiasts throughout Europe, and the institution they now began to recognize as a more permanent source of legitimacy and order than the unstable crowns of the *ancien régime* – the papal tiara. The resurgence of papal authority and self-confidence was marked in 1814 by the reestablishment of the Jesuits throughout the world, and by the presence at the Congress of Vienna the next year of Cardinal Ercole Consalvi, the able papal Secretary of State, who brought the papacy back into the arena of European diplomacy after an absence of nearly two centuries. A new Vatican department was set up to tighten the bonds between the Holy See and Catholics throughout Europe, and fresh concordats or similar arrangements were made with all the Catholic states. Thus we have the paradox that the convulsion which threatened to engulf Roman Christianity ended by endowing a dying papacy with a new cycle of life. And the papacy, thus reborn, returned to an ancient theme but with a modern orchestration – populist triumphalism.

To see clearly how this phenomenon came to dominate modern Christianity we must first return to Enlightenment England. The system of belief constructed by Locke, and applied by the Whig Establishment of the Church of England, went a long way towards satisfying the needs of the commercial middle classes of the towns, and it did so without driving a wedge between science and learning on the one hand, and institutional religion on the other. But it had nothing to offer to the lower orders, in particular to the swelling proletariat of the new industrial cities. Moreover, in its anxiety to dispel dangerous 'enthusiasm' and avoid any kind of fanaticism, it presented a Christianity which was part cerebral, part ceremonial, and wholly purged of emotion. To the magistrates and the squirearchy, the release of personal emotions in religious expression – the Montanist or millenarian impulse – was necessarily a form of protest against the existing social order. Memories of the egalitarian, Munster-like Civil War sects were long; and authority was determined, if possible, to restrict the religious dynamic within the prescribed forms of the statutory Church. But of course this was a dangerous strategy, with the risk that the popular forces thus confined might, as in France, eventually break out in a secular, political, even revolutionary direction. This did not happen. The existing order was not only saved but greatly reinforced by a man the authorities first thought of as an arch-enemy: John Wesley.

Like so many others, Wesley came to active religion by re-reading St Paul to the Romans, in his case in the light of Luther's preface. This was in 1738, and Wesley was thirty-five and an Anglican clergyman. 'I then testified openly to all there what I now first felt in my heart.' His Christianity was almost totally devoid of intellectual content. It had no doctrinal insights. It was wholly ethical and emotional. If anything, Wesley was an Arminian. He thought: 'God willeth all men to be saved.' Among his associates were strict Calvinists, like the great preacher George Whitfield, who subscribed to double predestination, accused Wesley of the heresy of universalism, and told him: 'Your God is my devil'. It was necessary to 'rouse the soul out of its carnal security' which Wesley's 'assurances of salvation' induced. But Wesley did not concern himself much with such matters. Right to the end he thought of himself as an Anglican: 'I live and die a member of the Church of England. None who regard my judgment or advice will ever separate from it.' But he believed he had been appointed by God to assume the role of a modern Paul, and 'proclaim the glad tidings of salvation' among a supposedly Christian people who had forgotten them. This meant breaking the conventions of the Anglican parochial system and preaching wherever he could find an audience. He travelled over 250,000 miles, and spoke to gatherings in the open air of up to 30,000 people. On forty-two occasions he crossed the Irish Sea, and it is calculated he preached over 40,000 sermons, some of which lasted for three hours.

Moreover, Wesley was not just a Montanist charismatic: he had the organizing ability of a Gregory the Great or a Benedict. He discovered that religious enthusiasm was an ephemeral thing unless it was harnessed to a carefully defined structure, periodically galvanized by meetings, and given a chance to express itself in regular, planned and arduous activities. He started with 'societies' and 'classes'. Then he introduced the Methodist Conference, 'circuits or rounds', quarterly meetings, then district meetings. Lay leadership was organized in the shape of 'class leaders', stewards, trustees, and local preachers. Every member was drawn into a corporate life, giving (or receiving) financial support, and all pledged themselves to take part in activities such as Bible-meetings, sewing for charity, and so forth. He produced regulations about clothes, food and drink, ornaments, money, buying and selling, and language. There was strict corporate and personal discipline; victories and defeats were reported at class meetings, and offenders excommunicated. Thus at Newcastle in 1743, Wesley himself expelled sixty-four members for a variety of sins ranging from swearing and Sabbath-breaking to vaguer categories such as 'idleness, railing, lightness, etc.'.

In short, Wesley despite his disclaimers was creating an alternative Church, especially among the lower orders; and there was a natural and widespread belief it would be a radical one. Like the early Christians, whom they resembled in some ways, especially in their charitable organizations, they fell victims both to official disapproval and popular prejudice. As with the early Christians, their use of the expression 'love-feast' was unfortunate. At their noctural gatherings behind closed doors, Methodists were believed to take part in orgies; it was reported, wrote Nicholas Manners, 'when they were assembled together, they put out the candles and committed lewdness.' Their conversions often divided families, and this was particularly resented: it was the direct cause of the Wednesday riots of 1744. They were also accused of robbing widows of their savings; and their habit of inducing fits and convulsions among the 'elect' was thought to be due to conjuring or witchcraft.* Among recorded crowd-cries aimed at Methodists were: 'You make people go mad; and we cannot get drink or swear, but every fool must correct us, as if we were to be taught by them.' 'After May-day we shall have nothing but preaching or praying; but I will make noise enough to stop it.'

Hence the gentry often had no difficulty in stirring up a mob against the Methodists. They had their preaching-houses pulled down at St Ives, Sheffield, Arborfield, Wolverhampton, Nantwich and Chester. John Smythe, known as 'the Conjuror' – he was an expert at inducing fits – had the reputation of the most mobbed Methodist in Ireland, and was eventually murdered; so were several others, including William Seward, first blinded, then torn to pieces at Hay in 1741. Wesley's first biographer, Henry Moore, thought: 'The lower orders of the people would never become riotous on account of religion, were they not excited to it under false pretences by persons who have some influence over them and who endeavour to keep behind the scenes.' Wesley himself said it was a case of 'the great Vulgar stirring up the small'. Incitement came from clergymen, the gentry or 'some blustering, influential farmer'. Often, free ale was laid on at the local inn. Church accounts at Illogan, Cornwall, show the entry: 'expenses . . . on driving the Methodists, nine shillings'. Men in livery frequently figured at the head of mobs; at Barnard Castle, the gentry provided a gold-laced hat and sword for the local mob leader; at Teesdale, the vicar persuaded the Earl of Darlington to set his servants on the Methodists; and gentlemen's bailiffs often organized the violence. Mobs were also led, on occasions, by Anglican clergy in full canonicals. At Otley, the magistrate told them: 'Do what you will to them so long as you break no bones.' Wesley maintained that immediately the law was enforced the mobs melted away – many having joined them on the assumption that it was the Methodists who were breaking the law or that 'there is no law for the Methodists'. The gentry often thought Wesley preached community of goods, and there was a case at Middleton in Yorkshire of a gentleman picking up a stick and joining the mob himself, swearing 'most dreadfully that the Methodists should not take his lands from him'.

This combination of upper-class hostility and lower-class prejudice had the effect, as it undoubtedly did with many of the early Christian groups, of strengthening the conventional and conservative forces within the movement. This was Wesley's own inclination (he was a Hanoverian Tory), and he used popular reactions to repress any tendency for Methodists to drift to

---

* Wesley deplored the decline in witch-hunting. Virtually all the Methodists believed in witches, and the Primitive Methodists engaged in titanic battles against spirits. The *Journals of William Clowes* (London, 1844) show him defeating the notorious Kidsgrove Bogget; and in 1810 Hugh Bourne's *Journal* records: 'I visited Clowes. He had been terribly troubled by the woman we saw . . . I believe she will prove to be a witch. These are the head labourers under Satan . . . So we are fully engaged in the battle . . . It appears that they have been engaged against James Crawfoot ever since he had a terrible time praying with and for a woman who was in witchcraft. For the witches throughout the world all meet and have connection with the power-devil.' See W. R. Ward, 'Popular religion and the problem of control, 1790–1830', in *Studies in Church History* (Cambridge, 1972).

millenarianism. Not only did his sermons endorse the existing order of society; he urged his converts to strive actively to prevent economic or political discontent breaking out into violence, and to obey the law in all its rigour. His appeal was particularly powerful among the upper echelons of the working classes – skilled craftsmen and journeymen – and small traders and shopkeepers, all those anxious to improve their status, inch their way up the social or commercial ladder, and to achieve respectability and modest affluence. Such groups could easily be detached from any revolutionary element among the proletariat, and used to emasculate it.

Wesley never had the slightest fear that he was stirring up social demons. On the contrary, he noted from the start that his converts tended to improve their social and economic situation, and his only anxiety was that this would lead to a loss of religious fervour:

> 'I fear, wherever riches have increased, the essence of religion has decreased in the same proportion. Therefore I do not see how it is possible, in the nature of things, for any renewal of true religion to continue long. For religion must necessarily produce both industry and frugality, and these cannot but produce riches. But as riches increase, so will pride, anger and the love of the world in all its branches. How then is it possible that Methodism, that is, a religion of the heart, though it flourishes now as a green bay tree, should continue in this state? For the Methodists in every place grow diligent and frugal; consequently they increase in goods. Hence they proportionately increase in pride, in anger, in the desire of the flesh, the desire of the eyes, and the pride of life. So, although the form of religion remains, the spirit as swiftly vanishes away. Is there no way to prevent this – the continual decay of pure religion? We ought not to prevent people from being diligent and frugal; we must exhort all Christians to gain all they can, and save all they can: that is, in effect, to grow rich.'

In 1773, he noted in his *Journal*: 'I went to Macclesfield, and found a people still alive to God, in spite of swiftly increasing riches. If they continue so, it will be the first instance I have known in above half a century.'

As the eighteenth century progressed, Methodism accordingly identified itself with the established order of society, and after its break with the Anglican Church it became an institution on its own. Like the primitive Church itself, it became immersed in the problems and responsibilities of finance, it built expensive churches, and virtually abandoned itinerant preaching – it underwent the subtle transformation from awakening and enthusing to teaching and ruling. As Methodism changed itself from a revival to an established sect, the more militant sections of the movement hived off. In 1807, when the Methodist Conference voted against camp-meetings, a group broke away to form the Primitive Methodist Connection in which revivalism was institutionalized. Among the poorer elements of the working class, it provided religious fireworks as a substitute for political activism. At Redruth in Cornwall, in 1814, a revival went on for nine successive days and nights: 'Hundreds were crying for mercy at once. Some remained in great distress of soul for one hour, some for two, some six, some nine, 12 and 15 hours before the Lord spoke peace in their souls – then they would rise, extend their arms and proclaim the wonderful works of God with such energy that bystanders would be struck in a moment and fall to the ground and roar for the disquieture of their souls.'

This wild revivalism, known in Britain as 'Ranterism', was an international phenomenon during the French Revolutionary and Napoleonic period, and was particularly common in Germany. In the Middle Ages and the sixteenth century, revivalism was always liable to transform itself into political violence. Now, in Britain, the two forms of activism became alternatives. It is true that the sons of strict Methodists sometimes became political revolutionaries: six out of seventeen Luddites hanged at York in January 1813, for instance, came from Methodist families. But Methodist radicals were more likely to be political reformers – the beginning of a tradition which made Methodism and other nonconformist sects the allies first of the Liberals, then of the Labour Party. And the Methodist organization itself almost invariably sided with law, order and property during difficult times. In 1812, the rich Burton family, leading Methodists who were said to be exceptionally generous to their workers, summoned cannons to defend their print-works at Rhodes and, aided by the prayers of Methodist preachers, mowed down the factory hands. In 1818 the preachers took the conformist title of 'Reverend', thus defying an earlier ruling; and three years later, one of them, John Stephens, put their social philosophy plainly: 'The objects we have to keep in view are: (1) to give the sound part of society a decided ascendancy . . . (2) To put down the opposition . . . (3) To cure those of them that are worth saving. (4) To take the rest one by one and crush them . . . They are down and we intend to keep them down . . . Methodism stands high among the respectable people.'

Of course it did, though it did not primarily interest itself in 'respectable people'. Or, rather, it was designed – and in this it was highly successful – to convert a significant section of the upper working-class to moral 're-spectability'. Wesley ignored the upper classes. He told his preachers: 'You are no more concerned to have the manners of a gentleman than a dancing-master.' Yet indirectly Methodism was to have a powerful influence on the ruling class. A number of wealthy families were associated with the movement; and when it split from the Anglicans they remained within the Establishment and sought to evangelize it from within. They were primarily concerned with moral reform, but also to some extent with social reform, since they believed that poverty, squalor and cruelty were enemies of the Ten Commandments. They wanted to make society more moral by making it more bearable; but of course they did not want to change its structure.

Most of the Evangelicals were Tories. Their real founder was John Thornton of Clapham, who was born in 1720 and who became the wealthiest merchant in England. After his death in 1790, the leadership devolved on William Wilberforce, the heir to a Hull merchant fortune, a diminutive orator and friend of William Pitt, the Prime Minister. He and his friend Hannah More constituted the nucleus of the Clapham Sect, which was not really a sect at all but a pressure-group within the Anglican Church and within the ruling class. The idea had met with Wesley's approval. He said to Hannah's sister: 'Tell her to live in the world – there is the sphere of her usefulness; they will not let us come nigh them.' While Methodism sought to make the working class respectable, reformist and tame, the Evangelicals sought to instil a spirit of *noblesse oblige* among their betters. They presented a 'change of heart' as a more moral, and acceptable, alternative to change of a more fundamental kind. They made a great point of their gentility. The first Evangelical in Parliament, Sir Richard Hill, was lovingly described by the Reverend Edward Sidney, his biographer, as 'a model of a Christian gentleman and an upright senator'. Hill quoted the Bible to the Commons to 'prolonged roars of laughter'. Willingness to face ridicule was a hallmark of the group. After the French Revolution broke out, however, the laughter changed to tolerance: fear of radicalism and its consequences brought the Evangelicals a widening foothold among the upper and middle classes; its programme gave many influential people an object in life when the road to political reform was barred, or seemed too dangerous.

Hence Wilberforce and his group prospered. He carried earnest religion from Wesley's fields to the public hall, and to the hearing of what the papers always termed a 'noble and respectable gathering'. In Parliament the Tory Evangelicals voted against suffrage reform, and in favour of the government's repressive legislation, such as the Combination Laws against trades unions, and the notorious Six Acts. Their own legislative programme was also in many respects repressive, since it included heavy taxes on sporting guns, prints, music, visiting cards, theatres, operas, playhouses, masquerades, cards, dice, races, magazines, Sunday newspapers and Sabbath travel. Hill even wanted actors licensed; and during the scarcity of 1800 he told the Commons that it was much better to have a dearth of earthly food than a famine of the word of God. The Evangelical-run Proclamation Society Against Vice and Immorality was founded to enforce the law when the authorities were slow or unwilling to act, and it instituted prosecutions against writers, publishers and printers, brothel-keepers, prostitutes, unlicensed private theatricals, purveyors of obscene prints and objects, operators of illegal dance-halls and commercial Sabbath-breakers. On the other hand, Evangelicals campaigned very effectively to abolish first the slave-trade, and later slavery itself throughout the British Empire.* Nor was this the only instance in which Evangelical plans to improve society, and those of secular reformers

* The founder of the Quakers, George Fox, had condoned slavery, reflecting the prevailing wisdom of Protestantism in the mid seventeenth century. But Quakers began to oppose slavery from 1688 on. A growing number of mainstream Protestants swung into opposition with the eighteenth-century development of the idea of 'progressive revelation' and the 'benign Providence', which increasingly identified Christian action with

overlapped. Wilberforce subscribed to seventy societies, which embraced, besides purely religious objects, a huge spectrum of human grievance and misery. They included the Bible Society, the Church Missionary Society, the London Society for the Promotion of Christianity Amongst the Jews, the School Society, the Sunday School Society, various Irish Societies, the Climbing Boys (chimney-sweeps) Society, the Betting Society, societies to befriend or improve Blücher's Soldiers, French Refugees, Foreigners in Distress, Sick Strangers, Irish Serving-Girls, Orphans and Vagrants, Juvenile Mendicants, Youthful Sinners, Distressed Widows, Poor Clergymen, Infirm Gentlewomen, Degraded Females, those imprisoned for Small Debts, and Societies to build and maintain hospitals, fever-wards, asylums, lying-in homes, infirmaries, refuges and penitentiaries.

Wilberforce's letters recorded progress: 'It is delightful to witness the many accessions to the cause of Christian piety in the higher ranks of life' (1811); '... wide and more wide the blessed circle spreads in the elevated walks of life . . . a great increase in piety, especially among the higher classes' (1813). Gradually, the robust commercial rationalism of Locke ceased to be the main characteristic of middle- and upper-class religion, and yielded to the emotion-charged propriety which we associate with Victorianism, but which established its grip a whole generation before Victoria came to the throne. An Evangelical had to be 'converted', however long he had been a member of the Church, or even if he were in holy orders. In the movement, both sexes tended to wear black gloves. There were many other characteristics, especially the phrase 'Shall we engage?' as a prelude to discussing religion. Most amusements were banned. One of the Clapham Sect, John Venn, said of his children: 'They never go anywhere where cards and dancing are introduced, neither do they learn to dance.' His son banned dancing, cards, theatres and novel-reading amongst his family. Abner Brown recorded of one Evangelical parson's wife: 'When her fine and manly boys came home for the holidays, she would not allow them to stand at the window of their father's parsonage without making them turn their backs so as not to look at the romantic views by which the house was encircled, lest the loveliness of "Satan's Earth" should alienate their affections from the better world to come.' The Evangelical paper, the *Record*, set the tone. It suspected Handel's oratorios because they were performed at Ranelagh and Vauxhall; indeed, it called an oratorio 'an awful and impious desecration of holy things by a giddy and perishing world'; it wanted theatres 'shut altogether', since people went there 'to see a strumpet crowned with garlands and cheered to the echo by a demoralized multitude'; it deplored the idea of clergymen playing cards, and published the names of those present at balls and hunts; it thought Scott's novels 'in the highest degree injurious' and lamented the fact that even Wilberforce read them – several readers wrote in horrified disgust when they heard this news, one signing himself 'Flag of

reform. This was the theological impulse behind the Evangelical anti-slavery campaign. See Roger Anstey, *The Atlantic Slave Trade and British Abolition, 1760–1810* (London, 1975).

Distress'. As Evangelicalism penetrated down the social scale, meeting Methodist influence on the way, it tended to take on an additional middle- or lower-class colouring, and from the 1830s supported temperance and even prohibition. The Lord's Day Observance Society, founded in 1831, was another non-gentlemanly feature. But the wealthy Evangelicals had long campaigned to abolish Sunday work. In 1809 one of them, Spencer Percival, stopped Parliament sitting on Monday so that MPs would not have to travel on the Sabbath; and Evangelicals gave their servants the day off. This advertisement, for a coachman, was typical of many carried by the *Record*: 'High wages not given. A person who values Christian privileges will be much preferred.' Where Evangelicals of all classes united was in their opposition to any open treatment of the sexual or bodily functions. The Reverend Lewis Way's daughter, Drusilla, wrote home after seeing the Medici Venus: 'As to the Venus, she looks like what she *is*, and ought to be – *a naked woman thoroughly ashamed of herself!*'

Instead, they dwelt lovingly on the subject of death. Through their children's magazines, they popularized the child death-beds later immortalized by Dickens (for instance, the death of Paul Dombey in *Dombey and Son*). They thought it a public duty to publicize 'successful' deaths. Hannah More wrote in 1792: 'I, and indeed all of us, have been for nearly three weeks closely engaged in another triumphant death-bed scene.' When Bishop Horne died, she thought 'a more delightful or edifying death-bed cannot well be imagined' – 'two such dying beds, so near to each other, are not to be found.' They also enjoyed funerals. One of her correspondents, Miss Patty, wrote to her: 'The undertaker from Bristol wept like a child and confessed that, without emolument, it was worth going a hundred miles to see such a sight.' There were also bad deaths. It was an axiom of the Evangelicals that religious scoffers, atheists and so forth invariably died horribly. They frequently quoted the cases of Hume, Gibbon, Voltaire and Paine, without taking the slightest trouble to verify the accuracy of their accounts. Thus Paine's doctor, Manly, specifically denied that his patient changed his views while dying, or suffered moral distress. But Hannah More wrote an account of his death which was 'widely circulated among the lower classes of society' stating that in America he 'lived in brutal violence and detestable filthiness . . . during the whole of the week preceding his death he never failed to get drunk twice a day . . . His last words were: "*If ever a devil had an agent on earth*, I AM THAT MAN!"'

There was, too, an element of high-minded deviousness underneath the Evangelical disclaimers of wordly ambitions. Wilberforce had a doctrine of 'usefulness' which led him to concentrate on those who were influential or important in some way. He wrote to his son Sam, later Bishop of Winchester, that he had just contrived to introduce an 'excellent man' to the Archbishop of Dublin, 'in conformity to a principle I hold to be of first-rate importance . . . It is that of bringing together all men who are like-minded, and who may probably at some time or other combine and concert for the public good.

Never omit any opportunity, my dear Samuel, of getting acquainted with any good or useful man . . . More perchance depends on the selection of acquaintances than on any other Circumstance in life . . . Acquaintances, indeed, are the raw Materials, from which are manufactured friends, wives, husbands etc.' The Evangelicals believed in 'getting on' and pushing ahead anyone who agreed with them.

In particular, the way in which Evangelicals penetrated the Church of England was thoroughly worldly, and almost Jesuitical in its subordination of means to ends. In 1814, for instance, the Reverend Charles Sumner, a young Evangelical, went on a Continental tour with the two sons of the Marquess of Conyngham. To prevent the elder marrying the daughter of a Geneva professor, Sumner married her himself. In gratitude, Lady Conyngham, George IV's mistress, had Sumner made royal chaplain and historiographer, Deputy-Clerk of the Closet, Bishop of Llandaff in 1826, and the next year, aged thirty-seven, Bishop of Winchester, a see he held for forty-two years during which he nominated Evangelicals throughout the diocese. His brother, another Evangelical, got Chester in 1828 and, in 1848, Canterbury. Like-minded clergy were termed by Evangelicals 'religious' 'sincere' or 'pious'; the rest were 'Scribes and Pharisees', 'Fat Bull of Bashan' or 'priests walking in darkness'. Like the Puritans in the sixteenth century, they plotted hard to grab positions of power within the Establishment. In 1788, they captured Queens', Cambridge, by getting Isaac Milner elected President. Tutors who opposed him had to resign or accept country livings. The college expanded rapidly; Evangelicals sent their clever sons there; and it churned out large numbers of potential right-thinking clergymen.

From this bridgehead, the Evangelicals expanded their hold on Cambridge through a brilliant and wealthy organizer, Charles Simeon, who was 'converted' in 1779, at the age of nineteen, and who was minister at Holy Trinity Church, Cambridge, for fifty-three years. The aim was to exploit the existing, but under-utilized, propaganda resources of the Anglican Church itself. Cobbett argued shrewdly in 1802: 'The clergy are less powerful from their rank and industry than from their *locality*. They are, from necessity, *everywhere*, and their aggregate influence is astonishingly great. When, from the top of any high hill, one looks around the country, and sees the multitude of regularly distributed spires, one not only ceases to wonder that order and religion are maintained, but one is astonished that any such things as disaffection or irreligion should prevail.' With enough Evangelical Cambridge graduates, it was hoped in time to put the right kind of clergyman in every parish, or at least every centre of influence. Simeon used the movement's wealth and contacts in a number of highly practical ways. He got Evangelicals appointed to Church lectureships, by nomination of the founder, by nomination of livery companies and other institutions, and by election of the seat-holders. Others were given chaplaincies at hospitals, asylums and so forth, by working on the officers or large subscribers. Evangelicals also built churches, the right of presentation going to Simeon and his friends. Finally, Evangelical money was used both to buy up advowsons and 'next pre-sentations', which were sold on the open market, or to establish trusts to do this. Thus flagrant abuses in the old system were exploited in a direct and systematic manner to achieve other-worldly ends. Moreover, these carefully organized 'victories' were treated as the direct intervention of Providence on the side of the Evangelical cause, for it was one of their assumptions – they were tinged with Calvinism – that nothing was accidental.

Yet in the end Evangelicalism tended to be self-defeating. By its very pervasiveness and assiduity it forced large numbers of people, including large numbers of clergymen, to take religion seriously and to endeavour to clarify their own positions. It set up shock-waves in the placid Anglican sea, and thus caused cross- and counter-currents to flow. Moreover, Evangelicalism was not really a theological system. Though it was tinged with Calvinism, it was not based on any solid structure, like Calvin's *Institutes*. In fact it had no structure at all, other than the Bible, which it took quite literally.

Now here we come to a paradox. In the later Middle Ages, and throughout the Reformation period, the Bible had been the great strength of the Protestants. Christianity, as we have noted before, is essentially a historical religion; and in giving absolutely priority to the historical documents – the scriptures – the Protestants had appeared to be on infinitely stronger ground than the Catholics, who relied for their dogmatic justification on the unscriptural authority or *magisterium* of the Church – that is, the mere opinions of uninspired men – and who could justly be accused of trying to keep the text of the inspired Revelation from the hands of the multitude.

The Evangelicals, in particular, relied on the traditional strength of the Bible. Everything was to be found there; and nothing that was not found there was of consequence. Their standard textbook, the *Elements of Christian Theology* by Bishop George Pretyman Tomline, had a totally uncritical approach to scripture. Thus, the thirteenth edition (1820) noted: 'The great length to which human life was extended in the patriarchal ages rendered it very practicable for the Jews, in the time of Moses, to trace their lineal descents as far as the Flood, nay even to Adam'; Methuselah 'was 243 years contemporary with Adam, and 600 with Noah'; and so forth. Both the Old and the New Testaments were treated as historical records, and to question their literacy accuracy was to deny their inspirational status.

By the end of the eighteenth century, this position was beginning to be highly vulnerable. Science itself was not necessarily a threat to Christianity. Christianity could rationalize within its own assumptions changes in cos-mology and the discovery of new operative laws. Indeed, up to a point at least, the very existence of scientifically demonstrable laws was welcome to Christian apologists who could instance them to prove the workings of an all-powerful divine intelligence. But could religion withstand the invariable application of scientific methodology, that is the pursuit of truth for its own sake regardless of the consequences? Chritianity being a faith which identified itself with truth, it was essential that it should do so. Locke's presentation was based on this assumption. But then Locke had lived at a time when it had seemed more likely that scientific demonstration of truth would confirm rather than discredit Christian claims. A hundred years later the situation was changing radically. It then emerged that what Christianity had to fear was not so much science itself as scientific method applied historically. This worked in two ways. Geologists and astronomers on the one hand, and biologists and anthropologists on the other, combined to present a historical picture of the earth's origin, and of man's habitation of it, which was wholly incompatible with the historical account in the Old Testament. Secondly, study of the scriptural texts using the new methods of historical analysis, and with the assistance of philology and archaeology, revealed the scriptures as a much more complicated collection of documents than anyone had hitherto imagined, a bewildering compound of allegory and fact, to be sifted like any other ancient literature.

Could Protestantism, with its heavy dependence on scriptural documentation, survive this process? It was from Protestant Germany that much of the new scriptural scholarship came. And it was accompanied by new theological approaches and insights which in fact provided a way out of the dilemma. In the 1820s and 1830s, Friedrich Schleiermacher made the first real reappraisal of Christian theology since Calvin. He thought it possible to devise a theology valid for all time, subject to continual renewal through experience. Dogma, he argued, was not so much knowledge as the result of history; revelation was the sum total of individual conceptions of God; articles of Christian belief were not proofs so much as expressions furthering piety. What was essential to Christianity was the redemption, dependent on Jesus, who did not need to be redeemed. Heresies were departures from these affirmations; but the doctrine of two natures in Christ, and three persons in God, he believed to be misleading, and the resurrection, ascension and return in judgment inessential. The Church was a fellowship of believers. Election was determined by God's good pleasure, but not necessarily to exclude permanently a part of the human race. This analysis made it possible, in theory at least, to recruit Lutherans and Calvinists, and it opened the way for Christian theology to reconcile itself to science, modern biblical scholarship, and other disciplines more or less indefinitely. Indeed, it was in the tradition of 'minimum theology' established by Erasmus and continued by Locke.

Nevertheless, it was a line of defence few Protestants, at least initially, were prepared to adopt. The Evangelical fundamentalists simply averted their gaze both from science and German 'higher criticism', as it was termed. Others peered – and lost their faith. In 1835, almost coincidental with the most devastating revelations of geology, the German biblical scholar David Friedrich Strauss published the first volume of his *Leben Jesus*, which analysed the gospel narratives like any other collections of sources, and sought to detect the element of myth. Strauss argued that 'the supernatural birth of Christ, his miracles, his resurrection and ascension, remain eternal truths, whatever doubts may be cast on their reality as historical facts', and he claimed that 'the dogmatic significance of the life of Jesus remains inviolate'; yet the impact of the book was overwhelmingly to emphasize the contradictions, and minimize the accuracy, of the New Testament. One of the new agnostics, Arthur Hugh Clough, noted the event in his poem *Epi-Straussium*:

> Matthew and Mark and Luke and Holy John
> Evanished all and gone. . . .

The first big exodus from Christianity came in the 1830s; thereafter there was a steady drift away, especially in the 1850s and early 1860s, under the impact of Darwin. Some Protestants welcomed the challenge. The Reverend Charles Kingsley wrote of evolution: 'Men find that now they have got rid of an interfering God – a master-magician as I call it – they have to choose between the absolute empire of accident, and a living, immanent, ever-working God.' But the majority resisted theological change with varying degrees of anger. This raised special disciplinary difficulties for the Anglican Church. It was an Establishment, subject to Parliament. In fact, in the cause of institutional reform, Parliament was becoming more active in the affairs of the Church. Measures passed included the Established Church Act and the Tithes Act (1836), the Church Pluralities Act (1838), the Church Discipline Act and the Sinecures Act (1840), and a measure which transferred church appeals to the Judicial Committee of the Privy Council (1833). In fact the Church did not have charge of its own discipline and doctrine, except in so far as statute allowed; and Anglican theologians who offended against majority opinion could look for protection to the State. In 1832, the Reverend Reed Dickson Hampden gave the Bampton Lectures at Oxford, in which he took the German position that theology varies from age to age, and reflects contemporary philosophy, that doctrines are built on inspired facts by uninspired men, and that church pronouncements had been repeatedly inconsistent and could not be infallible. His *Observations on Religious Dissent* (1834) declared that dogma was unimportant compared to religion itself, and it pleaded for toleration, since on the essence of religion few Christians differed. In short, the line was again Erasmian. There were violent Anglican protests when Hampden was appointed Regius Professor of Divinity at Oxford in 1836; and when, in 1847, he was promoted to be Bishop of Hereford, an attempt to prevent his formal election was abandoned only after the Prime Minister, Lord John Russell, threatened to invoke statutory sanctions against the protestors.

There was, moreover, the further problem within the Anglican Church of reconciling a huge spectrum of theological opinion, which tended to widen in the light of the new scholarship. In 1847, the Bishop of Exeter refused to institute the Reverend G. C. Gorham to a living on the grounds that his

Calvinistic views on baptismal regeneration were inconsistent with the Thirty-Nine Articles. Gorham fought the case, was defeated in the Anglican Court of Arches in 1849, but was upheld when he appealed to the secular Judicial Committee of the Privy Council in 1850. The effect of these two cases, as it seemed, was to demonstrate that the Anglican Church did not control its own doctrines and could not prevent the rise to authority within it of men whom it considered heretics.

It was against this background that the High Church developed and began to turn in the direction of Rome. Here again, the Evangelicals were ultimately responsible, since the revivalist atmosphere they introduced inevitably stimulated hostile and contrary tendencies: it is a permanent characteristic of Christianity that emphasis on one of its matrices always leads to the development of a rival. In the 1820s, Oxford, and notably Oriel College, was undergoing an intellectual revival. The Oriel fellows included John Keble, John Henry Newman, Edward Pusey, the Regius Professor of Hebrew, and R. H. Froude. They began their campaign with Keble's Assize Sermon at Oxford in July 1833, on the theme of 'National Apostasy', and continued it by publishing tracts which took as the standard of what they believed the faith and practices of the early apostles of the Church. It is notable that whereas in the Reformation, the first Protestants had appealed to the early Church against papal triumphalism, and mechanical Christianity, this new group of Christian reformers employed the early Church to illumine a path back to Rome. Some of the members of the Oxford tractarian movement came from Evangelical families. Yet it was Evangelical Protestantism which they saw as the enemy within. Keble and Newman found the Evangelical way of talking about religion distasteful; Newman deplored 'the mechanical way . . . in which the great doctrine of His sacred death and the benefit of his blood-shedding is thrown to and fro, at best as if a spell or charm, which would surely convert men'. They wanted beauty and mystery. Keble thought it 'dangerous' to 'impart the oracles of God to profane and unworthy men'. 'New truth,' he added, 'in the proper sense of the word, we neither can nor wish to arrive at. But the monuments of antiquity may disclose to our personal perusal much that will be to this age new, because it has been mislaid and forgotten.' Both men denounced the 'low-minded school of Burnet and Hoadley' which 'robbed the church of all her most beautiful pronouncements'.

In a sense, the Oxford Movement was a repudiation of Erasmianism. If Newman and Keble had been privileged to follow in the steps of Colet and Erasmus, and visit the shrine of St Thomas before it was destroyed, they might have drawn precisely the opposite conclusions from the experience. *That* was the real Christian Church, not 'minimum theology'. Newman began to drift away from Anglicanism when he worked on his book about Arianism in the fourth century. He discovered on his own account how serious a threat history was to Protestantism because of its biblical fundamentalism. He wrote: 'To be deep in history is to cease to be a Protestant.' He saw history as an asset to

Catholicism in that its study reminded the believer of the incredible richness of its past, which Rome alone seemed fully to represent in the nineteenth century.

The movement began by assuming that they were safe within the Church of England, at any rate as they conceived it, 'a true branch or portion of the one Holy, Catholic and Apostolic Church of Christ'. It taught the truth, whereas the Nonconformists and Evangelicals taught only part of the truth, and Rome more than the truth. They rejected the Latitudinarian doctrine that 'every man's view of revealed religion is acceptable to God if he acts on it'; and they argued that religious truth was not part scriptural, part authority, as Rome maintained, but wholly scriptural – 'though it *is* in tradition, yet it can also be gathered from the communication of the scripture . . . the Gospel message or doctrine . . . is but indirectly and covertly recorded there, under the surface.' This was an exceptionally difficult half-way house to occupy. In the end many found themselves unable to maintain it, if only because they needed to rely more and more on the principle of authority to defend scripture from the 'higher criticism'. Thus Newman wrote in his *Apologia Pro Vita Sua*, attacking Protestant liberalism:

'Liberty of thought is in itself a good; but it gives an opening to false liberty. Now by Liberalism I mean false liberty of thought, or the exercise of thought on matters in which, from the constitution of the human mind, thought cannot be brought to any successful issue, and therefore is out of place. Among such matters are first principles of whatever kind; and of these the most sacred and momentous are especially to be reckoned the truths of Revelation. Liberalism then is the mistake of subjecting to human judgment those revealed doctrines which are in their nature beyond and independent of it, and of claiming to determine on intrinsic grounds the truth and value of propositions which rest for their reception simply on the external authority of the Divine word.'

Now this is a very clear and weighty statement, which effectively repudiates the Erasmian tradition and specifically denies Locke's insistence that truth must be pursued wherever it leads. Some Anglicans of the school, such as Samuel Wilberforce and W. E. Gladstone, believed that they could argue themselves successfully out of the problems raised by science, by new interpretations of the scriptures and by the impact of the modern world generally. Hence they remained Anglicans. Newman did not want to take that risk. On the contrary, he believed that there must be a cut-off point beyond which human inquiry was not allowed to penetrate. Up to that point, thought and argument were free; after it, prohibited. But who was to determine that point? And who was to decide what was to be believed beyond that point? Only one Church was really prepared to take on such responsibilities, and their draconian consequences, and that was Rome. Hence in the 1840s and 1850s, Newman and others crossed to Rome in the quest for authority.

Of course their decision did not revolve solely around this issue. The heart-searchings both of those who became converts and those of the movement who did not are fully documented in many thousands of letters. Since all these men knew each other, wrote to each other frequently and copiously, and could discuss their problems and views freely without fear of censorship, inquisition or punishment, the various factors which shape the changing beliefs of serious, educated Christians are fully revealed, as has perhaps happened at no other time, before or since. In this sense the episode was unique, and important. The letters show that reason, ambition, social factors, friendship, fashion, and innumerable aspects of Church life from aesthetics to pure theology, all played their part in varying degrees depending on the individual. They remind us that a change in religious belief is a very complicated process, more likely to resemble a Pascalian than a Voltairean sequence. 'It was not logic which carried me on,' wrote Newman, but 'the state of my heart'. 'Surely,' added Manning, 'if anything ever brought us to the Foot of the Cross it is confession, the altar and the sacrifice.'

Certainly there were Catholic converts for whom the use of the sacraments and ritual were the main motives. But for the great spirits, like Manning and Newman, it is hard not to conclude that the impulse was the need for a Church which not only accepted, but gloried in, the exercise of authority. To Manning, the effect of state control was to strip the Anglican Church of any claim to authority. When Hampden was made a bishop, Manning protested: 'It is monstrous and unspeakably irreverent towards Him who is the Head of the Body that the bishops of the church should be chosen by any layman who may chance to lead the House of Commons. It is worthy of the age when courtesans made popes.' A few years later, in 1851, when the Gorham judgment had pushed him over the brink, he was not so sure about the historical truth of courtesans making popes, which he now saw as a Protestant libel: '... may not the Catholic Church know its own history better, and by a lineal knowledge and consciousness, to which no individual can oppose himself without unreasonableness?' Moreover, in Manning's case there was no doubt, from the start, that authority must reside wholly in clerical hands; that its delegation should be strictly hierarchical; and that it ultimately resided solely with the Pope, whose person and role was mystical. He wrote of 'the firm belief that I have long had that the Holy Father is the most supernatural person I have ever seen. . . . The effect on me is of awe, not fear, but a conscious nearness to God and the supernatural agencies and sufferings of His church.'

Thus, at a time when the intellectual advances of the nineteenth century were thrusting some Protestants into agnosticism, others into mindless fundamentalism, and yet others into a heroic reappraisal of their theology, Catholicism and above all papalism developed a new power of attraction by characteristics which had once made it seem repellent. In 1846, Manning indicted Anglicanism: 'There seems about the Church of England a want of antiquity, system, fullness, intelligence, order, strength, unity; we have dogmas on paper; a ritual almost universally abandoned; no discipline, a divided episcopate, priesthood and laity.' The Roman Church was the opposite to this sorry picture – a triumphalist monolith, unchanged, unchangeable and, granted its assumptions, impervious to challenge. It alone, in practice, was prepared to accept wholeheartedly Newman's premise that inquiry into such assumptions was illegitimate, and exert ecclesiastical power to render it impossible. Thus on the darkening plain of nineteenth-century agnosticism and fading belief, the Church of Rome stood out like a fortress: once within, the drawbridge could be raised, and the solid walls would separate absolutely the true Christians from the rest. By comparison the walls of the Protestant citadel were crumbling, were, in fact, being rapidly demolished, since the enemy was already within. The images of safety, refuge and the flight to security abound in the writings of the converts. It gives us the essential clue to the reinvigoration of the nineteenth-century Roman Church, and the reassertion of papal power.

Of course, the presence within the Church of those who fled there for security and authority necessarily reinforced those burgeoning tendencies. A case in point was W. G. Ward, who, even before he left the Anglicans for Rome in 1845, had been working on his *Ideal of a Christian Church*, with its stress on the abdication of personal responsibility. 'Within the *magic circle* which it protects, we are saved from the pain of doubt, from the necessity of disputation, and are called upon but to learn and to believe.' What he called 'conscience' was the act of obeying Church authority; there was no role in it for the reason or the intellect. As a refugee from liberalism, he naturally fought fiercely against any attempt to establish it within the fortress. He strongly approved, in 1857, of the Vatican's condemnation of works by Anton Gunther, who held that there was no real cleavage between natural and supernatural truth, a position fundamental to the whole scientific argument. In 1863 Ward became editor of the influential *Dublin Review* and used it to urge that Rome should direct and control all scientific and historical research conducted by Catholics. This was the return to the medieval assumption of a total society, in which it was impossible to mark a point where the authority of the Church ended since spiritual considerations pervaded all material affairs. Ward argued that a separation between theology and other aspects of human knowledge was in practice impossible because the overlay was too great: 'We therefore see over how large a field of secular science the church's authority extends. She has the power . . . of infallibly pronouncing propositions to be erroneous if they tend by legitimate consequence to a denial of any religious doctrine which she teaches. But secular science contains a vast number of such propositions, and on all these, therefore, the church has power to pronounce an infallible judgment.'

This attack on the intellect and the free pursuit of knowledge was only one aspect of the reassertion of control which characterized Roman Christianity in the nineteenth century. Among the English converts there was an impressive attempt to apply the full rigours of a moral theology which claimed to deal with every minute aspect of human action and thought, and left the penitent wholly in the hands of the clerical supervisor. Once again, the habit of Victorians of committing everything to paper (and preserving the results) enables us to penetrate the details of their spiritual lives. F. W. Faber, the poet and hymnwriter, came from a social and religious background similar to that of the Wilberforces; as a convert and a Catholic priest, he was a good exemplar of the new triumphalist pastoralism. Here he is, for instance, writing to one of his penitents, Mrs Elizabeth Thompson (11 August 1851): 'All your faults turn on two things: you make yourself the centre of everything, and you are greatly wanting in simplicity. You have at present not the least notion of the literally desolating extent of this latter fault in your soul. Pray daily against these two faults and look particularly after them in your examen of conscience. You must read no high spiritual books. . . . Pray silence as much as you can – never . . . argue on religion. . . . There is at present no symptom whatever of God calling you to perfection. . . . So far your spiritual life has been no more than an unreal ambition and built on sand. Your work is to begin.'

We also have a note of remonstration, dating from 1860, which Fr Faber, in accordance with his invariable custom, slipped under the bedroom door of Fr William Morris, one of the priests in his charge:

'The absence of supernatural principles illustrated in your refusing to give Miss Merewether Holy Communion, because it *might* have shortened your breakfast by five minutes (1) Want of obligingness to one of your brothers and that when he was sick. (2) The example of what Jesus would have done obviously not your rule of action. (3) Want of penance, for even an almost microscopic inconvenience. (4) Want of silence in speaking of the breakfast. (5) Clear loss of spiritual sense in letting the length of breakfast be an obstacle, and in quoting it without any sense of shame or unspirituality. (6) Want of charity to an extern, and she sick. (7) Want of zeal of souls, depriving an invalid of the Fountain of Grace. (8) Want of love of Jesus, who longs to communicate Himself to souls, and you hindered Him, rather than curtail your breakfast five minutes, and His three hours on the Cross for you! You talk much of Our Lady – think of the want of love of her, who so jubilees in Communions. (9) Want of humility, in not doing so, if you thought you were being put upon. (10) Want of charity in judging, if you thought you were being put upon. (11) Plain absence of the saints' principle of always being on the look out to increase your merits, and to do something for God. (12) The extreme nastiness of this pettiness, as compared with the grand, large, kindly apostolic spirit of St Philip's Institute. (13) The disclosure of it is the absence of a life and spirit of prayer. (14) A token of fearful want of sensitiveness of conscience. (15) A proof of non-abiding presence of God: your first thought is self – and self's comfort. Only your selfishness is *prompt* and at home: supernatural principles not at all. My poor child, sad and shameful as this disclosure of your interior must be for you, it is what I have seen all along – but I cannot put aside the mists of self-love and self-occupation and hardened delusion in which you habitually live. Vileness . . . is your characteristic.'

This, it should be emphasized, is one intellectual writing to another.

The stress on authority, and the maintenance of detailed clerical control of the conscience of the individual, were almost necessarily accompanied by a continued insistence on eternal punishment. The retreat from Hell was a characteristic of the nineteenth century liberal Protestant churchmen, many of whom, claimed their opponents, were guilty of the heresy of universalism. The nearer a man moved to Rome, the more the need for Hell seemed to increase (though it was also marked on the extreme fundamentalist wing of Protestantism). The Tractarians insisted that burning by physical fire was an essential part of eternal punishments. In his sermon on Hell (1856) Pusey noted: 'This, then is the first outward suffering of the damned, that they are purged, steeped in a lake of fire. O woe, woe, woe! Woe unutterable, woe unimaginable, woe interminable!' He wrote to Keble: 'People risk too much now. They would risk everything, if they did not dread an eternity of suffering. A mere purgatory for the bad would not move them.' Newman, while believing in physical torture, gave a description of the plight of the damned soul, in the sermon reprinted in *Discourses to Mixed Congregations* which is far more imaginative and frightening. It was evidently a topic on which his mind frequently dwelt, and he emphasized the centrality of the doctrine: Hell was 'the great crux in the Christian system. . . . It is the turning point between pantheism and Christianity, it is the critical doctrine – you can't get rid of it – it is the very characteristic of Christianity. We must therefore look matters in the face. Is it more improbable that eternal punishment should be true, or that there should be no God? *For if there be a God there is eternal punishment (a posteriori).*'

Of course Rome itself had always insisted on the importance of Hell. It was the solidity of this, and similar, doctrines which attracted so many converts. But Rome's pastoral use of Hell was greatly augmented as a result of the work of St Alphonsus Liguori, who in 1732 founded the Order of the Re-demptorists. They specialized in Hell-fire sermons and made themselves available for retreats and Lenten missions in ordinary Catholic parishes. The order flourished; hence, at a time when Protestantism as a whole was pushing Hell into the background, it played a more colourful role for Catholics. Liguori published in 1758 a book called *The Eternal Truths*, which served as a handbook both for his own community and for parish priests generally. He thought that the stench of one damned person would be enough to asphyxiate all mankind. Oddly enough, he refused to describe Heaven, since he argued it was impossible to picture it for those who had experience only of earthly pleasures; but no such inhibition prevented him from conjuring up Hell: '... the unhappy wretch will be surrounded by fire like wood in a furnace. He will find an abyss of fire below, an abyss above, and an abyss on every side. If he touches, if he sees, if he breathes, he touches, sees, breathes only fire. He will be in fire like a fish in water. This fire will not only surround the damned, but it will enter into his bowels to torment him. His body will become all fire, so that the bowels within him will burn, his heart will burn in his bosom, his brains in his head, his blood in his veins, even the marrow in his bones; each reprobate will in himself become a furnace of fire.'

It was the Redemptorists who, in 1807, resurrected a remarkable seventeenth-century work by F. Pinamonti, *Hell Opened to Christians*, and reprinted it with horrific woodcuts. One edition was published in Ireland as late as 1889, and it has demonstrable links with the sermon on Hell described in James Joyce's *Portrait of the Artist as a Young Man*. Redemptorists often preached Hell-sermons at Catholic schools. One of them, the Reverend Joseph Furniss, wrote a number of books for children, in which Hell figured prominently. In *The Sight of Hell* he showed Hell as a mid-earth enclosure (thus following Liguori), with streams of burning pitch and sulphur, deluged with sparks and filled with a fog of fire. Tormented souls shrieked, 'roaring like lions, hissing like serpents, howling like dogs and wailing like dragons.' There were six dungeons, each with an appropriate torture – a burning press, a deep pit, a red-hot floor, a boiling kettle, a red-hot oven and a red-hot coffin. 'The little child is in the red-hot oven. Hear how it screams to come out; see how it turns and twists itself about in the fire. It beats its head against the roof of the oven. It stamps its little feet on the floor. . . . God was very good to this little child. Very likely God saw it would get worse and worse and never repent, and so it would have been punished more severely in Hell. So God in his mercy called it out of the world in early childhood.' About four million copies of Furniss's works were sold in English-speaking countries. But we must not suppose that Hell was directed chiefly at children. The Catholics, unlike some of the Protestants, had no 'double doctrine' on Hell; they taught it, in all its imaginative rigour, to all ages and all classes. Father Faber, who was greatly interested in death and its consequences ('O grave and pleasant cheer of death . . . the diligent, ubiquitous benignity of death'; 'Deathbeds form a department of the church . . . which belongs to her officially'), deplored any tendency to preach Hell-fire to the lower classes but not to their betters: 'I see real, good wholesome work to be done in real, good wholesome souls, by frequent meditation on Hell. . . .' Moreover, Catholic intellectuals were expected to subscribe to the doctrine, and, where appropriate, to reflect it in their writings. In 1892, Professor St George Mivart, a Catholic zoologist, suggested that the sufferings of the damned might gradually be ameliorated, a speculation Newman thought admissible. Cardinal Vaughan, Archbishop of Westminster, thought otherwise, and required Mivart to subscribe to a statement of orthodox doctrine. Mivart refused, and found himself outside the Church.*

The image of Rome as a repository of medieval certitudes, of social homogeneity, of a unitary view of life, exercised a marked appeal to a certain type of intellectual, and not only in England. In France, the current was, initially at least, much stronger, and it was linked to social and political forces which made nineteenth-century French Catholicism the driving force behind populist triumphalism. Châteaubriand's *Génie du Christianisme* was the harbinger of a new Catholic and papal apologetic. For the first time since the twelfth century, various vocal interests saw the papacy, potentially at least, as a popular force, as a protection against unwelcome secular claims, and as a far more acceptable defender of civilized tradition than the old royal houses. The decline of Gallicanism and localism in the Church, and the virtual eclipse of the old type of bishop-aristocrat, produced an abrupt and permanent decline in episcopal authority, and thus placed the Pope and the parish priests (and through them, their congregations) in a direct relationship. In 1819 de Maistre published his remarkable celebration of the papacy, *Du Pape*, which not only reasserted the complete doctrine of papal infallibility, which had been devalued in the eighteenth century, but advanced persuasive and modern secular reasons for keeping, and exalting, the papal institution, as a barrier against barbarism and proletarian terror. The French Revolution and its consequences had destroyed Christianity as a total society; but it gave it a new place as a huge and vocal minority movement, active against change, ardent for conservatism, fighting reason with romance and progress with tradition, appealing strongly to certain ineradicable emotions in the human spirit. Catholicism, as conservative intellectuals recognized, was the chief beneficiary of the Christian reinvigoration because it made the fewest concessions to the modern egalitarian world, and because it radiated its unshaken faith in hierarchy and authority. And it also had a single ruling figure, a charismatic or cynosure, holy and international, on whom could focus all the aspirations of traditionalists throughout the world. Why should not the Pope lead a great popular movement of faith, a triumphalism for the millions?

The idea was not entirely new. Gregory VII had seen himself interposing between the people and regal tyranny; Becket, and other prelates in conflict

---

*Apart from Manning and Ward, the converts did not flourish in the Catholic Church. Dean Church wrote of Frederick Oakeley on his death in 1880: 'The Romans made nothing of him, but sent him up to Islington to live poorly in a poor house with two Irish colleagues . . . a genuine bit of the old Balliol Common Room, set in the frame of this dingy Islington parlour.' Newman complained: 'I was made a humiliation at my minor orders and at my examination for them, and I had to stand at Dr Wiseman's door waiting for confession amid the Oscott boys. . . . We have been (necessarily) treated as children, being grown men.' The married converts were worse off. T. W. Allies was condemned to 'the drudgery of teaching dunces'. Henry Wilberforce, said Newman, was sentenced to a life of 'dull, listless inactivity, and of fitful, precarious employment'. The Catholic Church knew how to use masterful men like Manning, but had no employment for intellectuals. This wastage helps to explain why, in families divided by conversions, animosities lingered on. At Bishop Samuel Wilberforce's impressive funeral in 1873, the Catholic members of the family refused to join in the prayers but sat saying the *De Profundis* to themselves; though it was a Friday, the Protestant members insisted that cutlets be served for lunch – so the Catholics got nothing to eat. See David Newsome, *The Parting of Friends: a study of the Wilberforces and Henry Manning* (London, 1966).

with the State, had loudly appealed for popular support. The identification of the Church with one variety of freedom was an ancient doctrine, rooted in St Paul. But the French revolution seemed to give it new life, since it was a reminder that tyranny was multifarious – there could be tyrannies of reason and tyrannies of ideology, tyrannies of progress, and even tyrannies of liberty, equality and fraternity. An institution which upheld an international and timeless divine law was a necessary counterpoise to unbridled human assertion. In 1809, the Abbé Félicité de La Mennais began a new movement within the French Church with his *Reflections*, which put a distinctively Catholic case against the *philosophes* for the first time, and argued that Catholicism was indispensible to the well-being of the world; in *Tradition* (1814), a study of the episcopate and the papacy, he rejected Gallicanism and presented ultramontanism as the true and necessary face of modern Catholicism. La Mennais was an aristocrat, by birth, a Celt, a visionary, a weak, stunted man, with a thin body wrapped in a brown frock-coat, wearing a skull-cap; his friends said he looked like a sacristan. He was ordained priest in 1816 and set about compiling a huge four-volume restatement of Christian faith as opposed to the prevailing rationalism of the intellectuals, the first modern *summa*, but presented in the form of a personal statement. In the 1820s, he emerged as a natural leader, the centre of a group of young, intense Catholic propagandists and activists, a phenomenon unknown in France since the meridian days of the Jansenists. There was Lacordaire, the Bonapartist son of a Burgundy surgeon, a convert, a priest and a liberal; and Montalembert, a romantic aristocrat, wanting to get back to the Middle Ages, which had been destroyed, in his view, by Richelieu and Louis XIV. At the study-centre La Mennais set up at the College de Juilly, many of the future bishops, preachers, apologists and historians of the French Church gathered. They also met for long and highly emotional discussions at La Chenaie, in Normandy, where in 1828 he formed the voluntary Congregation of St Peter and operated a kind of spiritual dictatorship over the abler young clerics. The group was held together by La Mennais's strong personality, by personal links – 'the deep, generous friendship of the kind that is formed in youth and under enemy fire', as Lacordaire put it – and by the vision of a reinvigorated Church appealing and responding to all the noblest elements in European society and civilization.

In many respects, the group at La Chenaie resembled the Oxford Movement, which came together in the same decade, with La Mennais playing the role of Keble. There was the same romantic preoccupation with medievalism, the same tense atmosphere of male celibacy, of intellectual struggle overlaid with high-strung emotions. And there was the same instability of conviction. But whereas the Oxford Movement was primarily concerned with doctrine, La Mennais was obsessed with the social force of the Church. He wanted to make it a dominant element in European society, as it had been (so he thought) in the thirteenth and fourteenth centuries. 'Without the pope,' he argued, 'there can be no church, without the church no Christianity, and without Christianity no religion and no society, which implies that the life of the European nations is solely dependent on the power of the papacy.' This was the theory. How to make it the practice? As a young man, La Mennais wanted to revert to the Augsburg idea of the princes of Europe settling religion, and thus serving as the agents of a Catholic-papal revival: 'The people are what one makes of them, criminals or well behaved, peaceful or agitators, religious or unbelieving, according to the wishes of those who lead them.' He saw himself and those who felt as he did as the nineteenth-century equivalent of the Jesuits, redeeming the ravages of the Revolution, as the Jesuits had rescued Catholicism from the Reformation. He seems to have thought that the whole of Europe would be Catholic in ten years, if only the princes wished it that way. This Waterloo perspective of the *ancien régime* restored, or rather of a group of enlightened monarchs applying God's law to man under the direction of the Pope, did not survive the actual experience of the years 1815–30. La Mennais and his friends grew to hate the Bourbons and the other sovereign houses of Europe, and gradually their slogan changed from 'the Pope and the king', to 'the Pope and the people'. The new, direct relationship between papacy and individual Catholics, which the destruction of Gallicanism made possible, was to be used to align Catholicism with democracy and construct a social identity of interests between the spiritual influence of the Pope and the mass economic and political power of the ordinary people.

La Mennais launched his new Catholic social philosophy with a small paper called *L'Avenir* in 1830, just three years before Keble's Assize Sermon. The time was well-chosen, since the new bourgeois regime of Louis-Philippe was anxious, as the king put it, 'to keep my finger out of church affairs . . . for once you put it in you cannot pull it out, and there it has to stay.' La Mennais had now come to the view that the Vatican's policy of rebuilding Church-State relationships with the European powers, painstakingly pursued through innumerable concordats and agreements over the last twenty years, was mistaken. He now saw the State as an obstacle to religious truth, and urged that the Church should seek its freedom from it. It should have nothing more to do with the concept of 'legitimacy', which was a burden and an embarrassment. It should not seek privileges at the cost of tying its hands. It should not play safe by aligning itself with the old forces of Europe, but should turn to the people, the force of the future.

La Mennais did not actually coin the phrase 'Christian Democracy', but that was undoubtedly the concept towards which he was moving; and to which, indeed, the Catholic Church itself moved, more than a century later. At the time, however, it was hard to see the papacy reversing its historic conservative role – just at a time, too, when it had appeared to regain so much by maintaining its traditional posture so stoutly. The impact of La Mennais and his group was exceedingly powerful; but it was also narrow. *L'Avenir* had an impressive following among the younger clergy, but its total subscribers only numbered 2,000. Moreover, the French hierarchy and older Catholics tended to put their trust completely in the monarchy, the idea of legitimacy, and the established forces of the past; the privileges of a Church-State relationship, regarded by La Mennais as encumbrances, they felt to be essential to the defence of religion. We see here the emergence for the first time of the great debate in the modern Catholic Church – the policy of security versus the policy of risk. In 1831, *L'Avenir* ran into trouble with the French bishops, and La Mennais, Lacordaire and Montalembert decided to make a personal appeal to the Pope.

The gesture was naive. It would be hard to imagine a man less likely to be sympathetic to La Mennais's ideas, or indeed to any new ideas. Château-briand, the first to hail the new opportunities of Catholicism in the post-Revolutionary era, had sadly come to recognize Rome's limitations when he came to serve as ambassador there: 'Old men name an old man as their sovereign. Once in power he himself appoints old cardinals. Turning in a vicious circle the supreme power is exhausted and stands permanently on the edge of the tomb.' Bartolomeo Cappellari, elected Pope as Gregory XVI not long before the *L'Avenir* appeal, was an old-fashioned monk and in papal terms an embittered triumphalist – indeed, in 1799 he had written a book called *Il Trionfo della Santa Sede*. He belonged to what was called the Zelanti group, a freemasonry of Vatican right-wingers, and his Secretary of State, Lambruschini, the General of the Barnabites, was strongly anti-liberal and worked closely with the Jesuits. The natural conservatism of the two men was intensified by constant political unrest in the papal states. Indeed, Gregory thought he had no alternative but to support princely power everywhere, in the hope that his fellow-sovereigns would rally to his own if the need arose. His was a medieval mind, but not quite in the sense that the La Chenaie group understood. He was crudely superstitious – during a cholera epidemic, he led a propitiatory procession through the streets of Rome carrying a picture of the Madonna he believed had been painted by St Luke; and he accepted uncritically the rights of hereditary title and property, which to him were the very foundations of society. The idea that people had rights, or monarchs obligations, was foreign to him. To the Polish Catholics who rose for religious and national freedom against the oppressive rule of Orthodox Russia he flatly refused support or sympathy; they were, he wrote in an encyclical, 'certain intriguers and spreaders of lies, who under pretence of religion in this unhappy age, are raising their heads against the power of princes'. On 1 March 1832, Gregory granted La Mennais and his lieutenants an interview, but only provided religious topics were not mentioned; it took place in the hostile presence of their legitimist enemy, the Cardinal de Rohan, and was confined to cold platitudes. La Mennais found the Pope 'a cowardly old imbecile', and Rome 'a huge tomb in which there are nothing but bones'. Of the Vatican court he wrote: 'I saw there the most dreadful cesspit that it has ever been the lot of man to look upon. The great sewer of Tarquin itself would have been incapable of dealing with such a mass of filth.' Six months later, during a banquet given in La Mennais's honour by German progressive Catholics in Munich, he was handed the Pope's answer on a silver tray: it took the form of the encyclical *Mirari vos*, which totally condemned his ideas without mentioning his name.

This was effectively the end of the initiative. Lacordaire slipped away from La Chenaie in the night, without saying good-bye. La Mennais himself was ordered to submit openly, and he did so, saying afterwards: 'I signed, yes I signed. I would have admitted that the moon was made of green cheese.' But in fact he intensified, rather than repudiated, his radical ideas. As an anti-aristocratic gesture he henceforth wrote his surname as one word, Lammenais; and his *Paroles d'un Croyant* (1834) was a sustained attack on tyranny, an aggressive defence of democracy, and a plea for 'a free church in a free state' – he prophesied that God would shortly transform society by casting down the oppressors of the poor, and by inaugurating a new age of justice, peace and love. Thus Lammenais in his own lifetime had come full circle, from a legitimist condemnation of revolution to the hope of a Christian millenium. The book was the subject of an explicit papal condemnation, and for the rest of his life (he died in 1854) Lammenais, though never excommunicated, was pushed into the shadows of Catholic disapproval. The failure of his movement meant that the Church in France lost the romantic intellectuals – Victor Hugo, Alfred de Musset, Alfred de Vigny, Lamartine and many others. Thus at the very moment when the Oxford intellectuals – or some of them – were moving to Rome and even crossing the Tiber, the Paris intellectuals were moving out. Intellectually, they met on the drawbridge – some pursuing authority, others fleeing it.

But it would not be true to say that the Church, or even specifically the triumphalists, learned nothing from Lammenais. They accepted his view that the Church could become a popular institution, and the Pope a populist leader. What they denied was his assumption that the Church needed to compromise on its traditional social attitudes to win such support. Indeed some of them, if only dimly, grasped the important point that it was the very refusal of the papacy to compromise that, for many, formed its chief attraction. What repelled a Lammenais attracted a Manning; and not just Mannings but men and women of all classes and nations who saw the Vatican fortress as a security-symbol. It was this instinct which lay behind the success of Giovanni Mastari-Ferretti, who became Pope as Pius IX on the death of Gregory XVI in 1846. His life was a Lammenais-type pilgrimage in reverse. He was an aristocrat and a soldier, but epilepsy forced him to give up the army. He had been to Latin-America during the anti-colonial period, and he began his pontificate with a series of liberal reforms in the papal states. He visited prisons and released political prisoners, allowed some freedom of the press, reformed the criminal code, excused Rome's Jews from attending compulsory sermons, installed gas-lighting and built a railway. The desperate revolutionary year of 1848 turned him round completely: thereafter, for the next thirty years, he aligned himself totally with reaction in Church and State, and set his face steadily against liberalism in any form. In his old age, indeed, he seemed to have taken an almost physical delight in his personal struggle to hold the liberal world at bay, and a pride in epitomizing the traditions and characteristics of the *ancien régime*. He incarnated the papacy as de Maistre had conceived it; and, as de Maistre had perceived, this constituted part of his undoubted power to attract loyalty and devotion from very large numbers of people, including many who were his intellectual superiors. He was the first pope for centuries to become a popular symbol; and it was his very quality of intransigence which seemed to constitute his chief appeal. Sixteen centuries before, Tertullian had remarked with satisfaction that Christianity made outrageous demands on one's credulity – therein lay the glory and power of faith. The point was still valid: indeed, the seemingly relentless march of science and liberalism made it seem, to some, more valid than ever before.

There were also less paradoxical reasons for the success of populist triumphalism. 1848 had frightened other people besides the Pope. In France (and the movement can be paralleled elsewhere) there was a mid-century bourgeois rallying to the stable old faith. The motive was not so much religious as Voltairean: 'I like my lawyer, my tailor, my servants and my wife to believe in God because I can then expect to be robbed and cuckolded less often.' As Lacordaire's friend, Frederic Ozanam, put it (1849): 'Every Voltairean with a decent income is anxious to send people to mass, provided he does not have to go himself.' Ernest Renan called them 'Christians by fear'. (They nevertheless read his shocking and best-selling *Vie de Jésus*.) During the nineteenth century, the Church's economic and financial assets were steadily rebuilt. By the 1860s, especially in certain countries like France, Italy, Germany and Belgium, it had more schools and institutions than ever before, and all the religious orders, but especially the teaching ones, were expanding their numbers. The Church was a 'possessing' body, with which the bourgeois could feel strong affinities, economic if not intellectual. In the state schools, radical secular teachers aroused bourgeois fear and hostility. As Thiers put it: 'Their teachers are 35,000 Socialists and Communists. There is only one remedy: elementary education must be left in the Church's hands.' Such attitudes became the prevailing wisdom of French bourgeois society under the Second Republic of Napoleon III. Perhaps as much by accident as by design – certainly not as a result of deeply shared convictions – Napoleon and Pius IX became allies and, in a sense, partners. Each propped up the regime of the other. From the 1850s, Napoleon, while generally supporting the House of Savoy's anti-Austrian campaign to reunite Italy, used his ultramontane army to prevent the new crown, and its revolutionary supporters, from making Rome the capital of Italy and annexing the papal states by force. So Pius IX gloried in reaction by virtue of Napoleon's bayonets. Equally, the steady approval of the Church was a principal factor in keeping Napoleon in power.

The arrangement was more practical than edifying. Not only Montalembert found it distasteful when the Empress Eugénie, Napoleon's raffish consort, sent the Pope a present of £25,000 on his jubilee. The Bourbon Restoration had been a Catholic regime; the Second Empire was merely a clerical one, marked by cynical attention to the *quid pro quo* on both sides. When Napoleon visited Brittany in 1858, a bishop told him publicly that he was the most devoted Christian king of France since St Louis. The prelate was duly promoted to be archbishop, 'thus earning his tip, like a cab-driver'. This last remark was made not by a fierce anti-clerical but by the Viscomte de Falloux, author of the regime's pro-Catholic schools-laws. Indeed, it was among the Catholics that the alliance evoked the most irreverent comments. At election-time, the Pope's vast and obedient clerical army duly turned out Napoleon's voters; in return, the emperor was obliged to suppress his embarrassment when, in 1858, a three-year-old Jewish boy, called Mortara, baptized by a Catholic servant when in danger of death, was removed from parental control by the Holy Office as soon as he recovered. This was the law of Rome, upheld solely by French infantry. Hence Montalembert's sneer that the alliance was 'a coalition between the guard-room and the sacristy', capped by General Chargarnier's epitome of Napoleon's regime: 'A bawdy house blessed by bishops.'

Yet there was also a number of active and able French Catholics who upheld the new papalism with passionate devotion. Nearly all were converts, that is former agnostics or atheists who had turned to Rome after an emotional or intellectual crisis. As with the Oxford converts, what chiefly attracted them in their new Church was its authority, and its crude self-confidence in cutting through complex intellectual issues. They were not only ultramontanist but, in most cases, violent papalists. Among them was Louis Veuillot, who became editor of the Catholic daily *l'Univers*, and radiated the views of a W. G. Ward but on an incomparably greater scale, and in more virulent form. Veuillot was the son of a cooper, self-taught working-class in manner and outlook – totally unlike the well-heeled and highly-educated Oxford Tractarians, or, for that matter, the upper middle-class French Catholic liberals. He had turned himself into a barrister's clerk and so graduated to journalism, for which he had a kind of genius. He wrote magnificent French prose, and had a sharp eye for the sensational. His posture was one of aggressive enthusiasm, with his short, stocky body, huge head and bristling mane. Veuillot's views of religion and history were unsubtle, the crude prejudices of the traditionalist working-class *croyant*: 'If there is anything to be regretted, it is that they did not burn John Huss earlier, that Luther was not burned with him, and that, at the time of the Reformation, there was not one prince in Europe with enough piety and political sense to start a crusade against the countries it had infected.' On the other hand, he grasped the potentialities of working-class Catholicism. Just as, with a mass-suffrage, the Catholic parish clergy could prove themselves indispensible election-agents to the Right – one of the salient discoveries of the mid nineteenth century – so the advent of modern communications made it possible to organize and regiment the Catholic proletariat and peasantry into a huge force within the Church. The churchgoing masses and the Pope, in alliance, were an unbeatable combination. Veuillot's populism coincided with the growth, under papal impulse, of new forms of mass devotion associated with the Sacred Heart, the Virgin Mary, and the eucharist. Many of these were, in fact, a return to late medieval ideas, and were associated with visions, visitations and the ecstasies of mystics. The Madonna made her appearance twice in Paris, in 1830 and 1836, in Savoy in 1846 and, from 1858, at Lourdes. The two most celebrated religious figures of the age were both sensational, and both French: Bernadette herself, and J-B. Marie Vianney, the parish-priest of Ars, near Lyons. The Curé of Ars flogged himself unmercifully, fasted prodigiously, held all-night prayer sessions and wrestled physically with the Devil. He became a cult-figure, thousands travelling from all over France (and abroad) to confess to him.

Father Vianney was significant of a new trend to exalt the work of the priest and his contacts with the Catholic masses. Veuillot, the astute populist, reinforced this tendency in *L'Univers*. Nearly all the parish priests took it; it was sold outside their churches on Sunday. It reflected and amplified their simple views on religion: devotional piety, the cult of the papacy, and, concealed beneath a thick veneer of emotionalism and sentimentality, the mechanical Christianity of the Middle Ages, the credal climate in which populist triumphalism could flourish. Ozanam said of Veuillot and his friends: 'They are not trying to convert unbelievers but to rouse the passions of believers.' This was broadly true. The ultimate object of a total Christian society was not abandoned, but it was subordinated to the organization of the faithful for the purpose of exercising power. As Veuillot saw it, this would be achieved by readjusting the balance within the Church, by strengthening the links between the sole and autocratic power of the papacy, on the one hand, and the parish priests and the masses on the other; and by turning the episcopate into mere Vatican functionaries. *L'Univers*, and the spiritual atmosphere it created, was an important instrument in this process. It became extremely difficult for any French bishop, unless his personal position was exceptionally strong, to argue or act against a line taken by the paper, especially if, as was usual, it was supported by the Pope and a majority of the parish priests. When in 1853 the Archbishop of Paris and Bishop Doupanloup of Orléans, the outstanding individualist of the French hierarchy, condemned the paper, Veuillot appealed to the Pope. Pius exonerated him in the encyclical *Inter Multiplices*, in which he commanded the hierarchy to be 'generous in their encouragements and to show their goodwill and love towards those men who . . . devote the watches of the night to writing books and papers . . . so that the ancient rights of the Holy See and its acts may enjoy their full force, so that opinions and sentiments contrary to this Holy See may disappear, so that the darkness of error may be dissipated and the minds of men flooded with the blessed light of the truth.' And what was this 'blessed light of the truth'? *L'Univers* had the answer: 'Who is the Pope? He is Christ on earth.' This was the paper's theme throughout the 1850s and 1860s. It was also the theme of an increasing number of bishops. Trains and steamships made it possible for most of them to travel to the Vatican regularly, and they did so increasingly at the Pope's invitation; communications thus served to break down the 'Gallican' element in the Church, itself a product of isolation and distance as much as anything else, and to make it increasingly difficult for bishops to resist the papal inclination, even on quite minor matters. Many bishops, in fact, moved wholly into the triumphalist camp, and became the fuglemen and drum-beaters of the new populism. Bishop Mermillod went so far as to deliver a sermon on the three incarnations of Christ – in the womb of the Virgin Mary, in the eucharist, and in the person of Pius IX. As episcopal subservience developed, the resurrected conciliar theory of the eighteenth century was quietly buried again, and it became clear that Pius IX had very little, if anything, to fear from a council.

A council was necessary to crown triumphalism by giving the sanction of the Church Fathers to the doctrine of papal infallibility, long asserted but never formally pronounced as dogma. For many years Pius IX had been urged to take such a step by his supporters, led by Manning, now Archbishop of Westminster, for whom papal infallibility was the necessary and ultimate endorsement of the authoritarian principle. And much of Pius's reign had seemed a preparation for the event. In 1854, his bull *Ineffabilis Deus* plunged into the heady waters of theological adventurism by declaring 'the Blessed Virgin Mary to have been, from the first instant of her conception, by a singular grace and privilege of Almighty God, in view of the merits of Christ Jesus the Saviour of mankind, preserved free from stain or original sin'. Here was a case of a pious traditional belief turned into ineradicable dogma – and in the teeth of Protestant, and even liberal Catholic, hostility. Such gestures appealed to the faithful Catholic masses; they were part of the populist repertoire. So, too, were great gatherings of the clergy. In 1862, to mark the canonization of twenty-six missionaries martyred in Japan, Pius invited the entire episcopate to attend a Pentecostal celebration in Rome. The response was encouraging: 323 cardinals, patriarchs, archbishops and bishops, over 4,000 priests, and 100,000 Catholic lay-folk. In 1864, the Pope made a characteristically late-medieval gesture: he published an encyclical, *Quanta cura*, announcing that the following year would be a jubilee, in which a plenary indulgence might be gained by those strong in the Catholic faith. And by way of an appendix to the encyclical he included a document listing the propositions which a good Catholic was specifically enjoined not to hold. This 'Syllabus of Errors' was in fact an index, giving references to various views already condemned in papal speeches, letters, addresses and encyclicals. Its precise status and authority was not, therefore, entirely clear, but in the circumstances it appeared to be a defiant manifesto against the whole of the modern world. Sections 1–7 condemned pantheism, naturalism and absolute rationalism; 8–14 moderate rationalism; 15–18 indifferentism, latitudinarianism, socialism, communism, secret societies, Bible societies and liberal clerical groups. Sections 19–76 set out the rights of the Church, and of the Roman pontiff and his state, in the most uncompromising and triumphalist manner, and any infringements by civil society were roundly condemned. It was wrong to deny the Pope the right to 'a civil princedom' or to the use of force to defend it; Catholics were forbidden to accept civil education, or to deny the assertion that the 'Catholic religion was the sole religion of the state to the exclusion of all others'; and in Section 79 freedom of speech was condemned as leading to 'corruption of manners and minds' and 'the pest of indifferentism'. Finally, Section 80 summarized the document by condemning the assertion that 'the Roman pontiff can and should reconcile and harmonize himself with progress, with liberalism, and with recent civilization'.

The Syllabus was received with astonishment, not to say incredulity by many non-Catholics, and with dismay by liberal Catholics (and a number of bishops). Some governments, notably those of France, Austria and Bavaria, feared that it might be invested with full dogmatical authority at any forthcoming council. There was some attempt, on the part of those Catholics who thought it both theologically possible and socially essential, for the Church to adjust to the modern world, to organize opposition and put the brakes on the headlong progress to triumphalism. Among the leading English laity, the liberal historian Lord Acton, who had extensive academic and political contacts on the Continent, went on a tour of European state archives in the years 1864–8, which awoke him to what he termed 'the vast tradition of conventional mendacity', including the willingness of a triumphalist papacy to employ lying and violence to further essentially secular policies. In his travels he was able to consult with the critical Catholic element, especially in Germany. In France, too, Montalembert now became convinced that the ultramontanism he had once vigorously sponsored had been perverted to transform the Pope into a theological monster, what he termed 'a papal Louis XIV'. But it would be an error to suppose these opposition elements were significant either in numbers or influence. In Britain, the Catholic Church, for all practical purposes, was wholly controlled by Cardinal Manning, the most ardent of triumphalists; in France, the liberals were in a tiny minority – Montalembert's *Correspondent* was a monthly selling only 3,000 copies. In 1867, Pius summoned another gathering to Rome, to celebrate the eighteenth centenary of the great pontifical feast of SS Peter and Paul. This time over 500 bishops attended, with 20,000 priests and 150,000 lay-pilgrims. Finally, the invitations to the council went out. W. G. Ward, who had greeted the publication of the Syllabus with noisy approval, and who used to say 'I should like to have a fresh papal bull to read every morning with my breakfast', not only assumed that papal infallibility would be declared dogmatic, but publicly expressed the hope that it would be defined as widely as possible, that is, to include papal letters and encyclicals. A new Jesuit publication, the *Civilita Cattolica*, published in Rome and believed to be the semi-official organ of Vatican opinion, went further: in an attack on French progressives, it divided the faithful 'into two parties – one, simply Catholics, the other those who call themselves liberal Catholics'; the latter were not really Catholics at all, and were to be distinguished by their critical approach to papal infallibility. When the dogma was placed before the council, 'which it is hoped will be very shortly', the proper course would be for the Fathers 'to define it by acclamation', without debate or vote. This was also the position adopted by *L'Univers* and other ultramontanist organs. It clearly had the approval of Pius IX himself, who was fond of saying '*La tradizione sono io!*'

In the event, the dogma was defined in 1870 only after long debate and in a qualified form which limited the Pope's freedom from error only to matters of faith and morals defined *ex cathedra*. But in all other respects the council marked the apparent extinction of the liberal Catholics. It took place against the background of the Franco-Prussia war, the withdrawal of French military protection, the Italian seizure of Rome and the extinction of the papal states. But this eclipse of the Pope's temporal power served, in real terms, to emphasize the huge importance of his new and dominant position within the Church and, it seemed, within Christianity in consequence. The fortress had been constructed not in perishable stone but in ideas and populist notions. Its garrison was unanimous. Montalembert had turned his back on the council in disgust: 'I do not want to offer up justice, reason and history as a burnt offering to the idol that the lay theologians of Catholicism have set up for themselves in the Vatican.' Bishop Doupanloup protested in vain that Cardinal Barnabo, Prefect of the College of Propaganda, was 'driving the bishops like pigs'. Professor Johann von Dollinger, leader of the German anti-triumphalists, and Acton's close friend, rejected the dogma: 'As a Christian, as a theologian, as a historian and as a citizen, I cannot accept this doctrine.' A few, mainly academics, went with him, and formed the Old Catholic Church. Acton himself washed his hands of ecclesiastical politics. These desertions or renunciations caused scarcely a ripple within the Church, and were welcome to most of the triumphalists. Of the few bishops who initially voted against the dogma, or allowed their opposition to it to become known, some survived because of the strength of their personal position. Others were victimized, not indeed by the Vatican – that was unnecessary – but by their own triumphalist clergy. Thus Mgr de Marguerye, Bishop of Autun, after his return from the council, tried to justify his negative vote at a meeting of his diocesan clergy: they denied him a hearing by drumming their feet on the wooden boards of the chapter-house, and he felt he had no choice but to resign his see. A great silence descended on the Catholic Church.

By 1870, then, the papacy had achieved a position of total control within Roman Christianity which it had been unable to secure even in the thirteenth century, and it had achieved it in circumstances which seemed to suggest that the overwhelming majority of Christians who owed allegiance to Rome were not only willing, but eager, to accord the Holy See this unprecedented paramountcy. In the dawn of democracy, Rome had erected a popular despotism; and it had done so in a Christian Europe which, in the 1870s, was rapidly extending its dominion to cover virtually the entire civilized world. The papacy had constructed for itself a fortress against modernity: in 1870 it had seemed to enter the fortress with a united garrison, and raise the drawbridge. But the 'idol in the Vatican' assumed, and most of his supporters assumed with him, that a time would come when the garrison would issue forth and, in the name of a united European Christianity, complete its universalist mission. 'To the City and to the World' – the ancient papal phrase seemed to have acquired a new significance in 1870. But how real was this vision of global Christianity?

PART SEVEN

Almost-Chosen Peoples
(1500–1910)

ON 13 NOVEMBER 1622, the Virginia Company of London, then engaged in opening up the Atlantic Coast of North America, held a feast at the Merchant Taylors' Hall. The subscription was three shillings a head: 'And for that at such great feasts venison is esteemed a most necessary compliment, the Court hath thought fit that letters be addressed in the name of the Company unto such noblemen and gentlemen as are of this society to request this favour at their hands, and withall their presence at the said supper.' Before the feast, the Company listened to a sermon at St Michael's Cornhill, delivered by the Dean of St Paul's, John Donne. Dean Donne told the four hundred well-to-do merchants present that their object in crossing the Atlantic should not be so much the amassing of wealth as the recovery of souls, 'Act over the Acts of the Apostles; be you a light to the gentiles, that sit in darkness . . . God taught us to make ships, not to transport ourselves, but to transport Him.'. Let them all be missionaries, he concluded, 'And you shall have made this island, which is but the suburbs of the old world, a bridge, a gallery to the new; to join all to that world that shall never grow old, the Kingdom of Heaven.'

We have no means of knowing how seriously the Virginia merchants took Donne's exhortations to act in the spirit of the first Apostles. The universalist urge which had animated the early Christians had never wholly disappeared. But it had become inextricably mingled with other motives and often completely subordinated to them. Moreover, it appeared to have lost some of its dynamism. In the seventh century, Christianity's expansion to the south and east was sealed off by the various Monophysite heresies, and by Islam, which constituted, and indeed still constitutes, an almost impenetrable barrier to Christian progress. Byzantium abandoned its efforts in these directions, except in pursuit of purely political and military aims, and sent missions only to the northern pagans of Russia. The crusaders would not, or could not, proselytize in Africa or Asia, or even assist existing Christian communities to maintain themselves. The Latin mercantile cities were not primarily interested in converts, and certainly made few.

From the early thirteenth century, the Teutonic Knights, assisted by the Dominicans, undertook the systematic conversion of Prussia and the Baltic. Force was used. One of the treaties specified: 'All who are not baptized must receive the rite within a month.' Those who declined were banished from the company of Christians, and any who relapsed were to be reduced to slavery. Pagan rites were banned, monogamy enforced, and churches built. Neophytes were obliged to attend church on Sundays and feast-days and provide support for the clergy; and converts had to observe the Lenten fast, confess at least once a year and take Communion at Easter. But the prime object was conquest and settlement. So long as it instructed the pagans, the order was authorized to possess any lands it conquered; and when the new territories were divided into bishoprics, the bishops received a third. Thus paganism was finally eliminated from Europe, the process being completed in the last decades of the fourteenth century when Lithuania was settled. But during this long process, which had begun early in the sixth century, two propositions had become deeply rooted in Christian minds, both alien to Christian teaching or indeed to the practice of the early Church. The first was the association of conversion with conquest, or at any rate with economic penetration; the second was the identification of Christianity, or Christendom, with the European continent and its races. Just as the Latin crusaders had treated the eastern Christians (even when they were in communion with Rome) as inferiors, or even as enemies, so there was a tendency to regard non-European converts as second-class Christians.

This may help to explain the failure of the earliest European missions. For there were some, even though their ostensibly religious purpose was combined with the political and military object of weakening Moslem power. There were a number of Franciscan missions in both Central Asia and India in the thirteenth and fourteenth centuries, with the aim of reinforcing the semi-Christian element among the Mongol tribes. Early in the fourteenth century an 'Archbishop of the East' was established in or near Peking, and a team of fifty friars was despatched there in 1335. But the scheme was never very successful; and it collapsed when the Chinese retook Peking from the Mongols before the end of the century. Missions to Moslem and pagan Africa also proved ephemeral. In the late thirteenth century Raymond Lull worked out the first modern missionary programme, and established a college of oriental languages in Majorca. In 1311 the Council of Vienne asked the European universities to provide courses in modern oriental tongues. But very little came of these plans. There were Christian posts on the south side of the Straits of Gibraltar in 1415; in 1444 contact was made with the negro races of tropical Africa, in 1482 with the Congo, and five years later there was a landing at the Cape of Good Hope. In 1518 it appears that an African was consecrated a titular bishop and Vicar-Apostolic of West Africa; but we do not know whether he ever returned there. Virtually all the African missions seem to have died out by the mid sixteenth century.

The papacy took little part in these ventures. Indeed, it had no motive other than a purely altruistic one. In an age when power over the national churches was passing to princes, early missions, associated with trade or colonization, came under the crowns, and papal interference was almost invariably ruled out. It was a different matter for the great 'imperialist' orders, the Franciscans, Dominicans, Augustinians and, later, the Jesuits. To them missionary work was an enormous and valuable extension of their activities. They dominated the first phase of Christian colonization. The Protestants, having no orders, lacked the personnel and the means to undertake missionary work. And they were not sure of its value. Luther's mind was limited by national, almost provincial, horizons. He scarcely thought in continental, let alone global terms. He thought 'the faith of Jews, Turks and Papists is all one thing.' He was interested in reforming Christians rather than converting pagans. And the Calvinists were preoccupied with the élite. Their faith did not focus on the heathen masses. With some justice Cardinal Bellarmine attacked Protestants for their lack of missionary activity: 'Heretics are never said to have converted Jews or pagans, but only to have perverted Christians.' Some Protestants argued that the command of Christ to preach the gospel ceased with the apostles: the offer had been made once and for all, and there was no need to make it again. But this was a minority opinion. Donne's sermon reflects Anglican orthodoxy. Many of the English seamen and Atlantic traders were pious, even fanatical, Protestants who felt an obligation to proselytize. Sir Humphrey Gilbert's charter of 1583 refers to the compassion of God 'for poor infidels, it seeming probable that God hath reserved these gentiles to be introduced into Christian civility by the English nation'. Many early company charters express a similar conviction. But such missions were left in secular and mercantile hands. The Anglican church created no organization; nor did the state. Chaplains were appointed for the benefit of the merchant or settler communities. Conversions served the objects of commerce or were the work of individuals.

It was in territories occupied by the Spanish and Portuguese that the missions were taken seriously. The work was undertaken almost entirely by the orders, led by the Franciscans, on the instructions of the crown. Motives were mixed. The authorities needed a docile labour force and a sense of security. Conversion was an element of the conquest, as it had been in eighth-century Europe: the Indians, like the Saxons, were told that their gods had failed them in allowing the Spanish to win. Some of the *conquistadores* were pious; Cortes had a devotion to the Blessed Virgin, carried her image with him, and her standard; his orders were '... the first aim of your expedition is to serve God and spread the Christian faith ... you must neglect no opportunity to spread the knowledge of the true faith and the church of God among those people who dwell in darkness.' One of his earliest messages home was to ask for the dispatch of missionaries 'with as little delay as possible'. On the other hand, Pizarro admitted brutally: 'I have not come for any such reasons. I have come to take their gold away from them.' Was it a case of Cortes being hypocritical and Pizarro honest? Medieval Christian soldiers were curious and volatile combinations; often the most savage among them were the most generous in Christian charity and works, as the rise of the Cistercians suggests. The friars were also divided in themselves. They were motivated by inter-order rivalry, by the quest for spiritual and material power, but also, right from the start, by compassion for the Indians. In Hispaniola, on Christmas Day 1511, the Dominican Antonio de Montesimos preached a sermon to the settlers to the text 'I am a voice crying in the wilderness' in which he demanded: 'By what right or justice do you keep these Indians in such horrible servitude? . . . Are these not men? Have they not rational souls? Are you not bound to love them as you love yourselves?'

The first batch of twelve Franciscans arrived in Mexico in 1526: within thirty years there were 380 of them, plus 210 Dominicans and 212 Augustinians. By this time, it was claimed the Franciscans alone had baptized over five million natives, considerably more than the entire population of England at that time. There is no means of checking these figures or even of knowing how they were compiled. The whole conversion process was an extraordinary mixture of force, cruelty, stupidity and greed, redeemed by occasional flashes of imagination and charity. We have a copy of the first address by the original twelve Franciscans: 'We do not seek gold, silver or precious stones: we seek only your health.' Some Indians were baptized immediately after submission. Papal efforts to restrict defective ceremonies of baptism were failures. The catechism process was rudimentary. Moreover, we have an episcopal edict of 1539 forbidding missionaries to beat Indians with rods, or imprison them with irons, 'to teach them the Christian doctrine'. In Mexico there were six main languages and many minor ones, none of which the missionaries spoke at first. One witness, Munoz Camargo, says they pointed to the earth, fire, toads and snakes to suggest Hell, raised their eyes to Heaven, then spoke of a single God. More systematic conversion was attempted by seizing children, teaching them at missionary schools, and then using them as interpreters and proselytes.

The Aztecs were polytheists, practising human sacrifice and, in some areas, ritual cannibalism; but there were also points of comparison with Christianity – their chief god was born of a virgin, they ate pastry images of him twice a year, they had forms of baptism and confession, and a compass-point cross. Yet there was no attempt to build on these foundations, contrary to early Christian practice and, indeed, to the instructions of Gregory the Great. From the time of Juan de Zumarraga, first Bishop of Mexico, a great destroyer of religious antiquities, a systematic attempt was made to erase all trace of pre-Christian cults. Writing in 1531, he claimed that he personally had smashed over 500 temples and 20,000 idols. (It is true, of course, that temples were sometimes used as fortresses.) Little resistance is recorded. Some idols were taken away and hidden, and Indians refused to reveal them even under torture. But there is only one case in which they seem to have argued with the missionaries on theological grounds, defending their own religion. Usually they retreated to more remote areas, and only when this was impossible did they stage revolts. In settled areas, they were liable to prosecution by the Holy Office for concubinage, bigamy or heresy. Thus a chief was accused in 1539 of concubinage and idolatry; arms and idols were found in his house; and his ten-year-old son, as often happened in Inquisition trials, gave evidence against him. The chief, Ometochtzin, known as 'Don Carlos Mendoza', said in his deposition that the various orders of friars and seculars had different dress and rules; that everyone had his own way of life; so had the Indians, and they should not be obliged to give it up; he also argued that many Spaniards were drunkards and scoffed at religion. He was condemned to death.

Efforts were undoubtedly made to convey the subtleties and truth of Christianity. In teaching his converts, Maturino Gilberti tried hard to distinguish between devotion and image-worship – later he thought this was the chief reason why he was suspected of Protestantism. Francisco de Bustamente railed against the cult of the Virgin, because of the polytheistic confusion it produced. Most priests did not bother much. Luis Caldera, a Franciscan, who spoke only Spanish, taught the doctrine of Hell by throwing dogs and cats into an oven, and lighting a fire under it: the howls of the animals terrified the Indians. The difficulty was that the more imaginative or sensitive missionaries nearly always got into trouble with their superiors, ecclesiastical or secular. The most remarkable of the sixteenth century Franciscans, Barnadino de Sahagun, who spent over sixty years in Mexico, argued that it was vital to study the 'spiritual maladies' and 'the vices of the country' in order to effect Christianization. He employed native assistants and an original methodology to compile a gigantic *Historia general de las cosas de Nueva Espana*, whose twelve volumes covered the religion, customs, constitution, intellectual and economic life, flora, fauna and the languages of Mexico and its peoples. It was written in both Nahuatl and Spanish, and must be regarded as one of the greatest intellectual achievements of the entire Renaissance. But it aroused the opposition of his colleagues, and in 1577 Philip II ordered its confiscation, though one copy was to be sent to the Council of the Indies for examination; no one was to be allowed to 'describe the superstitions and customs of the Indians'. Barnadino died without knowing what had happened to his life's work, and the manuscript was not recovered until 1779; two similar studies were made, but none was printed until modern times. Nevertheless, some of the friars, especially the Franciscans, persisted in native studies; some could preach in three dialects, and by 1572 there were 109 publications (that we know of) in ten different native languages, most of them in Nahuatl, which the friars tried to raise to a *lingua franca*. The Holy Office seems to have disliked all publications for the Indians, even catechisms, especially if they were in translation; and the crown, too, tried to insist on Spanish, 'that the Indians be instructed in our Castilian speech and accept our social organization and good customs' (1550). The intrinsic difficulties of finding the exact translation for Christian concepts were greatly increased by fear of heterodoxy. The seculars, who took virtually no part in the missions, and who hated the friars, were always on the watch; and in each order there was a rigorist group in sly contact with the authorities at home. In 1555 the first Mexican synod ordered the seizure of all sermons in the native language; and ten years later a further synod forbade the Indians access to the scriptures, in any language.

We come here to some of the central problems which confronted mission work, which indeed have always bedevilled efforts to spread Christianity. To what extent should Christianity, in penetrating new societies and cultures, take on a native coloration and adapt its presentation of the essential truth? There is very good reason to believe, as we have seen, that the earliest Christian missionaries, spreading in Africa, Asia Minor and southern Europe, developed modulations and varieties which assisted the rapid dissemination of Christian ideas, and which were only later, in the course of three centuries, reconciled to a standard. It is hard not to believe that this was the apostles' intention; it is certainly adumbrated in Paul's Epistles. But by the sixteenth century, a millenium and a half of increasingly narrow doctrinal definition had deprived Christianity of its flexibility and ambiguities. And then, in its homeland, Christianity itself was locked in dispute over points of doctrine which had come to seem momentous. Any divergence was held to entail torture and death in this world and eternal horror in the next. Moreover, arrogant and insistent state power was involved: Christianity was identified with a national culture whose export was the whole point of the conquest.

In Spanish and Portuguese America, the missionary friars (and later the Jesuits) were far too closely supervised by state and church authorities to attempt, or permit, a marriage between Christian and local culture. They did what seemed to them the next best thing: attempted to effect a separation between the native Christians and the Spanish settlers and half-castes; and this was made possible because it was both official and ecclesiastical policy to gather the Indians in new villages. In Mexico all the orders, but especially the Augustinians, were enthusiastic founders of new villages and towns. This reorganization and separation of the people allowed the friars to impress their leadership on the Indians in their own way. Thus the Franciscan Antonio de Roa went barefoot, wore nothing but a coarse robe and slept on boards, took no wine, meat or bread, and in the sight of the Indians, threw himself on burning coals, had himself singed with a torch, and scourged himself every time he saw a cross. By such methods the Franciscans, says Suarez de Peralta, 'were almost worshipped by the Indians'. Scourging was one of the aspects of Christianity the Indians seem to have adopted eagerly. Missionaries were asked: 'Why do you not order me to be whipped?', after confession; and natives adopted the custom of scourging themselves in Lent, and in times of drought or epidemic. (Even today, in Tzintzuntlan, the natives scourge themselves, on occasion, for several hours with nail-studded straps.)

The new towns and villages enabled a specifically local way of life and decor to evolve, even if the faith presented was, and remained, alien. The friars laid out squares, streets and plantations, and built hospitals, convents and churches. Some of these places were huge, with 30,000 inhabitants, and involved major works. Near Mexico City, one friar, Francisco de Tembleque, took nearly two decades to build a gigantic aqueduct, 30 miles long, with 136 arches; he was the sole European engaged in this project, which worked for

126 years and is still virtually intact. In these places, the churches, like Aztec temples, took on the dual role of fortresses; they were often built in high or defensible places, as at Tepeaca, Tochimilco and Tula, for instance – huge, crenellated masses, with a single row of high windows, square buttresses and turrets, the roof a gun-platform. They had walled exterior enclosures, which could accommodate whole populations or up to 10,000 troops.

Some of these churches were gigantic. The Augustinians were the big builders. Often, three or four of them in a convent would cause thousands of Indians to set up churches bigger than Seville Cathedral. In 1554, one official, Lebron de Quinones, told Philip II that such churches were deliberately created 'of an extreme splendour and sumptuousness' to impress the Indians. Philip also got a complaint from the jealous cathedral chapter of Guadalajara that 'when the Augustinian friars built . . . a new monastery, the few natives left alive disappeared because of the splendour the friars aspire to in constructing their churches and convents.' This was denied. The Dominicans claimed that 'we see to it that the Indians work on them with their full consent and at their pleasure, without abuse or vexation of any kind.' It is hard to know where the truth lay, since specific charges usually flowed from inter-order rivalry, or, more often, from the hatred of the seculars. In 1561 two bishops brought a case against all three orders of friars because they had 'inflicted and are now inflicting many mistreatments on the Indians . . . they insult and strike them, tear out their hair, have them stripped and cruelly flogged, and then throw them into prison in cages and cruel irons.' All Christian organizations, lay or secular, flogged Indians at times. On the other hand, in some ways the Indians adapted themselves enthusiastically to mission civilization. Zummarago, writing to Charles V, noted: 'The Indians are great lovers of music, and priests who hear their confessions tell me they are converted more by music than by anything else.' In the enclaves, terrific religious ceremonies were developed. The Indians learned singing and especially plain-chant more easily than anything else, and they took rapidly to a wide variety of instruments – clarinets, cornets, trumpets, fifes, trombones, Moroccan and Italian flutes, drums, bowed guitars and many others. Juan de Grijalva wrote: 'There is not an Indian village even of 20 inhabitants which is without trumpets and a few flutes to enrich the services.' It is typical of Philip II's niggling attention to detail that he tried to reduce the numbers of singers and instrumentalists in these villages in 1561 – with no success. Equally futile were official bans on liturgical extravaganzas, including wild dancing, which grew up round religious fiestas.

But if these protected enclaves were intended (and the policy of the orders was never clear, even to themselves) to produce a distinctively native and self-sustaining form of Christianity, they were total failures. They necessarily involved the concept of tutellage. Travellers could not stay there for more than two days. In Mexico, no Europeans, mestizos, negroes or mulattoes were allowed to settle in them. In parts of Brazil and Paraguay, the Jesuits, with their customary efficiency, created entire colonies, or *reductiones* as they were called, stretching over thousands of square miles. By 1623 there were over a score of them, encompassing 100,000 inhabitants, and they continued to expand, especially after 1641 when the Portuguese authorities forebade access to these territories and allowed the Jesuits to maintain private armies to defend them. The friars also had their armed bands, and indeed were sometimes accused of fighting pitched battles with each other, with the seculars, and with the authorities themselves. In a way this idea of protecting vulnerable natives and their way of life from intruding European civilization is a modern one; but the instinct was paternalistic and necessarily condescending. 'All the Indians', Philip II was told, 'are like nestlings whose wings have not grown enough yet to allow them to fly for themselves . . . religious, as your Majesty should know, are their true mothers and fathers.' There was an invincible reluctance to admit that the fledglings might grow up, or assist them to do so. The Dominicans refused to found any secondary schools, and it was always against their policy to teach Latin – the key to advance of any kind – to Indians. The Franciscans and Augustinians were less dogmatic, and they in fact discovered that the natives took to Latin more easily than Spaniards. But the College of Santiago Tlatelolco, where the Franciscans taught it, did not produce a single native priest. Even so attempts to educate the Indians met bitter criticism. Jeronimo Lopez wrote in 1541 : 'It is a most dangerous error to teach science to the Indians and still more to put the Bible and the holy scriptures into their hands. . . . Many people in our Spain have been lost that way, and have invented a thousand heresies.' Teaching Latin bred insolence and, worse, exposed the ignorance of European priests. (Bishop Montufar quoted an instance in which, of twenty-four Spanish Augustinians brought to him for ordination, only two knew Latin.) One complaint was that 'reading the holy scriptures, [the Indians] would learn that the old patriarchs had many wives at the same time, just as they used to have.' Eventually the college was accused of teaching heresy, and entrance to Indians was forbidden; thus it lost its purpose and decayed. Synods repeatedly made it clear, in any case, that natives were not to be ordained, or indeed admitted to monastic orders except as servitors. We know of one case in which an Indian. Lucas, was refused admission to the Dominicans, despite 'his virtues and exemplary life', the reason being stated bluntly 'because he is an Indian'. If individual friars favoured Indian priests, the policies of their orders remained adamant until quite recent times. The Jesuits in South America were no more enlightened. They protected their Indian charges jealously but never accorded them the status of adult Christians. Hence, when the society was suppressed in the late eighteenth century, the *reductiones* had no native cadres to sustain them, and were quickly and ruthlessly pillaged by the settlers.

The failure to produce self-sustaining Christianity among the natives was paralleled among the Latin-American communities of European descent. In the Roman empire distinctive regional schools of Christianity had soon emerged, both before the development of orthodoxy, and after: Alexandria, Antioch, Carthage, Spain, the Rhone Valley – all had made their cultural and doctrinal contributions to Christian richness within a few generations of receiving the faith. The process had been repeated again and again as Christianity spread over Europe. But the transplantation to Latin America bore no such fruit. This huge continent, where paganism was quickly expunged, where great cities, universities and sub-cultures were soon established, where Christianity was united and monopolistic, carefully protected by the State from any hint of heresy, schism or rival, and where the clergy were innumerable, rich and privileged, made virtually no distinctive contribution to the Christian message and insight in over four centuries. Latin America exuded a long, conformist silence. This is not entirely surprising. Spain, as we have seen, had staged its own orthodox reformation before the Lutheran schism. It possessed powerful and popular institutional machinery to stifle clerical initiatives of any kind. Ecclesiastical control was, if anything, even more effective in the crown colonies than at home. And then, too, the clergy has always been employed by the Spanish kings as royal agents, just as their councils had served as legislative assemblies. The Catholic Church was a department of the Spanish government, and never more so than in the Americas. Right from the start Charles v and Philip ii used clerics to check abuses and limit the independence of early colonists and officials, the precedent being set by the appointment of Fr Bernado Boil to represent the crown's interests in newly discovered Hispaniola, the first settlement. In return, the Church required protection, privilege, and the crown's unswerving devotion to the orthodox faith. In these circumstances, there was no place or opportunity for experiment or deviation. Steadfast and united against change, both Church and crown liked this working arrangement, whereby the Pope was excluded along with heresy, and the crown ruled – but vicariously, through the hierarchy. The system was remarkably successful, and cheap. The royal garrisons were tiny. The clergy mesmerized Spaniards and natives alike. They could always be brought in to quell riots when soldiers failed.

The system broke down only when the crown itself, in the eighteenth century, deserted the orthodox Catholic camp and initiated reforms. This was all very well for enlightened despots in Europe, but it was fatal in the Americas, where the Church, not the army, was the instrument of control. The first warning came in 1769, when the Jesuits were suppressed, arrested and deported. Mobs of angry Indians tried to break into the barracks where the Jesuits were held, in an effort to release them; and a large military escort was required to march 500 Jesuits to the coast at Veracruz. The crown was repeatedly advised that moves against the clergy would weaken its grip on the colonies. There was need, the king was told for 'constant vigilance to preserve suitable conduct and healthy principles of obedience and love for Your Majesty among the clergy' (1768); 'the conduct of the people depends in large part on that of the clergy' (1789). The most effective way of quelling unrest, he was informed, was 'to station a friar with a holy crucifix in the nearest plaza'. In 1799 the cathedral chapter of Pueblo wrote to the king of the 'fanatical devotion' of the Indians to the clergy, whose hands 'they always knelt to kiss', and whose advice they 'blindly followed'. The same year an Indian crowd attacked a Pueblo gaol where a priest was imprisoned. The Indians, the king was warned, 'resented royal reforming efforts to remove ecclēsiastical privileges'.

It was the failure of the Spanish crown and government to hᵤᵤᵢ these warnings which led to the colonial revolution, under the cry 'America is the only refuge left for the religion of Jesus Christ.' The Latin-American clergy did not want an uneasy mixture of Bourbonism and Voltaire, and when they were given it they revolted, and carried the masses with them. It was the famous decree of 1812 abolishing clerical immunity which detonated the independence movement. The clergy provided many of the political and military leaders of the insurrection. Priests persuaded their entire parishes to 'pronounce' for the revolution. It was the clergy who drew up the first scheme for separation from Spain, in 1794, and provided most of the press propaganda. They were active politically throughout Spanish America, but in Mexico they also provided the military leadership. The rebellion of September 1810 was started by a village curate in the small town of Dolores in Michoacan. Among active rebels who had been captured or convicted, the government identified 244 secular priests and 157 monks and friars. One official wrote (1812): '. . . the ecclesiastics were the principal authors of this rebellion . . . one can count by the hundreds the generals, brigadiers, colonels and other officers, all clerics, in the bands of the traitors, and there is scarcely a military action of any importance in which priests are not leading the enemy.' As the Bishop of Pueblo told the king, Mexico was a nation which hid 'a profound malice and irreconcilable hatred towards its conqueror underneath the most humble and abject exterior'; Spain had controlled its colonies with only a token force for 300 years because the clergy had constantly preached obedience to the king. For a time, the bishops, the cathedral clergy and the Inquisition officials (most of them born in Spain) remained loyal, though their efforts to rally the lower clergy to the crown were ineffective. The last straw came in 1820, when the triumph of the liberals in Spain, followed by anti-clerical legislation, brought all the prelates, with two exceptions, out on the side of independence. Fr Mariano Lopez Bravo told Ferdinand vii in 1822 that Spain lost Mexico because the clergy had persuaded the people that their choice lay between loyalty to the crown and 'defending their religion from destruction, their priests from persecution and their churches from despoliation'. He said that when he had attempted to preach against independence 'they branded me as a heretic'. Thus Spain forfeited the New World by reforming its colonial pillar, the Church. The attempt failed; the Church emerged stronger; it retained its political and financial privileges. But it now reigned in isolation, without the support of the crown, and so in turn has tended to fall victim to the violent anti-clericalism of the nineteenth and twentieth centuries, until, quite recently, it has resumed its revolutionary role in defence of a new orthodoxy.

The case of Latin America is without parallel. Yet it directs attention to what might be called the dynamic weakness of all the missions sponsored by mature Christianity. From the sixteenth century, Christian attempts to evangelize the world were continuous in one theatre or another, and at times extremely vigorous. But they have never set off a chain-reaction. They have tended to require continual reinforcement, guidance and creative stimulation. The lack of self-sustaining growth in Latin America was not fatal to the Church there since its only local opponents were primitive forms of paganism. But when Christianity had to compete with well-established and sophisticated religious cults in Asia it was a very different matter, especially when it lacked the political and military support of a colonial government. The western mercantile penetration of the Asiatic seaboard in the sixteenth century was extremely rapid, and was closely followed by the erection of an ecclesiastical structure. The Portuguese set up a bishopric in Madeira in 1514, Cap Verde in 1532, Goa 1533, Malacca 1557, and Macao in 1576. By this time the Spanish were in Manilla, which got its first bishop three years later. Yet Christianiz-ation was slow and remained unspectacular. Only the Philippines, which the Spaniards conquered in the 1560–70s, and where they imposed their religion virtually by force, became a predominantly Christian country. And there the missionaries had to deal only with primitive pagan cults, or a debased form of Mohammedanism. This was the pattern for the next three hundred years. Where Islam was firmly and fully established, as in west Asia, northern India, Malaya and Java, the Christians made little progress, even when they disposed of overwhelming political, economic and military power. Where Islam merged into animism, as in some of the Indonesian islands, Dutch Protestant missions enjoyed some success. It was, broadly speaking, the same with the other great eastern religions, Hinduism, Buddhism and Confucianism. Wherever they were well-established and mature, and associated with the cultural, social and racial consciousness of the locality, Christianity could not penetrate in depth. In short, it could not succeed, or at least did not succeed, against other imperial religions. But in the economically backward regions, in tribal areas of low cultural achievement, and indeed almost anywhere where primitive paganism was the predominant cult, Christianity quickly became established, especially where it had the backing of a colonial power.

Was the failure of Christianity to supplant other imperial religions intrinsic? Might the story have been different? The question is historically very important. If Asia had been Christianized in the period 1550–1900, during the European military and economic paramountcy, the twentieth century would have to be entirely rewritten; and indeed Christianity itself must have been radically changed. But therein perhaps lies the key: it was the inability of Christianity to change, and above all to de-Europeanize itself, which caused it to miss its opportunities. Far too often the Christian Churches presented themselves as the extensions of European social and intellectual concepts, rather than embodiments of universal truths; and, equally important, the Churches as institutions, and their clergy as individuals and as a collectivity, appeared merely as one facet of European rule. Though Christianity was born in Asia, when it was reexported there from the sixteenth century onwards, it failed to acquire an Asian face.

The mistakes that were made varied from country to country. Sometimes the dilemma was complex, and it is not clear how error could have been avoided. There was never a uniform policy on any great, central issue of missionary endeavour. Indeed, how could there have been? There was no one centre of authority even in the Catholic Church. Throughout the sixteenth century, and for much of the seventeenth, the papacy had virtually no control over the missions, which were entirely in the hands of the Spanish and Portuguese crowns, and of the bishops they appointed. Or, rather, 'entirely' should be qualified, since the actual missionary work was chiefly in the hands of the friars and (from the 1540s) the Jesuits, who were often semi-autonomous and acted independently of both crown and pope. But these, in turn, all hated each other, and often deliberately and systematically attempted to frustrate each other's efforts. Unable to control the local bishops, the papacy used the device of appointing Vicars-Apostolic; but this, as often as not, was a further cause of friction and divided authority. And, finally, from the seventeenth century there was conflict with the rival efforts of the Protestant sects, usually envenomed by a background of European war and commercial competition.

These conflicts and divisions, exported from Europe, were compounded by local differences of opinion among missionaries as to the best way to proceed. In India the Christians were confronted by the caste system, which raised dilemmas they were never able to resolve. Basically, there are two possible forms of proselytization of a society. One is to evangelize the lowest and least privileged elements, capture their allegiance in huge numbers, and so work upwards from the base. This was the method followed by the first Christians within the Roman empire. The second is to aim at the élite, or even at the individuals at the head of the élite, obtain recognition or adoption of the faith as a matter of state policy, and then work downwards, by authority, example or force (or all three). This was the method followed in the conversion of the Germanic and Slavonic tribes of the Dark Ages, and to some extent in Spanish America. In India, the caste system presented the choice in its most acute form, for it made a combination of the two approaches, at any rate in the same area, almost impossible. The religious instinct of the missionaries was to go for the masses, for, in the absence of military and state sanctions, Christianity is most successful when it appeals to the underdogs and the deprived, and so comes closest to its earliest pastoral attitudes. But their social instinct, coming from a European background where the will of the prince was paramount in matters of faith, was to go for the élite. Both were tried, but neither successfully.

Some of the most intelligent of the missionaries, especially among the Jesuits, believed passionately in the élitist approach. It was their proven method in Europe, and it gave the widest possible scope for their gifts as educators and scholars. It also reflected Jesuit admiration for many of the customs (including religious customs) and cultural achievements of the Asian societies. To capture the élite it was necessary not only to accept their culture but many quasi-religious assumptions and ways of presenting ideas. There was really no other way to do it successfully. But this posed the risk of conflict with superiors at home (and, of course, with other, rival orders, and the seculars). In South India, the Jesuit Robert de Nobili insisted to the high-caste Indians among whom he worked that he was not a low-caste *Parangi* (European). He accepted the caste system entirely, and placed himself in its highest rank as a Brahmin. He adopted Brahmin dress and diet, shaved his head, and wrote Christian poems in the form of Vedic hymns. These compromises might have been acceptable to authority. But De Nobili allowed India to penetrate his presentation of Christianity. He wrote Tamil poems which reconciled Christian doctrine with Hindu wisdom; he allowed his high-caste converts to wear the sacred thread and to observe certain Hindu feasts, and perhaps most important of all he administered communion to inferior castes by holding the wafer on the end of a stick. As a result, he was repeatedly denounced in Rome. In 1618 he was summoned to the archiepiscopal court in Goa, and appeared in a Brahmin robe. In 1623, Rome refused to condemn him 'until further information is available'. But the effect of the campaign against De Nobili was to inhibit his own efforts and discourage others. The Church, in practice, was never able to go as far towards reconciliation as the Brahmins required, and the élitist campaign was almost totally unsuccessful. De Nobili's efforts over many years brought him only twenty-six Brahmin converts. By 1643, the Jesuits calculated that no more than 600 high-caste Indians had been baptized in thirty-seven years.

Nor was this surprising, since, apart from a handful of enthusiastic missionaries, the Europeans, either lay or ecclesiastical, would not accord even high-caste converts equality. The educated Brahmin Matthew de Castro (his Portuguese baptismal name) was refused ordination by the Archbishop of Goa. He went to Rome where he was received into the priesthood. But his orders were not acknowledged when he returned to Goa. Back in Rome, he was consecrated a bishop in 1637, and given the see of Idalcan, which was outside Goa's jurisdiction. He was nonetheless suspended by the archbishop, who actually imprisoned priests whom Bishop de Castro had ordained. He spent the last nineteen years of his life in Rome as adviser on Indian affairs. By this time there were something like 180 Indian priests in Goa, but there was no prospect of promotion for them in the Church, then or for the next 200 years, since most European priests would not serve under Indian bishops, of whatever caste. Nor was there any prospect of the Brahmins making any impact on Christian rites or dogma.

The irony in De Nobili's case is that the low-caste converts to whom he handed the eucharist on a stick were far more numerous even in his mission than any other Indian element. The low-castes often welcomed Christianity enthusiastically; only among them was it possible to effect mass-baptism. Hence some of the friars, especially Franciscans, wanted to concentrate on this approach. But for this to be successful meant the presentation of Christianity in its primitive, revolutionary form (as, of course, St Francis would have wished). Neither the hierarchy in the East, nor Rome – nor indeed most of the missionary clergy – wanted the millenium. The Portuguese secular authorities and merchants (and, later their French and British successors) had no desire to subvert society, which would have meant conflict with the Mohammedans as well as the Indian princes; on the contrary, they were anxious to work through, and reinforce, the existing structure and hierarchy. Hence the missionary effort fell neatly between two stools: neither 'Asian' Christianity nor 'pure' Christianity was offered. Instead, the Indians were presented with European Christianity, and rejected it.

In China the missionaries did not face the problem of caste. But this meant there was less chance of adopting the strategy of conversions from the base. Indeed, it is hard to see how it could have been used unless as part of a deliberate plan to subvert the whole of Chinese government and society, something the sixteenth century Catholic Church could not have contemplated. In any event, it was not considered, since the first on the scene were the élitist Jesuits, in the steps of St Francis Xavier, who regarded China as the key to the Christianization of Asia. They deemed it essential to work through the imperial court. But that meant a confrontation with one of the oldest, most arrogant and least adaptable civilizations in the world, whose moral philosophy was permeated with powerful concepts such as Confucian ancestor-worship. The alternative to confrontation was alliance, in which Christianity would have to play the role of junior, and humble, partner. This, in effect, was the strategy the Jesuits tried to adopt.

Chinese imperial policy admitted only subject tribute-payers, Mohammedan merchants, and foreigners 'lured by the good fame of Chinese virtues'. They did not welcome European Christians. A local south China chronicle, c. 1520, gives their first recorded experience of the Christians (in fact Portuguese):

'Some time near the end of Ching-Te's reign, a people not recognized as tributary to China known as the Feringhis, together with a crowd of riff-raff, filtered into the harbour between T'un Mun and Kwait Ch'ung and set up barracks and forts, mounted many cannons to make war, captured islands, killed people, robbed ships and terrorized the population by their fierce dominion over the coast.'

Hence the first Jesuit to penetrate to the imperial court, Father Matthew Ricci, spent seventeen years, 1583–1600, insinuating his way there, and his approach was suitably supplicatory: 'Despite the distance, fame told me of the remarkable teaching and fine institutions with which the imperial court has endowed all its people. I desire to share these advantages and live out my life as one of Your Majesty's subjects, hoping in return to be of some small use.' The Jesuits and other Christians in China had to accept that the Chinese ruling class regarded them as learners, not teachers; and, initially at least, the only tolerable form of instruction the Chinese would take was in practical matters rather than the realm of ideas and concepts. The Jesuits operated through science, mathematics and mechanics. Ricci presented the Emperor Wan-Li with a clock in 1601, and then drew a map showing China as the centre of the world. By the time he died in 1610 he had established himself at the court. The salient was enlarged by Father Adam Schall over nearly half a century. He was able to demonstrate errors in the calculations of the Moslem astronomers at court, and was eventually made director of the Chinese observatory and minister for mathematics, with the title 'Master of the Mysteries of Heaven'. To the Chinese court Christianity was 'the religion of the great Schall', thus making its appearance as an epiphenomenon of physical science in an age when the papacy had condemned Galilean astronomy. His successor, Father Verbiest, made a series of long-range cannon for the Emperor, with the name of a saint engraved on each; and he dedicated them wearing stole and surplice.

In this way, Chinese congregations emerged in the big cities. It was claimed in 1664 that there were 254,980 Chinese converts. But this figure included multitudes of tiny children baptized at death. More important, there were virtually no Chinese priests; and the only Chinese prelate, Lo Wen-Tsao, made Vicar-Apostolic for North China in 1674, spent eleven years trying to find bishops who would consecrate him. (He had no successor as a Catholic bishop until the twentieth century.) The problem of a native clergy would have been formidable in any case. But there was no prospect of mass conversion until Christianity adapted itself to a whole range of Chinese assumptions. Ricci, studying the long history of China, pointed out that a wholesale revision of the Old Testament was required. The Christian assumption that the world was about 5,000 years old (Archbishop Ussher of Armagh, in his *Annales Veteris et Novi Testamenti,* 1650–4, calculated that the date of Creation was 4004 BC, and this was widely accepted, especially in the Protestant world) was belied by Chinese chronology. If the Chinese were right on this point, might they not be right on others? To what extent could their burial customs or prayers, so crucial in almost every religion, be reconciled to Christian theory and practice? The Chinese were clearly not prepared to abandon what Europeans crudely termed 'ancestor worship', but which might be reinterpreted and adjusted to the doctrine of the resurrection and the first and second coming. An elementary system on these lines was worked out by Ricci and his successors. They incorporated Chinese nuances in references to God, and used the same Chinese word for mass as was customarily used for ancestor-ceremonies. The compromise was secretly noted by Franciscans and

Dominicans in 1631, and a triumphant complaint made to Rome.

The subsequent controversy over Asian rites was gradually broadened to include a number of other variations and translations, and became an explosive issue, as indeed it deserved to be. Was Christianity to throw off its European chrysalis and become at last the world religion, united in its central truth, infinitely varied in its presentation, which Christ implicitly and Paul explicitly had always intended? There was a time when the papacy seemed to be ready to grasp the opportunity. In 1615 Paul v had authorized a Chinese liturgy, and translations were made. In 1622 Gregory xv created a new Vatican Department of Propaganda, with the object of universalizing the missionary movement and freeing it from the narrow national horizons of Spain and Portugal. Francesco Ingoli, the first Secretary of Propaganda until his death in 1649, had a personal vision of global, post-European Christianity, and his philosophy was still reflected in instructions on propaganda sent out a decade after his death:

> 'Do not regard it as your task, and do not bring any pressure to bear on the peoples, to change their manners, customs and uses, unless they are evidently contrary to religion and sound morals. What could be more absurd than to transplant France, Spain, Italy or some other European country to China? Do not introduce all that to them but only the faith, which does not despise or destroy the manners and customs of any people, always supposing that they are not evil, but rather wishes to see them preserved unharmed. . . . It is the nature of men to love and treasure above everything else their own country and that which belongs to it. . . . Do not draw invidious contrasts between the customs of the peoples and those of Europe; do your utmost to adapt yourselves to them.'

The intention of this document was wise, indeed admirable; but of course the qualifying phrases laid it open to argument. How ruthless was Rome prepared to be in backing it up, against the protests of the conventional and orthodox? Or, to put it another way, how powerful was Rome's imagination in the vital process of reinterpreting Christian dogma in the light of strange cultures? In the event, Rome always proved more susceptible to European pressures, and to the arguments of colonial viceroys, bishops and vicars-general, than to the more creative of the missionaries. The kind of battles that Paul won, Ricci and his successors and emulators lost. Latin was re-established as a universal requirement for the liturgy. The controversy lasted over a century, with repeated rulings, both curial and local, some flatly contradictory, with the 'Europeans' gradually prevailing. In both India and China, the Jesuits put up a stiff resistance; and they were backed by the Chinese court. But in 1742, Benedict xiv, in the bull *Ex quo singulari*, finally ruled decisively against any permission to relax the strict European rites, and condemned their Asian substitutes: '. . . we condemn and detest their practice as superstitious . . . we revoke, annul, abrogate and wish to be deprived of all force and effect, all and each of those permissions, and say and announce that they must be considered for ever to be annulled, null, invalid and without any force or power.' These injunctions, repeated against 'Malabarian' rites two years later, effectively ended any hopes that a specific form of Asian Christianity might develop, as a prelude to a Christian conquest of the continent.

Indeed, by 1742, those hopes had perished anyway. The great chance for Christianity came in the sixteenth century, when its impact was new and tremendous, when the Christians themselves were still astonished by the boundless opportunities which seemed open to them, and when they possessed, in the Jesuits, an instrument of extraordinary adaptability and youthful vigour. Moreover, in the late sixteenth century, when the Jesuits reached the Far East, there was coming into existence for the first time as a united state and culture the perfect agent – perhaps the only one – for the Asianization of Christianity and so for the Christianization of Asia. This was Japan. The country already had twenty million inhabitants and a reputation throughout the area for bellicosity and imperial ambitions. It had only one language, albeit a complicated and primitive one, and was in the process of transforming itself from a vast number of fragmented lordships into a national state under military rule. It had two religions, in violent conflict: Shintoism, indigenous, crude and sinister, and Buddhism, imported and corrupt. Christianity had, perhaps, a unique opportunity to offer itself to Japan as the national creed of the new, unified state. And in the Japanese people it had a race astonishingly gifted in receiving and mutating ideas.

Francis Xavier was excited by reports of Japanese intelligence two years before he managed to get there, in 1549. He could not speak more than a few words of the language (the 'Apostle of the Indies' was a poor linguist), but he had with him three Japanese who had been taught Portuguese at Goa, and so he was able to preach and converse. He assumed, wrongly, that Buddhism was the key to Japan, and that therefore it might be necessary to convert China first. In fact the more successful war-lords who were coming to power were often violently anti-Buddhist – and consequently open to Christianity if, as was possible, it could expose the essentially primitive nature of Shinto. But Xavier noted of a Buddhist abbot: 'In many talks which I had with him, I found him doubtful and unable to decide whether our soul is immortal or whether it dies with the body; sometimes he told me yes, and sometimes no, and I fear the other wise men are all alike.' Xavier perceived that the Japanese had no answer to the question Christians had always been able to face fully and confidently: what happened to us after death? So he was full of hope: 'The people whom we have met so far are the best we have yet discovered anywhere, and it seems to me that we shall never find another heathen race to equal the Japanese.'

In the late 1560s, the Jesuits arrived in strength, to insert themselves into the fissures opened by a religious-civil war, at a time when the war-lord

Nobunaga, an agnostic who was willing to let them preach, was emerging as the chief force. Moreover, they had in Alessandro Valignano, their Vicar-General in the Orient, perhaps the greatest of the missionary statesmen. He came to Japan first in 1579, aged forty, a Neapolitan noble, over six feet tall, immensely energetic, with clear, challenging ideas. Like St Paul, he saw missionary work as an opportunity for spiritual adventure; like Xavier, he found the Japanese exciting. His views on race were a curious mixture of prejudice and enlightenment. From his own experience he thought the Indians 'base and bestial people'. There could be no question of making them Jesuits because 'all the dusky races are very stupid and vicious, and the basest spirit, and likewise because the Portuguese treat them with the greatest contempt.' He did not like the Portuguese or the Spanish either; but he had, to his fury, to bow to their ruling that no one of Jewish (and, by extension, mixed) blood be admitted to the Jesuit order, as they could be classified as 'New Christians' or crypto-Jews.

But the Japanese were a different matter. Valignano delighted in 'these most cultivated and intelligent people'. He quickly grasped that Japan was totally different from anything Christianity had hitherto encountered: 'It is impossible either in India or in Europe to evaluate or settle the problems of Japan. Nor can one even understand or imagine how things happen there – it is a different world.' From the first he favoured a Japanese clergy, and on his third visit had two native priests ordained. Leaving aside Chinese culture, which he respected, 'this people is the best and most civilized of all the East, and it is the most apt to be taught and to adopt our holy law, and to produce the finest Christianity in the East, as it is already doing.' Three years later he boasted that Japanese converts numbered 150,000 and included a high proportion of the nobility and gentry, something which had not happened anywhere else in the East. The existence of a single language, he thought, made all the difference in staging a national mission. And then, he added, the Japanese appeared to be the only eastern people who accepted Christianity from disinterested motives, moved by faith and reason alone. 'We have no jurisdiction whatsoever in Japan. We cannot compel them to do anything they do not wish to do. We have to use pure persuasion and force of argument. They will not suffer being slapped or beaten, or imprisonment, or any of the methods commonly used with other Asian Christians. They are so touchy they will not brook even a single harsh or impolite word.' He liked their spirit. He admired their courage – 'the most warlike and bellicose race yet discovered on the earth'. He thought Japanese Christians would willingly die for their faith, and, in sum, he concluded that Japan was the only mission which held any prospect of soon becoming a healthy and self-supporting Christian kingdom with a trustworthy native hierarchy and clergy of its own. Other Jesuits shared his view; among them, Japan was by far the most popular posting.

Unfortunately, neither Rome nor Portugal was willing to take the risk of a native clergy. Neither was ready to treat Japan as a special case, and accord its inhabitants chances and privileges denied elsewhere. Nor did they accept Valignano's estimate of Japan's desire and capacity to preserve its political, economic and cultural independence. The Pope saw no reason to make concessions; and from 1580 the Portuguese were ruled by Philip II of Spain, and their policy thus submerged beneath an expanding imperialist system. What followed could be called one of the great tragedies of history. Of course, within the Church, the Jesuits were suspect: to outsiders it looked as though they were asking to be granted a monopoly of Japan's spiritual and economic welfare. In his report of 1580 Valignano emphasized that the Japanese derived enormous benefit from the Portuguese 'great ship' which called annually at Nagasaki. The Portuguese then had a virtual stranglehold over the trade in valuable goods between the Persian Gulf and the Yellow Sea, and as there was a ban on direct trade between China and Japan, the Jesuits acted as intermediaries, especially as bullion-brokers, from Nagasaki, which they made their headquarters. Trade and religion were inextricably mixed, not to say confused. It is not clear whether the Japanese authorities permitted Jesuit evangelism to continue because they feared that, if the Jesuits left, the great ship would no longer call. But they were certainly highly suspicious of western motives, as Valignano realized and warned. On the whole, the Japanese trusted the Jesuits but no one else. Unfortunately, no one else trusted the Jesuits. They needed the profit from their bullion-broking in order to finance their missions in Japan, which were run at a considerable loss. Valignano had drawn up a formal contract in 1578 with the Macao mercantile ring, which had been approved by Pope Gregory XIII – 'this could not properly be called trade, since it was done out of pure necessity' (1582). But if the Pope knew the facts he seems to have made little effort to convey them to other interested clerical bodies. The Jesuits were actually in debt; but the Franciscans, the Dominicans, the secular clergy and the Protestants were quite sure the trade had made the Society fabulously rich. Moreover the Dominicans had great influence over the Spanish government, which of course controlled Portuguese possessions after 1580. Although the thrones had been united on the clear understanding that the two empires should be separately administered and independent, in fact the Spanish lay and ecclesiastical authorities, operating from Manila, never recognized an exclusive Portuguese sphere of influence east of Malacca.

In 1583 Valignano devoted a whole section of his report to the topic 'Why it is not convenient that other religious orders should come to Japan'. So far, he argued, the Christians had had a great advantage in Japan because they were under unitary command, whereas the Buddhists were splintered. Admitting the friars would lead to similar splits among the Christians, since experience showed they always ganged up on the Jesuits (as well as quarrelling among themselves). He particularly feared the Spanish Dominicans and Franciscans, and the *conquistador* methods they and the Spanish army commanders had employed against the Aztecs and the Filippinos. That would be disastrous

with the Japanese: 'Japan is not a place which can be controlled by foreigners
... and the King of Spain does not and cannot have any power or jurisdiction
here. There is no alternative to relying on training the natives in the way they
should go, and then leaving them to manage the churches themselves. For this,
a single religious order will suffice.' He added, truthfully:

'In the past, many of the Japanese lords had a great fear that we [Jesuits]
were concocting some evil in Japan, and that if they allowed the conversion
of Christians in their fiefs we would afterwards use them to raise a rebellion
on behalf of the [Spanish] king who supports us; for they could not
understand why these monarchs should spend such vast sums on the
mission if it was not with the ultimate intention of seizing their lands. . . .
Now they know the Kingdoms of Spain and Portugal are united, this
existing suspicion will be vastly strengthened by the arrival of new foreign
religious. . . .'

The argument was deployed with passionate conviction. But to outsiders it
looked like special pleading. Why should the Jesuits have a monopoly of the
profits? In fact Valignano's request was formally endorsed by both the papal
and the Spanish authorities, but from 1592 the Franciscans began to break in
with the assistance of disgruntled merchants and adventurers, and they at
once began to proselytize and celebrate mass openly. In 1597 a row broke out
over the cargo of a wrecked Portuguese ship. The Spanish governor sent a
threatening note to the Japanese tyrant, Hideyoshi, pointing out with
unbelievable ineptitude that missionaries preceded *conquistadors*; and in
response Hideyoshi promptly crucified six Franciscans, three Jesuit lay-
brothers, and nineteen Japanese neophites.

What grounds were there for Japanese fears? Valignano himself was sincere
in his belief that Japan should retain its political independence. But even he
did not see this as unconditional. In response to the 1597 martyrdoms, he
urged Philip II to cancel the 'great ship' the next year as a reprisal, in the belief
that such a move would provoke economic crisis and unrest in Japan. He was
not against force everywhere. Writing of India in 1601, he recalled that Xavier,
'with his customary spirit and prudence, realized how rude and incapable
[Indians] are by nature in the things of God, and that reason is not so effective
with them as compulsion.' As a group, the Jesuits were not above acting from
nationalistic motives. In 1555 Father Balthasar Gago said he taught his
Japanese converts to pray for Joao III of Portugal as their potential protector.
Father Charlevoix, the Jesuit historian of the Society in Canada says they
persuaded their Indian converts to 'mingle France and Christ together in their
affections'. Some Spanish Jesuits actively engaged in Far Eastern power-
politics. In 1586, Father Alonso Sanches SJ produced a proposal for the
conquest of China and its re-education to Christianity. He calculated that
10,000–12,000 men should be sent from Europe, 5,000–6,000 natives recruited
in Manila, and a similar number in Japan. The main invasion force was to set

out from Manila, while a concerted attack was to be launched by the Portuguese from Macao and Canton. This project, conceived at almost the same time as the Armada against England, was supported by the governor, bishop and council of Manila, and by a number of Japanese merchants, which lends colour to the suspicion that it had been canvassed in Japan. Sanches was quite sure the Jesuits would cooperate in recruiting the Japanese volunteers. (The Spanish actually used Japanese mercenaries in their expedition to Cambodia in 1595, and to suppress the Chinese rebellion at Manila in 1603.) The Bishop of Manila begged Philip II to give his approval: 'Not even Julius Caesar or Alexander the Great had an opportunity such as this. And on the spiritual plane, nothing greater was ever projected since the time of the Apostles.' The Japanese leaders were not privy to Spanish official correspondence but they knew perfectly well that such schemes were being discussed. All along they proved much better informed than even the Jesuits supposed. They saw the connection between religion and politics perfectly clearly. In a letter to Don Francisco Tello, Governor of the Philippines, Hideyoshi pointed out that Shinto, which the Franciscans in Japan had crudely attacked, was the basis of the Japanese social structure: 'If perchance religious or secular Japanese proceeded to your kingdoms and preached the law of Shinto there, disturbing the public peace, would you, as lord of the soil be pleased? Of course not; and therefore you can see why I acted.'

The massacre of 1597 was intended as a warning. Having made their point, the Japanese authorities allowed the Jesuit mission to proceed, and the number of converts increased steadily, reaching an estimated 750,000 in 1606. Valignano ordered all Jesuits to conform as closely as was ethically possible to Japanese life. They showed no approval of Buddhist or Shinto rites but they did not preach against them, and they avoided crucifixes, associated in Japanese minds with the shame of criminal punishment. What they were not allowed to do, however, was to ordain large numbers of Japanese priests; and the papacy, and the Jesuit general, Aquaviva, ruled that even lay-brothers might be recruited only in sufficient numbers to disarm Japanese criticism. Thus the Jesuit aim of attaining rapid self-sufficiency, which would have allowed them to depart, leaving Japanese Christians in control of the mission, was made unattainable. Worse, despite the appeals of all the civil and ecclesiastical authorities of Portuguese India, the papacy and the Spanish crown proved unable, or unwilling, to keep the friars out. Friar Jeronimo de Jesus proclaimed in 1598 that he and his team would stay in Japan despite pope, king, prelate or governor. They preached openly against 'pagan cults'. They flourished their crucifixes. They fuelled the suspicions of the feudal class by proselytizing among what the Jesuits called 'the poxy rabble'. And, despite Jesuit advice, they insisted on treating the victims of 1597 as honoured martyrs. In 1608 Paul V gave in and threw Japan open completely to the friars. This coincided with another blow the Jesuits had long feared but could not avert – the arrival of the Dutch Calvinists, with the English not far behind. By

1613 both Protestant groups were active in Japanese waters, making the annual great ship obsolete and the Jesuits no longer indispensible, or even necessary, as commercial brokers. The English promptly engaged in anti-Spanish propaganda, preying on the very insecurity the Japanese already nursed. Had they not heard of Jesuit subversive plans in England, concerted and timed to assist Spanish naval plans to invade? That, said the English captain Richard Cocks, was exactly why his government had expelled Catholic clerics from England: 'Hath not the Emperor of Japan as much reason to put your Jesuits and friars out of Japan and to withstand the secret entrance of them, knowing them to be stirrers up of sedition, and turbulent people?' It was the last straw.

On 27 January 1614 the Japanese government published an edict which accused the Christians of coming 'to disseminate an evil law, to overthrow true doctrine, so that they may change the government of the country and obtain possession of the land.' The attachment of the Christians to the cross was explicitly cited as grounds for believing they approved of criminal acts. All European Christians were to leave, and Japanese Christians were to renounce their faith. The reaction to the expulsion order took the form of a tremendous outbreak of mass religious fervour in Nagasaki, with ritual flagellations and mutilations, several Japanese Christians dying of self-inflicted wounds. This disgusted and infuriated the Japanese authorities. The Jesuits later blamed the Franciscans for setting off this frenzy, and it is true that the Franciscans often encouraged flagellation while the Jesuits hated it. But the truth is that the Japanese converts, as Valignano had perceived, made Christians of unrivalled determination and courage. Had the mission been allowed to proceed under the right conditions, the Japanese would have changed the face of world religion. As it was, they became the victims of one of the most ruthless and prolonged persecutions in the long, bloody story of confessional cruelty.

From 1614–43, up to 5,000 Japanese Christians were judicially murdered, nearly always in public. The exact total is not known, but 3,125 individual cases are recorded, 71 of them Europeans. About 46 Jesuits and friars contrived to 'go underground', but in the long run this merely served to prolong the agony, since the mission could not be effectively reinforced and fugitives were systematically and relentlessly hunted down. The most appalling tortures were inflicted on those, usually Japanese, who refused to recant. Some died of starvation in gaol. Others were tortured to death. Europeans were sometimes beheaded. Most of the Japanese were burned alive, loosely tied by one arm to a stake in the middle of a circle of fire. Some were mothers with small children in their arms. The local governors stepped up the horrors when mere burning failed to secure apostasy. Many victims were killed by water-torture at the sulphur hot springs at Unzen – boiling water being slowly poured into slits in their flesh. From 1632, the martyrs were suspended upside down over a pit, some of them living up to a week. One young Japanese woman endured it for fourteen days, while the aged Jesuit provincial, Christova Ferreira, recanted after six hours. The Jesuits produced manuals teaching the faithful how to endure martyrdom: '. . . prepare yourself with confession. . . . Never cherish an evil thought towards the official passing the sentence of death or the executioner. . . . While being tortured visualize the Passion of Jesus.' In 1637 there was a rebellion, provoked by officials torturing the daughter of a Japanese Christian before his eyes. It was suppressed with the armed help of the Dutch, who were thereby able to end the Portuguese trade for good. Christianity survived for some time underground, though even in hiding the Jesuits and the friars quarrelled. In 1657–8, 600 Christians were rounded up in the countryside around Nagasaki: 411 were executed, 77 died in prison, 99 apostasized. One girl, arrested at the age of eleven, remained a Christian until she died in prison in 1722. At Urakami a crypto-Christian community contrived to survive until it was brought to light in 1865, still baptizing correctly and insisting on clerical celibacy. But the episode as a whole seems to indicate that persecution, if applied with sufficient ruthlessness, intelligence and pertinacity, will eventually succeed, even against the most courageous. Thus a notable and poignant chapter in Christian history ended.

At precisely the time when Japanese Christianity was being exterminated, Presbyterians and Independents (Congregationalists) were establishing another élitist religious state on the east coast of North America. It was to be the greatest, indeed the only, realized experiment in post-European Christianity. It was also the first and only instance in which we can watch a major Christian community coming into independent being by the light of documentary sources. The birth of Protestant America was a deliberate and self-conscious act of Church-State perfectionism. As Donne said, in his Virginia sermon: 'You shall add persons to this kingdom, and to the Kingdom of Heaven, and add names to the books of our chronicles, and to the book of life.' Governor Winthrop, sailing the Atlantic on board the *Arbella*, wrote proudly: 'For we must consider that we shall be as a city upon a hill, the eyes of all people are upon us.' These dissenting groups were fleeing an Anglican Jacobean England of whose 'reformation' they had despaired. But they were not fleeing to religious liberty and diversity. On the contrary: like the Carolingians, they were seeking to create a total Christian society, where the divine instructions on every aspect of life would be obeyed to the letter, and a city of earth created as the antechamber or prelude to entry into God's city. The original vision of America was Augustinian, rather than Erasmian. There could be no question of religion being 'private': civil and religious society were one, inseparable. William Penn, in his *Preface to the Frame of Government of Pennsylvania*, wrote in 1682: 'Government seems to me a part of religion itself, a thing sacred in its institution and end . . . it crushes the effects of evil and is as such (though a lower yet) an emanation of the same divine power that is both author and object of pure religion . . . government itself being otherwise as capable of kindness, goodness and charity as a more private society.' The founding of a colony was an individual and collective contract with the deity to set up a Church-State: 'We whose names are underwritten. . . .' reads the *Mayflower* Compact of 1620, 'having undertaken, for the glory of God, and advancement of the Christian faith, and honour of our king and country, a voyage to plant the first colony in the northern parts of Virginia, do by these presents solemnly and mutually in the presence of God, and of one another, covenant and combine ourself together in a civil body politic, for our better ordering and preservation, and furtherance of the ends aforesaid. . . .' The Church was also formally constituted, as at Salem 1629: 'We covenant with the Lord and one with another; and do bind ourselves in the presence of God, to walk together in all his ways, according as he is pleased to reveal himself unto us in his blessed word of truth.'

The official religion, set out in the Cambridge Platform of 1648, was based on the English Westminster Confession of 1643–5, and was Independent rather than Presbyterian – that is, councils and synods had advisory and admonitory powers, but no coercive authority. But there was no toleration either: the magistrates or 'nursing fathers' were to tackle heresy, schism and disobedience, 'to be restrained and punished by civil authority'. A man could not be a member of the State without being a member of the Church, exactly as in medieval society, since the beliefs and objects of the two were necessarily identical. As Uriah Oakes, later President of Harvard, put it (1673):

'According to the design of our fathers and the frame of things laid by them, the interests of righteousness in the commonwealth and holiness in the churches are inseparable. . . . To divide what God hath joined . . . is folly in its exaltation. I look upon this as a little model of the glorious kingdom of Christ on earth. Christ reigns among us in the commonwealth as well as in the church and hath his glorious interest involved and wrapt up in the good of both societies respectively.'

Was New England, then, to expand into a gigantic Geneva? Not exactly. It was not a theocracy. It gave the clergy themselves less actual authority than any other government in the western world at the time. The minister's power lay in determining Church membership. Moreover, the churches were, right from the start, managed by laymen. The religious establishment was popular, not hieratic. This was the foundation of the distinctive American religious tradition. There was never any sense of division in law between layman and cleric, between those with spiritual privileges and those without – no jealous juxtaposition and confrontation of a secular and ecclesiastical world. America was born Protestant, and did not have to become so through revolt and struggle. It was not built on the remains of a Catholic Church, or an Establishment; it had no clericalism or anti-clericalism. In all these respects it differed profoundly from a world shaped by Augustinian principles. It had a traditionless tradition, starting afresh with a set of Protestant assumptions, taken for granted, self-evident, as the basis for a common national creed.

In any case, the idea of a gigantic Geneva was quickly rendered impossible by events. A Calvinist Church-State could not maintain itself without a terrifying apparatus of repression: even Geneva had had to expel people. Some of the problems of the Old World rapidly reproduced themselves in the New. Dissidents like Roger Williams and Anne Hutchinson emerged, were ejected and took refuge in the future Rhode Island, termed by the orthodox 'the sewer of New England'. Founding Providence, Williams wrote: 'I desired it might be for a shelter for persons distressed for conscience.' In 1644 he published his defence of religious freedom, *The Bloody Tenent of Persecution for the Cause of Conscience Discussed*, and his new instrument of government declared that 'the form of government established in Providence Planations is DEMOCRATICAL, that is to say, a government held by the free and voluntary consent of all, or the greater part, of the free inhabitants.' To its laws and penalties for transgressions, it added: 'And otherwise than thus, what is herein forbidden, all men may walk as their consciences persuade them, every one in the name of his God. And let the saints of the Most High walk in this colony without molestation, in the name of Jehovah their God, for ever and ever.' This was confirmed by royal charter in 1663: 'No person within the said colony, at any time hereafter, shall be in any wise molested, punished, disquieted or called in question, for any differences in opinion in matters of religion, and who do not actually disturb the civil peace of our said colony; but that all . . . may from time to time, and at all times hereafter, freely and fully have and enjoy his and their own judgments and consciences, in matters of religious concernments.' This was the first commonwealth in modern history to make religious freedom, as opposed to a mere degree of toleration, the principle of its existence, and to make this a reason for separating Church and State. Its existence, of course, opened the door to the Quakers and the Baptists, and indeed to missionaries from the Congregationalists of the north and the Anglicans of the south.

In fact, once this decisive breach had been made, it was inevitable that America, with its lay predominance, should move steadily towards religious liberty and the separation of Church and State, and that the vision should cease to be Augustinian and become Erasmian. Economic factors pushed strongly in this direction. The later waves of emigrants had not, for the most part, experienced 'conversion' and 'saving grace'; they tended, increasingly, to be a mere cross-section of Englishmen (and later of Northern Irish and Scottish Presbyterians). A New England synod of 1662 declared that baptism was sufficient for church membership, but not for full communion. This 'half-way Covenant' was the beginning of the end of a pure Church, which went into a period of what was woefully termed 'declension'; calamitous events, such as Indian attacks, were seen as divine punishments. In 1679 it was decided to make 'a full inquiry . . . into the cause and state of God's controversy with us'. Thus a 'Reforming Synod' was called and reported: 'That God hath a controversy with his New England people is undeniable, the Lord having written his displeasure in dismal characters against us.' A new covenant and confession of faith were produced, but everything, it seemed, conspired to frustrate the elect. James II's attempt to reintroduce Catholicism, the Glorious Revolution, and the subsequent settlement, imposed toleration, an Anglican element, and a franchise based on property rather than church membership. Church leadership was discredited by the witchcraft mania at Salem in 1692, and weakened by the powerful backlash of public remorse which followed it. And the merchant element of Boston, who loathed the strict interpretation of the scriptures, especially the commercial restrictions derived from the Pentateuch, published a 'manifesto' in 1699 for a new Church 'on broad and catholick' lines, which accorded full status to any who professed Christian belief. The liberal elements captured Harvard College in 1707, and founded Yale at New Haven nine years later. To the Calvinist élite, these hammer-blows threatened to destroy their theory that they had been appointed a chosen people to do divine work in America. In 1702 Cotton Mather published his *Magnalia Christi Americana*, documenting 'Christ's great deeds in America' and was forced to conclude: '*Religion* brought forth *prosperity*, and the *daughter* destroyed the *mother*. . . . There is danger lest the *enchantments* of this world make them forget *their errand into the wilderness*.' But by this time the original Calvinist monopoly in New England had gone for good.

The South, too, which had had an Anglican confession but a Puritan ethic and Church-State assumptions, had surrendered to diversity and economics. Tobacco and negro labour, rather than biblical institutionalism, became the determining factors. In 1667 Virginia laid down that 'Baptism doth not alter the condition of the person as to his bondage and freedom.' In 1731 George Berkeley said that American slaveholders held blacks in 'an irrational contempt . . . as creatures of another species, who had no right to be instructed or admitted to the sacraments'. Religious belief had to be adjusted to fit social and economic realities, rather than vice versa. As Commissary James Blair reported in 1743: 'From being an instrument of wealth, [slavery] has become a moulding power, leaving it a vexed question which controlled society most, the African slave or his master.'

Yet the collapse of the total Christian society did not lead to a growth of secularism. In America as a whole, religion continued to be the dynamic of society and history. The difference was that Christianity now became a voluntary movement, or series of movements, rather than a compulsory framework. And it was these movements which determined the shape of America's constitutional and social development. The multiplicity of America's religious structure, and the continuance of the millenarian ideal, gave revivalism the opportunity to act as a unifying, national force. Moreover, the establishment of the voluntary principle led to an identification, in the minds of all reglious groups, of Christian enthusiasm with political liberty. As John Adams put it in 1765, in his *Dissertation on the Canon and Feudal Law:*

'Under the execrable race of the Stuarts, the struggle between the people and the confederacy of temporal and spiritual tyranny became formidable, violent and bloody. It was this great struggle that peopled America. It was not religion alone, as was commonly supposed, but it was a love of universal liberty, and a hatred, a dread, a horror of the internal confederacy of ecclesiastical, hierarchical and despotic rulers that projected, conducted and accomplished the settlement of America.'

That being so, revivalism tended to precede political action; and it was the so-called Great Awakening of the 1730s and after which prepared the American Revolution.

The Awakening was a much more complicated phenomenon than Wesley's revival in England, since it combined rumbustious and unsophisticated mass-evangelism with the ideas of the eighteenth-century Enlightenment. Both shared a distrust of doctrinal ideas, a stress on morality and ethics, an ecumenical spirit. The Awakeners would agree with Wesley: 'I . . . refuse to be distinguished from other men by any but the common principles of Christianity. . . . Dost thou love and fear God? It is enough! I give thee the right hand of fellowship.' But Jonathan Edwards, who first preached the revival in Northampton, Massachusetts, in 1733, was also in the mainstream of the Erasmian intellectual tradition. He was the pupil, at New Haven, of Samuel Johnson, whose work reflected the liberation from the ancient theological system as it was still taught in the seventeenth century – 'a curious cobweb of distributions and definitions', as he termed it. Johnson traced his own intellectual birth to the reading of Bacon's *Advancement of Learning*, which he says left him 'like one at once emerging out of a glimmer of twilight into the full sunshine of open day'. He read and admired Bishop Berkeley's attempt to reconcile idealism, reason and Christian belief, and he defended 'natural' law, holding morality to be 'the same thing as the religion of Nature', not indeed discoverable without revelation but 'founded on the first principles of reason and nature'. Edwards says he himself read Locke's *Essay Concerning Human Understanding* with more pleasure 'than the most greedy miser finds when gathering up handfuls of silver and gold from some newly-discovered treasure'. But he brought to Locke's methods of reasoning the warmth and the emotionalism they lacked. This might be termed providential: Locke was writing after a successful revolution, Edwards before one, at a time when unifying and energizing emotions were necessary to create a popular will for change. Much of his writing is capable of a political, as well as a theological interpretation. He sought in his preaching to arouse what he called 'affections', which he defined as 'that which moves a person from neutrality or mere assent and inclines his heart to possess or reject something'. In his very widely read *Treatise Concerning Human Affections* (1746) he quoted from the Cambridge Platonist John Smith a passage which should be read in the light of subsequent political history: 'A true celestial warmth is of an immortal nature; and being once seated vitally in the souls of man, it will regulate and order all the motions in a due manner; as the natural head, radicated in the hearts of living creatures, hath the dominion and economy of the whole body under it. . . . It is a new nature, informing the souls of man.' Edwards argued strongly that the deeds of men were caused by God's will. There was thus no essential difference between a religious and a political emotion, both of which were God-directed. Within Edwards's rational theology there was a strident millenarian struggling to get out. In human history, he wrote, 'all the changes are brought to pass . . . to prepare the way for that glorious issue of things that shall be when truth and righteousness shall finally prevail.' Men must know the hour when God 'shall take the kingdom' and he looked towards 'the dawn of that glorious day'. In his last work, on original sin (1758), he prophesied: 'And I am persuaded, no solid reason can be given, why God, who constitutes all other created union or oneness, according to his pleasure . . . may not establish a constitution whereby the natural posterity of Adam, proceeding from him, much as the buds or branches from the stock or root of a tree, should be treated as *one* with him.'

It was against this eschatological background that the Great Awakening 'took off', being reanimated whenever it showed signs of flagging by the advent of new and spectacular orators, such as Wesley's friend George Whitefield, the 'Grand Itinerant'. A German immigrant woman who heard Whitefield in New England said that though she understood no English, she had never been so edified in her life. He preached, as he put it, 'with much Flame, Clearness and Power . . . Dagon falls daily before the Ark'; and when he left Boston he handed over to a native evangelist, Gilbert Tennent. 'People wallowed in snow, night and day', wrote a jealous Anglican, 'for the benefit of his beastly brayings'. Another 'awakener' who served to 'blow up the divine fire lately kindled' was John Davenport from Yale, at one point arrested and judged mentally disturbed when he called for wigs, cloaks, rings and many works on religion to be burned. It was the beginning of American personal evangelism. Not everyone liked it. Its roots were in the country areas, where it helped to democratize society and arouse opposition to the restrictions of royal government, but it took fire in the towns, where hearers fainted, wept, shrieked and generally gave vent to their 'affections'. Charles Chauncy, who might be termed an Erasmian or an Arminian, and who reflected the eighteenth-century rationalist spirit in his *Seasonable Thoughts on the State of Religion in New England* (1743), disapproved of these antics; he considered even Edwards a 'visionary enthusiast', and warned: 'There is the Religion of the Understanding and Judgment, and Will, as well as of the Affections; and if little account is made of the former, while great Stress is laid on the latter, it can't be but People should run into Disorders.'

In fact, it was the marriage between the rationalism of people like Chauncy, and the Great Awakening spirit, which enabled the potential 'Disorders' to be channelled into the political aims of the Revolution, which was soon plainly identified as the coming eschatological event. Neither force could have succeeded without the other. Nor is the Revolution conceivable without this religious background. As John Adams was to put it afterwards (1818): 'The Revolution was effected before the war commenced. The Revolution was in the minds and hearts of the people; and change in their religious sentiments of their duties and obligations.' We must remember that until the 1740s America was a collection of disparate colonies with little contact with each other and often (as with all Latin America) more powerful links with cities and economic interests in Europe than with other colonies. Religious evangelism was the first continental force, an all-American phenomenon which transcended colonial differences, introduced national figures and made state boundaries seem unimportant. Whitefield was the first 'American' public figure to be well-known from New Hampshire to Georgia, and his death in 1770 evoked comment from the entire colonial press. Thus ecumenicalism preceded, and shaped, political unity. And by crossing in many ways the sectarian religious barriers, just as it crossed the colonial-state ones, it helped to bring into being the real ethic of the American Revolution, which might be termed the Protestant consensus, the beliefs and standards and attitudes which the American majority had in common. If it was no longer possible, or necessary, to imagine the American people making a binding covenant with God for their Church-State, the Protestant consensus nevertheless had a definite utilitarian and civic purpose. As John Adams, who had lost his original religious faith, put it in his diary:

> 'One great advantage of the Christian religion is that it brings the great principle of the law of nature and nations, love your neighbour as yourself, and do to others as you would that others should do to you – to the knowledge, belief and veneration of the whole people. Children, servants, women and men are all professors in the science of public as well as private morality. . . . The duties and rights of the man and the citizen are thus taught from early infancy.'

The diversity of American religion thus seemed no barrier to its social and political unity since it rested on a Christian ethic which was infinitely more important than the dogmatic variations of the sects. Indeed, the key state in the formation of the union, Pennsylvania, was also the most diverse in religions. Philadelphia, its 'City of Brotherly Love', saw the last great flowering of Puritan political innovation. It was the city of the Quakers, a Presbyterian stronghold, the headquarters of the Baptists, an Anglican centre, and the home of a number of German pietistic groups, and of Moravians, Memmonites and other sects, as well as a place where Catholicism was tolerated and flourished. What mattered were not doctrinal differences but the fact that all were able to live there in harmony, alongside the seat of the American Philosophical Society – and at the centre of America's system of communications and economic traffic. The Declaration of Independence and the Constitution were thus framed in a highly appropriate and prophetic setting. What is tremendously significant and new about the American Revolution is that its victory for religious freedom and the separation of Church and State was won not so much by left-wing millenarian sects revolting against magisterial churchmen, but by the denominational leaders and statesmen themselves, who saw that pluralism was the only form consonant with the ideals and necessities of the country.

Thus for the first time since the Dark Ages, a society came into existence in which institutional Christianity was associated with progress and freedom, rather than against them. The United States was Erasmian in its tolerance, Erasmian in its anti-doctrinal animus, above all Erasmian in its desire to explore, within a Christian context, the uttermost limits of human possibilities. It was Christianity presented not as a total society, but as an unlimited society. De Tocqueville, in *Democracy in America* (1835), says the attitude of and towards the churches was the first thing that struck him in the United States: 'In France I had almost always seen the spirit of religion and the spirit of freedom pursuing courses diametrically opposed to each other: but in America I found that they were intimately united, and that they reigned in common over the same country.' He concluded: 'Religion . . . must be regarded as the foremost of the political institutions of that country; for if it does not impart a taste for freedom, it facilitates the use of free institutions.' And Americans, he added, held religion 'to be indispensible to the maintenance of republican institutions'.

Some of them saw it as much more than this. In the period 1750–1820, Presbyterianism and Congregationalism, the two formative sects of American Protestantism, ceased to be dominant, and, in numbers at any rate, the Baptists and Wesleyans took over. In New England, as indeed in England itself, many well-educated Presbyterians, under the impact of the Enlightenment, became Unitarians; and it was the New England Unitarians who created the so-called American Renaissance, centred round the *North American Review* (1815) and the *Christian Examiner* (1824), papers whose editors included William Emerson, the father of the poet, Edward Everett, George Ticknor, Jared Sparks, Richard Henry Dana, Henry Adams, James Russell Lowell and Edward Everett Hale. Harvard, whose staff included John Quincy Adams, Longfellow, Lowell and Oliver Wendell Holmes, was largely Unitarian. Unitarianism was, to a great extent, the religion of the élite – critics joked that its preaching was limited to 'the fatherhood of God, the brotherhood of man and the neighbourhood of Boston'. In fact it had its ultimate roots in Arminianism and the third force, and could trace its pedigree not so much to the Founding Fathers as to Erasmus himself, who saw true Christianity in full alliance with the Renaissance. One could even push it back further, for the idea of human rebirth, the 'new man' was the central point of St Paul's moral theology. 'Christianity', wrote William Ellery Channing, '. . . should come forth from the darkness and corruption of the past in its own celestial splendour and in its divine simplicity. It should be comprehended as having but one purpose, the perfection of human nature, the elevation of men into nobler beings.' The declaration of the American Unitarian Association (1853) spoke of God 'forever sweeping the nations with regenerating gales from heaven, and visiting the hearts of men with celestial solicitations'.

The prime instrument in this progressive process was the American Republic itself. Jonathan Edwards had predicted in 1740: 'It is not unlikely that this work of God's spirit, that is so extraordinary and wonderful, is the dawning, or at least the prelude, of that glorious work of God so often foretold in scripture, which in the progress and issue of it shall renew the world of mankind. . . . And there are many things that make it probable that this work will begin in America.' To the Unitarian élite, the work had already, manifestly, begun. The old Calvinist theory of the Elect Nation infused nineteenth-century American patriotism. Thus Longfellow:

> Sail on, O Union, strong and great!
> Humanity with all its fears,
> With all its hopes for future years,
> Is hanging breathless on thy fate.

Within the framework of this early nineteenth-century concept of the chosen people, or what was termed the 'favouring providence', at work by using America as the 'melting pot' – a new nation arising from the debris of the old – American Christianity and the Republic it infused acquired their modern characteristics. America's most typical churches tended to leap back straight from the nineteenth century to the age of the New Testament, and to seek to combine both. The Middle Ages, the age of religious wars, were dismissed as nightmares, and the association of Christianity with force ('compel them to come in') was broken. The assumption of the voluntary principle, the central tenet of American Christianity, was that the personal religious convictions of individuals, freely gathered in churches and acting in voluntary associations, will gradually and necessarily permeate society by persuasion and example. It is not so much the instrumentation of the good doctrine, as the agency of the good man, which will convert and reform the world. Thus the world was seen primarily in moral terms. This became a dominant factor whether America was rejecting the Old World and seeking to quarantine herself from it (a concept used as recently as 1963 during the Cuban Missile Crisis), or whether America was embracing the world, and seeking to reform it. It was characteristic of the American State, first to reject espionage on moral grounds, then to undertake it through the Central Intelligence Agency, a moralistic institution much more like the Society of Jesus than its Soviet equivalent.

In American religion, the reflective aspect of Christianity was subordinated, almost eclipsed. The Catholic-medieval emphasis on the perfection of God –

and man's mere contemplation of Him – was replaced by the idea of God as an active and exacting sovereign, and man's energetic service in his employment. Augustinian pessimism was rejected, and Pelagianism embraced. It was not the Christian's duty to accept the world as he found it, but to seek to make it better, using all the means God had placed at his disposal. There was little mysticism, little sacramentalism or awe before the holy. There was no place for tragedy, dismissed as an avoidable accident, and its consequences as remediable. American religion, in its formative period, owed nothing to Pascal. Indeed, for essential purposes, it had no theology at all. Theological matters were points, all agreed, on which the various religions and sects happened to differ. This aspect of religion was important to individuals but not to society and the nation, since what mattered to them was the deep Christian consensus on ethics and morality. So long as Americans agreed on morals, theology could take care of itself. Morals became the heart of religion, whether for Puritans or revivalists, orthodox or liberal, fundamentalist or moralist – the eccentric hot-gospeller at the street-corner shared in this consensus as much as the episcopalian prelate. Moreover, this was a consensus which even non-Christians, deists and rationalists, could share. Non-Christianity could thus be accommodated within the national framework of American Christendom. It could even (the argument is ironic) accommodate Roman Catholicism. Both American Catholicism and American Judaism became heavily influenced by the moral assumptions of American Protestantism, because both accepted its premise that religion (meaning morality) was essential to democratic institutions.

Now here we come to an important stage in the argument around modern Christianity. The Augustinian total society had come into being in Carolingian times in great part because the Christian clergy operated a monopoly of education, which they only began to lose just before the Reformation. How could the total voluntary society of American Christianity come into being if Church and State were separated, and education were a secular concern? The Founding Fathers saw education and faith as inseparable. Schools were established in Boston as early as 1635, and in 1647 the Massachussetts General Court passed an act requiring towns within its jurisdiction to set up public schools. Harvard itself had been founded eleven years earlier. These institutions were run entirely by religious bodies, were instruments of the Church and were designed to serve religion. The pattern varied, but the principle was the same throughout the early states. Virginia set up the future William and Mary College in these terms (1661): 'Whereas the want of able and faithful ministers deprives us of those great blessings and mercies that always attend upon the service of God, be it enacted that for the advance of learning, education of youth, supply of the ministry, and promotion of piety, there be land taken up or purchased for a college and free school.' This tendency was reinforced during the Great Awakening of the 1730s and 1740s.

However, at about the same time, American Christian rationalists were finding a way out of the dilemma. Benjamin Franklin's *Proposal Relating to the Education of Youth in Pennsylvania* (1749) put forward a scheme to treat religion as one subject in the curriculum, and relate it to character-training. Similar theories were advanced by Jonathan Edwards when President of Princeton. This was the solution adopted when the modern American public school movement, directed by Horace Mann, came into existence in the nineteenth century. The State took over financial responsibility for the education of the new millions by absorbing all primary and secondary education but not (after the Dartmouth decision of 1819) of higher education, where independent colleges survived side by side with state universities. Thus the true American public school was non-sectarian from the very beginning. But it was not non-religious. Mann thought religious instructions should be taken 'to the extremest verge to which it can be carried without invading those rights of conscience which are established by the laws of God, and guaranteed by the constitution of the state'. What the schools got was not so much non-denominational religion as a kind of generalized Protestantism, based on the Bible. As Mann put it, in his final report: 'That our public schools are not theological seminaries is admitted. . . . But our system earnestly inculcates all Christian morals; it founds its morals on the basis of religion; it welcomes the religion of the Bible; it allows it to do what it is allowed to do in no other system, *to speak for itself*.' Hence, in the American system, the school supplied Christian 'character-building' and the parents, at home, topped up with sectarian trimmings.

Naturally there were objections. The Reverend F. A. Newton, on behalf of some episcopalians, argued that 'a book upon politics, morals or religion, containing no party or sectarian views, will be apt to contain no distinctive views of any kind, and will be likely to leave the mind in a state of doubt and scepticism, much more to be deplored than any party or sectarian bias.' This kind of point could be brushed aside. More serious, however, as America increasingly took on the characteristics of a secular state, which she was, *ab initio*, by definition, and as she accepted millions of non-Protestants, especially Catholics and Jews, was the association of moral character-building in the schools with specifically Protestant labels. Gradually, and especially in the big cities, religion as such was eased out of the schools. As the Presbyterian Samuel T. Spear wrote (1870): 'The state, being democratic in its constitution, and consequently having no religion to which it does or can give any legal sanction, should not and cannot, except by manifest inconsistency, introduce either religious or irreligious teaching into a system of popular education which it authorizes, enforces and for the support of which it taxes all the people in common.' But something had to supply the cultural machinery by which the immigrant millions were turned into Americans; and, Spears added, the schools had to have some spiritual foundation. Therefore, since the State was not Christian but republican, republicanism should constitute it. The solution was neat, since in effect republicanism was based on the Protestant ethical and moral consensus, which was what the schools already taught – the two concepts stood or fell together. So in this way the American way of life began to function as the operative creed of the public schools, and it was gradually accepted as the official philosophy of American state education, which it remains. Horace Mann Kallen, writing in the *Saturday Review* (July 1951) under the title 'Democracy's True Religion', summarized the theory: 'For the communicants of the democratic faith, it is the religion *of* and *for* religion. For being the religion of religions, all may freely come together in it.' The case was pushed a little further by J. Paul Williams in *What Americans Believe and How they Worship* (1952):

> 'Americans must come to look upon the democratic ideal . . . as the Will of God, or, if they please, of Nature . . . Americans must be brought to the conviction that democracy is the very Law of Life . . . government agencies must teach the democratic idea as *religion*. . . . Primary responsibility for teaching democracy might be given to the public school.. . . The churches deal effectively with but half the population; the government deals with all the population. . . . It is a misconception to equate separation of church and state with separation of religion and state.'

It was on the basis of such assumptions, imperfectly carried out though they might be, that the two great non-Protestant religions of America, the Catholic and the Jewish, became to some extent Protestantized, and the political ideals and practices of the United States were aligned with a broad-based form of Christianity. The process was already operating even in the seventeenth century, and it began to come to maturity after 1800. As Conrad Moehlman was to put it in 1944 (in *School and Church*): 'The religion of the American majority is democracy.' Hence religion and government were tied together rather as, in the Dark Ages, the State was personalized in the pontifical king, anointed at his coronation so that he might possess regal characteristics. The American people were anointed, as children, and filled with the ethics and morality of standardized Protestant Christianity so that, as adults and voters, they might rule wisely. The institutions were different but the assumption that the spiritual and secular worlds were interdependent was exactly the same.

The system could work granted two preconditions. The first was what might be termed a high level of religiosity in the nation. Religious enthusiasm must be continually replenished to make the ethical and moral ideology seem important. This was supplied by the American system of credal plurality. Having abandoned the advantages of unity, the Americans sensibly turned to exploit the advantages of diversity. And these proved to be considerable. It was the very competitiveness of rival religions in the United States, acting by analogy to the free enterprise system, which kept the demands of the spiritual life constantly before the people. Whereas unity, it was argued, led to mechanical Christianity, apathy and, eventually, atheism, religious competition produced an atmosphere of permanent revival. And this to some extent was true, especially along the expanding frontier and in the areas of nineteenth-century settlement. The second Great Awakening, starting in the 1790s, continued until the middle decades of the new century. The Wesleyans and Baptists spawned multitudes of cults and sub-cults, and the camp-meeting became, for several decades, the characteristic form of American religious experiment.

The atmosphere as one might expect, was Montanist, second-century – the reinterpretation of the central ideas of Christianity by a multitude of exalted individuals, 'speaking with tongues'. A Maryland presbyterian, Barton Stone, who held a great meeting at Cane Ridge, Kentucky, in August 1801, described the actions of the 'saved', which he strongly approved, in great detail. Thus, there was the 'falling exercise' – 'the subject of this exercise would, generally, with a piercing scream, fall like a log on the floor, earth or mud, and appear as dead. . . .' Then there were the jerks: 'When the head alone was affected, it would be jerked backward and forward, or from side to side, so quickly that the features of the face could not be distinguished. When the whole system was affected, I have seen the person stand in one place, and jerk backwards and forwards in quick succession, their head nearly touching the floor behind and before.' The barking exercise: 'A person affected with the jerks, especially in his head, would often make a grunt or bark, if you please, from the suddenness of the jerk.' The 'dancing exercise' was 'indeed heavenly to the spectators . . . the smile of heaven shone in the countenance of the subject.' The 'laughing exercise' was 'loud, hearty laughter . . . it excited laughter in none else. The subject appeared rapturously solemn, and his laughter excited solemnity in saints and sinners. It is truly indescribable.' There was also a running exercise, the subject motivated, apparently, by fear, and a singing exercise, 'not from the mouth or nose but entirely in the breast, the sounds issuing from thence – such music silenced every thing.'

Such descriptions conjure up, not only the realities of many medieval (and, indeed, sixteenth-century sects), but forms of religious enthusiasm visible in Tertullian's day – run by the same kinds of prophets, attracting the same categories of people, criticized by the same kinds of purists and for similar reasons. But of course in America they were allowed to manifest themselves, for the first time in history, virtually without supervision by the State or by a State Church. Most of the cults sprang from Methodist or Baptist trees; and they were a spontaneous rediscovery of ancient forms of Christian enthusiasm. But some could trace a long history. Thus a French medieval sect of Shakers, which became Huguenot in the sixteenth century, and was expelled by Louis XIV after 1688, settled in England, where they re-christened themselves the 'Shaking Quakers', and were brought to the United States in the eighteenth century by the visionary daughter of a Manchester blacksmith, Anne Lee Stanley. They profited from the second Great Awakening to establish a number of utopian centres, distinguished by separation of the sexes and community spiritualist séances, and they continued to shake, in the form of a wild group dance derived from Huguenot *camisards*.

Hundreds of such communities were founded in the nineteenth century. As Emerson wrote to Carlyle in 1840: 'We are all a little wild here with numberless projects of social reform. Not a reading man but has a draft of a new community in his waistcoat pocket.' One of the more rational ones was Brook Farm, in West Roxbury, founded by a Unitarian minister from Boston, George Ripley. It included Nathaniel Hawthorne on its agriculture committee, produced books, pottery and furniture and ended in bankruptcy. Carlyle wrote its epitaph by describing Ripley as 'a Socinian minister who left the pulpit to reform the world by growing onions'. Many central and east European sects successfully established themselves, and still flourish today. Others proved unstable: the German pietist group, under George Rapp, which settled at Harmony, Pennsylvania in 1804, practised auricular confession, opposed procreation and marriage, and contrived to dogmatize itself out of existence. And the Oneida Community of western New York State, which combined socialism with free love or 'complex marriage' – procreation as distinguished from other sexual 'transactions' was decided communally, and the children brought up in a *kibbutz* – flourished by making steel-traps, lost its faith and eventually became a prosperous Canadian corporation, thus justifying Wesley's worst fears.

As in the first and second centuries, some groups of enthusiasts ceased to belong to the prophetic or Montanist type and moved into forms of gnosticism, that is, claimed to have discovered secret codes, texts or systems of knowledge which provided keys to salvation. As such, they tended to part company with Christianity since they replaced Revelation with arcane documents of their own. In about 1827, for instance, Joseph Smith Junior was given by the Angel Moroni a new Bible in the form of golden plates inscribed in 'reformed Egyptian' hieroglyphics, with a set of seer-stones, called Urim and Thummim, with which to read them. The Book of Mormon, as Smith translated it, was put on sale in 1830, after which the angel removed the original plates. Its 500-page text describes the religious history of America's pre-Columban people, who originally crossed from the Tower of Babel in barges, surviving only in the form of Mormon and his son, Moroni, who buried the golden plates in AD 384. The text clearly derived from the King James Bible, but it fitted into some of the social realities of the frontier, and its early rejection, harassment by authority, and difficulties created by 'wicked men', followed by great success, soon gave the movement a genuine tribal history. Smith was providentially murdered by a mob in Illinois in 1844, after which Brigham Young was able to take the sect on a great exodus to Salt Lake City in 1847. Even at this stage Mormonism had crossed the farthest frontiers of Christianity, but it did so in a more obvious sense when Young introduced polygamy. Under the controlling provision of the First Amendment, 'Congress shall make no law respecting an establishment of religion, or prohibiting the free exercise thereof . . .', sects did not become illegal if they offended

Christian dogma. But Christian morals and social customs were a different matter, and Mormonism was in continuous battle with the state until polygamy was renounced in 1890. Gnosticism was thus perfectly acceptable within the American total, and voluntary, Christian society, but only provided it genuflected to Protestant morality.

It was subject to this qualification that Catholicism was tolerated. It was not so much forced to change iself as to develop a highly defensive posture, which to some extent came to the same thing. Although American Christianity escaped religious warfare, the witchcraft frenzy showed that it was not immune to fanatical infection, and at times the development of Protestant horror-literature aimed at Catholics came close to bringing about a break- down in the consensus. Of course, to many Protestants, a number of Catholic institutions infringed the moral consensus in spirit, even if they did not actually defy it legally, as the Mormon polygamists did. One example was convents, the objects of a campaign by the *Protestant Vindicator*, founded in 1834. The next year saw the publication in Boston of *Six Months in a Convent*, and, in 1836, *Maria Monk's Awful Disclosures of the Hotel Dieu Nunnery in Montreal*, written by a group of New York anti-Catholics. This was followed by *Further Disclosures* and *The Escape of Sister Frances Patrick, Another Nun from the Hotel Dieu Nunnery in Montreal*. Maria Monk herself was arrested for picking pockets in a brothel and died in prison in 1849; but her book had sold 300,000 copies by 1860 and was termed 'the *Uncle Tom's Cabin* of Knownothingness'. (It was reprinted as recently as 1960.) An Ursuline convent was burned down by a Boston mob in 1834 and those responsible were acquitted – Protestant juries believed Catholic convents had sub- terranean dungeons for the murder and burial of illegitimate children.

There were also widespread fears of a Catholic political and military conspiracy – fears which had existed, in one form or another, since the 1630s, when they were associated with Charles I. In the 1830s, Lyman Beecher's *Plea for the West* revealed a plot to take over the Mississippi Valley, the Emperor of Austria being in league with the Pope. Samuel Morse, the inventor of the telegraph, made the conspiracy more plausible by suggesting that the reactionary kings and emperors of Europe were deliberately promoting Catholic emigration to America as a preliminary to a take-over. (Morse was not particularly Protestant, but, during a visit to Rome, he had been outraged by a papal soldier who had knocked off his hat when Morse failed to doff it to a religious procession.) In fact, during the 1850s, America's population rose from 23,191,000 to 31,443,000, or almost fifty per cent, more than a third of the increase being due to immigration. This brought the Catholic issue into politics with the emergence of the secretive ultra-Protestant American Party, whose 'I don't know' answer to a key question led to their popular title, the 'Know Nothings'. The party became a national force before being merged into the Republican Party in 1854; and it was a matter of note that, whereas the Republican Party became identified with the anti-slavery campaign, the

Roman Catholic hierarchy remained non-committal on the issue, and took virtually no part in the crusade.

This brings us to the second precondition needed to make the American politico-religious system work. As we have seen, there was no difficulty about the level of religiosity. But the second precondition was a level of agreement on certain basic moral and ethical notions as interpreted in public institutions. It was here that the system broke down, for American Christianity could not agree about slavery. One sees why St Paul was chary of tackling the subject head-on: once slavery is established, religious injunctions tend to fit its needs, not vice versa. In the United States, the dilemma had been there right from the start, since 1619 marked the beginning both of representative government and of slavery. But it had slowly become more acute, since the identification of American moral Christianity – its undefined national religion – with democracy made slavery come to seem both an offence against God and an offence against the nation. Political and religious arguments reinforced each other.

On the other hand, weren't the Southern slave-owners Christians too? Indeed they were. There had been a strong anti-slavery movement among the churches, particularly the Baptists and Quakers, in the 1770s; it had petered out because the churches came to terms with Southern practice. But this did not, indeed, could not, remove religion from the slavery question. The doctrinal position might be arguable, but the moral position – which was what mattered – became increasingly clear to the majority of American Christians. The Civil War can be described as the most characteristic religious episode in the whole of American history since its roots and causes were not economic or political but religious and moral. It was a case of a moral principle tested to destruction – not, indeed, of the principle, but of those who opposed it. But in the process Christianity itself was placed under almost intolerable strain.

The movement which finally destroyed American slavery was religious in a number of different senses. It reflected a degree of extremism in the northern Christian sects. William Lloyd Garrison, a Baptist converted to activism by Quakers, who founded the *Boston Public Liberator and Journal of the Times*, wrote in its first issue: 'I will be as harsh as truth and as uncompromising as justice. On this subject I do not wish to think, or speak, or write, with moderation. . . .' Extremists on this issue had many links with revivalism, which gave it a nationwide platform and constituency. Then, too, the cause was watered with the blood of martyrs, especially by Elijah Lovejoy, murdered in Illinois in 1837 while defending his printing-press. (The printing-press had had a special symbolic significance in the minds of Anglo-Saxon Protestants since the sixteenth century, being equated with liberty and anti-papal propaganda.) Finally, there was the theology of abolition which, as one would expect, was primarily a moral theology. In 1845 Edward Beecher published a series of articles on what he termed the nation's 'organic sin' of slavery, which invested the abolitionist cause with a whole series of evangelical insights, mostly ethical. Theology, but again of a moral nature, was the background to *Uncle Tom's Cabin* which appeared seven years later, Harriet Beecher Stowe being the wife of a Congregationalist Old Testament professor, and a lay-theologian herself.

The defence of the South was sociological rather than doctrinal. Nevertheless there was little internal opposition to slavery among white Southern Christians, and a notable closing of Christian ranks after the black preacher Nat Turner led the Virginia slave revolt of 1831, in which fifty-seven whites were killed. Revivalism, which in the North was used to strengthen the mass following of abolition, was put to exactly the opposite use in the South, where it was, if anything, more powerful. The South Carolina Baptist Association produced a biblical defence of slavery in 1822, and in 1844 John England, Bishop of Charleston, provided a similar one for Southern white Catholics. There were standard biblical texts on negro inferiority, patriarchal and Mosaic acceptance of servitude, and of course St Paul on obedience to masters. Both sides could, and did, hurl texts at each other. In fact revivalism, and the evangelical movement generally, played into the hands of extremists on both sides. Of course, it could be argued that the slavery issue could just as easily have split the Christian movement in the first century AD, if it had not been side-stepped by Paul; his evasions – so the argument might continue – made it possible for the issue still to be unresolved in the nineteenth century. But the answer to this was that the bulk of Christian opinion and teaching had been anti-slavery for more than a millenium, that Christianity was the one great religion which had always declared the diminution, if not the final elimination, of slavery to be meritorious; and that no real case for slavery could be constructed, in good faith, from Christian scripture. The fact that Southerners from a variety of Christian churches were prepared to do so, in the second half of the nineteenth century, was a shocking and flagrant stain on the faith.

What followed when war came was even worse. The Presbyterians from North and South tried to hold together by suppressing all discussion of the issue, but split in the end. So did the Wesleyans. (In 1843, 1200 Methodist clergy owned slaves, and 25,000 church members collectively owned over 200,000.) So did the Baptists. The Congregationalists, because of their atomized structure, remained theoretically united, but in fact were divided in exactly the same way as the others. Only the Lutherans, the Episcopalians and the Catholics successfully avoided public debates and voting, but the evidence suggests that they, too, were diametrically opposed on a salient matter of Christian principle. The parallel was not exactly with the wars of religion, but rather with the papal schisms and the papal-imperial contests of the Middle Ages, with both sides operating from precisely the same assumptions and using the same agreed texts, but reaching diametrically opposed and dogmatically asserted verdicts.

Having split, the churches promptly went to battle on opposing sides, exactly like feudal bishops. Leonidas Polk, Bishop of Louisiana, immediately entered the Confederate army as a major-general: 'It is for constitutional liberty, which seems to us to have fled for refuge, for our hearthstones and our altars that we strike.' Thomas March, Bishop of Rhode Island, told the militia on the other side: 'It is a holy and righteous cause in which you enlist . . . God is with us . . . the Lord of Hosts is on our side.' The Southern Presbyterian Church resolved, 1864: 'We hesitate not to affirm that it is the peculiar mission of the Southern Church to conserve the institution of slavery, and to make it a blessing both to master and slave.' (It also justified its separation from the Northern Church on the grounds that otherwise 'politics would be obtruded on our church courts'.) The dogma that slavery was inherently sinful was 'unscriptural and fanatical . . . one of the most pernicious heresies of modern times'.

To judge by the many hundreds of sermons and specially-composed church prayers which have survived, ministers were among the most fanatical on both sides. The churches played a major role in the dividing of the nation, and it is probably true that it was the splits in the churches which made a final split of the nation inevitable. In the North, such a charge was often willingly accepted. The Northern Methodist Granville Moddy said in 1861: 'We are charged with having brought about the present contest. I believe it is true we did bring it about, and I glory in it, for it is a wreath of glory around our brow.' Southern clergymen did not make the same boast, but it is true that of all the various elements in the South they did the most to make a secessionist state of mind possible. Both sides claimed vast numbers of 'conversions' among their troops, and a tremendous increase in church-going and prayerfulness as a result of the war; and Southern clergymen were mainly responsible for prolonging the futile struggles. Thus Christianity on both sides contributed to the million casualties and 600,000 dead.

The clerical interpretations of the war's lessons were equally dogmatic and contradictory. Robert Lewis Dabney, the Southern Presbyterian theologian, blamed the 'calculated malice' of the Northern Presbyterians, and he called on God for a 'retributive providence' which would demolish the North. Henry War Beecher said the Southern leaders 'shall be whirled aloft and plunged downward for ever and ever in an endless retribution'. The New Haven theologian Theodore Thornton Munger declared that the Confederacy had been 'in league with Hell'; the South was now suffering 'for its sins' as a matter of 'divine logic', the North being the 'sacrificing instrument'. He worked out that General McClellan's much-blamed vacillations were an example of God's hidden cunning, since they made a quick Northern victory impossible and so ensured that the South would be much more heavily punished in the end. But this sort of thing was mere theologian's Billingsgate, the sort of abuse with which St Jerome cheered himself up in his Jerusalem monastery. More intelligent people tended to see the war as a national purging process, or, more optimistically, as a preparation, through self-redemption, for America's coming role in advancing world freedom. In his Second Inaugural, the Baptist Abraham Lincoln tried to rationalize God's purpose. America was 'the almost-chosen people'; the war was part of God's scheme, a great testing of the nation by an ordeal of blood, showing the way to charity and thus to rebirth. Less sophisticated Christians did not want to rationalize, but to indulge their feelings. Some Northern churchmen clamoured to destroy the dissident Southern branches. The *Independent*, an influential church paper, wrote in 1865: 'The apostate church is buried beneath a flow of divine wrath; its hideous dogmas shine on its brow like flaming fiends; the whole world stands aghast at its wickedness and ruin. The Northern church beholds its mission.'

In fact, nothing happened. As in the Middle Ages, once peace had broken out, the rival prelates came together again, provided they were white. Southern Baptists, Methodists, Presbyterians and Lutherans continued to proclaim their loyalty to the lost cause, but otherwise resumed standard Christian attitudes. The liberated slaves formed their own churches, chiefly Baptist and Methodist. These flourished, encompassing more than a third of the black population by 1900. The fact that white Baptist and Methodist ministers had recently preached slavery (and still defended it, *sotto voce*) seems to have made no difference to black Baptists and Methodists, so long as they could run their own churches. Nor, in a wider sense, does any sect appear to have suffered from the fact that its clergy and members were on both sides or that, institutionally, it evaded the issue. What was necessarily damaged, or at any rate challenged, was the identity between the political aims of the nation and its religious beliefs. For the first time America began to miss the Pascalian element in its Christian philosophy, and to feel the lack of theodicy.

Yet the majority of American Christians came to look on the Civil War not as a Christian defeat, in which the powerlessness or contradictions of the faith had been exposed, but as an American-Christian victory, in which Christian egalitarian teaching had been triumphantly vindicated against renegades and apostates. It fitted neatly into a world vision of the Anglo-Saxon races raising up the benighted and ignorant dark millions, and bringing them, thanks to a 'favouring providence' into the lighted circle of Christian truth; thus the universalist mission of Christ would be triumphantly completed. For, by the 1860s, the United States, along with Britain, was in the forefront of a huge missionary effort whose aim was no less than the evangelization of the globe.

It must be said that it took the Protestant powers, and Protestantism generally, a very long time to get themselves into this posture. Until the early nineteenth century, Protestantism cannot be called a missionary faith. It is true that some efforts were made. As early as 1622, the Dutch set up a seminary in Leyden to train missionaries for work in the East Indies and Ceylon. But the chief object, linked to economic and political penetration, was to combat Spanish and Portuguese efforts to Catholicize the islands, and when Catholic power declined, Dutch efforts slackened too; in the eighteenth century the Dutch claimed many converts, but less than one in ten of them were admitted to communion, and in 1776 only twenty-two ministers (five of whom spoke a native language) looked after the entire East Indies.

The English were even less energetic in the East. In the whole of the seventeenth century, there is only one recorded case of an Anglican baptism in India, though the English had been active there from 1600 – and this was a Bengali boy brought back to London in 1616, for whom James I chose the name Peter Pope. In fact the Anglicans did not have a service for adult baptism until 1662. The Puritans did, and in 1648 a Calvinist House of Commons had recorded: 'The Commons of England assembled in parliament, having received intelligence that the heathens of New England are beginning to call upon the name of the Lord, feel bound to assist in this work.' The Presbyterian John Elliot, following the practice of Catholic friars, learned the Iroquois language and founded 'praying towns'; by 1671 he had gathered 3,600 Christian natives into fourteen settlements. But these, and similar, efforts were ruined by the Indian wars and the Anglo-French struggles, and today none of the surviving Indians can even read Elliot's 'Moheecan' Bible. The Anglican Society for the Propagation of the Gospel in Foreign Parts, founded in 1701, claimed that its activity 'doth chiefly and principally relate to the conversion of heathens and infidels', but in fact most of its missionaries worked among the English settler communities, both in New England and in the West Indies. Indeed, Protestant settlement, and Protestant missions, in the true sense, were mutually exclusive, or at least incompatible, for where Europeans found it climatically and economically possible to settle in large numbers, the natives were expelled or exterminated. (This happened in Catholic areas too: for example, the French settlements in Canada, and the Spanish in Argentina.)

The first sophisticated Protestant missionary work was a product of late seventeenth-century German pietism. In 1706, the Lutheran Frederick IV of Denmark started a carefully organized but small-scale mission in the little Danish settlement of Tranquebar on the Coromandel Coast of south-east India. He employed two German pastors, Bartholomew Ziegenbald and Henry Plutschau, who based their work methodically on a number of assumptions which became standard. The mission church must be associated with a mission school (and later a hospital or clinic). The gospels (and preferably the whole of the Bible) must be translated. Missionaries must possess an accurate knowledge of the native mentality and language. Conversions must be made of individuals not of groups. And native missionaries and ministers must be trained as rapidly as possible. The last two of these principles raised controversy of a type which had already puzzled the Jesuits. The earliest Christians had made individual conversions, partly because they had no state power behind them. In the Dark Ages, missionaries had worked through kings and tribal leaders; the Germans and Slavs had become Christians in entire social units, sometimes indeed at the point of the sword. Both methods had worked. In India, it could be argued that only personal conversion enabled the adult neophyte to understand the true meaning of the Christian message and the privileges and responsibilities he was receiving. On the other hand, he thereby became detached from his social group – hence the practice of transplanting converts and bringing them together in new settlements, a method used, with variations, by Catholics and Protestants alike, all over the world. Others argued that it was much better to work on a whole community, and bring them over together when the moment was ripe, without damaging the social structure. Christianity then became fully integrated with the native way of life. But against this it was urged that the whole object of Christianity was to change the way of life. As a new religion, or cult, it necessarily involved the adoption of new cultural and social norms. This was the meaning of Paul's expression, becoming 'a new man'. Polygamy was a case in point. Enforcing Christian monogamy meant a huge and unwelcome change in the social structure. But this was unavoidable unless it was seriously proposed that Christianity should accept polygamy. If polygamy, why not cannibalism?

The argument remained unresolved throughout the period – that is up to the end of the nineteenth century – when collective conversions were a possibility, at least in some areas. It was the same with the debate over a native clergy. As in the Catholic missions, the Protestants became divided, and usually in the same way. The home and secular authorities, and the hierarchies, were less anxious to train and promote natives than the men on the spot. Native clergy were regarded as incompatible with colonial rule; or with doctrinal orthodoxy. Some of the actual missionaries were much more ready to try experiments. One of the earliest Baptists in India, William Carey, wrote in 1805 that his chief object was 'the forming of our native brethren to usefulness, fostering every kind of genius, and cherishing every gift and grace in them; in this respect we can scarcely be too lavish in our attention to their improvement. It is only by means of native preachers we can hope for the universal spread of the Gospel through this immense Continent.' Again, one of the Protestant pioneers in East Africa, Lewis Krapf, from the Basel Seminary, who worked for the Christian Missionary Society in the 1830s, thought the training of black clergy would bring about a qualitative change. 'When the colour of a man's skin no longer excludes him from the office of an evangelist, the traffic in slaves will have had its knell. A black bishop and a black clergy of the Protestant church may ere long become a necessity to the civilization of Africa.' But then he was against colonialism too: 'Banish the thought that Europe must spread her protecting wings over East Africa, if missionary work is to prosper in that land of outer darkness. Europe would, no doubt, remove much that is mischievous and obstructive out of the way of missionary work, but she would probably set in its way as many, and perhaps still greater checks.' Examples of similar views could be produced from all the missionary territories.

The missions themselves were divided. Those, like Carey and Krapf, who identified themselves with the natives and gave high priority to creating an independent clergy and Church, included most of the ablest and most sensitive of the missionaries, but constituted only a minority of the workers in the field. Most of those who lived among the natives, both in India and Africa, were more struck by their ignorance than by their potentialities. Whereas the Acts of the Apostles, for example, while drawing attention to gentile wickedness, never refers to cultural and economic inferiority of a kind to make the reception of Christianity difficult or the emergence of fully-fledged Christians impossible, the European evangelists tended to feel themselves confronted with a different, and inferior, kind of being. The New Testament seemed to give them no guidance on this point. Charles Grant, who cannot fairly be accused of prejudice against non-European races, who was one of the prime organizers of the anti-slavery campaign, and who strongly urged the case for missions, formed a very pessimistic view during the many years he spent in India. Writing in 1797, just eight years before Carey, he admitted: '... we cannot avoid recognizing in the people of Indostan a race of man lamentably degenerate and base; retaining but a feeble sense of moral obligation; yet obstinate in their disregard of what they know to be right, governed by malevolent and licentious passions, strongly exemplifying the effects produced on society by a great and general corruption of manners, and sunk in misery by their vices.' Here, one feels, there is an almost total confusion between economic, cultural and moral 'inferiority'. This was very common. The missionaries were not anthropologists or sociologists; they found it exceedingly difficult to think in terms of relative scales of moral values. They did not see European-Christian notions of right and wrong as the indices of a particular culture and society but as absolutes, springing from divine revelation. A man's conscience was a kind of direct line to the Deity. Everyone had such a thing. The Baptist George Grenfell wrote of the Congo: 'The chief characteristics of the Bolobo people appear to be drunkenness, immorality and cruelty, out of each of which vice spring actions almost too fearful to describe. In hearing of these, anyone living out here almost gets to feel like calling the people terrible brutes and wretches, rather than poor miserable heathen. The light of their consciences must condemn them in most of their sins.' Another missionary, Holman Bentley, commented on cannibalism: 'To this awful depth have these children of the Heavenly Father fallen, until they have indeed become children of the devil. ... This is how they live up to their light! Again we say, if the light that is in them be darkness, how great is that darkness!'

It was hard indeed for missionaries with such feelings, and they formed by far the majority, to visualize the emergence of a predominantly native clergy, or indeed to visualize natives as fully-fledged Christians at all. They were seen to approximate to Christianity in so far as they succesfully imitated European modes of behaviour. Thus missionaries found themselves exporting not so much Christianity as European or western culture – including, of course, its moral culture. The idea of Christianity as a series of matrices, capable of being applied to all societies, and indeed to all individuals, tended to be smothered in the cultural packaging. When it came to selecting native converts for training as clergy – and very few missionaries objected to the idea in principle – the most Europeanized tended to be chosen. Naturally, the influence they had among the unconverted diminished *pari passu* with their departure from native norms; they were, not unjustly, regarded as poor imitations of European missionaries. Thus experiments in training native clergy were liable to be classified as failures, or as not justifying the amount of trouble and debate they involved.

These points are worth a digression because it is important to realize that the methods adopted by the early German missionaries in India, though they became standard, always remained subjects of debate. Missionaries differed greatly and sometimes violently among themselves on virtually every issue. There was no such thing as a missionary 'attitude', and it is hazardous indeed to generalize about missionary history. All one can do is to try to indicate certain salient features. Of course, missionary effort tended to reflect the level of religious commitment and enthusiasm in the Christian West. The Catholic missions undoubtedly decayed after the Treaty of Westphalia and the end of religious warfare. During the eighteenth century they virtually ceased in most areas, especially after the dissolution of the Jesuits led to the enforced withdrawal of over 3,000 of the best field-workers, and by far the most efficient international organization. In the eighteenth century, then, the Protestants were left with virtually a clear field. They were slow to take advantage of their opportunities. In Protestant countries too, the flame of faith burned low. Not only were German freelances the first in India; for a long time they were the only ones. The British upper classes and the Anglican Church were very slow to endorse missionary work. The East India Company did not want missionaries at all, and approved of clergymen only to minister to the European community. The most famous of the south Indian missionaries, Christian Friedrich Schwartz, who served there for forty-eight years ending in 1798, was not only a German but was not even validly ordained by Anglican standards. One British officer wrote of him: 'The knowledge and integrity of this irreproachable missionary have retrieved the character of Europeans from imputations of general depravity'. But this was the view of an enthusiast. The British establishment did not want such people. The first Anglican bishop sent out to India, Thomas Fanshawe Middleton, consecrated Bishop of Calcutta in 1814, did not know what to do with his largely German missionaries: 'I must either license them or silence them.'

Indeed, the first positive missionary efforts by the British had nothing to do with government, officialdom, the ruling class or the Anglican Church. They were essentially lower middle-class, dissenting ventures. The first modern missionary society, 1792, was Baptist, and was followed by the largely

Congregationalist London Missionary Society in 1795. These people actually got missionaries working in the field. Carey, for instance, was a Northampton shoemaker, the son of a weaver; his companion in India, William Ward, was a printer. Such men were not necessarily ill-educated. Carey, who was self-taught, spoke Latin, Hebrew, Greek and Dutch, and he produced a Sanskrit grammar of 1,000 pages; his 1792 pamphlet, *An Inquiry into the Obligation of Christians to use Means for the Conversion of the Heathen*, was the most influential of all tracts in getting a large-scale missionary movement going. Again, his printer friend Ward wrote a book on *Manners and Customs of the Hindus*; and together they created Serempore College for the Instruction of Asiatic, Christian and Other Youth, in Eastern Literature and European Science. But, as a rule, they were impelled more by simple Bible-reading enthusiasm than by any knowledge of the peoples and territories involved. The first mission to the Pacific, sent out by the Congregationalists in the ship *Duff* to Tahiti in 1796, consisted of four ministers, six carpenters, two shoemakers, two bricklayers, two weavers, two tailors, a shopkeeper, a harness-maker, a servant, a gardener, a surgeon, a blacksmith, a cooper, a butcher, a cotton-manufacturer, a hatter, a draper and a cabinet-maker. This class and occupational composition was characteristic. Very few of the early missionaries had educational qualifications. The effort was earnest but it was unsophisticated and often wildly off target. What Protestantism lacked was an élite organization like the Jesuits, which could develop a thorough under-standing of the cultural and social structure of the mission-territory, appeal to its intellectual leaders, and argue from its own assumptions rather than from European ones.

From the 1780s, a section of the British upper classes became interested in the global responsibilities of British Christianity, but they concentrated almost exclusively, at first, on the slave trade; in other words, their focus was on English vice rather than the spiritual demands of the black heathen. In a way this was natural. Slave-trading had become a huge English industry by the 1780s. In four centuries, the European slave trade carried over ten million slaves from Africa, over sixty per cent of them between 1721 and 1820. Some of them went east. Thus the East India Company had a few slaves, but left the business in 1762. By then the trade had become largely transatlantic, shipping an average of 60,000 a year, with Portuguese America the chief market, followed by the West Indies and the United States. The trade was shared out between the French, British and Portuguese, with Britain taking half. After 1792, the French dropped out, and the British took up the slack, making 1798, for instance, a record year, with 160 British slaving ships operating, mostly from Liverpool. Slaving was one of the largest, and certainly the most profitable, sectors of the British economy. In England, 18,000 people were employed simply on making goods to pay for slaves in Africa; this trade alone formed 4·4 per cent of British exports in the 1790s. The trade had been traditionally tolerated by Anglican divines. It was defended even by some missionaries. One of the founders of the Society for the Propagation of the Gospel in New England, Thomas Thompson, who had worked among negroes in New Jersey, and then spent four years in Guinea, 'to make a trial with the Natives', wrote *The African Trade for Negro Slaves shown to be Consistent with the Principles of Humanity and the Laws of Revealed Religion*, setting out the kind of case made by southern state Christians in the 1840s and 1850s. In fact the SPG itself actually owned slaves in Barbados.

Of all the Christian sects, the Quakers were the first to adopt the view that slavery was intrinsically wrong in all circumstances. Indeed in 1780 they forced the Pennsylvania legislature to make slavery illegal in the state. It had already been declared illegal in England in 1772, when Lord Mansfield ruled against it not on religious but on Common Law grounds. Thereafter the change of Christian opinion in England was steadily brought about, as all the Christian groups were forced to declare themselves. The movement coincided with the first full-blossoming of upper-class evangelicalism, and William Wilberforce became its leader and made ending the slave-trade the principal object of its enthusiasm. Without this conjunction, slavery would undoubtedly have persisted for much longer. As it was, Britain made the trade illegal in 1807, and in 1824 it was legally ranked with piracy, and punishable by death; nine years later slavery was outlawed in all British territories. The preoccupation with slavery and the slave-trade explains why British upper-class Christians were slow to engage in the missionary venture. But of course the two were closely related, above all in Africa. So long as slaving continued, it was very difficult in practice for missionaries to get into the African interior. But once it was illegal, and the British Navy, consuls, and other agents and agencies instructed to enforce the law, the missionaries found themselves propelled powerfully forward on a ubiquitous secular force. For the first time, in effect, the British empire was giving practical, even if indirect, support to missionary endeavour.

This big change coincided with the development of missionary societies not only as a huge middle-class movement but as a global Protestant phenomenon. The Anglican Church Missionary Society was formed in 1799, the British and Foreign Bible Society (Anglican and Free Church) in 1804, the American Board of Commissioners for Foreign Missions (mainly Congregational) in 1810, the American Baptist Missionary Board in 1814, the Berlin Society in 1824, the Basle Mission in 1815, and mission-boards in Denmark (1821), France (1822), Sweden (1835), and Norway (1842). These societies were the first evangelical wave, to be followed by a second, much bigger one, which in the 1850s came from across the Atlantic. The United States began to take the lead in missionary enthusiasm, especially in the Far East. For the first time, women were dispatched as missionaries, eventually coming to outnumber the men; and for the first time, too, missions began regularly to operate medical as well as educational services, and so to become associated with the developing secular idea that the white man held colonies in a form of trusteeship.

Inevitably, then, large-scale missionary effort became involved with colonialism and commerce. In Asian and African eyes it was inextricably involved. As the century progressed, Indian intellectuals, for instance, came to see Christianity as nothing more than an epiphenomenon of western political and commercial expansion. Westerners put it a different way. Grant, in his *Observations on the State of Society among the Asiatic Subjects of Great Britain* (1797) observed:

'Those distant territories . . . were given to us not merely that we might draw an annual profit from them, but that we might diffuse among their inhabitants . . . the light and benign influence of the truth, the blessing of well-regulated society, the improvements and comforts of active industry. . . . In every progressive step of this work, we shall also serve the original design with which we visited India, that design so important to this country – the extension of our commerce.'

The point was made more crudely by Holman Bentley: 'So, with the opening up of Africa, Manchester may take heart; not only are there thousands more to wear its cloth, but thousands more to be buried in it.' Yet here again, the western mind was not unanimous, or even quite sure of itself. Officially, the British empire, for instance, was not a proselytizing organization. The proclamation which replaced the East India Company by direct British rule began: 'Firmly relying ourselves on the truth of Christianity, and acknowledging with gratitude the solaces of religion, We disclaim alike the right and the desire to impose Our convictions on any of Our subjects. . . .' This prolegomena was only agreed after much argument. Again, the 1854 provision of state aid to Indian schools, from which missionary establishments chiefly benefited, was defended by Sir Charles Wood, first Viscount Halifax, with notable ambivalence, on the grounds that 'it will strengthen our empire. But . . . even if the result should be the loss of that empire, it seems to me that this country will occupy a far better and prouder position in the history of the world, if by our agency a civilized and Christian empire should be established in India, than if we continued to rule over a people debased by ignorance and degraded by superstition.'

Sometimes it is extremely hard for the historian, trying to peer into a nineteenth-century mind, to decide exactly how important the Christian impulse was among so many others. Was David Livingstone, for instance, primarily a Christian evangelist, an imperialist – or an egoist? It is possible to make out a case for all three. (His father-in-law, Robert Moffat, was also a puzzling figure: in 1857 he finished the vast work of translating the Bible into Tswana, but he seems to have had no interest in the African background, believing quite wrongly, for instance, that the Bechuna had no word for God.) Livingstone's initial motive was almost wholly spiritual: 'Can the love of Christ not carry the missionary where the slave-trade carries the trader?' His life can be quite plausibly interpreted as a sacrifice. Yet after fame came to him, he left the London Missionary Society for a consulship in East Africa, the government backing his venture with £5,000. He told the University of Cambridge in 1857: 'I beg to direct your attention to Africa. I know that in a few years I shall be cut off in that country, which is now open. Do not let it be shut again! I go back to Africa to try to make an open path for commerce and Christianity. Do you carry on the work which I have begun. I leave it with you' – the speech ending in a shout. Again, the next year, he wrote to Professor Sedgwick:

'That you may have a clear idea of my objects, I may state that they have more in them than meets the eye. They are not merely exploratory, for I go with the intention of benefiting both the African and my own countrymen. I take a practical mining geologist to tell us of the mineral resources of the country, an economic botanist to give a full report of the vegetable productions, an artist to give the scenery, a naval officer to tell of the capacity of river communications, and a moral agent to lay a Christian foundation for anything that may follow. All this machinery had for its ostensible object the development of African trade and the promotion of civilization; but what I can tell to none but such as you, in whom I have confidence, is that I hope it may result in an English colony in the healthy high lands of Central Africa! . . . I have told it only to the Duke of Argyll.'

In some cases, the missionaries regarded colonialism (and commerce) with open hostility. New Zealand, which the missionaries first penetrated in 1814, was a battleground between the Church, which wanted to create an independent, self-sustaining Maori Christian state – rather like the Jesuits in Japan – and the colonizing interests, which recognized the country as an ideal area for European settlement. Darwin, who was there in 1835, warmly praised the missionaries' work: '. . . all this is very surprising when it is considered that five years ago nothing but the fern flourished here. . . . The lesson of the missionary is the enchanter's wand.' Five years later, the declaration of British sovereignty marked the victory of the settlers and colonists, and was the prelude to Maori wars. Yet the defeat of mission policy, and the Maori-European conflict does not seem to have sullied the Christian image: by 1854 it was reported that ninety-nine per cent of the Maoris were Christian. In the Far East, by contrast, the missionaries undoubtedly supported the use of force by the great western powers to open up opportunities. In 1839–42, the consequence of the first Opium War was the cession of Hong Kong to Britain, and the transfer to the great powers of five treaty ports. Missionaries took the view that the deplorable war had been in some way manipulated by divine providence to make China accessible to the gospel. Missionary societies from the main sects sent teams to all six places. The Perry ultimatum to Japan in 1853 was followed, five years later, by the arrival of the first Christian mission since the destruction of Japanese Christianity in the seventeenth century. The same year, the end of the Second Chinese War brought the further concession of toleration for Christianity throughout China, and in effect ensured the protection of missionaries and their penetration of the interior. In both countries the ability of missionaries to operate was conditional on western military preponderance, and the willingness to exert it.

In Africa, the process was taken a stage further when the British government (followed by others) became directly involved in missionary enterprise. This was, to some extent, inevitable because government needed missionary help in suppressing the slave-trade, and the churches were eager to supply it. But it was in Africa, too, that the British ruling establishment first became fully involved in the evangelizing effort. The upper-class Evangelicals moved straight from anti-slavery to missions. Thomas Fowell Buxton, who succeeded Wilberforce as leader of the anti-slavery campaign, coined the phrase: 'It is the Bible and the plough that must regenerate Africa.' The Reverend Charles Simeon, the key figure in the Evangelical take-over of bishoprics and parishes, also began to deal in colonial appointments, and to send out his protegés to be, as he put it, 'princes in all lands'. The Evangelicals dominated the Anglican Church Missionary Society, and in 1840 they launched the new African campaign with an enthusiastic meeting at Exeter Hall, attended by Prince Albert, Sir Robert Peel, Mr Gladstone, Lord Shaftesbury, the French Ambassador, the leader of the Irish Nationalists, Daniel O'Connell and, among others, the young David Livingstone. Archdeacon Wilberforce, William's sonorous son, told the distinguished throng that their purpose was to make sure 'that every ship laden with commerce might also bear the boon of everlasting life, that from no part of the earth should they receive only, without giving for the gold of the west and the spices from the east the more precious wealth – the more blessed frankincense of Christ their master'.

Fowell Buxton persuaded the government to turn this pledge into reality by providing £80,000 for an expedition to open up the Niger in West Africa. It set off in 1841 in three iron ships, the *Albert*, the *Wilberforce* and the *Soudan*, but was defeated by malaria, which struck down 130 out of the 145 European members of the expedition, and killed 40 of them. But two more sorties were made, under Admiralty protection, and Christianity was established permanently under the aegis of a British presence which inevitably turned into a series of colonies. Some of the local African rulers, such as Eyo Honesty II, king of Greek Town in Old Calabar, were inclined to welcome Christian evangelism, believing it would strengthen their authority. In fact the missionaries tended sooner or later to provoke violence, leading to armed European intervention, a constitutional crisis, and outright annexation. The pattern was not necessarily deliberate, but it was remarkably similar in various parts of the African coast. The missionaries might seek to dissociate themselves from European colonization, but the fact is that most of them, in Africa at least, found it far more convenient (and safe) to operate with whites in control.

In Calabar the missions soon focussed their hostility on the Old Town and Duke Town, described as 'an African Sodom and Gomorrah', where obnoxious customs, such as infanticide, were said to flourish. They promptly formed a Society for the Abolition of Inhuman and Superstitious Customs and for Promoting Civilization in the area, and the British Consul was signed up as a founder member. The missionary stationed in the Old Town, the Reverend Samuel Edgerley, made no secret of his anxiety to change the habits of those he termed 'a degraded and heathen people'. In 1849 he kicked over a religious drum; and in 1854, following an alleged massacre of fifty slaves by the deposed king of Old Town, Willie Tom, Edgerley smashed up images in a local shrine and broke its sacred egg; he also removed various objects as souvenirs. In the ensuing trouble, the missionaries, seconded by European traders, persuaded the Consul that he would be 'forwarding the work of civilization' if he got HMS *Antelope* to bombard Old Town; and this was done. A CMS missionary, the Reverend C. A. Gollmer, commented: 'I look upon it as God's intervention for the good of Africa.' Two years later,· Gollmer instigated another naval attack, this time on the Ijebu tribe. Vessels like HMS *Scourge* were repeatedly used on the coast and river to frighten chiefs into complying with missionary demands to operate freely. Local by-laws soon reflected the needs of Christian evangelism. Thus Greek Town legislated for the Sabbath: 'Henceforth, on God's day, no market to be held in any part of Greek Town territory; no sale of strong drink, either native or imported, in doors and verandahs; no work; no play; no devil making; no firing of guns; no Egbo processions; no Palaver.' From this it was a short step to the permanent deposition of kings and the assumption of all executive power in the hands of white officials.

On the other hand, as experience in both Central and East Africa showed, without European rule, one of two things was likely to happen. The missionaries nearly always found a demand for Christian teaching. Many of the Africans were looking for a new and less primitive religion, and for a refuge from the often appalling cruelties of cults centred on tyrannical chiefs. It was comparatively easy for missionaries, even in territories where Europeans exercised no direct power, to set up new Christian villages, thus falling into a form of evangelization with strong social and political (and indeed economic) implications. They then rapidly found themselves becoming *de facto* chieftains. Dan Crawford, in a thoughtful survey of mission problems called *Thinking Black* (1912), wrote: 'Many a little Protestant pope in the lonely bush is forced by his self-imposed isolation to be prophet, priest and king roled into one.' He himself founded a new inter-Christian tribal city (he was a Plymouth Brother) and was known to the Africans as *konga vantu*, 'the gatherer of the peoples'. The alternative, which was worse, was for the missionaries to become, as it were, agents of powerful kings whom they could not control or even influence. Discussing the local tyrant in Katanga, an English vice-consul reported in 1890: 'The missionaries treat Msidi as a great king, do nothing without first asking his permission, and are at his beck and call, almost his slave. . . . They dared not come to see me on my arrival for several days, because Msidi told them not to come. They live like natives, on corn porridge, and occasionally stinking meat.' Msidi was eventually shot by British mercenaries in the Belgian service, and Crawford complained: 'The stupid and mischievous notion has got currency that since Msidi's death *we* are the chiefs of the country.' Mischievous, yes; but scarcely stupid, since Africans were often right to associate the downfall of their kingship with the coming of the missionaries.

This was also, perhaps especially, true when kings tried to preserve their independence by playing off one faith against another. It became a possible tactic as the nineteenth century progressed, and the Catholics once again became active in the missionary field. By 1815, the Catholic missions had been virtually extinguished; they had only 270 field-workers in the entire world. The recovery was due not so much to the restoration of the Jesuits in 1814 as to the emergence of popular French ultramontanism, and its close alliance with a reinvigorated papacy. New mission orders were founded: the Oblates of Mary Immaculate in 1816, the Marists in 1817, the Salesians in 1859, the Scheut Fathers in 1862, the White Fathers in 1868. French diplomacy pushed missionary work far more ardently than any other major power – French missionaries in China, for instance, were provided with special diplomatic passports – and the growth, from the 1820s, of a huge French African empire provided a natural field of endeavour. France did not hesitate to back up missions with force. It was attacks on missionaries which led to Napoleon III's Indo-China expedition of 1862, and in 1885 to the occupation by France of the entire country; and in North and Central Africa, missionaries, most of whom had served in the French army, worked closely with the military commanders, nearly all of them *bien-pensant* Catholics.

Moreover, in Charles Lavigerie, Bishop of Nancy at the age of thirty-eight, and later Cardinal-Archbishop of Algiers, French colonialism found an enthusiastic spiritual leader, and the Vatican a superb international propagandist. Lavigerie was a flamboyant French patriot from Bayonne, a region where the Gallic spirit was forged in fierce combat with Basque nationalism. He was a Frenchman first, an ultramontane second, but his attachment was to France as a culture rather than a crown, and he took the lead in reconciling the papacy and the French hierarchy to republican institutions. Marshal McMahon picked him for the Algiers job, and the papacy doubled his powers by making him Apostolic Delegate for the Sahara region. Colonel Playfair, British consul in Algiers, noted: 'We have St Augustine amongst us again.' The comment was shrewd: Lavigerie clearly saw himself in the role of a Constantinian patriarch, knitting together the ecclesiastical infrastructure of a new African empire. In Carthage, on the site of the ancient citadel, he built a cathedral bigger even than Augustine's basilica at Hippo, and installed in it, ready for his own reception, an elaborate and grandiose tomb. He held strongly to the Elect Nation theory: 'God has chosen France to make of Algeria the cradle of a great and Christian nation . . . our country is watching . . . the eyes of the whole church are fixed upon us.' He thought of Algeria as 'the open port of entry to a barbaric continent with 200 million inhabitants.' The White Fathers were created by him as a Jesuit-style élite of priests, bound to mission-work by special lifelong vows. To assist them, Lavigerie became the first prince of the Catholic Church to take a vigorous line against the slave-trade, and swung France, and the other Catholic powers, into line. At the 1884 Berlin Conference on Colonial Questions, the Protestants at last got Catholic backing on this issue, and all the powers undertook to suppress slavery and to exterminate the traffic; they agreed, too, to adopt full religious liberty in colonial territories and to guarantee special protection for Christian missions. Five years later, at the Brussels Conference for the Abolition of the Slave Trade, Lavigerie got a definitive international agreement drawn up and signed.

There is no doubt that Lavigerie's initial aim was to Christianize the Arab peoples, and thus begin to reverse the ravages introduced by the Monophysite schism over 1300 years before. He sent his White Fathers into the desert (where they were often murdered by Tuaregs) and for a time ran his own 'Christian Militia' to protect them. But like Raymond Lull before him, and indeed everyone else, he found it impossible to make any real headway against Islam. The French could conquer Arab territories, and annex them, or establish protectorates; and they planted huge numbers of Christian settlers in Algeria; but they could not make Moslem converts. It was this failure which led them (later followed by the Belgians) to push south of the Sahara into black Africa, and the easy missionary pickings among the pagans. Here they did exceedingly well; on the whole, much better than the Protestants. Lavigerie's advice was: 'Be all things to all men.' He told his Fathers: 'Love the poor pagans. Be kind to them. Heal their wounds. They will give you their affection first; then their confidence; and then their souls.' The Catholic missions had a number of distinct advantages in competition with Protestants. Their unmarried missionaries were much cheaper to maintain, between one-fifteenth and one-twentieth of the cost of a full-time Protestant (even in 1930, Catholic missionaries cost, on average, only £35 a head a year; the CMS paid a married European missionary £650 a year, and an African clergyman £10–£25). They were better educated than the largely lower middle-class Protestants. They lived much closer to native living standards, were less identified with European social and cultural absolutes, and were often much more flexible in their approach.

Superficially, at least, Catholicism tended to be more attractive to Africans than most brands of Protestantism. Protestants often made war on images – Holman Bentley recorded: 'My dinner . . . was cooked with the wood of a fetish image four feet high, which was publicly hacked to pieces without a word of dissent by one of our new church members' – and their barter-stores, which stocked virtually everything, often including guns, never sold dolls. The Catholics, with their multiple statues of saints, seemed to offer an easier bridge to Christianity than the overwhelmingly Low Church Anglicans and Noncon- formists. Moreover, the Catholics were not internally divided, for the removal of crown control, and the discipline of the new papacy, made inter-order squabbles of the old kind virtually impossible. As in the sixteenth and seventeenth centuries, the Catholics vigorously pursued the policy of creating Christian villages, and of removing converts or prospective converts from what were termed 'the temptations of tribal life'. They set up scores of very large orphan settlements, and units known as *ferme-chapelles*, in which groups from the main villages were hived off into farming colonies. Where they failed to compete effectively with the Protestants was in the training of native priests: if the Protestants were slow, the Catholics were positively backward. For most of the nineteenth century their policy on this issue was less enlightened than it had been in sixteenth century Japan.

Of course neither side talked in terms of competition. When Lavigerie launched his missions into areas where Protestants were already established, his orders were that the White Fathers must never be nearer than eight to ten kilometers to Protestant mission-stations. But these instructions were widely ignored, as perhaps Lavigerie knew they would be. When he decided to penetrate East Africa he did so in the knowledge that conflict was virtually certain, and despite remonstrances and appeals by R. N. Cust of the CMS. He was also aware that on the upper Nile, and to the south of it, French and British political interests were on the point of contact. In fact in Uganda, where the trouble came to a head, the clash was three-sided since the Moslems had been proselytizing there first, since 1844. The explorers Speke and Grant had arrived in 1862, and impressed King Mutesa of the Baganda: 'I have not heard a white man tell a lie yet ... the time they were in Uganda they were very good.' When H. M. Stanley arrived, he was encouraged by Mutesa to bring missionaries, and he appealed for them in a letter to the *Daily Telegraph*. The first came in 1877, and within five years were followed by a Catholic mission. Baganda society was in some ways orderly and sophisticated, but royal rule was arbitrary and savage. Mutesa ordered summary executions almost every day, and he had the largest collection of wives on missionary record. As Britain, through the presence of military and naval units to the East, through the operations of the British East Africa Company – which evolved from Livingstone's trading organization – and through the projected railway, was the power most closely involved, the Protestants felt the obligation to protest against royal depravity fell on them; at any rate, that is what they did. Thus the royal house came to fear the Protestants, and to align itself with the Catholics (and, on occasion, with the Moslems). Both Christian groups built up parties, which armed themselves.

The climax came under Mutesa's heir, Mwanga. In 1885 he had James Hannington, an Anglican bishop, speared to death; and when Christian boys refused to submit to his sodomitic practices – learnt from the Arabs, so the missionaries claimed – he murdered thirty-two of them, three being roasted alive. From the coast, Captain Lugard and a detachment of Askaris were summoned; and in 1892 they fought, and won, the so-called Battle of Mengo against the royalists and their Catholic allies. The event took place perhaps appropriately on a Sunday, and was decided by Lugard's new Maxim gun. He did not blame the missionaries, but the Africans (probably rightly): 'My own belief was that the Baganda were par excellence the greatest liars of any nation or tribe I had met or heard of, and that it appeared to be a point of honour that each side should out-lie the others, especially to their missionaries.' In the House of Commons, Sir Charles Dilke said that the only person who had benefited from the British presence in East Africa was Mr Hiram Maxim; and Sir William Lawson claimed that Uganda was being 'turned into the Belfast of Africa'. Two years later, Anglican pressure led Britain to take Uganda into protective custody. The Mengo affair caused great scandal at the time, but largely among agnostics and professional anti-Christians. It does not seem to have damaged the image of any of the Christian sects among the Africans; on the contrary, Catholics and Protestants alike reported an increase in converts; and it was a Baganda, Canon Apolo Kivebulaya of Kampala Cathedral, who translated the Gospel of St Mark into pidgin. Indeed, it is a curious and perhaps melancholy fact that violence seems nearly always to have stimulated Christian evangelism. Thus, from 1835 in Madagascar, the native Christians were ferociously persecuted by Queen Ranavalona for more than a quarter of a century. At least two hundred were killed, by being thrown over a cliff, burned alive or scalded to death in pits. But during this time the Christians increased four-fold, and eventually reached forty per cent of the population.

It was, with variations, the same story all over the world. Despite difficulties, Christianity appeared to have made advances everywhere during the second half of the nineteenth century. To the shrewd and analytical observer the salient fact remained the almost unrelieved failure of the missions to penetrate the heartlands of the great imperial cults: Islam, the Hindu family, Confucianism, Buddhism or for that matter, Judaism. But among the primitives and the pagans, the hills tribes and the mountains, in swamps and islands – everywhere where cultural standards were low or imperial religions had not yet penetrated – Christianity made spectacular conquests. And even in India, China and Japan, and in cities throughout the Moslem world, the Christians could boast of flourishing, if select, Christian communities, well-staffed and amply-financed missions, and an air of confidence and hope for the future.

It is true there were critics, eager to pounce on any missionary detected in an un-evangelical posture. Missionaries tended to take too easily to fire-power. Francis McDougal, first Bishop of Labuan, reported of an attack by pirates in 1862: 'My double-barrelled Torry's breechloader proved a most deadly weapon for its true shooting and certainty and rapidity of firing.' In

East Africa, the year before, Bishop Mackenzie's battles against the slave-trading Ajawa, which involved burning villages, brought haughty protests from the High Church party, which kept aloof from missionary work. 'It seems to me a frightful thing,' grumbled Pusey, 'that the messengers of the Gospel of Peace should in any way be connected, even by their presence, with the shedding of human blood. . . . The Gospel has always been planted not by doing, but by suffering. . . .' The missionaries retorted that this was bad history, and most of them were only too glad to invoke military aid on occasion. The Reverend Denis Kemp, from the Wesleyan Gold Coast mission, asserted, in *Nine Years at the Gold Coast* (1898): 'I should consider myself worse than despicable if I failed to declare my first conviction that the British army and navy are today used by God for the accomplishments of His purpose.' They were also under fewer illusions than those at home about the virtues of their 'charges'. The Reverend Colin Rae, from the Anglican South Africa mission, spoke for the majority: 'The native must be kept under control, and subjected to discipline, and the keynote must be work! work! work!'

How much discipline? There was constant criticism of Catholic missions for inflicting corporal punishment on natives. But then, so did all colonial (and native) governments; and, it soon emerged, so did Protestant missions, especially the Scots ones. In 1880 there was much criticism of the Free Church of Scotland mission in Nyasaland, which had a pit-prison, and where a man died after receiving over two hundred lashes. Andrew Chirnside reported to the Royal Geographical Society: 'Flogging with the whip is an everyday occurrence, three lads in one day getting upwards of 100 lashes; and it is a fact that after being flogged on several occasions, salt has been rubbed on their bleeding backs.' He claimed he had seen a man executed without trial. In 1883 there was a similar case in Nigeria where a woman died after she had been beaten and had red pepper rubbed in her wounds. These cases were rare, and caused uproar. More damaging, in the long run, was the gentle deprecation of missionary work by travellers like Mary Kingsley, whose *Travels in West Africa* (1897) was a huge success; she hinted that the natives were probably better if left alone, polygamy and all, and she poured scorn on missionary efforts to dress African women in the asexual 'Mother Hubbard'.

In general, though, missionaries were held in high esteem, and reporting on their work was almost universally favourable. The pattern of hero-worship was set by the Livingstone legend, and in the late nineteenth century they provided a new type of hero for European, and still more American, society. Their competitors for fame, imperialists and business tycoons, had their opponents; but to all except a tiny minority, the missionaries seemed harmless as well as valiant. Biographies of well-known missionaries sold in large editions, and formed a special department of literature. S. W. Partridge, the leading performer in the field, wrote no less than thirty-six; and they often had children's editions. For the Catholics, the missionary became a new type of saint, and even the Protestants indulged in hagiography. There were children's games, such as *The African Picture Game*; *What Next?*, which had thirty-six cards, four series of nine each devoted to famous missionaries; *A Missionary Tour of India*, like snakes and ladders; *Missionary Outpost*, 'an instructive round-game for children'; missionary jigsaws and painting-books, and, for adults, *Missionary Lotto*. In Catholic countries there were elaborate money-raising schemes, run by convent schools, by which schoolgirls could buy stamps and 'adopt' African orphans. The climax of missionary expectations coincided with the climax of European imperialism, and it was very widely supposed that the entire world would be Christianized in the process of being westernized – that is, incorporated politically, economically, or at any rate culturally, in a system which was still wholly identified with Christendom.

It is this optimistic background of global predominance which helps to explain the triumphalism of the age. For it is important to realize that there were two kinds of triumphalism. As we have seen, there was the populist triumphalism of the reinvigorated papacy, whose new victories in the missionary field were seen as adumbrating an ultimate – if still far distant – reinstallation of Rome as the world centre of a ubiquitous Christian creed; every baptized black and yellow baby was bringing that inevitable day nearer. But there was also, during these decades, a species of Protestant triumphalism, linked closely to the huge industrial paramountcy of the Protestant powers, to their burgeoning economic and political empires, and to the very widespread conviction that Protestant theology and moral teaching were intimately, indeed organically, linked to worldly achievement.

The picture we have, then, is of two forms of Christianity struggling, peaceably but persistently, for a world religious supremacy which both believed was inevitable. Nowhere was this conviction more strongly held than in the United States. The American Christian Republic was a gigantic success. It was a success because it was, essentially, Protestant; failure was evidence of moral unworthiness. In the 1870s, Henry Ward Beecher used to tell his congregation in New York: 'Looking comprehensively through city and town and village and country, the general truth will stand, that no man in this land suffers from poverty unless it be more than his fault – unless it be his *sin*. . . . There is enough and to spare thrice over; and if men have not enough, it is owing to the want of provident care, and foresight, and industry and frugality and wise saving. This is the general truth.' And a related general truth was that God's will was directly related to the destiny of a country where success-breeding virtue was predominant. The dynamic of Protestant triumphalism was American triumphalism. George Bancroft, in his *History of the United States* (1876 edition) began: 'It is the object of the present work to explain . . . the steps by which a favouring providence, calling our institutions into being, has conducted the country to its present happiness and glory.' Was it not, as Jonathan Edwards had termed it, 'the principal kingdom of the Reformation'? Sooner or later the world would follow suit – it was urged to do so, in

1843, by the American missionary Robert Baird, in his *Religion in America*, projecting the principal of Protestant voluntarism on to a global frame. History and interventionalist theology were blended to produce a new kind of patriotic millenarianism, as in Leonard Woolsey Bacon's *History of American Christianity* (1897): 'By a prodigy of divine providence, the secret of the ages (that a new world lay beyond the sea) had been kept from premature disclosure. . . . If the discovery of America had been achieved . . . even a single century earlier, the Christianity to be transplanted to the western world would have been that of the Church of Europe at its lowest stage of decadence.' Hence he saw 'great providential preparations as for some "divine event" still hidden behind the curtain that is about to rise on the new century.'

The 'divine event' could only be, in some form, the Christianization of the world according to American standards. Hence in the period 1880–1914 America, too, developed its own form of Christian imperialism, linked generally to missionary endeavour but sometimes embodying armed Christian – indeed Protestant – force. In the McKinley-Roosevelt era, the Protestant churches were vociferous supporters of American expansion, especially at the expense of Spain, since they saw it as a God-determined process by which 'Romish superstition' was being replaced by 'Christian civilization'. President McKinley justified the American seizure of the Philippines – where Philip II had imposed Catholicism by the sword – in Christian evangelical terms: 'I am not ashamed to tell you, Gentlemen, that I went down on my knees and prayed Almighty God for light and guidance that one night. And one night late it came to me this way. . . . There was nothing left for us to do but to take them all and to educate the Filippinos and uplift and civilize and Christianize them, and by God's grace do the very best we could by them, as our fellow men for whom Christ also died.'

It was among the evangelical sects, with their predominance in the missionary field, that the consciousness of a national or racial destiny was strongest. In 1885, when the movement was just getting under way, Josiah Strong, General-Secretary of the Evangelical Alliance, argued in *Our Country: its Possible Future and its Present Crisis*:

'It seems to me that God, with infinite wisdom and skill, is here training the Anglo-Saxon race for an hour sure to come in the World's future . . . *the final competition of races, for which the Anglo-Saxon is being schooled* . . . this race of unequalled energy, with all the majesty of numbers and the might of wealth behind it – the representative, let us hope, of the largest liberty, the purest Christianity, the highest civilization – having developed peculiarly aggressive traits calculated to impress its institutions upon mankind, will spread itself over the earth. And can any one doubt that the result of this competition of the races will be the survival of the fittest?'

In 1893, in *The New Era: or, The Coming Kingdom*, he pushed the argument further. 'Is it not reasonable to believe that this race is destined to dispossess many weaker ones, assimilate others, and mould the remainder, until in a very true and important sense, it has Anglo-Saxonized mankind?'

Such racial theories were not uncommon in the 1890s: they reflected popular misconceptions of Darwin. What was significant in the United States was that they radiated from a Christian context, and could be, and were, presented in less strident and offensive terms as part of a scheme to Christianize the world. Just as America was now the leading missionary force, so the Anglo-Saxons in particular, but the white races as a whole, would succeed in bringing to reality Christ's vision of nearly two millennia before – a universal faith. The nineteenth century had been a period of such astonishing, and on the whole welcome, progress that even this great dream now seemed possible. In the 1880s, the young American Methodist John Raleigh Mott had coined the phrase 'The evangelizing of the world in one generation.' He repeated it in 1910 at Edinburgh, when the First World Missionary Conference, of which he was chairman, met to give ecumenical shape, and a specific programme of action, to Protestant triumphalism. Here was the modern and Protestant alternative gathering to the Vatican Council of 1870.

Of course, by evangelization in one generation Mott did not mean actual conversion; he meant that Christian preaching would be made available to everyone in the world during that period – the rest was up to the spirit. And the proposition, he argued, was hard-headed. It is true that the Catholics and the Greek Orthodox churches had boycotted the conference. But the rest of Christianity was there – including eighteen of the 'new' churches from missionary territories. Except in Tibet and Afghanistan, two places which, it was hoped, would soon be opened, missionaries were at work in every country in the world. The discoveries of tropical medicine had made it possible for white Christian preachers to be present in strength even in the harshest climates. There were now more missionaries than ever before. There were as many recruits as could be handled. Finance was no problem. The language barriers were being progressively removed. The New Testament had been translated into all the main living languages, and the entire Bible would soon follow. The worst opposition, as in China and Japan, had been broken down. There were converts in every single area, and from all religions; no missionary now stood alone. There were 45,000 missionaries, backed up by more than ten times that number of national workers, and a wonderful generation of native Christian leaders was beginning to emerge. The tone of the summary was optimistic; but much of its factual content was solid and unarguable. It did not seem wholly absurd, at Edinburgh in 1910, to predict that the work of St Paul would be brought to its culmination, within the lifetime of some of those present: a hard-headed, calculated and costed millenium.

PART EIGHT

The Nadir of Triumphalism (1870–1975)

ON 20 OCTOBER 1939, Eugenio Pacelli, who had become Pope Pius XII six months earlier, published his first encyclical, *Summi Pontificatus*. The Second World War had just begun. Hitler had completed the conquest of Poland, which he and his temporary ally Stalin had now dismembered and extinguished. The prospects for humanity looked infinitely sombre, and the theme of the letter, which supplied its English title, was 'Darkness over the Earth'. Yet its tone was not shocked or indignant; it was, rather, reproachful. Pius XII was a triumphalist aristocrat, born into the 'black nobility' of Rome and destined almost from birth to occupy the throne of St Peter. Slightly built, austere, autocratic, single-minded to the point of obsession, confident in his own powers and superbly sure of the rights of his Church and office, he identified himself wholly with the divine wisdom. Surveying a tragic and violent world from the serene, uncontaminated walls of the papal fortress, he judged that the Catholic Church had been absolutely right to reject modern civilization and to retire within its citadel.

The horrors of 1939, wrote Pius, were not fortuitous or unexpected. They arose inevitably from mankind's decison to reject the truth as expounded by an infallible papacy: '. . . the reason why the principles of morality in general have long since been set aside in Europe is the defection of so many minds from Christian doctrine of which Blessed Peter's See is the appointed guardian and teacher.' In the earliest medieval times the nations of Europe 'had been welded together by that doctrine, and it was the Christian spirit which formed them'. In turn, they could pass it on to others. Then came the Reformation, the beginning of tragedy, 'when many of the Christian family separated themselves from the infallible teaching of the church'. This opened the way to the 'general deterioration and decline of the religious idea'. Christianity, 'the truth that sets us free', had been exchanged for 'the lie that makes slaves of us'. By rejecting Christ, men had been 'handing themselves over to a capricious ruler, the feeble and grovelling wisdom of man. They boasted of progress, when they were in fact relapsing into decadence; they conceived they were reaching heights of achievement when they were miserably forfeiting their human dignity; they claimed that this century of ours was bringing maturity and completion with it, when they were being reduced to a pitiable form of slavery.' In medieval Christian Europe there had been quarrels and wars, but at least 'men had a clear consciousness of what was right and what was wrong, what was allowable and what was forbidden.' Now there was total moral confusion, 'which allows all the canons of private and public honesty and decency to be overthrown'. There had never been an age like the present when 'men's spirits are broken by despair' and they searched in vain to provide 'any remedy for their disorders'. In fact the remedy had been there all along, and was available still: the return to Christianity under papal guidance. Pius would continue to proclaim it: 'To bear witness of the truth is the highest debt we owe to the office we hold and the times we live in.'

This had been the theme of papal triumphalism for some seventy years, since Pius IX had issued his Syllabus of Errors; in a sense, it was a theme inherent in the whole of Augustinian Christianity. Gregory VII and Innocent III had called on the world to align itself with the policies and precepts of the imperial papacy, and had anathematized those of its rulers who declined to do so. When the world refused to obey him, the Pope looked on it with sorrow, and predicted doom. It was a natural and traditional pontifical attitude. But of course there was another form of Christianity in the nineteenth and twentieth centuries – Protestant triumphalism, which we have seen proclaiming itself at the Edinburgh world mission conference in 1910. It identified Christianity with modern progress and democracy, and the burgeoning success of the American ideal and system with its Protestant ethics. One rejected the modern world; the other not only accepted it but to some extent claimed paternity. Both of these Christian theories were based on the assumption that the acceptance or rejection of Christianity was the only real formative element in society, and the criterion by which it should be judged. Both evolved against a cultural background in which Christianity inevitably dominated any dis-cussion of truth and falsehood, right or wrong, good and evil. It was the moral air in which all-powerful western man lived, and adjusted his perspectives. Should Christians fight the modern world and by a supreme spiritual effort wrench it from its disastrous course? Or should they take advantage of the boundless opportunities offered by modernity to deliver the Christian message afresh? These questions were regarded not merely as relevant but as absolutely essential to the whole future of human society. The history of twentieth-century Christianity is the history of the attempt to answer them but equally of the effort to prevent them from seeming academic.

In October 1939, Pius XII delivered his admonition from his citadel on the assumption, in which he profoundly believed, that Christianity in general, and pontifical Christianity in particular, were ideologically, and indeed in-stitutionally detached from the horrors of the modern world. But here he was deceived by analogy. Immediately after the declaration of papal infallibility in 1870, the Italian crown had seized Rome and the papal territories had been incorporated in the new Italian State. Successive popes had refused to accept this situation, inevitable though it was, and had remained entrenched in the Vatican, refusing to recognize the Italian regime, or its government and parliament, or to set foot in the usurped eternal city. The fortress image had, as it were, become an actual one – of the defiant 'prisoner in the Vatican'; and it remained vivid even after papacy and State were reconciled in the Lateran

Treaty of 1929. The Pope, reduced to the Vatican redoubt, was cut off from the world outside and in no way responsible for it. Yet the image was false because incomplete; for beyond the Vatican lay the whole of Catholic Christianity, which not only dealt with the world but to a great extent *was* the world; and the Pope, as its leader, was necessarily and continually involved in the shaping of that world. Like any other power, it had done its utmost to advance its policies and extend its influence. There had, in fact, been no renunciation; the papacy too had helped to make the modern world what it was.

Indeed, from 1870 onwards, the papacy, acting in conjunction with the hierarchies and Catholic lay organizations throughout the world, had been as busy as at any time in its history, and had certainly wielded more effective power than it had done since the sixteenth century. Populist triumphalism never fulfilled all its expectations, but it often won battles and sometimes whole campaigns. Indeed, the papacy was the only institution to inflict a defeat, if a qualified one, on Bismarck's Germany. For Bismarck, who was anxious to subordinate every element in German society to the control of the State, gave covert backing to the Independent Catholic Church which came into existence after the Vatican decree of 1870. It was mainly an academic group, which had little chance of capturing a mass following among German Catholics, but he was anxious to keep it in play; hence in 1871 he forbade Catholic bishops to remove Old Catholic professors and lecturers from their jobs. This quickly widened into a conflict with the papacy and official Catholicism in Germany over the whole field of education, and the influence international Catholicism exerted on German national culture. Bismarck called it a *Kulturkampf* or culture-war; he was not going to submit to another Canossa, and he said so publicly. A law forbade clergymen to discuss matters of state from the pulpit, and in 1872 a programme was launched to bring all schools under the State. The Jesuits were expelled, and diplomatic relations with the papacy were broken off. As a result of Bismarck's penal laws, several bishops and hundreds of priests were imprisoned, seminaries were closed and Catholic newspapers suspended.

The *Kulturkampf* was a product of the last years and decline of Pius IX. Pius died in 1878 and was succeeded by Luigi Pecci, a former Bishop of Perugia, as Leo XIII. Leo was as conservative as his predecessor, but he was more of a realist, and he believed in making minor adjustments to the world if it was to the Church's advantage. He was quite happy to do a deal with Bismarck if only the anti-Catholics laws were withdrawn. In 1874 Bismarck had said that to do so would mean a papal triumph and 'we non-Catholics must either become Catholics or emigrate or our property would be confiscated, as is usual with heretics.' But by 1887 he was tired of the struggle and looking for allies; Leo XIII persuaded some of the Catholic Centre party to support Bismarck in the Reichstag, and got as his reward the withdrawal of the laws. Bismarck, who had put them through to preserve national unity from papal interference now said: 'What do I care whether the appointment of a Catholic priest is notified to the state or not – Germany must be united' – a reversal of position which marked his discomfiture.

The truth is that, in practice, the papacy did not so much turn its back on the world as seek to nudge it in a conservative direction. It did not object to the modern state so long as it had a traditionalist posture. Leo, one of the few modern popes to write elegant Latin, spent a great deal of time publishing encyclicals which purported to lay down Catholic principles; but nearly all of them reflected the views of a conservative empiricist. In Italy, he refused to recognise the regime and forbade Catholics to take any part in it – they were to be 'neither electors nor elected'; on the other hand he encouraged the systematic creation of a network of Catholic clubs, associations and congresses, which the Church could control much more easily than Catholic deputies, and which could exert almost as much pressure behind the scenes. In 1885 his encyclical *Immortale Dei* was a move towards recognizing popularly-elected governments where there was really no alternative: he laid down that 'the greater or less participation of the people in government has nothing blamable in itself'. This document set out his political philosophy, such as it was. Both Church and State have their authority from God. The Church has power of judgment over all that relates to the salvation of souls and the worship of God, and of course there can be only one true Church. He denounced the 'rage for innovation'. Freedom of thought and publication was 'the fountain-head of many evils'. It was 'not lawful for the state . . . to hold in equal favour different kinds of religion'; on the other hand 'no one should be forced to embrace the Catholic faith against his will', a retreat from the papal position held at least until the 1820s, when toleration had been again condemned as 'madness'.

Leo had attacked socialism as long ago as 1878, in his *Quod apostolici muneris*, and he denied the right of any state, whatever its composition, to dissolve Christian marriage (*Arcanum* 1880). The right to rule came from God: civil power did not come from men as such (*Diuturnum illud* 1881). But in *Sapientiae Christianae* (1890) he conceded that the Church did not oppose any particular system of government, provided it promoted justice, and did nothing to harm religion or moral discipline. In 1888, noting that Brazil had finally abolished slavery, he aligned the Church with what was now the conventional wisdom: *In plurimis* declared the Church 'wholly opposed to that which was originally ordained by God and nature', thus neatly reconciling the Church's new alignment with majority opinion with her failure to condemn slavery before. In general, Leo wanted systems of government and policies which conformed as closely as possible to the ideals of the Middle Ages and the practical sagacity of Thomas Aquinas, a pundit he admired almost to the point of idolatry. In *Rerum novarum* (1891), which dealt with the working classes, he accepted authorized trades unions and arbitration boards to fix wages, but lamented the disappearance of the old medieval guilds. Both socialism and usury were wrong; private property was essential to freedom and the 'classless society' was against human nature. Workers should never resort to violence. Employers should adopt a paternal attitude to their labourers, pay them a just wage, guard them from occasions of sin, and use any wealth 'left over from maintaining their standing' to promote 'the perfection of their own natures' and act as stewards 'of God's providence for the benefit of others'. He said it was the Church's desire that 'the poor should rise above poverty and wretchedness and better their condition in life' – even to own property. He thought that 'Christian morality, when adequately and completely practised, leads of itself to temporal prosperity'; hence the State's duty was 'to see to the provision of those material and external helps, the use of which is necessary to virtuous action' – it must 'safeguard private property' but also regulate conditions of labour; and employers must pay wages adequate for 'a frugal and well-behaved wage-earner, wife and children'.

The power of the papacy lay in the degree to which such guidelines were in fact followed by Catholic populations in the chief states, and the extent, therefore, to which their governments heeded or feared papal pressure. The papacy used the bargaining power of a national Catholic pressure group to strike a good bargain with its government; but sometimes it ignored the pressure-group to do a deal. Leo found it convenient to adopt a slightly more liberal line in France than the French ultramontanists wished; he could afford to do so – they had nowhere else to go. Thus, having authorized Lavigerie to persuade his fellow-bishops to recognize the Third Republic, he published *Inter innumeras solicitudines* (1892) which enjoined French legitimists to drop their opposition, and join in the fight to get anti-religious laws repealed. This was more easily advised than accepted. It was typical of French Catholics that, having switched from Gallicanism to Ultramontanism they should become more papalist than the Pope, almost to the point of embarrassment. This, in turn, led to a reaction on the Republican side, in the form of anti-clericalism – in some ways more bitter than during the Revolution since it was aimed at clerics as such rather than as privileged enemies of the State. Archbishops of Paris were murdered in 1848 and again in 1857. Napoleon III's 'bawdy house blessed by bishops' led to a fresh wave of anti-clericalism in the 1860s under Peyrat's slogan: 'Clericalism – there's the enemy'; and when the Commune took power in Paris, Mgr Darboys, the comparatively liberal archbishop, was dragged before Raoul Rigaud at the Prefecture of Police. His remonstrance: 'What are you thinking of, my children?' was answered by 'There are no children here, only magistrates.' Darboys, too, was murdered; and the Catholic Right took its revenge, when the Commune collapsed, by mass shootings without trial. The republic and Catholicism thus seemed natural enemies. 'My aim', said Jules Ferry, speaking for the republic, 'is to organize humanity without God and without kings.' His Catholic opponent, Count Albert de Mun, accepted the dichotomy: 'The church and the revolution are irreconcilable. Either the church must kill the revolution, or the revolution will kill the church.'

In an age of mass electorates, when even a pope was driven to advise
Catholics to accept a republic, Catholicism had to be identified with popular
issues: that was what the new triumphalism was about. It possessed its own
machinery for evangelizing the workers. In 1845 the ultra-Catholic Père
d'Alzon had founded the Assumptionist order specifically to work among the
lower classes. They had their own publishing house and printing-presses and
took a rabid right-wing populist line. There were other Catholic extremist
papers, like L'Autorité, run by Paul de Cassagnac, which proclaimed that it
did not matter whether the country were run by a legitimist king or a
Napoleonic emperor 'provided the bastard [republicanism] is crushed'. But
the Assumptionists' La Croix, a daily from 1883, became the most powerful,
its circulation boosted by salesmen called 'Les Chevaliers de la Croix', and its
leaders written by Père Vincent de Paul Bailly under the pseudonym 'Le
Moine'. It was not the only Catholic publishing house in France but it was the
only one to make money, and this gave it a good deal of freedom from the
hierarchy.* In the 1880s the anti-republicans, searching for a popular issue,
began to whip up anti-semitism. The tone was set by Edouard Drumont's La
France Juive, which concluded: 'At the end of this history, what do you see? I
myself see but one thing, the figure of Christ, insulted, covered with
opprobrium, torn by the thorns, and crucified. Nothing has changed in 1800
years. It is the same lie, the same hate, and the same people.' The Jews were
behind the Republic, its financial scandals, the betrayal of the army at Sedan,
the success of Jew-controlled Germany, and of course behind the campaign
against the Church. La Croix took up the theme with energy, and the truth
seemed miraculously confirmed when, in October 1894, the only Jew ever to
have been on the general staff of the army, Captain Dreyfus, was arrested for
high treason and spying for Germany.

In fact the Dreyfus case proved a disaster for the French Catholic Church.
The activities of the Assumptionists identified Catholics as a body with the
worst aspects of the anti-semitic campaign. Le Moine wrote at the time of the
Zola trial: 'Thus it is free thought, defender as it is of Jews, protestants and all
the enemies of the church, that is at the bar with Zola, and the army is forced,
despite itself, to go over to the attack.' The Jesuit La Civilta Catholica
commented in 1898: 'If a judicial error has indeed been committed, the
Assembly of 1791 was responsible when it accorded French nationality to
Jews.' The Jesuit intervention was particularly unfortunate since it led to

* The most meritorious of the Catholic publishing houses was the one set up by the Abbé J. P. Migne to
provide scholars with cheap editions of the Greek and Latin Fathers of the Church. His workshop did its own
type-founding, stereotype, satinage, brochure, reliure and everything except paper-making. Between 1844–64,
Migne published 217 volumes plus four volumes of indices of his Patrologia Latina, plus two series of Patrologia
Graeca in 161 volumes, making 382 volumes in all. This stupendous undertaking left Migne practically
bankrupt and got him into trouble with the Archbishop of Paris and Rome. Edmond and Jules de Goncourt
noted in their Journal, 21 August 1864: 'A queer figure is the Abbé Migne, this manufacturer of Catholic books.
He has started a printing works at Vaugirard, crammed full with priests who are under interdict, unfrocked
rascals, devil-dodgers, fellows lost to all grace. If ever a police-officer appears, there is a stampede for the door.'
See the Appendix in G. G. Coulton, Fourscore Years (Cambridge, 1945).

accusations of an élitist anti-republican conspiracy, particularly in the army, where many of the senior officers were practising Catholics. Attention centred on the Jesuit Père du Lac, headmaster of the Society's leading Paris school, who had converted Edouard Drumont, and was the confessor of Albert de Mun and General de Boisdeffre, chief of the army general staff. Joseph Reinarch, the most impressive of the Dreyfusard propagandists, described his study and its central importance in the campaign to deny Dreyfus justice: 'The orders of the day emanate from Pere du Lac's simple cell. In it, there is a crucifix on the wall, and on the writing table an annotated copy of the *Army List*.'

The Church's problems were compounded by the fact that some of the most vociferous and embarrassing anti-semites were not themselves Catholics but were, rather, authoritarian ideologues in the de Maistre tradition who regarded Rome as a natural defence against the Left. Thus Jules Le Maitre, prominent in the anti-Dreyfus League of Patriots, wrote: 'We want to make love of the fatherland a kind of religion... the equivalent of the denominational faith which Frenchmen no longer hold.' Again, Charles Maurras, who founded the anti-Dreyfus Action Française in 1898, was an agnostic, but virtually all his followers in the movement were passionate Catholics, and its so-called Institute had a professorial chair endowed in honour of the Syllabus of Errors. Maurras had no scruples in taking the supposedly Jesuitical line that the end justified the means. He had nothing but praise for Major Henry, whose anti-Dreyfus forgery was exposed and who committed suicide on the eve of arrest, and only regretted that his crime had been unsuccessful: 'Colonel, there is not a drop of your precious blood that does not cry out wherever the heart of the nation beats.' And *L'Action française* added: 'We need money to buy all the tools we require and to provide the necessary bribes. We must buy women and consciences, and we must buy disloyalty.' This was just what the anti-clericals wanted to hear.

The tragedy was that a number of young, thoughtful Catholics were strongly pro-Dreyfus. Charlés Peguy wrote that, so long as Dreyfus remained condemned unjustly, France was 'living in a state of mortal sin'. How could Catholics, of all people, and the Church, of all institutions, deny justice in the name of patriotism? He argued powerfully that the Church, in its anti-Dreyfus posture, was being un-Catholic, since it was denying its own mystical spirit: '... the political forces in the church have always been against what is mystical, and particularly what is mystical in a Christian sense.' Leo XIII was also upset by the French Church's anti-Dreyfus posture, but for a more realistic reason: he thought they were backing a loser, since the facts were bound to prevail in the end. In an interview with the pro-Dreyfus *Figaro* in March 1899, he made the point that, since it was now obvious Dreyfus was innocent, it was the institutions of the republic, rather than the Jew, which were on trial; and he added: 'Happy is the victim whom God recognizes as sufficiently just to confound his cause with that of his own son who was sacrificed.' Coming from anyone else, the remark would have been denounced as blasphemous, since in effect it compared Devil's Island with Golgotha and Dreyfus with Christ. But Leo was now ninety, and French Catholics too embattled and angry to take much notice of him.

In any case, the papal intervention, such as it was, did not alter the fact that the bulk of identifiable Catholic opinion was anti-Dreyfus. When the right-wing League for the French Fatherland was formed in 1899, as a response to the Dreyfusard League of the Rights of Man, the prominent Catholic members of the Académie Française joined it *en bloc*. Hardly any well-known Catholics supported Dreyfus; the bishops kept silent with one exception – and he championed the discredited army. Hence, when the Dreyfusard politicians triumphed under Emile Combes, in 1902, the machinery of the State was turned against the Church as in the 1790s. Combes was a former Catholic teacher who had lost his faith – though he was more of a heretic than a renegade. When Théodore Ribot said to him: 'You cannot confine the policy of a great country to a mere struggle against the religious orders', he replied: 'I took office solely for that purpose.' As Paul Deschanel put it, the idea of a neutral state was dropped: 'They look upon Catholicism as error.... They turn upon the principle announced by Bossuet when he said "The prince must use his authority to destroy false religions."' The grip of the French Church on education was broken, never to be restored; the concordat was ended, Church and State separated; and the ideologies and strategies of the Dreyfus affair became models for other anti-clerical regimes, in Portugal and Spain, and throughout Latin America.

The danger of European Catholics becoming locked in a struggle against a republican form of government was that it imperilled the position of Catholics in the United States who, thanks to emigration, were becoming one of the largest (and certainly by far the richest) Catholic communities in the world. Leo XIII, in his special encyclical to the United States, *Longinqua oceani*, (1895), tried hard to straddle the horns of the dilemma:'. . . it would be very erroneous to draw the conclusion that in America is to be sought the hope of the most desirable status of the church, or that it would be universally lawful or expedient for state and church to be, as in America, dissevered and divorced... [the church] would bring forth more abundant fruits if, in addition to liberty, she enjoyed the favour of the laws and the patronage of public authority.' He added that 'unless forced by necessity to do otherwise, Catholics ought to prefer to associate with Catholics.' This effusion struck anti-republicans in Europe as feeble and compromising, but it infuriated Americans and made the position of the Catholic hierarchy there very difficult. They had always emphasized that the republic and the Church were virtually soul-mates. As the most influential of them, John Ireland, Arch-bishop of St Paul, put it: 'There is no conflict between the Catholic church and America. I could not utter one syllable that would belie, however remotely, either the church or the republic, and when I assert, as I now solemnly do, that the principles of the church are in thorough harmony with the interests of the republic, I know in the depths of my soul that I speak the truth.' But many Americans did not accept this assurance. How could they, when there was so manifest a gulf between Protestant triumphalism, and the triumphalism of the Vatican? The feeling was established, and it persisted for more than half a century, that no Catholic must be allowed to become President of the Republic. What was, perhaps, more important, was the effect on American Catholics. At times they feared that the papacy would simply condemn 'Americanism' as a modern 'error', and thus quarantine the Catholics within American society. The American bishops were constantly obliged to head off the Vatican from this direction, and though they were successful, the concession was bought at the price of servile conformity on virtually everything else. Thus American Catholics did not play the progressive role within the Church which their membership of the millennial society made natural.

A Vatican assault on American ideology came very near when the ninety-three-year-old Leo XIII was succeeded by Guiseppe Sarto, as Pius X, in 1903. Pius X was remarkable in a number of ways. He came from a very poor family: his father had belonged to the lowest and most despised grade of the municipal civil service, a process-server and debt-collector. There had been popes from poor backgrounds in the Middle Ages, but none in recent centuries, virtually all coming from aristocratic families. Pius was also the first pope for many generations to have had pastoral experience as an ordinary priest. He was, finally, the first pope to achieve canonization since Pius V, the Dominican monk who had excommunicated Queen Elizabeth I in 1570. Pius X's election might be said to have completed the revolution which, in the nineteenth century, raised the parish priest to collective importance (at the expense of episcopal independence) in a church dominated by populist triumphalism. But Pius had no particular sympathy with the poor. The background of his father's work had given him a low opinion of their merits, and his seventeen years of parish work did not dispose him to sympathize with the political aspirations of the masses. What he shared with the poor was an intense superstition. He convinced himself, and others, that he possessed second sight and other supernatural powers; and it was reports of such miracles which ensured him posthumous honours. Pius was a big, handsome man, with a fine presence and enormous feet (his giant papal slippers can still be seen in Rome). He used to lend his red pontifical socks to sufferers from foot complaints, and the device sometimes worked; though Pius could not cure his own uricaemia. Pius had a passionate devotion to the cult of saints and relics, and other aspects of mechanical Christianity, and a corresponding distrust of more intellectual approaches to religion. He saw the universe in black and white terms. The Tridentine papacy and the Church it represented was white; the rest was black, and in the rest he mingled democracy, republicanism, science, modern biblical exegesis, communism, atheism, free thought and any form of

Christianity which was not clerical-directed. He believed Protestantism to be a mere staging-post on an inevitable progression to atheism. His career had been embattled. As Bishop of Mantua he had been involved in a bitter dogfight with municipal socialists and freemasons. Appointed Patriarch of Venice, he had been prevented from taking up his post for three years by the Italian government, which refused to issue its *exequator*.

Pius was elected pope after a protracted political struggle. The favourite at the Conclave had been Cardinal Rampolla, Secretary of State since 1887, who exhibited mildly liberal tendencies. The French Foreign Minister asked the French cardinals who, as usual, voted *en bloc*, to give their votes to him, and they apparently did so; at the first ballot Rampolla emerged clearly the leader with twenty-nine votes out of sixty-two. But Rampolla, as the French choice, was unacceptable to the central powers, and before the second ballot, Cardinal Puzyna, Archbishop of Cracow, on behalf of the Habsburg emperor, exercised the 'Aulic Exclusiva', the veto on a papal candidate which traditionally belonged to Austria as the residual legatee of the Holy Roman Empire. The Conclave did not formally accept the validity of the veto, but its secretary, Archbishop Merry del Val, who managed the ballot, ensured that in fact it did so. Rampolla's vote rose to thirty on the fourth ballot, but thereafter fell; and Sarto passed the two-thirds majority required on the seventh.

Pius x's appointment of Merry del Val as his Secretary of State, at the very early age of thirty-eight was not so much a reward for services rendered as a complementary alliance between an elderly self-made reactionary and a conservative intellectual aristocrat. Del Val was the wealthy son of a Spanish diplomat and an English lady, a well-known figure in European society and a staunch and resourceful defender of the *ancien régime*. This combination at the Vatican reversed the accommodationist policies of Leo XIII and Rampolla – unadventurous though they had been – and introduced a reign of terror against liberalism in the Church. Pius believed in right-wing fireworks. His first consistorial allocution, in November 1903, appeared to be a gloss extending the infallibility decree: '... the Sovereign Pontiff, invested by Almighty God with the supreme magistrature, has no right to remove political affairs from the sphere of faith and morals' – and this was followed by a reassertion of the *cuius regio, eius religio* principle, or at any rate a genuflexion to de Maistre: 'People are what their governments wish them to be.' Pius was soon embroiled with the Combes government. In 1903 the liberal Bishop of Dijon, Mgr Le Nordez, had been shown consorting with freemasons in a compromising photograph published by the scurrilous anti-Dreyfus paper, *La Libre Parole*. Most of the diocesan clergy and seminarians boycotted him, and the Pope, after a perfunctory investigation, ordered his removal. But this was a breach of the concordat, the French government rushed to the bishop's defence, the photograph was shown to be a forgery (as the less excitable had already guessed) and it was the uproar over this issue which led to the end of the concordat and the separation of Church and State in France. However, the

Combes government, too, overreached itself. It was defeated in 1904 when it emerged that the War Ministry maintained a card-index of officers divided into two categories: 'Corinth' and 'Carthage'. This was based on information supplied by the Secretary to the Grand Orient, the most influential of the French freemasons' organizations. 'Corinthians' were freemasons and atheists in good standing; 'Carthaginians' were officers whose children attended religious schools and whose wives went to mass – and who were to be denied promotion accordingly.

The card-index affair persuaded the more militant triumphalists in the Vatican that there was in existence a huge international conspiracy to destroy the Roman Catholic Church. It was the piece of evidence for which they had been waiting. Moreover, they believed that the most important part of the conspiracy was within the Church, masquerading as progressive or liberal Catholicism, but in reality linked to freemasonry and atheism. They termed the conspiracy 'modernism' and they linked it in particular to the efforts by Catholic scholars to catch up with the German Protestant historians and scriptural exegesists who had dominated biblical and ecclesiastical studies since the end of the eighteenth century. In all essentials, the new campaign was a resumption of the warfare waged by the orthodox scholastic theologians against the Renaissance textual scholars of the Erasmian age, warfare which had eventually degenerated into a witch-hunt. 'Modernism' was associated with the study of history which (as we have seen) was really a more dangerous enemy of orthodoxy and triumphalism than science as such.

The orthodox had long had their eye on the historians. It was the German ecclesiastical historians, especially those from the Catholic faculty at Tübingen University who, with one exception (he was made a cardinal) condemned the infallibility decree; it was Lord Acton, the English historian, who had tried to organize international opposition to the decree; and it was the five French Catholic Institutes, founded in 1875, with their emphasis on historical studies, which harboured the more adventurous Catholic academics. Of course biblical studies had always been dangerous. Heresies arising from them were as old as Marcion, older indeed than the canon. Many of the most distinguished Renaissance biblical scholars, from Erasmus down, had subsequently had works condemned in Tridentine times. On the other hand, the Catholic Church could not simply abandon biblical studies to the Protestants – that would be to betray the orthodox tradition stretching back to Papias and including all the great doctors of the Church.

In 1893, in his encyclical *Providentissimus Dei*, Leo XIII had issued a severe warning to the more enterprising scholars. 'All those books,' he insisted, 'and those books in their entirety, which the church regards as sacred and canonical were written with all their parts under the inspiration of the Holy Spirit. Now, far from admitting the coexistence of error, Divine inspiration by itself excludes all error, and that also of necessity, since God, the Supreme Truth, must be incapable of teaching error.' Taken literally, this astonishing statement virtually imposed a veto on scholarship, since it asserted as dogmatic fact what historical scholarship had already in 1893 demonstrated to be in great part a matter of argument and speculation. The truth is that very few people of importance in the Vatican (or, often, in national hierarchies) knew enough to understand the premises and methodology of modern biblical exegesis and its related disciplines. Like the theologians Erasmus despised, they condemned from ignorance. Those few who did understand were already – *eo ipso*, as it were – suspect. Cardinal Meigan summed it up neatly in correspondence with the Abbé Alfred Loisy of the Paris Catholic Institute: 'Rome has never understood anything about these questions. The whole of the Catholic clergy are profoundly ignorant about the matter. In trying to draw them out of their ignorance one runs grave risks, for our theologians are ferocious.' The words might have been uttered by Erasmus himself; in this respect Rome seemed to have learned nothing in 400 years.

Leo had not followed up his 1893 warning by systematic persecution. Pius x did. There were many victims, great and small. Indeed virtually everyone engaged in biblical studies, unless they were purely mechanical, came under suspicion during this pontificate. One victim was Albert Lagrange, the Dominican founder of the Biblical Study Centre in Jerusalem. He was forced to make a full submission to Pius. Another was Louis Duchesne, whose *History of the Early Church* was condemned; he, too, was driven to abject submission. More combative was Loisy, a Hebrew and Assyrian scholar. His *Gospel and the Church* (a reply to *What is Christianity?* by the great Protestant church historian Adolph von Harnack) led to no less than five of his works being placed on the Index in 1903; unwilling to recant, he was excommunicated by Pius in 1908. Pius was determined to prevent the Catholic clergy from being contaminated by the errors, as he saw them, of the historical and physical sciences. In his very first enyclical, *E Supremi Apostolatus Cathedra*, he promised: 'We will take the greatest care to safeguard our clergy from being caught up in the snares of modern scientific thought – a science which does not breathe the truths of Christ, but by its cunning and subtle arguments defiles the mind of the people with the errors of Rationalism and semi-Rationalism.' Hence the hunt did not stop at the biblical scholars: the net was spread pretty wide. Father George Tyrrell, an Irish convert, Jesuit and Thomist scholar, was attacked because he upheld 'the right of each age to adjust the historico-philosophical expression of Christianity to contemporary certainties, and thus to put an end to this utterly needless conflict between faith and science which is a mere theological bogey'. Tyrrell was pushed out of the Jesuits in 1906 and suspended from the sacraments the next year; he was given extreme unction on his deathbed (1909) but denied burial in a Catholic cemetery. His was one of many tragic cases.

In 1907 Pius formalised the campaign by publishing the decree *Lamentabili*, which distinguished sixty-five propositions of what was termed the 'Modernist Heresy'. The United States Catholic hierarchy were mightily relieved to discover that 'Americanism' was not one of them. Broadly speaking, modernism, as Pius conceived it, was the attempt to illuminate the history and teaching of Christianity (and of Judaism) by the objective use of academic disciplines which had been developed during and since the Enlightenment. By denying objectivity in study, it inhibited the pursuit of truth wherever it might lead, and thus appeared to draw a distinction between faith and truth which is the very essence of the Pauline message. Whether *Lamentabili* was itself heretical was, therefore, a matter of argument; but it was not an argument which could be put at the time. Indeed, the decree was followed, two months later, by the encyclical *Pascendi dominici gregis* which imposed a compulsory anti-modernist oath on all Catholic bishops, priests and teachers. It was this which began the anti-modernist terror, conducted with venom at many Catholic teaching establishments, and especially seminaries. There were large numbers of victims, who had their ecclesiastical careers wrecked; and many 'suspects', whose future appointments were affected, were totally unaware of the charges against them, held on the files of the Holy Office. One such was Angelo Roncalli, then at the Bergamo seminary, who did not find out about the information lodged against him until he became pope in 1958 and demanded to see his Holy Office file.

Pius x and others may have believed there was an actual modernist conspiracy, emanating from France. Every day, Merry del Val read a digest of the French press, equipped with a 'commentary' prepared by a rabid Assumptionist, Père Salvien; the conspiracy theory was well documented by 'information' carried in *Action française* and *La Libre Parole*. In fact no evidence of such a conspiracy has ever been found. What did emerge, however, when the Germany army intelligence captured a *cache* of ecclesiastical documents in Belgium in 1915, was the existence of an anti-modernist secret society in the Vatican, with offshoots elsewhere in Europe. Ostensibly it was a devotional group known as the Sodalitium Pianum (nicknamed *la sapinière*, the fir-tree plantation); in fact it was a pressure-group to further the careers of 'reliable' clerics in the Church bureaucracy, and an information network which gathered damaging material about 'unreliable' clerics and then delated them to the Holy Office. Its organizer was Mgr Umberto Benigni, a former Professor of Diplomatic Style at the Pontifical Academy for Noble Ecclesiastics, which provided the bulk of the Vatican diplomatic service, and of which Del Val was an *alumnus*. It is not clear how far Del Val was privy to its activities. It communicated with its agents in code: thus, Pius was 'Michael', Del Val was 'George' and so on, methods used in the age of Philip II – indeed, the whole organization had the flavour of the late sixteenth century. On the other hand it had its own publication, *La Correspondence de Rome*, which tended to give part of the game away. Del Val broke up the group, at least above the surface, when it drew hostile attention to itself in 1913; and of course there was a row when the Germans published their discoveries. But the Sodalitium was not formally dissolved until 1921. Some years later, Pius xi sent Father Salvien to end his days in a punishment monastery. There is no evidence that Holy Office files were ever cleansed of information supplied by the group, and indeed this is most unlikely. The anti-modernist terror as such was only halted when Benedict xv succeeded Pius x in 1914.

Pius x's campaign against Catholic scholarship was accompanied by a series of political moves, organized by Del Val, to extinguish any spirit of independence among the progressive-minded Catholic laity, and in particular to curb the development of a Christian democrat movement. In Italy this had taken the form of the Opera dei Congressi, a nationwide series of clubs, societies, charities and unions, organized by laymen to provide a machine for Catholic penetration of the political system the moment the papacy ended the *non-expedit* policy and allowed Catholics to participate in the public life of the state. On 28 July 1904, without warning, but with Pius's approval, Del Val sent out letters dissolving the Opera, and transferring all their activities to the diocesan bishops. The movement was replaced by a Vatican-organized right-wing pressure group, Azione Cattolica. Much the same procedure was followed in France, where Christian democracy was being organized around a group called Le Sillon ('the furrow'), founded by Marc Sagnier in 1898. This too was primarily a lay organization, and outside the control of the bishops. By 1908, ten archbishops and twenty-six bishops had forbidden their clergy to join it, and Pius gave it sentence of death by condemning it in its existing form, and ordering it to be reorganized by the bishops at a diocesan level. What made the attack on Le Sillon, which was doctrinally quite orthodox, more reprehensible was that an extraordinary tolerance was shown to its extreme right-wing rival, Action Française. Though controlled by an atheist, and wildly eccentric in its teaching, the movement enjoyed the protection of the Vatican, and continued to recruit French Catholics, including clergy. Pius called Maurras 'a doughty defender of the church and the Holy See'. When his books were delated to the Holy Office, it had no alternative (within its own terms of reference) but to condemn them as heretical. But Pius vetoed a public condemnation, saying they were *'Damnabilis, non damnandus'* – worthy of condemnation but not to be condemned; and he forbade any action against the movement. In technical terms, the condemnation was drawn up in 1914, but suspended by the Pope's wish. A few years later, all the papers relating to the case were discovered to have been 'lost' by the Holy Office, and it may be that Pius and Del Val ordered them to be destroyed. The conclusion which many drew from these unseemly proceedings was that, to the Vatican, orthodoxy in doctrine was less important that orthodoxy in politics, and that the object of crushing both biblical scholarship and the Christian democrat movement was not so much a concern for the purity of Christian truth as a hatred of any challenge to the existing order of society, and the imposition of authority from above. As one French prelate put it, in attacking Le Sillon, '. . . membership . . . quickly engenders, especially among the young, a critical, disrespectful and undisciplined spirit'.

The drift of the populist papacy to the right necessarily widened the gulf between Catholics and Protestants. In the United States, the Catholic hierarchy, thankful at least that the Pope had not asked them to subscribe to a condemnation of the American way of life, avoided any kind of controversy, and any kind of contact with other Christians. In Germany, the more independent-minded Catholics had been driven back into regimented orthodoxy by the ravages of the *Kulturkampf*. In Britain, the 'second Spring' of Catholicism, which some thought was beginning with the conversion of Newman and Manning, passed straight into Autumn; there was no mass-movement of Anglicans to Rome, and the conversion of the élite dwindled to a trickle. Instead there were attempts in the 1890s to bring the two churches together, but these were quickly crushed by the disdainful posture of the Vatican, and by the open and avowed hostility of the English restored Catholic hierarchy, led by Cardinal Vaughan, who duplicated Anglican sees and would, therefore, have been eliminated in the event of reunion. The attempts, sponsored by a pious High Church layman, Lord Halifax, came to grief over the question of Anglican orders, the validity of which Rome had challenged on both historical and theological grounds. In 1894, Vaughan publicly announced that Anglican bishops and clergy 'can only be considered as so many laymen'; privately, he begged Leo XIII to pronounce definitively against Anglican orders. Leo was divided in his mind. As usually, he was searching for the advantageous empirical solution. But he was persuaded by Vaughan's plea that Rome's acknowledgement of a validly-ordained Anglican clergy would make his own shadow-hierarchy look ridiculous; and he also seems to have believed Vaughan's assurance that outright condemnation would bring a flood of Anglican converts to Rome. Hence in 1895 he issued an encyclical to the English, *Ad Anglos*, which simply invited the English, collectively, or individually, to make their submission to 'the Church', and followed it a year later with the bull *Apostolicae Curae*, which called Anglican orders 'absolutely null and utterly void'. The tone and implications of these two documents could not have been more insulting to and condemnatory of Anglicanism and, by inference, a huge spectrum of Protestantism throughout the world. And the breach was further widened, and envenomed, by the anti-modernist terror under Pius X.

The Church of England had its modernists, too, and its anti-modernists; and it was deeply divided by the question-marks modern Protestant scholars had placed against the Virgin Birth, the miracles of the New Testament, and even the resurrection itself. These included *The Miracles of the New Testament* (1911) by J. M. Thompson, Dean of Divinity at Magdalen, *Foundations* (1912), a book of clerical essays edited by Canon Streeter, and Canon Hensley Henson's *The Creed in the Pulpit* (1912). The response of the Vatican, in dealing with its modernists, had been simply to invoke discipline. A huge number of books were condemned, and Catholic scholarship in this field virtually halted. Some Anglicans, too, wanted action against the liberals

(Thompson actually had his licence withdrawn by his bishop). But Archbishop Randall Davidson of Canterbury contrived to reach a sensible compromise. At a meeting of Convocation in 1914 he accepted the dictum of Archbishop Temple, 'If the conclusions are prescribed, the study is precluded'. Truth had to come first. 'I would say to every honest student in these matters: "Follow the truth, do your utmost to find it, and let it be your guide, whithersoever it may lead you. . . . Do not let your study be hampered by a single thought about what the consequences of this or that conclusion may be to you or to others. If it be true, go forward to that truth." ' At the same time, he insisted that Anglican clergymen, as accredited spokesmen of the Christian faith, had to subscribe to certain beliefs; and he persuaded Convocation to pass unanimously a resolution which 'places on record its conviction that the historical facts stated in the Creeds are an essential part of the faith of the Church'.

The Anglican solution placed the onus on the individual, and remained faithful to the teaching of St Paul. A scholar was to pursue the truth; but it might lead him to a stage at which he passed the bounds of Christianity, which had defined limits. If so, it was better to face the fact, in the light of his own mind and conscience, rather than try to suppress it, since Christianity itself was identical with truth. The implication of this line of argument was that ultimately the problem would be resolved by scholarship, which would reconcile historical truth and scripture – or that Christianity would disappear, having been shown to be untrue. The implication of the papal attitude was that man was too frail a vessel to be left to wrestle with truth individually; he needed the collective guidance of the Church, which was divinely directed, and which he must follow even against the apparent evidence of his senses and conscience. The controversy thus served to demonstrate that nothing essential had changed in the Catholic-Protestant argument since the sixteenth century.

In 1914, then, Christians still could not reach a consensus about how their creed was to absorb the new knowledge pouring in from all directions, or even about how Christians were to acquire it. This depressing conclusion ran counter to the spiritual euphoria of the times. There were still plenty of triumphalists in 1914. The papalists assumed an eventual submission of all Christians to Rome, followed by a redirection of the world under papal guidance; a return, as it were, to Innocent III's thirteenth century, but with steamships, radio and aircraft. The Protestant triumphalists looked forward to the evangelization of the world along the lines of American voluntaryism. Their rival future projections were thus very different. But they rested on similar assumptions. The paramountcy of the West – intellectual, economic, military and political – would be maintained. Indeed, it would be fortified. And Christianity would continue to be the beneficiary of western strength. The West still rested on an essentially Christian framework of beliefs and ethics. And Westerners, as individuals, were overwhelmingly Christian in their outlook and expectations.

The historical process begun by the First World War has demonstrated the fragility of all these certitudes. If 1914 was a watershed in the history of monarchy and legitimacy, of privilege and liberal capitalism, of western imperialism and the domination of the white race – if it foreshadowed the destruction of all these institutions – it was also a devastating blow to Christianity. In one respect it demonstrated the futility of the type of rearguard action conducted by Pius x, since the march of change was seen to be less the work of conscientious scholars than of huge implacable forces beyond the control of any pontiff or Holy Office. More damagingly, though, the war also drew attention to the superficial hold Christianity appeared to possess over the passions of multitudes or the actions of their governments. European Christianity, supposedly based on a common moral foundation, proved no more able than the network of marriage relationships among the royal families to prevent Armageddon, or to stop it degenerating into mutual genocide. The doctrinal and ecclesiastical divisions of Christianity, so rich in history, so stridently debated and defended, proved equally, if not more, irrelevant. All the participants claimed they were killing in the name of moral principle. All in fact pursued purely secular aims. Religious beliefs and affiliations played no part whatever in the alignments. On one side were ranged Protestant Germany, Catholic Austria, Orthodox Bulgaria and Moslem Turkey. On the other were Protestant Britain, Catholic France and Italy, and Orthodox Russia.

Thus divided, the Christian churches could, and did, play no part in transcending the struggle and bringing about reconciliation. Clergymen were unable, and for the most part unwilling, to place Christian faith before nationality. Most took the easy way out and equated Christianity with patriotism. Christian soldiers of all denominations were exhorted to kill each other in the name of their Saviour. Some clergy went further. The provision in canon law forbidding priests to bear arms, or shed blood, was in effect suspended, and about 79,000 Catholic priests and nuns were mobilized. Of these, 45,000 came from France alone, and over 5,000 French priests were killed in action. In Britain, clergy were exempt but served the war effort in any capacity they could. Hensley Henson, future Bishop of Durham, noted of the outbreak of war: 'We hastened back to Durham, and were soon immersed in the excitements and activities of bellicose preparations' – in his case a tour of the county with the Lord Lieutenant to raise recruits for the Durham Light Infantry. Dr Garbett, later Archbishop of York, rejoiced that three out of six of his curates, serving as chaplains at the Front, had won the Military Cross (one with bar). The Anglicans organized a 'National Mission of Repentance and Hope', which William Temple, later Archbishop of Canterbury, termed 'hardly an adequate way of meeting the end of a world'. The Mission enlisted the support of Horatio Bottomley, the commercial fraud and rabble-rouser, who specialized in recruiting campaigns; he took tea with the Bishop of London, but afterwards wrote in *John Bull* that British troops at the Front had no need of 'hope and repentance', since they were all 'heroes and saints'. Clergy who revealed themselves unenthusiastic for the war were victimized. Cosmo Gordon Lang, Archbishop of York, quite inadvertently fell into this category. Lang was an incorrigible snob, and in a recruiting address in the Empire Music Hall at York, he could not resist dropping the name of the Kaiser, whom, he said, he had last seen kneeling and weeping at Queen Victoria's deathbed – the sight, he said, was a 'sacred memory', and he 'resented extremely the coarse and vulgar way in which the Emperor of Germany had been treated in some of the newspapers and so-called comic illustrations'. This was interpreted as a pro-German remark; Lang received thousands of abusive letters (plus twenty-four Iron Crosses), was cut in the Yorkshire Club and, 'worst of all', detected 'a coolness at Windsor and Balmoral'. The incident pursued him for the rest of his days. More deliberately, Benedict xv invoked hatred by working through diplomatic means to try to prevent the conflict from spreading. His unsuccessful efforts to keep Italy out earned him the hostility of the French Catholics, who termed him 'the boche pope'. In August 1917, his proposal for a truce was denounced by a leading Dominican, Père Sertillange, from the fashionable Paris pulpit of the Madelaine: 'Like the apparent rebel in the Gospel, we are sons who reply "No, no!"' (At the time, Sertillange was supported by his archbishop, Cardinal Amette; after the war, the Vatican took its revenge, and the friar was kept a prisoner in religious houses in Palestine, Italy and Holland, regaining his freedom of expression only just before the Second World War.)

It was, not surprisingly, America, as the millenarian Christian state, which made the bravest, or at least the loudest, attempts to identify its national cause with religious principle. As a neutral, the United States had failed to detect any moral distinction between the belligerents. Indeed, President Wilson had noted privately that for America to join the Allies 'would mean that we should lose our heads along with the rest and stop weighing right and wrong'. His attitude changed immediately the war was joined. 'We entered the war', he declared publicly, 'as the disinterested champion of right.' Christian pulpit rhetoric supplied the colourful details, as it had during the Civil War. 'It is God who has summoned us to this war,' said the Reverend Randolph H. McKim in his Washington church. 'This conflict is indeed a crusade. The greatest in history. The holiest. It is in the profoundest and truest sense a Holy War.... Yes, it is Christ, the king of righteousness, who calls us to grapple in deadly strife with this unholy and blasphemous power.' The Reverend Courtland Meyers preached in Boston: 'If the Kaiser is a Christian, the devil in Hell is a Christian, and I am an atheist.' Newell Dwight Hillis, minister of the Brooklyn Plymouth church, advocated a plan for 'exterminating the German people... the sterilisation of 10 million German soldiers and the segregation of the women'. Henry B. Wright, the evangelical YMCA director, and former Professor of Divinity at Yale, assured soldiers with qualms about bayonet drill that he could 'see Jesus himself sighting down a gun-barrel and running a bayonet through an enemy's body'. Albert C. Dieffenbach, Unitarian, also thought Christ would 'do the work of deadliness against that which is the most deadly enemy of his Father's Kingdom in a thousand years'. Shailer Mathews, of the Chicago Divinity School, thought a conscientious objector should be spared persecution,'provided he does not speak with a German accent', but added that 'for an American to refuse his share in the present war . . . is not Christian'.

Organized Christianity in America did at least attempt to retrieve some ethical results from the débâcle by demanding peace terms which conformed to Christian principles. In his book *Christian Ethics in the World War* (1918), W. Douglas MacKenzie, of the Hartford Seminary Foundation, 'Christianized' the conflict as a campaign against German militarism, and argued that a Christian outcome would be the replacement of the nation state by the League of Nations. The League, indeed, was the way out of the dilemma which the war posed for Christians. Christianity had been powerless to stop the war, or to shorten it, or to mitigate the 'frightfulness', or to prevent both sides – with scarcely a dissenting clerical voice – from invoking the aid of the same God. But at least Christianity could be identified with the peace-solution. This was the spirit in which Woodrow Wilson came to Versailles, as John Maynard Keynes noted at the time: '. . . if the President was not the philosopher-king, what was he? . . . The clue, once found, was illuminating. The President was like a Nonconformist minister. . . . His thought and his temperament were essentially theological. . . . He had no plan, no scheme, no constructive ideas whatever for clothing with the flesh of life the commandments he had thundered from the White House. He could have preached a sermon on any of them, or have addressed a stately prayer to the Almighty for their fulfilment, but he could not frame their concrete application to the actual state of Europe.' Nor, as it turned out, could Christian leadership deliver American policy. The righteous Wilson wanted the League; and official religious opinion in America was overwhelmingly in favour of American participation. It greeted the Senate rejection with dismay, but was unable to reverse it. Thus Christian impotence in war was confirmed by Christian impotence in peace.

The First World War, a civil war among the Christian sects, opened a period of tragedy and shame for Christianity. The war, and the peace that followed, demonstrated the weakness of the churches; but at least none of them positively identified themselves with evil. That was to come. During the 1920s a mood of pessimism and discouragement set in among Christian leaders. Triumphalism was quietly laid on one side. Ostensibly, there was no decline – at least no dramatic decline – in Christian numbers. But visions of a Christianized world faded, and a defensive posture was adopted. Rome set the tone. As always, in periods of uncertainty, it looked for reliable, conservative allies. In 1922, Achille Ratti, a middle-class archivist, was elected pope as Pius XI. Unlike his predecessor, Benedict XV, he was narrow-minded, unimaginative and reactionary. He feared communism and socialism and saw Soviet Russi. as the supreme enemy. He did not want the Church to get itself mixed up in workers' movements. Hence he would have nothing to do with Christian Democracy. In France he was reluctantly persuaded to condemn Action Française in 1927, but only after Maurras's provocative atheism had made such a step inevitable. He gave no corresponding encouragement to Catholic social movements. In Italy, Don Sturzo's mass party of Christian Workers, the Partito Populare, had received the help and blessing of Pope Benedict; Pius reversed the policy, and instead backed Mussolini, with the object of settling the 'Roman Question'. This was achieved with the signing of the Lateran Treaty in 1929 which, Pius said, had 'given Italy back to God'. Mussolini, in return, called the Pope 'a good Italian'. In the meantime, Sturzo had been forced into exile, his successor Alcide de Gasperi imprisoned, and the Christian Democrats broken up. In Germany, Pius backed the conservative forces of the right, and gave no countenance to Christian socialists, whom he refused to distinguish from Marxists.*

If the papacy, while discouraging Christian democracy, had been completely consistent and held itself aloof from all political contacts, it would have been in a position simply to uphold and expound Christian principles and identify those who broke them. But it did not do this. While in theory denouncing the whole of the modern world, and remaining within its fortress, in practice it came to terms with established authority. It acted thus out of very deep reflexes, which in fact went back to the alliance with the Roman imperial power. Augustinian Christianity was based on the assumption that the Church was in concert with the civil authorities. The Church was protected, its commandments and moral teaching were broadly speaking embodied in civil law, its property was secured, its bishops and priests accorded honourable status, and its words were listened to (if not always heeded). For 1500 years the Church had come to accept this as the norm. Whether or not Church and State were formally linked, the Church was accustomed to operate in a favourable civil environment. The exceptions to this rule had been brief, and had been treated as periods of crisis. Indeed, history seemed to point to the gloomy conclusion that the Church could not sustain the active hostility of the State for very long – at the most, a generation or two. The idea of the Church conducting a long campaign within a hostile society – as it had done for 250 years within the Roman empire – was not regarded as feasible. Hence a long war with the State was to be avoided if possible. Of course, with the Marxists there could be no question of compromise or mutual toleration. Alliances should therefore be sought with those forces in society which were most

---

* In Spain Civil War was made possible by the failure of a Christian Democrat party to emerge. Gil Robles's Catholic Accion Popular was a right-wing party which did not oppose the fascist overthrow of the Republic; the nearest approach to a Christian Democrat leader was Aguirre, the Basque; the Catholic authorities classified him along with 'Jews, Masons and Communists'. See Xavier Tusell, *Historia de la Democracia Cristiana en España* (Madrid, 1975).

committed to the anti-Marxist struggle. Of course, ideally, the Church preferred to cooperate with legitimist Catholic monarchies, with whom a full-blown concordat could be signed. But it was prepared to settle for the next best thing, or even the next one after that, so long as the one absolutely unworkable situation – the Marxist state – was held at bay. It was this kind of consideration which motivated Catholic strategy between the wars: the desire for practical convenience, and a huge fear, based on a pessimistic assessment of the Church's ability to withstand prolonged attrition.

These considerations applied most strongly in Germany, where the Catholic Church was still conditioned by its experiences in the *Kulturkampf*. This had been more damaging than perhaps either the papacy, or even Bismarck, had realized. His accusations that German Catholics were not truly Germans, since their cultural assumptions were hostile to the spirit of German nationalism, had struck very deep, and inflicted lasting harm on the Catholic community. In its subsequent relations with the State, and other Germans, it became infused with an intense eagerness to demonstrate its loyalty to German ideals and aims and its total identification with Germanic society. It had been encouraged to do so by its clergy. In 1914 the Catholics had outbid the Lutherans in their anxiety to endorse the war. No one on either side had excelled the patriotic rhetoric of the German Catholic hierarchy. Cardinal Faulhaber had even gone so far as to say that the war, which he defined as undertaken to avenge the murder at Sarajevo, would enter the annals of Christian ethics as 'the prototype of the Just War'.

It was the continued anxiety not to expose themselves to the charge of being anti-German which led the Catholic Church to come to terms with Hitler and the Nazis. They were terrified of another *Kulturkampf*. There was a common fear shared by the German bishops, the papal nuncio, Archbishop Pacelli, and the Vatican itself, that a second campaign, waged much more ferociously – and perhaps for much longer – than the first would in effect destroy the Catholic Church in Germany. They feared that Hitler would create a separatist church, subordinate to the State, and that the vast majority of German Catholics (and clergy) would adhere to it, thus exposing the weakness of loyalty to the papacy, undermining the whole concept of populist triumphalism, and inflicting incalculable damage on international Catholicism elsewhere.

The strength of this fear can be measured when we consider what the Catholics had to lose by accepting Hitler. The Weimar republic had ended the official Lutheran predominance in Germany. Catholics no longer had to reckon with the hostility of a Protestant state. In fact they flourished under Weimar. The Protestants, with forty million adherents, had only 16,000 pastors; the Catholics, with twenty million, had 20,000 priests. The last traces of Bismarck's restrictive legislation had been erased. The Catholic church had more money than ever before. New schools, monasteries and convents were being opened every year. There were literally hundreds of Catholic papers and

magazines, and thousands of clubs. Karl Bachem, the historian of the
Catholic Centre Party, boasted in 1931: 'Never yet has a Catholic country
possessed such a highly developed system of all conceivable associations as
today's Catholic Germany.' There was a large, prosperous, growing and vocal
Catholic intellectual community.

Yet the Catholics felt no loyalty to Weimar; it was not 'nationalist' enough.
And towards Hitler, who was, they were ambivalent. It is true some bishops
were initially hostile to the Nazis. In 1930, for instance, Cardinal Betram of
Breslau called Nazi racism 'a grave error', and described its fanatical
nationalism as 'a religious delusion which has to be fought with all possible
vigour'. The same year, an official statement by Dr Mayer, Vicar-General of
the Mainz archdiocese, confirmed that Catholics were forbidden to vote Nazi
because of the party's racial policy. The Bavarian bishops also attack Nazism,
and a statement by the Cologne bishops drew attention to the parallel with
Action Française, officially condemned by the Holy Office three years before.
But this comparison was a foolish one to make, since Rome's long hesitation
about Action Française was notorious – evidently it was by no means in the
same category as communism, or even socialism. (In fact, Pius XII revoked the
ban on Action Française, without any retraction on their part, as soon as he
became pope in 1939.) In any case, some of the bishops flatly refused to take
a stand against the Nazis, and especially against Hitler, who was becoming
increasingly popular. Cardinal Faulhaber drew a clear distinction between
'the Führer' whom he thought was well-intentioned and basically a good
Christian, and certain of his 'evil associates'. (This was a common illusion,
based entirely on wishful-thinking, among German clergy of all sects.) Some
bishops went further: Shreiber of Berlin dissociated himself from the Mainz
condemnation, and when an attempt was made at Fulda in August 1931 to get
a unanimous condemnation of Nazism by all the Catholic bishops, the
resolution was voted down. The fact is that most of the bishops were
monarchists. They hated liberalism and democracy much more than they
hated Hitler. So an ambiguous statement went through instead; worse, on this
as on other occasions, it was accompanied by fervent balancing assertions of
German patriotism, and by rabid complaints at Germany's unfair treatment
and sufferings, so that the net effect of the declaration was to help the Nazis,
and incline Catholic voters to support them. By trying to trump Hitler's
patriotic ace, the Catholic bishops played straight into his hands, and thus
encouraged the faithful to give him their votes.

Moreover, once Hitler attained power, German Catholicism dropped its
'negative' attitude and assumed a posture of active support. This was carried
through by the bishops as early as 28 March 1933, on a firm indication from
Rome (advised by Pacelli) that there would be no Vatican support for a policy
of opposition. In the summer, Rome signed a concordat with Hitler, which in
effect unilaterally disarmed German Catholicism as a political and social
force, and signalled to rank-and-file Catholic priests and laymen that they

should accept the new regime to the full. The Church accepted that only avowedly non-political Catholic societies and clubs had the right to exist in Hitler's Germany; the rest – trades unions, political parties, discussion groups, pressure-groups of every kind – were promptly disbanded. The surrender was amazing; a century of German Catholic social activity was scrapped without a fight, and all the principles which had been passionately defended during the *Kulturkampf* were meekly abandoned. Moreover this was done at a time when the Nazis had already begun to demonstrate their hostility, by searching priests' houses, forcing Catholic clubs and organizations to liquidate themselves, dismissing Catholic civil servants, confiscating diocesan property, censoring Catholic papers, and even attempting to close Catholic schools – all these actions had been undertaken before Rome signed the concordat. On 28 June 1933, over two hundred prominent Bavarian Catholics, a hundred of them priests, were arrested, and not released until the Catholic Bavarian People's Party had agreed to dissolve itself. Pacelli's defence of his advice to Rome to sign the concordat at all costs was that 'a pistol had been pointed at my head'; he had to choose 'between an agreement on their lines and the virtual elimination of the Catholic church in Germany'. But if the Catholics did not dare fight for what they had just yielded, what then would they fight for?

One factor in the Catholic capitulation was undoubtedly fear of the Lutherans. For if the Catholic attitude to Hitler was apprehensive and pusillanimous, many of the Protestant clergy were enthusiastic. The collapse of 1918 and the end of the Protestant monarchy had been a disaster for the Lutherans. Article 137 of the Weimar Constitution laid down that there was to be no state church. The necessary legislation to bring this about had never, in fact, been enacted, so church tax continued to be collected and paid. But most Lutherans were afraid their church would collapse once state support was completely removed. So they hated Weimar. Even as it was, the decline of the Evangelical Church in the 1920s filled them with terror. They had no confidence in their ability to survive even with a neutral state, and like the Catholics they were deeply pessimistic on their chances against systematic persecution. In short, they had lost faith. Some of them, therefore, looked on Hitler and his movement as saviours.* In the 1920s, a group of right-wing Lutherans had formed the Federation for a German Church, aimed at obliterating the Jewish background to Christianity and creating a national religion based on German traditions. They made great play with Luther's anti-semitic statements, and his hatred of democracy. Under the influence of the former Lutheran court-preacher, Adolf Stocker, they taught that Luther's

---

* The Evangelical churches thought they would regain lost ground under Hitler. Otto Dibelius wrote: 'To the church leaders it seemed that this presaged the dawning of a new era in which the church would become a national institution.' Karl Barth said the Church 'almost unanimously welcomed the Hitler regime, with real confidence, indeed with the highest hopes.' See James Bentley, 'British and German High Churchmen in the Struggle Against Hitler', *Journal of Ecclesiastical History* (1972).

reformation would be at last completed by a national reassertion of Germany's spiritual power and physical strength – thus Luther had been, as it were, a John the Baptist to Hitler. An even more extreme group, the Thuringian German Christians, actually acclaimed Hitler as 'the redeemer in the history of the Germans ... the window through which light fell on the history of Christianity'; the Fuhrer was 'God-sent'. A third group, the Christian German Movement, was the first to welcome uniformed Nazi units to their churches and to assign chaplains to the SA. At Hitler's suggestion, in April 1932, the three groups joined forces in the Faith Movement of German Christians, Pastor Joachim Hossenfelder being made 'reich leader'. He quickly offered his services to the Nazi hierarchy.

If the behaviour of the German Protestants seems incredible, it must be remembered that they had no anti-state tradition. They had no dogmatic or moral theology for an opposition role. Since Luther's day they had always been in the service of the State, and indeed in many ways had come to see themselves as civil servants. Unlike the High Anglicans, for instance, they had not been able to develop a doctrinal position which enabled them to distinguish between being part of a national church, and totally subservient to the government. Hence, once Hitler came to power, he benefited from Protestant history. On 3 April 1933 the first National Conference of the Faith Movement passed a resolution: 'For a German, the church is the community of believers who are under an obligation to fight for a Christian Germany. ... Adolf Hitler's state appeals to the church: the church must obey the appeal.' Otto Dibelius, in a broadcast to America two days after the first anti-Jewish measures, appeared to justify them, and claimed the boycott of Jewish businesses was conducted 'in conditions of complete law and order', as though that was the whole point. In the summer of 1933, the offices of the Prussian Evangelical Church were taken over as a prelude to setting up a state protestant church directly aligned to the party. But this Hitler did not want. He had the church officers reinstated. Unlike Mussolini, he was unwilling to be burdened with a state church. He refused the German Christian organization any status in his regime; and he declined to give Hossenfelder any office, or even to receive him. He disliked Christians, not least those prepared to grovel at his feet. On 14 July 1933, at a cabinet meeting, Hitler expressed satisfaction, as well he might, at the progress of events over the whole of the 'Christian front', especially the concordat. He was delighted that the Vatican had 'abandoned the Christian labour unions', and he ordered the publication of the proposed sterilization law to be held up until the concordant was actually signed on 20 July.

Meanwhile, at the Protestant Church elections, with the help of the Nazi propaganda machine, the German Christians won an overwhelming victory. Their motto was: 'The Swastika on our breasts, the Cross in our hearts.' At synods, the pastors dressed in Nazi uniforms, and Nazi hymns were sung. Nazis, some picked by Hitler, were installed as bishops, and the synods passed

Aryan legislation. Hitler chose Ludwig Muller as 'Reich Bishop', and he was duly elected; in his acceptance speech he referred to Hitler and the Nazis as 'presents from God'; on the same occasion, Pastor Leutheuser intoned: 'Christ has come to us through Adolf Hitler. . . . We know today the Saviour has come. . . . We have only one task, be German, not be Christian.' Actually, this last injunction more or less represented Hitler's own position. He gave no further encouragement to the group. They aroused hostility among the anti-Christian Nazis, and they went against his policy of having no other official centres of power. Moreover, he did not trust the discretion of his Evanglical admirers. In November 1933, at a mass-meeting in the Berlin Sports Palace, presided over by Bishop Muller, Dr Reinhold Krause called for 'a purge of the Old Testament with its Jewish morality of rewards, and its stories of cattle-dealers and concubines'; he also urged the censorship of the New Testament, and the removal of 'the whole theology of the Rabbi Paul' – instead a 'heroic Jesus' was to be proclaimed. This speech provoked a number of pastors into joining a semi-opposition group called the Pastors' Emergency League, formed by Martin Neimoller. Hitler was annoyed, and thereafter did not attempt to work directly through a Christian movement. The enthusiasm had always been on their side, rather than his.

Nor was this odd. Despite the attempts of both Protestant and Catholic clergy to delude themselves, Hitler was not a Christian, and most of the members of his movement were avowedly anti-Christian. Of course Hitler was sometimes deceptive. He never officially left the Church; he sometimes referred to 'providence' in his speeches, and he attended church several times in his first years of power. In the 1920s he told Ludendorf that he had to conceal his hatred of Catholicism, because he needed the Bavarian Catholic vote as much as he needed the Prussian Protestants – 'the rest can come later'. His party programme was deliberately ambiguous: 'We demand freedom for all religious denominations in the state so far as they are not a danger to it and do not militate against the customs and morality of the German race'. These careful qualifications ought to have been enough to have alerted any intelligent Christian. Yet the belief persisted, especially among Protestants, that Hitler was a very pious man. They accepted his smooth assurances when he dissociated himself, or if convenient the movement, from the writings of his men – thus he pointed out that Rosenberg's anti-Christian tract, *The Myth of the Twentieth Century*, which the Catholics put on the Index, was a personal view, not official party policy. In fact he hated Christianity and showed a justified contempt for its German practitioners. Shortly after assuming power, he told Hermann Rauschnig that he intended to stamp out Christianity in Germany 'root and branch'. 'One is either a Christian or a German. You can't be both.' He thought the method might be to 'leave it to rot like a gangrenous limb'. Again: 'Do you really believe the masses will ever be Christian again? Nonsense. Never again. The tale is finished . . . but we can hasten matters. The parsons will be made to dig their own graves. They will betray their God to us.

They will betray anything for the sake of their miserable little jobs and incomes.'

This harsh judgment comes close to the truth. Neither the Evangelical nor the Catholic Church ever condemned the Nazi regime. Yet the Nazis as a whole did not even go through the motions (as Hitler did at first) of pretending to be Christians. They fiercely rejected accusations that they were atheists. Himmler declared that atheism would not be tolerated in the ranks of the SS. They claimed, rather, to believe in the 'religion of the blood'. They were in the millenarian tradition, and had something in common with the experimental pseudo-religions of the 1790s in revolutionary France, but with an added racialist content. Like the revolutionary cults, they tried to develop a liturgy. The Nazi publishing house put out a pamphlet describing 'forms of celebrations of a liturgical character which shall be valid for centuries.' The main service consisted of 'a solemn address of 15–20 minutes in poetical Language', a 'confession of faith recited by the congregation', then the 'hymn of duty'; the ceremony closed with a salute to the Führer and one verse of each of the national anthems. The Nazi creed, used for instance at harvest festivals, ran:

'I believe in the land of the Germans, in a life of service to this land; I believe in the revelation of the divine creative power and the pure blood shed in war and peace by the sons of the German national community, buried in the soil thereby sanctified, risen, and living in all for whom it is immolated. I believe in an eternal life on earth of this blood that was poured out and rose again in all who have recognised the meaning of the sacrifice and are ready to submit to them. . . . Thus I believe in an eternal God, an eternal Germany, and an eternal life.'

Essentially, then, Nazism, unlike communism, was not materialist; it was a blasphemous parody of Christianity, with racialism substituted for God, and German 'blood' for Christ. There were special Nazi feasts, especially 9 November, commemorating the *putsch* of 1923, the Nazi passion and crucifixion feast, of which Hitler said: 'The blood which they poured out is become the altar of baptism for our reich.' The actual ceremony was conducted like a passion-play. And there were Nazi sacraments. A special wedding service was designed for the SS. It included runic figures, a sun-disc of flowers, a fire-bowl, and it opened with the chorus from *Lohengrin*, after which the pair received bread and salt. At SS baptismal ceremonies, the room was decorated with a centre altar containing a photograph of Hitler and a copy of *Mein Kampf*; and on the walls were candles, Nazi flags, the Tree of Life and branches of young trees. There was music from Grieg's *Peer Gynt* ('Morning'), readings from *Mein Kampf*, promises by the sponsors and other elements of the Christian ceremony; but the celebrant was an SS officer and the service concluded with the hymn of loyalty to the SS. The Nazis even had their own grace before meals for their orphanages, and Nazi versions of famous hymns. Thus:

> Silent night, holy night,
> All is calm, all is bright,
> Only the Chancellor steadfast in fight,
> Watches o'er Germany by day and night,
> Always caring for us.

There was also a Nazi burial service.

The existence of this cult was, of course, well known. The Catholic hierarchy tried to excuse their failure to remonstrate by fostering the belief that these pagan ceremonies were unknown to Hitler, and 'the work of enthusiasts'. They raised no objection to Nazi youth-camps, attended by hundreds of thousands of young Catholics, though Hitler made no secret of his aims: 'I want a powerful, masterly, cruel and fearless youth.... The freedom and dignity of the wild beast must shine from their eyes ... that is how I will root out a thousand years of human domestication.' At no point were Catholics given, either by their own hierarchy or by Rome, the relaxation from their moral obligation to obey the legitimate authority of the Nazi rulers, which had been imposed on them by the 1933 directives of the hierarchy. Nor did the bishops ever tell them officially that the regime was evil, or even mistaken. The turning point, even for the most blind, should have come on 30 June 1934, when the Nazi State carried out its mass-purge. Among those murdered were, for example, Dr Erich Klausener, General-Secretary of Catholic Action, Adalbert Probst, Director of the Catholic Sports Organization, Dr Fritz Gerlich, editor of a Munich Catholic weekly, and Father Bernard Stempfle, editor of an anti-semitic Bavarian newspaper; Hitler refused to hand over their bodies to relatives and had them cremated in defiance of Catholic teaching. But the Catholic bishops made no protest, no statement at all. Nor did the Evangelicals. What reaction there was was favourable. Dr Dietrich, Evangelical bishop of Nassau-Hessen, sent Hitler a telegram of 'warmest thanks for the first rescue operation', followed by a circular letter claiming that the blood-bath 'demonstrated to the world' the 'unique greatness of the Führer'; 'he has been sent to us by God'. The failure of the churches at this great turning-point, which demonstrated the essential criminality of the regime and opened the way for all the horrors ahead, proved Hitler was right in his estimate of organized Christianity in Germany. 'Why should we quarrel?' he asked. 'They will swallow everything in order to keep their material advantages. Matters will never come to a head. They will recognise a firm will, and we need only show them once or twice who is the master.' The churches were on Hitler's pay-roll. Both Evangelicals and Catholics, as state churches, benefited from public taxation. Hitler pointed out, in a speech in January 1939, that the two churches were, after the State, the largest landowners in Nazi Germany, and that they had accepted state subsidies which rose from 130 million marks in 1933 to 500 million in 1938; during the war they further increased to over 1,000 million.

In fact, both churches, in the main, gave massive support to the regime. The Catholic bishops welcomed 'the new, strong stress on authority in the German state'; Bishop Bornewasser told the Catholic youth in Trier Cathedral: 'With raised heads and firm step we have entered the new reich and we are prepared to serve it with all the might of our body and soul.' In January 1934, Hitler saw twelve Evangelical leaders, and after this meeting they withdrew any support for the Pastors' Emergency League and issued a communiqué which pledged 'the leaders of the German Evangelical Church unanimously affirm their unconditional loyalty to the Third Reich and its leader. They most sharply condemn any intrigue or criticism against the state, the people or the [Nazi] movement, which are designed to endanger the Third Reich. In particular they deplore any activities on the part of the foreign press which seek falsely to represent the discussions within the church as a conflict against the state.' The Evangelicals provided both the most craven supporters of Hitler and the only element in the state churches to oppose him. Resistance, of a sort, began with the Evangelical 'Barmen Confession' of May 1934, rejecting 'the false doctrine that the state, over and above its special commission, should and could become the single and totalitarian order of human life, thus fulfilling the church's vocation as well.' But this was a theological not a political statement; the 'Confessing Church' never attempted political opposition. Even in Neimoller's church, Nazi flags hung from the walls, and the congregation gave the Nazi salute. And the courage of the pastors was limited. When some of them sent a private protest to Hitler in 1936, which was later published in Switzerland, the public outcry – Hitler was growing in popularity at the time – led the signatories to backtrack. When the Olympic Games were over, Dr Weissler, who had authorized publication (and had then been disowned by the 'Confessing Church') was put into Sachsenhausen, and beaten to death a few months later.

The first, and virtually the only, protest gesture by the Catholics was Pius XI's German encyclical, *Mit Brennender Sorge*, smuggled into Germany and read out on Palm Sunday in 1937. It attacked not merely violations of the concordat but Nazi state and racial doctrines, and was taken by Hitler to be a declaration of war. He suppressed it without difficulty and there is no evidence it stirred Catholic opposition to the regime. Indeed, he dealt with the state churches without really raising his voice. He used the currency laws, from 1935, to punish priests or nuns with contacts abroad, a device later adopted by the Communist states. The Gestapo carried out repression when necessary. It rarely needed to be severe. Except for a few individuals, the clergy were hardly ever imprisoned for long. Of 17,000 Evangelical pastors, there were never more than fifty serving long terms at any one time. Of the Catholics, one bishop was expelled from his diocese, and another got a short term for currency offences. There was no more resistance, despite the fact that, by summer 1939, all religious schools had been abolished. Only the free sects stuck to their principles enough to merit outright persecution. The bravest were the Jehovah's Witnesses, who proclaimed their outright doctrinal opposition from the beginning and suffered accordingly. They refused any cooperation with the Nazi state which they denounced as totally evil. The Nazis believed they were part of the international Jewish-Marxist conspiracy. Many were sentenced to death for refusing military service and inciting others to do likewise; or they ended in Dachau or lunatic asylums. A third were actually killed; ninety-seven per cent suffered persecution in one form of another. They were the only Christian group which aroused Himmler's admiration: in September 1944 he suggested to Kaltenbrunner that, after victory, they should be resettled in the conquered plains of Russia.

Of the well-known Christians, Dibelius was arrested in 1937, but acquitted. So was Neimoller in 1938, but he was nonetheless held in concentration camps. As Hitler consolidated his hold on German emotions, resistance grew weaker. Gestapo reports 1938–9 noted that the Evangelicals were giving up the struggle. In Austria, Hitler's annexation was welcomed by the churches. The Austrian Catholic hierarchy greeted the imposition of Nazi restrictions with relief on the grounds that 'the danger of an all-devastating atheistic bolshevism was averted by the actions of the National Socialist Movement. They therefore welcome these measures for the future and bestow their blessing, and would instruct the faithful in this sense.' The Austrian Evangelicals, though less important, were equally enthusiastic. Hitler's response to the grovelling of the Austrian bishops was to revoke their concordat, close their schools, and loot and burn the palace of Cardinal Innitzer, their leader. Despite this, Pius XII, elected pope in March 1939, could hardly wait to send Hitler a friendly letter. He refused to condemn the absorption of Czechoslovakia a few days later, although he knew this meant the Czech Catholics – whom the Jesuits had fought so hard to save for Catholicism three hundred years before – would immediately lose their schools. He described the seizure as one of the 'historic processes in which, from the political point of view, the church is not interested'. In April 1939, Protestants and Catholics rang their bells for Hitler's birthday, and Cardinal Bertram, the Catholic primate, sent him a greetings-telegram.

The churches played no part in the events leading to the outbreak of the Second World War. Both the state churches urged Germans to obey the Führer and fight for victory. The only exception was Preysing, Catholic bishop of Berlin. The German bishops do not seem even to have discussed whether a war started in pursuit of Hitler's expansionist aims was justified or not. Archbishop Grober's line was that the church had 'never left it to the judgment of the individual Catholic, with all his shortsightedness and emotionalism, to decide, in the event of war, its permissibility or lack of it.' Instead, this final decision has always been in the province of lawful authority.' But what did lawful authority have to say? Nothing. The only relevant statement was made right at the end, in January 1945, when Archbishop Jager, calling for further Catholic sacrifices, wrote of Germany's two great enemies, 'liberalism and individualism on the one side, collectivism on the other'. The rest simply told their flocks to obey Hitler. The Pope gave no guidance. Pius XII advised all Catholics everywhere to 'fight with valour and charity' on whichever side they happened to find themselves. Later, he defended his early war-statements by claiming that both sides construed them to be in their favour. In that case, what was the point in issuing them? It is against this whole background that his encyclical quoted at the beginning of this section should be read. Curiously enough, it contains no condemnation of the Nazi-Soviet carve-up of Catholic Poland. The topic was not even mentioned.

During the war, the churches' attitude to Hitler became, if anything, more servile. There was wholesale confiscation of church property of all kinds, each ministry taking what it wanted. There was anti-Christian propaganda in the armed forces. But the churches continued to greet Nazi victories by ringing their bells, until they were taken away to be melted down for the war-effort. Only seven Catholics in the whole of the German Reich refused to perform military service; six were executed, the seventh was declared insane. The sacrifices of the Protestants were more considerable, but still insignificant. In June 1940, their leader, Kerrl, offered to donate all Evangelical property to the State, and make Hitler its 'supreme head' and *Summus Episcopus*. Hitler contemptuously refused. When he heard of Kerrl's death in 1941, he remarked: 'Pure Christianity, the Christianity of the catacombs, is concerned with translating the Christian doctrine into fact. It leads simply to the annihilation of mankind. It is merely wholehearted Bolshevism under a tinsel of metaphysics.' Thus Hitler, whom Pius XII saw as the indispensible bastion against Russia, himself equated true Christianity with communism.

In the end he intended to exterminate the Christians. But first he wanted to deal with the Jews. Here he rightly believed he could get German Christian support, or at least acquiescence. 'As for the Jews,' he told Bishop Berning of Osnabruch in April 1933, 'I am just carrying on with the same policy which the Catholic church had adopted for 1500 years.' It was true there was an anti-semitic element in nineteenth-century German Catholicism. In the 1870s, Bishop Martin of Pederborn had asserted his belief in stories of Jewish ritual murders of Christian children. The Catholics had used anti-semitism when German Jews supported the *Kulturkampf*. One Catholic encyclopaedia (1930) asserted that 'political anti-semitism' was permissible provided it utilized morally acceptable means. Bishop Buchberg called it 'justified self-defence' against 'too-powerful Jewish capital' (1931). Archbishop Grober, editing a handbook on religious problem, included an article on 'race' which stated:

'Every people bears itself the responsibility for its successful existence, and the intake of entirely foreign blood will always represent a risk for a nationality that has proven its historical worth. Hence, no people may be denied the right to maintain undisturbed their previous racial stock and to enact safeguards for this purpose. The Christian religion merely demands that the means used do not offend against the moral law and natural justice.'

What did this mean in practice? Many Jews became Catholics to avoid persecution; thus the old Spanish problem of 'new Christians' cropped up again in a different form. The Nuremberg Laws of September 1935 dealt with this by forbidding two Catholics to marry if one were racially non-Aryan. By and large the Church bowed to this new law, which she had earlier termed an inadmissible infringement of her spiritual jursidiction. One Catholic bishop, Hudel, actually defended the Nuremberg laws. The clergy made some effort to protect Catholics of Jewish birth; but it was unsystematic and unsuccessful. They claimed credit for forcing the Nazis to drop the compulsory divorce of people who had made racially mixed marriages, but this was probably achieved, rather, by demonstrations by Aryan wives. When the bishops condemned 'killing', as they occasionally did, they did not mention words like 'Jews' or 'non-Aryan', and never made it clear precisely what they were calling sinful. Thus Catholics engaged in the extermination processes were never told specifically by their clergy that they were doing wrong. The point is academic since they must have known already. The Church excommunicated Catholics who laid down in their wills that they wished to be cremated, or who took part in duels; but it did not forbid them to work in concentration or death-camps – and at the end of 1938, 22.7 per cent of the SS were practising Catholics. Provost Lichtenberg of Berlin was one of the very few Catholic priests who made a real protest against Hitler's Jewish policy; he died on the way to Dachau in 1943. The laity were not much better, and the behaviour of the German bishops contrasted shamefully with that of their colleagues in France, Holland and Belgium. In 1943, the Prussian Synod of the Confessing Church pointed out that liquidation of the Jews was against the Fifth Commandment; this was a statement which the German Catholic bishops could not bring themselves to echo.

The most that can be said in their favour is that they received no guidance from the Pope. When French cardinals and archbishops objected to Pétain's 'Jewish statutes' in June 1941, the Vichy Ambassador, Léon Berard, reported that the Vatican did not consider them in conflict with Catholic teaching. It resisted a good deal of pressure to come out against anti-Jewish atrocities. In the autumn of 1943, Bishop Hudel, head of the German Catholic community in Rome, asked the German military commander to stop the arrest and deportation of 8,000 Jews, not on the grounds that it was wrong to exterminate them, but because 'I fear that otherwise the Pope will have to make an open stand which will serve the anti-German propaganda as a weapon against us.' Both he and the German ambassador, Ernst von Wiezsacker, took it for granted that Pius would not protest willingly, but only under pressure – they knew their man. In fact he did nothing at all, though 1,000 Jews were sent off for extermination. The only action taken was a statement in *Osservatore Romano*, the official Vatican paper, describing the treatment of Jews in concentration camps, and the confiscation of their property, as 'too harsh'. What would have been adequately harsh? The paper did not say. What made Pius keep silent, apart from natural timidity and fear for the safety of the Vatican itself, was undoubtedly his belief that a total breach between Rome and Hitler would lead to a separatist German Catholic Church. Like the Protestant pastors, he was a man of little faith. The Frenchman, Cardinal Tisserant, who watched this sad story unfold in Rome, said at the time: 'I fear that history will reproach the Holy See with having practised a policy of selfish convenience and not much else!'

Would the Germans have resisted a similar campaign to exterminate active Christians? Hitler was susceptible to pressure. There is no record of church protests against such Nazi activities as human stud-farms, breeding and sex experiments conducted at Himmler's Lebensborn Institute and elsewhere. But in August 1941, Bishop Galen of Munster preached a sermon on the sanctity of human life, aimed at the compulsory euthanasia programme, of which he gave details. This sermon was widely circulated and talked about. Not only was the bishop not punished – despite demands from Nazis that he be hanged – but Hitler ordered the operation to be halted. (He later allowed it to be resumed secretly, and in 1943 the system was extended to include orphan children.) The euthanasia issue was the only one on which the German people seem to have felt strongly, apart from the special case of the wives who protested against compulsory divorces; in each case Hitler gave way, at any rate in public, which indicates that he was less intransigent in such matters than either the Pope or the German Christian clergy supposed. But it is notable that when the same gas-chambers intended for the euthanasia victims were in fact employed on Jews of all ages, and in vast numbers, no Christian protest was heard.

What the papacy failed to realize was that the Nazis were more serious enemies of Christianity than even the Communists. They exposed the ambivalence and weakness of Christians, and their cowardice, whereas Communism brought out their strength. And, in the last resort, the Nazis were much more implacably determined to stamp out Christianity. When the Christian aristocrats who had taken part in the July 1944 plot were brought to trial, the president of the court, Roland Freisler, told their leader: 'Count Moltke, Christianity and we Nazis have one thing in common and one only: we claim the whole man.' The real threat of Nazism to Christianity was proclaimed far more loudly by the Nazis themselves than by the official Catholic leaders, who largely ignored it – at any rate in Germany, Austria and Italy. Hitler's plans for Christianity were more draconian than anything envisaged by the Russians. He told his entourage on 13 December 1941: 'The war will be over one day. I shall then consider that my life's final task will be to solve the religious problem. . . . The final state must be: in the pulpit, a senile officiant; facing him, a few sinister old women, as gaga and poor in spirit as anyone could wish.' Anti-Christian activities undertaken in Poland and elsewhere were more ferocious than anything contrived by the Russians, and applied equally to Catholic, Protestant and Orthodox churches. Himmler said: 'We shall not rest until we have rooted out Christianity.' The Nazi image of the future was adumbrated in the experimental area of the Warthegau, carved out of former Polish territories and handed over completely to party control as a *tabula rasa*. The plan involved not merely the separation of Church and State but the progressive and systematic destruction of religion. Did Pius XII know of this? He was usually well-briefed on what was going on. Eventually, Pius made a speech to the College of Cardinals. Nazism he said was 'a satanic spectre . . . the arrogant apostasy from Jesus Christ, the denial of his doctrine and of his work of redemption, the cult of violence, the idolatry of race and blood, the overthrow of human liberty and dignity'. But it was then June 1945, the Germans had surrendered and Hitler was safely dead.

Thus the Second World War inflicted even more grievous blows on the moral standing of the Christian faith than the First. It exposed the emptiness of the churches in Germany, the cradle of the Reformation, and the cowardice and selfishness of the Holy See. It was the nemesis of triumphalism, in both its Protestant and Catholic forms. Yet the Christian record was not entirely shameful. Christian resistance to Hitler and the Nazis had been weak and ineffectual, yet it did exist – it was more persistent and principled than that of any other element in German society. Some Christians in the West recognized its existence and tried to strengthen it; there was a slender line of Christian communication across the abyss of war. During the 1930s George Bell, Anglican Bishop of Chichester, had been in touch with the anti-Nazi group in the Evangelical Church, and in particular with Pastor Dietrich Bonhoeffer. When war broke out he tried hard to combat the mindless Christian patriotism which, in 1914, had reinforced the hatreds on both sides. Indeed, he was one of the few Christian prelates in either of the world wars who tried to think out what a Churchman ought to do in these circumstances. In November 1939 he published an article, 'The Church's Function in Wartime', in the *Fortnightly Review*, which argued that it was essential that the Church should remain the Church, and not 'the state's spiritual auxilliary'. It should define basic principles of conduct, and 'not hesitate . . . to condemn the infliction of reprisals, or the bombing of civilian populations, by the military forces of its own nation. It should set itself against the propaganda of lies and hatred. It should be ready to encourage the resumption of friendly relations with the enemy nation. It should set its face against any war of extermination or enslavement, and any measures directly aimed to destroy the morale of a population.'

Bell did his best to live up to these principles, all of which were broken by the Allies with the knowledge and encouragement of the churches. In early summer 1942 he contrived to get to Sweden where he made contact with the German resistance and Bonhoeffer. The latter had told his friends in 1940, after Hitler's success in France: 'If we claim to be Christians, there is no room for expediency. Hitler is the anti-Christ. Therefore we must go on with our work and eliminate him, whether he be successful or not.' Bonhoeffer's last message, smuggled out of prison just before his execution in April 1945, was to Bell: '... with him I believe in the principle of our Universal Christian Brotherhood, which rises above all national interests, and that our victory is assured.' For his part, Bell tried to set limits to Allied ferocity. He thought 'the church cannot speak of any earthly war as a crusade'. He advocated an international agreement against night-bombing, but got no support from the Archbishop of Canterbury, Cosmo Gordon Lang. All he obtained from the government was a public statement that their aim was not the total destruction of the German people; and on bombing he was sharply rebuked by Lang's successor, Archbishop Temple, in July 1943: 'I am not at all disposed to be the mouthpiece of the concern which I know exists, because I do not share it.' Bell was horrified by the mass terror raids on German cities conducted by the British, and later by the Americans also. He wrote in the *Chichester Diocesan Gazette* in September 1943: 'To bomb cities as cities, deliberately to attack civilians, quite irrespective of whether or not they are actively contributing to the war effort, is a wrong deed, whether done by the Nazis or by ourselves.' This unexceptionable Christian observation won virtually no support at the time, and led to Bell being asked by the Dean of Chichester to withdraw from a Battle of Britain Sunday service in his own cathedral. Bell continued to condemn indiscriminate bombing, and forced a debate in the House of Lords on 9 February 1944. The speech he then made did not succeed in halting the bombing, but it aroused much comment and forced many complacent people to think. It also brought, at the time, a comment from Liddell Hart, the military analyst: '... the historian of civilisation, if that survives, is likely to regard it as better evidence for Christianity and common decency, than has been provided by any other spokesman. It represents the longer view and the higher wisdom.'

The longer view and the higher wisdom: to what extent did these characterize Christianity in the twentieth century? There was no striking evidence of far-sighted Christian statesmanship in the Protestant camp. The triumphalist euphoria which marked the first decade of the century slowly disappeared. In Britain, the last real (as opposed to commercially organized) Christian revival took place in Wales, 1904–5. It was essentially Noncon-formist, and was promoted by anger against the status and privileges of the established Church in Wales. Its leader, Evan Roberts, was a young miner studying for the ministry, but the movement seems to have been entirely spontaneous and repudiated ministerial guidance. Roberts thought he was guided by the spirit; his helpers did not organize meetings, and he did not prepare his sermons. Sometimes he would remain silent in the pulpit for one and a half hours. But when he spoke he provoked contortions, prostrations and outcries, and his mere presence at a mass political meeting was sufficient to turn it into a religious one: at the 1906 General Election, Lloyd George, the most charismatic politician of the day, begged Roberts not to come to Caernarvon. At the end of 1906, Roberts suddenly collapsed and went into retirement, and the movement quickly subsided. The Nonconformist churches had more MPs in the House of Commons in the 1906 Parliament than at any time since the 1640s; but their legislative programme was a failure, and thereafter their representation declined sharply. Indeed, Nonconformity had been in decay for some time. The main period of growth for the Wesleyans and Baptists had ended by 1845; and even the Primitive Methodists slackened after 1854. For the Church of England, attendances had begun to fall by the 1880s. The last public victory for British Protestantism came in 1911, and was characteristically a negative one. The Reverend F. B. Meyer, the minister of Regent's Park Baptist Church, and organizing secretary of the Free Church Movement, launched a nationwide campaign to stop the staging of the Jack Johnson–Bombardier Wells prize fight in Earls Court. Under pressure from the Protestants, the Director of Public Prosecutions began an action against the two fighters for 'contemplating a breach of the peace': but this proved unnecessary when the railway company which owned the freehold of Earls Court forbade the fight by legal injunction.

In the United States, Protestant triumphalism persisted much longer. American Protestants, too, were campaigning against prizefighting; in 1910 they had succeeded in banning the Jack Johnson-Jim Jeffries fight in California. But their chief preoccupation was with alcoholic liquor. It was the great Protestant crusade of the twentieth century. In 1900, thanks to Protestant pressure-groups, twenty-four per cent of the population lived in dry territory; by 1906 this had been extended to forty per cent. In 1913, the Protestants won their first victory at the Federal level, when the Webb-Kenyon law prohibited the sending of liquor into dry states; by 1917 there were twenty-nine dry states and over half the American people lived on dry territory. The famous Eighteenth Amendment came on top of 1918 laws prohibiting the manufacture and sale of liquor after June 1919, and in October the Volstead enforcement act went through Congress, so total prohibition became a fact on 16 January 1920. The trouble with the legislation, however, was that it was undiscriminating and too comprehensive; it bore the marks of an unreasoning religious fanaticism, and it ignored much sympathetic and wise advice. Hence the movement failed to make prohibition stick, and it was not merely defeated but routed. This was a disaster for organized American Protestantism. It was followed by a rapid decline in its domestic political power. Traditional Protestant moral theology had no answer to the Depression. It regarded the New Deal and similar interventionist schemes as unscriptural and sinful. Hence the great majority of Protestant periodicals and ministers, except in the South, favoured the Republicans and opposed

Roosevelt. One survey showed that in the 1936 Roosevelt landslide, over seventy per cent of 21,606 Protestant ministers polled voted for Roosevelt's Republican opponent. Landon, who also received the majority of the votes of all Protestant church members. Among the Congregationalists, the élite of the traditional Protestant dominance, the vote for Landon was as high as seventy-eight per cent. Thus the 1930s and 1940s marked a Protestant political retreat, before a Democratic coalition in which Jews and Catholics and progressives all had increasing roles to play.

Yet it was some time before the weakening in Protestant ability to influence events, or set the tone of society, was translated into figures of church attendance, or was recognized as merely one aspect of a general contraction of Christianity. The number of those actually affiliated to particular churches appeared to be rising. It was calculated at forty-three per cent of the population in 1910, and almost exactly the same in 1920. By 1940 it had risen to forty-nine per cent, and there appears to have been an impressive post-war 'revival' to fifty-five per cent in 1950 and sixty-nine per cent in 1960. The phenomenon was not easy to explain. Within academic Protestantism there had, indeed, been an intellectual revival. It sprang originally from Switzerland, where Pastor Karl Barth, the latest in a long line of innovatory theologians who have found inspiration in the Epistle to the Romans, published his *Commentary* in 1918, followed by his *Church Dogmatics* in the 1930s. This neo-orthodoxy, as it is termed, reversed the liberal and rationalist attempt to translate Christianity into a formula for progress and reform – the *raison d'être* of Protestant triumphalism – and emphasized the fact that the Christian hope or *kerygma* is essentially other-worldly. The new theological philosophy, as it might be called, was Germanic in origin, and in a sense was an attempt to understand or explain the hateful fact of world war. But it proved powerfully attractive to American Christian intellectuals in the 1930s – themselves trying to understand the hateful fact of the Depression – who no longer equated Christianity with the American way of life and capitalist democracy. They believed Christianity was millenarian, but not in a materialist sense at all. Reinhold Niebuhr's *Introduction to Christian Ethics* (1935) denied 'the illusion of liberalism that we are dealing with a possible and prudential ethic in the Gospels. . . . The ethic of Jesus does not deal at all with the immediate moral problems of every human life. . . . It transcends the possibilities of human life . . . as God transcends the world.' The manifesto published by the neo-orthodox group the same year was entitled *The Churches Against the World*, and it emphasized withdrawal rather than crusade.

It would, however, be idle to pretend that this essentially theological revival had much to do with high attendances at church in the postwar period. On the contrary, American popular religion was becoming increasingly divorced from its doctrinal basis, and ordinary churchgoers less and less inclined to read the New Testament – as the neo-orthodox scholars urged – to discover what it actually says. As long ago as 1831 de Tocqueville had noted of

American preachers: 'It is often difficult to ascertain from their discourse whether the principal object of religion is to procure eternal felicity in the other world or prosperity in this.' Religion and church-going served almost as a national talisman to ensure that economic expansion continued into the 1950s and 1960s; it was an insurance policy against the end of affluence. And it was marked by the adaption of psychological concepts to induce tranquility and felicity, a debased modern form of mysticism. Thus Americans read *Peace of Mind* (1946) by a Boston Reformed Rabbi, Joshua Loth Liebman, the Rev. Norman Vincent Peale's *Guide to Confident Living* (1948) and *Power of Positive Thinking* (1952), Mgr Fulton J. Sheen's *Peace of Soul* (1949), Billy Graham's *Peace with God* (1953) and Erich Fromms's *Art of Loving* (1956). These were, in effect, variations on harmonial or gnostic themes which had always flourished in the United States, and which had produced such phenomena as Christian Science, Theosophy, American Rosicrucianism, and the Christian therapies of Dale Carnegie, the speech-trainer and author of *How to Win Friends and Influence People* (1936). It could be argued that many of these cults were in the tradition of Jesus Christ as a miracle-worker and faith-healer, just as many of the revivalist sects were in the tradition of the early charismatics and 'speakers with tongues'. They were thus Christian. Some, indeed, were insistently so. Norman Vincent Peale's best success-story, in his *Power of Positive Thinking*, which sold two million copies during the Eisenhower years, were Maurice Flint and his wife, who after being 'reached' by Peale built up a successful business marketing 'mustard-seed re-membrancers' worn as an amulet and recalling Matthew 17: 20. But many of the cults, such as Theosophy and Rudolf Steiner's 'Esoteric Movement of the Reformation', had virtually no common dogmatic ground with Christianity. And the religious afflatus shaded off into domestic revivals of other imperial religions – Indian Vedanta, Persian Baha'i, Zen Buddhism, and, for American blacks, the prison-cult of Black Power, which is pseudo-Islamic. Indeed, even in President Eisenhower's Washington, which symbolized the Christian revival in the 1950s, and where the tone was Protestant, the actual content was patriotic moralism and sentimentalized religiosity rather than specifically Christian. 'Piety on the Potomac', as it was termed, had something of the quality of classical Roman religion. It was kept up officially, as befitted a great imperial state with world-wide responsibilities and the consciousness of a global mission. In 1954, the phrase 'under God' (as used by Lincoln in the Gettysburg Address) was added to the United States Pledge of Allegiance, and in 1956 the device from the coinage, 'In God We Trust', became the nation's official motto. Which God? God as defined by whom? No answer was required. President Eisenhower, himself the archetype of the generalized *homo Americanus religiosus*, asked the nation only for 'faith in faith'. He told the country in 1954: 'Our government makes no sense unless it is founded on a deeply-felt religious faith – and I don't care what it is.'

In any event 1960 marked the high-water mark of ostensible religious growth, and thereafter all the indices, for what they were worth, showed continuous decline. As in Britain, popular Christianity had been associated with the imperial mission; as in Britain, the questioning of religious certitudes seemed to grow *pari passu* with doubts about geopolitical ones. The only difference was that in the United States the sceptical dawn came a generation later. Moreover, Christianity and the western paramountcy were directly linked in the mission field: Protestant triumphalism, as a global phenomenon, rested essentially on Anglo-Saxon imperialism in its various forms. It lost its self-confidence as the West lost its will (and ability) to rule.

In sheer size, the missionary effort continued to expand both between the wars and even after 1945. The number of white Protestant field-workers increased from 4,102 in 1911 to 5,556 in 1925 and 7,514 in 1938; Catholic numbers increased even faster. But income fell, and has continued to fall in comparative terms. Moreover, there was an almost complete failure to speed up the recruitment of local clergy and, above all, their promotion to higher ranks. Thus East Africa did not get its first Catholic bishop until 1939, and the black Anglicans had to wait until 1947. After the Second World War, all the main groups changed their policies and made frantic attempts to produce native clergy in large quantities. But by then it was, in a sense, too late; the colonial revolution was beginning. A confident native Christian clergy, running their own national churches, might have played a formative role in the construction of the new societies, as Christianity and the Christian clergy did in western and central Europe between the fifth and ninth centuries. But in the 1950s the clergy did not yet exist; and though they have since been created, the moment appears to have passed. Locally recruited and trained missionaries now dominate the movement, and form the great majority of the 60,000 Catholic and 42,000 Protestants now active in Asia, Africa and Latin-America. But their influence on Third World governments, never extensive, declines steadily; and in a great part of Asia missionary work has been halted by Communist governments.

More serious, in the long run, has been the failure, or the unwillingness, of the European Christian movements to allow local insights into Christianity to develop. This failure reaches right back into the sixteenth century, when the Jesuits were first discouraged from allowing cultural reinterpretations of Christian teaching to develop. It explains the inability of Christianity to establish more than a foothold in China, India or Japan. Where syncretistic forms of Christianity have made their appearance, 'official' Christianity has promptly stamped on them. Thus in China, the so-called 'Worshippers of Shang-ti', in the 1850s, developed a Christian political reform programme, linked to a new set of commandments – their seventh commandment, for instance, included a ban on opium. Here was a case of Christianity rising up from the depths, since the 'Worshippers' led a rebellion against the Manchu dynasty. One missionary, Griffiths John of the LMS, wrote in 1860: 'I fully believe that God is uprooting idolatry in this land through the insurgents, and that he will by means of them, in connection with the foreign missionary, plant Christianity in its stead.' But the movement allowed polygamy; and it inconvenienced western political arrangements. So it was categorized as non-Christian and destroyed by General 'Chinese' Gordon. In Japan, too, there have been several tentative syncretistic cults, such as Kanzo Uchimua's Mukyokai or 'Non-Church' movement. None has received encouragement from official Christian sects.

In India, an indigenous Christian Church existed when the first Portuguese missionaries arrived around 1500. These native Christians, mainly around Kerala, and numbering about 100,000, believed they sprang from the evangelizing of India by St Thomas in the first century AD. They had a Syriac liturgy and, apparently, a true apostolic succession. But they were, of course, Nestorians. Hence both the Catholic Europeans, and then, in turn, the Protestants, instead of building on this native tradition, sought instead to convert its representatives to their own Continental varieties. Hence the Thomas Church of India, far from expanding, has in fact contracted under the battering of the Western proselytizers, split into five branches. There are now Romo-Syrians of the Syriac rite (plus those of the Latin rite), Malankarans, Monophysite and Unreformed; Nestorians; the Mar Thomas, or the Reformed Syrian Church, and Thomas Anglicans.

The stresses of Christian teaching have produced similar religious abortions elsewhere. Thus in California, there are Wesleyan and Baptist branches of both the Northern anti-slavery Church, and the Southern segregationalist one, though the issue which once split the churches has no meaning in western America. Again, in the Central Provinces of India, there are native branches of the Scottish Original Seceders, though none of their members has been to Scotland or seceded from anything; as primitive Presbyterians they have inherited a disembodied religious tradition. Unassimilated Christianity can also produce entirely new but powerful and creative religions whose origin springs from linguistic and cultural misunderstanding. 'Where is the road that leads to Cargo?' asked the natives of parts of Papua and New Guinea. These peoples are unable to accept the white Christian's distinction between sacred and secular knowledge. The believe that western goods and technology originate in the worlds of gods and spirits. They also think, rationalizing bitter experiences, that the intruding white man prevents the material betterment of the native people, in particular by withholding from them, and keeping to himself, the religious secrets by which they are obtained. Hence there arises a constant stream of prophets – one a month, on average – whose aim is to release the gods held in white bondage so that they will send possessions (Cargo) to the people.

Innovation in religion is essentially linked to prophecy. Here, perhaps, we have the key to the creative failure of non-European Christianity. The ferocious battles waged by the orthodox Church in the second and third centuries to stabilize Christian dogma and eliminate unlicensed prophets ended by killing prophecy as a means by which the Christian faith was expanded and interpreted – prophecy became a pseudo-science rather than a form of divine revelation. When therefore Christianity was exported by Europe from the sixteenth century onwards, prophecy was not recognized as a legitimate form of Christian activity. Yet it has made its appearance nevertheless, and has done so against a background of official Christian disapproval, thus leading to breakaway movements. Prophecy has, in fact, become the characteristic form of Christianity in Africa, the only large area (apart from Latin America) where Christian missions were faced not with other imperial cults but with primitive pagan religions which could be overborne. Christianity is thus making headway in Africa, but in ways which the official Christian churches find disturbing or even horrific.

The history of separatist native Christian churches in Africa now goes back nearly a century, to the Native Baptist Church (1888) organized in West Africa by David Vincent. The motive was, from the start, independence from white-controlled churches, and the emotional framework was nationalist and racialist. Vincent renamed himself Mojola Agbebi, and he wrote: '. . . when no bench of foreign bishops, no conclave of cardinals lord over Christian Africa, when the Captain of Salvation, Jesus Christ himself, leads the Ethiopian host, and when our Christianity ceases to be London-ward and New York-ward, but Heaven-ward, then will be an end to Privy Councils, Governors, Colonels, Annexations, Displacements, Partitions, Cessions and Coercions.' Vincent defended secret societies, human sacrifice and cannibalism, and he was plainly anxious to bring about a Christian absorption of African customs; but he was not strictly speaking prophetic since he did not claim a personal revelation. The Liberian episcopalian, William Wade Harris, did. He appeared on the French Ivory Coast about 1914, preaching orthodox morality but claiming a direct line to the Deity and urging immediate repentance, rather like John the Baptist. A French observer, Captain Marty, described him as 'an impressive figure, adorned with a white beard, of magnificent stature, clothed in white, his head enturbaned with a cloth of the same colour, wearing a black stole; in his hand a high cross and on his belt a calabash containing dried seeds, which he shakes to keep rhythm for his hymns.' The Prophet Harris was immensely successful, and set a completely new pattern for African Christianity. He himself did not attempt to found a personal church, and the orthodox Baptists were the beneficiaries of his converts when he disappeared. But those who followed in his wake had higher ambitions, or less altruistic ones. In the 1920s, Isiah Shembe created the black Nazarite Church, which flourished near Durban in South Africa, and from this point native churches multiplied. Christian native charismatics often fell foul of the colonial authorities. The Congolese baptist Simon Kimbangu, creator of the Church of Christ on Earth, which now has over three million members and is affiliated to the World Council of Churches, was sentenced by the Belgians to thirty years and died in gaol. John Chilembwe, founder of the Ajawa Providence Industrial

Mission of Nyasaland, was shot after capturing the land-grabber W. J. Livingstone, one of the Doctor's family, cutting his head off, and mounting it on a pole during a service. Some of these churches, on the other hand, gave no trouble in colonial times, but have been suppressed by nationalist governments – one example being the Lumpa ('Excelling') Church of Zambia, five hundred of whose adherents were killed in a riot, and whose founder, Alice Lenshina, was banished. Many African political leaders are charismatics themselves, and do not welcome rivals, even if their claims are confined exclusively to the spiritual field.

Nevertheless, the African churches are the one form of Christianity which is growing at spectacular speed. Their names are not arbitrary, and often encapsulate the emphasis of their doctrinal teachings which originally spring, as a rule, from the American Evangelical sects. They include the African Casteroil Dead Church, African Correctly Apostolic Jerusalem Church in Zion, Afro-Anglican Constructive Gaathly, Almighty God Church, Apostles Church of the Full Bible of South Africa, Apostolic Fountain Catholic Church, Bantu Customers Church to Almighty God, the Catholic Church of South Africa King George Win the War, Christ Apostolic Holy Spout Church, the Christian Apostolic Stone Church, the Church of Pleasant Living Congregation, the Ethiopian National Theocracy Restitution, the Fire Baptized Holiness Church of God, the Great George v National Church, the International Foursquare Gospel, the Remnant Church of God, the Sunlight Four Corners Apostolic for Witness of God Church, and so forth. Many of these churches teach there is a reverse colour-bar in heaven, with a black 'Holder of the Keys'. Sometimes they specify there are two gates into heaven, sometimes only one, but with a black Christ in control. The parables are often adjusted. Thus:

> 'There were ten virgins. And five of them were white and five were black. The five whites were foolish, but the five blacks were wise, they had oil in their lamps. All ten came to the gate but the five white virgins received the same answer as the rich man. . . . The white will go a-begging to dip the tip of their finger in cool water. But they will get as a reply: "Nobody can rule twice." '

Many of these religions or cults are associated with the desire for land, and reflect the traditional native leadership of priest-kings. In fact they are tribal churches. They are characterized by sacramental vomiting, water-rituals, and speaking with tongues, such as (a very common formula):

> Zzzzzzzzzzzzzzzzzzzzzzzzzzzzz
> Hhayi, hhayi, hhayi, hhayi,
> Sorry Jesus Sorry Jesus Sorry Jesus
> Spy spy spy spy, Naughty boy, Naughty boy
> Nhayi hhayi hhayi – Halleluja, halleluja,
>   Amen.

The big Western Christian communities do not know what they ought to do about these African churches. Significantly, they cannot even agree what, generically, they should be called. 'Separatist', 'messianic', 'prophetic', 'nativistic', 'syncretistic' have all, in turn, been discarded as offensive to African feelings (and to the feelings of American blacks, too, and West Indians, since many of the churches have international links, and some have outposts in London, Paris and elsewhere). The currently acceptable description is 'independent'. A number of these churches are broadly orthodox in their teaching. Some even belong to the World Council of Churches. But others are barely Christian and many are chronically unstable. It is the Montanist world of the second century again, though of course with important variations. Some students of these sects argue that their drift is ultimately anti-Christian in that they tend to form a bridge by which Africans pass back into paganism. They move, it is claimed, from the (orthodox) mission church to an 'Ethiopian' church, then to a Zionist, then by the nativistic or tribal Zionism back to the African animism of their parents or grandparents. This undoubtedly happens in some cases. On the other hand, some of the sects are startingly original and creative in their theological imaginings, and fervent in their enthusiasm. In any case, the phenomenon is growing. An analysis of these churches published in 1948 listed the names of 1023 distinct sects. An analysis published in 1968 was based on a survey of over 6,000. According to recent calculations, 'revival movements', usually leading to new churches, break out on average in seven new tribes each year. The expansion of African Christianity is not confined to the 'independent' churches, but they take the lion's share of the new recruits. At present, African Christians of all denominations are doubling in numbers every twelve years, and by the end of the century there may be over 350 million professing African Christians, thus forming the largest single group within the global Christian community, exceeding in numerical importance even the Latin Americans. A big majority of these Christians will be 'independents'. How they will be regarded by the churches of European origin may prove one of the most important ecclesiastical developments of our time.

Much will depend, of course, on how western Christianity organizes itself in the meantime; and this, in turn, will be determined very largely by the attitude of the Catholic Church. So long as Pius XII lived, world Catholicism was immobile, frozen in a posture which, in all essentials, had been assumed by Pius IX in the third quarter of the nineteenth century. While Protestant triumphalism was quietly abandoned, the populist triumphalism of the papacy remained intact, lovingly preserved like a precious heirloom from an earlier age. Pius XII was, indeed, the last of a long line of popes stretching back to Boniface VIII, Innocent III and Hildebrand himself. His vision of the Church was Augustinian in that, while he reluctantly recognized that it did not embrace all society, he upheld its authority as universal and omnicompetent. There was, in effect, no aspect of life on which the Church did not have the right, and usually the duty, to give its ruling. In November 1954, in an address to cardinals and bishops, later printed as *The Authority of the Church in Temporal Matters*, he insisted:

> 'The power of the Church is not bound by matters strictly religious, as they say, but the whole matter of the natural law, its foundation, its interpretation, its application, so far as their moral aspects extend, are within the Church's power. . . . Clergy and laity must realize that the Church is fitted and authorized . . . to establish an external norm of action and conduct for matters which concern public order and which do not have their immediate origin in natural or divine law.'

And of course by 'the Church' Pius meant essentially the papacy. Montalembert had protested vigorously against the idea of 'a Louis xiv in the Vatican'. Yet that was what Pius xii became. He had his own little court of admirers, officials, servants and relatives. He was his own Secretary of State. For nearly twenty years he reigned as the autocratic monarch of the last *ancien régime* court in history. Increasingly, as he grew older, he separated himself from the day to day business of the curia. It was often extremely difficult, even for the cardinals who were heads of the Vatican departments, to get an audience with him. Usually they had to solicit the favour of his all-powerful German housekeeper, Mother Pasqualina Lehnert. Pius came to dislike business meetings or committees, where he might be faced with uncongenial facts or arguments – even opposition. He was very conscious of his unique, and divinely warranted, powers as a supreme pontiff. These were reinforced, from the autumn of 1950, by supernatural visions which, it appeared, he saw on a number of occasions. Pius did not invite discussion. He dealt with subordinates directly, without using a secretary, giving his orders over his gold-and-white telephone, and replacing the receiver as soon as he had finished what he wanted to say. Officials, when they heard his voice – '*Qui parla Pacelli*' ('Pacelli speaking') – were trained to go down on their knees with the phone in their hands. Pius insisted on retaining traditional monarchical protocol. All but the most senior, or privileged, officials, on the rare occasions when they came into his presence, addressed him on their knees and left the room walking backwards. He reinstated the practice, which had been scornfully abandoned by Pius x, that the Pope always took his meal alone; not even his favourite relatives were allowed to sit down at the table with him. When he walked in the Vatican gardens, the workmen and gardeners were instructed to hide themselves behind trees so as not to break his solitude. The papal Cadillac, a present from Cardinal Spellman, Archbishop of New York, had solid gold door-handles and, in the back, a single seat, where Pius sat alone, communing with himself.

Yet Pius was not without energy. He understood the nature of the populist papacy, and reinforced it with striking success. He was the first pope to exploit the resources of modern mass-communications, and his figure and voice became familiar to hundreds of millions. Though he disliked private contacts, he enjoyed public appearances. He held many more public and semi-public audiences than any of his predecessors. He could deliver addresses in at least nine languages. He made it his business to receive Catholic representatives from virtually every profession and occupation. He read technical manuals avidly so that he was conversant with some of the details of each calling, and could display this vicarious expertise in the speeches he made. As the Catholic Church claimed to have the moral answers to all problems, and as he was its animating force, he thought it right to deliver his verdicts on as many aspects of human existence as possible. Thus he received, and addressed, men and women in the fields of medicine, law, dentistry, architecture, chemistry, printing, journalism, heating engineering, public health, acting, diesel engines, aeronautics, celestial navigation, radio engineering, and so forth. His encyclicals and published letters and speeches covered a vast range of subjects, usually in considerable technical detail. One of his last encyclicals, *Miranda prorsus* (1957), dealt with the movies, radio and TV, and laid down, for instance, the moral duties of a news announcer; the way in which regional censorship offices should be set up and operated; the moral responsibilities of cinema managers, distributors and actors; the duty of bishops to rebuke erring Catholic movie directors and producers, and if necessary to impose appropriate sanctions on them; the obligation of Catholic members of festival juries to vote for 'morally praiseworthy' movies, and even the moral criteria by which posters advertising movies were to be determined. In such ways Pius came into dogmatic contact, as it were, with an unnumbered host of Catholics throughout the world. Yet the confrontation was impersonal. Carried high on his *Sedia Gestatoria* – a form of monarchical transport inherited from imperial Rome – amid the cheering crowds, he remained a solitary figure, Montalembert's 'little idol in the Vatican'. Pius, wrote Guiseppe Dalla Torre, former editor of *L'Osservatore Romano*, 'separated himself from direct contact with life, though not, unfortunately, from people who abused his confidence'. The keynote of his pontificate was isolation.

The isolation was not merely personal. It was credal and political. Pius was a Tridentine pope. To him, the Greek Orthodox were simply schismatics, and the Protestants heretics. There was nothing more to be said or discussed. He was not interested in the ecumenical movement. The Catholic Church already was ecumenical in itself. It could not change, because it was right and always had been right. Indeed, fundamental change in the Catholic Church was to be avoided at all costs. Motion was dangerous: experience showed it invariably led in the direction of evil. Catholicism must stay exactly where it was: it was for the heretics and schismatics to submit as, in God's good time, they surely would. As for the world, Pius saw no reason to alter the analysis set out in his first encyclical. He learnt nothing from the war, or the phenomenon of the Nazis. He had made no mistakes. On the contrary: the war confirmed his initial judgment. International society, by ignoring the Vicar of Christ, was heading for disaster. The war had merely been a further stage of the descent into the abyss. Germany had been divided; the godless Communists controlled all eastern Europe, including the Catholics of Poland, Hungary, Czechoslovakia, Slovenia and Croatia – 'the church of silence'. This was the greatest disaster to Christianity and civilization, in Pius's view, since the end of the Wars of Religion. It seemed as though God, in his infinite wisdom, had condemned his Church to fight a perpetual rearguard action against change. But every inch yielded must be bitterly contested first. In political terms, this meant that the papacy had to present adamantine resistance to Communism, socialism or any philosophy which, whatever its other merits, had a basis in materialism. And to do this it must ally itself with the conservative elements in society wherever trustworthy ones could be found. At the same time, the papacy had constantly to remind the world of the claims of the Church, and exhort its leaders to repair the injustice inflicted by the war, especially in eastern Europe.

In international terms, Pius was a Cold Warrior. He thought a peace without justice was not a true peace. Therefore 'Peaceful Coexistence' was morally wrong, since it denied the opportunity to rectify the injustices of the past. He wrote: 'A nation which is threatened by, or already a victim of, unjust aggression, cannot remain passively indifferent if it wishes to behave in a Christian manner . . . the solidarity of the family of peoples forbids others to behave as mere spectators in an attitude of passive neutrality.' This was the sin of 'indifferentism'. Pius himself refused any contact with Communist states, and forbade the Catholic hierarchies of the 'church of silence' to compromise in any way with the state authorities. He did not want 'roll back' or open war, but, short of war, he saw the world in terms of a capitalist-Christian crusade against Marxist atheism. The least that Christendom could do, he thought, was to impose a total boycott of the Soviet world. Hence he had no sympathy for the United Nations, since Russia was one of its creators and a permanent member of the Security Council. He argued that the UN could not become 'the full and pure expression of international solidarity in peace' until it had 'cancelled from its institutions and statutes all traces of its origin, which was rooted in the solidarity of war'. Of course, this might take a long time to bring about. Indeed, Pius's whole analysis of Christianity and the world implied a long period of waiting. It would take time before heretics and schismatics came to their senses, and Marxists abandoned their godless materialism. The Church could wait, as it had waited before. It would remain in its fortress, avoiding contact with the evils of compromise, and from time to time lifting its admonitory voice. It was a policy of splendid isolation; or, if the isolation was not splendid, it was at least holy.

The policy changed, in almost all its aspects, from the end of 1958 when Angelo Roncalli succeeded Pius as Pope John XXIII. Roncalli was in his late seventies; he had been a popular patriarch of Venice and it was thought he would prove an acceptable and moderate transitional pope until the time came to hand over to a younger and more liberal generation. In fact he quickly inaugurated an era of rapid change. John, though conservative in such matters as liturgy and devotions, was a political liberal who had begun his career as secretary to Bishop Radini of Bergamo, a protégé of Cardinal Rampolla. He had spent most of his career as a papal diplomat *en poste* and had never involved himself in Vatican politics, but he had always remained loosely attached to the progressive forces within the Church. Unlike Pius XII he was an extrovert, a voluble and well-adjusted hedonist who loved human contact and enormously enjoyed pastoral work. He was a historian, not a theologian, and thus he was not afraid of change but rather welcomed it as a sign of growth and greater illumination. His favourite words were *aggiornamento* ('bringing up to date') and *convivienza* ('living together'). Not only did he immediately open the windows and let fresh air into Pius's musty and antique court, but he changed papal policy in three vital respects. First he inaugurated a new, Rome-centred ecumenical movement, which he placed under the direction of a secretariat headed by the German Jesuit-diplomat Cardinal Bea. Second, he opened up lines of communication with the Communist world, and ended the policy of 'holy isolation'. Third he set in motion a process of democratization within the Church by summoning a general council.

Of these the most important was the council – announced within three months of John's election to a stunned and silent group of curial cardinals – because it also embraced the other two aspects of the new policies. John was unable to make the council ecumenical in the true sense, since it proved impossible to arange an agreed representation of the Orthodox churches, and therefore the Protestants could not be invited either. But all were invited as observers, and by the end of the council there were over a hundred in this category, including, beside the Orthodox, accredited delegations from the Coptic church of Egypt, the Syrian Orthodox, the Ethiopian (Nestorian) Church, the Russian Orthodox Church in Exile, the Armenian Church and other Monophysite churches, the Old Catholics, the Lutherans, Presbyterians, Congregationalists, Methodists, Quakers, the Taize Community, the Disciples of Christ, and other Christian churches, besides the secretariat of the World Council of Churches, which the Vatican had hitherto ignored and instructed Catholics to boycott. The other Christian churches, now rechristened 'separated brethren', though not participating, were in fact, by private behind-the-scenes contacts, able to influence the debates and voting, and their very presence acted as a restraining force on religious bigotry during the sessions. The triumphalist rhetoric which had been so notable a feature of the First Vatican Council in 1870 was conspicuously absent. John also engaged in complicated negotiations to secure the presence at the council of full delegations from Communist countries (the term 'the church of silence' was now dropped). He failed with China, and also with Albania and Rumania, but he had a notable success in securing the release from prison, to attend, of Mgr Josef Slipyi, the Catholic archbishop of the Byzantine rite in

Lvov, who had been in gaol for seventeen years; and in the event there were, for the opening session, seventeen bishops from Poland, four from East Germany, three from Hungary, three from Czechoslovakia, and all the Yugoslav bishops.

John arranged and held the council, which opened in 1962, against strong and persistent curial opposition. His position was by no means all-powerful because, though personally popular at all levels of the Church, he was unable or unwilling to reorganize the Vatican bureacracy. It continued to operate as an independent and highly conservative force throughout John's pontificate. But he made his wishes clear, and he trusted to the bishops of the council to do the rest. His opening speech, setting out the new papal policy, was apparently provoked by a lecture given to the Lateran University, the stronghold of Roman orthodoxy, by a former head of the Holy Office, Cardinal Pizzardo, in the autumn of 1960. Pizzardo reiterated the message of 'holy isolation', the Augustinian theory of the Church and the world, as updated by Pius IX and his successors, and as maintained to the end by Pius XII. It was nonsense, he said, to speak or think of 'one world'. There were two worlds confronting mankind: the so-called 'modern world', which was the City of Satan' and the City of God, symbolized and represented by the Vatican – he used the old fortress image again. The world beyond the walls of the City of God, said the cardinal, was 'the new city of Babel':

'It rises on a basis of crude materialism and blind determinism, built by the unconscious toil of the conquered, and bathed in their tears and blood, like the old pagan Colosseum – a ruin washed over by the Christian centuries. It rises up monstrous, holding out before the eyes of the deluded mob of slaves – bringing bricks and pitch for its making – a vain mirage of perfect prosperity and terrestial felicity. . . . But at the same time on the glacis of the New Babel, there arise the launching ramps for missiles, and in its storehouse the ogival nuclear weapons pile up for the universal and total destruction to come.'

Pizzardo was virtually repeating the 1939 analysis of Pius's *Summi Pontificus*, though adding the new and terrifying image of a thermo-nuclear apocalypse – a *parousia* flying in on the wings of intercontinental missiles. The tone was the characteristic pessimism of populist triumphalism, with its Augustinian roots. John, in his opening speech, begged those attending the council to reject this analysis:

'We are shocked to discover what is being said by some people who, though they may be fired by religious zeal, are without justice, or good judgment, or consideration in their way of looking at matters. In the existing state of society they see nothing but ruin and calamity. They are in the habit of saying that our age is much worse than past centuries. They behave as though history, which teaches us about life, has nothing to teach them. . . .

On the contrary, we should recognize that, at the present historical moment, Divine Providence is leading us towards a new order in human relationships which, through the agency of man and what is more above and beyond their own expectations, are tending towards the fulfilment of higher and, as yet, mysterious and unforeseen designs.'

Pope John's speech was rightly seen as an incitement to action and an optimistic acceptance of change. Such, indeed, was the moral philosophy of John's two major encyclicals, *Mater et Magistra* (1961) and *Pacem in Terris* (1963), dealing with political and social theory, and international relationships. These introduced some very important developments in papal teaching, since the first implicitly rejected Pius IX's *Quanta Cura* and its appended Syllabus of Errors, and indeed a mass of other papal statements on politics going back to Gregory XVI's *Mirari Vos* and *Singulari Nos*. John not only accepted democracy, but took it for granted that most societies would move towards a welfare state. Indeed, he accepted the socialist argument that the assumption of social responsibilities by the State is an extension of human freedom: state intervention 'makes it possible for the individual to exercise many of his personal rights . . . such as the right to . . . preserve himself in good health, to receive further education and a more thorough professional training; the right to housing, work, suitable leisure and recreation.' He did not spell out his idea of the perfect form of government, but his advocacy of a written constitution, the separation of powers, and built-in checks on total government power indicated that he took the American system as his model – a system which, in his own lifetime, had very nearly been condemned by the papacy as immoral. In *Pacem in Terris* he accepted, for the first time in the history of the papacy, total liberty of conscience – an idea which Gregory XVI had dismissed as 'monstrous and absurd' and Pius IX as a cardinal error. Every human being, John wrote, should be able 'to worship God in accordance with the right dictates of his own conscience, and to profess his religion both in private and in public'. He also indicated a desire to come to terms with Socialism, Communism and other materialist philosophies. He distinguished between Communism as such, which he termed 'a false philosophy', and many of its aspects, which might be welcome in practical political programmes, 'even when such a programme draws its origins and inspiration from such a philosophy'. Such consequences, he argued, were more important than philosophical logic, since theory, as he put it, 'was subject to practical considerations' and the practice of Communist states might well contain 'good and commendable elements'. Communist leaders might be theoretically committed to world revolution but in concrete terms it was possible and even likely they would settle for peaceful coexistence; the Church should recognize this probability and turn it to good advantage. Statesmen should strive for disarmament, disputes should be settled through the United Nations, and all should work 'towards the establishment of a juridical and political organization of the world community'. He indicated that he was more concerned with the poor countries of the Third World than with the 'lost territories' of eastern Europe. He urged the rich nations to help underdeveloped countries 'in a way which guarantees to them the preservation of their own freedom'.

John brushed aside previous papal objections to the principle of national sovereignty. He argued that the collective right of a nation to national independence was merely an extension of the rights of an individual, which it was the duty of the Church to uphold. In Africa and Asia, the Church should not merely cease to oppose necessary changes, but should identify itself with them. And it should protest against the attempt to impose uniform western ideas; the countries of the Third World 'have often preserved in their ancient traditions an acute and vital awareness of the more important human values. To attempt to undermine this national integrity is essentially immoral. It must be respected, and as far as possible strengthened and developed, so that it may remain what it is: a foundation of true civilization.' To this John added, by way of concluding his political and international philosophy, a total condemnation of racialism: 'Truth calls for the elimination of every trace of racial discrimination, and the consequent recognition of the inviolable principle that all states are by nature equal in dignity. . . . The fact is that no one can be by nature superior to his fellows, since all men are equally noble in natural dignity. . . . Each state is like a body, the members of which are human beings.' In sum, the two encyclicals represented an attempt by John to align Catholic thinking with the progressive economic and political wisdom of his day, and they thus marked a benign revolution in papal attitudes.

John saw the council itself as the beginning of a transfer of power from the papal monarchy to the Church as a whole. It was a parliament of the episcopate and he was a constitutional sovereign. He wished to reverse the process whereby, during the nineteenth century, the bishops had been deprived of their independence and had become mere functionaries of a populist papacy. Indeed, he wanted to go further back still to the abortive conciliar theory of the fifteenth century. It had been argued, at the Council of Basle (1431–39), that Christ-delegated authority lay in the Church as a whole. 'Supreme power', said John of Segovia, '. . . belongs to the church continuously, permanently, invariably and perpetually.' Such power could not be alienated any more than a person could discard his own qualities: 'Supreme power resides first in the community itself like a personal sense or inborn virtue.' The Second Vatican Council was a reassertion of this view, and a denial that power could be permanently alienated to a monarchical pontiff; indeed, it took up where Basle had left off. The Vatican II Decree on the Church was, in effect, a denial of the dogma of papal infallibility since it asserted that the true source of authority was plural: 'The body of the faithful . . . cannot err in matters of belief. Thanks to a supernatural sense of the faith which characterizes the people as a whole, it manifests this unerring quality when, "from the bishops down to the last member of the laity", it shows universal agreement in matters of faith and morals.'

The revival of conciliar theory, of course, automatically opened up bridges to both the Protestants and the Orthodox, since in both cases the breach had come because of the failure to allow disputes to be settled by true ecumenical methods. Yet John did not overcome the weakness of conciliar method, a weakness which had been fatal to the theory in the fifteen century. Councils were *ad hoc* affairs. What was also required was the embodiment of conciliar theory in the permanent machinery of church government. Because of its absence, the Pope had wrested back his monarchical absolutism in the fifteenth century. The same process threatened to occur again. Indeed, even during the first session of the Council, John was made aware of a *lacuna* in his arrangements. The first series of propositions, or *schema*, to be debated by the Council dealt with the authority of faith, and the sources of revelation. The subject was absolutely crucial, since it determined the whole manner in which the Christian faith was asserted and interpreted, and transcended all the arguments between the Catholics and the other Christian churches. The *schema* prepared by the Curialists was Tridentine and asserted that the church's innate authority or *magisterium* was an alternative and equal source to that of revelation through scripture; it was, in effect, identical to the position adopted by Pius x at the height of the Modernist controversy. John had been officially classified as 'suspected of Modernism' then, and in a sense he proved it in 1962 by intervening on the side of the progressives to prevent the curialists exploiting procedural devices to get their *schema* through. This ultimately led to the adoption by an enormous majority of a definition of revelation which was eirenic and ecumenical. But it was disquieting that the Pope's intervention should have been necessary when it was quite clear what most of the bishops wanted.

Pope John did not live to remedy this defect in his machinery of change. He died in 1963, before the second session of the Council, and before he or it had the opportunity to tackle the whole question of power and government within the Church – indeed, he was already ill when the council first met. Thus, although John's intentions and aspirations were clear, and though he had set in motion a 'revolution of rising expectations' among many bishops and priests and among ordinary Catholic laymen, he had not in fact changed the manner in which the Church was ruled. He left the absolutist papal powers intact. Hence Cardinal Montini, the curialist who succeeded John as Paul vi, inherited a democratic spirit but an autocratic machine. Which should be allowed to prevail? Pope Paul attempted a compromise. He allowed the council to continue and complete its work. But he withdrew from its competence two subjects which he reserved for himself. This was an arrangement difficult to defend either in logic or on grounds of practical wisdom. Either the Council was sovereign in the Pope's eyes or not. If it was, then why should it not deal with all topics? If it could not deal with two topics considered so important and delicate that only the Pope had the divine wisdom to settle them, then why should it deal with any? The decision devalued the authority of the Council without reinforcing that of the Pope; indeed, it ended by devaluing the authority of the Pope too, by throwing doubt as to where the real source of power in the Church lay.

Moreover, the two subjects was both highly contentious, calculated to rouse emotions, and of a kind which a representative assembly (as opposed to a solitary individual) is peculiarly fitted to handle – clerical celibacy and contraception. Both concerned sex, a matter on which bachelor popes were notoriously liable to come to grief. Both tended to divide Catholics from the other Christian churches, a point which rendered a personal ruling by the Pope peculiarly odious to the 'separated brethren'. And both, as it happened, were matters on which the Pope himself found it difficult to make up his mind. Clerical celibacy had always caused trouble. It had never been enforced in the Eastern Church, except for higher clergy; and in the Latin West it had never been effectively enforced until the nineteenth century. It was pre-eminently a matter which should have been left for the clergy as a whole – or, in more practical terms, the episcopate – to settle themselves. As it was, Paul's ruling that the topic should not be opened, and that celibacy must stay, was seen by many of the younger clergy as neither equitable nor conclusive, and it became a source of disobedience, scandal and disaffection – and of ridicule to the secular world.

Contraception was even more serious, since it involved the morale and the discipline of the Catholic laity. The Latin Church had traditionally taught that birth control in any form was sinful. Yet the scriptural authority on which this ruling was based was meagre. There is nothing about the subject in the New Testament, and the only apparent reference in the Old is Genesis 38:8–10: '... and Judah said unto Onan, go unto thy brother's wife and perform the duty of an husband's brother unto her, and raise up seed to thy brother. And Onan knew that the seed should not be his; and it came to pass, when he went in unto his brother's wife, that he spilled it on the ground, less he should give seed to his brother. And the thing which he did was evil in the sight of the Lord: and he slew him also.' This is a very obscure passage. It is not clear whether the Lord killed Onan for spilling his seed, or for failing to give his brother's wife a child (a breach of the Levirate law). The implication may be that Onan would also have been killed if he had simply refused to 'go unto' the wife. Yet Augustine declared 'intercourse even with one's legitimate wife is unlawful and wicked where the conception of the offspring is prevented. Onan, the Son of Judah, did this and the Lord killed him for it.' In fact, that was precisely what Onan did not do, as the woman was not his 'legitimate wife'. Moreover, it is clear that Augustine's ruling sprang from his restrictive view of marriage as solely procreative in purpose. For a couple to have intercourse without actively willing conception was, in his view, sinful. He made his position gruesomely clear in *Marriage and Concupiscence*, a book which greatly influenced Christian teaching on sex for fifteen hundred years:

'It is one thing not to lie except with the sole will of generating: this has no fault. It is another to seek the pleasure of the flesh in lying, although within the limits of marriage: this has venial fault. I am supposing then that, although you are not lying for the sake of procreating offspring, you are not for the sake of lust obstructing their procreation by an evil prayer or an evil deed. Those who do this, although they are called husband and wife, are not; nor do they retain any reality of marriage, but with a respectable name cover a shame . . . sometimes this lustful cruelty or cruel lust, comes to this, that they even procure poisons of sterility, and, if those do not work, extinguish and destroy the foetus in some way in the womb, preferring that their offspring die before it lives, or if it was already alive in the womb to kill it before it was born.'

This position, as elaborated by Aquinas, and endorsed by Luther, Calvin and other theologians, remained orthodox teaching in all Christian churches until after the First World War. The Anglican Church reluctantly accepted artificial contraception at the Lambeth Conference of 1930, and shifted the moral theology to a consideration of whether the married couple's intention was selfish or not. This analysis was later adopted by most other Protestant churches. In his 1930 encyclical, *Casti Connubii*, Pius XI reiterrated the traditional view in the most forceful terms. But in 1951, Pius XII, in an address to Italian Catholic Midwives, stated that use of the so-called 'safe period' as a system of birth control was lawful, provided the intention was justified by circumstances. Such a compromise undermined the Augustinian teaching since Augustine had specifically denounced use of the safe period in his *The Morals of the Manichees*; and the concession was also fatal to Augustine's whole doctrine of marriage. Moreover, use of the safe period systematically tended to raise the question of whether it was legitimate to stabilize the period artificially; and if this were conceded, it became almost impossible to a draw a workable moral distinction between 'natural' and 'artificial' contraception.

The supposition among many Council members was that the Council would solve the problem by reformulating the doctrine of marriage; and Pope John set up an advisory committee of specialists. Some of the shrewder members were anxious that the Church should not get involved in giving detailed judgment in a field where medical science was moving fast, but should stick, like the Anglicans, to the safe ground of 'right intention'. As Cardinal Suenens of Brussels put it: 'I beg of you, let us avoid a new "Galileo Affair".' One is enough for the church.' In fact, despite the papal veto, the topic necessarily arose when the Council discussed marriage and the family as part of the *schema* on 'The church and the modern world' during the fourth and final session in Autumn 1965. The debate was interrupted on 24 November by a message from the Secretary of State insisting on the Pope's orders that certain changes in the text be made, that it should include explicit mention of *Casti Connubii* and the address of Pius XII to the midwives, and that 'it is absolutely necessary that the methods and instruments of rendering conception ineffectual – that is to say, the contraceptive methods which are dealt with in the encyclical letter *Casti Connubii* – be openly rejected; for in this matter admitting doubts, keeping silence, or insinuating opinions that the necessity of such methods is perhaps to be admitted, can bring about the gravest dangers to the general opinion.' The text of four amendments on which the Pope insisted were attached. The conservatives were delighted; one of them, Cardinal Browne, exclaimed: '*Christus ipse locutus est* – Christ himself has spoken.' This peremptory intervention, of course, made nonsense of the whole principle of the Council; and in fact after much behind-the-scenes negotiations, the Pope's message was itself amended, and the changes he proposed were relegated to a footnote in the final text of the schema. Here was a case of a pope willing to assert his authority, but also willing to withdraw it again under pressure: the pattern of a weak autocrat. The Council thus ended and dispersed with both the contraception issue, and the larger one of sovereignity within the Church, wholly unresolved. Nor has either been resolved since. In July 1968, Pope Paul finally made up his mind on contraception, ignored the majority view of his advisory commission, and published his encyclical *Humanae Vitae*, which stated that, while 'natural' contraception was licit, 'None the less the church calling men back to the observance of the norms of the natural law, as interpreted by her constant doctrine, teaches that each and every marriage act must remain open to the transmission of life' – thus ruling out artificial methods of birth-control. The encyclical aroused widespread criticism among the international Catholic community, not merely among laymen and women, but among the priesthood and the episcopate; and its teachings, to judge from opinion polls, are believed to have been generally ignored. *Humanae Vitae* effectively alienated the progressive wing of the Catholic Church from the papacy; and, at about the same time, the introduction of sweeping changes in the liturgy, including the compulsory use of the vernacular at most services, alienated many on the conservative wing. The reign of Paul VI thus signalled the end of populist triumphalism. It was marked by a general erosion of ecclesiastical authority, the assertion of lay opinion, the defiance of superiors, the spread of public debate among Catholics, the defection of many clergy and nuns, and the decline of papal prestige. And, for perhaps the first time since the Reformation, the number of practising Catholic Christians owing allegiance to Rome began to contract.* Catholicism appeared to have joined Protestantism and Orthodoxy in a posture of decline.

---

* Accurate figures are subject to arguments over definition. For Britain, the statistician A. E. C. W. Spencer, formerly director of the Newman Demographic survey, compiled a number of tables for the Pastoral Research Centre, summarized in the April 1975 issue of *The Month* (London). For England and Wales, he estimated the baptized Roman Catholic population at 5,569,000 in 1958; by 1971 he calculated that 2,600,000 had become 'alienated to the extent that they would not use the offices of the church at the three great turning-points in life: birth, marriage and death'; he estimated alienations by 1975 as 3,300,000.

Yet it must be asked: is the expression 'decline' appropriate? If the claims of Christianity are true, the number of those who publicly acknowledge them is of small importance; if they are not true, the matter is scarcely worth discussing. In religion, quantitative judgments do not apply. What may, in the future, seem far more significant about this period is the new ecumenical spirit, the offspring of the Second Vatican Council. On 7 December 1965, the Bishop of Rome, Pope Paul VI, and the Bishop of New Rome, the Ecumenical Patriarch Athenagoras, at a simultaneous ceremony in Rome and Istanbul, performed what was termed a 'joint act', and lifted the mutual excommunications imposed by their predecessors nine hundred years before in 1054. On 23 March 1966, the Bishop of Rome and the Archbishop of Canterbury, Dr Ramsay, exchanged the kiss of peace before the altar of the Sistine Chapel. Both these symbolic gestures have been followed by detailed and continuing negotiations. Progress has been made on marginal matters, such as the status of Anglican orders. Whether the churches reunite will depend entirely on the question of authority, which always has been, and remains, the real source of division within Christianity.* And the definition of authority between the churches cannot be settled until the Catholic Church determines the source of ecclesiastical power within itself – an issue which the Vatican Council raised but left unresolved. As we have seen, the argument about the control of the Christian Church is almost as old as Christianity itself; and it may be that it will continue so long as there are men and women who assert that Christ was God, and who await the *parousia*. Perhaps it is part of the providential plan that the organization of Christianity should be a perpetual source of discord. Who can say? We should remember the words of St Paul, towards the end of his letter to the Romans, the key document of the faith: 'O depth of wealth, wisdom and knowledge in God! How unsearchable his judgments, how untraceable his ways! Who knows the mind of the Lord? Who has been his counsellor?'

---

* The point can be illustrated by comparing the oaths sworn by bishops on their consecration. The oath of allegiance of all Roman Catholic bishops includes the promise: 'with all my power I will persecute and make war upon heretics'. The homage performed by Anglican bishops reads: I, ——, lately of ——, having been elected Bishop of ——, and such election having been duly confirmed, do hereby declare that Your Majesty is the only supreme governor of your realm in spiritual and ecclesiastical things as well as temporal and that no foreign prelate or potentate has any jurisdiction within this realm.'

Epilogue

IT SHOULD BE EVIDENT from this account of 2,000 years of Christian history that the rise of the faith, and its developing relationship with society, were not fortuitious. The Christians appeared at a time when there was a wide, and urgent, if unformulated need for a monotheistic cult in the Graeco-Roman world. The civic and national deities no longer provided satisfactory explanations for the cosmopolitan society of the Mediterranean, with its rising living standards and its growing intellectual pretensions; and, being unable to explain, they could not provide comfort and protection from the terrors of life. Christianity offered not only an all-powerful God, but an absolute promise of a felicitous life to come, and a clear explanation of how this was to be secured. Furthermore, it was disembodied from its racial and geographical origins, and endowed by its founder with a glittering variety of insights and guidelines calculated to evoke responses from all natures. It was, from the beginning, universalist in its scope and aim. St Paul, by giving it an internationalist thought-structure, made it a religion of all races; Origen expanded its metaphysics into a philosophy of life which won the respect of the intellectuals while retaining the enthusiasm of the masses, and so made Christianity classless as well as ubiquitous.

Once Christianity acquired the same profile as the Roman empire, it inevitably replaced the state religion. But of course it was more than a state cult – it was an institution in itself, with its own structure and cycle of growth. In the West it drained the empire of talent and purpose, and substituted its own Augustinian vision of society, in which Christian ideas penetrated every aspect of life and every political and economic arrangement. Europe was a Christian creation not only in essence but in minute detail. And therein lay Europe's unique strength, for Christianity proved a matchless combination of spirituality and dynamism. It offered answers to metaphysical questions, it provided opportunities and frames of reference for the contemplative, the mystic and the devout; but at the same time it was a relentless gospel of work and an appeal to achievement.

Moreover, Christianity contained its self-correcting mechanism. The insights provided by Christ's teaching are capable of almost infinite elaborations and explorations. The Christian matrices form a code to be translated afresh in each new situation, so that Christian history is a constant process of struggle and rebirth – a succession of crises, often accompanied by horror, bloodshed, bigotry and unreason, but evidence too of growth, vitality and increased understanding. The nature of Christianity gave Europe a flexible framework of intellectual and moral concepts, and enabled it to accommodate itself to economic and technological change, and seize each new opportunity as it arose. So Europe expanded into the western-dominated society of the twentieth century.

The account of Christianity presented in this book has necessarily stressed its failures and shortcomings, and its institutional distortions. But we have been measuring it by its own stupendous claims, and its own unprecedented idealism. As an exercise in perfectionism, Christianity cannot succeed, even by its internal definitions; what it is designed to do is to set targets and standards, raise aspirations, to educate, stimulate and inspire. Its strength lies in its just estimate of man as a fallible creature with immortal longings. Its outstanding moral merit is to invest the individual with a conscience, and bid him follow it. This particular form of liberation is what St Paul meant by the freedom men find in Christ. And, of course, it is the father of all other freedoms. For conscience is the enemy of tyranny and the compulsory society; and it is the Christian conscience which has destroyed the institutional tyrannies Christianity itself has created – the self-correcting mechanism at work. The notions of political and economic freedom both spring from the workings of the Christian conscience as a historical force; and it is thus no accident that all the implantations of freedom throughout the world have ultimately a Christian origin.

Of course human freedoms are imperfect and delusory. Here again, Christianity is an exercise in the impossible; but it is nevertheless valuable in stretching man's potentialities. It lays down tremendous objectives but it insists that success is not the final measure of achievement. Indeed, the primary purpose of Christianity is not to create dynamic societies – though it has often done so – but to enable individuals to achieve liberation and maturity in a specific and moral sense. It does not accept conventional yardsticks and terrestrial judgments. As St Paul says: 'Divine folly is wiser than the wisdom of man, and divine weakness stronger than man's strength . . . to shame the wise, God has chosen what the world counts folly, and to shame what is strong, God has chosen what the world counts weakness. He has chosen things low and contemptible, mere nothings, to overthrow the existing order.'

We must bear this in mind when we consider the future of Christianity, in the light of its past. During the past half-century there has been a rapid and uninterrupted secularization of the West, which has all but demolished the Augustinian idea of Christianity as a powerful, physical and institutional presence in the world. Of St Augustine's city of God on earth, little now remains, except crumbling walls and fallen towers, effete establishments and patriarchies of antiquarian rather than intrinsic interest. But of course

Christianity does not depend on a single matrix: hence its durability. The Augustinian idea of public, all-embracing Christianity, once so compelling, has served its purpose and retreats – perhaps, one day, to re-emerge in different forms. Instead, the temporal focus shifts to the Erasmian concept of the private Christian intelligence, and to the Pelagian stress on the power of the Christian individual to effect virtuous change. New societies are arising for Christianity to penetrate, and the decline of western predominance offers it an opportunity to escape from beneath its Europeanized carapace and assume fresh identities.

Certainly, mankind without Christianity conjures up a dismal prospect. The record of mankind *with* Christianity is daunting enough, as we have seen. The dynamism it has unleashed has brought massacre and torture, intolerance and destructive pride on a huge scale, for there is a cruel and pitiless nature in man which is sometimes impervious to Christian restraints and encouragements. But without these restraints, bereft of these encouragements, how much more horrific the history of these last 2,000 years must have been! Christianity has not made man secure or happy or even dignified. But it supplies a hope. It is a civilizing agent. It helps to cage the beast. It offers glimpses of real freedom, intimations of a calm and reasonable existence. Even as we see it, distorted by the ravages of humanity, it is not without beauty. In the last generation, with public Christianity in headlong retreat, we have caught our first, distant view of a de-Christianized world, and it is not encouraging. We know that Christian insistence on man's potentiality for good is often disappointed; but we are also learning that man's capacity for evil is almost limitless – is limited, indeed, only by his own expanding reach. Man is imperfect with God. Without God, what is he? As Francis Bacon put it: 'They that deny God destroy man's nobility: for certainly man is of kin to the beasts by his body; and, if he be not kin to God by his spirit, he is a base and ignoble creature.' We are less base and ignoble by virtue of divine example and by the desire for the form of apotheosis which Christianity offers. In the dual personality of Christ we are offered a perfected image of ourselves, an eternal pace-setter for our striving. By such means our history over the last two millennia has reflected the effort to rise above our human frailties. And to that extent, the chronicle of Christianity is an edifying one.

Select Bibliography

Addington, Raleigh, ed., *Faber, Poet and Priest. Selected Letters by Frederick William Faber from 1833–1863* (London 1974)

Ahlstron, Sidney A., *A Religious History of the American People* (New Haven 1972)

Aigrain, René, *L'Hagiographie: ses sources, ses méthodes, son histoire* (Paris 1953)

Albright, W.F., *From the Stone Age to Christianity* (Baltimore 1957)

Alphanery, A. and Dupront, A., *La Chrétienté et l'idée de la Croisade*, 2 vols. (Paris 1954–9)

Andreson, H., *Jesus and Christian Origins* (New York 1964)

Atiya, A.S., *A History of Eastern Christianity* (London 1968)

Atkinson, James, *Martin Luther and the Birth of Protestantism* (London 1968)

Attwater, Donald, ed., *The Penguin Dictionary of Saints* (London 1965)

Bailyn, Bernard, *The Ideological Origins of the American Revolution* (Harvard 1967)

Bainton, R., 'The development and consistency of Luther's attitude to religious liberty', *Harvard Theological Review* (1929)

Bainton, R., 'The parable of the Tares as the proof text for religious liberty to the end of the sixteenth century', *Church History* (London 1932)

Bainton, R.H., *Erasmus of Christendom* (London 1970)

Baker, Derek, 'Vir Dei: Secular sanctity in the early 10th century', *Studies in Church History* (Cambridge 1972)

Bald, R.C., *John Donne: A Life* (Oxford 1970)

Barley, M.W. and Hanson, R.C.P., eds., *Christianity in Britain, 300–700* (London 1957)

Barlow, Frank, *The English Church, 1000–1066* (London 1966)

Barnie, John, *War in Medieval Society: Social Values and the Hundred Years War 1337–99* (London 1974)

Baron, S.W. *The Social and Religious History of the Jews*, 12 vols. (Oxford 1952–67)

Barr, J. *The Semantics of Biblical Literature* (Oxford 1961)

Barrett, C.K., *The Holy Spirit and the Gospel Tradition* (London 1954)

Barrett, C.K., *New Testament Background: Selected Documents* (London 1956)

Barrett, David B., *Schism and Renewal in Africa: an analysis of 6,000 contemporary religious movements* (Oxford 1968)

Barrett, H.M., *Boethius: some aspects of his life and work* (London 1940)

Bataillon, Marcel, *Erasme et l'Espagne* (Paris 1937)

Bauer, Walter, *Orthodoxy and Heresy in Earliest Christianity*, trns. (London 1972)

Beckwith, J., *Early Medieval Art: Carolingian, Ottonian, Romanesque* (London 1964)

Benevisti, M., *The Crusaders in the Holy Land* (Jerusalem 1970)

Benevot, Maurice, 'The Inquisition and its antecedents', *Heythrop Journal* (1966–7)

Bennett, G.V., and Walsh, J.D., eds., *Essays in Modern English Church History* (London 1966)

Bentley, James, 'British and German High Churchmen in the struggle against Hitler', *Journal of Ecclesiastical History* (1972)

Berger, Peter L., *The Social Reality of Religion* (London 1969)

Berger, Peter L., 'The Secularisation of Theology', *Journal for the Scientific Study of Religion* (New York 1967)

Besterman, Theodore, *Voltaire* (London 1969)

Bethell, Denis, 'The Making of a 12th-century relic collection', *Studies in Church History* (Cambridge 1972)

Betternson, J., ed., *Documents of the Christian Church* (Oxford 1967)

Betts, R., 'Social and Constitutional Developments in Bohemia in the Hussite Period', *Past and Present* (April 1955)

Black, A.J., 'The Council of Basle and the Second Vatican Council', *Studies in Church History* (Cambridge 1971)

Black, M., *The Scrolls and Christian Origins* (London 1961)

Black, M., *The Dead Sea Scrolls and Christian Doctrine* (London 1966)

Blau, J., *The Christian Interpretation of Cabala in the Renaissance* (New York 1944)

Bloomfield, M. and Reeves, M., 'The penetration of Joachim into Northern Europe', *Speculum* (1954)

Boardmann, E.P., *Christian Influence upon the Ideology of the Taiping Rebellion* (London 1952)

Bonner, Gerald, *St Augustine of Hippo: Life and Controversies* (London 1970)

Boodyer, G.H., *Jesus and the Politics of His Time* (Salisbury, Rhodesia 1968)

Bornkamm, G., *Jesus of Nazareth* (London 1960)

Bornkamm, G., Barth, G. and Held, H.J., *Tradition and Interpretation in Matthew* (London 1963)

Borsch, F.H., *The Son of Man in Myth and History* (London 1967)

Bosher, R.S., *The Making of the Restoration Settlement* (London 1951)

Bouvier, André, *Henri Bullinger* (Neuchâtel 1940)

Bouwsma, W.J., *Venice and the Defence of Republican Liberty* (California 1968)

Bowker, John, *Jesus and the Pharisees* (Cambridge 1973)

Bowker, John, *Problems of Suffering in Religions of the World* (Cambridge 1970)

Bowker, M., *The Secular Clergy in the Diocese of Lincoln* (Cambridge 1968)

Boyer, Paul and Nissenbaum, Stephen, *Salem Possessed: the Social Origins of Witchcraft* (Harvard 1974)

Boxer, C.R., *The Christian Century in Japan* (London 1951)

Boxer, C.R., 'Portuguese and Spanish Rivalry in the Far East during the 17th century', *Transactions of the Royal Asiatic Society* (Dec. 1946, April 1947)

Brandi, Karl, *The Emperor Charles V*, trns. (London 1954)

Brandon, S.G.F., *The Fall of Jerusalem and the Christian Church* (London 1967)

Brandon, S.G.F., *Jesus and the Zealots* (Manchester 1967)

Broderick, James, *St Francis Xavier* (London 1952)

Brown, Ford K., *Fathers of the Victorians* (Cambridge 1961)

Brown, L.W., *The Indian Christians of St Thomas* (Cambridge 1956)

Brown, Peter, 'The Patrons of Pelagius', *Journal of Theological Studies* (1970)

Brown, Peter, 'Religious Dissent in the later Roman Empire: the case of North Africa', *History* (1963)

Brown, T. J., *The Stonyhurst Gospel of St John* (London 1969)

Bruce, F.F., *New Testament History* (London 1969)

Bruce-Mitford, R.L.S., 'The Art of the Codex Amiatinus', *Journal of the Archaeological Association* (1969)

Budd, S., 'The Loss of Faith: reasons for unbelief among the members of the secular movement in England', *Past and Present* (April 1967)

Bullogh, D.A., 'Europa Pater: Charlemagne and his achievement in the light of recent scholarship', *English Historical Review* (1970)

Bultmann, R., *The History of the Synoptic Tradition* (London 1968)

Burkitt, F.C., *The Religion of the Manichees* (Cambridge 1925)

Butterfield, H., *Christianity and History* (Cambridge 1949)

Callus, D.A., ed., *Robert Grosseteste, Scholar and Bishop* (Oxford 1955)

Campenhausen, H. von, *The Fathers of the Greek Church*, trns. (London 1963)

Campenhausen, H. von, *The Fathers of the Latin Church*, trns. (London 1964)

Campenhausen, H. von, *Ecclesiastical Authority and Spiritual Power*, trns. (London 1969)

Cappuynus, M., *Jean Scot Erigène* (Paris 1933)

Caraman, Philip: *The Lost Paradise: an account of the Jesuits in Paraguay, 1607–1768.* (London 1975)

Carpenter, H.J., 'Popular Christianity and the Theologians in the Early Centuries', *Journal of Theological Studies* (1963)

Chadwick, Henry, *The Early Church* (London 1967)

Chadwick, Henry, 'John Moschus and his friend Sophronius the Sophic', *Journal of Theological Studies* (1974)

Chadwick, Owen, *John Cassian* (Cambridge 1950)

Chadwick, Owen, *The Reformation* (London 1968)

Chapman, Guy, *The Dreyfus Case* (London 1955)

Chapman, Raymond, *The Victorian Debate: English Literature and Society, 1832–1901* (London 1970)

Charles, R.H., ed., *The Apocrypha and Pseudepigrapha of the Old Testament* (London 1963)

Cheyette, F.L., ed., *Lordship and Community in Medieval Europe* (New York 1968)

Cipolla, C.M., *Money, Prices and Civilisation in the Mediterranean World* (Princeton 1956)

Cohen, P.A., *China and Christianity: the Missionary Movement and the Growth of Chinese anti-foreignism* (London 1963)

Cohn, Norman, *The Pursuit of the Millenium* (London 1970)

Cohn, Norman: *Europe's Inner Demons* (Sussex 1975).

Cone, James H., *Black Theology and Black Power* (New York 1969)

Constable, G., *The Letters of Peter the Venerable* (London 1967)

Conway, J.S., *The Nazi Persecution of the Churches, 1933–45* (London 1968)

Conzelmann, Hans, *An Outline of the Theology of the New Testament*, trns. (London 1969)

Cook, G.H., *The English Cathedral through the Centuries* (London 1960)

Copleston, F.C., *Aquinas* (London 1965)

Coulton, G.G., *Medieval Panorama* (Cambridge 1938)

Coulton, G.G., *Five Centuries of Religion*, 4 vols. (Cambridge 1923–50)

Coulton, G.G., *Life in the Middle Ages*, 4 vols. (Cambridge 1967)

Cowdrey, H.E.J., 'The Peace and the Truce of God in the 11th century', *Past and Present* (1970)

Cragg, G.R., *The Church and the Age of Reason* (London 1960)

Cranston, Maurice, *John Locke: a Biography* (London 1957)

Craveri, Marcello, *The Life of Jesus*, trns. (London 1967)

Cross, F.L., *The Oxford Dictionary of the Christian Church* (Oxford 1957)

Cullmann, O., *Peter: Disciple, Apostle, Martyr* (London 1962)

Cullmann, O., *The Earliest Christian Confessions* (London 1949)

Cullmann, O., *The Christology of the New Testament* (London 1963)

Currie, Robert, *Methodism Divided* (London 1968)

Curtin, Thomas van Cleve, *The Emperor Frederick II of Hohenstaufen: Immutator Mundi* (Oxford 1972)

Daniel, N., *Islam and the West* (Edinburgh 1958)

Dansette, Adrien, *A Religious History of Modern France*, trns. 2 vols. (Horder-Frieborg 1961)

Daube, David, *Civil Disobedience in Antiquity* (Edinburgh 1972)

Daube, David, *Collaboration with Tyranny in Rabbinic Law* (Oxford 1965)

Davies, W.D., *The Setting of the Sermon on the Mount* (Cambridge 1964)

Davies, W.D. and Daube, D., eds., *The Background of the New Testament and its Eschatology: Essays in Honour of C.H. Dodd* (Cambridge 1956)

Deansley, M., *The Significance of the Lollard Bible* (London 1951)

Deansley, M., *The Pre-Conquest Church in England* (London 1961)

Decarreaux, Jean, *Monks and Civilisation,* trns. (London 1964)

Delehaye, Hippolyte, *Sanctus* (Brussels 1954)

Dell, R.S., *An Atlas of Christian History* (London 1960)

Devos, P., 'La mysterieuse épisode finale de la *Vita Gregorii* de Jean Diacre: la fuite de Formose', *Analecta Bollandiana* (Antwerp, Brussels 1964)

Dickens, A.G., *Reformation and Society in 16th century Europe* (London 1966)

Dickens, A.G., *Lollards and Protestants in the Diocese of York, 1509–58* (Oxford 1959)

Digard, G., *Philippe le Bel et le Saint-Siège,* 2 vols. (Paris 1934)

Dijk, S.J.P. Van, 'The Urban and Papal rites in 7th–8th century Rome', *Sacris Erudiri* (1961)

Dillon, Myles and Chadwick, Norah, *The Celtic Realms* (London 1972)

Dion, R., 'Viticulture ecclésiastique et viticulture princière au moyen age', *Revue historique* (Paris 1954)

Dodd, C.H., *The Apostolic Teaching and its Developments* (London 1956)

Dodds, E.R., *The Greeks and the Irrational* (Berkeley 1951)

Doney, William, ed., *Descartes: a collection of critical essays* (London 1968)

Donnelly, J.S., *The Decline of the Cistercian Brotherhood* (London 1949)

Douie, D., *The Nature and Effect of the Heresy of the Fraticelli* (Manchester 1932)

Downing, F. Gerald, *The Church and Jesus: a study in history, philosophy and theology* (London 1968)

Dudden, F. Holmes, *Gregory the Great,* 2 vols. (London 1905)

Dudden, F. Holmes, *The Life and Times of St Ambrose,* 2 vols. (Oxford 1935)

Duggan, C., 'The Becket Dispute and the Criminous Clerks', *Bulletin of the Institute of Historical Research* (Cambridge 1962)

Dunham, Chester F., *The Attitude of the Northern Clergy towards the South, 1860–5* (Toledo 1942)

Dunn, G.H., *Generation of Giants: the first Jesuits in China* (London 1962)

Dvornik, F., *Byzantine Missions among the Slavs* (New Brunswick 1970)

Eells, Hastings, *Martin Bucer* (New Haven 1931)

Ehrhardt, A., *The Apostolic Succession* (London 1953)

Erikson, Erik H., *Young Martin Luther* (London 1972)

Evans, R.F., 'Pelagius, Fastidius and the pseudo-Augustinian *de vita Christiana', Journal of Theological Studies* (1962)

Evans, R.F., *Pelagius: Inquiries and Reappraisals* (London 1968)

Evans, R.J.W., *Rudolf II and his World: a study in intellectual history, 1576–1612* (Oxford 1973)

Every, G., *The Byzantine Patriarchate* (London 1962)

Faludy, George, *Erasmus of Rotterdam* (London 1970)

Farmer, W.R., *Macabees, Zealots and Josephus* (New York 1956)

Farris, N.M., *Crown and Clergy in Colonial Mexico, 1759–1821* (London 1968)

Febvre, L., *Le Problème de l'incroyance au XVIe siècle: la religion de Rabelais* (Paris 1947)

Fedotov, G.P., *The Russian Religious Mind* (Cambridge, Mass. 1966)

Feiblemann, J.K., *Religious Platonism* (London 1959)

Fenlon, Dermot, *Heresy and Obedience in Tridentine Italy: Cardinal Pole and the Counter-Reformation* (Cambridge 1972)

Ferguson, W.K., 'The Attitude of Erasmus towards Toleration' in *Persecution and Liberty: Essays in Honour of G.L. Burr* (New York 1931)

Fischer, Bonifatius, 'The use of computers in New Testament studies', *Journal of Theological Studies* (1970)

Fischer-Galati, Stephen A., *Ottoman Imperialism and German Protestantism, 1521–55* (Harvard 1959)

Flender, H., *St Luke: Theologian of Redemptive History* (London 1967)

Folz, R., *L'Idée d'empire en occident du Ve au XIVe siècle* (Paris 1953)

Folz, R., *Le couronnement impérial de Charlemagne* (Paris 1964)

Fontaine, J., *Isidore de Séville et la culture classique dans l'Espagne wisigothique*, 2 vols. (Paris 1958)

Foss, Michael, *The Founding of the Jesuits* (London 1969)

Frame, Donald M., *Montaigne* (London 1965)

Frazier, Franklin E., *The Negro Church in America* (New York 1964)

French, R.M., *The Eastern Orthodox Church* (London 1951)

Frend, W.H.C., 'Heresy and schism as social and national movements', *Studies in Church History* (Cambridge 1971)

Frend, W.H.C., 'The archaeologist and church history', *Antiquity* (1960)

Frend, W.H.C., *The Donatist Church: a movement of protest in Roman North Africa* (Oxford 1971)

Frend, W.H.C., 'The Gnostic-Manichean Tradition in Roman North Africa', *Journal of Ecclesiastical History* (1953)

Frend, W.H.C., *Martyrdom and Persecution in the Early Church* (London 1965)

Frend, W.H.C., 'Popular religion and Christological controversy in the 5th century, *Studies in Church History* (Cambridge 1972)

Fuller, R.H., *Interpreting the Miracles* (London 1963)

Gairdner, W.H.T., *Edinburgh 1910: an account and interpretation of the World Missionary Conference* (Edinburgh and London 1910)

Ganshof, F.L., *The Imperial Coronation of Charlemagne: theories and facts* (London 1949)

Ganshof, F.L., *The Carolingians and the Frankish Monarchy*, trns. (London 1971)

Gartner, Brtil, *The Temple and the Community of Qumran and the New Testament* (Cambridge 1965)

Gasper, Louis, *The Fundamentalist Movement* (The Hague 1963)

Gay, Peter, *The Enlightenment, an Interpretation* (New York 1966)

Geanakoplos, D.J., *The Emperor Michael Palaeologus and the West* (London 1959)

Ghirshman, R., *Iran: the Parthians and Sassanians* (London 1962)

Giles, E., ed., *Documents Illustrating Papal Authority, AD 96–454* (London 1952)

Goodspeed, E.J., *A History of Early Christian Literature* (Chicago 1966)

Grant, Michael, *The Ancient Historians* (London 1970)

Grant, Robert M., *Historical Introduction to the New Testament* (London 1963

Grant, Robert M., *Miracle and Natural Law in Graeco-Roman and Early Christian Thought* (Amsterdam 1952)

Green, Robert W., *Protestantism and Capitalism: the Weber thesis and its Critics* (Boston 1959)

Hales, E.E.Y., 'The First Vatican Council', *Studies in Church History* (Cambridge 1971)

Hales, E.E.Y., *Pio Nono* (London 1962)

Hales, E.E.Y., *Pope John and his Revolution* (London 1965)

Hall, Basil, 'The Colloquies between Catholics and Protestants, 1539–41', *Studies in Church History* (Cambridge 1971)

Hall, Basil, 'The Trilingual College of San Ildefonso and the Making of the Complutensian Polyglot Bible', *Studies in Church History* (Leyden 1969)

Haller, W., *Liberty and Reformation in the Puritan Revolution* (New York 1955)

Hammerton-Kelly, R.G., *Pre-Existence, Wisdom and the Son of Man* (Cambridge 1973)

Hanke, L., *Bartolome de las Casas* (The Hague 1951)

Hare, D.R.A., *The Theme of Jewish Persecution of the Christians in the Gospel According to St Matthew* (Cambridge 1967)

Harrison, Brian, 'Religion and Recreation in 19th century England', *Past and Present* (1967)

Hart, A. Tindal, *The Life and Times of John Sharp, Archbishop of York* (London 1949)

Harvey, Van Austin, *The Historian and the Believer* (London 1967)

Hauser, A., *Mannerism,* 2 vols. (London 1965)

Hay, D., *Europe: the Emergence of an Idea* (New York 1965)

Heard, R.G., 'The Old Gospel Prologues', *Journal of Theological Studies* (1955)

Heath, Peter, *English Parish Clergy on the Eve of the Reformation* (London 1969)

Heath, R.G., 'The Western Schism of the Franks and the "Filioque"', *Journal of Ecclesiastical History* (1972)

Heimert, Alan E., *Religion and the American Mind from the Great Awakening to the Revolution* (Harvard 1966)

Hennell, Michael, 'Evangelicanism and Worldliness', *Studies in Church History* (Cambridge 1972)

Hennell, Michael, *John Venn and the Clapham Sect* (London 1958)

Henry, F., *Irish High Crosses* (Dublin 1964)

Hill, Rosalind, 'The Northumbrian Church', *Church Quarterly Review* (1963)

Hillgarth, J.N., 'Coins and Chronicles: Propaganda in 6th century Spain and the Byzantine Background', *Historia* (Chicago 1966)

Hillgarth, J.N., *The Conversion of Western Europe, 350–750* (New Jersey 1969)

Hinchcliff, Peter, 'African separatism: Heresy, Schism or Protest Movement?', *Studies in Church History* (Cambridge 1971)

Holt, E., *The Opium Wars in China* (London 1964)

Hoppen, K. Theodore, 'W.G. Ward and Liberal Catholicism', *Journal of Ecclesiastical History* (1972)

Hughes, Kathleen, *The Church in Early Irish Society* (London 1966)

Hughes, P., *The Reformation in England*, 3 vols. (London 1950–4)

Hunter-Blair, Peter, *The World of Bede* (London 1970)

Hussey, J.M., *The Byzantine World* (London 1961)

Hussey, J.M., 'Byzantine Monasticism, *Cambridge Medieval History, IV* (Cambridge 1967)

Jacob, E., 'Gerard Groote and the beginning of the "New Devotion" in the Low Countries', *Journal of Ecclesiastical History* (1952)

Jasper, Ronald C.D., *George Bell, Bishop of Chichester* (Oxford 1967)

Jedin, Hubert, *History of the Council of Trent*, trns., 2 vols. (London 1957)

Jeremias, J., *Infant Baptism in the First Four Centuries* (London 1960)

Jeremias, J., *The Problem of the Historical Jesus* (London 1964)

John, Eric, 'The social and political problems of the early English Church', *Agricultural History Review* (1970)

Johnson, S.M., 'John Donne and the Virginia Company', *Journal of English Literary History* (1947)

Jonas, H., *The Gnostic Religion* (London 1963)

Jones, A.H.M., *The Later Roman Empire,* 3 vols. (London 1964)

Jones, A.H.M., 'Were the ancient heresies national or social movements in disguise?', *Journal of Theological Studies* (1959)

Jones, A.H.M., 'Church finance in the 5th and 6th centuries', *Journal of Theological Studies* (1960)

Jordan, E.K.H., *Free Church Unity: A History of the Free Church Council Movement,* 1896–1941 (London 1956)

Jungmann, Joseph A., *The Early Liturgy to the time of Gregory the Great* (London 1960)

Kamen, Henry, *The Spanish Inquisition* (London 1965)

Kelly, J.N.D., *Early Christian Doctrines* (London 1958)

Kelly, J. N. D.: *Jerome: his Life, Writings and Controversies* (London 1975)

Kendrick, T., *St James in Spain* (London 1960)

Kent, John, *The Age of Disunity* (London 1966)

Kittler, G.D., *The White Fathers* (London 1956)

Kitzinger, Ernst, 'The Gregorian Reform and the visual arts', *Transactions of the Royal Historical Society* (London 1972)

Knowles, David, *Saints and Scholars* (Cambridge 1962)

Kummel, W.G., *The New Testament: the History of the Investigation of its problems*, trns. (London 1973)

Laistner, L.W., *Thought and Letters in Western Europe, 500–900* (London 1957)

Latouche, Robert, *The Birth of Western Economy: Economic Aspects of the Dark Ages*, trns. (London 1961)

Latourette, K.S., *History of the Expansion of Christianity*, 7 vols. (London 1937–45)

Latourette, K.S., *Christianity in a Revolutionary Age*, 5 vols. (New York 1957–61)

Lau, F. and Bizer, E., *A History of the Reformation in Germany to 1555* (London 1969)

Lawrence, Peter, *Road Belong Cargo: a study in the Cargo movement in the Southern Madang District, New Guinea* (Manchester 1964)

Lea, H.C., *A History of Auricular Confession and Indulgences in the Latin Church*, 3 vols. (London 1896)

Le Bras, Gabriel, *Introduction à l'histoire de la pratique religieuse en France*, 2 vols. (Paris 1945)

Lecler, Joseph, *Toleration and the Reformation*, 2 vols. (London 1960)

Le Guillou, M.J., *Christ and Church, a Theology of the Mystery*, trns. (New York 1966)

Lee, Robert and Marty, Martin E., eds., *Religion and Social Conflict* (New York 1964)

Lesne, E., *Histoire de la propriété ecclésiastique en France*, 6 vols. (Lille and Paris 1910–42)

Lewis, E., *Medieval Political Ideas*, 2 vols. (London 1954)

Lewy, Gunter, *The Catholic Church and Nazi Germany* (New York 1964)

Leyser, K., 'The German aristocracy from the 9th to the early 12th century: a historical and cultural sketch', *Past and Present* (1968)

Liebeschultz, W., 'Did the Pelagian movement have social aims?', *Historia* (Chicago 1963)

Lineham, Peter, 'Councils and Synods in 13th century Castille and Aragon', *Studies in Church History* (Cambridge 1971)

Little, David, *Religion, Order and the Law* (Oxford 1970)

Llewellyn, Peter, *Rome in the Dark Ages* (London 1971)

Luchaire, A., *Innocent III*, 6 vols. (Paris 1905–8)

Lynch, J., 'Philip II and the Papacy', *Transactions of the Royal Historical Society* (London 1961)

Mabbott, J.D., *John Locke* (London 1973)

MacFarlane, Alan, *Witchcraft in Tudor and Stuart England* (London 1970)

MacIntyre, A., *Secularisation and Moral Change* (London 1967)

Manuel, Frank E., *A Portrait of Isaac Newton* (Cambridge, Mass. 1968)

Maranon, Gregorio, 'El processo del Arzobispo Carranza', *Boletin de la Real Academia della Historia* (Madrid 1950)

Marcus, R.A., 'Gregory the Great and a papal missionary strategy', *Studies in Church History* (Cambridge 1970)

Markus, R.A., 'Christianity and dissent in Roman North Africa: changing perspectives in recent work', *Studies in Church History* (Cambridge 1971)

Markus, R.A., *Saeculum: History and Society in the theology of St Augustine* (Cambridge 1970)

Martin, D., *A Sociology of English Religion* (London 1967)

Martin, E.J., *History of the Iconoclastic Controversy* (London 1930)

Martyn, J.L., *History and Theology of the Fourth Gospel* (London 1968)

Matthews, Donald G., *Slavery and Methodism: a Chapter in American Morality* (Princeton 1965)

Mayr-Harting, Henry, *The Coming of Christianity to Anglo-Saxon England* (London 1972)

McDonnell, E., *The Beguines and Beghards in Medieval Culture* (New Jersey 1954)

McElrath, Damian, ed., *Lord Acton: the Decisive Decade, 1864–74* (Louvain 1970)

McManners, John, *French Ecclesiastical Society under the Ancien Régime: a Study of Angers in the 18th Century* (Manchester 1960)

McManners, John, *The French Revolution and the Church* (London 1969)

McMullen, Ramsay, *Enemies of the Roman Order: treason, unrest and alienation in the Empire* (Harvard 1966)

McNeill, J.T., *The History and Character of Calvinism* (Oxford 1954)

Mehl, Roger, *The Sociology of Protestantism* (London 1970)

Mew, James, *The Traditional Aspects of Hell* (London 1903)

Meyvaert, P., *Bede and Gregory the Great*, Jarrow Lecture (1964)

Michaelson, C., *Japanese Contributions to Christian Thought* (London 1960)

Milburn, R.L., *Early Christian Interpretations of History* (London 1954)

Miller, D. H., 'The Roman Revolution of the 8th Century', *Medieval Studies* (Toronto 1974)

Mollat, G., *The Popes at Avignon*, trns. (London 1963)

Mollet, M., 'Problemès navales de l'histoire des Croisades', *Cahiers de civilisation médiévales* (Paris 1967)

Momigliano, A.D., ed., *The Conflict Between Paganism and Christianity in the 4th Century* (Oxford 1963)

Momigliano, A.D., 'Popular religious beliefs and the late Roman historians', *Studies in Church History* (Cambridge 1972)

Momigliano, A.D., 'Cassiodorus and the Italian culture of his time', *Proceedings of the British Academy* (London 1955)

Moore, A.L., *The Parousia in the New Testament* (Leiden 1966)

Moore, G.F., *Judaism in the First Centuries of the Christian Era,* 3 vols. (London 1954)

Moore, R.I., 'The Origin of Medieval Heresy', *History* (1970)

Moore, W.J., *The Saxon Pilgrims to Rome and the Scuola Saxonum* (London 1937)

Moorhouse, Geoffrey, *The Missionaries* (London 1973)

Moorman, J., *History of the Franciscan Order* (London 1968)

Morris, Colin, 'A critique of popular religion: Guibert de Nogent on the relics of the Saints', *Studies in Church History* (Cambridge 1972)

Morris, J., 'Pelagian Literature', *Journal of Theological Studies* (1965)

Morrison, K.F., *Tradition and Authority in the Western Church, 300–1140* (Princeton 1969)

Morton, A.Q. and McLeman, J., *Paul* (London 1966)

Mounier, Roland, *The Assassination of Henri IV: the Tyrannicide Problem and the Consolidation of the French Absolute Monarchy in the early 17th Century,* trns. (London 1973)

Neill, S.C., *A History of Christian Missions* (London 1964)

Neill, S.C., *A History of the Ecumenical Movement, 1517–1948* (London 1954)

Neill, S.C., and Weber, H.R., eds., *The Layman in Christian History* (London 1963)

Nelson, Janet L., 'Society, theodicy and the origins of heresy: towards a reassessment of the medieval evidence', *Studies in Church History* (Cambridge 1971)

Nelson, Janet L., 'Gelasius I's doctrine of responsibility', *Journal of Theological Studies* (1967)

Nersessian, Surapie Der, *Armenia and the Byzantine Empire* (Cambridge, Mass. 1965)

Newsome, David, *The Parting of Friends: a study of the Wilberforces and Henry Manning* (London 1966)

Nichol, Donald M., *The Last Centuries of Byzantium, 1261–1453* (London 1972)

Nilsson, Martin P., *Greek Popular Religion* (New York 1954)

Oblensky, Dimitri, 'Nationalism and Eastern Europe in the Middle Ages', *Transactions of the Royal Historical Society* (London 1972)

O'Collins, Gerald, *The Easter Jesus* (London 1973)

Oldenbourg, Z., *Massacre at Montségur: a History of the Albigensian Crusade,* trns. (London 1961)

Oli, John C., ed., *Christian Humanism and the Reformation* (London 1965)

Oliver, R., *The Missionary Factor in East Africa* (London 1952)

O'Neill, J.C., *The Theology of 'Acts' in its Historical Setting* (London 1961)

Ozment, Stephen E., *The Reformation in Medieval Perspective* (Chicago 1971)

Patterson, W.B., 'King James I's call for an ecumenical council', *Studies in Church History* (Cambridge 1971)

Patterson, W.B., 'Henry IV and the Huguenot appeal for a return to Poissy', *Studies in Church History* (Cambridge 1971)

Pernoud, R., *Joan of Arc, by herself and witnesses*, trns. (London 1964)

Perowne, Stewart, *The End of the Roman World* (London 1966)

Pirenne, H., 'De l'état de l'instruction des laiques à l'époque mérovingienne', *Histoire économique de l'Occident médiévale* (Paris 1951)

Plinval, Georges de, *Pélage: ses écrits, sa vie et sa réforme* (Lausanne 1943)

Plongeron, B., *Les réguliers de Paris devant le serment constitutionel* (Paris 1964)

Popkin, Richard H., *The History of Scepticism, from Erasmus to Descartes* (Assen, Netherlands 1964)

Power, Eileen, *Medieval English Nunneries, 1275–1535* (Oxford 1922)

Prawer, Joshua, *The Latin Kingdom of Jerusalem: European Colonialism in the Middle Ages* (London 1972)

Purver, Margery, *The Royal Society: Concept and Creation* (London 1967)

Reeves, Margery, *The Influence of Prophecy in the Later Middle Ages: a study in Joachimism* (Oxford 1969)

Reumann, J., *Jesus in the Church's Gospels* (London 1968)

Riccard, Robert, *The Spiritual Conquest of Mexico*, trns. (Berkeley 1966)

Riley-Smith, J., *The Knights of St John in Jerusalem and Cyprus, 1050–1310* (London 1967)

Rowley, H.H., *The Relevance of the Apocalyptic* (London 1963)

Rowley, H.H., 'The Qumran Sect and Christian Origins', *Bulletin of the John Rylands Library* (Manchester 1961)

Runciman, Stephen, *A History of the Crusades*, 3 vols. (Cambridge 1951–4)

Runciman, Stephen, *Sicilian Vespers* (London 1958)

Rupp, Gordon, *Studies in the Making of the English Protestant Tradition* (Cambridge 1947)

Rupp, Gordon, 'Protestant Spirituality in the first age of the Reformation', *Studies in Church History* (Cambridge 1972)

Russell, J.B., *Dissent and Reform in the Early Middle Ages* (Berkeley 1965)

Samaran, C. and Mollet, G., *La Fiscalité pontificale en France au XIVe siècle* (Paris 1905)

Saint-Croix, G.E.M. de, 'Why were the early Christians persecuted?' *Past and Present* (1963)

Schoeps, H.J., 'Ebionite Christianity', *Journal of Theological Studies* (1953)

Schonfield, H.J., *The Passover Plot* (London 1965)

Schwartz, Marc L., 'Development of a lay religious consciousness in pre-Civil War England', *Studies in Church History* (Cambridge 1972)

Scott, Patrick, 'Cricket and the Religious World in the Victorian Period', *Church Quarterly* (October 1970)

Setton, K.M., ed., *A History of the Crusades*, 2 vols. (Philadelphia 1955–62)

Sherwin-White, A.N., *Roman Society and Roman Law in the New Testament* (London 1963)

Silver, James W., *Confederate Morale and Church Propaganda* (Tuscaloosa 1957)

Simon, M., *St Stephen and the Hellenists* (London 1958)

Smalley, Beryl M., *The Study of the Bible in the Middle Ages* (Oxford 1952)

Smalley, Beryl M., *The Becket Conflict and the Schools: a study of intellectuals in politics* (Oxford 1973)

Smart, Ninian, *The Religious Experience of Mankind* (London 1971)

Smith, John Holland, *Constantine the Great* (London 1971)

Smith, James Ward, and Jamison, A. Leland, eds., *Religious Perspectives in American Culture* (Princeton 1961)

Soulis, G., 'The legacy of Cyril and Methodius to the Southern Slavs', *Dunbarton Oaks Papers* (Cambridge, Mass. 1965)

Southern, R.W., *Medieval Humanism and Other Studies* (Oxford 1970)

Southern, R.W., *Western Society and the Church in the Middle Ages* (London 1970)

Southern, R.W., 'Aspects of the European Tradition of Historical Writing: History as Prophecy', *Transactions of the Royal Historical Society* (London 1972)

Spearing, E., *The Patrimony of the Roman Church at the time of Gregory the Great* (London 1918)

Stark, Rodney, and Glock, Charles Y., *American Piety* (Los Angeles 1968)

Steinmann, Jean, *Pascal,* trns. (London 1965)

Stendhal, K., *The School of St Matthew* (London 1954)

Stevenson, J., ed., *Documents Illustrative of the History of the Church to AD 461,* 2 vols. (London 1970)

Strauss, Gerald, ed., *Manifestations of Discontent in Germany on the Eve of the Reformation* (Indiana 1971)

Stridbeck, C.G., 'Breughel's "Combat between Carnival and Lent" ', *Journal of Courtauld and Warburg Institutes* (London 1956)

Sundkler, B.G.M., *The Christian Ministry in Africa* (London 1960)

Sundkler, B.G.M., *Bantu Prophets in South Africa* (London 1961)

Swanson, Guy E., *Religion and Regime* (Michigan 1967)

Syme, R., *Ammianus and the Historia Augusta* (London 1968)

Talbot, C.H., *The Anglo-Saxon Missionaries in Germany* (London 1954)

Talbot-Rice, David, ed., *The Dark Ages* (London 1965)

Taylor, J.V., *The Growth of the Church in Buganda* (London 1958)

Taylor, J. V., *Primal Vision* (London 1965)

Thomas, Keith, *Religion and the Decline of Magic* (London 1970)

Thompson, David M., 'The churches and society in 19th century England', *Studies in Church History* (Cambridge 1972)

Thompson, E. A., *The Goths in Spain* (London 1969)

Thompson, Rhodes, *Voices from Cane Ridge* (St Louis 1954)

Tisset, P. and Laners, Y., eds., *Procès de condamnation de Jeanne d'Arc* (Paris 1970–2)

Todt, H.E., *The Son of Man in the Synoptic Tradition* (London 1965)

Towler, Robert, *Homo Religiosus: sociological problems in the study of religion* (London 1974)

Trevor-Roper, Hugh, *Religion, Reformation and Social Change* (London 1967)

Trocmé, Etienne, *Jesus and his Contemporaries,* trns. (London 1973)

Turner, H.W., *History of an African Independent Church,* 2 vols. (Oxford 1967)

Ullmann, Walter, 'Public Welfare and Social Legislation in Early Medieval Councils', *Studies in Church History* (Cambridge 1971)

Ullmann, Walter, 'Julius II and the schismatic cardinals', *ibid.*

Ullmann, Walter, *Medieval Papalism: the Political Theories of the Medieval Canonists* (London 1949)

Ullmann, Walter, *Principals of Government and Politics in the Middle Ages* (New York 1961)

Vale, M.G.A., *Charles VII* (London 1974)

Verliden, Charles, 'Les origines coloniales de la civilisation atlantique: antecédents et types de structure', *Cahiers d'histoire mondiale* (1953)

Vermes, G., *The Dead Sea Scrolls in English* (London 1968)

Vicaire, M.H., *St Dominic and his Times,* trns. (London 1964)

Vlasto, A.P., *The Entry of the Slavs into Christendom* (Cambridge 1970)

Wakefield, Walter L., *Heresy, Crusade and Inquisition in Southern France, 1100–1250* (London 1974)

Walker, D.P., *The Ancient Theology* (London 1972)

Walker, D.P., *The Decline of Hell: 18th century discussions of eternal torment* (London 1974)

Wallace, Ronald S., *Calvin's Doctrine of the Christian Life* (Edinburgh 1959)

Wallace-Hadrill, D.S., *Eusebius of Caesarea* (London 1960)

Wallace-Hadrill, D.S., *Early Germanic Kingship in England and on the Continent* (Oxford 1971)

Wallace-Hadrill, D.S., *The Barbarian West, 400–1000* (London 1967)

Wallach, Luitpold, *Alcuin and Charlemagne* (Cornell 1969)

Walsh, John, 'Methodism and the Mob in the 18th century', *Studies in Church History* (Cambridge 1972)

Ward, W.R., 'Popular religion and the problem of control, 1790–1830', *Studies in Church History* (Cambridge 1972)

Ward-Perkins, J.B., 'The shrine of St Peter and its twelve spiral columns', *Journal of Roman Studies* (1952)

Ware, Timothy, *The Orthodox Church* (London 1963)

Warren, W.L., *Henry II* (London 1973)

Washington, Joseph R., *Black Religion: the Negro and Christianity in the United States* (Boston 1964)

Waterhouse, Ellis, 'Some painters and the counter-Reformation before 1600', *Transactions of the Royal Historical Society* (London 1972)

Watt, J.A., *The Theory of Papal Monarchy* (New York 1965)

Webster, J.B., *The African Churches among the Yoruba 1888–1922* (Oxford 1964)

Wedgwood, C.V., *The Thirty Years War* (London 1968)

Weiss, J., *Earliest Christianity* (London 1959)

Wells, G.A., *The Jesus of the Early Christians* (London 1971)

Wendel, François, *Calvin: the Origins and Development of his Religious Thought,* trns. (London 1963)

Werner, M., *The Formation of Christian Dogma* (London 1957)

Wheeler, H., *The Bible in its Ancient and English Versions* (Oxford 1940)

Whiteley, D.E.H., *The Theology of St Paul* (London 1964)

Williams, George Hunston, *The Radical Reformation* (London 1962)

Williamson, G.A., *The World of Josephus* (London 1964)

Wilson, Bryan R., *Religious Sects* (London 1970)

Winter, P., 'Josephus on Jesus', *Journal of Historical Studies* (1968)

Yates, Frances A., 'Paolo Sarpi's History of the Council of Trent', *Journal of Courtauld and Warburg Institutes* (London 1944)

Yates, Frances A., *Giordano Bruno and the Hermetic Tradition* (London 1964)

Yates, Frances A., *The Rosicrucian Enlightenment* (London 1972)

Zuntz, G., *The Text of the Pauline Epistles* (Oxford 1953)

Index

Aaron, 13, 16
abbeys, 236–9
Action Française, 474, 480, 482
L'Action française, 467, 473
Acton, Lord, 393, 394, 471
Acts of Paul, 4
Acts of the Apostles, *see* New Testament
'Acts of the Pagan Martyrs', 72
Adam and Eve, 45, 109
Adam of Usk, 221–2
Adamists, 293
Adams, Henry, 428
Adams, John, 427; *Dissertation on the Canon and Feudal Law*, 424–5
Adams, John Quincy, 428
Adiabene, 12
Admonitio Generalis, 160
Adriatic. 127
Ælfeah, St, 165–6
Æthelbert, King of Kent, 134, 160
Æthelnoth, Archbishop, 165
Æthelric, Bishop of Durham. 165
Æthelstan, Abbot of Romsey, 165
Æthelwine, Bishop of Durham, 165
Africa: Constantine's massacres in, 68; Constantinople tries to re-establish authority over, 127; conversion to Islam, 93, 179; missionaries in, 400, 442, 446–7, 448–51, 452–4, 498, 500; papal estates in, 133; separatist native Christian churches, 500–2; Vandals overrun North Africa, 113, 116, 121; Zealots and Essenes in, 48
Agapetus, Pope, 153
Agathias, 112
Agricola, St, 106
Aidan, St, 144, 146
Aimery, Arnold, 252
Alaric, 128, 129
Albert, Archbishop of Mainz, 280–1
Albert, Prince Consort, 448
Albertus Magnus, 240
Albigensian crusades, 252
Alcala university, 297
Alcobaca, 151
Alcuin, Abbot, 125, 160–1, 174, 175, 244
Aldus Manutius, 269
Alexander, Bishop of Alexandria, 51
Alexander, sectarian, 51, 93
Alexander, St, 165
Alexander I, Tsar of Russia, 362
Alexander II, Pope, 243
Alexander III, Pope, 166, 205, 211
Alexander IV, Pope, 249
Alexander VI, Pope, 280, 363
Alexander of Hales, 240
Alexander the Great, 7, 9, 99
Alexander's Isle, 73

Alexandria: church founded by Mark, 61; 'Gospel of the Hebrews', 53; as intellectual centre, 58, 80; and Islamic conversion of North Africa, 179, 243; Jewish diaspora, 10, 42, 53; monks, 94–5; sack of, 246; Septuagint, 11; Temple of Seramis attacked, 98; Therapeutics, 102; university closed, 112
Alexandrinus codex, 26
Alexius, Emperor, 187
Alfred, Canon of Durham, 165
Alfred, King of England, 157, 164, 177, 229n.
Allies, T.W., 384n.
alms-giving, 232
Alnwick, William, Bishop of Lincoln, 238–9
Alps, monasteries, 145
Alzon, Père d', 466
Ambrose, St, Bishop of Milan, 77, 103–10; and church music, 105; and confession, 230; and cult of relics, 161; *De Officiis*, 107; pessimistic about human condition, 111, 112; ruling on the Church and farming, 139; and St Augustine, 114; works transcribed in *scriptoria*, 157
Ambrosian rite, 168
America, *see* United States of America
American Baptist Missionary Board, 445
American Board of Commissioners for Foreign Missions, 445
American Philosophical Society, 427
Amette, Cardinal, 478
Amiens, 228, 256
Ammianus, 77, 78–9, 116, 157
Ammon, 140
Amorbach, 161
Ananias, 21
Anastasius, Emperor, 137
Andrew, Master, 224
Andrew, St, 23, 163
Andrew of Crete, St, 105
Angeli, 166
angels, in Judaism, 14
Angers, 129, 355, 356, 358
Anglican Church: in America, 423, 427; becomes principal religion of England, 331–2; and contraception, 512; and Evangelicals, 373; First World War, 477–8; and Glorious Revolution, 332; Gorham case, 376–7; and Hampden, 376; missionaries, 401, 443; relationship with Catholic Church, 475, 476; *see also* Church of England; Oxford Movement
Anglican Church Missionary Society, 445, 448
Anglican Society for the Propagation of the Gospel in Foreign Parts, 440
Anglo-Saxon chronicles, 138
Anicii family, 131, 132
Anna Comnena, 183–4, 245
Annals of St Bertin, 156

PAUL JOHNSON

Born in 1928 and educated at Magdalene College, Oxford, Paul Johnson was editor of the influential English weekly, *The New Statesman,* from 1964-1970, and is now Director, New Statesman Publishing Company. Mr. Johnson's prodigious scholarship and varied interests are evident in the themes of his books. Since publication of *A History of Christianity* he has written *Enemies of Society, The Civilization of Ancient Egypt* and *Civilizations of the Holy Land*.